PC Tools:
The Complete Reference,
Second Edition

PC Tools:
The Complete Reference
Second Edition

Hy Bender

Osborne **McGraw-Hill**

Berkeley   New York   St. Louis   San Francisco
Auckland   Bogotá   Hamburg   London   Madrid
Mexico City   Milan   Montreal   New Delhi   Panama City
Paris   São Paulo   Singapore   Sydney
Tokyo   Toronto

Osborne **McGraw-Hill**
2600 Tenth Street
Berkeley, California 94710
U.S.A.

For information on translations or book distributors outside of the U.S.A., please write to Osborne **McGraw-Hill** at the above address.

PC Tools: The Complete Reference, Second Edition

234567890 DOC 998765432

ISBN 0-07-881748-X

To Vera, Clara, and Tracey

Publisher ——————
Kenna S. Wood

Acquisitions Editor ——————
Elizabeth Fisher

Associate Editor ——————
Scott Rogers

Project Editor ——————
Laura Sackerman

Copy Editor ——————
Valerie Robbins

Proofing Coordinator ——————
Wendy Goss

Proofreaders ——————
Mick Arellano
Colleen Paretty
Jeff Barash

Word Processing ——————
Lynda Higham

Indexer ——————
Valerie Robbins

Director of Electronic Publishing –
Deborah Wilson

Production Supervisor ——————
Barry Bergin

Production Assistant ——————
George Anderson

Illustrator ——————
Susie C. Kim

Computer Designers ——————
Michelle Salinaro
Jani Beckwith

Typesetters ——————
Helena Charm
J. E. Christgau
Peter Hancik
Fred Lass
Stefany Otis
Lance Ravella

Cover Design ——————
Bay Graphics Design, Inc.
Mason Fong

Contents
at a Glance

Contents

Part V
Using PC Shell

Foreword

At Central Point Software, our goal is to make computing safer, simpler, and faster. Safer, so your valuable data is there when you need it. Simpler, so you can get to the job at hand as quickly as possible. And faster, so you can get more done in less time.

PC Tools 7 delivers all three benefits. Now in its seventh major release, PC Tools gives you the most popular utilities in one integrated package:

- Advanced data protection and recovery

- Safeguarding against destructive viruses

- Fast, versatile, and reliable hard disk backup

- An easy-to-use DOS shell with a built-in disk and file manager

- A comprehensive desktop organizer

- Remote computing via modem, LAN, or cable

- Programs to enhance your system's performance under both DOS and Microsoft Windows

In *PC Tools: The Complete Reference,* author Hy Bender teaches you how to take full advantage of this productivity tool.

Like the software it describes, *PC Tools: The Complete Reference* is comprehensive and thorough. Its 32 chapters and more than 850 pages are well organized and clearly written; they contain step-by-step examples and quick-reference sections to help you get the most from our software. Also included are detailed appendixes that guide you through installation and network usage, and provide time-saving reference sections on menu and function key commands.

May *PC Tools: The Complete Reference* speed you along to safer, simpler, and faster computing.

Corey Smith
President and CEO
Central Point Software, Inc.

Michael Brown
Chief Technical Officer
Central Point Software, Inc.

Acknowledgments

It took a number of excellent people to help make this book come together.

First and foremost, I want to thank Liz Fisher, who guided this book through its second edition, and Roger Stewart, who shepherded the book through its first edition, for their never-ending patience, warmth, and humor. Working with each of them was a privilege and a joy.

In addition, I want to thank Scott Rogers, Laura Sackerman, Matt Lafata, and Wendy Goss for their skilled work on the second edition; and Laurie Beaulieu, John Levy, and Harriet Serenkin for their valuable contributions to the first edition.

I also want to thank the topnotch support staff at Central Point Software. Paula Tremblay, Craig Froude, and Teresa Warsop provided critical information early on to help get this book going. Doug Whitney, Ken Creggar, Jeff Milburn, John Beals, and Bill Grogg (on the second edition), and Tim Elmer, Danny Cormak, Kyle Dodge, and Ken Turle (on the first edition) spent many hours educating me about various nooks and crannies in PC Tools, giving me the knowledge I needed to describe each feature clearly and fully. And Debbie Hess and Ellen Pfeifer were instrumental in a dozen different ways in helping me get the support and materials I needed, while always sparing an extra moment to offer an encouraging word. I couldn't have done this book without them.

Thanks are also due to Neil Rosenberg of Inner Media, who provided a customized version of Collage Plus for capturing the screen shots in this book; Mark Clifton and Chauncey Taylor of Colorado Memory Systems, who graciously provided a Colorado Jumbo 250 for the chapters on CP Backup; and Susan Breshears of Intel CEO, who provided an Intel SatisFAXtion board for the chapter on Desktop fax telecommunications.

Lastly, I want to thank ace programmer Tracey Siesser for her expert technical help; and Tracey, Elena Andrews, Ed Bungert, Adam-Troy Castro, Donna Ellis, Kent

Greene, Jennie Grey, Sharon Gumerove, Avril Hordyk, Lisa Nowak, and Judy Starger for their support and friendship.

Introduction

PC Tools is an amazing product. *PC Magazine* has called it "the most extraordinary bargain in the PC marketplace," deeming it "powerful enough for advanced users and simple enough for beginners." *InfoWorld* has proclaimed it "one of the most capable, feature-laden packages to be found at any price," concluding "it may be the only program some users need." These positive assessments are shared by computer owners around the world, who have purchased over a million copies of PC Tools, making it one of the most successful software products of all time.

Like PC Tools itself, this book covers a wide range of features. It is written to be understandable to new computer users, yet goes into enough depth for even the most advanced user. It contains hundreds of tutorials and screen shots, making it the most effective tool available for learning PC Tools. At the same time, its extensive use of command lists, subheadings, and cross-references make it an extremely effective reference work. In addition, the book is modular, so that you can opt to read only the chapters you're interested in.

This introduction first outlines the features of this book, explains how to use the book, and describes the conventions employed in the book. It then covers the capabilities of PC Tools 7, how to use common PC Tools elements, and how to get online help.

 When this book uses the term "PC Tools 7," it is referring to both version 7.0 and version 7.1. For more information, see the "PC Tools 7.0 Versus 7.1" section later in this introduction.

About This Book

This book is for anyone who wants to learn PC Tools 7. You'll find it useful regardless of your level of computer expertise.

If you're fairly new to PCs, you'll find the book doesn't assume you have any computer knowledge outside of a few fundamentals (such as understanding how to turn on your machine, knowing your A drive from your C drive, and recognizing the DOS prompt). Computer terms are always defined shortly after they're introduced, and explanations are as jargon-free as possible. You may have to go over certain sections dealing with advanced topics a few times to fully understand them. However, the step-by-step tutorials will guide you through even the most difficult features.

If you're an intermediate or advanced PC user, you'll find this book doesn't sacrifice depth for the sake of readability. Each of PC Tools' hundreds of features is covered, including all its advanced features. In fact, this is by far the most comprehensive book on PC Tools available.

Lastly, if you're upgrading from PC Tools Deluxe 6, you'll find this book especially useful because it points out which features are new to version 7. It details such changes in special sections in overview Chapters 1, 15, 19, and 29, and marks the discussion of each new feature in the other chapters with an icon like the one to the left of this paragraph.

How to Use This Book

PC Tools organizes its hundreds of features into several different programs so you can skip over the operations you're not interested in. Similarly, this book divides its coverage of PC Tools into eight independent parts so you don't have to read about the topics you aren't interested in. These eight parts are as follows:

Part	Chapters	Title
Part I	Chapters 1 through 3	Using CP Backup
Part II	Chapters 4 through 8	Using the Data Recovery Utilities
Part III	Chapters 9 and 10	Using the Speedup Utilities
Part IV	Chapters 11 through 14	Using the Security and Connectivity Utilities
Part V	Chapters 15 through 18	Using PC Shell
Part VI	Chapters 19 through 28	Using the Desktop Manager
Part VII	Chapters 29 through 32	Using the Windows Utilities
Part VIII	Appendixes A through E	Appendixes

For example, if you're only concerned about file and disk management, you can restrict your reading to Part V (Chapters 15 through 18); and if you only want to know how to back up your hard disk, you can just read Part I (Chapters 1, 2, and 3). You can therefore learn about any component of PC Tools in any order you want.

In addition, each chapter is designed to be as independent as possible. As a result, you can start reading from any chapter to learn about the topic it covers; extensive cross-referencing is employed to let you know when discussion of a particular feature requires you to be familiar with other chapters.

On the other hand, if you aren't sure which components of PC Tools you're interested in, you should use this book to help you decide. First, study the list of chapter headings in the Table of Contents. Next, turn to the chapters that sound useful. The beginning of each chapter is designed to let you know in very clear terms the purpose and benefits of the application that it's covering.

If you're in a hurry and just want to get a sense of what menu commands an application offers, you can refer to Appendix C for a brief description of each command. You can also find more detailed command reference sections for CP Backup at the end of Chapter 1, for Undelete at the end of Chapter 6, for Compress at the end of Chapter 9, for Commute at the end of Chapter 14, for PC Shell at the end of Chapter 15, and for the Desktop applications in Chapters 20 through 26.

This book's emphasis is on tutorial instruction. In other words, after explaining the nature of a particular feature, it generally provides a step-by-step example demonstrating how to use the feature. You'll get the most out of the tutorials if you work along with them on your PC. However, screen shots are provided with the tutorials, so you can often follow the effects of various steps even without executing them on your computer.

Conventions Used in This Book

This book uses several typographical conventions to set off special sections of text. In addition, it uses certain conventions for representing keyboard and mouse commands.

Special Text Sections

If a feature that's about to be covered is new to PC Tools 7, a "7" icon like the one to the left of this paragraph is used to mark where the discussion of the new feature begins.

If a section of text makes a point that's either tangentially related to previous sections or is especially noteworthy, the text is marked off by a "Note" icon like the one to the right of this paragraph.

If a section of text provides a useful tip, the text is marked off by a "Tip" icon like the one to the left of this paragraph.

If a section of text provides a warning to help prevent some serious data accident, the text is marked off by a "Caution" icon like the one to the left of this paragraph.

Keyboard Commands

Any PC Tools menu or option can be selected by pressing the highlighted letter in its name. This book indicates which letter is highlighted on screen by boldfacing the letter in the text. For example, if a menu named File can be selected by pressing the letter "F," the menu is represented as **F**ile; and if a dialog box option named Exit can be selected by pressing the letter "X," the option is represented as E**x**it.

In some PC Tools programs, you can select a menu or option by just pressing its highlighted letter. In these cases, to select the **F**ile menu, for example, you're instructed to press F. Similarly, to select the E**x**it option, you're instructed to press X.

In other PC Tools programs, selecting a menu or option requires holding down the ALT key and then pressing the highlighted letter. In these cases, to select the **F**ile menu, for example, you're instructed to press ALT-F. Similarly, to select the E**x**it option, you're instructed to press ALT-X.

Finally, in Desktop Manager applications, you can select a menu by pressing the ALT key, releasing ALT, and then pressing the highlighted letter of the menu. For example, to select the **F**ile menu, you're instructed to press ALT, F; and to select the **F**ile E**x**it option, you're instructed to press ALT, F, X. However, in such cases you also have the option of keeping ALT pressed down. For example, if you're instructed to press ALT, F, X, you can press ALT-F, X instead. Which you choose is entirely a matter of taste.

Mouse Commands

In this book, an instruction on selecting a command using your keyboard is often directly followed by a comparable instruction on selecting the command using your mouse. For example, to select the File Exit command, you'll typically be told to "press ALT, F, X, or click on the File menu and select Exit." The latter instruction is telling you that instead of using your keyboard, you can position your mouse pointer over the word "File" on the second line of the screen (called the *menu bar*, because it contains the names of application menus), click your mouse button to bring down the menu, position your mouse pointer over the Exit option on the menu, and then click your mouse button to select the option.

Several conventions are employed in mouse instructions. First, the highlighted letters in menu and option names are *not* boldfaced in such instructions. This helps emphasize that you're using your mouse, not pressing keys on your keyboard.

Second, instructions will usually not specify whether to press your left or right mouse button. That's because most PC Tools operations will work with a click from either button equally well. On the rare occasion when an operation requires you to use a particular button, this book will specify which button to click.

Third, instructions will sometimes ask you to *drag* your mouse. This means that instead of clicking your mouse button and then immediately releasing it, you should keep the button held down, move your mouse pointer to the specified location, and then release the button.

About PC Tools 7

The PC Tools 7 package consists of the following broad range of programs:

- CP Backup, a feature-packed hard disk backup application

- Mirror, Data Monitor, PC Format, and Install, a set of data safeguarding utilities that protect critical areas of your hard disk, deleted files, and formatted data

- Undelete, Unformat, Rebuild, DiskFix, and File Fix, a set of recovery utilities that restore deleted files, formatted data, defective disks, and damaged 1-2-3 and dBASE files

- Compress and PC-Cache, a pair of utilities for speeding up your hard disk and your access to frequently-used data

- PC Secure, Wipe, VDefend, and Commute, a collection of security and connectivity utilities

- PC Shell, an extremely powerful but easy-to-use file and disk manager, and its related programs Directory Maintenance, File Find, System Information, and View

- The Desktop Manager, a collection of over a dozen full-featured applications including a word processor, a dBASE-compatible database, telecommunications programs for both modems and fax cards, simulations of Hewlett-Packard calculators, and an appointment scheduler

- The Microsoft Windows utilities CP Launcher, CP Scheduler for Windows, CP Backup for Windows, Undelete for Windows, and TSR Manager

In a nutshell, PC Tools can protect and recover your data, manage your data, and provide virtually every type of major PC application, continuing what Ed

Mendelson of *PC Magazine* has called its "relentless quest to include every known utility in a single package." Tom Bigley of *InfoWorld* recently wrote, "It's amazing what you get for your money with the new PC Tools. If you make a list of the fundamental things you want to do with your computer, scratch off spreadsheets (but not sophisticated calculators) and graphics editors (but not a PCX viewer), you'll probably be able to find utilities in the PC Tools 7 package to handle most of your remaining tasks—all for well under $200. To top it off, version 7 adds a wealth of unexpected features."

PC Tools 7.0 Versus 7.1

PC Tools 7 was first released in May 1991. Several revised versions of this original release were then produced between May and September 1991. All these versions are now referred to as "version 7.0."

In September 1991, "version 7.1" of PC Tools was released. This version didn't introduce any new features, but it fixed a number of problems that were discovered in existing features. (Some of the most significant of these problems are discussed in appropriate sections of this book.)

In addition to relatively invisible fixes, version 7.1 created some conspicuous changes to help avoid problems. Most notably, it set PC Shell to use the file editor of PC Tools Deluxe 6 rather than the Desktop Manager's Notepads application, and to provide the directory maintenance commands of PC Tools Deluxe 6 as an alternative to the new Directory Maintenance program. For more information on these changes, see "Editing Text Files" in Chapter 16 and "Managing Your Directories" in Chapter 17.

Since in most cases versions 7.0 and 7.1 are identical, this book typically uses the term "PC Tools 7" to refer to *both* versions. In the rare instances when there are notable differences between the versions, however, explicit distinctions are made between them.

If you have PC Tools 7.0 (which you can determine quickly by checking to see if your file dates precede September 1991), you'll probably find that most of its features work perfectly on your system. However, if you *do* experience any problems, it's highly recommended that you upgrade to version 7.1, which is available *free* to any registered user of PC Tools 7.0. For more information, call Central Point Software, the publisher of PC Tools, at (503) 690-8090.

Using Windows, Menus, and Dialog Boxes

Most PC Tools programs are made up of windows, menus, and dialog boxes. The following sections briefly explain how to use these elements. More detailed information on this subject appears in appropriate spots throughout the book.

Using Windows

Most PC Tools applications place your data into a section of the screen called a *window*. Some programs only provide one window, while others (such as PC Shell and the Desktop Manager) allow you to open multiple windows. A window typically has the following elements:

- A *title bar* at the top identifying the application the window is associated with. You can move a window by clicking on its title bar and dragging it to another area on the screen.

- A *close box* in the upper-left corner. Clicking on this box closes the window.

- A *resize box* in the bottom-right corner. Clicking on this box and dragging changes the size of a resizeable window.

- A *zoom icon* in the upper-right corner. Clicking on this triangle symbol expands a resizeable window to fill the screen or contracts it to its previous size.

- *Scroll bars* along the bottom and/or right side. Clicking in the bottom bar scrolls the data in the window horizontally, while clicking in the side bar scrolls the data in the window vertically.

- *Scroll arrows* at both ends of each scroll bar. Clicking on a scroll arrow scrolls the data in the window a short distance in the direction of the arrow. If you click on the scroll arrow and keep your mouse button held down, the data scrolls continuously.

- A *scroll box* within the scroll bars. You can scroll to a particular section of a window's data by clicking on the scroll box and dragging. For example, to move to the middle of your data, drag the scroll box to the middle of its scroll bar.

Using these window elements and your mouse, you can easily resize and move windows on your screen, navigate the data in each window, and close windows.

If you don't have a mouse, you can also perform all these operations using your keyboard. This subject is covered in "The Control Menu" section that follows shortly.

Using Menus and Dialog Boxes

A PC Tools program typically provides dozens of commands. Rather than require you to memorize all these commands, the program divides them into organized lists called *menus*. For example, file-related commands are placed in a menu named **File**, editing commands are placed in a menu named **Edit**, and so on.

As explained previously, you can display a menu by pressing the menu's highlighted letter in combination with the ALT key, or by clicking on the menu's name. Once the menu is displayed, you can select any of its listed commands, or *options*, by pressing the highlighted letter of the option, or by clicking the option.

If the command doesn't lead to other options, it's executed immediately. However, if the command offers additional choices, a dialog box appears. You can move from option to option in the box by pressing TAB or SHIFT-TAB. You can also move to or select a particular option directly by simply clicking it.

The Control Menu

Menu names and options in PC Tools generally vary from program to program. However, there's one special menu, named *Control*, that's present in virtually all PC Tools applications. This menu is represented by a dash symbol in the upper-left corner of the screen, and is similar to the Control menu provided in Microsoft Windows applications. As in Windows, you can select it by pressing ALT-SPACEBAR or by clicking on its dash symbol.

The Control menu always contains at least two options: **V**ersion, which displays the version number of the application, and **C**lose, which exits the application. In addition, if a program has windows which can be adjusted, the menu typically also provides the options **S**ize, **M**aximize, and **R**estore to resize windows using the keyboard; the option **M**ove to reposition windows using the keyboard; the option **A**pplication Colors to change window colors; and the option **S**witch To to switch to a different open window.

For more information on using Control menu options, see "Using the Control Menu" in Chapter 15, "PC Shell Overview."

Getting Online Help

If you ever need more information about a PC Tools option, press the F1 function key. This brings up a help window with information relevant to what you're currently doing. If you need additional information, you can select the Index option to list all available help topics, and then select the topic you want to read about.

In addition, many PC Tools programs provide a **Help** menu. In such cases, pressing ALT-H or clicking on Help in the menu bar displays a list of subjects you can get information on. These topics typically include Keyboard, which provides explanations of such special keys as ALT, CTRL, and TAB; Basic Skills, which teaches how to choose commands, use windows and dialog boxes, and so on; and **Using Help**, which describes how to use the online help system itself.

When you're done using the help system, press ESC. You're returned to where you left off in your application.

Part I

Using CP Backup

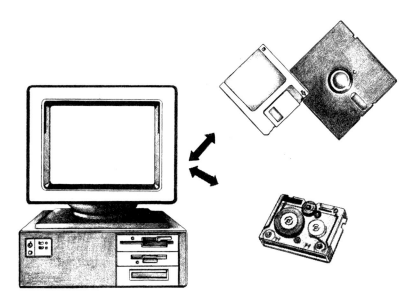

Chapter *1*

CP Backup Overview

CP Backup is a program that copies, or *backs up,* the data on your hard disk to another media for safekeeping. The most common backup media are floppy disks and tapes. However, you can also back up to another hard disk, a Bernoulli box, or any other kind of DOS device.

In PC Tools Deluxe 6, this program was called *PC* Backup. Its name has been changed to *CP* Backup to better identify it as a product of Central Point Software, the publisher of PC Tools. Like its previous version, CP Backup supports all of the following features:

- Dual memory access, or *DMA,* mode, which speeds the backup process by making your PC read and write data at the same time. Data can be transferred as quickly as 2.5MB per minute, backing up a 20MB hard disk in less than eight minutes.

- Compression of files during backup, which lets you use up to 60 percent fewer disks or tapes to store your data.

- Support for a number of popular tape drives, including drives from Colorado Memory Systems, Mountain, Irwin, and Tecmar.

- Extensive error checking, including both verification after writing to ensure readability and comparison with the original data to ensure accuracy. In addition, error protection information is saved with the data, so even if a backup disk or tape becomes damaged, its contents will typically be 100 percent recoverable.

- An easy-to-use directory tree display for selecting files to operate on, using either the keyboard or a mouse. Alternatively, you can select files using DOS wildcards and/or date ranges.

- Flexible backup options, including Full to copy the entire disk, and Incremental to incorporate new and revised files into the previous Full backup.

- A dynamic estimate of how much time, and how many disks or tapes, your backup requires as you select files and specify options.

- Setup files for preserving your file selections and menu settings so you can automate future sessions using batch files. You can create multiple setup files to cover multiple backup needs.

- Optional password-protection of your backup data.

- Three different user levels, so the program can be instantly adjusted to serve a beginner, an intermediate user, or an advanced user.

- Support for the Central Point Deluxe Option Board, which can speed the formatting of backup disks by as much as 40 percent.

In addition, the following *new* features are provided in CP Backup:

- A streamlined look and *Express* mode for quick operation.

- The ability to back up multiple drives in a single operation.

- Automatic scanning of your selected files for viruses before they are backed up.

- Sorting options for the display of files in the File List.

- Viewers for examining data files in their native formats. Thirty-eight different file formats are supported, including WordPerfect, Microsoft Word, dBASE, Lotus 1-2-3, and binary.

- Backup scheduling from within CP Backup itself, as opposed to from the Desktop's Appointment Scheduler. This feature works with either the Desktop (which takes up 25K when resident) or the new CP Scheduler program (which takes up only 5K when resident).

- The ability to search for backed-up files across all backup report (or *history*) files.

- Support for a number of new tape drives, including drives from Alloy, Tallgrass, and Wangtek.

- The ability to choose between the standard DOS format for disks and QIC 40/80 format for tapes versus CP Backup's own disk and tape formats, which use space more efficiently but are nonstandard.

- The ability to convert setup files from Norton Backup or Fastback Plus to CP Backup's format.

- Total data compatibility, and near-total keystroke and mouse click compatibility, with CP Backup for Windows, which is a Windows-based version of CP Backup also included in PC Tools 7 (see Chapter 31, "Using CP Backup for Windows").

In short, CP Backup is fast, easy to use, and feature-packed. By making the backup process relatively painless, it encourages you to create backups regularly and to protect yourself against the inevitable accidents that destroy data.

This chapter first discusses the importance of backing up data, some simple backup methods, and when it's best to use CP Backup. It next covers CP Backup's hardware support and software incompatibilities, starting CP Backup for the first time, understanding and using the different components of CP Backup screens, reconfiguring the program using menu commands, saving your settings as defaults, and exiting. Lastly, it describes CP Backup parameters, CP Backup files, new CP Backup features in version 7, and all the CP Backup menu commands.

After reading this chapter to get an overview of the program, read Chapter 2, "Backing Up Your Hard Disk," for complete information on performing backups, and Chapter 3, "Comparing and Restoring Backup Files," for complete information on comparing and restoring backup data to your hard disk.

Understanding the Importance of Backups

The most valuable component of your computer system isn't your monitor, or your printer, or your hard disk. All these physical devices are relatively affordable and can easily be replaced. Instead, the most valuable part of your system is your *data*.

For example, the information you accumulate and the work you compose over the course of six months can represent tens of thousands of dollars in time and effort. If this data is destroyed, though, no amount of money will bring it back.

Reconstructing lost data based on recollections and scattered bits of paper is a painstaking process. In the meantime, a business dependent on the data may be brought to a standstill. As a result, there is virtually no computer disaster greater than irrevocable data loss.

Because your files are so important, PC Tools provides a number of utilities for both safeguarding and recovering them. First, the Install, Mirror, Data Monitor, PC Format, Unformat, Rebuild, and Compress programs enable you to recover erased files, accidentally formatted disks, and damaged system data (see Chapters 4, 5, 6, and 9). Second, the DiskFix program detects and repairs defects that develop in your disks due to normal wear-and-tear usage (see Chapter 7). Third, the File Fix program repairs defects that can develop in dBASE- and Lotus 1-2-3-compatible data files (see Chapter 8).

These utilities are extremely capable, but they aren't infallible. For example, if a sudden power spike from an electrical outlet sends a surge of voltage through your hard disk; or your computer drops from a height of several feet while being moved; or your hard disk's read/write heads crash against the data platter (similar to a record player's needle scratching across a record, only much worse), the damage to certain files may be so severe that no utility will recover them. In addition, utilities offer absolutely no protection against such calamities as your computer being stolen or lost in transit. Therefore, the only surefire way to protect your data is to periodically back it up and store the backup copies in a safe place.

Determining Your Need for CP Backup

CP Backup isn't the only way to back up your data.

For example, if you're working for hours on a single file, it's recommended that you save the file every 15 minutes to your hard disk *and* save it every hour to a floppy disk. In addition to protecting against disk problems, the copy gives you a slightly older version of the file to fall back on in case you quickly regret making some major change. If you only work with a few files at a time, this procedure may provide you with most of the backups you need.

Also, if you typically work with only a few small directories of data, you may find it easiest to back up each directory by copying it directly to a floppy disk using the DOS COPY or XCOPY command.

Even in such cases, though, it's recommended that you use CP Backup occasionally to back up your entire hard disk. This will ensure the preservation of your programs, your batch files and device drivers, your older data, and the disk's overall structure, in addition to the data you're working with regularly.

On the other hand, if you frequently revise files all over your hard disk, or if you have a directory with more data files than a floppy disk can hold, or if your data fills many disks, it's recommended that you use CP Backup as your primary backup method.

A typical procedure is to perform a partial backup that covers only new and revised files every day, and then a full backup of the entire hard disk once a week. Detailed information about such backup techniques appears in Chapter 2, "Backing Up Your Hard Disk."

CP Backup Hardware Support

CP Backup has a number of outstanding features, but the area where it really shines is in its support of tape drives.

Unlike most backup programs, CP Backup provides explicit support for a wide range of popular tape drives. This is important, since these drives offer a convenient way to back up large amounts of data at a relatively low cost. For example, at the time of this writing the Colorado Jumbo 250, which can save up to 120MB on a single tape (meaning it can save the *compressed* contents of a 250MB hard disk), was selling through mail order dealers for under $320; and the Jumbo 120, which can save up to 60MB on a single tape (meaning it can save the *compressed* contents of a 120MB hard disk), was selling for under $240.

The tape drives supported by CP Backup are as follows:

- Alloy Retriever \120, \200, \525, \2000, and \2200

- ArchiveXL 5580

- CMS T2120

- Colorado Jumbo 120 and 250

- Compaq Internal 40MB and 80MB Tape Backup

- IBM PS/2 Internal Tape Backup (80MB)

- Irwin AccuTrak 2040, 2080, A120e, and A250e, and Irwin SX series

- Mountain FileSafe series FS4000 and FS8000

- Tallgrass FS120 and FS300

- Tecmar QT-40

- Wangtek 3040 and 3080

You should also note the following:

- Tape drive names tend to change quickly. As a result, drives with both older and newer names from the ones listed are in many cases also supported by PC Tools. To make sure a drive is supported, check with the manufacturer.

- In most cases, internal, external, and micro channel versions of the drives listed are all available and supported by PC Tools. However, to make sure a particular type of drive is supported, check with the manufacturer.

- Certain drives may be supported when connected to your floppy disk controller but *not* supported when connected to customized controller cards. (For example, at the time of this writing, the Colorado drives are supported when connected to a floppy drive controller, or to the AB-10 or FC-10 controllers, but not when connected to the more recent TC-15 controller.) Also, certain drives may not work with 8088 machines. For more information, check with the manufacturer.

- The numbers 40 and 80 in drive names typically represent 40MB and 80MB, which are the amounts of data the drive's tapes normally store. You can also use extra length tapes for 40MB drives that store 60MB, for 80MB drives that store 120MB, and so on.

If you have a tape drive that isn't explicitly supported by CP Backup, you can still use it with the program, but only by configuring the drive as a DOS device. Along the same lines, you can use a variety of other media for backup, such as another hard disk or a Bernoulli box, as long as they're defined as DOS devices. The drawback is that backups will take place at CP Backup's slowest speed setting (called *Low Speed/DOS Compatible*), as opposed to the *High Speed* setting available for explicitly supported devices. On the other hand, you can get around this problem by scheduling backups to take place when you're away from your machine. For more information, see "Scheduling Backups" in Chapter 2.

Lastly, if you opt to use floppy disks for backup, you may want to invest in Central Point's Deluxe Option Board. This card will work with CP Backup to format your backup disks from 20 percent to 40 percent faster (producing the greatest speed increases on advanced PCs, such as 80286 and 80386 machines). The card also lets you create archival copies of copy-protected disks, and transfer data between PC and Macintosh 3 1/2-inch disks. For more information, call Central Point Software at (503) 690-8090.

CP Backup Software Incompatibilities

Before using CP Backup, it's important that you know what programs aren't compatible with it or will create problems when running with it.

First, CP Backup is only partially compatible with PC Backup version 6. Specifically, CP Backup can restore any files backed up by version 6 at the High Speed or Medium Speed settings. However, it *cannot* restore version 6 files backed up at the Low Speed/DOS Compatible setting, because version 7 now employs a more efficient Low Speed compression scheme. Therefore, if you have previous Low Speed backup files, delete them if they're obsolete, or prominently mark their disks or tapes as being made with PC Backup 6, and store them separately from your new backup files.

Also, CP Backup doesn't provide any support for restoring its backup files with PC Backup 6. As a result, you should only use CP Backup to work with CP Backup files.

Second, if you're using any memory-resident programs, it's highly recommended that you turn them off before running CP Backup. You should especially avoid *invoking* any memory-resident program in the middle of the backup or restore process, as doing so may cause data errors.

Third, if you use a non-PC Tools disk caching program, it's highly recommended that you first experiment with a trial backup to make sure CP Backup is compatible with it (especially if the program is set to cache floppy drives). If you experience problems, you may need to discard the program you're using in favor of the PC-Cache program that comes packaged with PC Tools 7 (see Chapter 10, "Speeding Data Access Using PC-Cache").

Fourth, if you're using a fax card, it's highly recommended that you turn it off before running CP Backup. Otherwise, a fax could arrive in the middle of the backup or restore process, which could cause data errors.

Fifth, if you run CP Backup under multitasking software such as Microsoft Windows or DESQview, take care to avoid selecting open files that might change during the course of a backup or restore operation. If you're running Windows in Standard or Enhanced 386 mode, it's highly recommended that you instead use the CP Backup for Windows program included in PC Tools 7, which is specifically designed to work in a multitasking environment (see Chapter 31, "Using CP Backup for Windows").

Sixth, under certain circumstances you may experience problems using CP Backup with QEMM or 386Max. However, these problems can often be eliminated with a small change to your CONFIG.SYS file (see Appendix A, "PC Tools Installation and Configuration"). Specifically, if you're using QEMM and backing up to floppy disks, include the option DMA=20 on your DEVICE=QEMM line; if you're backing up to tape, include the option DMA=32 on your DEVICE=QEMM line. On the other hand, if you're using 386Max and backing up to either floppy disks or tapes, include the option DMA=32 on your DEVICE=386MAX.SYS line. If you still experience difficulties after revising your CONFIG.SYS file, contact the technical support staff at Quarterdeck for your QEMM problem or at Qualitas for your 386Max problem.

Lastly, if you're connected to a NOVELL NetWare or IBM LAN network, you can use CP Backup from a write-protected directory on the server. (For installation requirements, see Appendix B, "Installing and Using PC Tools on a Network.") However, on some networks you may encounter problems backing up due to a conflict with CP Backup's timer display. If this occurs, simply turn the timer off. For more information, see "Setting the Time Display" in Chapter 2.

Running and Configuring CP Backup

Before you can use CP Backup, you must copy its files to your hard disk using the Install program. For information on how to do this, see Appendix A, "PC Tools Installation and Configuration."

Also, as just mentioned in the previous section, it's recommended that you clear your system of all memory-resident programs other than PC Tools programs and your mouse driver. This is especially important the first time you run the program, because it helps ensure nothing interferes with CP Backup's initial equipment checking and backup testing.

When your system is set up properly, follow these steps to run CP Backup and configure it for your PC:

1. Type **CPBACKUP** (with no spaces) from the DOS prompt and press ENTER. If this is the first time you've run the program, the following message box appears:

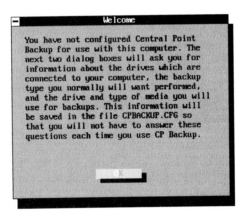

As the message explains, CP Backup needs to identify the type of devices your system has available for performing backups (for example, disk drives and tape drives), the type of media you'll use (for example, 1.44MB disks or 120MB tape cartridges), and the type of backup you'll typically perform. The program will then store the information in a configuration file for future sessions.

2. If you have a tape drive, make sure it's on and connected to your PC. Also, remove any cartridge in the drive, as this allows CP Backup to determine the drive's capacity more accurately.

3. Press ENTER or click OK. You're asked if you have a tape drive. If you don't, press ENTER or click No, and then skip to step 6. Otherwise, press Y or click Yes.

4. A message appears asking whether you want CP Backup to search your system for your tape drive's addressing information, or if you want to enter the information manually. First give the program the chance to search for the information itself by pressing ENTER or clicking Search. If your drive is connected to your floppy disk controller card, or if it's connected to a card that CP Backup recognizes, the needed data is found in a few seconds, and you're moved to the Define Equipment dialog box. In this case, go to step 6.

5. If CP Backup couldn't locate the data needed, a message box appears saying your drive couldn't be found. In this case, press ESC twice to exit the program; repeat steps 1 through 3 to run the program again; and this time press C or click Configure. The following dialog box appears requesting your controller card's port address, IRQ, DMA, and Data Rate:

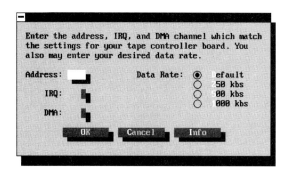

First check Table 1-1, which lists the I/O port addresses, IRQ channels, and DMA channels typically used by various popular tape drive controller cards, and then look up any additional information required from your controller card's manual. (You can also display addressing information by pressing ALT-I or clicking Info, and then exit the help screen by pressing ESC.) When you've found the data you need, move to each field using TAB or your mouse and type in the appropriate values. When you're done, press ALT-O or click OK to continue.

If you've changed the factory settings specified in Table 1-1, enter your revised settings instead. For the appropriate data rate, see your card's manual, or just accept the default setting. See also the ADDR=address-irq-dma parameter in the "CP Backup Parameters" section later in this chapter.

Tape Controller Card	Address	IRQ	DMA
Alloy FTFA Controller	340	3	2
Alloy Retriever 60e	340	3	2
Irwin 4100	370	3	2
Tecmar QT	300	3	1
Tecmar QT-40e	300	3	1
Mountain MACH2	3E7	6	2
Wangtek Lightning	300	3	1

Table 1-1. *Tape Drive Controller Card Addressing Data*

6. A Define Equipment dialog box like this appears, listing any backup drives detected in your system:

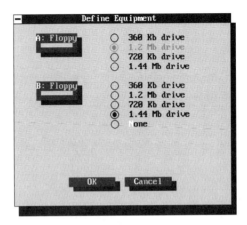

A dot appears next to each drive identifying its maximum capacity. If the appropriate option isn't selected (for example, if the 1.44MB option is marked for a 720K drive), correct the error by selecting the appropriate choice. You can move from option to option using TAB and the arrow keys, and then change a setting by pressing ENTER; or you can simply click on a different option using your mouse. When you're done, press O or click OK.

7. A Choose Drive & Media dialog box like this appears, listing the drives and media capacities you've specified:

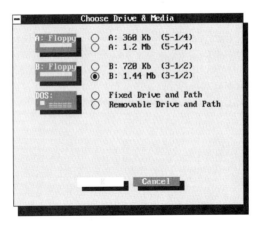

First, decide on the drive or drives you'll be using for backup operations. If all your drives are of different types (for example, a 1.2MB drive, a 1.44MB drive, and a tape drive), you can use only *one* of them for backup.

However, if your A and B drives are of the same type (for example, if they're both 1.44MB drives), you can use *both* of them. To do so, press T or click the Two Drive Backup option that appears at the bottom of the dialog box for same-drive systems. This sets CP Backup to prompt you to insert disks in both drives before a backup operation. As soon as the first backup disk is full, CP Backup will immediately begin writing to the second disk. You can then replace the first disk with your third one, and so on, with no backup time lost while you swap disks in and out.

8. When you've decided on your backup drives, select the media you'll use for backup. (For example, if you're going to be using 1.44MB disks in a 1.44MB drive, select that option instead of the 720K option.) If you selected the Two Drive Backup option in step 7, choose the media for only one drive; CP Backup will automatically apply your selection to both of your drives.

   When you're done selecting your backup drive and media, press O or click OK.

9. If you selected a Fixed Drive and Path (such as a hard disk) or a Removable Drive and Path (such as a Bernoulli box) in step 8, you're prompted to specify the path to use for backup and restore operations. A *path* is a line that specifies the drive and directory you want to work with. For example, to use the root directory of drive E, you'd type the path **E:**, while to use a directory named BACKUP on drive F, you'd type the path **F:\BACKUP**.

   Type an appropriate path for your drive, and then press ENTER or click OK. CP Backup will work with this drive at the Low Speed/DOS Compatible setting, so no further testing is required. Therefore, to finish the configuration procedure for your Fixed or Removable device, go to step 16.

10. If you selected a floppy drive or tape drive in step 8, you're told that a Backup Confidence Test is about to be performed to determine the highest backup speed your system is capable of. There are three available settings: High Speed, which is the fastest method for disks and tapes; Medium Speed, which is for computer systems that don't support DMA backups; and Low Speed/DOS Compatible, which is for generic DOS devices such as other hard disks and unsupported tape drives.

11. Locate a disk or tape that's either blank or contains obsolete data. If you're using a disk, be sure it's of the capacity you selected in step 7 (for example, 1.44MB if you designated your drive to back up to 1.44MB floppies). Also, be sure your disk or tape is in working order. Otherwise, CP Backup may attribute problems with the media to problems with your system and set CP Backup to Low Speed/DOS Compatible.

12. Insert the disk or tape into your designated backup drive. (If you selected the Two Drive Backup option in step 7, insert the disk in drive A.)

13. Press ENTER or click Continue. You're prompted to confirm that your floppy or tape doesn't contain any important data.

14. Press ENTER or click OK; and if your disk or tape contains data, press ENTER or click OK once more to confirm that it's all right to erase the data.

15. A sample backup session now begins. CP Backup first reads the directories and files on your hard disk, and then backs up arbitrary files to your floppy disk or tape, while a bar near the top of the screen shows the operation's progress. When the backup is completed, a compare operation is run to verify that the backup data on the floppy or tape conforms to the original data on your hard disk. If it does, a message appears that your system passed at the High Speed setting.

    Otherwise, the testing is repeated at the Medium Speed setting and, if necessary, repeated again at the Low Speed setting. If this occurs, it may be due to a software or hardware conflict, rather than inherent limitations in your system. For more information, see the "Using the Configure Menu" section later in this chapter.

16. When the testing is finished and a speed setting has been established, press ENTER or click Continue. The message "Saving defaults to configuration file" appears, and your settings are preserved in a file named CPBACKUP.CFG for future sessions.

You can revise the settings you've just made at any time through CP Backup's Configure menu. For more information, see "Using the Configure Menu" later in this chapter. You can also go through the entire configuration process again by deleting the CPBACKUP.CFG file, which is stored in either your PC Tools directory or, if you allowed the Install program to create DATA and SYSTEM subdirectories, in your DATA subdirectory. If you erase the file and then run CP Backup, the program will behave as if you're running it for the first time.

Once your configuration is completed, the CP Backup main menu in Figure 1-1 appears. It's from this menu that you'll begin your CP Backup activities.

Exploring the CP Backup Screens

As just mentioned, CP Backup starts you off with the main menu that appears in Figure 1-1. This menu lists the three principal options of the program:

- *Backup*   This option lets you back up the data from your hard disk to another media.

- ***Restore***   This option lets you restore your data from your backup media to your hard disk.

- ***Compare***   This option lets you compare the data on your hard disk with the data on your backup media to verify that the backup data is accurate.

The right side of the window describes each option verbally, and also describes it visually via icons representing a PC, data, and your backup drive. Notice that for the Backup option, arrows point from the PC to the backup drive. If you press DOWN ARROW to select the Restore option, the arrows switch direction to point to the PC. If you press DOWN ARROW again to select the Compare option, the arrows go in both directions (and include question marks) to indicate that data on one end is being checked against data on the other end. To return to the Backup option, press UP ARROW twice.

To select an option, you can move to it and press ENTER, or just press its first letter, or click on it. For example, select the **B**ackup option by pressing B. After a moment, you see the screen in Figure 1-2. This is called the *Express* screen, because it allows you to perform a backup with just a few keystrokes or mouse clicks. (You can also easily switch to the Tree and File List display used in PC Backup 6, as you'll see shortly.)

Figure 1-1.   *The CP Backup main menu*

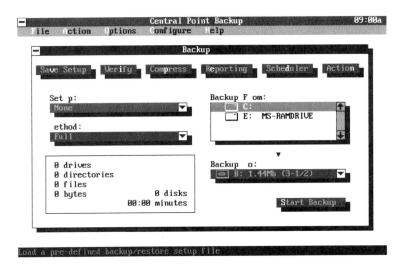

Figure 1-2.   *The Express Backup screen*

The Express screen is made up of the following elements:

- The title bar and menu bar at the top of the screen, which contain the Control menu and five CP Backup menus.

- The six command buttons near the top of the window, which let you quickly select the most commonly used backup options. (You can also select these commands through the CP Backup menus, but doing so requires a few extra keystrokes or mouse clicks.)

- The status boxes, which list the setup file currently loaded (if any); your backup method (which, by default, is Full); the drives, directories, files, and total number of bytes selected (which are initially all 0); the drive or drives to back up *from* (which is initially the hard disk you were set to when configuring CP Backup); and the drives to back up *to* (that is, the drives you specified during your CP Backup configuration).

- The command button in the lower-right corner of the window, which initiates a backup operation using the current settings.

- The message bar at the bottom, which displays a one-line description of whatever option you're currently on. (For more information on an option, press F1 to get context-sensitive help.) The bar also displays various messages as you perform CP Backup activities.

You can select any option on the screen by pressing its highlighted letter or clicking it. For example, select the Action command in the upper-right corner by pressing N or clicking Action. You're instantly returned to the main menu. This provides you with a quick way of switching between the Backup, Restore, and Compare screens.

Now switch to Restore mode by pressing R or clicking Restore. The screen in Figure 1-3 appears, which is very similar to the Backup screen. The main differences are

- The six command buttons near the top of the window now display the most commonly used restore options instead of backup options.

- The backup Method status box has been replaced by a History box. This displays your selected *history* file, which is a file that contains information on a particular backup operation, and is required to perform restore and compare operations.

- The box previously labeled Backup From is now labeled Restore To, and the box previously labeled Backup To is now labeled Restore From, to reflect the fact that restore operations reverse the data flow of backup operations.

- The command button in the lower-right corner has changed to initiate a restore operation instead of a backup.

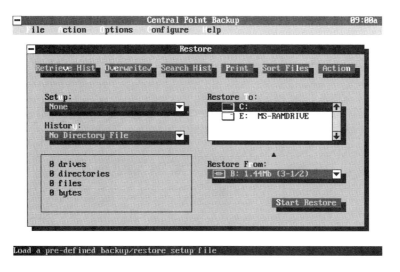

Figure 1-3. *The Express Restore screen*

Now switch to Compare mode by pressing N, C, or by clicking Action and Compare. The screen in Figure 1-4 appears, which is almost identical to the Restore screen. The only differences are the following (all in the right side of the window):

- The box previously labeled Restore To is now labeled Compare To, and the box previously labeled Restore From is now labeled Compare From.

- The command button in the lower-right corner now initiates a compare operation instead of a restore.

Lastly, to return to the Backup screen, press N, B, or click Action and Backup.

If you're familiar with earlier versions of PC Backup, you may wonder what happened to the Tree List and File List used to select directories and files. Actually, they're still available, and there are two ways to access them.

While in Express mode, you can bring up the Tree and File List windows by pressing R (which takes you to the Backup From or Restore From box), moving to the listed drive you want using the arrow keys, and pressing ENTER. You can also simply double-click on the drive you want in the Backup From or Restore From box.

If you're in the Backup screen, CP Backup reads the directories on the selected drive, organizes them into a directory tree, and then displays the Tree List screen shown in Figure 1-5. You can then select the directories and individual files you want (as explained in the next section). When you're done, you can return to the Express window by pressing F10.

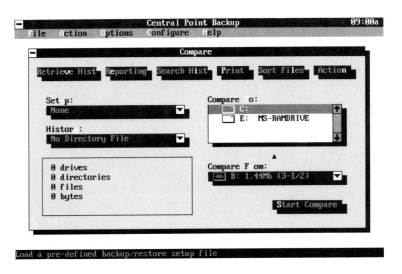

Figure 1-4.   *The Express Compare screen*

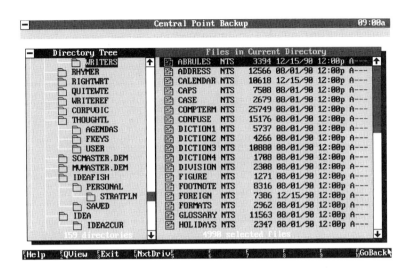

Figure 1-5.   *The Express Tree List*

If you're in the Restore or Compare screen, however, invoking the Tree List first brings up a list of the history files on the selected hard disk — or, if there are none, a prompt to insert the last disk or tape of your backup set. Once you select the history file you want, or insert the appropriate last disk or tape, a Tree List screen appears displaying the directories and files that were included in your specified backup operation. You can then select the data you want to restore or compare. When you're done, you can return to the Express window by pressing F10.

You can also switch to working exclusively in the Tree List screen by turning Express mode off. (This feature is *not* supported in CP Backup for Windows.) To do so, press C, U, E, O, or click on the Configure menu and select User Level, Express Mode, and OK. CP Backup displays the screen shown in Figure 1-6. This screen is made up of the following components:

- The title bar and menu bar at the top of the screen, which are identical to their counterparts in Express mode.

- The Settings status box, which displays the drive or drives you're backing up from or restoring to, your backup drives, and the setup file you've loaded (if any).

- The Statistics box, which displays the number of directories and files you've selected, as well as the total number of bytes selected.

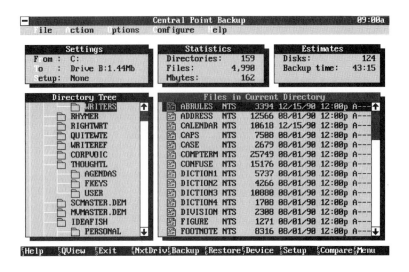

Figure 1-6.   *The Tree List Backup screen*

- The Estimates box, which estimates the number of disks or tapes, and the amount of time, the backup operation you're specifying requires. The display changes dynamically as you select files and menu options.

- The Tree List at the left, which displays the directories of the drive to be backed up or the drive to restore from.

- The File List at the right, which displays the files in the selected directory.

- The message bar at the bottom, which displays the commands assigned to function keys F1 through F10.

These screen elements are covered in the following sections.

If you prefer this display to Express mode, you can make it the default while you're using it by pressing F, D, or by clicking on the File menu and selecting Save as Default. For more information, see "Saving Your Settings as Defaults" later in this chapter.

The CP Backup Tree List and File List

The Tree List is a window that displays the current drive's directories. It's called a tree because it depicts your root directory (typically C:\) as having a trunk extending from it, and all your other directories as branching out from the trunk.

When you turn off Express mode, the Tree List is automatically activated, as indicated by its "Directory Tree" title being highlighted. Pressing DOWN ARROW or UP ARROW moves you along the Tree by directory; pressing RIGHT ARROW or LEFT ARROW moves you to the next or previous directory at the same level as your current one; pressing PGDN or PGUP moves you to the next or previous window; and pressing END or HOME moves you to the bottom or top of the Tree. You can also scroll the Tree vertically using your mouse.

Initially, all directories in the Tree List are highlighted, meaning they're selected for a backup or restore operation. To unselect a directory, and also all its sub-directories, move to it and press ENTER, or click it with your mouse. The highlighting of both the directory and its subdirectories disappears. Pressing ENTER or clicking again restores the highlighting.

Similarly, selecting or unselecting the root directory (that is, pressing HOME and ENTER) selects or unselects the entire Tree, because all other directories are subdirectories of the root.

When the cursor is on a directory in the Tree List, that directory's contents are displayed in the File List, which is the window on the right side of the screen. If the directory is selected, the files are highlighted; if it's unselected, they're not high-lighted.

To activate the File List, press TAB. The title highlighting shifts over from the "Directory Tree" heading to the "Files in Current Directory" heading.

Up to 14 rows of files are displayed at a time. By default, each row shows a single file's name, size, creation date and time, and attributes (see "Selecting Files by Attributes" in Chapter 2). You can alternatively restrict the display to filenames alone by pressing O, D, L, ESC, ESC, TAB, PGDN, PGUP. The space saved by not having to show file characteristics is used to display *three* files per row, or up to 42 (3 × 14) files in the window. To switch back to the long format display, press the same keystroke sequence again.

You can also sort the display in a variety of ways. To do so, first press O, D, O. This brings up a dialog box that lets you sort by Name, Extension, Date, or Size. In addition, you can specify your sort order to be ascending (lowest to highest) by leaving the Sort Descending option off, or descending (highest to lowest) by selecting the option to toggle it on and place a checkmark to its left. When you're done, pressing O puts your settings into effect.

After adjusting the display to your tastes, you can move by file using the arrow keys, by window using PGDN and PGUP, and to the last or first file using END or HOME. Alternatively, you can scroll the list of files vertically using your mouse.

When you're in the Backup screen, you can examine any file by moving to it and pressing F2. This brings up a window in the center of the screen showing the file's data. CP Backup draws upon 38 viewers to attempt to display the file in its native format. (For more information, see "Viewing Files" in Chapter 18.) If it selects the wrong viewer, you can choose a different one by pressing F6, moving to the viewer you want, and pressing ENTER. You can also search through the window using F7, expand and contract the window using F8, and view the previous or next file in the List using F9 or F10. When you're done with the View window, press ESC to close it.

You can also select and unselect individual files in the File List in the same way as individual directories in the Tree List. This enables you to back up or restore precisely the files you want. However, your individual file settings are retained only as long as you don't change the selection status of the files' directory. In other words, if you return to the Tree List and select or unselect a directory (even indirectly via a parent directory above it), that directory's individual file settings are discarded and all its files are changed to the new setting. Therefore, it's a good idea to make all your directory selections before making any file selections.

To get a feel for selecting and unselecting directories and files, follow these steps:

1. If you aren't in the Tree List, press TAB. The Directory Tree title should be highlighted.

2. Press HOME to move to the root directory.

3. Press ENTER to toggle the selection status of the entire Tree. If the Tree was highlighted, it's now unhighlighted; if it was unhighlighted, it's now highlighted. Also, the numbers in the Statistics box are revised to reflect the Tree's new status.

4. Press ENTER one or two more times, leaving the Tree unselected and the Statistics box filled with zeros. (If you previously selected other drives for a multidrive backup, the Statistics box will still indicate the selections from those drives.)

5. Press DOWN ARROW to move to the first directory below the root. Notice that the File List immediately changes to display the contents of the directory.

6. Press ENTER. The directory is selected, as indicated by the files to the right becoming highlighted. In addition, any subdirectories of the directory are selected and highlighted. The rest of the directories are unaffected.

7. Press TAB to move to the File List. The window's title is highlighted to indicate that you've chosen to work with it.

8. Press ENTER. The first file in the list is unselected.

9. Press END to move to the last file.

10. Press ENTER, and then press UP ARROW. This file is also unselected.

11. Press TAB to return to the Tree List.

12. Press ENTER to unselect the directory. Your individual file settings are discarded, and all the files are unselected.

13. Press HOME and ENTER. Your individual directory setting is discarded, and all the directories are selected again.

The Tree List and File List make it easy to select directories and files interactively. However, when it's more convenient to select files using DOS wildcards and/or date ranges, you can use the **S**election Options commands instead. For more information, see "Using the Options Menu" in Chapter 2.

The CP Backup Message Bar

The message bar displays information relevant to the CP Backup activity taking place. For example, if you're on a menu name, the bar provides a brief description of the menu's purpose, and if you're on a menu option, the bar tells you the option's function. (To get more extensive descriptions, press F1.) The bar also displays progress reports during backup, restore, and compare operations.

When no special activity is taking place, the message bar displays one-word descriptions of the operations assigned to the first ten function keys (F11 and F12 aren't supported). These are as follows:

Function Key	Action
F1 (Help)	Brings up context-sensitive help
F2 (QView)	Displays the contents of the selected file in its native format
F3 (Exit)	Selects **F**ile E**x**it
F4 (NxtDriv)	Displays the Tree List and File List for the next drive when you've selected a multiple drive backup
F5 (Backup)	Selects **A**ction **S**tart **B**ackup
F6 (Restore)	Selects **A**ction **S**tart **R**estore
F7 (Device)	Selects **C**onfigure **C**hoose Drive and Media
F8 (Setup)	Selects **C**onfigure **D**efine **E**quipment
F9 (Compare)	Selects **A**ction **S**tart **C**ompare
F10 (Menu)	Like ALT, activates the menu bar

Clicking on the function key description in the message bar has the same effect as pressing the function key.

The CP Backup Title Bar and Menu Bar

At the top of the screen are the title and menu bars, which contain the six menus available in CP Backup (along with, in the upper-right corner, the system time). Follow these steps to examine the menus:

1. Press F or click File to display the **F**ile menu, which lets you load and save setup files that preserve your file selections and menu settings, save your

current file and menu settings as defaults for future sessions, print a selected report about a backup operation, and exit the program.

2. Press RIGHT ARROW to display the **A**ction menu, which displays different options depending on whether you're in the Backup, Restore, or Compare screen. The menu lets you initiate a backup, restore, or compare operation; set the drives you want to back up from, or the drive to restore to or compare to; choose the directories you want to work with; schedule backups (in the Backup screen) or search for a particular history file (in the Restore and Compare screens); and switch to one of the two other screens.

3. Press RIGHT ARROW again to display the **O**ptions menu, which provides 1, 5, or 13 options, depending on your user level (see the next section). In Advanced mode, the menu lets you select your backup method, direct a backup report to printer or disk, select the degree of compression, set data verification, select standard or PC Tools formatting, set when formatting is performed, set error protection, set virus detection, select whether to direct backup reports to your hard disk in addition to the backup media, turn prompting about overwriting files on or off, turn the elapsed time display during backup on or off, set file selection options, and set display options.

4. Press RIGHT ARROW again to display the **C**onfigure menu, which lets you define your backup drive and media, define your backup equipment, set your backup speed, select a user level (to set the number of commands in the **O**ptions menu), and turn Express mode on or off.

5. Press RIGHT ARROW again to display the **H**elp menu, which displays a range of topics you can read about online. You can also get help anytime by pressing F1.

6. Press ESC and ALT-SPACEBAR to display the Control menu, which lets you display the program's version number and exit the program.

7. Press ESC to close the menu and return to the Tree List.

Of these menus (see Figure 1-7), **C**onfigure is covered in the next section, **O**ptions and the Backup commands in **A**ction are covered in Chapter 2, and the Restore and Compare commands in **A**ction are covered in Chapter 3.

Using the Configure Menu

When you ran CP Backup for the first time, you configured it by specifying your backup drives, backup media, and backup speed. These settings can be changed using the **C**onfigure menu. In addition, you can use the menu to change your user level, and toggle Express mode on or off. When you're done adjusting options, you

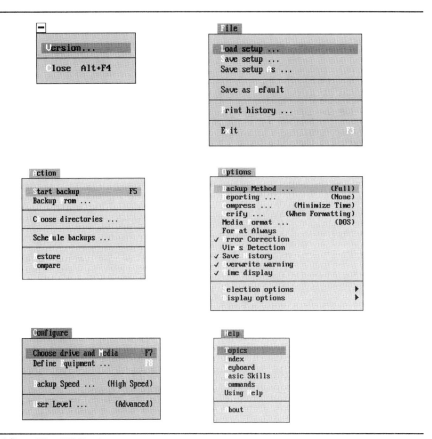

Figure 1-7.   *The CP Backup menus*

can save all your selections as new CP Backup defaults or as alternative settings in a setup file.

The menu provides the following four options: Choose Drive and Media, Define Equipment, Backup Speed, and User Level. These options are covered in the next three sections. In addition, be sure to read the section following them, "Saving Your Settings as Defaults."

Choosing Your Equipment, Drive, and Media

To revise your settings in the Define Equipment and Choose Drive & Media dialog boxes, press C, E or F8, or click on the Configure menu and select Define Equipment. As when you first ran the program, CP Backup asks if you have a tape drive. If you do, press Y, and then repeat steps 4 through 9 of the "Running and Configuring CP Backup" tutorial earlier in this chapter. Otherwise, press N, and then repeat steps 6 through 9 of the "Running and Configuring CP Backup" tutorial.

On the other hand, if you want to revise only the settings in the Choose Drive & Media box, press C, M or F7, or click on the Configure menu and select Choose Drive and Media. Select a different drive and/or backup media, and then press O or click OK.

When you're done changing settings, you're returned to the Configure menu. To complete the procedure, press ESC to close the menu.

Setting Your Backup Speed

To select a different backup speed, press C, B, or click on the Configure menu and select Backup Speed. The following dialog box appears:

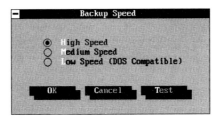

Set backups to proceed at the fastest (DMA-based) speed by pressing H or clicking High Speed; at the middle (non-DMA) speed by pressing M or clicking Medium Speed; or at the slowest (DOS device) speed by pressing L or clicking Low Speed/DOS Compatible.

Alternatively, make the program retest your system and select the appropriate speed for you by pressing T or clicking Test.

When you're done, press O or click OK to exit the dialog box, and press ESC to close the menu.

Setting Your User Level and Display Mode

To adjust the number of commands in the Options menu, press C, U, or click on the Configure menu and select User Level. The following dialog box appears:

If you expect to use only the CP Backup default settings, you can limit the **O**ptions menu to a single command (**R**eporting) by pressing B or clicking Beginner. If you want a bit more control over the program, you can limit the menu to 5 commands (**B**ackup Method, **R**eporting, **O**verwrite Warning, **S**election Options, and **D**isplay Options) by pressing I or clicking Intermediate. However, if you want all 13 menu options available, press A or click Advanced. This book concentrates on using CP Backup at the **A**dvanced level.

As an entirely separate option, you can also use this dialog box to toggle Express mode on or off. To do so, press E or click Express to make the checkmark next to the option appear or disappear. Whether you work in Express mode or Tree List mode is entirely a matter of taste, because all CP Backup commands and status data are available in both modes. (One consideration to keep in mind is that the Windows version of CP Backup doesn't support Tree List mode, so if you expect to frequently switch between the DOS and Windows versions, you may prefer to stick to Express mode for the sake of consistency.)

When you're done adjusting settings, press O or click OK to exit the dialog box, and press ESC to close the menu.

Saving Your Settings as Defaults

Any changes you make using the **C**onfigure menu—as well as any of your other menu selections, and directory and file selections—will normally last only as long as your current session. If you want your settings available for future sessions, you must explicitly save them. There are three ways to do so.

First, you can save them to a setup file. You can then override CP Backup's defaults at any time by loading the file using the *setup* parameter at the DOS prompt or the Load Setup command from the File menu. For more information, see "CP Backup Parameters" in this chapter and "Using Setup Files" in Chapter 2.

Second, you can define your current settings as new CP Backup defaults by pressing F, D, or clicking on the File menu and selecting Save as Default. This replaces the information in the CPBACKUP.CFG file with your current settings, so that CP Backup automatically starts up with these settings in future sessions.

Third, you can turn on the **S**ave Configuration option in the Close dialog box before exiting. This has the same effect as selecting the **F**ile Save as **D**efault command. For more information on this option, see the next section.

Exiting CP Backup

When you're done using CP Backup, you can exit the program by bringing up its Close dialog box, specifying whether you want to save your current settings as new defaults, and then actually exiting.

You can bring up the Close dialog box in a number of ways. If you're in a screen with a menu bar, you can press F, X; or ALT-F4; or ALT-SPACEBAR, C; or ESC twice; or F3 twice. You can also click on the File menu and select Exit, or on the Control menu and select Close, or (in an Express mode screen) double-click on the Control button.

Alternatively, if you're at the main menu, you can bring up the box by pressing ESC, or F3, or X; or by clicking on the menu's Close button; or by double-clicking on the Control button; or by clicking on the Exit button in the lower-right corner.

When you perform one of these actions, the following dialog box appears:

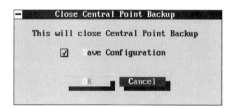

If you've changed your mind about quitting, press ESC or C, or click Cancel. The box closes and you're returned to the program.

Otherwise, decide whether you want to preserve your current settings (including your menu and dialog box settings, your file selections, and your screen selections) as defaults for future sessions, or if you want to retain the current defaults. For the former, a checkmark must appear to the left of the **S**ave Configuration option, while for the latter, the checkmark must *not* appear. You can toggle the checkmark on and off by pressing S or clicking to the left of Save Configuration.

When the **S**ave Configuration option is set appropriately, press ENTER or click OK. The program exits and returns you to the DOS prompt.

CP Backup Parameters

When you start CP Backup from the DOS prompt or modify its AUTOEXEC.BAT line, you can specify certain options, called *parameters*, following the program name. You can include any single parameter (for example, CPBACKUP /R) or combine a number of parameters (for example, CPBACKUP C:\DATA /FULL /DRIVE=TAPE) to achieve the effect you want. Keep in mind that parameters preceded by a slash require a *forward* slash (/, located on the bottom of the ? key) as opposed to the backslash (\) used to specify DOS directories.

The 26 parameters specific to CP Backup are as follows:

- /?   This "help" parameter lists and briefly describes each of CP Backup's parameters.

- **/VIDEO**   This "help" parameter lists and briefly describes the standard PC Tools video and mouse parameters. It should not be combined with any other parameters. For more information, see the "Video and Mouse Parameters" section in Appendix A, "PC Tools Installation and Configuration."

- *d:*   This parameter is a letter and colon specifying the drive you want to back up from or restore to. The parameter overrides any conflicting drive setting in CPBACKUP.CFG or a setup file.

- *filespec*   This parameter specifies the files you want to back up. It can include directory names, and the DOS wildcards ? (which represents any character) and * (which represents any group of characters). It can also consist of multiple file specifications. For example, **CPBACKUP \DATA*.DBF \WP*.TXT** would back up the dBASE-compatible files in your DATA directory and text files in your WP directory.

    If combined with the /R parameter (covered later in this section), this parameter instead restores the specified files. For example, **CPBACKUP /R *.DBF *.TXT** restores all dBASE and text files. See also the /DATE=*mmddyy-mmddyy* and /EXATTR=SHR parameters.

- *setup*   This parameter loads your specified setup file directly on startup (for example, **CPBACKUP FULL** would load a setup file named FULL.SET). Using this option is faster than selecting **File Load Setup** and typing the filename from within the program (see "Using Setup Files" in Chapter 2). In addition, it enables you to specify your setup file in a batch file, which is especially useful when you want to schedule backups to run while you're away from your PC (see "Scheduling Backups" in Chapter 2).

- **/ADDR=***address-irq-dma*   This parameter sets the three-digit port address, one-digit IRQ, and one-digit DMA for your tape drive's controller card, overriding the values you entered during your initial CP Backup configuration. You can also use the parameter /ADDR=0, which resets the values to the card's internal default settings. See also /RATE=*k*.

- **/COPY**   This parameter initiates a **F**ull **C**opy backup (see "Backup Methods and Strategies" in Chapter 2).

- **/DATE=***mmddyy-mmddyy*   When included following the *filespec* parameter (covered earlier in this section), this parameter restricts selection to those files falling within the specified date range, where *mm* is the month, *dd* is the day, and *yy* is the year.

- **/DIF**   This parameter initiates a **D**ifferential backup (see "Backup Methods and Strategies" in Chapter 2).

- **/DRIVE=***d:nnnn*   This parameter specifies the floppy disk drive and type of floppy to back up to. The *d* stands for the letter A or B, representing one of your first two disk drives; *nnnn* stands for 360 (for 360K disks), 720 (for 720K disks), 1200 (for 1.2MB disks), or 1440 (for 1.44MB disks). For example, /DRIVE=A:1440 backs up to the 1.44MB disk in drive A. See also /DRIVE=TAPE.

- **/DRIVE=TAPE**   This parameter directs the backup to use your tape drive. See also /DRIVE=*d:nnnn*.

- **/DOB**   If you have a Deluxe Option Board, this parameter turns it on to speed the formatting of disks during backup by up to 40 percent.

- **/ECC**   This parameter turns on the **O**ptions **E**rror **C**orrection switch (see "Setting Error Protection" in Chapter 2). This parameter is the default. See also /NOECC.

- **/EXATTR=SHR**   When placed after the *filespec* parameter (covered earlier in this section), this parameter excludes those files with system (S), hidden (H), and/or read-only (R) attributes from being backed up (see "Selecting Files by Attributes" in Chapter 2). You can include any combination of the letters representing the three categories; for example, /EXATTR=SH excludes system and hidden files, but not read-only files.

- **/FULL**   This parameter initiates a **F**ull backup (see "Backup Methods and Strategies" in Chapter 2).

- **/FULLERASE**   This parameter erases any of the previous contents of the backup tape, and then initiates a **F**ull backup (see "Backup Methods and Strategies" in Chapter 2).

- **/INC**   This parameter initiates an **I**ncremental backup (see "Backup Methods and Strategies" in Chapter 2).

- **/NO**   If your computer doesn't support DMA (as indicated by it freezing up or otherwise behaving strangely during backup or restore procedures), you can use this parameter to turn the DMA option in CP Backup off. You can achieve the same effect within CP Backup by selecting **C**onfigure **B**ackup **S**peed **M**edium **S**peed **OK**.

- **/NOECC**   This parameter turns off the **O**ptions **E**rror **C**orrection switch (see "Setting Error Protection" in Chapter 2). See also /ECC.

- **/NONSF**   When backing up, this parameter selects the CP Backup nonstandard format for disks (the default being the DOS format) and the CP Backup nonstandard format for tapes (which *is* the default, as opposed to the QIC 40/80 format). For more information, see "Setting Formatting" in Chapter 2. See also /SF.

- **/NOSAVE**   This parameter turns off the **O**ptions **S**ave **H**istory switch (see "Saving and Printing History Files" in Chapter 2). See also /SAVE.

- **/R**   This parameter starts CP Backup in Restore mode, bypassing both Express mode and the usual reading of the hard disk's directory for the Tree List, and prompts you to insert the last disk or tape of your backup set.

    If this parameter is followed by the *setup* parameter (covered earlier in this section), it makes CP Backup restore using the settings specified in the setup file; if this parameter is followed by the *filespec* parameter (covered earlier in this section), it makes CP Backup restore the specified files.

- **/RATE=***k*   This parameter sets the data transfer rate for tape controller cards in terms of kilobits per second, or *Kbps*. The possible values are /RATE=2 for 250Kbps, /RATE=5 for 500Kbps, and /RATE=1 for the top rate of 1000Kbps. Before using this parameter, check your controller card's manual for the highest rate the card can support. See also /ADDR=*address-irq-dma*.

- **/SAVE**   This parameter turns on the **O**ptions **S**ave **H**istory switch (see "Saving and Printing History Files" in Chapter 2). This parameter is the default. See also /NOSAVE.

- **/SEP**   This parameter initiates a **S**eparate Incremental backup (see "Backup Methods and Strategies" in Chapter 2).

- **/SF**   When backing up, this parameter selects the standard DOS format for disks (which is the default) and standard QIC format for tapes (as opposed to the default of CP Backup's tape format). For more information, see "Setting Formatting" in Chapter 2. See also /NONSF.

The general order of the command line is

CPBACKUP [*d:*] [/R] [*setup*] [*filespec*] [*all other parameters*]

The following are some examples of CP Backup command lines.

CPBACKUP WEEKLY

This command performs a backup based on the specifications in the setup file WEEKLY.SET.

CPBACKUP C:*.* /DATE=110191-120391 /FULL

This command performs a full backup on all files on drive C that were created or revised between November 1, 1991 and December 3, 1991 inclusive.

CPBACKUP C: /INC /DRIVE=TAPE /SF

This command performs an incremental backup on the files on drive C using your tape drive and the standard QIC 40/80 format.

CPBACKUP D: /R REPORT*.*

This command prompts you to insert the last disk or tape of your backup set, and then restores all files beginning with the name REPORT to your D drive. (However, if D is a floppy disk drive, this command will only work at the Low Speed/DOS Compatible setting.)

CP Backup Files

When you use the Install program to copy CP Backup to your hard disk, a number of files are generated. You may need to understand what each file represents in case a file gets damaged or you have to eliminate nonessential files to save disk space. You may also simply be curious about what all these files do. The following table lists each CP Backup file in alphabetical order and briefly describes it. In addition, if you allowed Install to create SYSTEM and DATA subdirectories in your PCTOOLS directory, it tells you in which directory each file resides.

The following "Directory" column will only be accurate if the line SET PCTOOLS=C:\PCTOOLS\DATA has been included in your AUTOEXEC.BAT file. If this line is left out, CP Backup will store certain files intended for the DATA directory into either your PCTOOLS directory or whatever directory is current instead. This does no harm, but it can make locating your various files difficult. For more information, see Appendix A, "PC Tools Installation and Configuration."

File	Directory	Description
CONVERT.EXE	PCTOOLS	Program for converting Norton Backup and Fastback Plus setup files to CP Backup files
CPBACKUP.EXE	PCTOOLS	Main program
CPBACKUP.HLP	SYSTEM	Online help
CPBACKUP.MSG	SYSTEM	Bottom-line screen help
CPBACKUP.TM	DATA	Data file for CP Backup scheduling
CPB.OVL	SYSTEM	CP Scheduler overlay file
CPB1.EXE	SYSTEM	DOS floppy disk backup subprogram
CPB2.EXE	SYSTEM	DOS floppy disk restore subprogram
CPB3.EXE	SYSTEM	DMA floppy disk backup subprogram
CPB4.EXE	SYSTEM	DMA floppy disk restore subprogram

File	Directory	Description
CPB5.EXE	SYSTEM	Backup directory creation subprogram
CPB6.EXE	SYSTEM	Floppy disk formatting subprogram
CPBDIR.EXE	SYSTEM	Floppy disk identification program
CPBH.EXE	SYSTEM	Help subprogram
CPBQ3.EXE	SYSTEM	DMA tape backup subprogram (QIC format)
CPBQ4.EXE	SYSTEM	DMA tape restore subprogram (QIC format)
CPBQ5.EXE	SYSTEM	Tape directory creation subprogram (QIC format)
CPBT3.EXE	SYSTEM	DMA tape backup subprogram (CPS format)
CPBT4.EXE	SYSTEM	DMA tape restore subprogram (CPS format)
CPBT5.EXE	SYSTEM	Tape directory creation subprogram (CPS format)
CPBV.EXE	SYSTEM	Virus identification and reporting subprogram
CPBX.EXE	SYSTEM	Express mode subprogram
CPSCHED.EXE	PCTOOLS	Memory-resident scheduler

In addition, when you begin using it, CP Backup creates certain files whose names are in the format *dyymmdds,* where *d* is the current drive, *yy* is the current year, *mm* is the current month, *dd* is the current day, and *s* is a sequence number. Also, the program creates a configuration file that stores data on your backup drives, selected files, and menu settings. These program-generated files are as follows:

File	Directory	Description
dyymmdds.DIR	DATA	History files
dyymmdds.INF	DATA	Information files for Low Speed backups
dyymmdds.RPB	DATA	Backup reports generated from history files
dyymmdds.RPC	DATA	Compare reports
dyymmdds.SET	DATA	Setup files containing program settings
CPBACKUP.CFG	DATA	Default configuration settings

Redirecting CP Backup Temporary Files

CP Backup also creates temporary files while executing. These files are ordinarily written to the same drive and directory CP Backup is executing from. However, you can redirect the files to another drive (such as a RAM disk to speed execution) by adding the following command in your AUTOEXEC.BAT file:

SET CPTMP=*d*:

with *d* representing the letter of the drive to redirect the files to. For example, **SET CPTMP=E:** would direct temporary files to be stored on drive E.

You should also determine whether the drive has enough space to hold the temporary files, because if it doesn't your operation will be interrupted by an error message. To calculate the amount of space needed, use the formula

$$70 \times \textit{number of drives selected} \times (\textit{number of files} + \textit{number of directories})$$

with *number of drives selected, number of files,* and *number of directories* representing the maximum number you expect to select for a backup or restore operation. For example, if you're likely to select up to 300 files in 10 directories on 2 different drives, you'll need $70 \times 2 \times (300 + 10)$ bytes, or 43,400 bytes, or about 42K.

New CP Backup Features in Version 7

If you're familiar with PC Backup 6, you'll find that CP Backup has been improved in version 7 through enhancements to existing features and numerous new features. The following sections briefly describe these changes and reference the section in this chapter, in Chapter 2, "Backing Up Your Hard Disk", or in Chapter 3, "Comparing and Restoring Backup Files," where they're covered more fully. Also, the new features are marked in Chapters 2 and 3 by the "7" icon to the left of this paragraph.

Improved Look

The most noticeable change in CP Backup is that its "look" has been significantly streamlined.

First, the program's default is to use Express mode screens, which hide the Tree and File Lists and instead emphasize status information and command buttons. These screens are less cluttered-looking and are easier to operate with a mouse. Also, if you tend to use default settings, these screens make it especially easy to initiate a backup, restore, or compare operation with a single keystroke or mouse click.

Second, instead of providing only one screen containing all of its commands, the program now provides a customized screen for backup operations, another for restore operations, and another for compare operations. This is true for both Express and Tree List modes, so there are actually six command screens available.

You can quickly switch from one screen to another in a particular mode by selecting one of the last two options in the **A**ction menu.

For more information on the program's new appearance, see "Exploring the CP Backup Screens" earlier in this chapter.

New Hardware and Software Support

CP Backup now provides explicit support for tape drives from Alloy, Tallgrass, and Wangtek. It also supports new tape drives from manufacturers supported in version 6. For more information, see Table 1-1.

CP Backup also lets you choose either a standard DOS format for backup disks and standard QIC 40/80 format for backup tapes, or the program's own nonstandard format for disks and tapes, which uses space more efficiently. For more information, see "Setting Formatting" in Chapter 2.

On the software side, you can now perform backups from Microsoft Windows using CP Backup for Windows, a separate but entirely compatible program packaged with PC Tools 7. For more information, see Chapter 31, "Using CP Backup for Windows."

In addition, you can use the new Convert program to translate setup files from CP Backup's competitors, Norton Backup and Fastback Plus, to CP Backup's format. To do so, simply go to the DOS prompt, type **CONVERT** followed by a file specification, and press ENTER. You can also display a list of Convert options by typing **CONVERT** by itself and pressing ENTER.

Lastly, you can now run scheduled backup sessions with the new CP Scheduler program, which takes up only 5K when resident as opposed to the 25K taken up by the PC Tools Desktop (see Chapter 23, "Using the Appointment Scheduler"). Also, your scheduling can now be set directly from within CP Backup. For more information, see "Scheduling Backups" in Chapter 2.

New Display and Scanning Options

CP Backup's new default is to display only one file per row in the File List. This provides enough space to display the file's name, size, creation date and time, and attributes. You can also switch to displaying three filenames per row by turning off the **O**ptions Display Options **L**ong Format switch.

In addition, you can now sort the File List display alphabetically, chronologically, by extension, or by size, and in ascending (lowest to highest) or descending (highest to lowest) order.

You can also now examine the data in any file—and often in its native format. That's because viewers are now included for 38 different file formats, such as WordPerfect, Microsoft Word, dBASE, Lotus 1-2-3, and binary.

For more information on all these display options, see "The CP Backup Tree List and File List" earlier in this chapter.

CP Backup also provides two new options for scanning data. First, it can scan all your selected files for a known virus before backing them up. It does this by matching file data against virus data patterns, or *signatures,* that are stored in a file named SIGNATUR.CPS. For more information, see "Setting Virus Checking" in Chapter 2, and Chapter 13, "Detecting Viruses Using VDefend."

In addition, the program can search for specified backup files across all your history files. For more information, see "Searching History Files" in Chapter 3.

New Parameters and Files

The number of command-line parameters you can use with CP Backup has increased from *10* in version 6 to *37* in version 7 (26 application-specific parameters, and 11 general video and mouse parameters). Most of these new parameters provide alternatives to selecting menu options. For more information, see "CP Backup Parameters" earlier in this chapter.

Also, the number of installed files connected to CP Backup has increased from *12* in version 6 to *23* in version 7. The extra files support such new features as Express mode screen handling, setup file conversion, scheduling, DOS formatting, QIC 40/80 formatting, and virus scanning. For more information, see "CP Backup Files" earlier in this chapter.

Expanded Help

The **Help** menu, which contained only one option in PC Backup 6, has been expanded in CP Backup 7 to offer seven subject headings. In addition, if you press F1 to expand on a message bar description, you'll find that the context-sensitive help in CP Backup has been significantly improved; the explanations displayed now tend to be much more informative about the specific feature you're examining. Therefore, if you ever get stuck while using the program, try pressing F1.

CP Backup Command Reference

Most of CP Backup's power lies in its menu commands, which let you adjust the program's settings, and initiate backup, restore, and compare operations.

Like a number of PC Tools programs, CP Backup's first menu is Control and its last menu is **Help**. These menus are covered in this book's Introduction.

The program also contains four additional menus: **File**, **Action**, **O**ptions, and **C**onfigure. The following sections cover the options in these menus. After the name of each option are the keystrokes that invoke it, its user level (for the **O**ptions menu only), a description of what the option does, and a reference to the section that discusses it in detail in this chapter, in Chapter 2, "Backing Up Your Hard Disk," or in Chapter 3, "Comparing and Restoring Backup Files."

The File Menu

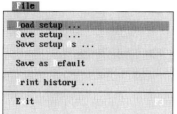

The **F**ile menu contains the following six options for loading and saving setup files, saving your current settings as new defaults, printing history files, and exiting the program:

Load Setup (F, L)

Loads a setup file to reset CP Backup to your previous option and file selections. Covered in "Using Setup Files" in Chapter 2.

Save Setup (F, S)

Saves your current option settings and file selections to the currently active setup file. Covered in "Using Setup Files" in Chapter 2.

Save Setup **A**s (F, A)

Saves your current option settings and file selections to a new setup file with the name you supply. Covered in "Using Setup Files" in Chapter 2.

Save as **D**efault (F, D)

Saves your current option settings and file selections as new CP Backup defaults to be used for future sessions. Covered in "Saving Your Settings as Defaults" in this chapter.

Print History (F, P)

Lets you print backup report information from the selected history file on either your hard disk or the last disk or tape of your backup set. Covered in "Saving and Printing History Files" in Chapter 2.

E**x**it (F, X or F3)

Brings up the Close dialog box. Pressing ENTER or O, or clicking OK, then quits CP Backup. Covered in "Exiting CP Backup" in this chapter.

The Action Menu

The Action menu's options change based on whether you're in the Backup, Restore, or Compare screen. It contains the following options for initiating a backup, restore, or compare operation; setting the drives to back up from or restore to; selecting the directories and files you want to back up, restore, or compare; scheduling backups (in the Backup screen only); searching your history files (in the Compare and Restore screens only); and switching to a different CP Backup screen:

Start Backup/Restore/Compare (A, S or F5/F6/F9)

Starts a backup, restore, or compare operation (depending on the screen you're in) using the currently selected files and option settings. Covered in "Performing a Full Backup" in Chapter 2, and the "Comparing Files" and "Restoring Files" sections in Chapter 3.

Backup From (A, F)

Lets you select the drives to back up from. This option appears only in the Backup screen. Covered in "Performing a Full Backup" in Chapter 2.

Restore/Compare To (F, T)

Lets you select the drive to restore to or compare to. This option appears only in the Restore and Compare screens. Covered in "Comparing Files" and "Restoring Files" in Chapter 3.

Choose Directories (A, H)

In the Backup screen, reads and selects all the directories on your currently selected hard drive. In the Restore and Compare screens, lets you select directories and files from the history file you choose on your hard disk or the last disk or tape of your backup set. The latter is covered in "Choosing a Backup Set" in Chapter 3.

Schedule Backups (A, D)

Lets you schedule backups. This option appears only in the Backup screen. Covered in "Scheduling Backups" in Chapter 2.

Search History Files (A, A)

Lets you search for specified backup files via the history files on either your hard disk or the last disk or tape of your backup set. This option appears only in the Restore and Compare screens. Covered in "Choosing a Backup Set" in Chapter 3.

Backup/**R**estore/**C**ompare (A, B) or (A, R) or (A, C)

Switches to the selected screen, just as if you'd selected the option from the CP Backup main menu. The screen you're currently in is the only one *not* listed on the menu. Covered in "Exploring the CP Backup Screens" in this chapter.

The Options Menu

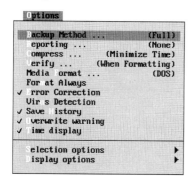

The **O**ptions menu contains a multitude of settings for adjusting the operation of backup, restore, and compare operations. The menu contains one command in Beginner mode, five commands in Intermediate mode, and 13 commands in Advanced mode. The following lists all 13 commands and specifies each command's user level:

Backup Method (O, B) (Intermediate)

Sets the backup to be **F**ull, **I**ncremental, **D**ifferential, **Fu**ll Copy, or **S**eparate Incremental. (If you're using a tape drive, **F**ull is replaced by two options, **F**ull/Append to Tape and Full/**E**rase Tape.) Alternatively, lets you scan your hard disk files for viruses. Covered in "Backup Methods and Strategies" in Chapter 2.

Reporting (O, R) (Beginner)

Directs a report on your backup operation to be sent to your printer or a text file (with a date-coded name and RPB extension) when the backup is completed. The report includes such information as the names, creation dates and times, sizes, and attributes of each backed-up file; which disk or tape each file is on; and the type of backup performed. Covered in "Saving and Printing History Files" in Chapter 2.

Compress (O, C) (Advanced)

Sets compression during backup to maximum to save space on your backup media; or to minimum to speed up the backup process; or to no compression at all. Covered in "Setting Compression" in Chapter 2.

Verify (O, V) (Advanced)

If on, verifies each track of a disk or tape during backup to ensure the data written is accurate. Covered in "Setting Error Protection" in Chapter 2.

Media Format (O, F) (Advanced)

Specifies whether to use **DOS** Standard Format or **CPS** Floppy Format for disks, and **CPS** Tape Format or **QIC** Compatible Format for tapes. The defaults are **DOS** Standard Format and **CPS** Tape Format. Covered in "Setting Formatting" in Chapter 2.

Format Always (O, M) (Advanced)

If on, formats every disk or tape during backup, even if it's already formatted. Covered in "Setting Formatting" in Chapter 2.

Error Correction (O, E) (Advanced)

If on, saves extra information on each disk or tape, which helps protect against data loss if defects later develop in the media. Covered in "Setting Error Protection" in Chapter 2.

Virus Detection (O, U) (Advanced)

Toggles on or off automatic scanning of your files for viruses before they are backed up. The default is *off*. Covered in "Setting Virus Checking" in Chapter 2.

Save History (O, H) (Advanced)

If on, saves a report about a just-completed backup to your hard disk in addition to your backup media. Covered in "Saving and Printing History Files" in Chapter 2.

Overwrite Warning (O, W) (Intermediate)

If on, alerts you when you're about to back up to a disk or tape that already contains data, or when you're about to overwrite an existing file during a restore. Covered in "Setting Overwrite Warnings" in Chapter 2.

Time Display (O, T) (Advanced)

If on (which is the default), displays a clock in a status line that times the backup process. If you find this is causing conflicts with your network system, turn it off. Covered in "Setting the Time Display" in Chapter 2.

Selection Options (O, S) (Intermediate)

This command leads to four options for selecting files to be backed up: Subdirectory Inclusion, which sets whether or not selecting a directory also selects its subdirectories; Include/Exclude Files, which lets you select files using DOS wildcards and overrides the Tree List and File List; Attribute Exclusions, which lets you exclude files based on their attributes; and Date Range Selection, which lets you narrow selections to files falling within a specified date range. The latter two options take effect only when the Include/Exclude Files command is active. All these options are covered in "Selecting Files" in Chapter 2.

Display Options (O, D) (Intermediate)

This command leads to two File List display options: Sort Options, which lets you sort the file display by name, extension, date, or size, and in ascending (lowest to highest) or descending (highest to lowest) order; and Long Format, which lets you switch between displaying one file per row and three files per row. Both of these options are covered in "The CP Backup Tree List and File List" in this chapter.

The Configure Menu

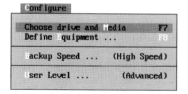

The Configure menu offers the following four options for defining your backup equipment and media, setting the backup speed, setting your user level, and setting Express mode:

Choose Drive and Media (C, M or F7)

Defines the media you're using for backup. Covered in "Choosing Your Equipment, Drive, and Media" in this chapter.

Define Equipment (C, E or F8)

Defines the drives you're using for backup. Covered in "Choosing Your Equipment, Drive, and Media" in this chapter.

Backup Speed (C, B)

Sets backup speed to High Speed (DMA), Medium Speed (non-DMA), or Low Speed/DOS Compatible. Covered in "Setting Your Backup Speed" in this chapter.

User Level (C, U)

Sets the program's user level to Beginner (**O**ptions menu displays 1 option), Intermediate (**O**ptions menu displays 5 options), or Advanced (**O**ptions menu displays all 13 options). Also, turns Express mode on or off. Covered in "Setting Your User Level and Display Mode" in this chapter.

Chapter 2

Backing Up Your Hard Disk

In Chapter 1, "CP Backup Overview," you learned how to start CP Backup, configure it for your system, and use such screen elements as the Tree List, File List, and menu bar. In this chapter, you'll learn how to use the program to back up your hard disk.

The chapter first explains the different backup methods and strategies available. It then guides you through performing a backup, changing program settings using the Options menu, saving your settings using setup files, scheduling backups, and solving typical backup problems.

Backup Methods and Strategies

CP Backup offers up to six backup methods, each of which has particular advantages and disadvantages. The following sections will help you determine the combination of methods that best fits your needs. Before you proceed, however, you need to understand two terms: *archive bit* and *history file.*

The archive bit is an indicator within every file that gets turned on, or *set,* when the file is created and every time the file is revised. The bit is typically turned off, or *cleared,* every time the file is backed up. The archive bit therefore provides a quick way of identifying files that have been created or revised since you performed your last backup.

A history file is a record of a backup operation that's automatically generated at the end of the operation. It contains the name, size, creation date and time, attributes, disk or tape location, and compression status of every file that's been backed up. It also contains the name, size, and creation date and time of the entire backup; the backup media used; and the settings of such program options as **Backup Method** and **Backup Speed**.

The history file is always saved to the last disk or tape in your set of backup disks or tapes (or *backup set*). If the **O**ptions Save **H**istory command is on (which is the default), and you're backing up at the High or Medium speed, a copy of the file is also saved to your hard disk. You can use history files to print reports on your backups, compare backup files with your hard disk files, and restore backup files to your hard disk.

To display the available backup methods, follow these steps:

1. If you aren't already in CP Backup, type **CPBACKUP** (with no spaces) from the DOS prompt and press ENTER.

   If a message appears saying you haven't configured CP Backup, first work through "Running and Configuring CP Backup" in Chapter 1.

2. Move to the Backup screen. If you're at the main menu, press B or click Backup. If you're in a Restore or Compare screen, press A, B, or click on the Action menu and select Backup.

3. Press C, U, A, O, ESC to set the program to the Advanced user level. As explained in "Setting Your User Level and Display Mode" in Chapter 1, this sets the **O**ptions menu to make all of its commands available.

4. Press O, B, or click on the Options menu and select Backup Method.

If you *don't* have a tape drive attached to your system, a dialog box like this appears:

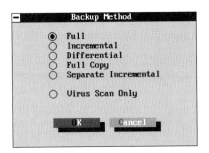

Otherwise, a similar box appears that substitutes two tape methods—Full/Append to Tape and Full/Erase Tape—in place of the Full option. All possible options offered by the box are as follows:

- *Full*   This method backs up all selected files, regardless of their archive bit settings, and clears their archive bits. This option is the default.

- *Full/Append to Tape*   This method performs a Full backup to a tape, starting at the point where the previous backup on the tape ends.

- *Full/Erase Tape*   This method first erases the tape in your tape drive, and then performs a Full backup to the tape.

- *Incremental*   This method backs up only files that have been created or revised since the last backup and clears their archive bits. It then merges its history file with the history files of previous backups. (This option is available only if you're set to back up to a floppy drive, or to a supported tape drive using the CPS format. For more information on the latter, see "Setting Formatting" later in this chapter.)

- *Differential*   This method backs up only files that have been created or revised since the last Full backup and leaves their archive bits unchanged. It replaces old versions of backup files with their revised versions so that you can use the same backup disks or tapes over and over again.

- *Separate Incremental*   This method, like Incremental, backs up only files that have been created or revised since the last backup and clears their archive bits. However, unlike Incremental, it keeps each history file separate.

- *Full Copy*   This method, like Full, backs up all selected files, regardless of their archive bit settings. However, unlike Full, it leaves archive bits unchanged.

- *Virus Scan Only*   This option isn't a backup method at all. Instead, it scans your files for viruses, just as the **O**ptions Vir**u**s Detection command does when it is turned on before a backup operation. For more information, see "Setting Virus Checking" later in this chapter.

These backup methods are detailed in the following sections. The differences between the methods are sometimes subtle, so it's recommended that you first read about all of them, and then go back and study the ones you're most interested in.

The Full Backup Method

The Full method backs up *all* selected files, regardless of their archive bit settings (that is, regardless of whether or not they've been revised since the last backup), and then clears their archive bits. This method is the default.

Full is the most thorough backup method, and it's the one you should always start off with. However, constantly backing up files that haven't changed wastes a lot of time and backup media. Therefore, it's recommended that you combine the Full method with a partial backup method that saves only new and revised files, such as Incremental, Differential, or Separate Incremental. For example, you might want to perform a Full backup every week and a partial backup every day.

When you perform a Full backup and then begin using a partial backup method, you must stick with that method until your next Full backup. For example, if you start with the Incremental method, don't switch to Separate Incremental for your subsequent backup, or the restore process won't work properly. After you've done another Full backup, you can start fresh and use a different partial backup method.

The Full/Append Tape and Full/Erase Tape Backup Methods

The Full/Tape Backup methods (which are new to CP Backup 7) are virtually identical to the Full method described in the previous section. The only differences are that they work exclusively with tape, and that they specify how to handle existing data on the tape.

Specifically, the Full/Append to Tape method starts saving backup data at the point where the previous backup on the tape ends. This is useful if you have lots of room on your tape and want to preserve your previous backup data.

On the other hand, the Full/Erase Tape method first erases the tape in your tape drive, and then performs the backup to the tape. This is useful if you have limited room on your backup tape and/or don't need its old backup data.

The Incremental Backup Method

The Incremental method backs up only the selected files that have their archive bits *set* (that is, new and revised files), and then clears the archive bits.

When using the Incremental method, you begin by backing up to the last disk or tape of your previous Full backup. After the backup is completed, the Incremental history file is *merged* with the Full history file. Therefore, even though their data are separate, the two backups can be treated as a single backup, greatly simplifying the restore process.

When performing subsequent Incremental backups, you begin by backing up to the last disk or tape in the Full/Incremental backup set. The history files of each of these Incremental backups are *also* merged into the original history file, keeping records of all the data consolidated.

At the same time, though, information is retained about each individual Incremental backup, so you also have the option of restoring data from any particular Incremental session.

The Incremental method always adds data to your backup set, as opposed to replacing old files with new ones. This allows you to restore files that are several versions old. However, this also means your set of disks or tapes can quickly grow to the point where it's unwieldy. When this happens, store the backup set away. You can then start fresh with a new Full backup on a new set of disks or tapes, and then begin a new cycle of Incremental backups.

You should continue storing the previous backup set until you're sure the older versions of files it contains won't be needed. You can then reuse the media for your next round of backups.

The Incremental method is an elegant one, as it provides large measures of both security and convenience. If you don't have large files that change frequently or if you're backing up to tapes, you may find a Full and Incremental backup combination to be ideal.

The Incremental method is only available if you're set to back up to a floppy disk drive, or to a supported tape drive using the CPS format. For more information on the latter, see "Setting Formatting" later in this chapter.

The Differential Backup Method

The Differential method backs up only the selected files that have their archive bits set. However, it leaves the archive bits unchanged. As a result, it always backs up the new and revised files since the last *Full* backup, as opposed to the last Differential backup.

The main way in which Differential differs from the other methods is that it doesn't save a version of each backup it performs. Instead, it *replaces* existing versions of backup files with new versions from the hard disk. This means that you can use a set of backup disks or tapes over and over. This is especially convenient if you're backing up to floppy disks or have large files that change frequently.

To use this method, pick out two sets of disks or tapes. Begin by performing a Full backup using the first set, and then store the set away in a safe place to keep it both secure and out of the way.

Next, perform a Differential backup using the second set. This saves all new and revised files since the Full backup.

Lastly, continue using the second set to perform subsequent Differential backups. Each backup *fully replaces* the files from the previous one. Not accumulating old versions of files keeps the backup set from constantly growing larger, so this method allows you to use significantly fewer disks or tapes.

When your backup set eventually *does* grow unwieldy, or your media starts wearing out, you can start fresh by performing a new Full backup, and then a new cycle of Differential backups.

To restore data after using this method requires two steps: first supplying the Full backup set, and then supplying the latest Differential backup set. The procedure is therefore only a bit more involved than restoring under the Incremental method.

Because it doesn't maintain older versions of files, the Differential method is somewhat riskier than the other methods. For example, if a file becomes corrupted on your hard disk and you don't know it, backing it up to your Differential set may destroy your only uncorrupted version. In addition, if you're using tapes, constantly backing up to the same tapes will tend to wear them out quickly.

To lessen such risks, you may want to perform your Differential backups on several different sets of disks or tapes that you alternate. You may also want to perform Full backups on a regular basis, regardless of whether or not the Differential backup set has grown in size. For a schedule that incorporates both these suggestions, see the "Tape Backup Strategies" section, which follows shortly.

The Separate Incremental Backup Method

The Separate Incremental method, like the Incremental method, backs up only the selected files that have their archive bits set (that is, new and revised files), and then clears the archive bits.

However, a Separate Incremental backup doesn't interact in any way with previous backups. Specifically, it doesn't merge its history file with those of previous backups the way the Incremental method does, and it doesn't replace old versions of files with new ones the way the Differential method does. Instead, each Separate Incremental backup is independent. As a result, you can perform such backups using *any* set of disks or tapes.

A typical strategy for using this method is to perform a Separate Incremental backup every day (making sure to label and date each backup), and then a Full backup at the end of the week. This spares you from accumulating more than seven Separate Incremental backups at a time.

To restore all your data, you must first restore your previous Full backup, and then *each* subsequent Separate Incremental backup in its order of creation.

If this method sounds more tedious than the other methods, that's because it is. Separate Incremental used to be the standard method for performing backups. However, with the recent availability of more sophisticated methods such as Incremental and Differential, there's a lot less reason to choose this option.

Separate Incremental's main strength is that it keeps its backups distinct, so you always have the freedom of choosing between backing up to the end of the previous Full backup, or backing up to fresh disks or tapes. If this kind of flexibility is useful for your backup needs, and you can don't mind managing multiple independent backup files, then the Separate Incremental method may be your option of choice.

The Full Copy Backup Method

The Full Copy method, like the Full method, backs up *all* selected files, regardless of their archive bit settings. However, Full Copy leaves the archive bits unchanged. It's therefore unsuitable for use in combination with partial backup methods such as Incremental, Differential, and Separate Incremental.

Full Copy is actually not a general usage method, but rather one provided for special occasions when you don't want to change the archive bits of the media you're backing up. For example, it's appropriate for backing up a CD-ROM drive, which can't be written to; a damaged hard disk, where writing to the disk could exacerbate its problems; or a hard disk whose contents you want to simply copy for transferral to another hard disk.

Tape Backup Strategies

Tape is an extremely convenient backup medium. A single cartridge can store from 40MB to over 250MB of data, which is usually enough to back up an entire hard disk. This huge capacity saves you the time and effort involved in swapping backup media in and out of drives. It also enables you to schedule tape backups to take place even when you're not at your computer (as detailed in the "Scheduling Backups" section later in this chapter).

However, tapes have a couple of disadvantages when compared to floppy disks. First, they tend to wear out more quickly than disks, especially when you use them continually. As a result, it's a good idea to alternate between at least three sets of backup tapes. For example, if you're combining Full backups with Incremental or Separate Incremental backups, you might use a three-week schedule like the following:

Week	Backup Method	Tape Set
Start of Week 1	Full/Erase Tape backup	Tape set 1
Week 1	Incremental backup	Tape set 1
Start of Week 2	Full/Erase Tape backup	Tape set 2
Week 2	Incremental backup	Tape set 2
Start of Week 3	Full/Erase Tape backup	Tape set 3
Week 3	Incremental backup	Tape set 3
Start of Week 1	Full/Erase Tape backup	Tape set 1
Week 1	Incremental backup	Tape set 1

On the other hand, if you're combining Full backups with Differential backups, you might use a two-week schedule like the following:

Week	Backup Method	Tape Set
Start of Week 1	Full/Erase Tape backup	Tape set 1
Week 1	Differential backup	Tape set 2
Start of Week 2	Full/Erase Tape backup	Tape set 3
Week 2	Differential backup	Tape set 4
Start of Week 1	Full/Erase Tape backup	Tape set 1
Week 1	Differential backup	Tape set 2

In both schedules, you can repeat each cycle over and over. When a set of tapes finally gets worn out, simply replace it with a fresh set.

Another disadvantage of tapes is that they must undergo several time-consuming formatting processes before they can be used.

Preparation Process	40MB	60MB	80MB	120MB
Servo-writing	36	54	51	76
Formatting	18	27	33	50
Certification	18	27	33	49
Total without servo-writing	36	54	66	99
Total with servo-writing	72	108	117	175

Table 2-1.   Tape Preparation Times (in Minutes)

First, if you have an Irwin tape, it must be *servo-written*. This process lays down information to help guide the tape drive read/write mechanism along the proper data areas of the tape.

Second, all tapes must be *formatted*. This process maps out how data will be divided among the different areas of the tape.

Third, all tapes must be *certified*. This process checks the tape for unreadable areas and marks any such areas it finds as unusable.

CP Backup can perform all three processes, but requires from *one to three hours* to do so. It's therefore usually a good idea to buy tapes that are already servo-written (if necessary), formatted, and certified. If you don't, be sure to take the time required to prepare a new tape into account in your backup schedule.

A complete list of the times required to prepare new tapes using CP Backup appears in Table 2-1. The four types of tapes listed are 40MB, 60MB (also called 40MB XL), 80MB, and 120MB (also called 80MB XL). All tapes are CD-2000 1/4-inch tapes.

Backup Methods Summary

In summary, you should always start a backup cycle with a Full backup. You can then do a series of Incremental backups (especially appropriate if you work with small files or back up to tapes); Differential backups (especially appropriate if you don't want old versions of files, back up to floppy disks, or work with large files that change frequently); or Separate Incremental backups (especially appropriate if you need to keep each backup distinct from previous ones). When you've begun using one partial backup method, be sure not to switch to another method until you've performed another Full backup.

When you've decided on a method you want, first invoke the Backup Method dialog box by pressing O, B, or clicking on the Options menu and selecting Backup Method. You can then choose the method by pressing its highlighted letter or by clicking its name. When you're satisfied with your choice, press O or click OK to exit the dialog box, and then press ESC to close the menu.

Performing a Full Backup

To get a feel for performing backups, work through the following steps to make a Full backup of your hard disk using the **O**ptions menu defaults. If you experience any difficulties not covered in this tutorial, see the "Troubleshooting Backup Problems" section at the end of this chapter.

1. You should be at the Backup screen. To begin, select the **F**ull method by pressing O, B, F, O, ESC, or select the Full/**E**rase Tape method by pressing O, B, E, O, ESC.

2. Select the single drive you want to back up; or select multiple drives, which is a new option in CP Backup 7. To do so, first press A, F, or click on the Action menu and select Backup From. All the drives in your system other than your A and B drives are displayed.

3. Use the TAB key to move to a drive you want to back up and press ENTER, or click the drive. Repeat this process for each drive you want to back up. (If the option in the lower-right corner reads **A**llow Multiple Drive Backups, you must first select it by pressing **A** or clicking the option. The command then changes to read **A**llow Single Drive Backups, which means you can proceed to select more than one drive.) When you're done, all the drives you selected should be highlighted.

4. Press ALT-O or click OK. After a few moments, all the directories of your chosen drives are read into memory. Also, status indicators show the number of directories, files, and bytes selected, as well as the estimated number of disks or tapes, and number of minutes, the specified backup will require.

5. If you're satisfied with the default data selections (which, the first time you use the program, will be *all* directories and files on all your selected drives), go to step 8.

    Otherwise, use the Tree List and File List to select only particular directories and files. If you're in Express mode, first display the Tree List for the topmost selected drive by pressing R, moving to the listed drive using the arrow keys, and pressing ENTER, or by double-clicking on the listed drive in the Backup From box. The Tree List for the drive appears.

6. Press ENTER from the root a few times to clear all previous selections, and then select only the data you want to back up, using as a guide the tutorial in "The CP Backup Tree List and File List" in Chapter 1.

7. When you're done, press F4 to display the next drive and repeat step 6. Then repeat the process again, as many times as necessary, until you've selected the data you want on all your selected drives. When you're done, if you're in Express mode, press F10 to return to the Express screen. Notice that the status

indicators now show lower numbers for selected directories, files, bytes, estimated media, and estimated time.

8. Gather the disks or tapes specified by the estimate indicator, plus some extras in case the program has underestimated (although it typically *over*estimates). Label each disk or tape with a consecutive number, the type of backup you're using it for, and the date.

9. You're now ready to initiate the backup operation. If you're in Express mode, press S or click the Start Backup button in the lower-right corner. Otherwise, press A, S, or press F5, or click on the Action menu and select Start Backup.

10. You're prompted to enter a description and password. First, type a description for your backup of up to 30 characters (for example, "FULL BACKUP #1") and press ENTER. When you want to perform a compare or restore operation, this description will help you identify this backup from the other backups recorded in history files on your hard disk.

11. If you want to safeguard your backup from being used without your permission, create a password from one to eight characters long. The password should be easy for you to remember but hard for others to guess. No distinction is made between upper- and lowercase letters.

    When you're ready, enter the password. Each character appears on the screen as a small filled-in rectangle to prevent anyone looking over your shoulder from seeing what you're typing.

If your data requires a high degree of security, see Chapter 11, "Encrypting Data Using PC Secure."

12. Press ALT-O or click OK to accept your entries. If you entered a password, you're now prompted to confirm it. Type the password again, and press ALT-O or click OK again.

13. Your backup drive is now activated. At the same time, status indicators display the number of your current disk or tape, the percentage of the backup completed, the elapsed time of the backup, the degree of compression executed, and the area, or *track number*, of the disk or tape that's currently being written to.

    If you haven't already inserted a disk or tape into your backup drive, do so now as directed by the screen prompt.

14. If your disk or tape already contains data, a warning message appears. If you don't mind losing the data, press ENTER or click OK to proceed with the backup.

    Otherwise, remove the current disk or tape (the drive will keep running, which is OK), insert a different disk or tape, and then press R or click Retry.

15. If your disk or tape isn't formatted, a message on the bottom of the screen says "Formatting & backing up, press ESC to abort," and the formatting is begun automatically. If you're using a disk, the standard DOS format is used, which adds about an extra minute to the backup time.

    However, if you're using a tape, the process takes from one to three hours (as explained earlier in this chapter in "Tape Backup Strategies"). If you want to abort tape formatting, press ESC, and then press Q or click Quit to exit the current backup operation. You can then return to step 8 using an already-formatted tape.

16. Once your disk or tape is accepted, the program begins backing up your selected data. When the disk or tape is full, remove it and return to step 13.

The drive light will stay on as you're removing and inserting disks during the backup process. This is normal for CP Backup, and doesn't cause any harm to your drive or your disks.

17. When all your selected files are backed up, the message "Writing directory information, please wait" appears. This refers to the history file, which contains information on the files you backed up, the current date and time, and the backup method you used. The history file is always saved to your last disk or tape. In addition, if the **O**ptions Save **H**istory switch is on, and you were backing up at the High or Medium speed, a copy is also saved to the hard drive containing the CP Backup program. (For more information, see "Saving and Printing History Files" later in this chapter.)

    Lastly, a dialog box appears that tells you the number of directories and files backed up, the number of bytes they took up on your hard disk, the number of disks or tapes that were required to back them up, the amount of time the procedure took, and the number of kilobytes (thousands of bytes) transferred per minute. Press ENTER or click OK. The dialog box closes, and you're returned to either your previous Tree List screen or the Express main menu.

While you performed a Full backup in this example, the process is identical for the other backup methods. Once you go through it a few times, you'll find backing up an easy procedure to perform and, using the partial backups methods, often a fairly quick one as well.

Using the Options Menu

In the previous section, you performed a backup using the **O**ption menu's default settings. You can also take advantage of the menu's 13 commands to adjust CP

Backup to your particular needs. The following sections explain how to select files using DOS wildcards, attributes, time ranges, and subdirectory switches. They also explain how to adjust settings for compression, overwrite warnings, error-checking, virus checking, formatting, history files, and the time display.

Selecting Files

As explained in Chapter 1, "CP Backup Overview," you can select the files you want to back up, restore, or compare using the Tree List and File List. While these two windows are very effective at letting you select files visually, they don't allow you to select files based on specific criteria. The **O**ptions menu therefore provides commands for selecting files using DOS wildcards, attributes, and date ranges. In addition, the menu lets you fine-tune your selections by including or excluding subdirectories.

Selecting Files Using DOS Wildcards

Sometimes you'll want to select files based on their names or extensions. For example, you might want to specify a DBF extension to back up your dBASE files; or a BAT extension to back up your batch files; or names beginning with REPORT to back up such files as REPORT2, REPORT.PRT, and so on. You can do all this using the Include/Exclude Files box.

To begin, select the drives you want to work with (using the **Action Backup From** command), and then press O, S, I, or click on the Options menu and select Selection Options and Include/Exclude Files. A large box appears, which initially contains *.* on its top line. The asterisk is the DOS wildcard, representing any combination of characters. Therefore, *.* represents files with any name and extension, meaning all files on all your selected drives.

You can replace whatever is on the line by simply typing over it. For example, to specify dBASE files, type ***.DBF**; to specify batch files, type ***.BAT**; and to specify all files beginning with REPORT, type **REPORT*.***.

You can also use the wildcard ?, which represents any single character. For example, ??.* selects all files with two-letter names, *.? selects all files with one-letter extensions, and *.WK? selects all versions of Lotus 1-2-3 worksheet files.

You can also exclude files by preceding your specification with a dash. For example, -*.* unselects all the files on your selected drives, and -*.EXE unselects all EXE program files.

In addition, you can use the backslash key (\) to specify directories. For example, *.* specifies all files in the root directory, \PCTOOLS*.* specifies all files in the PCTOOLS directory, \PCTOOLS*.TXT specifies files with TXT extensions in the PCTOOLS directory, \PCTOOLS\DATA*.* specifies PC Tools data files, and so on.

As just mentioned, your specifications normally apply across all your selected drives. However, you can restrict a specification to a particular drive by simply preceding it with the drive's letter and a colon (for example, C:\PCTOOLS*.TXT).

You can also fine-tune your selections by specifying up to 16 different selection criteria simultaneously. For example, the following selects all dBASE files, 1-2-3 files, and TXT files that are *not* in the PCTOOLS directory:

```
-*.*
*.DBF
*.WK?
*.TXT
-C:\PCTOOLS\*.*
```

The list is processed from top to bottom. Therefore, the first line unselects all files, the next three lines select DBF, WK?, and TXT files, and the last line unselects any DBF, WK?, and TXT files in the PCTOOLS directory on drive C. Such multiple criteria give you a great deal of control over which files are selected.

Once you've entered the selections you want, press ALT-O or click OK to close the dialog box, and press ESC twice to close the **O**ptions menu. Your selections instantly take effect, totally *overriding* any previous selections. If you're in Tree List mode, you can immediately see your wildcard selections reflected in the Tree and File Lists (which is a new feature in CP Backup 7). You can now optionally fine-tune them even further by manually selecting and unselecting directories and individual files.

When the Include/Exclude Files box is active, you can further hone your file selections based on attributes and creation dates. These options are covered in the next two sections.

Selecting Files by Attributes

As you learned earlier in this chapter, every file has an archive bit, or *attribute,* that can be turned on or off by various programs. In addition, a file can have up to three other attributes turned on: *hidden, system,* and *read-only.*

Hidden files don't display when you list filenames from DOS or an application. They're usually generated as part of an application's copy protection scheme, and typically work only from a specific location on the hard disk. CP Backup's restore process has no control over placing files back in their original locations, so there's no point in backing up such files.

System files are special DOS files such as IBMBIO.COM and IBMDOS.COM, or MSBIO.SYS and MSDOS.COM. These files also work only from a specific location on the hard disk, so there's no point in backing them up, either.

Read-only files are normal files that have been protected from being altered. In other words, you can read them, work with them, copy their data, and so on, but you can't replace them with an updated version. This option is often used on network files. These files *should* be backed up.

When the Include/Exclude Files box is active, you can exclude files based on these three attributes. To do so, press O, S, A, or click on the Options menu and select Selection Options and Attribute Exclusions. The following dialog box appears:

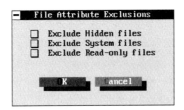

The box is initially set to include files with any of the three attributes, as indicated by the absence of checkmarks alongside the options. To toggle an attribute's exclusion on or off, press the first letter of the attribute (that is, H for **Hidden**, S for **System**, or R for **Read-Only**), or click to the left of the option. When you're done, press O or click OK to exit the dialog box, and press ESC twice to close the **Options** menu. Your settings are instantly applied to the Tree and File Lists.

Selecting Files by Dates

Sometimes you'll want to select files created within a certain range of time. For example, you may want to select only files created within the last two weeks, or created in the previous quarter, or created during May of last year. When the Include/Exclude Files box is active, you can narrow your file selections to any date range. To do so, press O, S, D, or click on the Options menu and select Selection Options and Date Range Selection. The following dialog box appears:

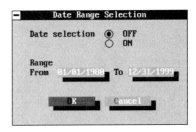

To set a date range, follow these steps:

1. If the Date Selection option is off (which is the default), press N to turn it on. You're moved to the Range From field.

2. Type the date from which you want to begin the range. (As soon as you type anything, the existing date will be replaced.) Dates should be entered in either *MM/DD/YYYY* or *MM/DD/YY* format, where *MM* are two month digits, *DD* are two date digits, *YYYY* are four year digits, and *YY* are the last two digits of the year 19*YY*. For example, December 3, 1991 should be entered as either 12/03/1991 or 12/03/91.

3. Press ENTER. You're moved to the Range To field.

4. Type the date at which you want to end the range, again using the *MM/DD/YYYY* or *MM/DD/YY* format, and press ENTER. You're moved to the **OK** button.

5. Press ENTER or click OK to exit the dialog box. Your settings are instantly applied to the Tree and File Lists.

6. Press ESC twice to close the Options menu.

Including and Excluding Subdirectories

When you select a directory in both the Tree List and the Include/Exclude Files box, you ordinarily also select all the subdirectories it contains. If you prefer to handle each directory individually, turn the Subdirectory Inclusion option off.

To demonstrate how the option works in the Tree List, follow these steps:

1. If you're in Express mode, turn it off temporarily by pressing C, U, E, O. You're switched to the root of the Tree List.

2. Press ENTER. The root directory is unselected. In addition, all the directories under it are unselected.

3. Press ENTER again. The root directory and its subdirectories are selected again.

4. Press O, S, or click on the Options menu and select Selection Options. Notice that the Subdirectory Inclusion option has a checkmark next to it, which indicates that it's on.

5. Press U or click on the Subdirectory Inclusion option. The checkmark disappears, indicating that the option has been turned off.

6. Press ESC twice to close the menu and return to the Tree List.

7. Press ENTER. The root directory is unselected again, as indicated by the files in the File List losing their highlighting. However, the rest of the Tree List is now unaffected.

8. Move to another directory that has subdirectories and press ENTER. Again, the directory is unselected, while its subdirectories remain selected.

9. Turn the option on again by pressing O, S, U, ESC, ESC.

Notice that the **Subdirectory Inclusion** option's effects aren't retroactive; in other words, changing its status doesn't affect subdirectories already selected or unselected in the Tree List. Similarly, if you change the option's status and want to affect the current selections in the Include/Exclude Files box, you must press O, S, I to bring up the box and press ALT-O to reprocess the box's selections.

Setting Compression

CP Backup ordinarily compresses files when backing them up so that you can use fewer disks or tapes to store your hard disk's data. To adjust the degree of compression, press O, C, or click on the Options menu and select Compress, or select the Compress button in Express mode. The following dialog box appears:

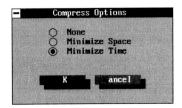

The box contains the following three options:

- *None*   This option shuts compression off completely to achieve faster backups. This is usually overkill unless you're in a big hurry.

- *Minimize Space*   This option sets maximum compression. It backs up files using up to 60 percent fewer disks or tapes, but slows down the backup process.

- *Minimize Time*   This option sets minimal compression. In other words, it compresses only when doing so doesn't slow down the backup process. The degree of compression achieved will largely depend on how fast your system is. For example, on computers with older chips such as the 8088, compression will be slight, while on 80286 and 80386 machines with swift hard disks, compression may be close to maximum. This option is the default.

Press N or click None for no compression; press S or click Minimize Space for maximum compression; or press T or click Minimize Time for a faster backup. When you're done, press O or click OK to exit the dialog box, and press ESC to close the menu.

Before and after you use the Compress command, check the display estimates of the number of disks or tapes needed and amount of time required for your backup. The numbers will often change dramatically based on the Compress method you select.

Setting Overwrite Warnings

During a backup, if a disk or tape already contains data, you'll ordinarily be warned about it. In addition, you'll be prompted to either verify that you want the data overwritten or replace the disk or tape with a blank one.

Similarly, during a restore, if a file on your hard disk has the same name as the file you're restoring, you'll ordinarily be given the option of overwriting the hard disk file, or overwriting it only if the restore file is newer, or skipping the restore of the file altogether. (You can additionally set whether your response should be applied automatically to all other such situations during the restore session.)

Rather than be prompted about overwriting, you may prefer to have CP Backup always overwrite files automatically. To choose this option, press O, O, or click on the Options menu and select Overwrite Warning. The checkmark next to the option disappears to indicate that it's off, and that backup and restore operations will now overwrite files without asking for verification. To close the menu, press ESC.

If you later want to turn the option back on, simply select **O**ptions **O**verwrite Warning again.

Setting Error Protection

CP Backup ordinarily performs two operations to help protect against data errors in your backup set. The first involves checking your backup media for defects and the second involves saving error-correction information.

While formatting a disk or tape, CP Backup checks the media to verify that it's free of defects that would make it unreadable. You can change this verify option by pressing O, V, or clicking on the Options menu and selecting Verify, or selecting the Verify button in Express mode. The following dialog box appears:

The default option is When Formatting, meaning that CP Backup will check a disk or tape for defects while formatting it.

If you press N or click None, no type of defect checking will be performed. This speeds the formatting process, but it isn't recommended.

Alternatively, if you press A or click Always, every disk or tape will always be checked for defects before being used. In addition, after a backup is completed, a tape is rewound and its backup files are compared with the hard disk files. (Tapes get this extra treatment both because they're more prone to errors than disks, and because they're easier to check than a set of floppy disks that need to be swapped in and out of drives.) This option slows down the backup process; however, if you're having problems with your media, it's recommended that you turn it on.

When you're done setting verification, press O or click OK to exit the dialog box, and press ESC to close the menu.

CP Backup ordinarily also provides another level of protection by saving error-correction information on each disk or tape. This process slows the backup process somewhat, and takes up to 11 percent extra space. However, it's highly recommended for tapes, which are prone to developing defects. It also allows recovery of all data from a disk with up to even 158 errors.

To turn the option off, press O, E, or click on the Options menu and select Error Correction. The checkmark next to the option disappears, indicating it's off. To turn the option on again, select it again. When you're done, press ESC to close the menu.

Setting Virus Checking

In addition to error checking, CP Backup 7 also provides a new security feature by letting you automatically check for known viruses in your selected files before backing them up. The checking is done by matching file data against virus data patterns, or *signatures,* that are stored in a file named SIGNATUR.CPS. If a virus is located, you're offered the following three options:

- *Continue*   This option continues with the backup procedure as if no virus was detected. It will therefore back up the suspect file along with your other files. This can be appropriate if a file you're *certain* is virus-free happens to contain data matching one of the patterns in the SIGNATUR.CPS file.

- *Rename*   This option renames the suspect file with a V*nn* extension, where *nn* is a number from 00 to 99. It also prevents the file from being backed up.

- *Cancel*   This option cancels the backup operation.

To turn automatic virus checking on, press O, U, or click on the Options menu and select Virus Detection. A checkmark next to the option appears. To close the menu, press ESC. You can later turn the option back off by simply selecting **O**ptions **Vir**us Detection again.

You can also explicitly check for viruses using the Virus Scan Only command in the Backup Method dialog box. For more information, see "Backup Methods and Strategies" near the beginning of this chapter.

For more information about viruses, see "Detecting Viruses Using VDefend" in Chapter 13.

Setting Formatting

If you're backing up to your A or B floppy drive, or to a supported tape drive, there are several options you can adjust concerning formatting. (If you're backing up to another drive, you must use preformatted media for backup.)

First, if you back up to disks, CP Backup 7 now lets you choose between a DOS format (which is the default) and a more space-efficient, but nonstandard, CP Backup format. If a disk is already formatted by DOS, selecting the CP Backup format will cause the disk to be reformatted.

Similarly, if you back up to tapes, you can now choose between the standard QIC 40/80 format or a more flexible, but nonstandard, CP Backup format. Unlike the situation with disks, selecting the CP Backup format will *not* force a QIC 40/80 tape to be reformatted. Instead, it will just cause CP Backup to write data to the tape differently. Therefore, there's no problem in using a preformatted QIC 40/80 tape with the CP Backup format. In fact, the CP Backup format is the default for tapes, and is required if you want to use the Incremental backup method.

To change formats, press O, F, or click on the Options menu and select Media Format. The following dialog box appears:

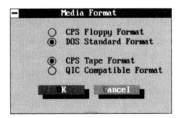

As just mentioned, the default option for disks is **DOS Standard Format**, while the default for tapes is CPS **T**ape Format. To switch to a different format, press F or click CPS Floppy format, or press Q or click QIC Compatible Format. When you're done, press O to close the dialog box and ESC to close the menu.

You can also select how often disks are formatted. CP Backup normally formats disks only when they aren't already formatted. However, if you press O, M, or click on the Options menu and select Format Always, the program will format the disks every time you use them. This "refreshes" each disk and so slightly increases the disk's chances of staying readable, but slows down the backup process considerably. To turn the option back off, select Format Always again. (This option also applies to tapes, but there are probably no circumstances under which you would want to repeatedly format a tape.)

Saving and Printing History Files

As mentioned previously, when a backup is completed, CP Backup generates a history file that contains such information as the name, size, date, attributes, and disk or tape location of each backed up file; the type of backup performed; and the date of the backup. The history file is always saved to the last disk or tape of the backup set.

In addition, if you're backing up at the High or Medium speed, an extra copy of the history file is normally saved to the hard disk containing the CP Backup program. The file is named *dyymmdds*.DIR, where *d* is the current drive, *yy* is the current year, *mm* is the current month, *dd* is the current day, *s* is a sequence number, and DIR is the extension that identifies it as a history file. If you allowed the Install program to create PC Tools subdirectories (see Appendix A), the file is saved to the DATA subdirectory. Otherwise, it's saved to the directory containing the CP Backup program (typically, the PC Tools main directory).

When you initiate a restore or compare operation, CP Backup first checks your hard disk to see whether it contains history files. If it does, the files are displayed and you're prompted to select the one you want. This process can be faster and more convenient than having to insert the last disk or tape from your backup set.

If you want to prevent history files from being saved to your hard disk after a backup, or prevent CP Backup from reading existing history files from the hard disk when a restore or compare has been initiated, press O, H or click on the Options menu and select Save History. The checkmark next to the option disappears, indicating it's off. To turn the option back on, just select it again.

You can also set each newly created history file to automatically generate a report specifying the names, creation dates and times, sizes, and attributes of each backed-up file; which disk or tape each file is on; and the type of backup performed. To do so, press O, R, or click on the Options menu and select Reporting, or select the Reporting button in Express mode. A dialog box appears that offers the options Report to **P**rinter (which sends the report to printer port LPT1), Report to **F**ile (which saves the report to a file with a date-coded name and RPB extension, typically within your PC Tools directory or DATA subdirectory), or **N**one (which simply saves new history files without having them generate their information for your examination). The default is **N**one. After you select the option you want, press O or click OK to exit the dialog box, and press ESC to close the menu.

You can also make an existing history file generate its information at any time using the File Print History command or the Print option in the Choose Directory box. For more information on the latter, see "Choosing a Backup Set" in Chapter 3.

Setting the Time Display

When a backup begins, the status line ordinarily displays a clock that keeps track of the amount of time the backup is taking. The clock makes use of a program (specifically, a timer interrupt handler) that may conflict with certain systems and networks. If you experience backup problems, try eliminating the timer by pressing O, T, or clicking on the Options menu and selecting Time Display. The checkmark next to the option disappears, indicating that it's off. To close the menu, press ESC.

If you later determine that the timer isn't a problem, turn it back on by selecting **O**ptions **T**ime Display again.

Using Setup Files

CP Backup provides dozens of settings, so reselecting options every time you run the program can take a lot of time and effort. As a result, the program allows you to save your current settings to a special file called a *setup* file. You can create as many setup files as you want. You can then load a particular file using the *setup* parameter from the DOS prompt (see "CP Backup Parameters" in Chapter 1) or the **L**oad Setup command from the File menu.

The settings stored by a setup file include all your **O**ptions menu settings, all your **C**onfigure menu settings, the drives you've selected to back up from, the drives you've selected to back up to, and the directories and files you've selected via the Tree and File Lists and/or the Include/Exclude Files box. The latter option is an improvement over PC Backup 6, which could not save Tree and File List selections.

To save your current settings, press F, A, or click on the File menu and select Save Setup As, or select the Save Setup button in Express mode. The following dialog box appears:

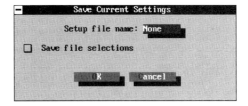

Type a filename of up to eight characters. Also, if you want to preserve your Tree and File List choices, press ALT-S or click Save File Selections to turn the checkmark on. When you're done, press ALT-O or click OK. The file is saved with the name you supplied and a SET extension. Also, if you turned on **S**ave File Selections, an additional file is saved for each selected drive with the name you supplied and an IE*d* extension, where *d* is the letter of the drive. To close the menu, press ESC.

To later load your setup file from within CP Backup, press F, L, or click on the File menu and select Load Setup, or select the Setup button in Express mode. A list of your setup files appears. Move to the file you want using the arrow keys, or click on the file with your mouse, and then press ALT- O or click OK. The current program settings are replaced by the file's settings, restoring your previous CP Backup environment.

You also have the option of revising a setup file. To do so, load the file; make the settings changes you want; and then press F, S, or click on the File menu and select Save Setup. Your current settings instantly replace the old ones in the file. (On the other hand, if you want to leave the old file unchanged, select File Save Setup As and simply save your current settings under a different setup filename.)

You can also save your current settings as new CP Backup defaults. For more information, see "Saving Your Settings as Defaults" in Chapter 1.

Scheduling Backups

If you have a tape drive, or if you have a floppy drive that can store a day's worth of incremental backups, it's a good idea to schedule backups to take place while you're away from your PC. This procedure provides you with consistent security at minimum inconvenience. You can set backups to take place on specific days and times via up to ten different schedules.

For scheduling to work, you must keep resident either the PC Tools Desktop (see Chapter 23, "Using the Appointment Scheduler") or the new CP Scheduler program. Both of these programs can regularly check a backup scheduling file you create within CP Backup.

To schedule a backup, follow these steps:

1. If CP Scheduler isn't already resident, exit CP Backup, load the Scheduler by typing **CPSCHED** at the DOS prompt and pressing ENTER, and run CP Backup again.

2. Switch to the Backup screen (scheduling isn't available in the Restore and Compare screens).

3. Press A, D, or click on the Action menu and select Schedule Backups, or select the Scheduler button in Express mode. A dialog box appears that lets you enter the name of a setup file to use with the backup, specify on which days you want the backup to occur, and specify a time for the backup.

4. Type in the name of the setup file you want to use; or press F4 to display the setup files available, use the arrows key or your mouse to move to the one

you want, and press O or click OK to have the filename entered into the field for you.

5. Move to a day you want to include in the schedule using TAB or SHIFT-TAB, and then press ENTER to select it. Alternatively, just click below the day. In either case, a checkmark appears to show the day has been selected.

   Repeat this procedure until you've selected every day you want to include in the schedule.

6. Use TAB or your mouse to move to the Run Time field.

7. Specify the time to perform the backup in *HH*:*MM*a or *HH*:*MM*p format, where *HH* represents hours, *MM* represents minutes, and "a" and "p" optionally represent A.M. and P.M. (For example, to specify 5:30 P.M., type either **5:30p** or **17:30**.)

8. When you're done specifying your schedule, press ALT-O or click OK. You're offered the options of specifying another backup schedule (you can have up to ten), modifying an existing backup schedule, deleting an existing backup schedule, saving the schedule you've just defined, or canceling the operation.

9. Press S or click Save. Your schedule is saved to the file CPBACKUP.TM. This file will be used by both CP Scheduler and the resident Desktop Appointment Scheduler (see Chapter 23, "Using the Appointment Scheduler").

When your scheduled backup time arrives, a 15-second notice appears. If you don't respond to the notice, any application currently running is interrupted and the backup takes place as specified (using the name "Unattended Backup"). When the operation is completed, CP Backup exits, and your system is returned to its previous state.

Troubleshooting Backup Problems

During the course of running CP Backup and using it to back up files, you may encounter some difficulties. The following are some of the problems most likely to come up and their probable solutions.

"Overlay Files" Error Message at Startup

If you see the message "Error at Loading CPBACKUP Overlay Files" when trying to run the program, it means you haven't copied all of its EXE program files into the same directory. For a list and description of all relevant CP Backup files, see "CP Backup Files" in Chapter 1.

Display or Mouse Problems

If the screen is fuzzy, or your mouse pointer seems to disappear, or you're experiencing any other type of display or mouse problem, see the "Video and Mouse Parameters" section in Appendix A, "PC Tools Installation and Configuration." This is a list of parameters that can be used with virtually every PC Tools program. The chances are that one of these options will solve your problem.

Major Problems Backing Up

If you're encountering any major difficulties while backing up, use the Configure Backup Speed command to switch from the High Speed (DMA) option to the Medium Speed (non-DMA) or Low Speed/DOS Compatible option. There's a good chance that this will eliminate the problems.

You should also check whether there are any non-PC Tools programs memory resident while CP Backup is running. If there are, try restarting your computer without the programs, and then run CP Backup again to see if it performs properly.

The Backup Time and Disk/Tape Indicators Are Wrong

You'll probably find that the status line indicators of the amount of time and number of disks or tapes a backup will require are *not* entirely accurate, only close estimates. This is because CP Backup can't tell precisely how fast your computer and hard disk are. For example, if your system is faster than CP Backup realizes, you may need fewer disks or tapes because greater compression will be performed, or the backup may take less time. Similarly, if your system is slower than CP Backup realizes, you may need more disks or tapes, or the backup may take more time. Therefore, the status line indicators should be treated as guides rather than 100 percent accurate predictions. However, they're generally pretty close to the mark.

"100% Complete" Appears and Then the Program Freezes

If you initiate a backup, the "100% Complete" message appears on a status line, and then the program suddenly freezes before writing the history file, you may have different DOS versions of the program COMMAND.COM on your hard disk. If this is the case, use PC Shell's File Locate command (see Chapter 16) to search for COMMAND.COM, and then delete every copy except the one you use for starting up your computer.

Otherwise, you may be running a conflicting memory-resident program (for example, a program called SEARCH.COM). If so, try restarting your PC without any memory-resident non-PC Tools programs, and then see if CP Backup works properly.

"Backup Complete" Appears but Nothing Was Backed Up

If you initiate a backup and the Backup Complete dialog box immediately appears (that is, without any files being transferred), there are a couple of possible reasons.

First, it may be that you haven't selected any files. You can easily check this by reading the Directories, Files, and Bytes indicators on the status lines.

Otherwise, you may be running a conflicting memory-resident program (for example, a program called LOG.COM). If so, restart your PC without any memory-resident non-PC Tools programs, and then see if CP Backup works properly.

Chapter **3**

Comparing and Restoring Backup Files

In Chapter 1, "CP Backup Overview," you learned how to start CP Backup, configure it for your system, and use such screen elements as the Tree List, File List, and menu bar. In Chapter 2, "Backing Up Your Hard Disk," you learned how to select backup methods, back up your hard disk, and change program settings using the **O**ptions menu.

In this chapter, you'll learn how to perform compare operations, which compare selected backup files against their hard disk counterparts, and restore operations, which copy selected backup files back to your hard disk.

The chapter first explains how to use the Choose Directory dialog box to select a backup set. It then covers comparing files, restoring files, restoring with damaged or missing disks, identifying disks, and solving common restore problems.

Choosing a Backup Set

Before you can perform a compare or restore operation, you must select a backup set and specify which of its files you want to work with. To do so, follow these steps (using the Restore screen to demonstrate):

1. If you aren't already in CP Backup, type **CPBACKUP** (with no spaces) from the DOS prompt and press ENTER.

If a message appears saying that you haven't configured CP Backup, first work through "Running and Configuring CP Backup" in Chapter 1.

2. Move to the Restore screen: If you're at the main menu, press R or click Restore. If you're in a Backup or Compare screen, press A, R, or click on the Action menu and select Restore.

3. If you're not already set to the Advanced user level and Tree List mode, press C, U, A, E, O, ESC.

4. If you're already set to the drive you want to restore to, skip to step 6.
   Otherwise, press A, T, or click on the Action menu and select Restore To. A display of all the hard disk drives detected in your system appears.

5. Use TAB and the arrow keys to move to the drive you want to restore to and press ENTER; or simply click the drive. Also, optionally enter a path to specify the directory on the drive where you want the files restored. When you're done, press ALT-O or click OK.

6. To specify the backup set you want to restore from, press A, H, or click on the Action menu and select Choose Directories. CP Backup searches your selected target drive for the history files of your various backup sets. If it doesn't find them, go to step 9.

7. If you allowed history files to be copied to your hard disk (that is, if you kept the **O**ptions Save **H**istory switch on during backups), representations of your various backup sets are listed in a Choose Directory dialog box. Each backup set entry shows the description you gave the backup when creating it, the date and time of the backup, the total number of bytes the backup files took up on the hard disk, and the media the files were saved to (Floppy or Tape).
   In addition, you're given the option of selecting a backup set to work with (**OK**), canceling the operation (**Cancel**), printing a backup report from the selected entry (**Print**), or ignoring the list and instead using the history file from the last disk or tape of a backup set (**Insert**).

8. If the history file of the backup set you want is listed, move to it or click it; press O or click OK; and then go to step 10.
   Otherwise, press I or click Insert to use the history file from a backup set you'll supply.

9. You're prompted to insert the last disk or tape of your backup set. Do so using the specified drive.

10. Your specified history file is loaded, and a Tree List and File List are generated from it. Also, the Statistics status lines display the number of directories, files, and bytes represented.

If the backup you selected was made with the Full, Full Copy, Differential, or Separate Incremental method, at the top of the Tree list is the letter of your first backup drive, followed by a backslash to represent the root directory. Below that is the date and time of the backup, and then the names of the backup directories.

However, if the backup you selected is a combination of Full and Incremental methods, first the date, time, and directories of the Full backup are listed, and then the date, time, and directories backed up in *each* Incremental session are listed. If you leave all directories selected, only the most recent version of each file will be used for compares and restores. Alternatively, you can choose to restore earlier versions of files, or all the files from a particular Incremental backup session.

Searching History Files

You can search through your history files for specified backup files, which is a new feature in CP Backup 7. This option is only available when you're in the Restore or Compare screen.

To use the option, press A, A, or click on the Action menu and select Search History Files, or select the Search Hist button in Express mode. A dialog box appears that prompts you for a file specification (for which you can use the DOS wildcards * and ?) and an optional date range. It also lists the history files on your hard disk and lets you select the ones you want to search using the SPACEBAR. Alternatively, you can select *all* the history files by pressing ALT-A or clicking Select All.

When you're ready to initiate the operation, press ALT-S or click Search. The files matching your specifications are located, and you're prompted to select Load to display them in the Tree List for a restore or compare operation. Alternatively, you can select **Search** to conduct a new search, or press ESC to cancel the operation.

Comparing Files

A compare operation checks each selected backup file against the file matching its directory and filename on your backed up hard disk. The operation then marks the backup file as being identical to its hard disk counterpart, or older, or newer, or internally identical but having a different date or time, or different but having the same date and time, or as not matching any file on the hard disk.

There are two basic reasons to compare files. First, if you're uncertain about whether a backup you've performed was successful, you can compare your backup files to the hard disk files to verify that they're identical. Second, if you aren't sure which files on your hard disk should be restored, you can first compare them to your backup files to determine which hard disk files are missing or need updating.

To compare backup files, follow these steps:

1. Follow the instructions in the "Choosing a Backup Set" section earlier in this chapter to display the backup set's directories in the Tree List.

2. If you aren't already in the Compare screen, switch to it now by pressing A, C, or clicking on the Action menu and selecting Compare.

3. Select the files you want to compare, using either the List windows (see "The CP Backup Tree List and File List" in Chapter 1) or the **O**ptions **S**election Options **I**nclude/Exclude Files command (see "Selecting Files" in Chapter 2). If your backup is Incremental and the **O**ptions **S**election Options Subdirectory Inclusion switch is on, you can specify a particular Incremental session by selecting its date and time in the Tree List.

4. Press A, S, or press F9, or click on the Action menu and select Start Compare. Your backup drive is activated. At the same time, the message bar at the bottom of the screen displays the message "Comparing, press ESC to cancel." Also, at the top of the screen a Compare Progress box monitors the number of your current disk or tape, the percentage of the compare completed, the elapsed time of the compare, and the track number of the disk or tape that's currently being read.

5. You're prompted to insert, one by one, each disk or tape that contains your selected files. Do so as directed. The directory and file being compared at any given moment are indicated by the highlight cursors in the Tree List and File List. When the operation is completed, each file is marked with a symbol to indicate the result of the compare.

When all your selected files are compared, a dialog box appears. If all the files were identical, the top of the dialog box says "All Files Compare!" However, if some of the files were not identical, a box like this appears:

The box identifies the number of files that were equal, missing, older, newer, equal internally but with different dates, or just mismatched. To close the box, press ENTER or click OK.

Each compared file in the File List is marked with a symbol to its left. The symbols and their meanings are as follows:

Symbol	Meaning
=	The backup file and hard disk file are identical.
<	The backup file is older than the hard disk file, and its contents are different.
>	The backup file is newer than the hard disk file, and its contents are different.
s	The date/time stamps of the backup file and hard disk file are different, but their contents are identical.
x	The date/time stamps of the backup file and hard disk file are identical, but their contents are different.
-	The corresponding hard disk file is missing (that is, either deleted or moved to a different directory).

If a file has no symbol next to it, it means you didn't select it for the compare operation and so it wasn't compared.

If you performed the compare directly after a backup and an "x" appears next to any of the files, your backups are not reliable. Eliminate any memory-resident programs in your system and try the backup again. If you still have problems, try using the **C**onfigure **B**ackup Speed command to switch to a slower speed and try again.

After the compare, all files whose contents are unchanged (indicated by "=" and "s" symbols) are unselected, while all other files remain selected. You can then proceed to restore the files that didn't match properly.

Restoring Files

A restore operation converts backup files from their CP Backup format to their original format, and then copies them from the backup set to your hard disk or another location.

There are two basic reasons to restore files. First, if some of your hard disk files are damaged or deleted, restoring their previous versions from your backup set will prevent any data from being lost. In fact, this is the main reason for using CP Backup.

Second, if you want to transfer large amounts of data from your hard disk to another location, you can use the backup and restore operations to do the job quickly and efficiently.

Performing a Partial Restore

You will probably seldom need to restore more than a few files or a directory. To perform a partial restore on a functioning hard disk, follow these steps:

1. Follow the instructions in the "Choosing a Backup Set" section earlier in this chapter to display the backup set's directories in the Tree List.

2. If you aren't already in the Restore screen, switch to it now by pressing A, R, or clicking on the Action menu and selecting Restore.

3. Select the files you want to restore, using either the List windows (see "The CP Backup Tree List and File List" in Chapter 1) or the **O**ptions **S**election Options Include/Exclude Files command (see "Selecting Files" in Chapter 2). If your backup is Incremental and the **O**ptions **S**election Options **S**ubdirectory Inclusion switch is on, you can specify a particular Incremental session by selecting its date and time in the Tree List.

4. Press A, S, or press F6, or click on the Action menu and select Start Restore. Your backup drive is activated. At the same time, the message bar at the bottom of the screen displays the message "Restoring, press ESC to cancel." Also, at the top of the screen a Restore Progress box monitors the number of your current disk or tape, the percentage of the restore completed, the elapsed time of the restore, and the track number of the disk or tape that's currently being read.

5. You're prompted to insert, one by one, each disk or tape that contains your selected files. Do so as directed. The directory and file being restored at any given moment are indicated by the highlight cursors in the Tree List and File List.

6. If the **O**ptions Overwrite Warning command is on, you'll be prompted to verify that you want to overwrite any existing hard disk files. If you're only interested in the newest versions of files, select the Overwrite With **N**ewer File Only and **R**epeat For all Later Files options, and then press O or click OK. This will save you from being prompted on such operations, while protecting new files from being replaced by old ones.

7. When all your selected files are restored, a dialog box appears displaying the message "Restore Completed!" and providing such information as the number of directories, files, and bytes restored. To close the box, press ENTER or click OK.

Performing a Full Restore

There's always a chance that *all* the data on your hard disk will be lost. In the event of such a disaster, first determine whether the hard disk is still sound. For example, if the data was lost because all the files were overwritten, the hard disk is still functional; but if the data was lost due to hard disk defects, first analyze and repair the disk using DiskFix (see Chapter 7, "Repairing Disks Using DiskFix").

If your hard disk is functional, follow these steps to perform a full restore:

1. Reinstall DOS following the instructions in your DOS manual or a book about DOS.

2. Reinstall CP Backup following the instructions in Appendix A, "PC Tools Installation and Configuration."

3. Run and reconfigure CP Backup following the instructions in "Running and Configuring CP Backup" in Chapter 1.

4. Switch to the Restore screen.

5. Press O, O, or click on the Options menu and select Overwrite Warning, to turn the command off. This will speed the restore process in replacing any defective files still on the hard disk.

6. Press A, S, or press F6, or click on the Action menu and select Start Restore. If the Choose Directory dialog box appears, press I or click Insert.

7. You're prompted for the last disk or tape of your backup set. To continue, read one of the following sections appropriate to your backup set.

Restoring a Full or Full/Incremental Backup

If your last backup was either Full or a Full and Incremental combination, insert the last disk or tape of the set. All the files are selected in the Tree List.

You're prompted to insert, one by one, each disk or tape, starting from the first. Do so as directed. After you insert the last disk, your hard disk should be completely restored, as indicated by the "Restore Completed!" dialog box. Press ENTER or click OK to close the box.

Restoring a Full/Differential Backup

If your last backup was a Full and Differential combination, first insert the last disk or tape of the Full backup set. All the files are selected in the Tree List.

You are prompted to insert, one by one, each disk or tape in the set, starting with the first. Do so as directed. After you insert the last disk, your hard disk should be restored up to the day you performed the Full backup. Press ENTER or click OK to close the "Restore Completed!" dialog box.

Next, press F6 (and, if necessary, select Insert) to perform a second restore. This time, insert the last disk or tape of the Differential backup. As before, all the files are selected in the Tree List. Once again, you're prompted to insert each disk or tape in the set, starting with the first. Do so as directed.

After you insert the last disk, your hard disk should be completely restored. Again, press ENTER or click OK to close the "Restore Completed!" dialog box.

Restoring a Full/Separate Incremental Backup

If your last backup consisted of a Full backup and several Separate Incremental backups, first insert the last disk or tape of the Full backup set. All the files are selected in the Tree List.

You're prompted to insert, one by one, each disk or tape in the set, starting with the first. Do so as directed. After you insert the last disk, your hard disk should be restored up to the day you performed the Full backup. Press ENTER or click OK to close the "Restore Completed!" dialog box.

Next, press F6 (and, if necessary, select Insert) to perform another restore. This time, insert the last disk or tape of the first Separate Differential backup you made following the Full backup, and then repeat the restore steps in the previous paragraph.

Next, perform another restore using your next oldest Separate Differential backup. Continue doing this until all the Separate Differential backups you created after the Full backup have been restored.

When you're done, your hard disk should be completely restored. Press ENTER or click OK to close the "Restore Completed!" dialog box one last time.

Restoring with Missing or Damaged Disks

Even if portions of your backup set are lost or irreparably damaged, you can still retrieve the files on the remaining disks.

To do so, follow the usual restore procedures described in the previous sections. When you come to a disk or tape that's missing or unusable, just skip over it and insert the next one. A dialog box will come up telling you that a disk or tape is out of sequence. Press O or click OK to proceed with the backup.

You won't be able to restore the files on the missing disk or tape, and you'll also lose any file that only partially exists on the previous disk or tape. However, you'll be able to restore all your other files without problems.

Rebuilding the History File

If your missing disk or tape is the *last* one of the backup set, and you don't have a copy of the set's history file on your hard disk, you must rebuild the history file before restoring.

To do so, insert the first disk or tape. A dialog box will appear with the message "Backup directory not found." Press B or click Rebuild. You'll be prompted to insert each disk or tape in order. CP Backup will then reconstruct the history file. To preserve the file, press S or click Save when prompted. When you're done rebuilding, you can proceed as usual with the restore operation.

Identifying Backup Disks

It's highly recommended that you label each of your backup disks with the date and its numerical order in the backup set. However, if you sometimes forget to do so, or if you're not sure that you labeled a disk correctly, you can quickly get this information from the disk by using the CPBDIR program.

To display a disk's backup date and its order in the backup set, follow these steps:

1. Insert the backup disk you want to identify into a disk drive. (If possible, use drive A, since that's the CPBDIR default.)

2. From the DOS prompt, move to the directory that contains the CPBDIR program. For example, if you let Install create subdirectories in your PCTOOLS directory, type **CD\PCTOOLS\SYSTEM** and press ENTER.

3. Type **CPBDIR** followed by a space, the letter of the drive your disk is in, and a colon, and then press ENTER. For example, if your disk is in drive A, type **CPBDIR A:** and press ENTER.

4. A list of information like the following appears:

```
Disk is number 2 of a CP Backup set, backed up at 10:13a on 07/20/1991.
Disk was created with release 6.0 or 7.0 of CP Backup
The directory starts on track 4 (4h) of this disk.
This disk is recorded in DOS standard format.
Advanced Error Correction was ON for this backup.
```

Remove the backup disk, and label it with the displayed date and order number.

5. If you have another disk you want to identify, insert it into the drive. If you're using drive A, press ENTER and return to step 4. Otherwise, type the letter of your drive and a colon (for example, **B:**), press ENTER, and return to step 4.

6. When you're done identifying disks, type **Q** and press ENTER. The CPBDIR program exits and returns you to the DOS prompt.

Troubleshooting Restore Problems

During the course of restoring backup files, you may encounter some difficulties. The following are some of the problems most likely to come up and their probable solutions.

1.44MB Backup Disks Aren't Restoring Data Properly

If you're having reliability problems backing up on 1.44MB disks, it may be that the disks are really 720K disks that have been formatted to a higher capacity than they can support. Be sure to only use factory certified 1.44MB disks for 1.44MB backups.

"Disk From Wrong Backup" Appears During Restore

The message "Disk From Wrong Backup" typically indicates that you've mixed up disks from different backup sets while restoring files. However, it can also occur if your backup file dates are inconsistent. If you don't have a clock in your computer and you aren't in the habit of setting the date and time, you can confuse CP Backup into thinking you've mixed up your disks. The short-term solution is to make the dates and times of your backup files consistent by using PC Shell's File Change File Attribute Change command (see Chapter 16, "Managing Your Files"). The long-term solution is to get into the habit of using the DATE and TIME commands at the DOS prompt to set your system clock properly.

CP Backup Won't Restore from Both Drives

If you have two drives of the same type (for example, drives that are both 360K, or both 1.2MB, or both 1.44MB), CP Backup can use both of them during backups, but only one of them (typically drive A) during compares and restores. This is a design decision, so there's no way to get around it.

There's No Drive Letter in the Tree List

If the top of the Tree List displays a lone "\" rather than "A:\," it's because you just rebuilt a history file to make up for a missing last disk or tape from your backup set. This is the result of a design decision that a Tree List constructed using the Rebuild command should be visually differentiated from Tree Lists created automatically by CP Backup. It makes no difference in the program's operation.

Part *II*

Using the Data Recovery Utilities

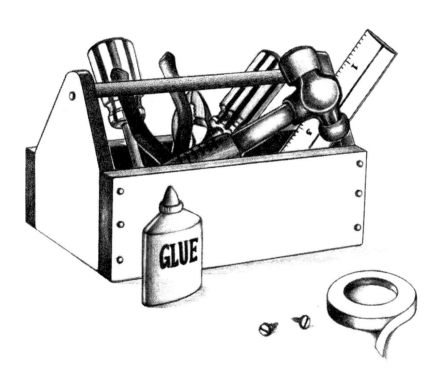

Chapter *4*

Data Recovery Overview

No matter how careful you are, you're occasionally going to experience data accidents.

For example, in the course of eliminating a group of obsolete files, you might end up also deleting some very important files. As another example, you might format an entire hard disk and then realize you still need much of the data it contains.

Even if you never make a mistake, disks spontaneously develop defects through normal wear-and-tear usage. When a defect occurs in an area where data is being stored, that data becomes unreadable.

PC Tools 7 can deal fully with all of these problems, and more. It does so by providing both programs that safeguard against data accidents and programs that recover lost data.

The data safeguard utilities include Mirror, which makes safety copies of critical information on your hard disk; Install (new to version 7), which creates a Recovery Disk containing important information about your system; Data Monitor (new to version 7), which preserves information about deleted files; PC Format, which formats disks without destroying their data; and DiskFix, which recognizes and repairs a variety of developing disk problems to prevent serious data loss.

The data recovery programs include Undelete, which quickly recovers deleted files; Unformat (new to version 7), which recovers the data on a formatted disk; Rebuild, which restores crucial system information; File Fix (new to version 7), which can repair common problems in dBASE- and Lotus 1-2-3-compatible files; and, again, DiskFix, which can often recover data by repairing areas of a disk that have become defective.

Coverage of these programs is divided among the next four chapters. Specifically:

- Chapter 5, "Safeguarding Your Data," covers protecting your files using the Mirror, Install, Data Monitor, and PC Format programs.

- Chapter 6, "Recovering Deleted or Formatted Data," covers using the Undelete program to rescue erased files, using the Unformat program to undo a disk format operation, and using the Rebuild program to restore a damaged partition table, CMOS data, or the boot record.

- Chapter 7, "Repairing Disks Using DiskFix," covers using the DiskFix program to mark or mend defective areas on a disk.

- Chapter 8, "Repairing dBASE and 1-2-3 Files Using File Fix," covers using the File Fix program to correct problems related to spreadsheet and database data files.

Each of these chapters requires that you have a basic understanding of how DOS handles disks and files. Therefore, this overview chapter is devoted to explaining how disks are laid out, the effects of formatting, and the processes behind file saving and deleting. After completing it, you'll have a solid foundation for knowing when and how to use the PC Tools recovery programs.

It's OK if you don't follow every detail of this chapter on your first reading. However, *do* try to understand the concepts behind the details. Also, pay special attention to the definitions of track, sector, cluster, boot record, FAT, root directory, and fragmentation, as these terms recur throughout the next four chapters (and, to a lesser extent, in Chapters 9 and 10, as well).

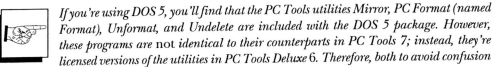

If you're using DOS 5, you'll find that the PC Tools utilities Mirror, PC Format (named Format), Unformat, and Undelete are included with the DOS 5 package. However, these programs are not identical to their counterparts in PC Tools 7; instead, they're licensed versions of the utilities in PC Tools Deluxe 6. Therefore, both to avoid confusion and to take advantage of the new features in PC Tools 7, it's recommended that you ignore these DOS 5 utilities and use the PC Tools 7 programs instead. In addition, it's recommended that you set the PATH statement in your AUTOEXEC.BAT file to list your PCTOOLS directory before your DOS directory. This will help ensure that whenever you run a program at the DOS prompt that's available in both directories, it's the PC Tools version that will be executed.

Understanding How Disks Are Organized

The main component of any disk is a magnetic platter like the one shown in Figure 4-1. The platter looks like a phonograph record, and there are actually several

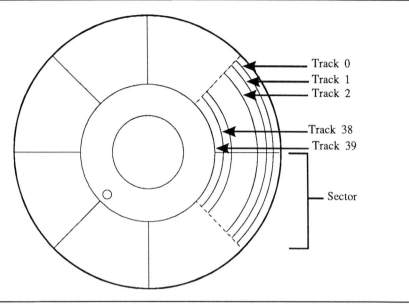

Figure 4-1.   *Disk Platter*

similarities. For example, just as a record holds music information, the platter holds all your computer data. (In fact, a hard disk's data is divided among several platters, but you can think of them as one large platter, which is how most PC Tools programs represent them.)

Also, just as a record has grooves around it to guide its needle, a disk platter needs concentric rings around it called *tracks* to guide the disk drive heads, which read and write data. A floppy disk might have as few as 40 tracks, while a hard disk might have 300 or more tracks.

Unlike a record, though, a disk is also conceptually divided by straight lines radiating out from the platter's center, as also shown in Figure 4-1. These lines split the disk up into pie-shaped wedges called *Sectors*. A floppy disk typically has from 8 to 16 Sectors, while a hard disk typically has from 17 to 30 Sectors.

Tracks and Sectors are numbered sequentially, starting with 0. For example, Figure 4-1 represents a floppy disk with 40 tracks numbered 0 to 39, and with 8 Sectors numbered 0 to 7. Just as you can refer to a spot on a map by using latitude and longitude, you can refer to a particular area of a disk by using its track number and Sector number. For example, the disk in Figure 4-1 begins at Track 0, Sector 0 and ends at Track 39, Sector 7.

The area defined by a track and Sector number is typically 512 bytes long. Somewhat confusingly, this area is *also* called a sector. Therefore, the word "sector" can refer to either an entire wedge of a disk or one arc of a track. You can usually tell which meaning is intended by the context in which the word appears. In addition, this book uses "Sector" (uppercase "S") for the wedge meaning and "sector" (lowercase) for the arc meaning.

To make things slightly more complicated, DOS splits a file's data into areas called *clusters,* whose size varies for different disks. For example, on 360K and 720K floppy disks, a cluster is two sectors long (1024 bytes), while on 1.2MB and 1.44MB floppy disks, a cluster is one sector long (512 bytes).

Cluster size also varies on different capacity hard disks. For example, on hard disks under 20MB, clusters are typically eight sectors long (4096 bytes), while on hard disks of 20MB or more, clusters are typically four sectors long (2048 bytes).

To make all this a bit more concrete, imagine that you are about to save a word processing file that is 4000 bytes long. If you stored the file on a 360K floppy disk, it would take up four clusters; but if you stored the file on a 32MB hard disk, it would take up two clusters.

It's not important that you remember such details as how big a sector is or how many clusters are on a certain type of disk. However, it *is* important that you understand the concepts these terms represent, so that you can comprehend such operations as repairing a defective sector or reorganizing a file's clusters.

Understanding Formatting

Virtually all floppy disks and many hard disks are sold unformatted. This means that they initially have no information on them and so are unreadable to DOS. The next two sections explain what happens when hard and floppy disks are formatted, and how formatting information can be protected and restored by PC Tools.

Understanding What Formatting Does

Hard disks are formatted in three steps: low-level formatting, partitioning, and high-level formatting.

The low-level format maps out the tracks and Sectors discussed in the previous section. It also marks off defective areas of the disk so that data won't be saved to them. This operation is typically performed for you by a program from the hard disk's manufacturer.

Partitioning defines the hard disk as one or more separate sections. For example, you can define a 40MB hard disk as a single 40MB partition, or as 32MB and 8MB partitions, or as four 10MB partitions, and so on. This operation is typically performed by the DOS program FDISK.

High-level formatting is what most people have in mind when they talk about formatting. This operation is performed by such programs as DOS FORMAT and PC Format.

High-level formatting does several things. Specifically:

- It checks the disk to verify that sectors have been mapped out properly and marks any defective ones it finds as unusable.

- It copies a small program for loading DOS, called the *boot record,* to Track 0, Sector 0. This program—in combination with hidden system files (these are typically named IBMBIO.COM and IBMDOS.COM, or MSBIO.SYS and MSDOS.COM) and the program COMMAND.COM (which contains DOS)—enables the disk to load DOS, starting up your PC. (However, these extra files are only copied when you format using the /S parameter by typing, for example, **FORMAT C: /S.**) Damage to the boot record will render the disk unable to load DOS, but won't cause any harm to the rest of the disk's files.

- It creates a *File Allocation Table,* or *FAT.* This table keeps track of which specific clusters each file's data are stored in, and which clusters are available for new files or for revised files that have grown in size. The FAT is extremely important; if it becomes damaged, you could lose access to all your data.

- It creates a *root directory,* which holds every file's name, size, creation date and time, and attributes. In addition, the root directory contains the location of each file's first cluster. The root directory is also extremely important, and damage to it can also result in your losing access to all your data.

When you format floppy disks, low-level and high-level formatting are combined in one step. In other words, when you use either DOS FORMAT or PC Format on an unformatted floppy, all the disk's tracks and Sectors are first mapped on the disk, and its defective areas marked. The disk's boot record, FAT, and root directory are then copied onto it.

You usually need to format a disk only once. However, you may occasionally reformat a disk to quickly wipe out all its contents, or to "rejuvenate" it if it's developed numerous defects. Once a disk is reformatted, its data can be very difficult to recover, so always think twice before formatting disks with files on them.

Using PC Tools to Preserve Formatting Data

All the effects of formatting are subject to defects. For example, a disk's sectors can become unreadable over time, its partition information or boot record can suffer injury, and its FAT or root directory can become damaged. As a result, PC Tools provides a number of programs for protecting and recovering disk data.

If a disk's sectors start to become unreadable, you can refresh them without harming the data on them by using either PC Format with the /R option (see "PC Format Parameters" in Chapter 5) or the DiskFix program (see Chapter 7, "Repairing Disks Using DiskFix"). Both programs also mark off unfixable sectors so that no new data is saved to them.

A hard disk's partition information is stored on a table on the disk, and is therefore as vulnerable as any other data. The same is true of the disk's boot record. You can save your partition and boot record data using either the Install or Mirror program (see "Creating a Recovery Disk" and "Saving Your Partition Table, CMOS Data, and Boot Record" in Chapter 5). If you then get a message such as "Invalid drive specification," you can restore the partition table and boot record using the Rebuild program (see "Restoring Your Partition Table, CMOS Data, and Boot Record" in Chapter 6).

Generally, however, the most serious threat to your data is damage to your disk's FAT or root directory (as detailed in the next section). If these areas start becoming defective, they can often be repaired by DiskFix (see Chapter 7 and "Restoring the FAT and Root Directory" in Chapter 6).

On the other hand, if you erase the contents of the FAT and portions of the root directory by reformatting the disk, your best chance of recovery is a combination of the Mirror and Unformat programs (see Chapters 5 and 6).

Understanding How Files Are Saved

When you save a new file, DOS first checks the disk's FAT to find the next cluster available, and it then writes to that cluster. If there is data left over once the cluster is full, DOS then writes to the next cluster, and then the next one, until all the file's data is saved.

If there is plenty of room on the disk, the clusters will all be adjacent to each other. Once the disk starts filling up, however, cluster organization gets more complicated.

For example, assume DOS saves a file named MEMO1 in two adjacent clusters, and saves a file named MEMO2 in the cluster directly following them. If you later revise MEMO1 so that it's ten clusters long, DOS will save the file's initial data back to the first two clusters, but will then have to look elsewhere because the cluster physically following them is still occupied by MEMO2. DOS will therefore check the FAT for the next available clusters, and proceed to use them to store the rest of the file's data. These other clusters could be *anywhere* on the disk. As a result, file MEMO1's contents will become physically separated, or *fragmented.*

Fragmentation isn't a major problem as long as the FAT keeps track of the location and order of each file's clusters. However, if the FAT becomes damaged, such fragmentation can instantly turn your disk into a jumble of disconnected data. Even if all your files are undamaged, without the FAT the fragmented files will often be unrecoverable.

You can protect the contents of the FAT by running the Mirror program regularly, and it's *highly* recommended that you do so. For more information, see "Using Mirror" in Chapter 5.

As an extra safeguard, you can eliminate most disk fragmentation by regularly running the PC Tools Compress program. For more information, see Chapter 9, "Speeding Your Disks Using Compress."

Understanding How Files Are Deleted

When you delete a file, its contents on the disk remain intact. However, in the root directory, the first letter of the file's name is replaced by a special character (typically σ, the Greek sigma), which marks the file as being deleted. Additionally, the FAT marks the file's clusters as being available for the storage of new files.

You can retrieve a deleted file in several ways. If the Data Monitor program was memory resident when you deleted the file, and either the Delete Sentry or Delete Tracker option was turned on, *and* you immediately run the PC Tools Undelete program, you generally won't have any problem recovering the file. The Monitor's Delete Sentry option actually preserves the file temporarily in a hidden directory, offering near-total protection. The Monitor's Delete Tracker option, on the other hand, allows the file to be deleted but saves its full name and cluster locations, so as long as you don't overwrite any of the file's clusters with new data before running Undelete, file recovery will be quick and complete.

If neither Data Monitor option was active when you deleted, but the file happened to be stored in consecutive clusters on the disk, immediately running the PC Tools Undelete program will also probably recover the entire file. That's because the disk's root directory still contains the location of the file's first cluster and the file's size. The Undelete program can read this information from the directory and then quickly reconstruct the file. The only information it won't have is the file's first letter (overwritten by the sigma character), which you can easily supply.

Lastly, if neither Data Monitor option was active when you deleted, and the file was fragmented into two or more areas on the disk, you may be able to recover the initial clusters of the file. However, you will find it difficult or impossible to recover the rest of the clusters because there's no longer any record of where they're located.

For more information on this topic, see "Monitoring Deleted Files" in Chapter 5 and "Recovering Deleted Files" in Chapter 6.

Data Recovery Overview Summary

You now have a solid grasp of how data is handled on your floppy and hard disks. This knowledge should prove useful as you work your way through the various inevitable data disasters that occur in the course of using your PC.

To obtain more detailed information, follow this guide:

- To learn the precise steps you should take to safeguard your data, read Chapter 5.

- To recover deleted files, formatted disks, defective partition tables, and other system data, read Chapter 6.

- To fix defective sectors and a number of other disk problems, read Chapter 7.

- To repair dBASE- and Lotus 1-2-3-compatible data files, read Chapter 8.

- For a summary of data safeguarding procedures, be sure to read the end of Chapter 5, and to heed its conclusion that in case all else fails, it's wise to back up your disks regularly using CP Backup (covered in Chapters 1, 2, and 3).

Chapter **5**

Safeguarding Your Data

In Chapter 4, you learned about the various disasters that can happen to your data. In this chapter, you'll learn how to safeguard against such disasters.

The following sections cover how to use Install to preserve critical system information; Mirror to save a disk's boot record, FAT, and root directory; the /PARTN option to save your hard disk's boot record, CMOS data, and partition table; Data Monitor to preserve information on a disk's deleted files; and PC Format to safely format disks. In addition, the end of this chapter lists and briefly describes *all* the PC Tools programs available for safeguarding your data.

Creating a Recovery Disk

PC Tools 7 includes a new program called Install, which handles the installation and configuration of all PC Tools utilities. In addition to these functions Install has the ability to copy critical system information and data restoration programs to a floppy disk. This disk can then be used to help you recover lost data, so it's referred to as a *Recovery Disk*.

If you followed the instructions in Appendix A, "PC Tools Installation and Configuration," you've already created a Recovery Disk. In this case, unless your system information has changed, you can skip the rest of this section and move on to the "Using Mirror" section.

On the other hand, if you didn't choose to create a Recovery Disk during installation, or if your partition table, CMOS data, or version of DOS has changed, it's highly recommended that you create a Recovery Disk now. The floppy will contain the following programs and data:

- Your DOS system files, which allow you to start your PC, or *boot*, from the floppy instead of your hard disk. This is useful if you suddenly develop problems booting from your hard disk. It's also useful if you need to start your PC "clean," that is, without all the drivers and memory-resident programs you ordinarily include in your hard disk's AUTOEXEC.BAT and CONFIG.SYS files.

- The DOS SYS program, which can restore damaged DOS system files. This is useful if your hard disk has suddenly developed problems with starting up your system.

- A minimal CONFIG.SYS file, which only contains commands such as FILES=35, BUFFERS=35, and STACKS=32,128 to ensure that your system runs properly.

- Your hard disk's partition table, which you can use to restore damaged partition data (see Chapter 4, "Data Recovery Overview," and also "Saving Your Partition Table, CMOS Data, and Boot Record" later in this chapter).

- Your CMOS data, which provides an 80286, 80386, or 80486 computer with such information as the type of memory it contains, and the number and type of hard and floppy drives it has installed. The CMOS (which stands for Complementary Metal-Oxide Semiconductor) is a small memory chip powered by a battery so that it can maintain its information independently of your PC's status. However, when its battery begins wearing out (which typically happens in about two years), the CMOS starts to lose data and may cause your system to behave erratically. The Recovery Disk allows you to restore any lost CMOS data (preferably after you've installed a new battery).

- The PC Tools utilities Unformat, Undelete, and Rebuild (see Chapter 6, "Recovering Deleted or Formatted Data"), which let you recover accidentally formatted disks, deleted files, and partition table and CMOS data; and the PC Tools program MI (see Chapter 18, "Using Advanced PC Shell Features"), which lets you display your system's memory usage. Having these recovery tools on the floppy safeguards against your being unable to access them on your hard disk.

To create a Recovery Disk after you've already installed PC Tools, follow these steps:

1. Locate a blank floppy disk that's in the proper format for your A drive, put a label on the floppy, and write "PC Tools Recovery Disk" and the current date on the label (or use the label supplied in your PC Tools package). Also,

if the disk isn't already bootable, format it using the /S option. (If you aren't sure how to format, proceed with steps 2 through 9.)

2. Insert your PC Tools Disk 1 installation disk into a floppy drive.

3. Go to the DOS prompt and set it to the drive that contains your PC Tools disk. (For example, if the disk is in drive A, type **A:** from the DOS prompt and press ENTER.)

4. Type **INSTALL /RD** and press ENTER. After a moment, a message appears saying that the program is about to build a Recovery Disk, and that it assumes you've already installed *at least* the Mirror program (which is needed to save your partition table, CMOS data, and boot record).

5. Press ENTER or click OK. You're asked to specify the drive and directory containing your PC Tools 7 files.

6. If the default path (typically C:\PCTOOLS) is correct, press ENTER twice or click OK. Otherwise, first edit the path appropriately, and then press ENTER twice. The message "Analyzing your hard disk" appears.

7. If your Disk 1 installation floppy is in your A drive, you're now requested to remove it. (On certain systems, you may see this request even if the floppy isn't in drive A.) Do so, and return the disk to storage with your other PC Tools disks. When you're ready, press ENTER or click OK.

8. You're asked to select the drive that contains your AUTOEXEC.BAT file and is used to start up, or boot, your system. Press the letter of the appropriate drive and press ENTER, or click on the drive's icon and click OK. The following dialog box appears:

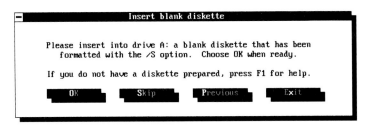

9. Insert your Recovery Disk into your A drive. (If the floppy hasn't already been formatted with the /S option (making it bootable), press F1 and ENTER to display information on how to format; write down the command that applies to your system; press ESC, ESC, ENTER to exit to DOS and format your disk; and then repeat steps 2 through 9.)

10. Press ENTER or click OK. Install now writes to the floppy the program files CONFIG.SYS, REBUILD.COM, MI.COM, UNFORMAT.EXE, and SYS.COM, and the data file PARTNSAV.FIL (via the command MIRROR

/PARTN), which stores your partition table, CMOS data, and boot record. A message then appears telling you the Recovery Disk has been successfully created.

11. Press ENTER or click OK. You're returned to the DOS prompt.

12. If your hard disk requires a device driver, use the DOS COPY command or PC Shell's **F**ile **C**opy option (see Chapter 16, "Managing Your Files") to transfer the driver to the Recovery Disk. Also, edit the floppy's CONFIG.SYS file to specify the driver; or, if you aren't sure how to do so, just copy the hard disk's CONFIG.SYS file to the floppy. If you need more information about your hard disk driver, contact your hard disk vendor or manufacturer.

13. Put your Recovery Disk in a safe place. If you later have some sort of data accident, see Chapter 6, "Recovering Deleted or Formatted Data," for instructions on how to use the files on the Recovery Disk to restore what was lost.

Using Mirror

As explained in Chapter 4, the Mirror program backs up the contents of the three most critical areas of a disk: its FAT, its root directory, and its boot record. If any of these areas become damaged or erased, you can restore them using your Mirror data and the Unformat program (see Chapter 6). Furthermore, the Mirror data is used by DiskFix (see Chapter 7, "Repairing Disks Using DiskFix"), which compares it against the current FAT and determines which is more accurate. Running Mirror is therefore a vital component to safeguarding your hard disk.

In addition to its normal usage, you can also run Mirror with the parameter /PARTN to save your hard disk's partition table, CMOS data, and boot record to a floppy disk for safekeeping. In fact, MIRROR /PARTN is the command used by the Install program to save this data to the Recovery Disk.

In PC Tools Deluxe 6, Mirror also included a Delete Tracking option, which preserved the full name and cluster locations of every file deleted. In PC Tools 7, however, this option has been renamed Delete Tracker and made part of an entirely new program named Data Monitor. For more information, see the "Monitoring Deleted Files" section later in this chapter.

To run Mirror, you can simply go to the DOS prompt, set the prompt to the drive you want to safeguard, type **MIRROR**, and press ENTER.

Alternatively, you can specify the drive you want to operate on by including it and a colon on the Mirror command line. For example, to safeguard drive C, type **MIRROR C:** from the DOS prompt and press ENTER.

In addition, you can specify running Mirror on multiple drives at a time. For example, to safeguard the disks on drives A, B, and C, type **MIRROR A: B: C:** from the DOS prompt and press ENTER.

For each drive specified, Mirror first copies the contents of the disk's boot record, FAT, and root directory to a read-only file named MIRROR.FIL in the disk's root. If a previous version of MIRROR.FIL already exists, Mirror renames it MIR-ROR.BAK. The old file is preserved so that if you accidentally run Mirror on the disk directly *after* a major data accident occurs, thus filling the new Mirror file with inaccurate information, you'll still have the old file to fall back on.

If you're especially short of disk space, you have the option of running Mirror with a /1 parameter. This causes the previous version of MIRROR.FIL to be overwritten rather than saved as MIRROR.BAK. Also, if a copy of MIRROR.BAK already exists on the disk, the parameter causes it to be deleted. (For example, to run Mirror on drive A, you'd type **MIRROR A: /1**.) *However, in most cases it's recommended that you avoid this parameter and allow the BAK file to exist for the extra protection it provides.*

After Mirror saves its data files, it creates or updates a hidden file named MIRORSAV.FIL in the last cluster of the disk. This file stores the cluster locations of MIRROR.FIL and MIRROR.BAK. Lastly, Mirror exits and returns you to the DOS prompt.

On the vast majority of systems, this operation is quick and trouble free. However, if the last cluster of your disk is defective, Mirror will make a number of attempts to save MIRORSAV.FIL to it before giving up and saving to the next to last cluster instead. This will occur *every time* you run Mirror.

If you experience this rare problem, first try to repair the defective cluster by running Diskfix (see Chapter 7). If that doesn't work, you may want to consider the drastic solution of backing up your entire disk using CP Backup (see Chapter 1, "CP Backup Overview"), then using FDISK to repartition the disk to exclude the defective last sector (see your DOS manual), and then restoring all your files. The only other alternatives are to put up with a long wait every time you run Mirror, or to give up using Mirror on the disk. Fortunately, again, this problem is fairly rare.

Running Mirror from Batch Files

It's a good idea to run Mirror every time you turn on your computer. You can make this happen automatically by entering the MIRROR command into your AUTO-EXEC.BAT file, or by having the Install program enter it for you. For more information, see Appendix A.

If you're dealing with especially sensitive data, or you're in an environment where it's likely that accidents will occur to your disk, you may want to additionally run Mirror every time you finish working with an application. You can do so by creating a series of batch files that run your various applications and then run Mirror after you exit to DOS. For example, a WPM.BAT batch file to run the word processing program WordPerfect could read as follows:

```
CD\WP51
WP
MIRROR
```

This batch file switches to the WordPerfect 5.1 directory, runs WordPerfect, and pauses until you exit the program. It then runs Mirror to preserve whatever FAT and root directory changes you created by revising your WordPerfect document files.

Saving Your Partition Table, CMOS Data, and Boot Record

As explained in Chapter 4, before your hard disk was high-level formatted, it was partitioned. The partition information is saved in a special table on the hard disk, and it's as vulnerable to damage as any other data. The Mirror program therefore provides a /PARTN parameter that lets you copy the contents of the table to a file named PARTNSAV.FIL on a floppy disk.

In addition, this parameter saves your system's CMOS data, which—as explained in "Creating a Recovery Disk" earlier in this chapter—provides an 80286, 80386, or 80486 computer with such configuration information as the type of memory it contains, and the number and type of hard and floppy drives it has installed.

The parameter also saves your hard disk's boot record, which is used by the disk to start up your PC.

If any problem occurs later with the partition table or your CMOS data (usually indicated by the DOS message "Invalid drive specification"), or if you've trouble starting up your PC from your hard disk, you can overwrite any defective data that may be causing the problem by using the PARTNSAV.FIL file and the Rebuild command (see Chapter 6).

The MIRROR /PARTN command is designed to save only a standard DOS partition table created by FDISK. It cannot save partition data created by programs such as Disk Manager from On-Track, SpeedStor from Storage Dimensions, or V Feature or V Feature Deluxe from Golden Bow Systems. If you use such a program, see your manual or contact the manufacturer to learn how to save partition information.

If you've created the Recovery Disk discussed at the beginning of this chapter, that floppy already contains your system's partition table, CMOS data, and boot record. However, if you ever use FDISK to alter your partitions or logical drives, or if you ever change your system's CMOS configuration, you should save the revised data. To do so, follow these steps:

1. Locate your Recovery Disk (or, if necessary, any formatted floppy disk), write the current date on the disk's label, and insert the disk into a drive.

2. From the DOS prompt, type **MIRROR /PARTN** and press ENTER. The following message appears:

```
Mirror V7
(c)1987-1991 Central Point Software, Inc.

Disk Partition Table saver.

The partition information from your hard drive(s) has been read.

Next, the file PARTNSAV.FIL will be written to a floppy disk.  Please
insert a formatted diskette and enter the name of the diskette drive.
What drive? A
```

3. Type the letter of the drive containing your floppy disk and press ENTER. (For example, if it's in drive B, type **B** and press ENTER. If it's in drive A, just press ENTER.) After a moment, the partition table, CMOS data (if any), and boot record are saved, the message "Successful." appears, and the Mirror program exits.

4. Type **DIR**, a space, the letter of the floppy drive, and a colon, and press ENTER. (For example, if the floppy is in drive A, type **DIR A:** and press ENTER.) You should see the file PARTNSAV.FIL listed with today's date as its creation date.

5. Store the floppy disk in a safe place.

Monitoring Deleted Files

When you delete a file, its contents are unaffected. However, as explained in Chapter 4, the first letter of the file's name and the locations of all but its first cluster are discarded. Therefore, if the file happens to be fragmented, it will be difficult or impossible to totally recover it. To increase your chances of restoring deleted files, PC Tools 7 includes a new memory-resident program called Data Monitor.

To run Data Monitor, type **DATAMON** at the DOS prompt and press ENTER. The following main menu appears:

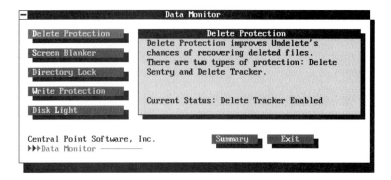

The menu lists five options: Delete Protection, Screen Blanker, Directory Lock, Write Protection, and Disk Light. The latter four options concern data security or general convenience, and they're therefore covered in Chapter 12, "Shielding Data Using Data Monitor." However, the Delete Protection option is a critical component of PC Tools' data recovery strategy.

If you select **D**elete Protection by pressing ENTER or clicking on it, a dialog box like this appears:

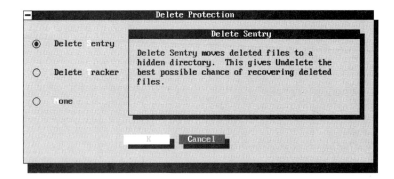

The box lists two protection options: Delete Sentry, which preserves all deleted files in a hidden directory; and Delete Tracker, which saves the names and cluster locations of deleted files. These options are covered in the following two sections.

Using Delete Sentry

Delete Sentry provides near-complete protection for deleted files at the cost of a portion of your disk space.

When Delete Sentry is active, it first creates a directory in your disk's root named SENTRY. This directory is "hidden" (that is, it has its "hidden" attribute turned on), so you won't see it listed when you use the DOS DIR command.

If you want to, you can view the SENTRY directory and its files by using the PC Shell or Directory Maintenance program (see Chapter 17, "Managing Your Directories and Disks"). Also, if you're using DOS 5 and are at the DOS prompt, typing **DIR\ /ADH** *and pressing* ENTER *will display the SENTRY directory name, and typing* **DIR\SENTRY** *and pressing* ENTER *will list the files in the directory. The files will* not *be listed with their original names, but they* will *be listed with their original sizes and creation dates.*

Delete Sentry then constantly monitors your system for a delete file command. When one occurs, it throws the command away and instead simply changes the directory path of the file to \SENTRY. This has the effect of "moving" the file to the SENTRY directory, even though the file's physical location on the disk has not changed. As far as DOS is concerned, no deletion has taken place, only a move operation. As a result, the file's clusters remain allocated in the FAT, preventing them from being overwritten by new files.

Next, to indicate that you *did* delete the file, Delete Sentry intercepts all your DOS DIR commands and makes DOS subtract whatever space the files in the SENTRY directory are taking up before it reports the amount of room left on your disk. In this way, Delete Sentry creates the appearance that the files you deleted have actually been removed from the disk. (To have the SENTRY directory *included* in a disk space total, you can use the CHKDSK command instead of DIR.)

Finally, if Delete Sentry detects that you're beginning to run out of disk space, it will begin to *really* delete, or *purge,* the files in the SENTRY directory, starting with the least-recently deleted files. However, it will perform all this disk space monitoring and purging automatically, so that you never have to be aware of what's actually going on.

In addition, you can set Delete Sentry to purge SENTRY files after a specified number of days or after they exceed a specified percentage of your disk's space. Furthermore, you can specify precisely what types of deleted files you want preserved (for example, data files) and/or what types of files you *don't* want preserved (for example, BAK files). In other words, Delete Sentry is flexible enough to be useful even if you don't have a great deal of disk space to devote to your SENTRY directory.

To summarize, Delete Sentry provides your deleted files with the most complete protection possible, because it actually preserves the files in a special directory. At the same time, the program does such a good job of unobtrusively hiding and managing your deleted files that you can forget about it—except when you need to recover deleted data.

To turn on and configure the Delete Sentry utility, follow these steps:

1. If Data Monitor is already resident in memory (which you can check by typing **MI** from the DOS prompt and pressing ENTER), first unload it so that you can start from a fresh slate. To do this, clear any memory-resident programs you ran after Data Monitor, and then type **DATAMON /U** at the DOS prompt and press ENTER.

2. Type **DATAMON** and press ENTER. The Data Monitor main menu appears.

3. Press ENTER or click Delete Protection.

4. Press S, O, or click Delete Sentry and OK. A dialog box like this appears:

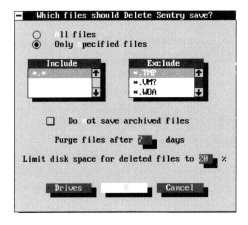

The box offers the following options:

- *All files*   This option sets Delete Sentry to preserve *all* deleted files.

- *Only specified files*   This option sets Delete Sentry to preserve only the files you specify in the Include and Exclude boxes (see the next two options). This is the default.

- *Include*   This box sets the files that Delete Sentry will preserve when "Only specified files" is selected. You can use the DOS wildcard ? to represent any single character and the DOS wildcard * to represent any group of characters. For example, to specify all dBASE and 1-2-3 files, you'd include the lines *.DBF and *.WK?. You can enter up to 20 lines. The default is *.*, which specifies all files.

- *Exclude*   This box sets the files that Delete Sentry will *not* preserve when "Only specified files" is selected. For example, the line *.BAK would make Delete Sentry skip preserving backup files. The defaults are *.TMP, *.VM?,

*.WOA, *.SWP, *.SPL, *.RMG, *.IMG, *.THM, and **.DOV,* which all specify various temporary files used by PC Tools and other software packages.

- *Do **not** save archived files*   If on, this option prevents Delete Sentry from preserving any files whose archive bits are cleared, indicating they've been backed up by a program such as CP Backup. If you perform regular backups and save your backup files for at least a week, you can use this option to reduce the space you provide to the SENTRY directory and/or to allow your non-archived deleted files more time on your disk before they're purged. The default setting is *off,* preserving files regardless of their archive status.

- *Purge files after* n *days*   This option sets a cutoff period for how long files are permitted in the SENTRY directory before being purged. You can select any period from 1 to 999 days, or enter 0 to *never* purge files based on their age. The default is 7 days.

Delete Sentry only checks the system date when it's initially loaded (typically from your AUTOEXEC.BAT file). Therefore, if you leave your PC on continuously for weeks at a time, no deleted files will be purged based on their age during that period regardless of the time limit you specified. To get around this, simply reboot your PC every now and then.

- *Limit disk space for deleted files to* n%   This option sets a cutoff for the percentage of the disk that will be allocated to the SENTRY directory. Once the directory reaches this limit, Delete Sentry begins purging the files that have been in SENTRY the longest. When choosing a percentage, take into account your hard disk's size, the number of files you normally delete, and the typical size of those files (for example, if a file is larger than your SENTRY directory, the file will *not* be protected in any way). In most cases, a number between 1 and 20 is appropriate. The default is *20* percent.

- *Drives*   This option lets you select the drives Delete Sentry will protect. To use it, press ALT-D or click Drives. A dialog box like this appears:

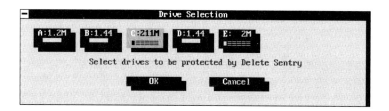

Your hard disk drives are already selected by default. To select additional drives and/or unselect drives, press the letter of each drive you want to affect, or click the drive's icon. When you're done, press ALT-O or click OK to accept your settings and return to the Delete Sentry dialog box.

- *OK*   This option accepts your settings and returns you to the Data Monitor main menu.

- *Cancel*   This option cancels your settings and returns you to the Data Monitor main menu.

After you adjust the box's settings, press ALT-O or click OK. You're returned to the Data Monitor main menu. To save your settings, first press X or click Exit to bring up the Close dialog box. If a checkmark does *not* appear next to the **S**ave Configuration option, press S or click next to the option. When the checkmark appears, press ENTER or click OK. Your new settings are saved to disk and will stay in effect for future Data Monitor sessions.

Lastly, you should install the Data Monitor program in your AUTOEXEC.BAT file so that it loads every time you start up your PC. You can do this by using the Install program (see Appendix A); or you can do it directly by inserting the line DATAMON /LOAD, which loads the program into memory based on your settings in its dialog boxes.

 If you're a NOVELL network supervisor, you can set Delete Sentry for use on your network by using the steps just discussed, and in addition assigning NetWare 286 users all rights to the \SENTRY directory except Parental, or NetWare 386 users all rights to \SENTRY except Access Control and Supervisory. The Delete Tracker option, on the other hand, will not *work on networks.*

Using Delete Tracker

As explained in the previous section, Delete Sentry provides the best protection for your deleted files, but to work properly it requires a significant portion of your disk. Therefore, if your disk is tight for space, use Delete Tracker instead. This utility saves the full name and cluster locations of each file that's deleted.

Specifically, when Delete Tracker is active, it constantly monitors your system for a delete file command. When one occurs, the utility pauses the deletion procedure, saves the file's full name and cluster locations to a hidden file named PCTRACKR.DEL in the disk's root directory, and then allows the deletion to proceed.

If you try to recover the deleted file *immediately* after the deletion occurs (which is the typical scenario for most people), the data in PCTRACKR.DEL virtually ensures that you'll succeed. However, if you try to recover the file after you've saved other files, you may find that the deleted file was overwritten by your new data and irretrievably destroyed.

Therefore, as soon as you realize you've deleted a file by accident, you should be very careful not to write to the disk until the file has been undeleted.

To keep PCTRACKR.DEL from taking up too much space, Delete Tracker imposes a default limit on the number of deleted files it maintains information on. The limit varies with the type of disk being tracked, as shown in Table 5-1. The first column of Table 5-1 lists the type of disk, the second lists the maximum number of deleted files that will be tracked, and the third lists the approximate amount of space PCTRACKR.DEL itself takes up when filled to its default capacity for the disk. When PCTRACKR.DEL reaches the limit, it simply erases its oldest entry to make room for its newest entry.

If you ever want to delete the PCTRACKR.DEL file itself, you must first unload Delete Tracker from memory, or the utility won't allow you to affect the file.

To turn on and configure Delete Tracker, follow these steps:

1. If Data Monitor is already resident in memory (which you can check by typing **MI** from the DOS prompt and pressing ENTER), first unload it so that you can start from a fresh slate. To do this, clear any memory-resident programs you ran after Data Monitor, and then type **DATAMON /U** at the DOS prompt and press ENTER.

2. Type **DATAMON** and press ENTER. The Data Monitor main menu appears.

3. Press ENTER or click Delete Protection.

4. Press T, O, or click Delete Tracker and OK. A dialog box appears that lets you select the drives Delete Tracker will protect. Your hard disk drives are already selected by default.

5. To select additional drives and/or unselect drives, press the letter of each drive you want to affect, or click the drive's icon. When you're done, press ALT-O or click OK. Your settings are accepted, and you're returned to the Data Monitor main menu.

6. To save your settings, first press X or click Exit to bring up the Close dialog box. If a checkmark does *not* appear next to the **S**ave Configuration option,

Disk Type	File Tracking Limit	PCTRACKR.DEL Size
360K	25	5K
720K	50	9K
1.2MB	75	14K
1.44MB	75	14K
20MB	101	18K
32MB	202	36K
Over 32MB	303	55K

Table 5-1. *Delete Tracker Default Limits*

press S or click next to the option. When the checkmark appears, press ENTER or click OK. Your new settings are saved to disk and will stay in effect for future Data Monitor sessions.

7. Install the Data Monitor program in your AUTOEXEC.BAT file so that it loads every time you start up your PC. You can do this by using the Install program (see Appendix A); or you can do it directly by inserting the line DATAMON /LOAD, which loads the program into memory based on your settings in its dialog boxes.

Using PC Format

PC Format is an alternative to the FORMAT program packaged with versions of DOS prior to DOS 5. PC Format is just as effective as FORMAT, but much safer to use because its effects can be undone and the data it has operated on recovered. In fact, it's *so* effective that for DOS 5, Microsoft licensed the PC Tools Deluxe 6 version of the program as a replacement for its own FORMAT program.

However, the PC Tools 7 version of PC Format is even *better*. That's because, in addition to supporting all its previous command line options, it now offers an easy-to-use visual system for selecting formatting options. This interactive mode is ideal for beginners, mouse users, people who use lots of formatting options, and anyone who enjoys a more attractive display.

The following sections first explain the advantages of using PC Format on floppy disks and hard disks. They then discuss how to install PC Format, run both the command line and interactive versions of PC Format, and use PC Format parameters.

For the rest of this chapter, the term "DOS FORMAT" is used to refer to versions of the program previous to DOS 5. As just mentioned, the FORMAT program in DOS 5 is really a version of PC Format 6 and so includes all the safeguards of PC Format.

PC Format Versus DOS FORMAT for Floppy Disks

When you format a floppy disk using the standard DOS FORMAT program, virtually every byte on the disk is overwritten by the hexadecimal characters F6. This totally destroys all your files, making any recovery of data impossible.

When you format a floppy disk using PC Format, however, a much more careful procedure is followed. First, the program checks Track 0 and Track 1 (where the boot record, FAT, and root directory are stored) for existing data. If it doesn't find anything, it concludes the disk has never been formatted and so doesn't contain any data. In this case, like DOS FORMAT, PC Format overwrites the disk with F6 characters to lay down tracks and Sectors.

However, if PC Format *does* find any data on the disk, it will first display the message "Are you SURE you want to do this?" and prompt you for verification. If you do anything other than type **YES** and press ENTER, the format will be canceled.

Furthermore, even if you verify, PC Format does only two things that are destructive in order to clear the disk for new files. First, it erases the first letter of each file's name in the root directory to mark the file as deleted. (At the same time, however, it saves each first letter 16 bytes from where it originally was, in a reserved area of the root directory.) Second, it clears the FAT so that all clusters on the disk are marked as available for use by new files.

Otherwise, PC Format leaves the disk's data intact. As a result, as long as you don't write new data to the disk, you can use the Unformat program to recover all of its files (if you recently ran Mirror to save the disk's FAT and root directory) or all of its defragmented files (if you didn't run Mirror). For more information, see Chapter 6.

PC Format Versus DOS FORMAT for Hard Disks

When you format a hard disk using the DOS FORMAT program, what happens depends on the type of DOS you're using. Certain versions—such as Compaq DOS up through version 3.2, AT&T DOS up through version 3.1, and some versions of DOS from Burroughs—provide a destructive FORMAT program that overwrites virtually every byte on the hard disk. This totally destroys all the disk's files, making any recovery of data impossible.

However, most versions of DOS FORMAT are more conservative when dealing with hard disks. Typically, FORMAT will just clear the FAT, and erase the names of all the files and first-level directories in the disk's root. All the disk's files are therefore left intact.

PC Format's procedure is identical to the nondestructive DOS FORMAT program's, except that instead of erasing the entire names of root files and first-level directories, it erases only their first letters. At the same time, it saves each first letter 16 bytes from where it originally was, in a reserved area of the root directory.

As a result, after using either DOS FORMAT or PC Format on a hard disk, as long as you don't write new data to the disk you can use the Unformat program to recover all of its files (if you recently ran Mirror to save the disk's FAT and root directory) or all of its defragmented files (if you didn't run Mirror). However, if you used DOS FORMAT, Unformat will be forced to make up new names for your root files and first-level directories. You'll then have to try to remember their real names, and rename them one by one. For more information, see Chapter 6, "Recovering Deleted or Formatted Data."

To summarize, PC Format is much less destructive on floppy disks and somewhat less destructive on hard disks than DOS FORMAT. At the same time, it's just as effective as DOS FORMAT. Therefore, it's highly recommended that you always use PC Format in place of DOS FORMAT.

Installing PC Format

You can copy PC Format to your hard disk using the Install program (see Appendix A). When you do, you actually get two files: PCFORMAT.EXE, a 78K file that contains the code for the new easy-to-use interactive system; and PCFORM.EXE, a 21K file that contains the standard command line version of PC Format. When you're at the DOS prompt, if you type **PCFORMAT** with no options and press ENTER, the interactive system comes up. However, if you include a command line option— for example, if you type **PCFORMAT A:** at the DOS prompt and press ENTER—it's assumed you don't want the visual system, and the larger program will run PCFORM to handle the formatting. You can also run the smaller program directly by typing **PCFORM** followed by the options you want and pressing ENTER. More information about both the interactive and command line versions appears in the following sections.

In addition to copying the PC Format files, Install (after you give it permission) searches your hard disk for the DOS FORMAT program, which is named FORMAT.COM, and renames it FORMAT!.COM to ensure you don't run it accidentally. Also, Install creates a simple batch file named FORMAT.BAT, which types out the **PCFORMAT** command for you if, out of habit, you type **FORMAT** instead.

As an additional precaution to accidentally running DOS programs instead of their PC Tools equivalents, it's recommended that you revise the PATH line in your AUTOEXEC.BAT file to make your PC Tools directory precede your DOS directory. It's also recommended that you use PC Shell's File Locate and File Delete commands (see Chapter 16, "Managing Your Files") to find and remove all copies of the DOS file FORMAT.COM from your hard disk.

Running Command Line PC Format

Once PC Format is installed, you can run it just as you would DOS FORMAT. However, PC Format provides you with more information and options. To get a feel for using the command line version of the program, follow these steps to format a floppy disk in drive A:

1. Insert a floppy disk that needs to be formatted into drive A. For this example, make sure the disk's capacity matches that of the floppy (for example, insert a 1.2MB-capacity floppy into a 1.2MB drive).

2. Type **FORMAT A:** and press ENTER to begin the formatting process. PC Format displays the drive you've selected, the type of disk in the drive, and the number of Sectors, cylinders, and sides it will format.

    (It isn't important to know these terms, but if you're curious, the term *cylinder* refers to a track on a particular side of a disk. A floppy disk has two sides—its top and bottom—while a hard disk with several two-sided platters has numerous sides. The term *head,* on the other hand, is just another word for "side." For example, one side of a floppy disk may be referred to as head 0 and its other side as head 1.)

3. Press ENTER to continue. PC Format now checks to see if the disk already contains data. If it doesn't, the formatting proceeds.

4. If the disk *does* contain data, the message "Are you SURE you want to do this?" appears. If you don't mind losing the data, type **YES** and press ENTER to begin formatting. Otherwise, press ENTER twice to abort the operation.

Once formatting begins, the program reads each track of the disk to see if it's been previously formatted and if it contains any defective sectors. The program constantly informs you which particular head and cylinder (that is, track) is being examined, and of the percentage of the format completed. After going through all the tracks, it clears the disk's FAT and the first letter of each filename in the root directory.

When PC Format is done, it tells you the maximum number of bytes the disk can normally hold, the number of bytes in defective sectors on the disk (if any), and the number of bytes on the disk available for use. If the disk is sound, only the first and last values will appear, and they'll be identical.

The program then asks if you want to format another disk. If you do, remove the current floppy, insert a new one, press Y and ENTER, and repeat steps 3 and 4.

Otherwise, press ENTER. PC Format exits and returns you to the DOS prompt.

Running Interactive PC Format

As mentioned previously, PC Format 7 also provides an easy-to-use visual mode as an alternative to the command line. This interactive system takes you through the formatting process step by step, and can be used with either the keyboard or a mouse. To try it out, follow these steps:

1. Insert a floppy disk that needs to be formatted into drive A.

2. Type **FORMAT** and press ENTER. The following dialog box shows your system's drives and their capacities:

3. Press A and press ENTER, or click the A drive icon and click OK. The following dialog box lists your formatting choices:

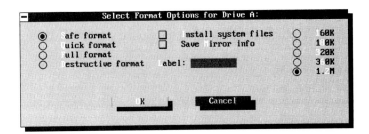

The box offers the following options:

- *Safe format*   This option performs a standard PC Tools format, meaning that it reformats every unused or defective track (marking unfixable tracks as unusable), rewrites any data on tracks it's formatted back to the disk so that they can later be recovered with Unformat (see Chapter 6), and clears the FAT and first letters of the files in the root directory. This option is the default.

- *Quick format*   This option, which works exclusively on already formatted disks, doesn't ask for confirmation about proceeding with the format and doesn't format any tracks. Instead, it just swiftly clears the FAT and first letters in the root directory, thus deleting all the disk's files and directories. This option works on Bernoulli boxes and RAM disks in addition to floppy and hard disks.

- *Full format*   This option is identical to Safe format except that it reformats *every* track on the disk, not just unused or defective ones. Specifically, it reads the data from each track into memory, formats the track, and then writes the data back to the track. This slows the formatting process, but refreshes any areas on the magnetic platter that have started to become defective (indicated by "read error" messages).

- **Destructive format**   This option, which can only be used with floppy disks, operates like DOS FORMAT; that is, it formats every track on the disk and *destroys* all the data by overwriting it. This option is only useful if you need to make a disk's data unrecoverable for security reasons. (See also "Destroying Data Using Wipe" in Chapter 11, "Encrypting Data Using PC Secure.")

- **Install system files**   This option copies DOS system files to the disk after it's been formatted, thus making the disk "bootable" (that is, able to start your PC).

- *Save Mirror info*   If you've already run Mirror on the disk, this option runs it again before formatting. This improves your chances of recovering data if you later need to use Unformat, but it takes extra time.

- *Label*   This option lets you give the disk a name consisting of up to 11 characters, or edit the disk's existing name.

- *Formatting capacity*   If you've selected a floppy drive, this last column of options is displayed to let you select the capacity of the disk you're formatting. The choices will depend on the drive; for example, for a 1.2MB drive they'll be 160K, 180K, 320K (all obsolete formats), 360K (the low capacity format), and 1.2M (the highest capacity the drive supports). Be sure to select the appropriate option; formatting a disk for a higher capacity than it can handle (for example, a 720K disk as 1.44MB) may sometimes work initially but later result in data loss.

When you've set your formatting options, press O or click OK. If your disk has data on it, and you've selected any option *except* Quick Format, a box appears that shows you the disk's files and asks you to verify that you want them deleted. If you press ENTER or click OK, the formatting begins, and you see a dialog box like this:

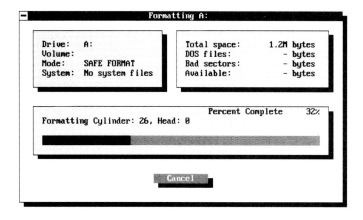

The box displays your formatting choices and the operation's progress. When the procedure is complete, the box also displays its results in the upper-right corner.

When your disk is formatted, press ENTER or click OK. You're returned to the Format Options box. You can now repeat your previous steps to format another disk. Otherwise, exit PC Format by pressing ESC twice, and then pressing ENTER. You're returned to the DOS prompt.

PC Format Parameters

When you want to run PC Format in its command line mode, you must specify the drive you're working with by following FORMAT with a space, the drive's letter, and a colon (for example, FORMAT A:). You can also include an additional parameter (for example, FORMAT A: /S) or a number of compatible parameters (for example, FORMAT A: /4 /F /P) to achieve a particular effect. Keep in mind that parameters preceded by a slash require a *forward* slash (/, located on the bottom of the ? key) as opposed to the backslash (\) used to specify DOS directories.

There are 18 parameters specific to PC Format. They are as follows:

- **?**   This "help" parameter lists and briefly describes every parameter specific to PC Format. It won't work unless you type either PCFORMAT or PCFORM (as opposed to FORMAT). However, it *will* work both with and without a slash in front of it. It should not be combined with any other parameter.

- **/VIDEO**   This "help" parameter lists and briefly describes the standard PC Tools video and mouse parameters. It should not be combined with any other parameter. For more information, see the "Video and Mouse Parameters" section in Appendix A, "PC Tools Installation and Configuration."

- **d:**   This parameter is a letter and colon specifying the drive you want to format on. You *must* include this parameter or PC Format will automatically run in interactive mode.

- **/1**   This parameter limits formatting to one side of a floppy disk.

- **/4**   This parameter formats a floppy disk as 360K in a 1.2MB drive, which is useful if you need to share data with someone who has 360K drives. (Not all 1.2MB drives do a good job of formatting readable 360K disks, so you should experiment with this option before coming to rely on it.) See also the /F:*nnnn* parameter.

- **/8**   This parameter formats a floppy disk to have eight Sectors (a standard before DOS 2.0) rather than the modern standards of nine Sectors for 360K disks and 15 Sectors for 1.2MB disks. See also the /N:*nn* parameter.

- **/DESTROY**   This parameter forces PC Format to operate like DOS FORMAT, destroying all the data on a floppy disk.

- **/F**   The format operation normally just reads a disk's tracks to verify that they're already formatted and not defective. This parameter performs a full format on a floppy disk by reading the data from each track into memory, formatting the track, and then writing the data back to the track. This slows the formatting process, but refreshes any areas on the magnetic platter that have started to become defective (indicated by "read error" messages). See also the /R parameter.

- **/F:*nnnn***   This parameter formats a floppy disk to the size specified by the *nnnn* code number. The codes are 160, 180, or 320 for disks that need to be compatible with versions of DOS before 2.0; 360 for 360K disks; 720 for 720K disks; 1200 for 1.2MB disks; 1440 for 1.44MB disks; and 2880 for 2.88MB disks (a new option in PC Tools 7). See also the /4 parameter.

- **/N:*nn***   This parameter lets you format 8, 9, 15, or 18 sectors per track on a floppy disk. It must be used in combination with the /T:*nn* parameter. See also the /8 parameter.

- **/P**   This parameter prints to your printer whatever information PC Format displays on your screen. Your printer must be attached to port LPT1 (which most printers are) and online for this option to work.

- **/Q**   When you're formatting a disk that is already formatted, PC Format normally scans the disk for data, asks for verification to proceed, and reads all the disk's tracks to verify that they're already formatted and not defective. This parameter skips the initial disk scan, the verification question, and the track reading, and goes straight to clearing the FAT and first letters in the root directory. Using PC Format with this parameter is generally the quickest way of deleting all of a disk's files and directories.

- **/R**   This parameter revitalizes a floppy disk by reading the data from each track into memory, formatting the track, and then writing the data back to the track. This refreshes any areas on the magnetic platter that have started to become defective (indicated by "read error" messages). Unlike the /F parameter, this option does *not* change the disk's FAT or root directory, so all the disk's data remains intact. The effects of this option are identical to those of the DiskFix program's **R**evitalize a Disk option (see Chapter 7).

- **/S**   After formatting is complete, this parameter places hidden DOS system files (typically named IBMBIO.COM and IBMDOS.COM, or MSBIO.SYS and MSDOS.COM) and the program COMMAND.COM (which contains DOS) directly following the disk's boot record. These programs enable the disk to load DOS, starting up your computer.

- **/T:*nn***   This parameter lets you format 40 or 80 tracks on a floppy disk. It must be used in combination with the /N:*nn* parameter.

- **/TEST**   This parameter simulates a format without actually performing one. In other words, it allows all the usual messages to be displayed and read operations to proceed, but doesn't allow any changes to be written to the disk. This option can be combined with any other parameters, so you can use it to become familiar with the effects of various parameter combinations.

- **/V** This parameter prompts you to supply the formatted disk with a name, or *volume label,* to identify it. The label can consist of up to 11 characters.

- **/V:***label* This parameter names the formatted disk with the label specified. This option is new to PC Tools 7.

Only nine of PC Format's 18 parameters apply to hard disks. These are ?, /VIDEO, d:, /P, /Q, /S, /TEST, /V, and /V:label. Also, nine of PC Format's disk parameters are unique to the program (that is, aren't provided by DOS FORMAT). These are ?, /VIDEO, /DESTROY, /F, /P, /Q, /R, /TEST, and /V:label.

Combining PC Format Parameters

The PC Format parameters can be combined in a variety of ways. The following are some examples.

FORMAT A: /DESTROY /S

This command formats the disk in drive A, destroying all its data. It then copies DOS system files to the disk to enable it to start up your computer.

FORMAT A: /R /F:720

This command rewrites the tracks of the 720K disk in 1.44MB drive A, refreshing any sectors that the drive's read/write heads may have had trouble reading. However, it leaves all the disk's data (including its FAT, root directory, and files) intact.

FORMAT A: /Q /V

This command performs a very quick format on the already-formatted disk in drive A by just clearing the FAT and first letters in the root directory to mark all files and directories as deleted. It then prompts you to assign the disk a name consisting of up to 11 characters.

FORMAT A: /4 /P

This command formats the disk in 1.2MB drive A as a 360K disk and directs all screen messages to be printed on your printer.

FORMAT A: /N:9 /T:40 /TEST

This command goes through the motions of formatting the disk in drive A with nine Sectors and 40 tracks, but doesn't actually alter the disk in any way.

Data Safeguarding Summary

To sum up, it's recommended that you follow these procedures to help prevent major data losses:

- If you haven't done so already, run the Install program's Recovery Disk option to preserve your system's partition table, CMOS data, and boot record (see "Creating a Recovery Disk"). Whenever this information changes (for example, when you use FDISK on your hard disk), use the MIRROR /PARTN command to save the revised data (see "Saving Your Partition Table, CMOS Data, and Boot Record").

- Run the Mirror program at least daily to back up your hard disk's boot record, FAT, and root directory (see "Using Mirror").

- Always keep Data Monitor resident, and either its Delete Sentry or Delete Tracker option turned on, to safeguard against losing accidentally deleted files (see "Monitoring Deleted Files").

- Always format disks using PC Format instead of DOS FORMAT (see "Using PC Format").

It's recommended that you also perform the following procedures using the rest of the PC Tools data safeguard programs to help prevent *any* data loss:

- Run the Compress program at least weekly to defragment your hard disk (see Chapter 9, "Speeding Your Disks Using Compress").

- Run the Diskfix program at least monthly to maintain and repair your hard disk (see Chapter 7, "Repairing Disks Using DiskFix").

- Before installing and running a new program, load VDefend to scan for known viruses (see Chapter 13, "Detecting Viruses Using VDefend").

- Run the CP Backup program daily to back up your hard disk files (see Chapters 1, 2, and 3). You should always have these backups available as a last resort.

Chapter **6**

Recovering Deleted or Formatted Data

If you've just deleted a number of important files, or even accidentally formatted your hard disk, *don't panic.* There's a good chance that most or all of your data can be recovered. This chapter will show you how.

Alternatively, if you tried to access your hard disk and got an "Invalid drive specification" message, or your system setup information was damaged or lost, or you suddenly can't start up your PC from your hard disk, this chapter will guide you in restoring your partition table, CMOS data, and boot record.

Lastly, if your disk's FAT or root directory was damaged, this chapter will help you to decide on the best method for repairing it.

If your data loss occurred on your hard disk, continue on to the following "Preparing for Hard Disk Recovery" section. Otherwise, skip to the "Preparing for Floppy Disk Recovery" section.

Preparing for Hard Disk Recovery

The first and most important rule you should follow is

Don't save or copy data to the hard disk.

That's because new files may overwrite and destroy the files you want to rescue.

In addition, be wary of performing actions that *indirectly* write data. For example, if you've installed a memory-resident program (such as PC Shell or the PC Tools Desktop), *don't* invoke the program now. Doing so may write temporary, or *overlay,* files to the hard disk that destroy the data you want to recover.

Similarly, if you haven't installed the PC Tools recovery programs, now is *not* the time to do so. Instead, insert the single 3 1/2-inch disk, or one of the two 5 1/4-inch disks, labeled "Data Recovery Utilities" into a floppy drive. (If you have 5 1/4-inch disks, insert whichever one contains the program you need—for example, UNDEL.EXE for deleted files or UNFORMAT.EXE for formatted disks.) You can run the recovery programs directly from this drive.

Lastly, if you formatted your hard disk and then turned your computer off, restart your PC from a floppy disk to ensure you don't corrupt your hard disk's Mirror file. If you can, do so using your Recovery Disk (see Appendix A or "Creating a Recovery Disk" in Chapter 5, "Safeguarding Your Data"). Otherwise, locate a floppy that is formatted with the /S option and the same version of COM- MAND.COM as your hard disk's so that it contains the appropriate system files (see "Using PC Format" in Chapter 5). In addition, if the hard disk requires a device driver, the floppy must also contain both the driver and a CONFIG.SYS file specifying the driver for the recovery process to work properly.

You're now ready to begin the recovery process. To proceed:

- If you need to undelete files, read the "Recovering Deleted Files" section.

- If you need to unformat your hard disk, read the "Recovering Formatted Disks" section.

- If you need to restore your partition table, CMOS data, or boot record, read the "Restoring Your Partition Table, CMOS Data, and Boot Record" section.

- If your disk's system area has been damaged, read the "Restoring the FAT and Root Directory" section.

Preparing for Floppy Disk Recovery

If you've formatted a floppy disk using any version of the DOS FORMAT program previous to DOS 5, then unfortunately there's no way to restore the disk's data. Your only options are to locate backup copies of the files, find printouts of their data, or reconstruct them from memory.

On the other hand, if you formatted the disk using the PC Format program or the DOS 5 Format program (see "Using PC Format" in Chapter 5), or if you only deleted files, your chances of recovering at least some of your data are very good.

First, to ensure the security of your lost files,

Don't save or copy data to the floppy disk.

That's because new files may overwrite and destroy the files you want to rescue. Use your hard disk and other floppy disks for any disk-writing operations you need to perform.

You'll find it most convenient to run the PC Tools recovery programs from your hard disk. Therefore, if you haven't already installed these programs, you may want to do so now (see Appendix A, "PC Tools Installation and Configuration"). Alternatively, you can run the programs directly from the single 3 1/2-inch disk, or one of the two 5 1/4-inch disks, labeled "Data Recovery Utilities." (If you have 5 1/4-inch disks, use whichever one contains the program you need—for example, UNDEL.EXE for deleted files or UNFORMAT.EXE for formatted disks.)

It's also a good idea to make an exact copy of your problem disk and then work only with the copy. That way, if anything goes wrong with the recovery process, your original disk will remain intact and able to generate additional copies that you can experiment with. To copy your floppy, follow these steps:

1. Write-protect your problem disk. If it's a 5 1/4-inch disk, place a write-protect tab (one of the tiny, sticky black strips of plastic packaged with new disks) over the notch on the disk's upper-right side. If it's a 3 1/2-inch disk, push the small switch in the back side of the disk's upper-left corner all the way to the top.

2. Locate a disk that's either blank or contains only obsolete data. Put a label on the disk, and write "Restore Disk #1" and the date on the label.

3. Perform the copy. If you've installed PC Shell on your hard disk, use its **Disk Copy** command, which will step you through the process (see "Copying Floppy Disks" in Chapter 17). Otherwise, use the DOS DISKCOPY command, following the instructions in your DOS manual. Regardless of the method you use, be *extremely* careful not to get confused and insert the wrong disk while copying (although, if you've write-protected your problem disk, no serious harm should be done).

4. When you're done, put the problem disk away in a safe place. You can now work with the copy.

You're ready to begin the recovery process. To proceed:

*   If you need to undelete files, read the following "Recovering Deleted Files" section.

*   If you need to unformat your floppy disk, read the "Recovering Formatted Disks" section.

*   If your disk's system area has been damaged, read the "Restoring the FAT and Root Directory" section.

Recovering Deleted Files

If you've accidentally deleted files, you can typically recover most or all of them. How successful you are depends on three factors: whether the Data Monitor program's Delete Sentry or Delete Tracker option was active when the files were deleted (see "Monitoring Deleted Files" in Chapter 5); whether you wrote to the disk after deleting; and whether the files were fragmented.

- If Delete Sentry preserved the deleted files, you'll recover all of them quickly and easily.

- If Delete Tracker recorded the deleted files, you'll recover all of them *unless* you wrote to the disk after deleting. In that case, there's a chance that some or all of your deleted data was overwritten and destroyed.

- If neither Data Monitor option was active during your deletions, PC Tools uses the disk's FAT and root directory to recover them. As explained in "Understanding How Files Are Deleted" in Chapter 4, the root directory retains the location of each deleted file's first cluster, and also all but the first letter of the file's name. Undelete can use this information to entirely recover each file that isn't fragmented, and the initial data of each file that *is* fragmented, after you supply the appropriate first letter of the file's name. You can then try to recover the rest of the data from your fragmented files using somewhat laborious manual procedures.

The success of both the Delete Tracker and DOS methods is dependent on your not copying or saving any new data to the problem disk, since doing so may overwrite your deleted files. It's therefore highly recommended that you undelete as soon as you realize that you need to.

To recover your files, use the new PC Tools 7 Undelete program. This version has several notable differences from the Undelete program in PC Tools Deluxe 6:

- The program filename has been shortened to UNDEL.EXE. This change helps prevent conflicts with the PC Tools Deluxe 6 UNDELETE.EXE program, which is now included in all copies of DOS 5. (As mentioned near the beginning of Chapter 4, it's recommended that you always *ignore* the Central Point-licensed programs in DOS 5, and also set the PATH statement in your AUTOEXEC.BAT file to list your PCTOOLS directory *before* your DOS directory to further ensure that no conflicts occur with the DOS 5 utilities.)

- The new Undelete program can be run in both command line mode and interactive mode. In PC Tools Deluxe 6, the standalone version of Undelete could run only in command line mode.

- The interactive version of Undelete now provides many more features. For example, it tells you at a glance the chances of recovering each listed file;

displays deleted file data; locates deleted files based on their names, contents, and/or protection status; locates Lotus 1-2-3, Symphony, dBASE, and/or text data clusters; can save a recovered file to a different location than the deleted file; and can purge selected files in the \SENTRY directory.

- The interactive mode of Undelete can also be run via PC Shell's File Undelete command (see Chapter 16, "Managing Your Files"). Previously, this PC Shell command executed a version of Undelete that was significantly different from the standalone version of the program.

Unless your deleted files were preserved by Delete Sentry, you should not *hotkey into PC Shell to undelete. That's because doing so may write overlay files to your hard disk, potentially destroying the data you want to recover. Instead, run UNDEL.EXE directly from the DOS prompt.*

- Undelete can now work with network drives. However, it can only recover files protected by Delete Sentry on such drives.

The following sections first cover using the command line version of Undelete to quickly recover an erased file, and then the interactive version of Undelete to perform a broad range of file recovery operations.

Using Command Line Undelete

To quickly recover files with the command line version of Undelete, follow these steps:

1. Set the DOS prompt to the drive containing the UNDEL.EXE program. For example, if the program is on your floppy disk drive A, type **A:** and press ENTER; if it's on your hard disk drive C, type **C:** and press ENTER.

2. Type **UNDEL** followed by a space, the letter of the drive you want to work with, a colon, the directory that contains your deleted files, and the names of the files you want. The latter can be indicated by using the DOS wildcard ? to represent any character and the DOS wildcard * to represent any group of characters.

For example, if you want the chance to recover all files in the root of drive A, type **UNDEL A:*.*** and press ENTER. As another example, if you're interested in all erased dBASE files in directory DATA on drive C, type **UNDEL C:\DATA*.DBF** and press ENTER. Alternatively, to specify all files in the current directory, just type **UNDEL *.*.**

Undelete first reports the number of deleted files it's found that fit your specifications. It also divides these files into three categories: those deleted while

Delete Sentry was active, those deleted while Delete Tracker was active, and those deleted while no protective program was active (referred to as being "recorded by DOS"). A typical display might look like this:

```
C:\PCTOOLS>undel *.*

Undelete V7 (c)1990-1991 Central Point Software, Inc.

Directory: C:\PCTOOLS

    12 deleted files.
     4 recorded by Delete Sentry.
     7 recorded by Delete Tracker.
     1 recorded by DOS.
```

Undelete then shows you the first deleted file's name, size, creation date and time, and chances for recovery, as in this example:

```
SAMPLE  .TXT    5184  7/07/91 11:42p  Perfect
Do you want to recover this file? (Y/N)
```

If only one undeleted file meets your command line specifications and the entire file is recoverable, Undelete skips asking whether you want to recover it and just undeletes it automatically.

The way the file's name appears is determined by its protection status. Specifically, if the file was protected by Delete Sentry or Delete Tracking, its full name appears. However, if it wasn't protected, the first letter of its name is missing and will have to be supplied by you when you undelete it.

The last word on the line is also determined by the file's level of protection. For example, "Perfect" indicates the file was protected by Delete Sentry and has 100 percent chance of recovery; and "Excellent" indicates the file was protected by Delete Tracker, or wasn't protected but is stored in contiguous clusters, and so has 100 percent chance of recovery *if* you didn't overwrite any of its deleted data. However, the word "Good" indicates the file can only be partially recovered in command line mode, and the word "Poor" or "Destroyed" indicates the file can't be recovered at all in command line mode. For complete descriptions of what these words mean, see the "Understanding File List and Status Information" section later in this chapter.

If the file's recovery chances are Perfect, Excellent, or Good, following the file information is the question "Do you want to recover this file? (Y/N)." If you don't, press N. The file remains deleted, and the next file is listed.

However, if you *do* want to undelete, press Y. If the file wasn't protected, you're also prompted to supply a first letter for the file's name. Do so.

The recovery procedure now executes automatically, and one of the following scenarios takes place:

- If the file was protected or is contiguous (that is, had its recovery chances described as "Perfect" or "Excellent"), and it hasn't been overwritten, the file is quickly undeleted, the message "Recovered" appears, and the next deleted file is listed.

- If the file was both unprotected and fragmented (that is, had its recovery chances described as "Good"), Undelete recovers as much of the initial data as it can, and then displays the message "Recovered" and lists the next deleted file. However, it's recommended that after you're done recovering your other files, you immediately examine this file, because you'll probably find it's not *fully* recovered. If this is the case, first try getting the missing data from an earlier version of the file. If no such file is available, however, try locating the rest of the deleted data by using one of the disk scanning commands in the interactive version of Undelete. You can then merge the data into the file using your application program, the DOS COPY command (using the /A or /B parameter; see your DOS manual for details), or one of Undelete's manual recovery methods. For more information, see the sections "Using Interactive Undelete," "Finding Free Clusters and Lost Files," and "Recovering Files Manually" later in this chapter.

- If some of the file's clusters have been overwritten, Undelete doesn't even attempt to recover the file, but instead just tells you to use the manual method of recovery. First, however, it's recommended that you try to locate a recent version of the file and determine what data you still need from the deleted file. Then, as just explained, you can search for this data using one of the disk scanning commands in the interactive version of Undelete, and merge that data into the earlier file using your application program, DOS COPY, or one of Undelete's manual recovery methods. For more information, again, see "Using Interactive Undelete," "Finding Free Clusters and Lost Files," and "Recovering Files Manually."

When all the deleted files you were interested in have been listed, press ESC to end the Undelete procedure and return to the DOS prompt. Alternatively, continue until all the deleted files you specified are listed. At that point, Undelete ends automatically and returns you to the DOS prompt.

Lastly, examine the files you undeleted to verify that they've been restored successfully. If they haven't, use the methods just discussed for recovering missing data.

Undelete Parameters

When you run Undelete in command line mode, you must specify certain options, or parameters, following the program name. Keep in mind that parameters preceded by a slash require a *forward* slash (/, located on the bottom of the ? key) as opposed to the backslash (\) used to specify DOS directories.

The 12 parameters specific to Undelete are as follows:

- **?**   This "help" parameter lists and briefly describes every Undelete command line option. It will work both with and without a slash. It should not be combined with any other parameters.

- **/VIDEO**   This "help" parameter lists and briefly describes the standard PC Tools video and mouse parameters. It should not be combined with any other parameter. For more information, see the "Video and Mouse Parameters" section in Appendix A, "PC Tools Installation and Configuration."

- *d*:   This parameter is a letter and colon specifying the drive containing the files you want to undelete. If this parameter is left out, the current drive is used.

- *path*   This parameter is a path specifying the directory containing the files you want to undelete. If this parameter is left out, the current directory is used.

- *filespec*   This parameter is a DOS filename, or a file specification using the DOS wildcards ? (representing any single character) and * (representing any combination of characters) to indicate the files you want to undelete. If this parameter is left out, *.* (meaning all files in the specified directory) is assumed.

- **/ALL**   This parameter lets you undelete all specified files regardless of their level of protection. This setting is the default, so it isn't necessary to include /ALL for it to take effect. See also the /DOS, /DT, and /S parameters.

- **/DT**   This parameter lets you undelete only the specified files that were protected by Delete Tracking. If no such files are found, it aborts execution and exits. See also the /ALL, /DOS, and /S parameters.

- **/DOS**   This parameter lets you undelete using DOS FAT and root directory information exclusively (or using Mirror data, if the /M parameter is also included). It therefore ignores any existing PCTRACKR.DEL file and any existing \SENTRY files. This is generally only useful if your PCTRACKR.DEL file or \SENTRY directory was somehow corrupted.

- **/LIST**   This parameter lists all available undeleted files. Its results can be adjusted by combining it with the *d:*, *path*, and *filename* parameters, and the /DOS, /DT, or /S parameter. Pressing CTRL-PRTSC before using /LIST will direct its results to your printer, and pressing CTRL-S will pause and unpause its display.

- **/S**   This parameter lets you undelete only the specified files that were protected by Delete Sentry. If no such files are found, it aborts execution and exits. See also the /DOS, /DT, and /ALL parameters.

- **/M**   For files that weren't protected by Delete Sentry or Delete Tracker, this parameter sets Undelete to use the disk's Mirror data instead of its FAT and root directory information. This will sometimes improve your chances of recovering a fragmented file.

- **/NC**   This parameter automatically undeletes all specified files without asking for confirmation. When recovering unprotected files, it supplies # (the number/pound sign) as the first character of each filename. If using # results in a name already used by another file, Undelete then tries the next character in a predefined sequence, and then the next, until it finds one that doesn't create a conflict. The character sequence used is

    #%&-0123456789ABCDEFGHIJKLMNOPQRSTUVWXYZ

    It's recommended that you first use the /LIST parameter to determine the effects /NC will produce. It's also a good idea to press CTRL - PRTSC before using /NC to direct its results to your printer. You can additionally press CTRL-S to pause and unpause the display.

The /ALL, /DOS, /DT, and /S parameters are mutually exclusive, so you can include only one of them in the Undelete command line. If you don't include any *of them, the /ALL parameter is used by default, and each file is recovered based on the protection method in effect when it was deleted.*

The following are some examples of Undelete command lines:

UNDEL C:\REPORTS*.*

This command lets you undelete all files on drive C in the REPORTS directory.

UNDEL C:\REPORTS*.TXT /M

This command lets you undelete on drive C in the REPORTS directory only those files with TXT extensions. In addition, it sets unprotected files to be recovered using the disk's Mirror data, as opposed to the disk's FAT and root directory information.

UNDEL C:\REPORTS\R*.* /S

This command lets you undelete on drive C in the REPORTS directory only those files that begin with the letter "R" and were protected by Delete Sentry.

UNDEL A:*.* /NC

This command undeletes all files in the root of drive A automatically (that is, without prompting), and then exits. When recovering unprotected files, it automatically supplies a default first character for the file's name (usually #).

Using Interactive Undelete

To display deleted files and be presented with a number of recovery options, follow these steps to run the interactive version of Undelete:

1. Set the DOS prompt to the drive containing the UNDEL.EXE program. For example, if the program is on your floppy disk drive A, type **A:** and press ENTER; if it's on your hard disk drive C, type **C:** and press ENTER.

2. Type **UNDEL** and press ENTER. A screen like the one in Figure 6-1 appears.
   The Undelete screen is very similar to the PC Shell screen (see Chapter 15, "PC Shell Overview"). The main difference is that instead of displaying existing files, it displays *deleted* ones. The screen is split into six parts:

   • The Tree List at the left, which displays the existing directories of the current drive. It's called a tree because it illustrates your root directory (typically C:\) as having a trunk extending from it, and all your other directories as branching out from the trunk.

   • The File List at the right, which displays the deleted files in the selected directory.

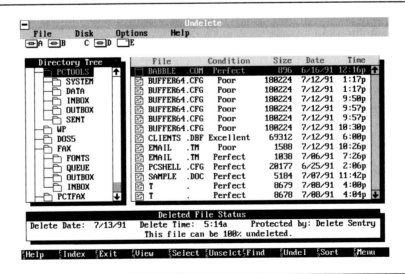

Figure 6-1.   The Undelete screen

- The message bar at the bottom, which displays function key definitions and information on Undelete's activities.

- The status lines above the message bar, which display information about the current file.

- The menu bar at the top, which lets you access the four main Undelete menus; and the Control button in the upper-left corner, which lets you access the Control menu.

- The drive bar directly below the menu bar, which displays your available drives and highlights your current drive. You can switch to a different drive by pressing CTRL and the drive's letter, or by clicking the drive's letter in the drive bar.

The following sections explain how to use these different screen elements.

Navigating the Tree List and File List

To move around in the Tree List, first activate it by pressing SHIFT-TAB or clicking it. The border highlighting shifts over from the File List, indicating that the Tree List is active. You can move along the Tree by directory using DOWN ARROW or UP ARROW; by 14 directories at a time using PGDN or PGUP; and to the bottom or top of the Tree using END or HOME. You can also scroll the Tree vertically using your mouse.

As you move to each directory, its deleted files (and any deleted subdirectories) are displayed in the File List. When you see the files you want to recover, activate the File List by pressing TAB or clicking the List window. You can move by file using the arrow keys, by 14 files at a time using PGDN and PGUP, and to the last or first file using END or HOME. You can also scroll the list of files vertically using your mouse.

Initially, whatever file the highlight cursor is on is considered to be selected. Therefore, if you want to work with a single file, simply move to it or click it with your right mouse button. You can also select multiple files at a time by moving to each file using the arrow keys and pressing ENTER, or by clicking each file with your left mouse button, or by pressing F5 to enter a file specification with DOS wildcards.

You can also unselect a highlighted file by again moving to it and pressing ENTER, or by again clicking on it with your left mouse button, or by pressing F6 to enter a file specification with DOS wildcards. You can also unselect all files simultaneously by simply moving to another directory in the Tree List.

Understanding File List and Status Information

The File List provides five columns of information about each deleted file. The heading and an explanation for each column follow.

- *File*   This column displays the file's name. If the file was deleted without protection, the first letter of its name is missing.

- *Condition*   This column displays a one-word description of the file's chances for recovery. This is based on such factors as the file's protection method (if any), whether it's fragmented, and whether any of its data has been overwritten. More information about this column appears following this list.

- *Size*   This column displays the file's size in bytes.

- *Date*   This column displays the file's creation date (*not* its deletion date).

- *Time*   This column displays the file's creation time (*not* its deletion time).

As just mentioned, the Condition column shows a file's chances of recovery. The one-word descriptions that can appear in the column are as follows:

- *Perfect*   This description indicates that the file was protected by Delete Sentry and has a 100 percent chance of recovery.

- *Excellent*   This description indicates that the file was protected by Delete Tracker, or was unprotected but is stored in contiguous clusters. If you didn't overwrite any of the file's deleted data (for example, if you've run Undelete immediately after deleting the file), it has a 100 percent chance of recovery.

- *Good*   This description indicates that the file was both unprotected and fragmented. The file's initial data can be recovered automatically, but the rest of its data will probably require a hands-on recovery method (see "Finding Free Clusters and Lost Files" and "Recovering Files Manually").

- *Poor*   This description indicates that the file was unprotected and *at least* its first cluster has been overwritten. As a result, no automatic recovery is possible. However, you may be able to salvage some of the data using a hands-on recovery method (see "Finding Free Clusters and Lost Files" and "Recovering Files Manually").

- *Destroyed*   This description indicates that *all* of the file's data has been overwritten. As a result, there's no longer any data left to recover.

- *None*   This description indicates that the file never contained any data (that is, had 0 bytes). As a result, there's nothing to recover.

- *Purge*   This description indicates that the file was purged from the \SEN-TRY directory during the current session via the **F**ile **P**urge Delete Sentry File command.

- *Lost File*   This description indicates that the file belongs to a deleted directory and is being displayed via the **D**isk Scan for **L**ost Deleted Files command.

- *Existing*   This description indicates that the file is a normal existing file. Such files are listed when you select the **O**ptions S**h**ow Existing Files command. (This command is used when you need to change the name of an existing file because it's the same as the name of a deleted file you want to recover. It's also used when you want to add deleted clusters to an existing file.)

- *Recovered*   This description indicates that the file has just been undeleted.

In addition to the File List columns, information about the file that the highlight cursor is currently on appears on the status lines near the bottom of the screen. These lines show the date and time the file was deleted (unless the file was unprotected, in which case the word "Unknown" is displayed); the protection in effect when the file was deleted (the possibilities being Delete Sentry, Delete Tracker, or DOS); and a sentence describing the file's chances for recovery.

The Undelete Message Bar

At the bottom of the screen is the message bar. When an Undelete activity is taking place, the bar displays appropriate definitions or instructions. Otherwise, it displays the following commands assigned to the function keys:

Function Key	Action
F1 (Help)	Brings up context-sensitive help
F2 (Index)	Brings up the online help index
F3 (Exit)	Performs the same functions as ESC
F4 (View)	Selects File View File
F5 (Select)	Selects **O**ptions Select **b**y Name
F6 (Unselct)	Selects **O**ptions Unselect by Name
F7 (Find)	Selects File Find Deleted Files
F8 (Undel)	Selects File Undelete File
F9 (Sort)	Selects **O**ptions Sort By
F10 (Menu)	Performs the same functions as ALT

Navigating the Undelete Menus

At the top of the screen are the five menus available in Undelete. To examine them, follow these steps:

1. Press F or click File to display the File menu, which lets you undelete the selected files; undelete and save to a different drive and/or directory; search for deleted files based on their names, contents, and/or protection status; view the data of the selected files; display information about the selected files;

purge files from the \SENTRY directory; manually recover deleted data; and rename the selected existing files.

2. Press RIGHT ARROW to display the **D**isk menu, which lets you search for free clusters containing Lotus 1-2-3, Symphony, dBASE, and/or text data; search for free clusters containing a specified text sequence; search for deleted files that belonged to a now-deleted directory; restrict searches to a specified cluster range; and continue an interrupted search.

3. Press RIGHT ARROW again to display the **O**ptions menu, which lets you reorder the File List display; select and unselect specified files; display existing files in addition to deleted ones; and undelete unprotected files using the disk's Mirror data instead of its FAT and root directory information.

4. Press RIGHT ARROW again to display the **H**elp menu, which lets you read about various Undelete topics online.

5. Press ESC and ALT-SPACEBAR to display the Control menu, which lets you display Undelete's version number and exit Undelete.

6. Press ESC to close the menu and return to the Undelete screen.

The following sections cover the options in these menus (shown in Figure 6-2). In addition, each menu option is listed and described at the end of this chapter.

Undeleting Files

To undelete one or more files, follow these steps:

1. Use the Tree List to select the directory of the files you want to delete.

 If the file's directory is also deleted, use these steps to first undelete the directory, and then repeat the steps to undelete the file. Alternatively, select the Disk Scan for Lost Deleted Files command to find the file. For more information on the latter option, see "Finding Free Clusters and Lost Files."

2. Press TAB or click the File List.

3. Use the arrow keys and ENTER, or use your left mouse button, to select the file or files you want to undelete. Alternatively, select the files using DOS wildcards by pressing F5, entering a file specification, and pressing ENTER.

4. If you selected more than one file, press F9, T, ENTER; or click on the Options menu and select Sort By, Condition, and OK. This ensures that the files with the best chances for recovery are undeleted first.

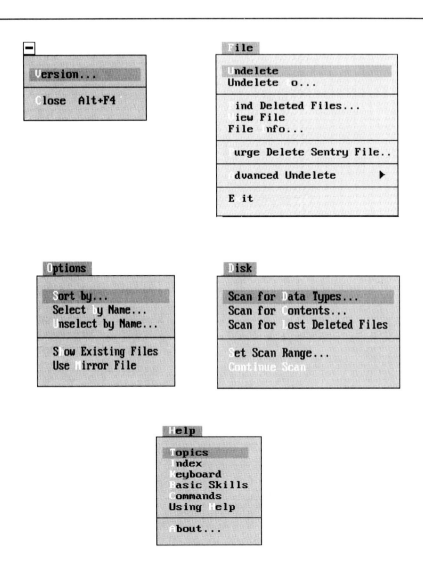

Figure 6-2. *The Undelete menus*

5. If your files all have a high chance of total recovery (indicated by the conditions Perfect or Excellent), you'll probably find it most convenient to save their recovered versions to their current location. In this case, press F, U, or press F8, or click on the File menu and select Undelete; and then go to step 9.

6. If you've selected files that are unprotected and fragmented (indicated by the condition Good), or that you suspect are partially overwritten, it's safest to

save their recovered versions to a different location. This allows you to examine the automatically recovered data and, if the results are unsatisfactory, use a manual method to try and recover the still undisturbed deleted data. To go this route, first press F, T, or click on the File menu and select Undelete To.

7. A display of all drives *except* your current one appears. Press the letter of the drive you want to save to and press ENTER, or click the drive's icon and click OK.

8. You're prompted for the directory you want to save to. Press LEFT ARROW and type the directory name, or accept the default of the drive's root. When you're done, press ENTER twice or click OK.

9. Undelete now attempts to automatically recover each selected file (beginning with the topmost file and then working its way down the File List). If any selected file was unprotected, you're prompted to supply the first letter of its name. If this occurs, do so, and then press ENTER twice or click OK to allow the recovery process to proceed.

For each selected file, one of the following scenarios now takes place:

- If the file was protected or is contiguous (that is, had a condition of Perfect or Excellent) and it hasn't been overwritten, the file is quickly undeleted, and its condition is changed to Recovered in the File List.

- If the file was both unprotected and fragmented (that is, had a condition of Good), as much of the file's initial data is recovered as possible, and its condition is changed to Recovered in the File List. However, it's recommended that after the undelete operation is over, you select the file and press F4 to view its contents, because you'll probably find that it's not *fully* recovered. If this is the case, first try getting the missing data from an earlier version of the file. If no such file is available, however, try locating the rest of the deleted data by using one of the **Disk** scanning commands (see "Finding Free Clusters and Lost Files"). You can then merge the data into the file using your application program, the DOS COPY command (using the /A or /B parameter; see your DOS manual for details), or one of the **File Advanced** Undelete manual recovery methods (see "Recovering Files Manually").

- If some of the file's clusters have been overwritten, Undelete doesn't even attempt to recover the file, but instead just tells you to use the manual method of recovery. First, however, try locating a recent version of the file and determining what data you still need from the deleted file. Then, as just explained, search for the data using a **Disk** scanning command, and then merge the data into the file using your application program, DOS COPY, or one of the **File Advanced** Undelete manual recovery methods.

When the recovery process is completed, you're returned to the main Undelete screen. You can then continue to use Undelete (for example, by using F4 to examine your recovered files), or exit the program by pressing ESC and ENTER.

Finding Deleted Files in Existing Directories

There may be times when you don't remember which directory contains your deleted files, or when you don't remember the names of the deleted files themselves, or when the files you want are scattered among a number of different directories. Undelete therefore provides you with a variety of ways to specify and locate such files contained in existing directories.

To begin such a file search, press F, F, or press F7, or click on the File menu and select Find Deleted Files. The following dialog box appears:

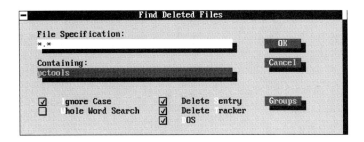

The box provides the following options:

- *File Specification*   This field lets you specify the names of the deleted files you want using the DOS wildcard ? to represent any single character and the DOS wildcard * to represent any group of characters. For example, to find all deleted batch files on the disk, type ***.BAT**; to find all deleted dBASE files, type ***.DBF**; and to find deleted files beginning with REPORT in the root-level directory WP, type **\WP\REPORT*.***. The default is **.**, specifying all deleted files.

  You can also enter multiple criteria. For example, to find all deleted program files, you'd type ***.EXE *.COM *.BAT**. Furthermore, you can exclude certain files by using the minus sign. For example, the specification **.TXT -\LETTERS*.** locates text files in all directories *except* the LETTERS directory.

- *Containing*   This field lets you search for files containing a specified text sequence, or *string,* up to 128 characters long. It can be used by itself when you don't remember a file's name, or in conjunction with the File Specification option to further narrow your search criteria.

- *Ignore Case*   If on (which is the default), this option allows the search to include occurrences which *don't* precisely match the upper- and lowercase differences in the specified text string.

- *Whole Word Search*   If off (which is the default), this option allows the search to include occurrences of the specified text string in larger words (for example, matching the word "form" in "uniform" and "formulate").

- *Delete Sentry/Delete Tracker/DOS*   For each of these options that's on, the search includes files protected by the option. The default is for each option to be on as long as Undelete detects at least one deleted file on the disk protected by the option.

- *Groups*   This option lets you select, edit, or create *search groups,* which are predefined file specifications. The Install program automatically created search groups for applications it found on your hard disk during the installation process (see Appendix A). You can also create your own, which saves you the bother of having to type in file specifications you use frequently. Search groups are also a feature in the PC Shell and File Find programs. For more information, see "Using Search Groups" in Chapter 16, "Managing Your Files."

When you've finished adjusting your settings, press ALT-O or click OK to execute the search. After scanning all your specified files, Undelete displays a box that either lists the deleted files that matched your criteria or the message "No files found." In the former case, you can select any or all of the displayed files, and apply any Undelete command to them *except* another Find Deleted Files command. To return to the main Undelete screen, press F, F, or press F7, or click on the File menu and select Tree & File List.

The File Find Deleted Files command will not locate deleted files whose directories have also been deleted. To find such files, use instead the Disk Scan for Lost Deleted Files command, which is covered in the next section.

Finding Free Clusters and Lost Files

In addition to finding deleted files in *existing* directories, you can locate ones in *deleted* directories (which are sometimes called "lost" files). You can also find data in free clusters—that is, clusters that are no longer associated with existing files in the FAT—which is especially useful when you're trying to reconstruct a fragmented file.

There are three **Disk** menu commands available for locating free clusters and lost files:

- *Scan for Data Types*   This option finds free clusters containing Lotus 1-2-3, Symphony, dBASE, and/or ASCII text data. It's especially useful for reconstructing a fragmented data file from a spreadsheet, database, or word processing application. To select it, press D, D, or click on the Disk menu and select Scan for Data Types.

- *Scan for Contents*   This option finds free clusters containing a specified text string up to 128 characters long. The search does *not* distinguish between upper- and lowercase. This option is especially useful for reconstructing a fragmented file that contains a unique word or phrase that you remember. To select it, press D, C, or click on the Disk menu and select Scan for Contents.

- *Scan for Lost Deleted Files*   This option lets you search exclusively for deleted files that belong to deleted directories and so can't be made to appear in the File List. You can specify whether or not the search includes files protected by Delete Sentry, Delete Tracker, and/or DOS. To select the option, press D, L, or click on the Disk menu and select Scan for Lost Deleted Files.

After you've selected one of these three commands, a dialog box appears that prompts you to select, respectively, the free clusters data types, free clusters text string, or lost files protection categories you want to search for. After choosing the appropriate options, press ALT-O or click OK. A dialog box like this appears:

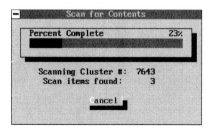

The box shows you the cluster number currently being scanned, the number of clusters or files found, and the percentage of the search procedure that's been completed. You can interrupt the procedure at any time by pressing ESC or clicking Cancel. If you do so, the clusters or files found up until that point are listed. You can continue the operation by pressing D, O, or by clicking on the Disk menu and selecting Continue. Alternatively, you can simply work with the data already listed.

When the scan is either interrupted or 100 percent complete, the specified free clusters (listed with filenames created by Undelete, such as CPS00001.FIL) or the specified lost files are displayed. You can select any or all of the files listed, and apply any Undelete command to them (*except* the Find Deleted Files command). For example, you can examine each listed cluster by selecting it and pressing F4. If the cluster contains the data you want, you can then undelete it by pressing F8, and later merge it with another file using either an appropriate application program or the DOS COPY command (using the /A or /B parameter; see your DOS manual for details).

When you're done working with the listed free clusters or deleted files, press F, F, or press F7, or click on the File menu and select Tree & File List. You're returned to the main Undelete screen.

The **Disk** menu's free cluster scans can take a long time to execute. Therefore, you also have the option of restricting searches to a limited range of clusters. To do so, press D, S, or click on the Disk menu and select Set Scan Range. You're prompted to enter starting and ending cluster numbers within a specified range for your current drive. After you do so, press ALT-O or click OK. Any further **Disk** scans you perform for the rest of the session will be restricted to the range you specified.

Examining Files

As mentioned previously, you can view a selected file's data. This is useful both *before* you undelete the file, because it allows you to make sure the file contains the data you're looking for, and *after* you undelete the file, because it lets you verify that the recovery process was successful.

To view a file, first highlight it in the File List, and then press F, V, or press F4, or click on the File menu and select View File. The bottom half of the screen becomes a View window, which displays the beginning of the file's contents.

Undelete will attempt to show the data in its native format. For example, if the selected file is a spreadsheet, its data will be displayed in rows and columns, while if it's a text file, its data will be displayed as a document with a tab ruler at the top. If you want to change to a different format, first move to the View window using TAB or click the window using your mouse, and then press F6. A list of 37 different application formats appears. Scroll through the list using the arrow keys or your mouse until you highlight the format you want, and then select it by pressing ENTER or double-clicking on it.

You can also scroll through the View window itself. To do so, use the arrow keys, PGDN and PGUP, and END and HOME; or click on the window's vertical scroll bar. You can additionally use F5 to jump to a specified line, F7 to locate a specified text string, and F8 to toggle the display between taking up half the screen and the entire screen. You can also press F9 or F10 to respectively display the contents of the previous or next file in the File List.

When you're done examining files, press ESC if the View window is selected, or press F4 if the window is *not* selected, or simply click on the window's Close box. The window closes, and you're returned to the main Undelete screen.

In addition to viewing a file's contents, you can display information about the file itself. This is useful because while the Directory Tree, File List, and status lines already provide a great deal of information about the currently selected file, that data is scattered among several areas of the screen. To gather it all into one spot, press F, I, or click on the File menu and select File Info. A dialog box like this appears:

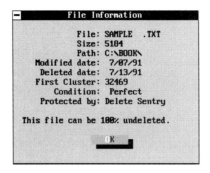

The box provides such details as the file's size (or the description <dir> if it's a deleted directory), and the number of its first cluster (which can be useful for manual recovery). After examining the information, press ENTER or click OK to close the box.

Recovering Files Manually

If a deleted file is both unprotected and fragmented, Undelete will only be able to automatically recover the file's initial clusters. Furthermore, if an unprotected file's initial clusters have been overwritten, Undelete won't be able to automatically recover *any* of the file's data. However, you may be able to locate and restore additional data from the file by using one of Undelete's manual recovery methods. These procedures are among the most technical and difficult in PC Tools 7, so they're recommended only as a last resort. It's also recommended that you take your time in experimenting with these options before you use them to restore any critical data.

To begin, select the file you want to work with (unless you're constructing an entirely new file), and then press F, A, or click on the File menu and select Advanced Undelete. The following submenu is displayed:

The submenu offers these options:

- *Manual Undelete*   This command lets you try to undelete the selected deleted file by locating and adding appropriate clusters to it.

- *Create a File*   This command lets you construct an entirely new file. It first prompts you for a filename, and then lets you locate and add appropriate clusters to it.

- *Append to Existing File*   This command lets you try to complete an existing file by locating and adding its missing clusters to it. To use it, you must first choose the **O**ptions **Sh**ow Existing Files command and select the existing file you want to revise.

- *Rename Existing File*   This command simply renames an existing file so it doesn't conflict with a file with the same name that you want to undelete. To use it, you must first choose the **O**ptions **Sh**ow Existing Files command and select the existing file you want to rename.

After you select **M**anual Undelete, **C**reate a File, or **A**ppend to Existing File, and you respond to any pertinent prompts, a screen like the one in Figure 6-3 appears. The screen's upper-left corner displays the selected file's name, size, and creation date and time, as well as the number of the next available cluster. The screen's lower-left corner displays options for adding clusters to the file, skipping to the next cluster, viewing the file as it currently stands, undeleting the file with the clusters you've added, and canceling the operation.

In the right corner of the screen is a box showing the starting cluster of the file, the number of clusters the file is still missing, and the number of clusters added. It also lists the clusters you've selected to add, and offers options for rearranging or deleting the listed clusters.

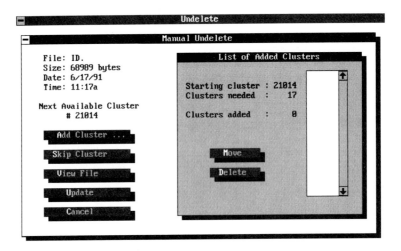

Figure 6-3.   *The Undelete manual recovery screen*

To proceed, first press A or click Add Cluster. The following additional dialog box appears:

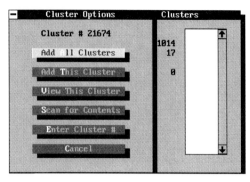

The box offers these six options:

- *Add All Clusters*   This option (which is only available in **Manual Undelete**) adds the next *n* free clusters to the file, where *n* is the number of clusters missing from the file. You can then examine each cluster to see if it really belongs.

- *Add This Cluster*   This option adds the next free cluster, that is, the cluster whose number appears at the top of the dialog box.

- *View This Cluster*   This option displays the data in the next free cluster.

- *Scan for Contents*   This option searches through all free clusters for a specified text string.

- *Enter Cluster #*   This option adds the cluster associated with the number you specify.

- *Cancel*   This option aborts the operation.

After you're done adding all your desired clusters, and revising your cluster list using the **Move** and **Delete** commands, select **Update** to undelete the file with the clusters you've specified. You're returned to the main Undelete screen, and your file is listed as "Recovered" in the File List. You can now press F4 to examine the file and verify that it's been reconstructed successfully.

Using Undelete on a Network

Undelete can now work with a network drive. When it does so, the Tree List is suppressed and the File List is expanded across the screen. Also, a Path column is added to the end of the File List to show the drive and directory of each listed file.

Undelete can quickly and fully recover files protected by Delete Sentry on a network drive. However, it *cannot* recover (or even display) unprotected files or files protected by Delete Tracker.

In addition, many of Undelete's commands are unavailable while it's operating on the network drive. These include the **File Advanced Undelete** commands, the **Options Show Existing Files** command, and all the **Disk** menu options.

Recovering Formatted Disks

If you've accidentally formatted a disk, you can usually recover most or all of your data using the Unformat program. How successful you are depends on four factors: the format program you used; whether the format was on a floppy or a hard disk; how recently you backed up the disk's FAT and root directory using Mirror; and how fragmented the disk is.

- If you used PC Format or the Format program in DOS 5 (see "Using PC Format" in Chapter 5), then you can recover all the files that aren't fragmented. If you also used Mirror on the disk recently, you can recover all of its fragmented files, as well.

- If you used a version of DOS FORMAT prior to DOS 5 on a floppy disk, all of your data has been destroyed. Your only options are to locate backup copies of the files, find printouts of the files' contents, or reconstruct the files from memory.

- If you used a version of DOS FORMAT prior to DOS 5 on a hard disk, your results will depend on the type of DOS. Certain versions (such as Compaq DOS up through version 3.2, AT&T DOS up through version 3.1, and some versions of Burroughs DOS) destroy all files when formatting. In these cases, you can only turn to backup copies, printouts, or your recollections.

   The vast majority of versions of DOS FORMAT, however, preserve hard disk files. If you used a nondestructive FORMAT and you *didn't* run Mirror on the disk recently, you can recover everything except your fragmented files, your root-level files, and the original names of your root-level directories. If you *did* run Mirror on the disk recently, you can recover virtually all your data.

- If you used Mirror on the disk, but you created or revised a number of files after doing so, you need to weigh several factors before deciding whether to unformat using the Mirror data. This subject is explored in the next section.

Deciding Whether to Unformat Using Mirror Data

If you unformat a disk using its Mirror data, you'll recover only the files whose cluster locations have stayed the same since you last ran Mirror. In other words, you will *not* recover any files that you created or significantly revised after the Mirror file was generated. To restore the latter data, you'll have to use backup files and/or the interactive version of Undelete covered earlier in this chapter.

On the other hand, if you unformat a disk without using its Mirror data, you'll recover only its unfragmented files. If you've been running Compress regularly (see Chapter 9), then the disk may not contain much fragmentation; but if you haven't, scores of files could be fragmented. Furthermore, if you used a version of DOS FORMAT prior to DOS 5, you'll lose your root-level files and the original names of your root-level directories.

If you're unformatting a floppy disk, you can have the best of both worlds by simply creating two *copies of the problem disk (see "Preparing for Floppy Disk Recovery" earlier in this chapter). You can then unformat the first disk using its Mirror data and the second disk ignoring its Mirror data. Between the two disks, you'll probably recover all of your files.*

If you're unformatting a hard disk, you should therefore weigh priorities, taking into account the date of your Mirror file (displayed when you run Unformat), the number and importance of the files you've saved since then, the number and importance of your older files, and the likelihood of significant disk fragmentation.

In most cases, it's recommended that you unformat using the Mirror data. This is generally the surest way of recovering the vast majority of your files.

The procedures for unformatting with and without Mirror data are covered in the next two sections.

Unformatting a Disk Using Mirror Data

To unformat a disk using the FAT and root directory information in its Mirror file, follow these steps:

1. If you're unformatting a floppy disk, insert it in a disk drive. On the other hand, if you're unformatting a hard disk, insert a disk containing the UN-FORMAT.EXE program (such as your Recovery Disk) into a drive.

2. Set the DOS prompt to the drive containing the UNFORMAT.EXE program. For example, if the file is on drive C, type **C:** and press ENTER; if it's on drive A, type **A:** and press ENTER.

3. Type **UNFORMAT** and press ENTER. Icons representing all the drives in your system are displayed.

4. Press the letter of the drive you want to unformat and press ENTER, or click the icon of the drive and click OK. The message "Please wait while drive is being validated" briefly appears.

5. If files are found that were saved to the disk *after* it was formatted, the files are listed and you're warned that they'll be destroyed. If you want to save these files, exit the program by pressing ESC, ESC, ENTER, or by clicking Cancel, Exit, and OK; copy the files to a different disk; and then return to step 1. However, if you don't mind losing the files, just press ENTER or click OK to proceed.

6. You're now asked whether you used Mirror on the disk. Press Y or click YES to unformat the disk using Mirror data.

7. Unformat first uses the MIRORSAV.FIL file in the disk's last cluster to locate MIRROR.FIL and, if it exists, MIRROR.BAK. It then displays the Mirror file creation date stored inside each file. If no prior Mirror file is found, simply press ENTER or click Last to tell Unformat to use the only existing Mirror file.

   If a MIRROR.BAK file *does* exist, you're asked to select between it and the current file. The only reason you should select the BAK file is if you accidentally ran Mirror on the disk *after* the format occurred, filling the current file with useless data. Press ENTER or click Last to work with the current Mirror file, or press P or click Prior to work with the BAK file.

8. A map of the disk like the one shown in Figure 6-4 now appears, and the recovery begins. This process is entirely automatic; it will continue uninterrupted until all files specified by the Mirror data have been recovered.

   When it's over, a message appears telling you the unformatting is complete. Press ENTER or click Exit. Unformat exits, and you're returned to the DOS prompt.

9. If you unformatted a hard disk, it's a good idea to restart your computer by pressing CTRL-ALT-DEL, both to verify that the disk is back in working order and to restore your usual working environment.

10. Use the DOS DIR command, PC Shell, and/or your application programs to examine your restored files and directories. Also, run DiskFix (covered in Chapter 7) to detect and repair any problem areas that may have resulted from the recovery process.

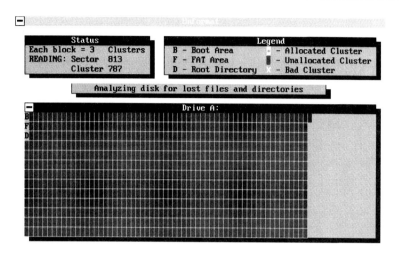

Figure 6-4.   *The Unformat recovery screen*

Unformatting a Disk Without Mirror Data

To unformat a disk that either doesn't contain a Mirror file or contains a Mirror file that's too old to be used effectively, follow these steps:

1. If you're unformatting a floppy disk, insert it in a disk drive. On the other hand, if you're unformatting a hard disk, insert a disk containing the UN-FORMAT.EXE program (such as your Recovery Disk) into a drive.

2. Set the DOS prompt to the drive containing the UNFORMAT.EXE program. For example, if the file is on drive C, type **C:** and press ENTER; if it's on drive A, type **A:** and press ENTER.

3. Type **UNFORMAT** and press ENTER. Icons representing all the drives in your system are displayed.

4. Press the letter of the drive you want to unformat and press ENTER, or click the icon of the drive and click OK. The message "Please wait while drive is being validated" briefly appears.

5. If files are found that were saved to the disk *after* it was formatted, the files are listed and you're warned that they'll be destroyed. If you want to save these files, exit the program by pressing ESC, ESC, ENTER, or by clicking Cancel, Exit, and OK; copy the files to a different disk; and then return to step 1. However, if you don't mind losing the files, just press ENTER or click OK to proceed.

6. You're now asked whether you used Mirror on the disk. Press N or click No to unformat the disk without using Mirror data.

7. A map of the disk like the one shown in Figure 6-4 now appears, and Unformat proceeds to read every sector of the disk to analyze its lost files and directories. A Status section in the upper-left corner constantly shows you the number of the sector and cluster currently being read. When the process is completed, a dialog box appears telling you "The next phase of the operation writes to the disk. Are you sure you want to continue?" Press O or click OK to initiate the actual recovery process.

8. Each file is now checked for fragmentation. When none exists, the file is restored automatically. Otherwise, a message appears asking whether the file should be truncated or deleted. You're also given the option of setting Undelete to automatically truncate or delete all fragmented files found.

   Truncating a file will recover its initial clusters but not the clusters following fragmentation. It could be that the majority of the file's data is contained in its initial clusters. However, it's equally possible that most of its data is in the fragmented clusters. You can tell which is true for each file by comparing its full size (listed after the file's name) against the number of bytes that can be recovered (listed at the end of the information line). In most cases, it's recommended that you mark down the filename and file size and then accept the truncation option, because it recovers at least *some* data for you automatically. You can later try to recover whatever data is still missing using the Undelete program (see "Using Interactive Undelete" and "Finding Free Clusters and Lost Files" earlier in this chapter). To truncate the current file, press T and ENTER, or click Truncate. You can alternatively set Unformat to automatically truncate all the fragmented files it finds by pressing R and ENTER, or clicking Truncate All; but this isn't recommended, because it doesn't give you the opportunity to write down the name and size of each partially recovered file.

   The other options, **Delete** and **Delete All**, don't recover *any* file data. However, once the unformat process is over, they enable you to list all deleted files using the Undelete program, and then try and manually recover each file's missing data cluster by cluster (see "Using Interactive Undelete" and "Recovering Files Manually" earlier in this chapter). If you want to delete the current file, press ENTER or click Delete; while if you want to set Unformat to automatically delete all the fragmented files it finds, press E and ENTER, or click Delete All.

9. When all the files found by Unformat have been fully restored, truncated, or deleted, the program tells you how many files have been recovered (including truncated files) and displays the message "Unformatting complete." Press ENTER or click OK. You're returned to the DOS prompt.

10. If you unformatted a hard disk, it's a good idea to restart your computer by pressing CTRL-ALT-DEL, both to verify that the disk is back in working order and to restore your usual working environment.

11. Use the DOS DIR command, PC Shell, and/or your application programs to examine your restored files and directories. If you recovered from formatting your hard disk with a version of DOS FORMAT prior to DOS 5, you'll also need to rename your root-level directories. Lastly, run DiskFix (covered in Chapter 7) to detect and repair any problem areas that may have resulted from the recovery process.

12. If fragmented files were found during the Unformat procedure, use the Undelete program to try and recover their missing data. For more information, see "Using Interactive Undelete," "Finding Free Clusters and Lost Files," and "Recovering Files Manually" earlier in this chapter.

Unformat Parameters

When you run Unformat, you can include several parameters following the program's name.

First, you can include a space, drive letter, and colon to specify the drive to unformat (for example, **UNFORMAT C:**).

Second, you can include a number of video and mouse parameters. For a complete list, type **UNFORMAT /VIDEO** at the DOS prompt and press ENTER, or see the "Video and Mouse Parameters" section in Appendix A, "PC Tools Installation and Configuration."

Third, you can type **UNFORMAT /?** to display the two parameters just mentioned.

Restoring Your CMOS Data, Partition Table, and Boot Record

If you're suddenly unable to start up your PC from your hard disk, or if you try to access the hard disk and get a DOS message such as "Invalid drive specification," the cause is likely to be defects in your partition table, CMOS data, or boot record. You can repair all such defects using the information stored on the Recovery Disk you created with the Install program (as covered in Appendix A and in "Creating a Recovery Disk" in Chapter 5). To do so, follow these steps:

1. Insert your Recovery Disk into drive A.

2. Restart your PC from the Recovery Disk by pressing CTRL-ALT-DEL.

3. When your PC has finished rebooting, type **REBUILD** from the DOS prompt and press ENTER.

4. You're prompted to insert the disk that contains PARTNSAV.FIL, which is the file that holds your partition table. Since your Recovery Disk contains this file, simply press ENTER.

5. Your partition table information is now displayed. (If more than one screen of information is available, press ENTER to display the second screen.)

6. If your system does *not* use a CMOS chip (that is, if you're running an 8088 PC rather than an 80286, 80386, or 80486), skip to step 10.

   Otherwise, initiate the restoration of your CMOS data by typing **C** and pressing ENTER. You're prompted for confirmation.

7. Type **YES** and press ENTER. The data in PARTNSAV.FIL is copied to your system's CMOS memory to overwrite any defects. A message then appears saying that your system is ready to be rebooted.

8. Press ENTER to restart your PC with its restored CMOS data. Once again, the computer boots from your Recovery Disk.

9. Repeat your previous steps by typing **REBUILD** from the DOS prompt and pressing ENTER, and pressing ENTER again in response to the drive prompt.

10. Initiate the restoration of your partition table and boot record by typing the number of the drive you're repairing (typically **1**) and pressing ENTER. You're prompted for confirmation.

11. Type **YES** and press ENTER. The data in PARTNSAV.FIL is copied to the hard disk's partition table and boot record to overwrite any defects. A message then appears saying your system is (again) ready to reboot.

12. Remove the Recovery Disk from the A drive and store the disk in a safe place. When you're done, press ENTER to restart your PC (which is necessary to let DOS know that your partition information has changed). The computer should now successfully start up from your hard disk.

13. If you continue experiencing hard disk problems; or if Compress (see Chapter 9) suddenly reports an unusually large number of hard disk defects; or if you begin having problems with the system date and time; or if the SI program (see Chapter 18) displays different system configuration information at different times, then it's likely that your CMOS chip needs a new battery. In this case, replace the old battery, repeat steps 1 through 6, press ENTER to exit Rebuild, remove the Recovery Disk and reboot your PC, and then see if your system problems disappear.

Rebuild supports several parameters, such as /L for listing PARTNSAV.FIL's partition data. For brief descriptions of these parameters, type **REBUILD /?** *at the DOS prompt and press* ENTER.

Restoring the FAT and Root Directory

If you get a message indicating that your disk's FAT or root directory has become defective, how you proceed depends on how recently you updated the disk's Mirror file.

If you haven't saved any important files to the disk since the last time you used Mirror on it, then the most effective restoration method is the Unformat program. Specifically, you should treat the disk as if you'd accidentally formatted it and follow the directions in the "Unformatting a Disk Using Mirror Data" section earlier in this chapter.

If you've saved a number of important files to the disk since the last time you updated its Mirror file, or if you've never used Mirror on the disk, then the most effective restoration method is the DiskFix program. In other words, in cases where a disk hasn't been formatted and lacks a recent Mirror file, DiskFix does a better job of restoring the FAT and root directory than Unformat does. For information on using the DiskFix program, see Chapter 7.

Undelete Command Reference

Most of Undelete's power lies in its menu commands, which control how deleted files are displayed, located, and recovered. Like a number of PC Tools programs, Undelete's first menu is Control and its last menu is **Help**. These menus are covered in this book's Introduction.

Undelete also contains three additional menus: **F**ile, **D**isk, and **O**ptions. The following sections cover the options in these menus. After the name of each option are the keystrokes that invoke it, a description of what the option does, and a reference to the section in this chapter that discusses the option in detail.

The File Menu

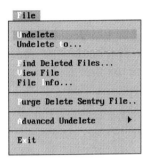

The **F**ile menu performs such operations as undeleting files, finding deleted files, displaying the data in undeleted files, purging the \SENTRY directory, and manually recovering free clusters. It contains the following eight options:

Undelete (F, U or F8)

Undeletes the selected files. Covered in "Undeleting Files."

Undelete **T**o (F, T)

Undeletes the selected files to a different drive and/or directory. Covered in "Undeleting Files."

Find Deleted Files (F, F or F7)

Finds deleted files based on their names, contents, and/or protection status. Covered in "Finding Deleted Files in Existing Directories."

View File (F, V or F4)

Displays the contents of the selected deleted files. Covered in "Examining Files."

File **I**nfo (F, I)

Displays information about the file currently selected by the highlight cursor in the File List. Covered in "Examining Files."

Purge Delete Sentry File (F, P)

Purges (that is, deletes beyond recovery) specified files or all files in the \SENTRY directory. This command can be used to clear out obsolete files so there's more room for other protected files. However, it's generally best to leave the \SENTRY directory alone and simply allow Delete Sentry to purge its files automatically.

Advanced Undelete (F, A)

Lets you select among the Manual Undelete, Create a File, or Append to Existing File commands to reconstruct files by recovering free clusters; or select the Rename Existing File command when an existing file's name is the same as that of a file you want to undelete. Covered in "Recovering Files Manually."

Exit (F, X)

Exits Undelete, returning you to the DOS prompt.

The Disk Menu

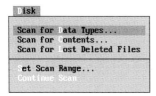

The **Disk** menu lets you find free clusters containing specified application data or a specified text string, or deleted files belonging to deleted directories. It provides the following five options:

Scan for **D**ata Types (D, D)

Finds free clusters containing Lotus 1-2-3, Symphony, dBASE, and/or text data. Covered in "Finding Free Clusters and Lost Files."

Scan for **C**ontents (D, C)

Finds free clusters containing a specified text sequence. Covered in "Finding Free Clusters and Lost Files."

Scan for **L**ost Deleted Files (D, L)

Finds deleted files that belong to deleted directories. The search can be restricted to files protected by one or two specified methods. Covered in "Finding Free Clusters and Lost Files."

Set Scan Range (D, S)

Restricts **D**isk menu searches to the specified cluster range. Covered in "Finding Free Clusters and Lost Files."

Continue Scan (D, O)

Continues an interrupted **D**isk menu search. Covered in "Finding Free Clusters and Lost Files."

The Options Menu

The **O**ptions menu contains the following five options for sorting the File List, selecting and unselecting files using DOS wildcards, displaying existing files, and setting Undelete to use Mirror data when recovering unprotected files:

Sort By (O, S or F9)

Sorts the File List by **N**ame, **E**xtension, **S**ize, **D**eleted Date and Time, **M**odified (that is, creation) Date and Time, Directory, or Condition. The Directory option is only for "lost" files listed by the **D**isk Scan for **L**ost Deleted Files command; files with the same date are sorted by their deletion time; and the Condition option should be selected before undeleting files to increase the chances for full automatic recovery. Mentioned in "Undeleting Files."

Select By Name (O, B or F5)

Selects specified files using DOS wildcards. Covered in "Navigating the Tree List and File List."

Unselect By Name (O, U)

Unselects specified files using DOS wildcards. Covered in "Navigating the Tree List and File List."

Show Existing Files (O, H)

Displays existing files in addition to deleted files in the File List. This is necessary if you want to use the **F**ile **A**dvanced Undelete **R**ename Existing File or **F**ile **A**dvanced Undelete **A**ppend to Existing File command. Covered in "Recovering Files Manually."

Use **M**irror File (O, M)

For files that weren't protected by Delete Sentry or Delete Tracker, sets Undelete to use the disk's Mirror data instead of its FAT and root directory information. This will sometimes improve your chances of recovering a fragmented file.

Chapter 7

Repairing Disks Using DiskFix

If you need to recover deleted files, a formatted disk, a partition table, CMOS data, or a FAT or root directory recently backed up with Mirror, use the programs described in Chapter 6, "Recovering Deleted or Formatted Data."

However, if you have any other kind of disk-related problem, use DiskFix. DiskFix is a powerful utility that can perform such diverse tasks as:

- Nondestructively low-level formatting a floppy or hard disk to make seemingly unreadable areas useable again. (The hard disk option is new to PC Tools 7.)

- Changing the spacing of data across a hard disk, or its *interleave,* to improve the disk's data access speed. (This feature is new to PC Tools 7.)

- Repairing a defective boot record so that your hard disk is able to start up your computer again.

- Eliminating cross-linked files, which are two or more files using the same cluster at the same time, by determining which file the cluster really belongs to.

- Eliminating lost clusters, which are clusters the FAT has marked as in use but which aren't allocated to any file.

- Correcting other cluster assignment errors, such as pointers to nonexistent clusters.

- Repairing a defective FAT or root directory even if no Mirror data exists (see "Restoring the FAT and Root Directory" in Chapter 6).

- Fixing problems reported by the DOS program CHKDSK. Don't let CHKDSK even attempt to solve the problems it discovers, because DiskFix will do a much better job of handling them.

If you get a disk error message, you should first determine that it isn't the result of something simple, such as a disk being full; or a floppy disk not being inserted properly in the drive; or a floppy disk having a write-protect tab on its notch, preventing your computer from writing data to it.

Once you've eliminated such possibilities, try using DiskFix. There's a good chance the program will correctly analyze the problem. If you then give it the go-ahead, it will fix the problem automatically.

You shouldn't just use DiskFix when errors occur, however. It's recommended you also use it as a maintenance utility, running it about once a month on your hard disk. This will let DiskFix search for developing problems and fix them before they become more serious. In addition, it will allow DiskFix to rejuvenate your hard disk's tracks to ensure they stay readable, and mark tracks that have become irreparably defective so that no further data is saved to them.

It's also recommended you maintain your hard disk by running the PC Tools Park program whenever you're ready to turn off your computer. This utility helps reduce the wear and tear that creates defects on the disk.

This chapter first covers running DiskFix, and then using it to analyze and fix general disk problems, find and repair defective tracks, and low-level format disks. The last section covers running the Park program to maintain your hard disk.

Running DiskFix

Before you can use DiskFix, you must transfer it to your hard disk or a floppy disk. You can do this by using the Install program (see Appendix A, "PC Tools Installation and Configuration"), or by copying the program directly from the PC Tools floppy labeled "Data Recovery Utilities" which contains the file DISKFIX.EXE.

When DiskFix is installed, run the program by following these steps:

1. Unload any memory-resident programs you're running other than PC Tools 7 programs and your mouse driver. This is *very important*. If you leave any programs in memory that conflict with DiskFix, they may cause it to diagnose your disk incorrectly and create serious problems in its attempts to perform repairs.

If you have Microsoft Windows or DESQview resident, DiskFix will analyze your disk, but it will refuse to execute any repair operations. DiskFix will only attempt to fix your disk when it doesn't detect any conflicting memory-resident programs.

2. Set the DOS prompt to the drive containing the DISKFIX.EXE program. For example, if the file is on your hard drive C, type **C:** and press ENTER; if it's on drive A, type **A:** and press ENTER.

3. Type **DISKFIX** and press ENTER. A message appears warning you about memory-resident programs.

4. Press ENTER or click OK. A message flashes by to indicate initial system testing, which includes checking your system's BIOS; your system's CMOS memory (on 80286, 80386, and 80486 machines only); and your hard disk's partition table, boot record, and FAT (which DiskFix compares against the disk's Mirror file).

5. If any problem is detected, a specific message about it is displayed, and you're prompted to allow DiskFix to effect repairs. If this occurs, and you believe the analysis is sound, press ENTER or click OK to let DiskFix try to eliminate the problem. (Also, be sure to accept any offer to save "undo" information, since this lets you return the disk to its previous state if the repairs aren't successful.) Alternatively, press ESC or click Cancel to make DiskFix skip repairs and continue with its system checking.

When DiskFix has completed its system checks, the following main menu appears:

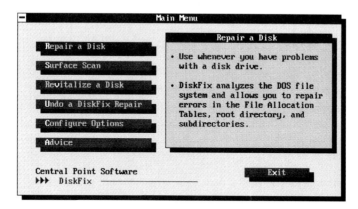

The menu offers these options for fixing floppy and hard disks:

*   ***Repair a Disk***   This option analyzes and repairs a wide range of disk-related problems. It's the first option you should try when experiencing difficulties accessing a disk or specific data on the disk. To use it, read the "Repairing a Disk" section.

- *Surface Scan*   This option checks a disk's tracks for defects, and repairs each defective track or marks it as bad. To use it, read the "Scanning a Disk" section.

- *Revitalize a Disk*   This option is similar to Surface Scan, except that in addition to fixing or marking defective tracks, it low-level formats *every* track on the disk. This refreshes any tracks that have started to become defective or misaligned with your disk drive heads (indicated by "read error" messages). Also, it gives you the opportunity to change a hard disk's interleave factor, which affects disk speed. To use this option, read the "Revitalizing a Disk" section.

- *Undo a DiskFix Repair*   This option lets you revert a disk to the state it was in before DiskFix attempted to repair it *if* you allowed DiskFix to save "undo" information preceding the repairs. To use it, read the "Undoing a DiskFix Repair" section.

- *Configure Options*   This option lets you change the tests that DiskFix runs automatically and the message it displays when it finds an error. To use it, read the "Customizing DiskFix" section.

- *Advice*   This option provides online help on a variety of disk-related subjects. To use it, press A or click Advice, and then select one of the listed topics you're interested in. You can also get help on DiskFix itself at any time by pressing F1.

- *Exit*   This option exits DiskFix and returns you to the DOS prompt.

Repairing a Disk

From the DiskFix main menu, follow these steps to analyze and repair a floppy or hard disk:

1. Press R or click Repair a Disk. Icons representing the different drives in your system appear.

2. Select the drive of the disk you want to repair by pressing its letter and pressing ENTER, or by clicking the drive's icon and clicking OK.

3. DiskFix first checks the disk's initial sectors. If any problem is found, an error message appears. If this occurs, press ENTER or click OK to allow DiskFix to handle the problem.

4. When the initial check of the disk is completed, the Repair Drive dialog box in Figure 7-1 appears. The box displays a list of tests DiskFix will automatically perform, the particular test being performed, the percentage of the test that's been completed, and the drive being tested.

    The eight tests listed are Boot Sector, which checks the area used to start up your computer; FAT Integrity, which checks the readability of the two

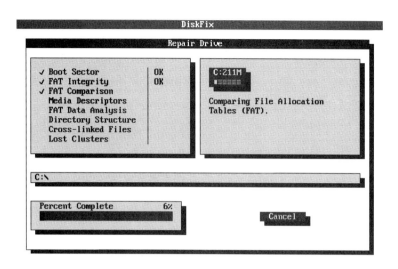

Figure 7-1.   *The Repair Drive dialog box*

copies of the FAT on the disk; FAT Comparison, which compares the two
copies of the FAT to ensure they're identical; Media Descriptors, which checks
that the FAT contains the proper ID number for the type of disk you have;
FAT Data Analysis, which checks for invalid data in the FAT; Directory
Structure, which checks the root directory for defects; Cross-linked Files,
which checks for clusters that are allocated to two or more files at the same
time; and Lost Clusters, which checks for clusters that aren't allocated to any
file but are marked by the FAT as being in use.

   DiskFix tests each item and, as before, displays an error message if it detects
a problem. If this occurs, press ENTER or click OK to allow DiskFix to effect
repairs and then continue testing.

5. DiskFix places a checkmark to the left and the word "OK" to the right of each
   item after finding it free of defects. When the testing is complete, you're asked
   if you want a report of the results. If you don't, press ENTER or click Skip, and
   then go to step 8.

6. Press O or click OK to create a report. You're asked if you want the report
   sent to your printer or a disk file.

7. If you want the report printed, make sure your printer is on and online, and
   then press ENTER or click Printer. After a moment, the results of the testing
   are printed.

8. Alternatively, press F or click File. A default filename of DISKFIX.RPT in the disk's root directory (or, under some circumstances, in DiskFix's directory) is suggested. You can optionally edit the line to save the report to a different drive, directory, and/or filename. When you're done, press ENTER. If it turns out that the file already exists, press O to overwrite the previous file, or press P to append the data to the end of the previous file. The report is saved.

9. The Fix a Disk procedure ends, and you're returned to the DiskFix main menu. To continue using DiskFix, select another menu option. Otherwise, press X or click Exit to quit the program and return to the DOS prompt.

Scanning a Disk

From the DiskFix main menu, follow these steps to find, and then repair or mark as unusable, the defective tracks on a floppy or hard disk:

1. Press S or click Surface Scan. Icons representing the different drives in your system appear.

2. Select the drive of the disk you want to test by pressing its letter and pressing ENTER, or by clicking its icon and clicking OK. The message "Reading System Areas" appears.

3. If any problem is found in the disk's initial sectors, an error message is displayed. If this occurs, press ENTER or click OK to allow DiskFix to effect repairs and then continue testing.

4. After DiskFix has finished its initial check, complete the procedure by going to the "Completing Scanning or Revitalizing" section. If you selected a hard disk, begin with step 1 of the section, while if you selected a floppy disk, begin with step 2.

Revitalizing a Disk

Follow these steps to low-level format a floppy or hard disk:

1. If this is the first time you're using DiskFix with your hard disk, it's recommended that you exit the program and *back up* the disk before proceeding (see Chapter 1, "CP Backup Overview"). While it's unlikely DiskFix will create any damage, it's generally wise to act cautiously when using powerful software such as a low-level formatter for the first time. When you're done backing up, run DiskFix again to return to the main menu.

2. Press V or click Revitalize a Disk. Icons representing the different drives in your system appear.

3. Select the drive of the disk you want to test by pressing its letter and pressing ENTER, or by clicking its icon and clicking OK. The message "Reading System Areas" appears.

4. If any problem is found in the disk's initial sectors, an error message is displayed. If this occurs, press ENTER or click OK to allow DiskFix to effect repairs and then continue testing.

5. After DiskFix has finished its initial check, a Testing System Integrity dialog box appears. This box shows DiskFix's progress as it tests such system components as the memory, controller card, and timer; and whether all hardware and software caches are turned off. (If you have PC-Cache resident, DiskFix turned it off automatically on startup and will reactivate the cache upon exiting.)

   When all the test items in the list are checked, the message "System Integrity testing finished" appears. If you're revitalizing a floppy disk, this is all the testing DiskFix needs to ensure it can low-level format the disk safely. In this case, press ENTER or click OK, and then go to step 2 of the "Completing Scanning or Revitalizing" section.

6. Press ENTER or click OK to continue testing your hard disk. A Testing Disk Timing Characteristics dialog box appears, which shows DiskFix determining the time it takes to move the drive's head from one track to the next (Track to Track); from the first track to the last track (Full Stroke); and, on average, from one track to any other track (Random Seek). When all three test items are checked, the message "Seek Timings Completed" appears.

7. Press ENTER or click OK. A Determining Physical Parameters dialog box appears, which shows DiskFix establishing a number of technical facts about your disk's speed and type. When all the test items are checked, the message "Physical parameters determined" appears.

8. Press ENTER or click OK. At this point, you may see a message telling you that the type of hard disk DiskFix has determined you're using *cannot* be low-level formatted. If this occurs, it's probably because you're using a modern hard disk, such as an IDE drive, that contains its own internal technology for correcting errors. If your drive is incompatible with low-level formatting programs, it would be *severely damaged* by continuing with the Revitalize a Disk procedure. Therefore, press ESC twice to return to the main menu. If you still want to use DiskFix on the drive, you can now select the **S**urface Scan option, which will at least detect bad tracks, move their data, and then mark the tracks as unusable. If your drive continues to exhibit problems after that, contact your dealer or the manufacturer.

9. If DiskFix has determined your drive is capable of being low-level formatted, it now analyzes how your disk's sectors should be spaced out, or its optimum interleave, as shown in Figure 7-2. To understand what this means, keep in

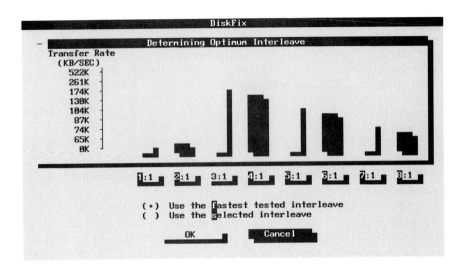

Figure 7-2. *The Determining Optimum Interleave dialog box*

mind that your disk is constantly spinning. If by the time your drive heads have finished reading one sector of data, your drive has spun past the following sector, then the heads will have to wait for an entire new revolution to access that second sector. Such a situation would take a great toll on your drive's performance. Spacing sectors out so your drive heads can read one after the other immediately therefore increases the data access speed of your hard disk. If your disk has an inefficient interleave, low-level formatting it for an optimal interleave can increase its effective speed by as much as 500 percent.

To choose to set your drive for its optimal interleave, simply press ENTER or click OK. However, if you want to maintain the drive's current interleave (although there typically isn't any reason to do so), press S and press ENTER. (If your current interleave is the same as the optimal interleave, it doesn't matter which of the two options you choose.)

10. DiskFix has now completed all the testing it needs to ensure it can low-level format your disk safely and efficiently. To continue, go on to the following "Completing Scanning or Revitalizing" section.

Completing Scanning or Revitalizing

To complete your Surface Scan or Revitalize a Disk procedure, follow these steps:

1. A screen appears prompting you to select the degree of testing you want DiskFix to perform when checking your hard disk's tracks for defects.

   The option that takes the least time is **R**ead/Write Only, which tests by simply reading the data from each track and then attempting to write the data back. If it encounters problems doing so, it either fixes the track and then writes the data back to it, or marks the track as unusable and moves whatever data it could recover to a different, problem-free track. In addition, if you've selected the Revitalize a Disk option, it low-level formats each track. This option is the default.

   If you want more thorough checking, select **M**inimum Pattern Testing, which performs 20 tests on each track; **A**verage Pattern Testing, which performs 40 tests; or Ma**x**imum Pattern Testing, which performs 80 tests. Each option takes twice as long as the one before it; for example, Maximum Pattern Testing typically takes *hours* to complete execution.

   Choose an option depending on your current experience with the disk. For example, if this is the first time you're testing the disk, or if you've been encountering a number of problems with it lately, select Maximum Pattern Testing; but start it at the end of your work day so that it can run uninterrupted for the several hours it will require.

   After you've selected an option by pressing its highlighted letter or clicking it, press ENTER or click OK.

2. A map of your disk like the one in Figure 7-3 is displayed. Each area, or *block*, on the map represents a certain number of tracks. The precise tracks-to-block ratio varies depending on disk size and is specified for your disk directly below the map's left side.

   DiskFix then proceeds to test each track and, if necessary, repair it or mark it as unusable. The status box in the bottom right of the screen constantly tells you which track number is being read or written to, and the percentage of the operation completed.

   In addition, the status of each block is indicated by one of the symbols in the Legend box in the lower left of the screen. For example, ▒ (confusingly identified as "Partition space" in the Legend box) means the block hasn't been tested yet; a double-headed arrow means the block is being read from or written to; .oO means DiskFix is using various testing patterns on the block; means the block was found to be defective, and its data is being moved to another location; and (if you've selected Revitalize a Disk) a skinny asterisk indicates the block is being low-level formatted.

   Once DiskFix has finished working with a block, it marks it on the map as ◨ to indicate it's problem free; "C" to indicate it was defective and contains data, and its problem's been corrected (or a small "c" if it doesn't contain data); "U" to indicate it's defective and contains data, and its problem is uncorrectable (or a small "u" if it doesn't contain data); a number from 1 to

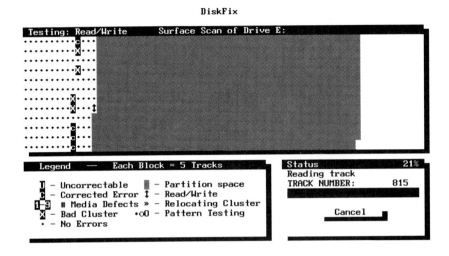

Figure 7-3.   *The DiskFix disk scanning screen*

9 to indicate that an unused sector in the block contained the specified number of defects ("9" meaning nine *or more*); or "X" to indicate the block was already marked bad in the FAT, so DiskFix didn't bother checking it.

If you want to interrupt the procedure at any point, press ESC or click Cancel. You can then press ESC to exit and return to the DiskFix menu, or press ENTER or click OK to continue from where you left off. However, *never* simply turn off your machine, as doing so could create data losses.

3. If the testing is allowed to finish, eventually all the disk's tracks are checked, and this message appears:

If you don't want a log report, press S or click Skip, and then go to step 5. Otherwise, press ENTER or click OK. You're asked if you want the report sent to your printer or a disk file.

4. If you want the report printed, make sure your printer is on and online, and then press ENTER or click Printer. After a moment, the results of the testing are printed.

Alternatively, press F or click File. A default filename of DISKFIX.LOG in the disk's root directory (or, under some circumstances, in DiskFix's directory) is suggested. Optionally edit the line to save the report to a different drive, directory, and/or filename, and then press ENTER. The log report is saved.

5. The procedure ends, and you're returned to the DiskFix main menu. To continue using DiskFix, select another menu option. Otherwise, press X or click Exit to quit DiskFix and return to the DOS prompt.

Undoing a DiskFix Repair

If you allowed DiskFix to save "undo" data before repairing a problem, and you now find you're dissatisfied with the job DiskFix did, follow these steps to return your disk to its previous state:

1. From the DiskFix main menu, press U or click Undo a DiskFix Repair. Icons representing the different drives in your system appear.

2. If you saved your "undo" information to a floppy disk (which is recommended), insert that floppy into a drive.

3. Select the drive by pressing its letter and pressing ENTER, or by clicking its icon and clicking OK. DiskFix now proceeds to change your repaired disk back to its original state.

4. When DiskFix is done, it returns you to the main menu. To continue using the program, select another menu option. Otherwise, press X or click Exit to quit DiskFix and return to the DOS prompt.

Customizing DiskFix

If you want to speed DiskFix slightly on startup by turning off its initial testing, or if you want to create a custom message box, go to the DiskFix main menu, and then press C or click Configure Options. The following dialog box appears:

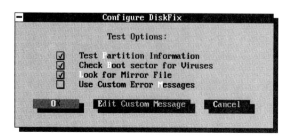

The box offers the following four options, the first three of which are initially selected:

- *Test Partition Information*   This option sets DiskFix to test your hard disk's partition table and boot record before displaying the main menu. If you run DiskFix with great frequency (for example, if you run it from your AUTO-EXEC.BAT file), turning this option off saves a little bit of time.

- *Check Boot sector for Viruses*   This option sets DiskFix to test your hard disk's boot record for known viruses before displaying the main menu. It's only in effect when the Test Partition Information option is also turned on.

- *Look for Mirror File*   This option sets DiskFix to compare your disk's Mirror data file (MIRROR.FIL) with its FAT to determine which has the fewest errors. Unless you don't use Mirror (which is *not* recommended), leave this option on.

- *Use Custom Error Messages*   This option prevents DiskFix from executing any repairs for problems it finds, and displays your single customized message (for example, "Contact your PC supervisor") in place of any specific DiskFix message about the problem. To create your message, press E or click Edit Custom Message.

DiskFix Parameters

You can run DiskFix from a batch file or your AUTOEXEC.BAT file by using certain options, called parameters, following DiskFix's program name. The ten parameters specific to DiskFix are as follows:

- /?   This "help" parameter lists and briefly describes each parameter specific to DiskFix. It should not be combined with any other parameter.

- /VIDEO   This "help" parameter lists and briefly describes the standard PC Tools video and mouse parameters. It should not be combined with any other parameter. For more information, see the "Video and Mouse Parameters" section in Appendix A, "PC Tools Installation and Configuration."

- *d*:   This parameter runs DiskFix on the specified drive, with *d* representing the letter of the drive.

- /TEST   This parameter selects the **Repair a Disk** option for the specified drive.

- /SCAN   This parameter selects the **Surface Scan** and **Read/Write Only** options for the specified drive.

- **/RA:*filename***   This parameter saves a report or log file on the DiskFix operation to the disk's root using the specified filename. If the specified file already exists, this command adds the information to the end of the old file.

- **/RO:*filename***   This parameter saves a report or log file on the DiskFix operation to the disk's root using the specified filename. If the specified file already exists, this command overwrites the old file with its new information.

- *path\filename*   This parameter specifies the directory and/or filename under which the DiskFix report or log should be saved. (If none is specified, the current directory and default name are used.)

- **/HCACHE**   This parameter turns off a HardCache card cache while DiskFix is running.

- **/HCARD**   This parameter turns off a HardCard card cache while DiskFix is running.

As an example, the command

DISKFIX C: /TEST /RO:DISKFIX.RPT

makes DiskFix automatically run its general analysis routines on drive C, and then save a report on its results to file DISKFIX.RPT in the root directory of drive C, overwriting any earlier version of the file.

Parking Your Hard Disk

An additional action you can take to maintain your hard disk is to run the PC Tools Park program just before you turn off your computer. This utility positions, or *parks,* all read/write heads over an unused portion of the disk. This has three benefits.

First, it guarantees you don't turn off your machine while your hard disk is still operating. This is important, because powering off while your hard disk is writing data could cause serious damage to both the data and the disk itself. Getting into the habit of parking makes certain you don't turn your machine off without paying attention to the hard disk's status.

Second, it helps to ensure that no data is lost during the somewhat tumultuous process your hard disk goes through when you turn on your computer. For example, if you typically turn your machine off from the same directory, the drive heads will constantly start up from that directory when you power your PC back on. This may eventually wear out the directory area and destroy its data. Parking positions the heads over an unused area of the disk, restricting the wear and tear of startup to that area.

Third, it protects your data whenever your computer is being moved. That's because when your PC is jostled around, the drive heads may brush against the disk. When the heads are parked, they can only contact an unused portion of the disk and so won't damage any data.

To run Park, follow these steps:

1. Ready your computer for shutdown by saving your files and exiting any application programs you're running.

2. From the DOS prompt, type **PARK** and press ENTER. After a moment, the following message appears:

```
PARK UTILITY
COPYRIGHT 1987-89 by Central Point Software, INC. All Rights Reserved.

The hard drive heads are now parked.
You may now turn off your computer
and transport it. If you continue,
the heads will no longer be parked.
```

3. If you've changed your mind, you can continue using your computer normally; the drive heads will automatically unpark.

   Otherwise, turn your computer's power switch off. Your hard disk data is now protected from the rigors of your next startup.

 You can also park your hard disk using the PC Shell program's Disk Park Disk Heads command. For more information, see Chapter 17, "Managing Your Directories and Disks."

If you always park your hard disk before powering off and also test it with DiskFix about once a month, you'll greatly reduce the odds of your hard disk developing defects and losing data.

Chapter *8*

Repairing dBASE and 1-2-3 Files Using File Fix

In addition to the general data problems covered in Chapters 6 and 7, you may occasionally encounter problems that are specific to files generated by a particular application. PC Tools 7 therefore includes a new program, called File Fix, that analyzes and repairs the data files of three widely used database and spreadsheet applications: dBASE, Lotus 1-2-3, and Symphony.

File Fix can recover databases from dBASE II, III, III Plus, and IV, and from any program that uses the dBASE data format, such as FoxPro, Clipper, and the Databases component of the PC Tools Desktop. The utility analyzes and fixes such dBASE problems as damaged file headers, zapped files, record frame errors, embedded end-of-file codes, and the presence of "junk" characters.

File Fix can also recover spreadsheets from any version of Lotus 1-2-3 (that is, versions 1.*x* through 3.*x*); from Symphony version 1.*x*; and from any other program that uses the 1-2-3 data format. (The only exception is password-protected WK3 files, because those files are heavily encrypted.) File Fix automatically analyzes and repairs damage to spreadsheet formats, password-protected files, global settings, and formula cells and recalculation sequences; and detects and eliminates invalid cell entries and invalid version numbers.

Running File Fix

It's safest if you don't write anything to the disk that contains your damaged data. Therefore, if this data is on your hard disk and you haven't installed File Fix yet, don't do so now. Instead, insert the single 3 1/2-inch disk, or the second of the two 5 1/4-inch disks, labeled "Data Recovery Utilities" into a floppy drive. You can execute the program directly from this drive.

On the other hand, if you've already installed File Fix using the Install program (see Appendix A, "PC Tools Installation and Configuration"), then you'll be able to conveniently run the recovery utility from your hard disk.

To use File Fix to repair your defective application files, follow these steps:

1. Set the DOS prompt to the drive containing the FILEFIX.EXE program. For example, if the program is on your hard drive C, type **C:** and press ENTER; if it's on drive A, type **A:** and press ENTER.

2. Type **FILEFIX** (with no spaces) and press ENTER. The following main menu appears:

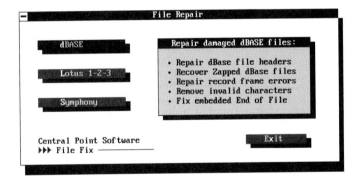

3. To recover a dBASE-compatible file, press D or click dBASE; to recover a 1-2-3-compatible file, press L or click Lotus 1-2-3; to recover a Symphony file, press S or click Symphony.

4. A File Load dialog box appears. The Files box at the left lists files in the current directory with the appropriate extension for your selection (DBF, WK*, or WR*). You can use TAB and the arrow keys, or use your mouse, to select a different drive in the Drives box, a different directory in the Directories box, and the file you want in the Files box. You can also simply type a different path and filename in the Filename field at the top. Once you've specified the file to recover, press ALT-O or click OK.

5. If you've selected a dBASE file, continue on to the following "Recovering dBASE Files" section. If you've selected a 1-2-3 or Symphony file, skip to the "Recovering Spreadsheet Files" section.

Recovering dBASE Files

After selecting the dBASE-compatible file you want to recover, you see the following dialog box:

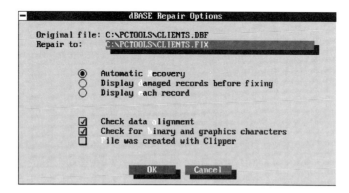

To repair your file, follow these steps:

1. Select the Repair To field by pressing TAB twice or by clicking the field with your mouse. This field specifies the path and filename for your repaired file. Its default is the same path and name as your damaged file, but with the extension FIX instead of DBF (for example, C:\DATA*filename*.FIX).

2. Revise the drive letter and directory to specify a different path (for example, A:*filename*.FIX). This ensures that you don't accidentally overwrite any of the data you're trying to recover. When you're done, press TAB or ENTER.

3. If you want your data lined up properly as the file is repaired, leave the Check Data Alignment option turned on. However, if your file is large and you believe it contains only a few bad records, press A or click the option to make repairs execute more quickly.

4. If you want graphics characters replaced with spaces when recovery is automatic, or to pause on such characters when you're performing manual checking, leave the Check for Binary and Graphics Characters option turned on. However, if your file is supposed to contain graphics characters (for example, if you're repairing an SBT Database Accounting Library SYS-DATA.DBF file), press B or click the option to ignore such characters.

5. If your file was created with Clipper, press F or click the File was Created With Clipper option.

6. You can now select one of three recovery options. The default is Automatic Recovery, which lets File Fix try to effect repairs automatically. This method is always the one you should try first.

   The other options are Display Damaged Records Before Fixing, which is the next one to try if you end up dissatisfied with the job Automatic Recovery does, and Display Each Record, which is useful if you find File Fix is including too many "junk" records in the repaired file. Both options prompt you to accept or reject each specified record before the repaired file is created.

7. Press ALT-O or click OK to begin the analysis of the file. A dialog box appears informing you of the status of the structural, or *header,* information at the start of the file.

8. If the message "No Bookkeeping Errors" is displayed, press ENTER or click OK to begin the automatic repair, and then go to the "Completing the dBASE Repair" section.

   Otherwise, when you're asked for missing header information (for example, the version of dBASE the file was generated from), answer each question appropriately, and then press ALT-O or click OK.

9. Eventually, you'll see a message such as the following:

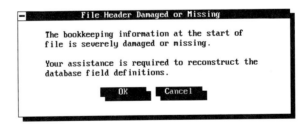

   Press ENTER or click OK to continue.

10. You're asked to choose between two structural recovery methods: Edit the Existing Structure (the default), which allows you to make changes manually; and Import the Correct Structure from Another dBASE File, which is the far superior option as long as you have an older, problem-free copy of the file that contains the appropriate structure.

    To select manual editing, press E and ENTER, and then go to the "Modifying the Database Manually" section. To select importing, press I and ENTER, and then continue on to the following "Importing a Database Structure" section.

Importing a Database Structure

1. If you chose the Import the Correct Structure from Another dBASE File option, the File Load dialog box appears and prompts you to enter the name of the other file. As before, use the Drives, Directories, and Files boxes to select it, or just type its name into the Filename field. When you're ready, press ALT-O or click OK.

2. If your source file was sound, the message "Imported Header OK" appears. Press ENTER or click OK, and then go to the "Completing the dBASE Repair" section.

Modifying the Database Manually

1. If you chose the Edit the Existing Structure option, a dialog box displays the first portion of your file, and you're prompted to scroll the data horizontally until the first field is at the beginning of the data window. To scroll past any inappropriate characters, press TAB three times to highlight the two-headed arrow box, and then press LEFT ARROW and RIGHT ARROW; or click on the arrows in the box with your mouse. When the data is positioned correctly, press ALT-O or click OK.

2. A dialog box now appears that prompts you to adjust the record size by scrolling the displayed data until they are aligned into neat columns. To do so, again, press TAB three times to highlight the two-headed arrow box, and then press LEFT ARROW and RIGHT ARROW; or click on the arrows in the box with your mouse. When the data is perfectly aligned, press ALT-O or click OK.

3. A dialog box now appears that displays each field's name and type, and the corresponding data for the first record. If necessary, use the Name, Type, Width, and Decimals options to change the selected field. Also, if necessary, use the **A**dd option to add a field directly below the selected field, and the **D**elete option to delete the selected field (which doesn't delete any data, but just shifts the data in the deleted field to the next field). You can also select the **R**evise option to return to step 1 and readjust your data's starting position and record size.

4. When the database looks correct, press ALT-O or click OK. If a message such as "The sum of the field sizes do not agree" or "The field definitions do not agree" is displayed, press N or click NO, and then go back to step 1 to try again. Otherwise, continue on to the next section, "Completing the dBASE Repair."

Completing the dBASE Repair

1. File Fix now finishes recovering the file's data, and saves a repaired version of the file to the path and filename you specified. In addition, the dialog box tells you the number of records recovered, bytes recovered, bytes replaced, bytes discarded, and sections discarded. Press O or click OK to continue.

2. A new screen appears that tells you the number of records recovered and the number lost. It also offers to let you view the fixed file. To do so, press O or click OK, scroll through the file using the arrow keys or your mouse, and press ESC when you're done. Otherwise, to skip viewing the file, press ENTER or click Cancel.

3. You're asked if you want a report of the repair results printed or saved to a disk file. To print, make sure your printer is on and online; and then press P and ENTER, or click Report to Printer and OK. After a moment, the results of the repair operation are printed.

4. Alternatively, press F and ENTER, or click Report to File and OK. A default of *filename*.RPT in the current directory is suggested. You can edit the line to save the report to a different drive, directory, and/or filename. When you're done, press ENTER. If it turns out the specified report file already exists, press O to overwrite the previous file; or press ESC to bring back the report file field, then revise its name and/or path, and press ALT-O. The report is saved.

5. You're now returned to the File Fix main menu. To continue using File Fix, select another menu option. Otherwise, press X or click Exit to quit the program and return to the DOS prompt.

6. Rename your repaired file so it has a DBF extension, and then examine it using your dBASE-compatible database program. If you aren't satisfied with the way the file turned out, you can try running File Fix on the original damaged file again using different option settings. (For example, if it has too many "junk" records, try using the Display Each Record option, which will prompt you to accept or reject each record before the repaired file is generated.) Alternatively, if there aren't too many problems left, you may prefer to simply fix the remaining defects manually from within your application.

Recovering Spreadsheet Files

After selecting the spreadsheet file you want to recover, you see this dialog box:

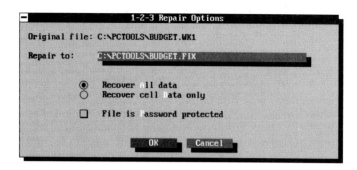

To repair your file, follow these steps:

1. Select the Repair To field by pressing TAB twice or by clicking the field with your mouse. This field specifies the path and filename for your repaired file. Its default is the same path and name as your damaged file, but with the extension FIX instead of WK? or WR? (for example, C:\DATA*filename*.FIX).

2. Revise the drive letter and directory to specify a different path (for example, A:*filename*.FIX). This ensures that you don't accidentally overwrite any of the data you're trying to recover. When you're done, press TAB or ENTER.

3. If this is the first time you're trying to recover the file, accept the default Recover All Data option, which sets File Fix to restore as much of your spreadsheet as it can. If you later find you can't open the repaired file, you can re-run File Fix and select the alternative Recover Cell Data Only option, which creates a new file that contains your cell values and labels, but no formatting information.

4. If your file was protected with a password, press P or click File is Password Protected. (As mentioned previously, File Fix will *not* be able to recover password-protected WK3 files, which are encrypted.)

5. Press ALT-O or click OK to accept your settings.

6. If you selected the File is Password Protected option, you're prompted for the password. Type it in, keeping in mind that distinctions are made between upper- and lowercase. When you're done, press ENTER twice.

7. The automatic repair procedure now begins, and a dialog box appears to show File Fix's progress. When the repair is completed, you're told the number of cells recovered. (In PC Tools 7, the screen incorrectly displays the

word "records" instead of "cells," but that's just a dialog box typo.) If the count seems too large, it's because blank cells are also included. To continue, press ENTER or click OK.

8. You're asked if you want to view the fixed file. If you do, press O or click OK, scroll through the file using the arrow keys or your mouse, and press ESC when you're done. Otherwise, to skip viewing the file, press ENTER or click Cancel.

9. You're asked if you want a report of the repair results printed or saved to a disk file. To print, make sure your printer is on and online, and then press P and ENTER, or click Report to Printer and OK. After a moment, the results of the repair operation are printed.

10. Alternatively, press F and ENTER, or click Report to File and OK. A default of *filename*.RPT in the current directory is suggested. You can edit the line to save the report to a different drive, directory, and/or filename. (The report describes the status of each cell entry in the repaired file, and therefore will be two to three times as large as the spreadsheet itself. Therefore, make sure you save it to a disk that has enough room for it.) When you're done, press ENTER. If it turns out the specified report file already exists, press O to overwrite the previous file; or press ESC to bring back the report file field, then revise its name and/or path, and press ALT-O. The report is saved.

11. You're now returned to the File Fix main menu. To continue using File Fix, select another menu option. Otherwise, press X or click Exit to quit the program and return to the DOS prompt.

12. Rename your repaired file so that it has the appropriate WK? extension, and then examine it using your 1-2-3- or Symphony-compatible spreadsheet program. If it turns out you can't open the file, run File Fix again, select your original damaged file again, return to step 1, and this time select the Recover Cell **D**ata Only option in step 3.

   However, if you *can* open the file, simply reenter whatever data and/or formatting was lost. The symbols L, F, and N are inserted in place of missing labels, formulas, and number values to help guide you in your reentry.

Part III

Using the Speedup Utilities

Chapter *9*

Speeding Your Disks
Using Compress

As explained in Chapter 4, "Data Recovery Overview," a disk is divided into small areas called clusters. DOS starts out saving files in adjacent, or *contiguous,* clusters. However, as files are repeatedly saved, revised, and deleted, each file's clusters start to get scattered all over the disk. This scattering is called *fragmentation.*

A fragmented file has two negative effects. First, it forces your drive's read/write heads to roam all over your disk to locate the file's various separate groups of clusters. If many files are fragmented, they will slow down your drive significantly and so degrade the performance of your entire system.

Second, if the locations of the various clusters of a fragmented file are lost, the file may be impossible to retrieve if you aren't using the Data Monitor program's Delete Tracking or Delete Sentry options (see Chapter 5, "Safeguarding Your Data"). These locations, which are kept in the disk's File Allocation Table, or FAT, are erased as a matter of course when you delete the file or format its disk. They may also be lost if the FAT develops defects.

Fortunately, you can eliminate disk fragmentation by using the PC Tools Compress program. Compress totally reorganizes a floppy or hard disk by storing each file's data in a single group of contiguous clusters. This allows your drive to locate all the data in each file very quickly. In addition, Compress moves all the files near the front of the disk, because this is the area your drive can access fastest. It even gives you the option of moving the particular files and directories you tend to use most frequently closer to the front than those you seldom access.

Compress also arranges all clusters not currently in use into one big, contiguous area at the back of the disk. This helps cut down on future fragmentation, since it provides a large number of consecutive clusters for the storage of new files.

In addition, Compress can sort your files at the same time it's defragmenting them. Based on your specifications, it will arrange them by name, creation date, size, or extension, and in ascending (lowest to highest) or descending (highest to lowest) order.

The Compress program actually isn't named very accurately. In the computer field, the term "compress" typically refers to compacting files so that they take up less space. PC Tools does provide this type of compression, but only through its PC Secure program (covered in Chapter 11). The Compress program instead packs a fragmented file's data together into a single area. This simplifies the file's organization, but it doesn't make the file take up any less room. Therefore, when the word "compress" is used in the program's commands and messages, keep in mind that what it's actually referring to is defragmentation, not compression.

Compress can be run interactively through menus or automatically through parameters. This chapter first explains the steps to follow before using Compress. It then explores the Compress menu options, and explains how the options can be represented by command line parameters.

If you used Compress in PC Tools Deluxe 6, you'll find that many of the commands in the new version have been renamed and reorganized. However, they still perform the same basic functions. The only significant command that was left out from version 6 is Surface Analysis, which is now performed exclusively by the DiskFix program (see Chapter 7, "Repairing Disks Using DiskFix").

Preparing Your System for Compress

Before you run Compress, you should follow these steps to prepare your system:

1. Unload any memory-resident programs you're running other than PC Tools 7 programs. This is *very important.* If you leave any programs in memory that conflict with Compress, they may cause it to reorganize your files incorrectly, turning your disk into an incomprehensible jumble of clusters. There is no practical way to recover your files from this kind of disaster unless you backed them up previously (see step 4).

2. If your disk has any deleted files on it you want to recover (see Chapter 6), you must undelete them *now.* That's because the defragmentation process will destroy most deleted files in the process of reorganizing disk space.

3. If your disk hasn't been tested within the last month with DiskFix (see Chapter 7), run DiskFix now and select the **R**epair a Disk option to thoroughly check the disk's critical areas and scan its sectors for defects. This ensures that Compress doesn't compound any problems that already exist in the disk's

FAT or Directory, or destroy data by moving it from readable clusters to unreadable ones. When you're done, exit DiskFix and return to the DOS prompt.

4. If you've never used Compress on your system before, there's a chance that some unexpected conflict will cause your files to be lost. Therefore, before proceeding, back up your disk using CP Backup (see Chapters 1 through 3). This ensures that if anything goes wrong, you can restore your files back to the disk.

   Once you become familiar with Compress and are sure it works on your system without problems, this step is unnecessary (although it's a good idea to back up regularly, anyway).

You're now ready to run Compress. The next section explains how to do so.

Running and Exploring Compress

To run Compress interactively (as opposed to through command line parameters, which are covered later in this chapter), go to the DOS prompt, type **COMPRESS**, and press ENTER.

First, the background portion of the compress screen appears. Messages then inform you that the program is "Reading File Allocation Table" (a procedure that, upon completion, displays a map of your hard disk), then "Processing directory and file areas from disk to memory" (which means Compress is reading the names and locations of all your directories and files into RAM so they can be analyzed rapidly), and then "Tracking directory and file chains to calculate compression technique" (which means Compress is analyzing your disk information for the extent and type of fragmentation present).

When it has finished, Compress tells you the degree of fragmentation it's found and what course of action it recommends. For example, if all your data is contiguous, the message will read "NO fragmented files. No compression is necessary." In this case, close the dialog box by pressing ENTER, and then exit Compress by pressing ESC and ENTER.

On the other hand, if fragmentation was detected, you'll get a message such as "Target disk has 5% fragmentation. The Unfragment Files technique is recommended." In addition, you're asked to choose between two options: Compress, which immediately begins the Compress operation; and Configure, which closes the box and places you in the standard Compress screen so that you can customize the program's settings before defragmenting. The first time you use the program, choose Configure by pressing O or clicking on the option. On many systems, Compress will respond by opening the Options menu. If this occurs, press ESC to close the menu for the moment.

You now see a screen like the one in Figure 9-1. The screen is split into four basic parts: the disk map, the Status and Legend boxes, the message bar, and the menu bar.

The Compress Disk Map and Legend Box

In the middle of the screen is the disk map, which is a representation of the current disk's clusters. As indicated by the Legend box in the upper right, areas of the disk are represented by the following symbols:

- *Boot Sector*   This is the area holding the boot record, which is used to start up your computer. It's always at the beginning of a disk and is represented on the map by the letter "B."

- *FAT Sector*   This is the area holding the FAT. It follows the boot record and is represented on the map by the letter "F."

- *Root Directory*   This is the area holding the root directory. It follows the FAT and is represented on the map by the letter "D."

- *Allocated*   This is an area that's currently in use by a file. It's represented on the map by a diamond symbol.

- *Unallocated*   This is a free area that's available for new files. It's represented on the map by a dotted rectangle symbol.

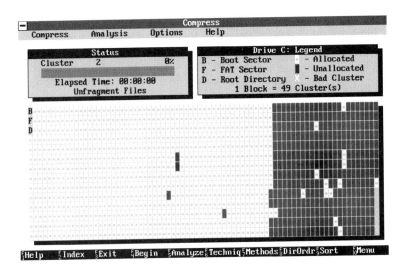

Figure 9-1.   *The Compress screen*

- *Bad Cluster*   This is an area on the disk that's physically damaged and has been marked as unusable. It's represented on the map by the letter "X."

If the disk is nearly full, its map will consist mostly of diamonds. If the disk is nearly empty, the map will consist mostly of dotted rectangles.

The proportions of the map are automatically scaled down to fit your screen. For example, the map of a 32MB disk might display a symbol for every 16 clusters, while the map of a 200MB disk might display a symbol for every 50 sectors. The scale being used always appears on the last line of the Legend box, and the letter of the disk represented always appears at the top of the box.

The Compress Message Bar and Status Box

At the bottom of the screen is the message bar. When no activity is taking place, it displays the following commands assigned to the function keys:

Function Key	Action
F1 (Help)	Brings up context-sensitive help
F2 (Index)	Brings up the online help index
F3 (Exit)	Performs the same functions as ESC
F4 (Begin)	Selects Compress Begin Compress
F5 (Analyze)	Selects Analysis Disk Statistics
F6 (Techniq)	Selects Options Compression Technique
F7 (Methods)	Selects Options Ordering Methods
F8 (DirOrdr)	Selects Options Directory Order
F9 (Sort)	Selects Options File Sort Options
F10 (Menu)	Like ALT, activates the menu bar

However, when a Compress activity is taking place, the bar displays appropriate definitions or instructions instead.

Another screen area that displays information about your activities is the Status box, which appears in the upper left. When you begin the defragmentation process, this box shows the compression technique you're using, the amount of time that's gone by, and what percentage of the process has been completed.

Navigating the Compress Menus

At the top of the screen is the menu bar, which contains the five menus available in Compress. Follow these steps to examine the menus:

1. Press C or click on Compress to display the Compress menu, which lets you choose a different drive to work with, initiate the defragmentation process, and exit Compress.

2. Press RIGHT ARROW to display the **Analysis** menu, which lets you examine statistics about your disk's clusters and files, view the cluster size and fragmentation of individual files, and identify the files contained in a particular spot on the disk map.

3. Press RIGHT ARROW again to display the **Options** menu, which lets you select which defragmentation technique to use, specify the general ordering of your files and directories, specify the ordering of specific directories, specify the ordering of specific files, specify the files you want to remain in place during defragmentation, set the order in which files are sorted within each directory, and request a printed report following defragmentation.

4. Press RIGHT ARROW again to display the **Help** menu, which lets you get information about various Compress features.

5. Press ESC and ALT-SPACEBAR to display the **Control** menu, which lets you bring up a Compress copyright notice or exit the program.

These menu options (shown in Figure 9-2) are covered in the following sections. They are also defined in the "Compress Command Reference" section at the end of this chapter.

Analyzing the Disk

If you'd like more information about your disk's status, you can obtain it using the three options in the Analysis menu: **Disk Statistics**, **File Fragmentation Analysis**, and **Show Files in Each Map Block**.

Disk Statistics

To display an analysis of your disk's cluster use and fragmentation, press A, D, or press F5, or click on the Analysis menu and select Disk Statistics. After a few seconds, a dialog box like this appears:

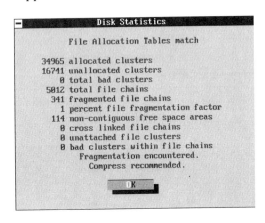

The box first reports the number of clusters that are in use (allocated), available for new files (unallocated), and defective (bad).

It then lists the disk's total number of files (confusingly called file chains), its number of fragmented files, and its percent of fragmented clusters. The latter is derived by dividing the number of fragmented clusters (which is not listed) by the total number of clusters on the disk.

Next, the number of noncontiguous free space areas is shown. This refers to the number of unallocated areas on the disk that aren't adjacent to each other. If there are many such free pockets of clusters, they'll cause new files to be fragmented when saved.

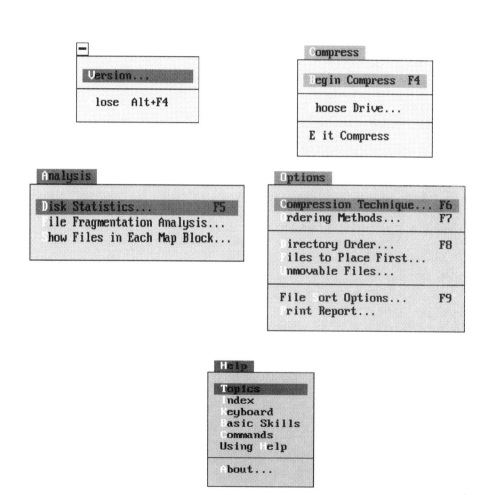

Figure 9-2.   *The Compress menus*

Three types of disk errors are then reported on: cross-linked files, which are two or more files using the same cluster at the same time; unattached file clusters, which are clusters marked as in use but not assigned to any file; and bad clusters within file chains, which are defective clusters currently holding file data.

Lastly, a recommendation is displayed about whether or not you should defragment the disk.

If there's any number but 0 in front of the three disk error categories, *don't* initiate defragmentation. Instead, exit to DOS by pressing ESC twice and pressing ENTER, use DiskFix to repair the disk (as covered in Chapter 7), and then start Compress again.

Otherwise, if there's even 1 percent fragmentation reported, it's recommended that you defragment. This will keep your disk at peak efficiency and will also avoid long Compress sessions later by inhibiting fragmentation from building up to high levels.

When you're done reading the analysis, press ENTER or click OK. The box closes, and you're returned to the Compress screen.

File Fragmentation Analysis

To display an analysis of the cluster size and fragmentation of individual files on the disk, press A, F, or click on the Analysis menu and select File Fragmentation Analysis. After a few seconds, a screen with a Directory Tree on the left and a File List on the right appears. To display the files you want, first highlight the directory they appear in by using the arrow keys or your mouse, and then press TAB or click to move to the File List. If the files you want aren't already displayed, scroll through the List using the arrow keys, PGUP and PGDN, and HOME and END; or click on the List's scroll bar with your mouse. The File List shows each file's name, the number of clusters the file occupies, the number of separate areas the file's clusters take up (for example, for a entirely contiguous file the number is 1), and the percent of the file's data stored in the fragmented clusters as opposed to its initial contiguous clusters (for example, for an entirely contiguous file the percent is 0).

When you're done examining file fragmentation, press ESC or ENTER. The dialog box closes, and you're returned to the Compress screen.

Show Files in Each Map Block

To display information about any particular area on the disk map (which is a new feature in PC Tools 7), press A, S, or click on the Analysis menu and select Show Files in Each Map Block. A blinking rectangular cursor appears over the first area on the map (that is, the boot sector). Use the arrow keys to move the cursor to the spot on the map you want to examine, and then press ENTER.

The message "Processing Map Block Entries to determine fragmentation" appears, and then for each cluster represented by the spot you selected, a box lists the cluster's number, the name of the file the cluster is a part of (if any), and whether the file is Optimized (that is, entirely contiguous) or Fragmented. You can scroll through the list using the arrow keys, PGUP and PGDN, and HOME and END; or click on its scroll bar with your mouse. When you're done examining the clusters, press ESC or ENTER. The box closes, and you're returned to the Compress screen.

Ordering Data While Defragmenting

At the same time Compress is reorganizing your disk to eliminate fragmentation, it can sort your files to make them easier to find, and it can move selected files and directories to the front of the disk so they can be accessed more quickly. None of these options are critical to the use of Compress, so if you find them confusing or uninteresting, just skip over them to the next topic, "Selecting a Compression Technique."

You can specify ordering preferences using four commands in the **O**ptions menu: File **S**ort Options, **O**rdering Methods, **D**irectory Order, and **F**iles to Place First. Your settings take effect when you initiate defragmentation with the **C**ompress **B**egin Compress command.

File Sort Options

If you want the files within each directory sorted while your disk is being reorganized, press O, S, or press F9, or click on the Options menu and select File Sort Options. The following dialog box appears:

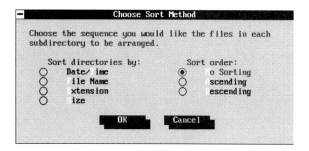

The box gives you the option of sorting your files chronologically, alphabetically, by type, or by size; and in ascending or descending order.

To sort files chronologically (that is, based on when they were created), press T or click Date/Time.

To sort files alphabetically (that is, based on their names), press F or click File Name.

To sort files by type (that is, based on their extensions, such as TXT for text files, DBF for database files, and so on), press E or click Extension. Within each extension, the files will be sorted alphabetically by filename.

To sort files by their size in bytes, press S or click Size.

In addition, you can specify your sort to be ordered from lowest to highest (1,2,3,...) by pressing A or clicking Ascending; or from highest to lowest (...,3,2,1) by pressing D or clicking Descending. The default order is **A**scending.

Lastly, if you decide you'd prefer not to sort your files in any way, press N or click No Sorting. This option is the default.

When you're done selecting options, press O or click OK. The box closes, and you're returned to the Compress screen.

Ordering Methods

To help your disk access certain directories and files more quickly, or alternatively to help speed the defragmentation process itself, press O, O, or press F7, or click on the Options menu and select Ordering Methods. You're presented with four options: **S**tandard, **F**ile Placement, **D**irectories First, and **D**irectories with Files.

- *Standard*   This option moves all directories *without* their files to the front of the disk, followed by their files in no special order. The directories are arranged based on your PATH statement, unless you specified a different arrangement with the **D**irectory Order command (covered in the next section). Standard can make your future defragmentation sessions run a lot faster, since it doesn't require Compress to perform any significant reorganization of your files. However, it won't significantly speed your disk's performance. This option is the default.

- *File Placement*   This option, like **S**tandard, moves all directories without their files to the front of the disk, ordering them by either your PATH statement or your specifications. However, it then moves the files based on the order you specified with the **F**iles to Place First command (covered in the next section; the command's default setting is to place all your COM and EXE program files first). If you tend to use certain types of files frequently, this will help speed your disk's performance.

- *Directories First*   This option, like **S**tandard, moves all directories without their files to the front of the disk, ordering them by either your PATH statement or your specifications. However, it then moves the files ordered by the directories they're associated with. If you tend to work with several files in the same directory simultaneously (for example, if you keep a program and the data files it generates in the same directory), this will help speed your disk's performance because it keeps files you access at the same time close together.

- *Directories with Files*   This option keeps directories and their files together, placing each directory right before its files. The directories are ordered based on either your PATH statement or your specifications. If you tend to create and delete whole directories at a time, this will help speed your disk's performance.

If your disk is typical, none of these options will create an enormous increase in your disk's access speed. However, if you choose an inappropriate option, it may noticeably slow down future defragmentation sessions. Therefore, if you aren't sure which option is right for your disk, accept the Standard default, which is certain not to slow down Compress.

When you're done selecting an option, press O or click OK. The dialog box closes and you're returned to the Compress screen.

Specifying Directory and File Placement

As just explained, certain options in the **O**rdering Methods command are affected by the directory and file placement order that you specify. To enter these specifications involves two **O**ptions menu commands: **D**irectory Order and **F**iles to Place First. Both commands are new to PC Tools 7.

Directory Order   To arrange your directories, press O, D, or press F8, or click on the Options menu and select Directory Order. After a few seconds, a screen appears with a Directory Tree on the left; an "ordering" box on the right (which initially contains the directories specified in your PATH statement); and the options **A**dd, **D**elete, **M**ove, OK, and **C**ancel. You can move between these elements by pressing TAB and SHIFT-TAB, or by clicking on the element you want with your mouse.

To specify a directory you want moved to the very front of the disk, first highlight it in the Directory Tree using the arrow keys or your mouse, and then press A or click Add. The directory's name is copied to the ordering box. Continue this process until all the directories you're concerned about are listed in the ordering box.

You can remove a directory in the ordering box by first selecting the directory, and then pressing D or clicking Delete. You can also change a directory's placement in the ordering box by first selecting the directory, then pressing M or clicking Move, then moving to the spot you want in the box using the arrow keys or your mouse, and then pressing O or clicking OK.

When the directories appear in the sequence you want in the ordering box, press O or click OK. The box closes, and you're returned to the Compress screen. If you then select any of the first three options of the **O**ptions **O**rdering Methods command, the directories will be set to be moved to the very front of your disk in the order specified; if you select the fourth option, Directories with Files, the directories will be set to be spread out over the disk, but in the particular order you've specified. Your settings take effect when you defragment using the **C**ompress **B**egin Compress command.

Files to Place First   To move certain type of files to the very front of your disk, press O, F, or click on the Options menu and select Files to Place First. A dialog box appears that contains a file ordering list on its left side, and **D**elete, **OK**, and **C**ancel options on the right.

You can designate files by using the DOS wildcard **?** to represent any character and the DOS wildcard ***** to represent any group of characters. For example, the list initially displays *.COM and *.EXE to specify program files with COM and EXE extensions. You can remove these specifications by first selecting them, and then pressing ALT-D or clicking Delete. You can also add new specifications by simply typing them in. When you're done, press ALT-O or click OK. The box closes, and you're returned to the Compress screen. However, your settings will take effect *only* if you also select the File Placement option from the **O**ptions **O**rdering Methods commands, and then defragment using the **C**ompress **B**egin Compress command.

Selecting a Compression Technique

Before you initiate the defragmentation process, you should select a particular defragmentation method. To do so, press O, C, or press F6, or click on the Options menu and select Compression Technique. This dialog box appears:

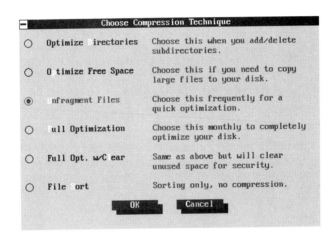

The box offers the following six choices:

- *Optimize **D**irectories*   This option moves directories to the front of the disk so you can access them more quickly. However, it does *not* defragment your disk, and it ignores your directory settings in the **O**ptions menu. This technique's main advantage is that it takes a relatively short amount of time to execute.

- *Optimize Free Space*   This option moves all data clusters to the front of the disk so you can access them more quickly. However, it does *not* defragment your disk, and it ignores your directory and file settings in the **O**ptions menu.

This technique's main advantage is that it takes a relatively short amount of time to execute.

- *Unfragment Files*   This option defragments all your files. However, it ignores your directory and file settings in the **O**ptions menu. In addition, it does *not* collect all free clusters together at the back of your disk, thus failing to provide a large number of consecutive clusters for the storage of new data. As a result, your newly saved files could quickly become fragmented. This technique is the default.

- *Full Optimization*   This option defragments all your files, arranges them following your directory and file settings in the **O**ptions menu, and collects all free clusters together at the back of your disk. This technique therefore performs all the functions most people desire from Compress.

- *Full Opt. w/Clear*   This option does everything **F**ull Optimization does, and in addition destroys all data in the free clusters grouped at the back of the disk by overwriting them (specifically, with the hexadecimal characters F6). This is useful if you need to eradicate any trace of deleted files for the sake of security, but the process takes extra time to execute. Also, this method will *not* erase deleted files protected by Data Monitor's Delete **S**entry command (see Chapter 5, "Safeguarding Your Data").

- *File Sort*   This option arranges files based on your specifications in the **O**ptions File **S**ort Options command. However, it does *not* defragment your disk, and it ignores your directory settings in the **O**ptions menu. This technique's main advantage is that it takes less time to execute than **F**ull Optimization.

For most people, the best method to select is **F**ull Optimization. If you're in a hurry, the next best technique is **U**nfragment Files; but if you settle on this method, use it frequently to prevent fragmentation from building up.

When you've selected the technique you want, press O or click OK. The dialog box closes, and you're returned to the Compress screen.

Specifying a Report

You can set Compress to generate a report when it has finished defragmenting a disk. To do so, follow these steps:

1. Press O, P, or click on the Options menu and select Print Report. You're asked if you want to direct the report to your printer or to a disk file.

2. To get a printout of the report, press P or click Printer. Alternatively, to save the report, press D or click Disk; the report will be stored in a file named COMPRESS.PRT in your disk's root.

When Compress is done defragmenting your disk, a report on its activities will be generated as specified.

Performing the Defragmentation

After you've prepared your system for Compress, optionally run your fragmentation analyses, optionally selected directory and file ordering settings, selected a defragmentation method, and optionally selected a report setting, you're ready to perform the actual defragmentation procedure.

To do so, first press C, B, or press F4, or click on the Compress menu and select Begin Compress. A dialog box appears warning you to unload non-PC Tools programs and recommending you back up your data before proceeding. Assuming you've already done so, press ENTER or click OK.

Compress first analyzes the disk based on your Option menu settings, and displays messages such as "Updating Directories/Sorting complete" and "Compress Status/Building tables in preparation for DISK OPTIMIZATION," while showing highlighted bars to indicate the percentage of the analysis that's been completed.

After the analysis, Compress commences defragmenting and ordering files, as indicated by the letters "R" and "W" (for Reading data and Writing data) quickly flashing around different areas of the disk map. You can also follow the procedure's progress through the Status box, which displays the defragmentation method being used, the current cluster being read from or written to, the elapsed time of the operation, and the percent of the operation completed. In addition, the message bar at the bottom of the screen occasionally flashes messages such as "Rewriting File Allocation Tables" and "Rewriting sub-directory." This entire process is automatic, so you can simply walk away from your PC and do something else until it's completed.

When Compress is done, it displays the following message offering to run the Mirror program (see Chapter 5, "Safeguarding Your Data"):

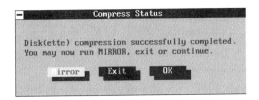

If you've installed Mirror on your system (which is highly recommended), press ENTER or click Mirror. Mirror executes, backing up the disk's new FAT and Directory. (Otherwise, press ESC or click Exit.) The box closes, and you're returned to the Compress screen.

You're now done with the program, so press ESC to bring up the Close dialog box. You're asked if you want to save your current settings. If you're happy with the choices you've made in the **O**ptions menu, press S or click Save Configuration to turn the checkmark *on*. This preserves your settings for future Compress sessions.

When you're done, press ENTER or click OK. The following message now appears, recommending you restart your computer:

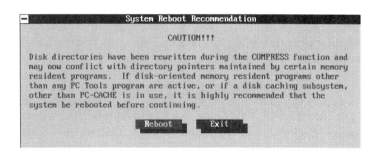

It's highly recommended that you follow the box's advice, as this ensures that the changes on your disk won't confuse any of your memory-resident programs and cause them to damage your data. To do so, press ENTER or click Reboot. After a moment, your PC is restarted.

Compress Parameters

Once you're familiar with the Compress menu options, you may find it faster and easier to specify the options you want directly at the DOS prompt or in a batch file. The batch file method is especially convenient, because it saves you from having to reselect options every time you run Compress.

To run Compress from the DOS prompt, first follow all the steps in the "Preparing Your System for Compress" section, then go to the DOS prompt, type **COMPRESS** followed by the parameters you want, and press ENTER.

Alternatively, to run Compress from a batch file, create an ASCII text file that contains the word **COMPRESS** followed by the parameters you want, save the file with a BAT extension, and then type the name of the file at the DOS prompt and press ENTER. For example, you could open a text file with a word processor such as Notepads (see Chapter 20, "Using Notepads"), type a line such as **COMPRESS C: /CF /SF** (which specifies using full compression and sorting by filename on drive C), and save the file under the ASCII option and the name FULLCOMP.BAT. You could then run the program from the DOS prompt by simply typing **FULLCOMP** and pressing ENTER.

If you include the /CU, /CF, /CC, /CS, or /CD parameter, Compress begins defragmenting immediately using your specified settings. Otherwise, it brings up its screen with your settings already selected in its menus.

Compress supports 17 parameters. You can include any single parameter (for example, COMPRESS /CF) or combine a number of parameters (for example, COMPRESS C: /CF /OD /SF) to achieve the effect you want. Keep in mind that parameters require a *forward* slash (/, located on the bottom of the ? key) as opposed to the backslash (\) used to specify DOS directories.

Compress parameters fall into five categories: General, Compression Techniques, Ordering Methods, File Sort Options, and Display and Mouse Settings. The first four categories are covered in the following sections, while the latter is universal to PC Tools programs and is covered in Appendix A.

General

Compress supports four general parameters that provide information on Compress parameters, provide information on display and mouse parameters, specify your drive, and suppress the running of Mirror. They are as follows:

- **/?**   This "help" parameter lists and briefly describes all parameters specific to Compress. It should not be combined with any other parameters.

- **/VIDEO**   This "help" parameter lists and briefly describes the standard PC Tools video and mouse parameters. It should not be combined with any other parameter. For more information, see the "Video and Mouse Parameters" section in Appendix A, "PC Tools Installation and Configuration."

- *d***:**   This parameter is a letter and colon specifying the drive you want to defragment. It should precede any other parameters. If you don't include it, the current drive is used.

- **/NM**   When you perform defragmenting from a command line, Compress ordinarily runs the Mirror program after it's done to back up your new FAT and Directory. This parameter suppresses the automatic running of Mirror. However, it's virtually always best to allow Mirror to run.

Compression Techniques

Compress supports five parameters that perform the same functions as the **O**ptions **C**ompression Techniques commands. Including any one of them begins defragmentation immediately. The parameters are as follows:

- **/CD**   Like Optimize Directories, this parameter moves directories to the front of the disk but doesn't defragment the disk.

- **/CS**   Like Optimize Free Space, this parameter moves all data clusters to the front of the disk but doesn't defragment the disk.

- **/CU**   Like **U**nfragment Files, this parameter defragments files but doesn't group free clusters together at the back of the disk.

- **/CF**   Like **F**ull Optimization, this parameter both defragments files and groups all free clusters together at the back of the disk.

- **/CC**   Like Full Opt. w/**C**lear, this parameter defragments both files and free clusters, and also destroys any data in the free clusters.

You can include only one of these parameters at a time.

Ordering Methods

Compress supports four parameters that perform the same functions as the **O**ptions **O**rdering Methods commands. They are as follows:

- **/OS**   Like **S**tandard, this parameter moves all directories to the front of the disk, and then their files in no special order.

- **/OF**   Like **F**ile Placement, this parameter moves all directories to the front of the disk, directly followed by the files specified in the **F**iles to Place First command (the default being COM and EXE files), and then all other files.

- **/OO**   Like **D**irectories First, this parameter moves all directories to the front of the disk, and then their files ordered by directory.

- **/OD**   Like **D**irectories with Files, this parameter places each directory right in front of its files.

You can include only one of these parameters at a time.

Sorting Files Within Directories

Compress supports six parameters that perform the same functions as the **O**ptions File **S**ort Options commands. They are as follows:

- **/ST**   Like Date/**T**ime, this parameter sorts files chronologically.

- **/SF**   Like **F**ile Name, this parameter sorts files alphabetically.

- **/SE**   Like **E**xtension, this parameter sorts files by type (and, within each type, alphabetically).

- **/SS**   Like **S**ize, this parameter sorts files by their size in bytes.

- **/SA**   Like **A**scending, this parameter sets sorting to be in lower to higher (1,2,3,...) order.

- **/SD** Like **D**escending, this parameter sets sorting to be in higher to lower (...,3,2,1) order.

You can include only one of the /ST, /SF, /SE, and /SS parameters at a time, and then either /SA or /SD.

Compress Command Reference

Most of the power of Compress lies in its menu commands, which control how files and directories are defragmented, sorted, and ordered. Like a number of PC Tools programs, the first Compress menu is Control and the last menu is **Help**. These menus are covered in this book's Introduction.

Compress also contains three additional menus: Compress, Analysis, and **Op**tions. The following sections cover the options in these menus. After the name of each option are the keystrokes that invoke it, a description of what the option does, and a reference to the section in this chapter that discusses the option in detail.

The Compress Menu

The **C**ompress menu lets you choose a different drive to work with, initiate the defragmentation process, and exit Compress. It contains the following three options:

Begin Compress (C, B or F4)

Launches the defragmentation process. Covered in "Performing the Defragmentation."

Choose Drive (C, C)

Lets you select a different drive to map, analyze, and defragment.

E**x**it Compress (C, X)

Quits Compress and returns you to the DOS prompt.

The Analysis Menu

The **A**nalysis menu allows you to display statistics about your disk's clusters and files, view the cluster size and fragmentation of individual files, and identify the files contained in a particular spot on the disk map. It contains the following three options:

Disk Statistics (A, D or F5)

Provides an analysis of the selected disk's cluster use and fragmentation. Covered in "Disk Statistics."

File Fragmentation Analysis (A, F)

Provides an analysis of the cluster size and fragmentation of each file on the disk. Covered in "File Fragmentation Analysis."

Show Files in Each Map Block (A, S)

Displays the cluster numbers, associated files, and fragmentation status of any specified area on the disk map. Covered in "Show Files in Each Map Block."

The Options Menu

The **O**ptions menu enables you to select which defragmentation technique to use, specify the general ordering of your files and directories, specify the ordering of specific directories, specify the ordering of specific files, specify the files you want to remain in place during defragmentation, set the order in which files are sorted within each directory, and request a printed report following defragmentation. It contains the following seven options:

Compression Techniques (O, C or F6)

Sets the disk reorganization process Compress uses. Options include moving directories or data to the front of the disk without any defragmentation, sorting files without defragmentation, defragmenting files but not free clusters, and defragmenting both files and free clusters. Covered in "Selecting a Compression Technique."

Ordering Methods (O, O or F7)

Sets the order in which directories and files are moved on the disk during defragmentation. Covered in "Ordering Methods."

Directory Order (O, D or F8)

Sets the order in which specific directories are moved to the front of the disk during defragmentation. Covered in "Directory Order."

Files to Place First (O, F)

Sets specified files to be moved to the front of the disk (directly following all directories) during defragmentation. Covered in "Files to Place First."

Unmovable Files (O, U)

Forces Compress to leave specified files in place during defragmentation. This can be useful for copy protected files, which may no longer work if moved.

File **S**ort Options (O, S or F9)

Sets the files in each directory to be sorted chronologically, alphabetically, by type, or by size; and in ascending or descending order. Covered in "File Sort Options."

Print Report (C, P)

Sets a report to be printed following defragmentation on the results of the procedure. Covered in "Specifying a Report."

Chapter *10*

Speeding Data Access Using PC-Cache

Your computer has two basic mechanisms for handling data: its memory chips and its disk drives. Memory chips transfer data very quickly, but they lose their contents when you turn your computer off. On the other hand, disk drives can preserve data indefinitely, but they transfer it at considerably slower speeds than memory chips (typically 10 to 20 times slower with floppy disks, and 3 to 10 times slower with hard disks).

There's no popular media for the PC that can transfer data at memory chip speeds and preserve it at the same time. However, you can approximate this ideal by using a program called a *cache*.

A cache is an area in memory that sets itself up between you and your hard disk. When you initially load data from the disk, the cache stores a copy of the data in its own memory area before passing it on to you. If you then request to read the data again, the cache supplies it directly from its memory area, forgoing the necessity of accessing the disk. If you frequently return to the same data, this greatly speeds up your system's performance.

In addition, when you request to save data, the cache can intercept the data and wait until your system isn't busy before writing it to your hard disk. This further speeds your computer's operation.

The cache program provided by PC Tools is called PC-Cache. It's memory resident, residing invisibly in the background of your system as it monitors your hard disk read and write commands. All of PC-Cache's operations are automatic, so once it's loaded you can generally forget about it and just enjoy its benefits.

This chapter first discusses whether you should use PC-Cache. It then covers PC-Cache hardware support, how to install and run PC-Cache, and the many PC-Cache options you can specify from the DOS prompt.

Read through the entire chapter (and especially the "Size Parameters" section) before running PC-Cache. After you do some experimenting and find the proper cache size for your particular system, you should find that your computer is operating significantly faster than it did before.

Understanding When to Use PC-Cache

While PC-Cache will significantly enhance the performance of many computer systems, it isn't for everyone.

First, it usually requires at least 64K to produce noticeable speed increases. Therefore, if your system is short on memory, you may have to forgo using PC-Cache in order to run large applications or memory-resident programs.

Second, it's an inappropriate utility for memory-intensive applications. For example, spreadsheet programs typically take advantage of as much memory as possible, so a large cache can actually slow a spreadsheet down or limit the amount of data it can handle. PC-Cache performs best when you're using disk-intensive applications, such as word processors and databases.

Third, because a cache takes so much control of your system, it can often create conflicts with other memory-resident software and system utilities. If you find PC-Cache is creating problems with some of your other software, you may have to stop using it.

On the other hand, if you're already using a cache program, you might consider *switching* to PC-Cache. That's because this utility has been designed to work flawlessly with all PC Tools programs, in both their standalone and memory-resident modes. (For example, it's virtually the only cache that will work safely with the Compress program covered in Chapter 9.) Therefore, if you intend to use PC Tools applications frequently, PC-Cache is the cache most likely to run trouble free.

You should never *run PC-Cache at the same time as another cache (such as SMARTDRV.SYS). The two independent caches would conflict with each other, which could result in severe data losses. Therefore, no more than one cache should be resident in your system at any time.*

PC-Cache Hardware Support

PC-Cache fully supports conventional, extended, and expanded memory. However, it always takes up a small amount of conventional memory (typically 2K to 16K, depending on the size of the cache).

*If you're using a memory manager such as DOS 5's EMM386, you can load the conventional memory portion of PC-Cache into high memory by including the LOADHIGH option at the front of the program's command line (for example, **LOADHIGH PC-CACHE**).*

PC-Cache also supports up to four hard disks. You don't need to specify the disks to cache, as the program automatically detects them in your system. However, you can specify hard disks or particular drives you want the program to *ignore* by using the /In and /Id parameters. For more information, see "General Parameters."

PC-Cache does *not* support floppy disk drives. Also, version 7 doesn't support Bernoulli boxes.

Running PC-Cache

As mentioned earlier, before running PC-Cache you should unload any other cache program you may have installed. If you make PC-Cache share your system with another cache, conflicts will occur that could create serious damage to your hard disk's data.

Also, unlike most components of PC Tools, PC-Cache must be run in a particular order relative to other programs. Specifically, it must be loaded *after* you've run Mirror but *before* you've run memory-resident programs such as PC Shell or the Desktop. If this order isn't followed, PC-Cache may function improperly and end up losing some of your data.

To run PC-Cache, go to the DOS prompt, type **PC-CACHE** (optionally followed by one or more of the parameters described in the next section), and press ENTER.

You can automate this procedure by entering this command line into your AU-TOEXEC.BAT file; or by having the Install program do it for you. If you use Install, it will automatically insert the line in your file in the proper order, as well as include the parameters you specify. For more information, see Appendix A, "PC Tools Installation and Configuration."

When you run PC-Cache, it loads itself into memory and then displays a status window like this:

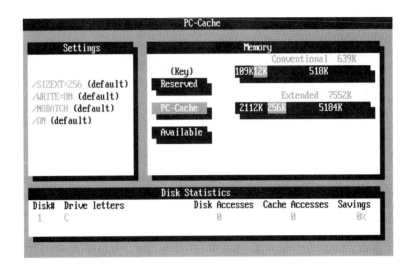

The window is split into three areas: a Settings box in the upper left, a Memory box in the upper right, and a Disk Statistics box at the bottom.

- *Settings* This box displays the parameters you used when running PC-Cache, as well as any default settings your parameters didn't override. The display will typically include the cache's size, whether the write delay switch is on or off, whether an extended memory cache will write in batch mode, and whether the cache is currently active (ON) or disabled (OFF). For explanations of these settings, see the "PC-Cache Parameters" section later in this chapter.

- *Memory* This box displays a "memory bar" representing your PC's conventional memory, as well as bars for any extended and/or expanded memory in your system. Each bar shows the amount of memory taken up by DOS and other programs, the amount taken up by PC-Cache, the amount that's still available, and (above each bar) the total amount of such memory present.

If you want to obtain even more information about your system's memory status, run the MI program, which is covered in Chapter 18, "Using Advanced PC Shell Features."

- *Disk Statistics* The left side of this box displays the number of hard disks currently being cached and the letters of all of the disks' drives. The right side of this box displays the number of times data was transferred between your applications and your hard disk (Disk Accesses), your applications and the cache (Cache Accesses), and the percentage of transfers that were diverted from accessing the hard disk by the cache (Savings).

After the status window is displayed, PC-Cache returns you to the DOS prompt, allowing you to resume your work. However, the program now invisibly monitors and caches your hard disk read and write operations.

In most cases, once PC-Cache is loaded, you can forget about it and just enjoy the performance benefits it brings. However, if you need to examine or adjust the program, there are parameters available for doing so. For example, if you need to remove PC-Cache from memory (say, to free up the space it's occupying for other programs), first unload any resident programs you installed after it, and then type **PC-CACHE /U** from the DOS prompt and press ENTER. The message "Cache and measurements reset; PC-CACHE program un-installed" appears. The program then exits, leaving the memory it occupied available again.

For more information about switches that affect PC-Cache when it's resident in memory, see the "Resident Parameters" section later in this chapter.

PC-Cache Parameters

You can specify certain options, called parameters, following PC-Cache's program name. You can include any single parameter (for example, PC-CACHE /SIZE=80) or combine a number of parameters (for example, PC-CACHE /SIZEXT=1024 /WRITE=OFF /WIN) to achieve the effect you want. Keep in mind that parameters require a *forward* slash (/, located on the bottom of the ? key) as opposed to the backslash (\) used to specify DOS directories.

PC-Cache supports 18 parameters specific to the program. These parameters fall into three categories: size, general, and resident. They are covered in the following three sections.

If you previously used PC Tools Deluxe 6, you should note that the parameter /MAX has been dropped, because PC-Cache is now smart enough to determine for itself the maximum amount of data it should load in a read operation. Also, the version 6 /PARAM, /PARAM*, /INFO, and /MEASURES parameters have all been replaced with /S, which brings up the new information-packed status window.

Size Parameters

Generally, the larger your cache is, the faster your system will run. At the same time, however, your cache must leave at least enough room in memory for DOS, any memory-resident programs you use regularly, and your main applications (including their data files).

In general, PC-Cache's performance increases very significantly as you increase its size up to 512K. Increasing the cache size from that point up to 1024K will yield more moderate, but still significant, performance increases. Any increase past 1024K will yield only minor performance benefits.

If you don't specify a cache size, a default is used. If your system has conventional memory exclusively, the default is 64K. However, if it has extended or expanded memory, the default is to use as much nonconventional memory as there is available up to 256K. (Also, as mentioned earlier, a small area is set up in conventional memory, generally ranging from 2K to 16K.)

To override the default and specify a cache size, include one of the following four parameters:

- **/SIZE=***nnnn*   This parameter sets the size of a cache installed in conventional memory (for example, /SIZE=64 sets the default of 64K). The minimum size is 8K.

- **/SIZEXP=***nnnn*   This parameter sets the size of a cache installed in expanded memory (for example, /SIZEXP=256 sets the default of 256K). If you use a size that isn't divisible by 16, your number is rounded up to the nearest 16K. The minimum size is 32K.

- **/SIZEXT=***nnnn*   This parameter sets the size of a cache installed in extended memory (for example, /SIZEXT=256 sets the default of 256K). The minimum size is 8K.

- **/SIZEXT*=***nnnn*   This parameter is identical to the previous one except that it makes PC-Cache check your system to see if the BIOS method of extended memory access is required. It should only be used if you have trouble getting the previous parameter to work.

General Parameters

PC-Cache provides ten general-purpose parameters, most of which can be combined with each other and/or with a size parameter when you run the program. They are as follows:

- **/?**   This "help" parameter lists and briefly describes each parameter specific to PC-Cache. It should not be combined with any other parameter.

- **/VIDEO**   This "help" parameter lists and briefly describes the standard PC Tools video parameters /BW, /MONO, and /LCD. It should not be combined with any other parameter. For more information, see the "Video and Mouse Parameters" section in Appendix A, "PC Tools Installation and Configuration."

- **/EXTSTART=***nnnn*   This parameter sets the location in extended memory that your cache should be loaded *above*. It's only necessary if the normal installation process is producing conflicts with other programs you're also loading in extended memory. The location you specify must be higher than 1024K.

- **/I*d*** This parameter forces PC-Cache to ignore the specified drive, with *d* representing the letter of the drive.

- **/I*n*** PC-Cache normally caches up to four of your hard disks. This parameter forces PC-Cache to ignore the specified hard disk, with *n* being the number of the disk (1, 2, 3, or 4) as identified in the lower-left corner of the status window.

- **/NOBATCH** If you're installing PC-Cache in extended memory, this parameter sets the maximum number of sectors transferred at a time (or in a single "batch") to *one*. This is useful if you're experiencing problems running certain applications such as telecommunications programs. The technical reason is that when PC-Cache transfers sectors in extended memory, it disables all interrupts, and that in turn confuses some programs. Reducing the number of sectors transferred in each batch makes the amount of time interrupts are disabled too short to affect other programs. However, it also slows down PC-Cache slightly, so don't use this parameter unless you actually experience software conflicts.

- **/PAUSE** This parameter pauses the status window when you run PC-Cache, thus allowing you to examine its display before you allow PC-Cache to load. This is especially useful when you're running PC-Cache from a batch file, since it enables you to examine the status window instead of just watching it flash by on your screen.

- **/QUIET** This parameter suppresses the PC-Cache status window from displaying when PC-Cache is loaded. Include it only if you're certain that you aren't experiencing any problems with PC-Cache.

- **/WIN** This parameter tells PC-Cache to shrink itself whenever you run Microsoft Windows. This is useful because Windows is designed to take maximum benefit of all available memory.

- **/WRITE=ON or OFF** When you tell an application to save data, PC-Cache normally intercepts the data and waits until your system isn't busy before writing it to your hard disk. This is more efficient than interrupting your system in the middle of some activity. However, it creates the risk that an accident will occur (for example, that your PC will freeze up, or its plug will get pulled out) before the data is actually written to disk. If you prefer ensuring your data's safety to some speed benefits, it's recommended that you include the parameter /WRITE=OFF to disable this delay feature. The default is /WRITE=ON.

Resident Parameters

Most PC-Cache parameters can only be used when you're loading the program into memory. However, a few parameters allow you to adjust the cache *after* it's been made resident. These five parameters, which should *not* be combined with each other, are as follows:

- **/FLUSH**   This parameter forces PC-Cache to immediately perform any writing to disk it was delaying, and then clear all the data in the cache to make room for new data.

- **/ON or /OFF**   The /OFF parameter temporarily disables PC-Cache, which is useful if you want to run a program that you know conflicts with the cache. When you're done with such a program, you can use the /ON parameter to make PC-Cache active again. If you have memory-resident programs loaded after PC-Cache, this procedure is much easier than having to unload and then reload the cache.

- **/S or /STATUS**   This parameter displays the status window, where you can use the Disk Statistics box to check the effectiveness of the cache, the Settings box to remind you of the cache's current parameter settings, and the Memory box to check on your memory usage.

- **/U or /UNLOAD**   This parameter forces PC-Cache to immediately perform any save operations it was delaying, and then removes the cache from memory, freeing up the space it occupied for other programs. However, it will only work if you've already cleared all memory-resident programs that were loaded after PC-Cache. Therefore, if you just want to turn off PC-Cache temporarily, it's easier to use the /OFF switch (described a few paragraphs earlier).

- **/WRITE=ON or OFF**   This parameter is identical to the one described in the previous "General Parameters" section. It's the only parameter that can affect PC-Cache both when you initially run the program and after the program is resident. For example, if you find the cache's write delay is causing significant lags between the time you save and the time your data is written to disk, use the /WRITE=OFF switch to eliminate any delay.

In addition, the /? and /VIDEO parameters continue to work when PC-Cache is resident.

Combining PC-Cache Parameters

PC-Cache parameters can be combined in a variety of ways. The following are some examples.

PC-CACHE /SIZE=128 /PAUSE

This command first displays the status window and pauses for confirmation that you want the loading process to proceed. If you press Y, it then installs a 128K cache in conventional memory.

PC-CACHE /SIZEXP=256 /QUIET

This command installs a 256K cache in expanded memory and suppresses the status window from being displayed.

PC-CACHE /SIZEXT=512 /NOBATCH

This command installs a 512K cache in extended memory. In addition, it restricts the amount of data the cache can transmit at a time to help ensure it doesn't conflict with certain applications such as telecommunications programs.

PC-CACHE /IE /SIZEXT=1024 /WIN

This command installs a 1MB cache in extended memory. In addition, it tells the cache to ignore drive E and to automatically reduce its size when Microsoft Windows is running.

PC-CACHE /I2 /WRITE=OFF

This command installs a cache of default size that ignores your second hard disk. It also forces the cache to execute any save commands immediately, rather than delay writing to the disk until the system isn't busy.

Part IV

Using the Security and Connectivity Utilities

Chapter 11

Encrypting Data Using PC Secure

Everyone has sensitive information they wish to keep private. For you, the information may be a personal diary, or salary payments, or a discovery not yet patented, or even military secrets. If no one inappropriate ever has access to your data, then your security needs are low. However, if you're in an office where people have potential access to your PC, or if you're transmitting data by modem through a public computer service, or if you're in some other situation where your information is vulnerable, you should safeguard your files by using PC Secure's *encrypt* command. Encryption scrambles files so that they can't be read or deciphered by anyone without the proper password. PC Secure can later *decrypt*, or unscramble, the files when you or another party needs to use them.

Additionally, if you have to create more room on your hard disk, or fit as many files as possible on a floppy disk, or transmit a lot of data with a modem, you can use PC Secure's compression command. This feature compacts files so they typically take up 25 percent to 60 percent less space. PC Secure can later expand the files to their original sizes when you or another party needs to use them.

You can also combine the encryption and compression features, creating files that are both secure and small.

There may also be times when you aren't interested in encrypting a file or directory, but just in irretrievably destroying it. You can do this using the Wipe program, which is new to PC Tools 7.

This chapter first provides an overview of encryption and compression. It then details how to get started, examines the PC Secure screen, explains how to use the various PC Secure options, and covers performing PC Secure operations from PC Shell. Lastly, it describes how to configure and run the Wipe program.

Encryption Overview

PC Secure encryption is based on the Data Encryption Standard, or *DES*, which is used by the U.S. Department of Defense (DOD) and other security-conscious institutions. It's virtually impossible to decrypt a DES file if you don't know the password used to generate it.

*PC Secure is such an effective encryption program that a Federal regulation prevents it, and other DES-based programs, from being shipped out of the country. As a result, if you're outside the U.S.A., you're using a version of PC Secure that can only compress. In this version, the Encrypt and Decrypt commands are renamed Compress and Decompress, and the encryption options are missing from the **Options** menu.*

PC Secure can encrypt virtually any kind of data file (such as TXT, DBF, WK1, and PIX) or program file (such as EXE, COM, and BAT). The one exception is a file that's copy protected. The same methods that make such a file difficult to copy (such as hiding important data in obscure places on the disk) make it difficult to properly encrypt and decrypt.

Encrypted files are normal DOS files that simply contain scrambled data. Therefore, they can be copied, renamed, deleted and recovered, backed up and restored, defragmented, and transmitted by modem, just like any DOS file. However, encrypted files should always be treated as nontext, or binary, files regardless of the type of encrypted data they contain; for example, when transmitting them via modem you should use binary protocols such as XMODEM.

Encrypted files can also be kept on standard DOS networks such as Novell. However, keep in mind that if you decrypt files on a file server, you make them vulnerable to unauthorized scrutiny. You should therefore decrypt files in a private directory or on a floppy disk.

The most important thing to remember about encryption, though, is *don't lose your password.* If you do, you may also lose all the data encrypted with that password. This subject is covered more thoroughly in the "Understanding Keys" section later in this chapter.

If you've encrypted files with an earlier version of PC Secure, you can still decrypt them with PC Secure 7. However, the files you encrypt with version 7 cannot be decrypted by any earlier version of the program.

You can choose to compress files at the same time you encrypt them without significantly slowing the operation. You can also choose to compress files without any encryption. These options are covered in the next section.

Compression Overview

PC Secure compression is based on a method called the block-adaptive Lempel-Ziv-Welch algorithm, or *LZW*. This technique typically reduces a file's size by 25 percent to 60 percent. After you perform a compression, you can view the particular space savings achieved by selecting the **File About** command.

LZW offers two significant advantages over rival methods such as Huffman coding. First, it reads and compresses a file in a single pass, as opposed to multiple passes. Second, it builds a translation table on the fly when decompressing, so it doesn't have to store the table with the compressed file. The only thing you really need to know about LZW, though, is that it works.

The degree of shrinkage achieved by PC Secure will vary depending on how repetitive a file's data is. For example, word processing files typically achieve high compression because their elements (letters, spaces, periods) tend to recur often. At the same time, EXE and COM program files typically achieve medium or poor compression because their elements (binary computer instructions and data) recur less frequently.

Along the same lines, you shouldn't try to compress files that are *already* compressed, such as ZIP files, ARC files, and spelling and thesaurus dictionaries. These files have had virtually all the repetition squeezed out of them, so the compression feature will just add some password protection data to them, making them *larger*.

If you turn on one of the two encrypt options and the **Compress** option, you can encrypt and compress files simultaneously. This is a convenient way to keep files both secure and small. Later, when you decrypt the files, they will also automatically be expanded.

If you turn both encrypt options off while keeping the **Compress** option on, you can compress files without encrypting them. However, PC Secure will still password protect the files.

If you want to compress files without imposing passwords on them, you should consider getting another program for this purpose. Recommended is the widely used "try-before-you-buy" shareware program PKZIP, which can be downloaded from most bulletin board services (see Chapter 26, "Using Telecommunications"). PKZIP's compression speed and results are comparable to PC Secure's. In addition, PKZIP provides extra compression features, such as the ability to temporarily combine a group of files into one file.

Getting Started

PC Secure is included in the PC Tools package in two forms: as a standalone application, and as an option in the PC Shell **File** menu. This chapter will concentrate on the standalone version. For information about using the PC Shell version, see "Encrypting and Decrypting from PC Shell" toward the end of the chapter.

PC Secure is initially composed of two files: PCSECURE.EXE, which contains the program itself, and PCSECURE.HLP, which contains related help information. Once you've begun using the program, a PCSECURE.CFG file is added to hold configuration information. If you allowed the Install program to create subdirectories in your PC Tools directory (see Appendix A, "PC Tools Installation and Configuration"), PCSECURE.HLP is in the SYSTEM subdirectory and PCSECURE.CFG is in the DATA subdirectory.

To start PC Secure from the DOS prompt, type **PCSECURE** (with no spaces) and press ENTER.

*You can also include a number of parameters following the **PCSECURE** command. For more information, see the "PC Secure Parameters" section towards the end of this chapter.*

If this is the first time you've run the program, the following message box appears:

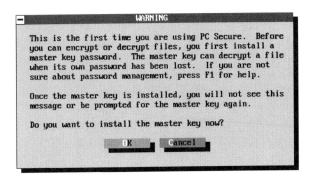

The box says that you must first supply a general password, or *master key*. If you press ENTER or click OK, a field for entering your password appears, while at the bottom of the screen the message bar prompts you to "Enter your Master Key; keep it safe." Before you proceed, there are a few things you need to understand about the use of passwords, or *keys* (the terms are interchangeable).

Understanding Keys

You must supply PC Secure with a key consisting of letters, numbers, and/or symbols when you want to safeguard a file against unauthorized inspection. The key is used to uniquely encrypt the file and to later decrypt the file.

It's important that you store keys in a secure place. If anyone without proper clearance gains access to a key, your data is vulnerable.

The most important thing to remember, however, is never lose a key. *If you do, the result could be the loss of all the files encrypted with that key.*

You can encrypt files in either Expert or Normal mode. In Expert mode, which provides greater security, a file can be decrypted *only* by the key used to encrypt it. If you lose that key, there is *no way* to recover any of the files it encrypted. In other words, you'll have *lost all the files* encrypted using that key, because you can no longer decrypt them. It's therefore vital that you store such keys in a safe place.

Under the default Normal mode, however, PC Secure is more forgiving and allows a backup password to help prevent this kind of irretrievable data loss. This backup is called a *master key.* Just as a door can be opened by both a key that's unique to the lock and a skeleton key that fits all locks, Normal mode allows a file to be decrypted by both its unique key and the master key. The screen you're currently looking at is prompting you to select this master key.

There are a number of variables to consider when choosing a key. These are detailed in the following section.

Choosing a Key

Your key can be any combination of letters, numbers, and symbols from 5 to 32 characters long. PC Secure pays attention to upper- and lowercase differences, so you should be careful to use a case sequence that you'll easily be able to duplicate in the future.

You also have the option of entering a hexadecimal (base 16) key by pressing F9 before typing. A hex password consists exclusively of the digits 0 through 9 and letters A through F (with no distinction made between upper- and lowercase). The key must be exactly 16 characters long.

Ideally, you should select a key that's easy for you to remember but hard for other people to guess. If your security needs are high, though, you may not be able to find a password that meets both these criteria, and you'll have to emphasize the "hard to guess" part. You can do so by using a random method.

For example, randomly choose two words from a dictionary or computer file. The words, combined with the random placement of some digits or symbols, can form your password.

Even better, choose a 16-digit hexadecimal random number. The best way to do this is pick a large number from a random number dictionary or PC random number generator, then translate the number to 16-digit hex using PC Tool's Desktop Programmer's Calculator (see Chapter 24, "Using the Calculators").

Entering a Key

If you've selected a nonhexadecimal key, enter it by following these steps:

1. Type each character carefully, paying attention to upper- and lowercase differences. To protect against someone reading over your shoulder, what you type is displayed as asterisks on the screen, like this:

```
┌──────────────────────────────────────────────────┐
│■               Master Key Password                │
│                                                    │
│  Please enter the password  :  ********            │
│                                                    │
└──────────────────────────────────────────────────┘
```

2. Press ENTER. The following verification prompt appears:

```
┌──────────────────────────────────────────────────┐
│■               Master Key Password                │
│                                                    │
│  Please verify the password :                      │
│                                                    │
└──────────────────────────────────────────────────┘
```

3. Type your key a second time to verify that you're entering it accurately, and then press ENTER. If what you typed matches your first entry, you're done.

4. If what you typed does *not* match your first entry, you'll see an error message saying "The keys are not equal." Press ENTER or click OK. You're returned to the initial password screen. Repeat steps 1 through 3 until you've entered the password correctly twice in a row.

If you've selected a hexadecimal key, follow these steps to enter it:

1. Press F9. The dialog box changes to the following prompt:

```
┌──────────────────────────────────────────────────┐
│■               Master Key Password                │
│                                                    │
│  Please enter the hex key :                        │
│                                                    │
└──────────────────────────────────────────────────┘
```

2. Type each character carefully. Because hex keys are complex, what you type is displayed on the screen to ensure you don't make a mistake. (If you

accidentally type a nonhex character, your PC will beep at you and will not accept the character.)

3. Press ENTER. If your key consists of 16 hex characters, you're done.

4. If you've entered fewer than 16 hex characters, an error message appears, saying "Key must be 16 Hex digits (0-9,A-F)." Press ENTER or click OK. You're returned to the blank hex key field.

5. Repeat steps 2 and 3 until you've entered the hex key correctly. Alternatively, press F9 and ENTER if you decide you want to use a nonhex key instead.

The PC Secure Screen

Once your key has been accepted, you're moved to the PC Secure screen, as shown in Figure 11-1. The screen consists of a message bar at the bottom of the screen, the title and menu bars at the top of the screen, and the currently blank area in between where PC Secure activities take place.

On many systems, PC Secure automatically starts with the File menu open. If the menu is currently open, press ESC to close it so you can examine the message bar.

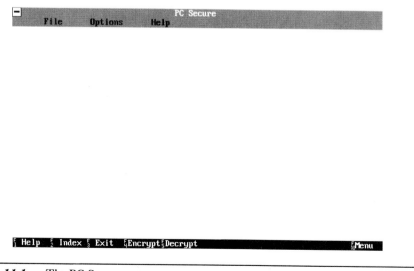

Figure 11-1.   *The PC Secure screen*

The PC Secure Message Bar

When a PC Secure activity is taking place, the message bar displays appropriate definitions or instructions. Otherwise, it displays the following commands assigned to the function keys:

Function Key	Action
F1 (Help)	Brings up context-sensitive help
F2 (Index)	Brings up the online help index
F3 (Exit)	Performs the same functions as ESC
F4 (Encrypt)	Selects File Encrypt File
F5 (Decrypt)	Selects File Decrypt File
F6	Undefined
F7	Undefined
F8	Undefined
F9	Undefined
F10 (Menu)	Performs the same functions as ALT

Navigating the PC Secure Menus

At the top of the screen are the four menus available in PC Secure. Follow these steps to examine the menus:

1. Press F or click on File to display the File menu, which lets you encrypt files, decrypt files, and exit PC Secure.

2. Press RIGHT ARROW to display the Options menu, which lets you set how files are encrypted, decrypted, compressed, and saved to disk.

3. Press RIGHT ARROW again to display the Help menu, which provides online help.

4. Press ESC and ALT-SPACEBAR to display the Control menu, which lets you bring up a PC Secure copyright notice or exit the program.

These menus are shown, with their default settings, in Figure 11-2. The next section explores the Options menu commands in depth.

Understanding the Options Menu

Before beginning a PC Secure operation, you should adjust the settings on the Options menu. When you bring the menu up by pressing O or clicking on it, the following nine options appear:

- *Full DES Encryption*   This option performs 16 rounds of scrambling a file's data versus the two rounds of the alternative Quick Encryption option. While it provides extra levels of protection for sensitive secrets pursued by decryption experts, this option is probably overkill for common office use, and takes at least twice as long to execute as Quick Encryption. Its default is *off*.

- *Quick Encryption*   This option performs two rounds of scrambling a file's data versus the 16 rounds of the alternative Full DES Encryption option. Unless you're dealing in extremely sensitive material, Quick Encryption is probably good enough. It takes about half as long to execute as Full DES Encryption. Its default is *on*.

- *Compression*   This option reduces a file's size by about 25 percent to 60 percent. It can be used in conjunction with either of the encryption options. It can also be used with both of the options turned off, in which case it compresses files without any encryption (although password protection is still imposed). This option's default is *on*.

- *One Key*   If turned on, this option lets you use the same initial key for your entire encryption/decryption session, saving you from being prompted to enter a key for each file. (However, when a file you're decrypting requires a different key from the one being used in your session, you still must provide that other key.) The default for this option is *on*.

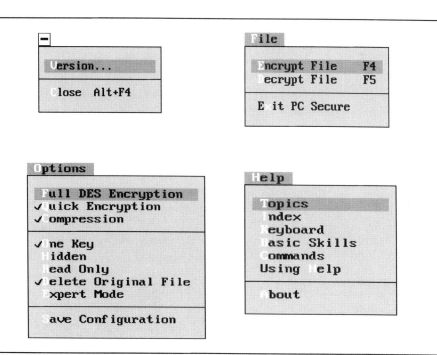

Figure 11-2.   *The PC Secure menus*

- *Hidden*   This option saves the encrypted and/or compressed file as a *hidden* file, meaning that it won't be visible to DOS commands such as DIR. For information on hidden files, see Chapter 16, "Managing Your Files." This option's default is *off*.

- *Read Only*   This option saves the encrypted and/or compressed file as a read-only file, meaning that it can be read, but not altered or deleted. For information on read-only files, see Chapter 16, "Managing Your Files." This option's default is *off*.

- *Delete Original File*   If on, this option causes your original file to be deleted after an encrypted and/or compressed version of it is created. (If you begin PC Secure with the /G parameter, the original is first overwritten several times to ensure that it's utterly unrecoverable, as explained in the "PC Secure Parameters" section.) If off, this option causes your original file to be preserved, and the encrypted and/or compressed version of it to be named with an SEC (for secure) extension. After decryption and/or expansion, the SEC extension will revert to the extension of the original file. This option's default is *on*.

- *Expert Mode*   As explained previously in "Understanding Keys," if on, this option provides extra security by setting a file's encryption to be based entirely on its supplied key. However, if the key is lost, there's no way to decrypt the file. If off, this option sets a file's encryption to be based on both its supplied key and your master key. This option's default is *off*.

- *Save Configuration*   This option saves your settings in the **O**ptions menu for future sessions, rather than just the current one.

To toggle an option on or off, press the first letter of the option or click on it. If an option is on, a checkmark appears to the left of it.

When you're done setting options, press ESC to close the menu. You can then proceed to process files based on your settings, as detailed in the next section.

Encrypting and Decrypting a File

To get a feel for safeguarding data using PC Secure, follow these steps to change **O**ptions settings and encrypt a file:

1. Press O or click on the Options menu. The settings should initially match the defaults in Figure 11-2.

2. Press ENTER or F, or click Full DES Encryption, to select the more rigorous type of encryption. A checkmark appears to the left of the option. Also, the checkmark next to **Q**uick Encryption disappears, since only one of these two options can be on at the same time.

3. Press O or click One Key to be prompted on every password operation. The checkmark to the left of the option disappears.

4. Accept the other settings, and press LEFT ARROW to move to the **F**ile menu. You're on the first option, **E**ncrypt File.

5. Choose the option by pressing ENTER or E, or by clicking Encrypt File. A File Selection dialog box like this appears:

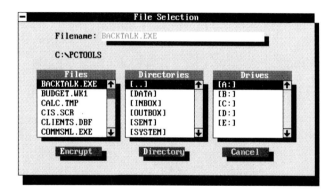

6. Select a file to encrypt. You can type the drive, directory, and name of the file you want in the text box. You can also search for its name in the Files box, scrolling individual files with DOWN ARROW and UP ARROW; displaying six files at a time with PGDN and PGUP; jumping to the bottom and top of the box with END and HOME; or scrolling vertically using your mouse.

7. When you've selected a file or typed a filename, press ENTER or click Encrypt. You're prompted to provide a key.

8. Type **ROSE?BUD** (paying attention to the use of uppercase) and press ENTER. You're asked to verify the password.

9. Again, type **ROSE?BUD** and press ENTER. The encryption now begins, and a dialog box like this comes up to track its progress:

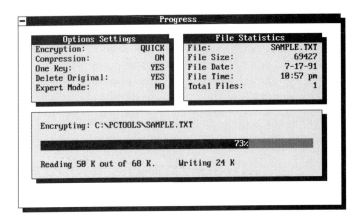

The box displays your **O**ptions menu settings; the selected file's name, size, and creation date and time (as well as a Total Files indicator for when you've specified more than one file at a time); how many bytes of the original file have been read and how many bytes of the encrypted copy have been written (the latter being a smaller number when the **C**ompression option is on); and the percentage of the operation that's been completed.

10. When the encryption is finished, press ENTER or click OK. The dialog box closes, and you're returned to the standard PC Secure screen.

If you now examined your encrypted file, you'd find its data scrambled beyond human comprehension. However, PC Secure can unscramble it using your password. To demonstrate, follow these steps to decrypt the file:

1. Press F or click on the File menu. Notice that the second option is **D**ecrypt File.

2. Choose the option by pressing D or clicking on it. The File Selection box appears.

3. Select or type the name of the file you just encrypted.

4. Press ENTER or click Decrypt. You're prompted for the file's password.

5. Type **ROSE?BUD** (again, paying attention to the use of uppercase) and press ENTER. The decryption begins, and the Progress dialog box appears again to track the procedure.

6. When the decryption is complete, press ENTER or click OK to close the dialog box. If you now examine the file, you'll find its contents have returned to normal.

Encrypting a Directory of Files

To get a feel for working with multiple files, follow these steps to encrypt and compress an entire directory of files:

1. Press O or click on the Options menu.

2. Press Q or click Quick Encryption to turn the option back on.

3. Press O or click One Key to turn the option back on.

4. Press D or click Delete Original File to turn the option off.

5. Press ESC to close the **O**ptions menu, and then press F4 to select the Encrypt command. The File Selection dialog box appears.

6. Type the name of a directory you want to encrypt; or press TAB twice to move to the Directories box and use DOWN ARROW to select a directory; or click on a directory with your mouse. Be sure to avoid choosing a directory with copy protected files or with system files vital to running your PC (such as COM- MAND.COM or, in this case, PCSECURE.EXE).

7. Press ALT-D or click Directory. The following dialog box asks you to verify that you want to affect multiple files:

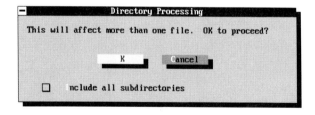

The box also contains an Include All Subdirectories option, which lets you affect all subdirectories in the directory. For this exercise, leave the option off, which is the default.

8. Press ENTER or click OK. Because the One Key option is on, your previous password is used automatically, and the encryption and compression process begins, file by file.

Since the **D**elete Original File option is off, copies of the original files with SEC extensions are produced, while the original files are unaffected.

If a name conflict arises (for example, if you have the files SAMPLE.EXE and SAMPLE.HLP, both of which would produce the encrypted file SAM- PLE.SEC), you'll be asked whether to overwrite the existing encrypted file or skip generating the new encrypted file. After you select **OK** or **C**ancel, the process continues.

When all the files have been processed, you see a box like this:

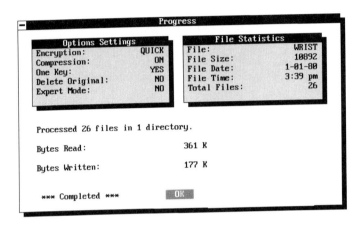

Notice that the box displays your option settings, information about the last file processed, the total number of files processed, the total number of bytes read, and the total number of bytes written (the latter being a smaller number because the **C**ompression option was on).

9. Press ENTER or click OK to close the dialog box.

10. Press ESC and ENTER to exit PC Secure.

11. Examine the new files' contents using a program such as PC Shell (see Chapter 18, "Using Advanced PC Shell Features"). Notice that, in contrast to their originating files, the SEC files are indecipherable.

12. Delete the SEC files, either by using PC Shell (see Chapter 16, "Managing Your Files"), or by moving to the directory in DOS, typing **DEL *.SEC**, and pressing ENTER.

If you want to keep certain directories encrypted all the time but also be able to work with their files conveniently, consider using the Directory Lock option in the new Data Monitor program. This utility automatically encrypts files you save to specified directories and automatically decrypts the files whenever you access them. However, it doesn't support DES encryption. For more information, see "Using Directory Lock" in Chapter 12, "Shielding Data Using Data Monitor."

PC Secure Parameters

When you start PC Secure from the DOS prompt or modify its AUTOEXEC.BAT line, you can specify certain options, called parameters, following the program name. You can include any single parameter (for example, PCSECURE /G) or combine a number of parameters (for example, PCSECURE /Q /KROSE?BUD C:\PAYROLL*.*) to achieve the effect you want. Keep in mind that parameters require a *forward* slash (/) as opposed to the backslash (\) used to specify DOS directories.

Most PC Secure parameters simply provide command-line equivalents to PC Secure menu commands to enable you to operate PC Secure from batch files. However, two parameters, /G and /M, provide security options that aren't available from the menus.

When you're encrypting with the **D**elete Original File option on, the /G parameter causes your original file to be overwritten several times according to DOD specifications to ensure that it's utterly unrecoverable. This procedure can take a while, but it's necessary if you're required to meet DOD security standards.

The /M parameter, on the other hand, provides additional decryption security by letting you encrypt a file using two or more passwords. This can be useful, for example, if you want to make it necessary for two or more people to participate in the decrypting of particularly sensitive data. When decrypting, the passwords must be supplied in the opposite order they were used for encrypting; in other words, the last key used for encrypting is the first key needed for decrypting, and so on. This parameter (as well as most of the other parameters) is new to version 7.

The following are the 12 parameters specific to PC Secure:

- **/?** or **/H**   This "help" parameter lists and briefly describes all parameters specific to PC Secure. It should not be combined with any other parameters.

- **/VIDEO**   This "help" parameter lists and briefly describes the standard PC Tools video and mouse parameters. It should not be combined with any other parameters. For more information, see the "Video and Mouse Parameters" section in Appendix A, "PC Tools Installation and Configuration."

- *d:\path\ filenames*   This parameter consists of the drive, directory path, and names of the files you want to encrypt or decrypt. You can use the DOS wildcards ? and * to specify groups of files.

- **/C**   This parameter turns the **C**ompression option off.

- **/D**   This parameter decrypts the files specified on the command line.

- **/F**   This parameter performs full DES encryption on the files specified on the command line.

- **/G**   When encrypting, this parameter overwrites the original file several times according to DOD specifications to ensure that it's utterly unrecoverable.

- **/K***ppppp*   This parameter specifies *ppppp* as the key to use when encrypting or decrypting. This saves you from having to respond to password prompts, which is useful for batch file execution.

- **/M**   This parameter lets you encrypt and decrypt files using two or more passwords.

- **/P**   This parameter prompts you for a password from the command line before running PC Secure.

- **/Q**   This parameter performs quick DES encryption on the files specified on the command line.

- **/S**   This parameter suppresses all messages (other than error messages) from appearing during encryption and decryption, which is useful for batch file execution.

The proper order for including these parameters is as follows:

PCSECURE [/Q *or* /F *or* /D] [/P *or* /K*ppppp*] [/C/G/M/S] [*d:\ path\filenames*]

Encrypting and Decrypting from PC Shell

In PC Tools 7, you can also perform most PC Secure functions from the PC Shell program. To do so, follow these steps:

1. Run PC Shell following the directions in Chapter 15, "PC Shell Overview."

2. Select the files you want to affect in the File Box. (To affect all the files in the directory, press ALT-F, S, or click on the File menu and select Select All Toggle.)

3. Press ALT-F, E, or click on the File menu and select Secure. You're offered the options of **Encrypt File**, **Decrypt File**, and **Settings**.

4. Select **Settings** to adjust the program's options, which are identical to the options in the standalone version's **Options** menu. When you're done, press ESC to close the box.

5. Press ALT-F, E again, and select either **Encrypt** or **Decrypt**. After you enter an appropriate password, the requested operation commences on your selected files.

The advantage of operating from PC Shell is that when the program is memory resident, you can pop it up at any time from any application. However, PC Shell doesn't support the standalone PC Secure's /G and /M options, and it can't be run in batch mode. Which form of PC Secure you use therefore depends on your personal tastes and needs.

Destroying Data Using Wipe

When you've finished using sensitive data, or you've moved the data to a different site, you may no longer be interested in keeping the files encrypted on your hard disk, but simply want to *destroy* them so no one else can view them. If you use the DOS DEL command, you won't actually eliminate the files, only mark their clusters as available (as explained in Chapter 4, "Data Recovery Overview").

To actually destroy files, you should instead use the Wipe program. This utility, which is new to PC Tools 7, can overwrite existing files, deleted files, the files in an entire directory and all its subdirectories, or an entire disk. It can perform this overwriting fairly quickly, or it can do it following DOD standards, making any data it erases impossible to recover.

In addition, Wipe can be set to delete precisely like the DOS DEL command. When it operates in this mode, it works with such protection programs as Data Monitor. Since Wipe can delete entire directories, and can even prompt for confirmation before deleting each file, you may therefore also want to use it as a more powerful version of DEL.

Wipe can be run both interactively and with command-line parameters.

Running Wipe Interactively

To run Wipe interactively, follow these steps:

1. Go to the DOS prompt, type **WIPE**, and press ENTER. The following Wipe main menu appears:

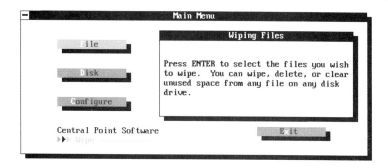

The menu offers selections for wiping files, wiping an entire disk, or configuring how data is wiped.

2. To begin, press C or click Configure. You're prompted to choose between two methods for overwriting data. The first is **Fast Wipe**, which simply overwrites with the number zero for a default of *1* time. If desired, you can specify a different repetition rate up to 999.

   The second is **DOD Wipe**, which overwrites your data with hexadecimal FF (a 1 for every bit), then hexadecimal zero (a 0 for every bit), and performs this operation a default of three times. It then finishes by overwriting your data with the default ASCII code 246, or hexadecimal F6. This satisfies minimum DOD standards for destroying data. If desired, you can specify a different repetition rate and ASCII code.

3. Select the option, repetition rate, and (if appropriate) ASCII code you want. When you're ready, press ALT-O or click OK to accept your settings for this session only; or press ALT-S or click Save Config to save your settings to disk for future sessions. You're returned to the main menu.

4. To wipe a disk, press D or click Disk. The following Disk Options dialog box appears:

First select the drive you want to wipe by pressing D or clicking Change Drive, pressing the letter of the drive, and pressing ENTER. If you then want to proceed to irretrievably destroy data, press W, O, W to overwrite all the data on the disk; or press U, O, ENTER to overwrite only the unused space on the disk (which may contain data from previously deleted files). A status box tracks the progress of the wipe operation. When it's done, you're returned to the main menu.

5. To wipe files, press F or click File. The File Options dialog box appears, as shown here:

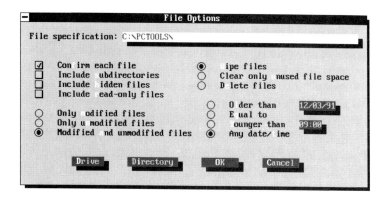

The box offers the following options:

- *File specification*   This field specifies the files to wipe. You can enter path names, and the DOS wildcards (? for any single character and * for any group of characters) to specify a group of files. For example, C:\DATA*.* would specify all files in your C drive's DATA directory.

- *Confirm each file*   If on (which is the default), this option prompts you for verification on each file before wiping.

- *Include subdirectories*   If on, this option wipes all files in subdirectories included in your file specification.

- *Include hidden files*   If on, this option wipes all hidden files included in your file specification.

- *Include read-only files*   If on, this option wipes all read-only files included in your file specification.

- *Only modified files/Only unmodified files/Modified and unmodified files*   These three options let you choose between wiping only the specified files that *have* changed since your last backup (the archive bit is set), only those that have *not* changed since your last backup (the archive bit is clear), or all your specified files (which is the default).

- *Wipe files/Clear only unused file space/Delete files*   These three options let you choose between wiping your specified files (which is the default), wiping only the unused clusters at the end of your specified files, or deleting files in the same way as the DOS DEL command.

- *Older than/Equal to/Younger than/Any date-time*   These three options let you choose between wiping only the specified files with creation dates older than, equal to, or younger than the specified date and time; or wiping the specified files regardless of their creation dates and times (which is the default).

- *Drive*   This option lets you select the drive containing the files you want to wipe. To use it, press ALT-D or click Drive; press the letter of the drive you want, or click the drive's icon; and press ENTER or click OK.

- *Directory*   This option lets you select the directory containing the files you want to wipe. To use it, press ALT-I or click Directory; use the arrow keys or your mouse to scroll through the directory list until the directory you want is selected; press ENTER or double-click to select the directory; and press O or click OK.

Select the options you want, and then press ALT-O or click OK. The wipe procedure you specified is performed, and you're returned to the main menu.

When you're done using Wipe, press X or click Exit. The program exits, and you're returned to the DOS prompt.

You can also wipe files from PC Shell. To do so, first run PC Shell and select the appropriate files (see Chapter 15, "PC Shell Overview"). When you're ready, press ALT-F, G, C, or click on the File menu and select Change File and Clear File. For each selected file, press W or click Wipe to destroy it using the current Wipe Configure settings; or press S or click Skip to leave it unaffected. When you're done, press O or click OK.

Wipe Parameters

Wipe can also be run using command-line parameters. However, combining these parameters can get complicated and may sometimes produce unexpected results. Since Wipe is a particularly destructive program, it's therefore recommended that you carefully experiment with the command-line version before you begin relying on it.

Keep in mind that parameters require a *forward* slash (/) as opposed to the backslash (\) used to specify DOS directories. In addition, Wipe requires that parameters be separated by spaces (most programs accept parameters both with and without space separators).

Wipe supports the following 16 parameters specific to the application:

- **/?**   This "help" parameter lists and briefly describes all parameters specific to Wipe. It should not be combined with any other parameters.

- **/VIDEO**   This "help" parameter lists and briefly describes the standard PC Tools video and mouse parameters. It should not be combined with any other parameters. For more information, see the "Video and Mouse Parameters" section in Appendix A, "PC Tools Installation and Configuration."

- **d:\\directory\\filenames**   This parameter consists of the drive, directory path and/or names of the files you want to encrypt or decrypt. You can use the DOS wildcards ? and * to specify groups of files.

- **/DELETE**   This parameter deletes the specified files (like the DOS DEL command) rather than wiping them.

- **/DISK**   This parameter wipes the entire disk of the drive specified by the d: parameter.

- **/GOVT**   This parameter wipes following minimum DOD standards. Specifically, it overwrites using a hexadecimal FF, then overwrites again using 00, then repeats the sequence two more times, and then overwrites a final time using hexadecimal F6 (ASCII 246).

- **/HIDDEN**   This parameter includes all hidden files in the file specification.

- **/MODIFIED**   This parameter restricts the file specification to files that have changed since your last backup (that is, that have their archive bits set).

- **/NOCONFIRM**   This parameter turns off the Confirm Each File switch so you don't have to confirm the wiping or deleting of each file. However, it allows the Wipe File Options screen to come up before the operation proceeds, requiring you to confirm the operation itself by selecting **OK**. If you want to wipe or delete without any confirmation, include the /QUIET parameter instead.

- **/QUIET**   This parameter suppresses all Wipe prompts, thus executing your Wipe command immediately (although status information will still be displayed). This option is ideal for speeding Wipe operations and for use in batch files. However, since it eliminates confirmation prompts, *use it with care.*

- **/READONLY**   This parameter includes all read-only files in the file specification.

- **/REP:n**   This parameter repeats overwriting n times. If this parameter is left out, the default is three times. See also the /VALUE:n parameter.

- **/SUB**   This parameter includes all files in subdirectories in the file specification.

- **/UNMODIFIED**   This parameter restricts the file specification to files that have not changed since your last backup (that is, that have their archive bits clear).

- **/UNUSED**   This parameter restricts wiping to the unused space in the specified files or disk.

- **/VALUE:n**   This parameter specifies the decimal number from 0 to 255 to be used to overwrite when wiping. If this parameter is left out, the default is *246* (hex F6). See also the /REP:n parameter.

Combining Wipe Parameters

Wipe parameters can be combined in a variety of ways. The following are some examples.

WIPE A: /DISK

This command first prompts you to choose between wiping all the data on the disk or wiping only the unused space. It then proceeds to wipe the disk in drive A following your choice, constantly informing you of the percentage of the operation completed.

WIPE A: /DISK /QUIET

This command immediately proceeds to wipe all the data on drive A without any prompting. It constantly informs you of the percentage of the operation completed.

WIPE C:\DATA*.* /SUB /NOCONFIRM

This command first brings up the File Options dialog box with the Confirm Each File option turned off and the Include Subdirectories option turned on. If you confirm the operation by selecting OK, it proceeds to wipe all the files on drive C in root directory DATA (and all its subdirectories) without asking for confirmation on each file. It constantly informs you of which file is currently being wiped.

WIPE C:\DATA*.* /SUB /QUIET

This command immediately proceeds to wipe the files in directory C:\DATA (and all its subdirectories) without any prompting. It constantly informs you of which file is currently being wiped.

WIPE C:\DATA*.* /DELETE /SUB /QUIET

This command immediately proceeds to nondestructively delete the files in directory C:\DATA (and all its subdirectories) without any prompting. It constantly informs you of which file is currently being deleted.

Chapter *12*

Shielding Data Using Data Monitor

 One of the most important new additions to PC Tools 7 is the memory-resident Data Monitor. This program provides several powerful utilities for protecting deleted files, keeping files secure, and preventing critical data areas from being overwritten. It also provides such convenience utilities as a screen blanker and a disk activity indicator.

Running and Configuring Data Monitor

To examine Data Monitor, follow these steps:

1. If Data Monitor is already resident in memory (which you can check by typing **MI** from the DOS prompt and pressing ENTER), first unload it so you can start from a fresh slate. To do this, clear any memory-resident programs you ran after Data Monitor, and then type **DATAMON /U** at the DOS prompt and press ENTER.

2. Type **DATAMON** from the DOS prompt and press ENTER. This Data Monitor main menu appears:

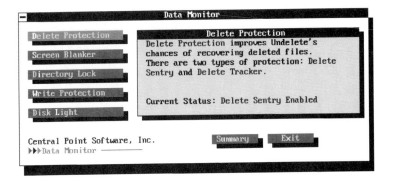

The menu lists the following utilities:

- **Delete Protection**   This option lets you choose between two powerful methods of protecting deleted files, Delete Sentry and Delete Tracker. These utilities aren't covered in this chapter; for complete information about them, see instead "Monitoring Deleted Files" in Chapter 5, "Safeguarding Your Data."

- *Screen Blanker*   This utility blanks your screen after your PC has been idle for awhile to prevent any static image from becoming permanently etched, or *burned,* into your monitor. It also lets you password-protect the blanked screen to prevent anyone from using your PC while you're away from it. For more information, read the "Using Screen Blanker" section.

- *Directory Lock*   This utility automatically encrypts all files saved to a designated directory, and automatically decrypts the files on the fly whenever you want to access them, thus providing convenient security. For more information, read the "Using Directory Lock" section.

- *Write Protection*   This utility prevents specified system areas, files, and/or entire disks from being deleted, overwritten, or otherwise altered in any way. It therefore provides protection against data accidents. For more information, read the "Using Write Protection" section.

- *Disk Light*   This utility displays the letter of the drive currently being accessed in the upper-right corner of your screen. This is useful if your physical drive lights aren't visible—for example, if you keep your PC under your desk, or if you access network drives. For more information, read the "Using Disk Light" section.

Once you're done configuring the utilities you want, go to the "Completing the Data Monitor Configuration" section.

Using Screen Blanker

If your PC is on but you don't perform any activity on it, whatever image is on its screen remains unchanged. If the image is left there long enough, there's a danger it will etch itself, or "burn," into the screen, leaving a permanent imprint. On modern monitors, it typically takes many hours, or even days, for a static image to create such damage. However, it's safest to eliminate even the possibility of such an accident occurring.

To do so, use the Screen Blanker. This utility constantly checks your system for keyboard, mouse, or disk activity. When no activity occurs after a specified period of time (the default being five minutes), it automatically turns your screen black and displays a constantly moving message that says "Press any key to resume...". When you press a key or move your mouse, your original screen reappears.

In addition, you can assign the Screen Blanker a password, so that anyone without the password will be prevented from accessing your blanked-out PC. You can also define a Screen Blanker keystroke that instantly blanks your screen when you press it.

To turn on and configure Screen Blanker, follow these steps:

1. From the Data Monitor main menu, press S or click Screen Blanker. The following dialog box appears:

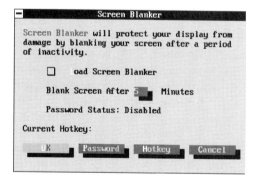

2. Press ALT-L or click Load Screen Blanker to place a checkmark by the option. You're moved to the Blank Screen After *n* Minutes field.

3. If you don't want to accept the default time period of 5 minutes, type a different number from 1 to 999 and press ENTER.

4. If you want the Screen Blanker to prevent others from using your PC in your absence, press ALT-P or click Password. You're prompted for a new password. (If you've previously entered a password, you must type that first.)

   Type a character sequence from 1 to 8 characters long that will be easy for you to remember but hard for others to guess. As you type, only asterisks are displayed so that anyone looking over your shoulder cannot see the password. When you're done, press ENTER twice. You're prompted to confirm by typing the password a second time. Do so, and then press ENTER twice again. Your password is accepted, and you're returned to the Screen Blanker options box.

5. If you want to specify a Screen Blanker keystroke, or *hotkey*, press ALT-H or click Hotkey. You're prompted for a CTRL or ALT keystroke (for example, CTRL-B or ALT-S). Press a keystroke that you don't ordinarily use in your other programs, and then press ENTER. After you've saved all your Data Monitor settings, pressing this keystroke will instantly blank your screen.

6. Press ALT-O or click OK to accept your Screen Blanker settings. You're returned to the Data Monitor main menu.

7. If you want to configure another Data Monitor utility, do so now. Otherwise, go to the "Completing the Data Monitor Configuration" section.

Using Directory Lock

If you have sensitive data on your hard disk that you want to prevent others from viewing, PC Tools offers two solutions. The first is PC Secure, which can encrypt any file or directory using the Data Encryption Standard, or DES. PC Secure is your best choice if you have high security needs, or if you seldom need to access the files you encrypt. For more information on this program, see Chapter 11, "Encrypting Data Using PC Secure."

The second solution is Directory Lock. This utility is ideal if your security needs aren't high and you access your sensitive files frequently. That's because it automatically encrypts all the files you save to a designated directory, and automatically decrypts those files on the fly when you want to use them. This procedure keeps the files constantly encrypted, while at the same time providing you with convenient access to them.

Directory Lock's encryption scheme is a quick and simple one created especially for PC Tools 7. It won't thwart a cryptographer, but it will make your files inaccessible to virtually anyone who isn't an encryption expert.

To use the files yourself, you simply supply your password the first time you try to access them after turning on your PC. You don't need to supply the password again *unless* no keyboard, mouse, or disk activity is detected for a specified period of time (the default being five minutes). After that time, Directory Lock assumes you've walked away from your PC and so protects access to the files until you return.

The most important thing to remember about Directory Lock is never lose your password. *That's because the password itself is used as part of the encryption scheme. If you lose your password, all the data encrypted with it will be effectively lost.*

To turn on and configure Directory Lock, follow these steps:

1. From the Data Monitor main menu, press 1 or click Directory Lock. The following dialog box appears:

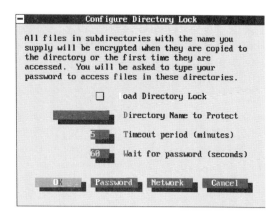

2. Press ALT-L or click Load Directory Lock to place a checkmark by the option. You're moved to the Directory Name to Protect field.

3. Type the name of the directory that will hold all your sensitive files. *Don't* include a drive letter, backslash, or path; Directory Lock will automatically act on *all* directories with the specified name on *all* of your drives. (For example, if your directory is named SAFE and your system contains the directories A:\SAFE, C:\SAFE, and C:\PAYROLL\SAFE, all three directories will be password-protected.)

4. Press TAB or ALT-T, or click Timeout Period (Minutes), to set the period of time your PC can be idle before you're again prompted for a password to access your protected directory. You can accept the default of 5 minutes, or type a different number from 1 to 9999. You can also type 0 (or press BACKSPACE to leave the field blank), which restricts Directory Lock to asking for a password once per session regardless of how long your PC is inactive.

5. Press TAB or ALT-W, or click Wait for Password (Seconds), to set the period of time Directory Lock will maintain its password prompt and await the entry of the correct password. This option is mostly useful as a safeguard against programs you've scheduled to run unattended (such as CP Backup) becoming stuck on the password prompt if they try to access your protected directory. You can accept the default of 60 seconds, or type a different number from 1 to 9999. You can also type 0 (or press BACKSPACE twice to leave the field blank), which keeps the password prompt up indefinitely. Regardless of your time

setting, however, the prompt will automatically disappear after three failed attempts have been made at entering the correct password.

If you're using PC Tools 7.0, typing 0 in steps 4 or 5 may create unexpected results. If this occurs, it's recommended that you upgrade to version 7.1. For more information, see the "PC Tools 7.0 Versus 7.1" section in this book's Introduction.

6. If you want to password-protect a network directory, press ALT-N or click Network, and then type the name of the directory. *Don't* include a drive letter, but *do* include a backslash and path name; for example, \HOME\SAFE. Directory Lock will automatically act on *all* directories with the specified name on *all* of the network drives you're logged onto. When you're done, press ALT-O or click OK.

7. Press ALT-P or click Password, and then type a character sequence from 1 to 8 characters long. The password should be easy for you to remember but hard for others to guess. As you type, only asterisks are displayed so that anyone looking over your shoulder cannot see the password.

8. When you're done, press ENTER twice. You're prompted to confirm your password by typing it a second time. Do so, and then press ENTER twice again. Your password is accepted, and you're returned to the Configure Directory Lock box.

9. Press ALT-O or click OK to accept your Directory Lock settings. Your hard disk may now be scanned for the directory you specified. If so, wait until the scan identifies the existing directories that will be protected, and then press ENTER or click OK. You're returned to the Data Monitor main menu.

10. If you want to configure another Data Monitor utility, do so now. Otherwise, go to the "Completing the Data Monitor Configuration" section.

If you ever want to permanently decrypt all the files in your password-protected directory, simply copy them to a different (that is, unprotected) directory. Directory Lock will automatically decrypt the files on the fly and generate the copies in their normal format.

Using Write Protection

There may be times when you want to protect areas of your disk from being altered in any way. For example, if you're a PC supervisor preparing a system for a novice user, you might want to protect all the program files and critical data files from being accidentally erased. As another example, if you're experimenting with an unstable program, you may want to protect your entire disk from being overwritten in case something goes wrong. The Write Protection program gives you the option of protecting your entire hard disk, or just its system areas, or just specified files. In addition, it lets you protect all the data on all your floppy disks. (This utility does *not* give you the option of protecting selected portions of your floppy disks; with floppies, it's everything or nothing.)

To turn on and configure Write Protection, follow these steps:

1. From the Data Monitor main menu, press W or click Write Protection. The following dialog box appears:

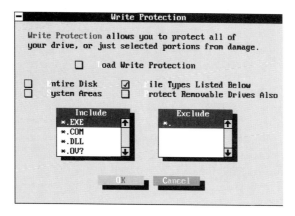

2. Press ALT-L or click Load Write Protection to place a checkmark by the option.

3. To write-protect all the data on your hard disk (including its system area and all its files), press ALT-E or click Entire Disk to place a checkmark by the option.

4. To write-protect all the data on all your floppy disks (including their system areas and all their files), press ALT-P or click Protect Removeable Drives Also to place a checkmark by the option. (If you're using PC Tools 7.0, click the Protect Floppy Drives option instead.) For your selection to take effect, however, you must also select at least one of the hard disk protection options; protection of floppy drives exclusively is not supported.

5. To write-protect your hard disk's system areas (for example, its boot record and FAT), press ALT-S or click System Areas to place a checkmark by the option. (This isn't necessary if you selected Entire Disk.)

6. To write-protect specified files on your hard disk, press ALT-F or click File Types Listed Below to place a checkmark by the option. (This isn't necessary if you selected Entire Disk.)

7. If you selected File Types Listed Below, specify the types of files you want protected in the Include box and the types you *don't* want protected in the Exclude box. You can use the DOS wildcards ? (to represent any single character) and * (to represent any group of characters). For example, to

specify all files, you'd enter *.* in the Include box and erase all lines in the Exclude box. The defaults for the Include box are *.EXE, *.COM, *.DLL, and *.OV? to specify program and overlay files. The default for the Exclude box is *., which specifies files with no extensions.

8. When you're done, press ALT-O or click OK to accept your Write Protection settings. You're returned to the Data Monitor main menu.

9. If you want to configure another Data Monitor utility, do so now. Otherwise, go to the "Completing the Data Monitor Configuration" section.

Using Disk Light

If your disk drive lights aren't in plain sight—for example, if you use a "tower" PC that you keep under your desk, or if you regularly access network drives—then you're not getting immediate visual confirmation that read and write commands to your drives are successful. If this bothers you, try using Disk Light. This utility displays the letter of the drive currently being accessed in the upper-right corner of your screen. In addition, it displays an "r" when the disk is being read and a "w" when the disk is being written to. (For example, if your drive C is being read, the letters "Cr" appear on your screen.)

To turn on and configure Disk Light, follow these steps:

1. From the Data Monitor main menu, press L or click Disk Light. The following dialog box appears:

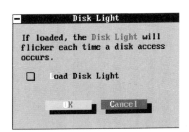

2. Press ALT-L or click Load Disk Light to place a checkmark by the option.

3. Press ENTER or click OK. You're returned to the Data Monitor main menu.

4. If you want to configure another Data Monitor utility, do so now. Otherwise, continue on to the following "Completing the Data Monitor Configuration" section.

If you find Disk Light showing network drives being accessed at times you didn't expect, it's probably because DOS is searching the drives specified in your PATH statement.

Completing the Data Monitor Configuration

When you're done configuring the Data Monitor utilities, follow these steps to save your settings:

1. From the Data Monitor main menu, press U or click Summary to display a summary of your configuration settings. After you've examined the screen, press ENTER or click OK to return to the main menu.

2. If you're comfortable with all your settings, press X or click Exit to bring up the Close dialog box.

3. If a checkmark does *not* appear next to the **S**ave Configuration option, press S or click next to the option. When the checkmark appears, press ENTER or click OK. Your new settings are saved to disk and will stay in effect for future Data Monitor sessions.

4. Install the Data Monitor program in your AUTOEXEC.BAT file so that it loads every time you start up your PC. You can do this using the Install program (see Appendix A, "PC Tools Installation and Configuration"); or you can directly insert the line DATAMON /LOAD, which loads the program into memory based on your dialog box configuration settings. You can also turn any Data Monitor utility on or off (both at startup and when Data Monitor is already resident) using the parameters covered in the next section.

Data Monitor Parameters

You can specify certain options, called parameters, following Data Monitor's program name. You can include any single parameter (for example, DATAMON /LOAD) or combine a number of parameters (for example, DATAMON /SENTRY+ /SCREEN+) to achieve the effect you want. Keep in mind that parameters require a *forward* slash (/, located on the bottom of the ? key) as opposed to the backslash (\) used to specify DOS directories.

Data Monitor supports 13 parameters specific to the program. They are as follows:

- /?   This "help" parameter lists and briefly describes each parameter specific to Data Monitor. It should not be combined with any other parameter.

- **/ VIDEO**   This "help" parameter lists and briefly describes the standard PC Tools video and mouse parameters. It should not be combined with any other parameter. For more information, see the "Video and Mouse Parameters" section in Appendix A, "PC Tools Installation and Configuration."

- **/ALL+** and **/ALL-**   This parameter turns on (+) or off (-) all Data Monitor utilities *except* Delete Tracker (which would conflict with Delete Sentry). When on, all the utilities conform to the options you specified when configuring Data Monitor.

- **/DATALOCK+** and **/DATALOCK-**   This parameter turns the Directory Lock option on (+) or off (-). When on, it conforms to the options you specified when configuring Data Monitor.

- **/LIGHT+** and **/LIGHT-**   This parameter turns the Disk Light option on (+) or off (-).

- **/LOAD**   This parameter loads Data Monitor based on your dialog box configuration settings.

- **/LOW**   If you're using a memory manager such as DOS 5's EMM386, this parameter prevents Data Monitor from loading into high memory.

- **/S** or **/STATUS**   This parameter displays your current Data Monitor settings.

- **/SCREEN+** and **/SCREEN-**   This parameter turns the Screen Blanker option on (+) or off (-). When on, it conforms to the time, password, and hotkey options you specified when configuring Data Monitor.

- **/SENTRY+** and **/SENTRY-**   This parameter turns the Delete Sentry option on (+) or off (-). When on, it conforms to the deleted file protection options you specified when configuring Data Monitor.

- **/TRACKER+** and **/TRACKER-**   This parameter turns the Delete Tracker option on (+) or off (-). When on, it tracks deleted files on the drives you specified when configuring Data Monitor.

- **/U** or **/UNLOAD**   This parameter removes Data Monitor from memory, freeing up the space it occupied for other programs. However, it will only work if you've already cleared all memory-resident programs that were loaded after Data Monitor.

- **/WRITE+** and **/WRITE-**   This parameter turns the Write Protection option on (+) or off (-). When on, it write-protects the drives and data you specified when configuring Data Monitor.

 The /ALL, /DATALOCK, /LIGHT, /SCREEN, /SENTRY, /TRACKER, and /WRITE parameters can all be used both when initially loading Data Monitor and after Data Monitor is already resident. However, before you turn on any utility from

the command line, you should configure it following the steps in the previous sections. Also, if you don't turn a utility on when Data Monitor is initially loaded (either explicitly or with the /LOAD parameter), you won't be able to turn it on later because it won't be available in memory.

The following are a few examples of using Data Monitor command-line parameters:

DATAMON /LOAD

This command loads Data Monitor based exclusively on your configuration settings.

DATAMON /LOAD /WRITE-

This command loads Data Monitor based on your configuration settings with the exception of Write Protection, which it turns off regardless of your settings.

DATAMON /SCREEN+ /DATALOCK+

This command turns on the Screen Blanker and Directory Lock utilities, but *only* those utilities. In other words, if this command is used to load Data Monitor, the other utilities you turned on during configuration will *not* be turned on; and if the command is used while Data Monitor is resident, it will have absolutely no effect on the status of the other three utilities.

DATAMON /ALL+

This command turns on all Data Monitor utilities (except Delete Tracker, which conflicts with Delete Sentry). However, it's only effective if you've previously configured all the utilities. In addition, if you run it when Data Monitor is resident, it will only turn on those utilities that were on when Data Monitor was initially loaded (since the rest of them won't be available in memory).

DATAMON /ALL-

This command turns off all Data Monitor utilities. If Data Monitor is resident and its utilities conflict with another program you want to run, you may find using this easier than clearing all programs loaded after Data Monitor and then unloading it with the DATAMON /U command.

Chapter *13*

Detecting Viruses Using VDefend

It's appropriate that Chapter 13 is devoted to viruses, both because of the misfortune they can bring, and because of all the superstition surrounding them.

A *virus* is a computer program that's designed to duplicate and attach itself to other programs. Some viruses are benign or mildly irritating. However, other viruses are quite destructive and capable of laying waste to all the data on a hard disk.

There are several ways a virus can spread. The most common method is for it to add portions of its viral code to other programs, so that it's run whenever any of its "host" programs is running. While executing in this way, the virus can attach itself to yet more program files.

Another method is for the virus to attach itself to the boot sector of a system's hard or floppy disk. This ensures that the virus is loaded into a system's memory before any other program. The virus can then spread to other files and disks at its leisure.

A third method is for the virus to be disguised as a legitimate program, also known as a "Trojan horse." These types of viruses tend to be especially pernicious, deleting files and even destructively low-level formatting hard disks while on the surface making a pretense of performing some useful or entertaining function.

How likely is it that your particular system will be hit with a virus? According to some experts, not very. For example, in his popular book *Dr. File Finder's Guide to Shareware* (Callahan: Osborne/McGraw-Hill, 1990), author Mike Callahan writes, "In over seven years of being online—having unpacked and tested thousands of programs from all over the United States, so that my collection of shareware consumes well over a gigabyte of space—I have never encountered even one program that was intentionally designed to do harm." Not everyone would be willing to make such an extreme statement, but it's fair to say that there's too much hysteria concerning viruses, and the odds of a typical system encountering one aren't enormous.

On the other hand, though, viruses *do* exist and are estimated to wreak havoc on thousands of PCs every year. As long as there's *any* chance that your system may one day become infected by some new program you've installed on your hard disk, you may want to take a few precautions. That's where the PC Tools utility VDefend comes in.

Using VDefend

VDefend, which is new to PC Tools 7, is a memory-resident program that constantly scans your system for signs of viruses. Specifically, it checks any program that you run or copy for the telltale code patterns, or *signatures,* of over 400 viruses that have been catalogued in the past decade. In addition, VDefend warns you whenever a program attempts to perform a low-level format, since this is a favored tool of intentionally destructive programs for eradicating all the data on a hard disk.

To load VDefend, you can simply type **VDEFEND** from the DOS prompt and press ENTER. This procedure is especially recommended right before you're about to install and run a program you haven't had any experience with.

Alternatively, if you install new programs frequently, or if you just prefer to have increased security, you can use the PC Tools Install program to insert VDefend into your AUTOEXEC.BAT file. The utility will then be loaded into memory automatically every time you start your PC.

*VDefend can monitor a NOVELL network if you include the parameter /N (that is, type **VDEFEND /N** in the system's AUTOEXEC.BAT file and place the command before the network drivers. However, this option may prevent you from later unloading certain memory-resident programs.*

*If you ever need to reclaim the 18K of conventional memory that VDefend takes up to make room for other software, you can unload the utility by first clearing any memory-resident programs you may have loaded after VDefend, and then typing **VDEFEND /U** from the DOS prompt and pressing ENTER.*

When VDefend is loaded, it invisibly and constantly scans your PC for signs of viruses. As long as your system appears secure, you won't notice VDefend's presence. The program will only make itself known under two circumstances.

First, if VDefend detects an attempt to low-level format your hard disk, it brings up a dialog box giving you the options of Continue, **S**top, and **B**oot. If you intentionally initiated a nondestructive low-level format via a disk optimizing program such as Gibson's SpinRite II or PC Tools' own DiskFix, select Continue to allow the operation to proceed undisturbed. However, if you did *not* initiate the low-level format, select **S**top to make VDefend thwart the program that did by sending back an error message saying the formatting couldn't be performed. If the offending program then tries again, select **B**oot to clear your system's memory by restarting your PC.

Second, if VDefend detects a virus, it brings up a dialog box informing you of the virus' presence, identifies the virus by the name it's commonly known by, and instructs you to use an anti-virus program to disinfect your disk.

Because new viruses crop up all the time, you should periodically update VDefend's list of known viruses. If you have a modem, you can do so by downloading the file SIGNATUR.CPS from either the Central Point BBS (503-690-6650) or the Central Point forum on CompuServe. For more information about using modems, see Chapter 26, "Using Telecommunications."

If you *do* encounter a virus, arguably the safest procedure to follow is to turn off your computer and call in a PC security consultant who's an expert in handling destructive software. If this isn't a cost-effective course of action for you, however, you can probably deal with the problem yourself.

First, delete any programs from your hard disk that you have reason to suspect are infected. If you believe the original copies of these programs are sound, copy them back to your hard disk from the original disks (but first place write-protect tabs over the disks to guard against *their* being infected).

Second, use CP Backup (covered in Chapters 1 through 3) to select *all* your files and then check them for viruses via the **O**ptions **B**ackup Method **V**irus Scan Only command. If any suspect files are found, select the **R**ename command to rename them with V*nn* extensions (*nn* being a number code from 00 to 99). When the scan is completed, exit CP Backup and use PC Shell's File **L**ocate and File **D**elete commands (covered in Chapter 16) to locate and delete the files.

Third, write-protect the Recovery disk you created when installing PC Tools 7, boot up from the disk, and use the Rebuild program to overwrite your hard disk's current boot sector and partition table with the versions on the floppy (as covered in "Restoring Your CMOS DATA, Partition Table, and Boot Record" in Chapter 6).

If you still experience problems after executing these steps, you might want to consider reformatting your hard disk using a write-protected DOS disk that you're certain is uninfected, and then restoring the hard disk data from a previous backup you've made with CP Backup.

A more elegant solution, however, is to try using one of the many antivirus packages now on the market. For example, Central Point Software, the publisher of PC Tools, also publishes a program called Central Point Anti-Virus.

PC Tools can sometimes mistake a normal file that coincidentally contains a viral code pattern for an infected one. Using a specialized program designed to deal with viruses in depth will help you better determine if a file is genuinely infected.

Of course, no program will ever make your PC entirely secure. Eugene Spafford is well known for remarking that "The only truly secure system is one that is powered off, cast in a block of concrete, and sealed in a lead-lined room with armed guards—and even then I have my doubts." Ultimately, what you should seek is a balance between a reasonable degree of security and a high degree of ease and comfort in using your system.

Both the CP Backup program (covered in Chapters 1 through 3) and the DiskFix program (covered in Chapter 7) can automatically scan your data for viruses using the same SIGNATUR.CPS file that VDefend does. Therefore, even if you never run VDefend, performing routine maintenance with these programs will provide you with some measure of security.

Chapter 14

Connecting Computers Using Commute

 If you've ever wanted to access programs on your office PC from home or while travelling; or if you often need to communicate with another workstation on your network; or if your job is to support PC users scattered among different locations, then you'll appreciate the usefulness of Commute, which is new to PC Tools 7.

Commute is a program that lets you control another PC from your own system, or give up control of your PC to another system. If your computer is the controlling PC, you'll see everything that appears on the other computer's screen, have access to all of the other computer's data, and be able to type commands and click on options as if you were physically sitting in front of the other PC. This makes it easy to transfer files between systems, diagnose someone else's system, walk someone through solving a software problem remotely, and so on. In addition, Commute provides a "chat" window that lets you and the person at the other PC type messages to each other simultaneously.

Commute works with two PCs that are physically connected in any of three ways:

- By modems attached to both PCs and hooked into telephone lines. This is typically the slowest connection method, but is fine for transferring files and for running programs that don't have a lot of graphics (which can take a long time to transmit to the controlling PC's screen).

- By a NOVELL or IBM Token Ring local area network, or *LAN*. This connection method is typically fast enough to provide a comfortable response rate.

- By a special cable, called a *null modem*, attached to both of the systems' serial ports. This is sometimes referred to as a *direct connection*, because it places nothing in between the two PCs except some wiring. It's typically the fastest method, and is best for performing such activities as running Microsoft Windows remotely from another system.

If you want to use the direct connection method, you must have a null modem that supports lines 2 (transmit data line), 3 (receive data line), 4 (request to send), and 5 (clear to send). Some null modems only support lines 2 and 3, which is good enough for the DeskConnect program (covered in Chapter 18), but is not sufficient for Commute. You can buy an appropriate null modem from almost any PC hardware supplier at a price ranging from about $10 to about $40. If you do, be sure to mention that you need all four of the data lines just specified.

This chapter first explains how to run and configure Commute, and how to use it to connect with other PCs. It then covers Commute menu commands and command-line parameters.

Running and Configuring Commute

To run Commute and configure it for your system, follow these steps:

1. Type **COMMUTE** from the DOS prompt and press ENTER. If this is the first time you've run the program, a dialog box like this appears asking for a Commute user name:

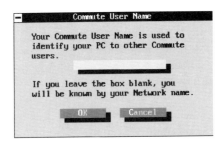

2. As the box explains, your user name will identify you to the other systems you'll be connecting with. If you're on a Novell network, your LAN login name appears as a default.

Accept any default name that's offered, or type a different name up to 20 characters long (optionally including spaces). When you're ready, press ENTER twice or click OK.

3. A dialog box like this asks for your connection type:

If you expect to use commute primarily with modems, press M or click the top option; if you expect to use it mostly with LANs, press L or click the middle option; if you expect to usually use a cable connection, press D or click Direct Connection. (This sets only your *default;* you can always choose a different connection type later on.) When you've made your selection, press ENTER or click OK.

4. If you selected the Direct Connection option, go to step 5; if you selected the LAN option, go to step 6.

   Otherwise, a dialog box appears listing the first of four screens of modem models. Go through the alphabetical list by selecting **Next** and **Prev** until you see either your model or the one most compatible with it (typically one of the Hayes selections that matches your modem's speed). When you're ready, select the appropriate model, and press ENTER or click OK.

5. The following dialog box appears, prompting you to select the port you'll be using:

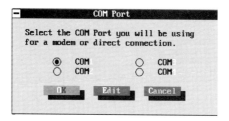

Press the appropriate COM number or click the appropriate option. In addition, if you select COM3 or COM4 and you don't have a PS/2 computer, select the Edit option, and enter the appropriate interrupt and port address numbers (unless they're already filled in for you). For more information on these values, see your modem or serial card manual. When you're done, press ENTER or click OK.

After you've made your COM port selection and any necessary addressing specifications, press O or click OK.

6. You should now see the screen in Figure 14-1. It's from this screen that you'll typically begin your Commute activities.

Exploring the Commute Screen

In the middle of the Commute screen are five command buttons (as well as a diagram to the right showing whether a selected command sets your PC or the other PC to initiate the connection). The five commands are as follows:

- *Call and Take Control*   This option lets you initiate a connection to another PC running Commute and take control of it.

- *Call and Give Control*   This option lets you initiate a connection to another PC running Commute and give control over to it.

- *Wait for Any Caller*   This option forces Commute to exit into the background (taking up about 48K of memory) and return you to the DOS prompt

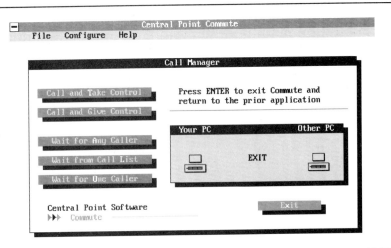

Figure 14-1.   The main Commute screen

so you can work in other applications. Commute will then constantly scan for *any* PC that's trying to initiate a connection and take control of your PC.

- *Wait from Call List*   Like the previous option, this forces Commute to exit into the background and scan for another PC trying to take control. However, it will ignore any PC that doesn't appear on the *Give Control List,* which is a directory of PC user names that you can create (as explained shortly).

- *Wait for One Caller*   Like the previous option, this forces Commute to exit into the background and scan for another PC trying to take control. However, it will ignore all PCs other than the one particular PC you previously selected in the Give Control List.

These commands form the foundation of your Commute operations. They'll be explored in more depth shortly.

Navigating the Commute Menus

In addition to the five command buttons, the top of the screen displays title and menu bars, which contain the four menus available in Commute. Follow these steps to examine the menus:

1. Press F or click File to display the File menu, which lets you set up directories of PCs you call frequently (Private Call List) and PCs that call *you* frequently (Give Control List). In addition, the menu lets you record and print information about your Commute sessions, ignore other PCs, temporarily exit to DOS, exit the Commute screen, and unload Commute from memory.

2. Press RIGHT ARROW to display the Configure menu, which lets you specify the hotkey, modem, COM port, baud rate, connection, user name, security options, schedules, and Auto-Call scripts you use with Commute. In addition, it lets you save your settings for future sessions, or return all settings to the program's initial defaults.

3. Press RIGHT ARROW again to display the Help menu, which lists a number of topics you can read about online.

4. Press ESC and ALT-SPACEBAR to display the Control menu, which lets you display the program's version number and exit the program.

5. Press ESC to close the menu. You're returned to the Commute screen.

Of these menus (shown in Figure 14-2), Control and Help are in most PC Tools programs and are discussed in this book's Introduction. However, Configure and File are specific to Commute and are covered in the following sections.

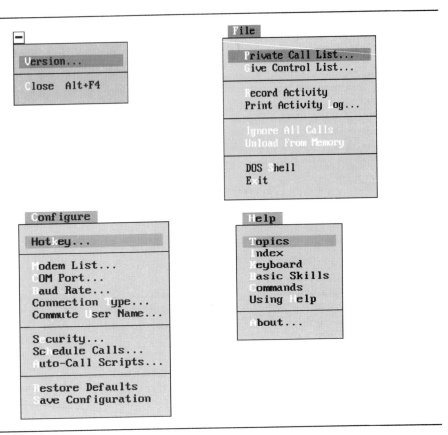

Figure 14-2.   *The Commute menus*

Conducting a Sample Commute Session

One of the most common uses for Commute is to dial into your office PC from a home computer or laptop. Follow these steps to set this up and to get a feel for using Commute:

1. First, bring up the Commute screen on your office PC. If you haven't previously set the connection type to be "modem," press C, T, M, O, or click on the Configure menu and select Connection Type, Connect by Modem, and OK.

2. If you haven't previously selected your modem model, COM port, and baud rate, do so now using the Configure menu options **Modem List**, **COM Port**, and **Baud Rate**. (For example, to set a baud rate of 2400, press C, B, 2, O.)

3. Set a security option to prevent anyone but you from taking control of your PC remotely. First, press C, E, or click on the Configure menu and select Security. The following Security Settings dialog box appears:

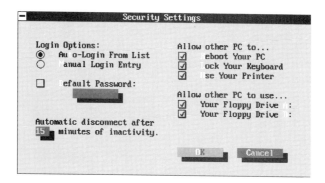

This box lets you set whether a calling PC logs into your PC automatically or manually, whether the calling PC must supply a password, the number of minutes of inactivity you'll allow before a session is disconnected, and the degree of control the other PC is allowed to have over your PC (for example, whether it can reboot your PC, and whether it can use its printer and floppy drives).

4. Turn on **Default Password** by pressing ALT-D or clicking the option, and then type a password up to ten characters long. Make sure the password is one that's very easy for you to remember, while difficult for others to guess. (Asterisks will appear as you type to ensure that anyone looking over your shoulder cannot see your password.) When you're done, press ALT-O or click OK. You're returned to the main Commute screen.

5. Make sure your modem is turned on and connected to your PC, and that a phone line is plugged into the modem. When your system is set up properly, press A or click the Wait for Any Caller command button. This allows your PC to respond to any caller. However, it will only give control to a caller providing the password you set in the previous step.

6. The Connection Type dialog box now appears to ensure that you've set it properly for this particular session. Your modem setting is still in effect, so just press ENTER or click OK.

7. A Configuration Settings box now appears, prompting you to save your settings for future sessions. If you want to do so, press ENTER or click Save Current Settings. (You can always return to the program's built-in default settings by selecting the Configure Restore Defaults option.) Alternatively, press E or click Exit Without Saving to use your settings for the current session only.

8. Commute now checks to make sure your modem is on and connected, and then exits to the background, displays the message "Restoring Application...," and returns you to DOS. Your office PC is now set up to await your call.

If you ever need to bring up the Commute screen while it's in the background, press ALT-RIGHT SHIFT *(that is, hold down the* ALT *key and press the right* SHIFT *key).*

9. From your home PC or laptop, repeat steps 1 and 2 to set up Commute on your calling computer properly.

10. From the Commute main screen, press T or click Call and Take Control. A Private Call List box like this appears:

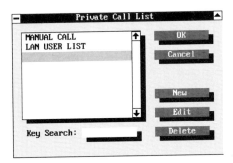

This List provides a directory of PCs you call frequently. (You can also bring this List up whenever you want to add or revise entries by selecting the **File Private Call List** option.)

11. Select MANUAL CALL. If you aren't already on the option, move to it using the arrow keys, and then press ENTER; or just double-click the option. The following dialog box prompts you to enter a phone number:

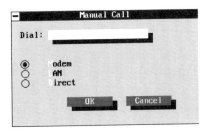

12. Type the phone number of your office PC. If you need to include a digit for an outside line, add a comma after the digit to pause briefly after it.

Furthermore, be sure to include any other necessary prefixes (for example, a 1 and an area code if you're dialing long distance). You can also optionally include spaces, dashes, and parentheses for readability, because these symbols are ignored by the program. For example, to dial a long distance number, you might type **1 (415) 555-5555**.

Also, if the connection type listed in the box isn't **M**odem, press ALT-M or click the top connection option.

13. Make sure your modem is on and connected to your PC, and that a phone line is plugged into your modem. When you're ready, make the call by pressing ENTER twice or clicking OK.

14. Commute dials from your current, or *local*, PC into your office, or *remote*, PC, and then displays a dialog box that shows the status of your connection. First, its "Initializing Communications" message changes to "Communications Initialized." Second, the "Calling *number*" message changes to "Call Answered—*nnnn* Baud." Third, the "Establishing Connection" message changes to "Connection Established." Fourth, a checkmark appears next to the "Waiting for Other PC" message. Finally, you're prompted for your password. When this occurs, type it and press ALT-O. After a moment, the screen of your other PC appears on your screen.

    You now have total access to your remote PC's resources. Using your keyboard or mouse, you can control the other PC as if you were actually sitting in front of it, and you can run any of its programs. (Meanwhile, if the other PC's keyboard has a SCROLL LOCK light, the light blinks to indicate that the system is being controlled remotely.)

15. Press ALT-RIGHT SHIFT (that is, hold down the ALT key and press the right SHIFT key). The Commute Session Manager menu in Figure 14-3 appears. This menu makes it easy to transfer files from one PC to the other, temporarily switch to your local PC's screen, and exit your session.

16. If you want to transfer files from the remote PC, press G or click Get Files from Other PC. A dialog box appears that prompts you for the *path* (meaning the drive and directory) and name (including the DOS wildcards * and ?) of the files you want to receive from your other PC, and the path you want to store them in on your current system. In addition, it provides you with the options of compressing files to make the transfer faster, overwriting existing files with the same names without being prompted for verification, checking transferred files for virus signatures (see Chapter 13), including subdirectories within the directory you've specified, copying on the basis of archive bit settings and clearing the bit after copying (see "Backup Methods and Strategies" in Chapter 2), and overwriting files with the same names only when the copies are newer than the originals. When you're done selecting the options you want, press ALT-O or click OK to execute the transfer. Alternatively, press ESC or click Cancel to abort the operation.

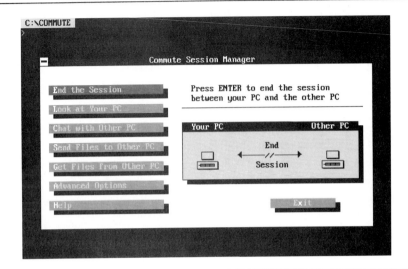

Figure 14-3.   *The Commute Session Manager menu*

17. If you want to transfer files *to* the remote PC, press S or click Send Files to Other PC from the Session Manager menu. A dialog box appears that is similar to the one described in step 16, except that it prompts you for the path and name of the files you want to send to (rather than receive from) your remote PC, and the path you want to store them in on your remote PC (rather than your local PC). Again, when you're done selecting the options you want, press ALT-O or click OK to execute the transfer; or press ESC or click Cancel to abort the operation.

18. If you want to temporarily use your local PC from the Session Manager, press L or click on Look at Your PC. You're switched to your local PC's screen, where you can run whatever DOS commands or programs you require. When you're done, type **EXIT** from the DOS prompt and press ENTER. After a moment, you're returned to the remote PC's display. To bring up the Session Manager again, press ALT-RIGHT SHIFT again.

19. If you have someone near your remote PC, you can communicate with him or her from the Session Manager by pressing C or clicking Chat with Other PC. This brings up a Chat box that lets you type comments in the top half and the other person type comments in the bottom half. (If necessary, first get the other person's attention by pressing F10 to make the remote PC beep.) Both of you can type simultaneously in the Chat box, so you don't have to

worry about waiting for each other or interrupting each other. When you're done chatting, press ESC to close the box.

20. If you want to explore additional Session Manager options, press A or click Advanced Options. The menu's main options are replaced by options to **Re**boot Other PC (only useful if Commute is set to load in the other PC's AUTOEXEC.BAT file); **L**ock Other Keyboard (useful if you want to prevent anyone from interrupting you); **P**rint Direction (which specifies whether to use your local printer or the remote printer); Redraw Your Screen (which refreshes your display when older graphic elements make it confusing to look at); **S**ave Current Screen (which saves your underlying screen in an ASCII text format); Screen **O**ptions (which lets you set your screen resolution, colors, and refresh rate); and **K**eyboard Level (which switches between Standard and Enhanced settings for the remote keyboard, and is useful when you encounter keyboard problems). You can also check the status of your current settings by simply moving to each option using DOWN ARROW and looking at the diagram display in the right side of the menu box.

    When you're done using the Advanced Options menu, press ESC or click Exit. You're returned to the Session Manager menu.

21. When you're done using your remote PC, press ALT-RIGHT SHIFT to bring up the Session Manager, and press ENTER or click End the Session. A Please Confirm dialog box appears asking you to verify that you want to disconnect. Press ENTER or click OK. The remote PC breaks contact and returns to its previous status of waiting for a call, while your local PC returns to the main Commute screen.

22. Press ESC and ENTER to exit Commute and keep it resident, or press F, U to exit Commute and unload it from memory. In either case, you're returned to the DOS prompt.

You now have a solid feel for using Commute with a modem connection. To use a direct cable connection instead, employ a similar procedure, but select the **Direct** Connection option in step 1, and leave the phone field blank and select the **Direct** option in step 12.

Similarly, to use a LAN connection, select the Connect by **LAN** option in step 1. Also, in steps 11 and 12, select the LAN USER LIST entry in the Private Call List box to display a list of login user names, and then select the workstation you want to connect to.

Using the Configure Menu

When you first ran Commute, you answered several prompts to complete a bare-bones configuration of the program. You can use the **Configure** menu to change these initial settings, and also to adjust other settings that give you greater flexibility in your use of Commute. To explore these options, follow these steps:

1. From the main Commute screen, press C or click on Configure to display the 11 Configure menu options.

2. Notice that the second group of options are Modem List, **COM** Port, **B**aud Rate, Connection **T**ype, and Commute User Name. These bring up the same configuration dialog boxes you saw earlier when running the program. For example, press T or click Connection Type. The Connection Type dialog box you filled in earlier reappears. You can use these options to change your initial settings at any time.

3. Press ESC, C to return to the Configure menu, and select the top option by pressing ENTER or clicking Hotkey. The following dialog box appears:

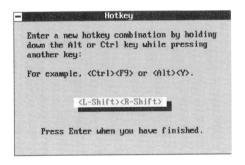

This box sets the keystroke that will bring up the Commute main screen when the program is waiting for a call, or the Commute Session Manager menu when a session is in progress. As noted in the previous section, its default is ALT-RIGHT SHIFT. You can set a different invoking keystroke, or *hotkey*, by pressing the keystroke and then pressing ENTER. However, make sure the keystroke you choose doesn't conflict with any other programs you're using, such as the PC Shell hotkey (see Chapter 15) or the Desktop Manager's hotkeys (see Chapter 28).

4. Press ESC, C to return to the Configure menu, and press A or click Auto-Call Scripts. An Auto-Call Scripts dialog box appears that lets you create a sequence of commands, called an *Auto-Call script*, that can run a Commute session automatically.

    To create a new script, press ALT-N, type a script name and press ALT-O, and then generate appropriate commands in the Script File Editor screen. Details on writing scripts are beyond the scope of this book, but you can get more information by pressing F1 from this screen. When you're done, press ALT-S to save your script and press ESC to close the Auto-Call Scripts box.

5. Press C to return to the **C**onfigure menu, and press H or click Schedule. A Schedule Calls dialog box appears that lets you schedule Commute sessions to take place at certain days and times, even if you're not at your PC. This is particularly effective when used in combination with an Auto-Call script, which can execute a number of commands automatically. For more information, see the following "Scheduling Commute" section.

6. Press ESC, C to return to the **C**onfigure menu, and press E or click Security. The dialog box used in the previous tutorial to set a password appears. As explained previously, this box provides you with the ability to shut out unauthorized callers and restrict the actions of authorized callers.

7. Press ESC, C to return to the **C**onfigure menu. Notice that the last two options are **R**estore Defaults and **S**ave Configuration. **R**estore Defaults clears all your settings and replaces them with the defaults originally built into the program. On the other hand, **S**ave Configuration preserves all your current settings to disk so that they'll be used by Commute in future sessions.

8. Press ESC to close the menu again.

Scheduling Commute

As mentioned previously, you can schedule Commute to run on specified days and times, even while you're away from your PC. This is useful if you need to make Commute available to a calling PC at certain times but prefer to keep it out of your system's memory the rest of the time. It's also convenient if you want to perform some procedure (such as transferring files between systems) automatically at specified times using an Auto-Call script. You can set up to ten different Commute schedules.

 For scheduling to work, you must keep resident either the PC Tools Desktop (see Chapter 23, "Using the Appointment Scheduler") or the new CP Scheduler program. Both of these programs will regularly check a scheduling file you create within Commute.

To schedule a Commute session, follow these steps:

1. If CP Scheduler isn't already resident, unload Commute, load the Scheduler by typing **CPSCHED** at the DOS prompt and pressing ENTER, and run Commute again.

2. From the main Commute screen, press C, H, or click on the Configure menu and select Schedule Calls. A dialog box appears that lets you enter the name

of an Auto-Call script file to run the Commute session. In addition, the box lets you specify on which days and time you want the session to occur.

3. Press ENTER or click New, and then type in the name of the Auto-Call script file you want to use.

4. Move to a day you want to include in the schedule using TAB or SHIFT-TAB, and then press ENTER to select it. Alternatively, just click below the day. In either case, a checkmark appears to show that the day has been selected.

   Repeat this procedure until you've selected every day that you want to include in the schedule.

5. Use TAB or your mouse to move to the Run Time field.

6. Specify the time to run the session in *HH:MM*a or *HH:MM*p format, where *HH* represents hours, *MM* represents minutes, and "a" and "p" optionally represent A.M. and P.M. (For example, to specify 5:30 P.M., type either **5:30p** or **17:30**.)

7. When you're done specifying your schedule, press ALT-O or click OK. You're now offered the options of specifying another session schedule (you can have up to ten); modifying an existing session schedule; deleting an existing session schedule; saving the schedule you've just defined; or canceling the operation.

8. Press S or click Save. Your schedule is saved to the file COMMUTE.TM, which is regularly checked by both CP Scheduler and the Desktop's Appointment Scheduler.

When your scheduled time arrives, a 15-second notice appears. If you don't respond to the notice, any application currently running is interrupted and your Commute session is executed as specified. When the operation is completed, Commute exits, and your system is returned to its previous state.

Using the File Menu

When you want to call a PC or accept a call from a PC, it's convenient to have the user names and phone numbers of these systems already available in a directory. To access these directories, as well as several other useful features, follow these steps:

1. Press F or click on File to display the eight **F**ile menu options.

2. Notice that the first option is **P**rivate Call List. If you select it by pressing ENTER or clicking it, a directory of PCs you can call appears. The directory initially consists of only two options, MANUAL CALL and LAN USER LIST, as shown here:

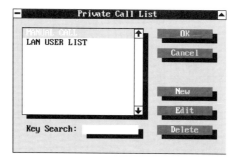

You can use the **N**ew option to add a new entry to the list. This makes the entry available for quick selection in future sessions when you choose the Call and **T**ake Control command.

3. Press ESC, F to display the **F**ile menu again, and this time select the second option by pressing G or clicking **G**ive Control List. A directory of PCs that you'll allow to take control of your PC appears.

   Initially, the directory consists of only your own user name. If you plan on dialing into your own system, you should select this and the **E**dit option to specify a phone number, password, and other security options. You can also add additional PCs to the List by selecting the **N**ew option.

4. Press ESC, F to display the **F**ile menu again. The third option, **R**ecord Activity, is a switch that you can toggle on or off. When on, it records the start and end times of each of your Commute sessions, who you were connected to, and which files were transferred. This information is stored in a compressed format in a file named COMMUTE.LOG. You can expand this file into a normal text file, or print it out on paper, by selecting the Print Activity **L**og option.

The last four options on the menu all involve activities peripheral to conducting Commute sessions. Specifically:

- The **I**gnore All Calls option is a switch that you can turn on to refuse callers while you keep Commute active for your own use.

- The DOS **S**hell option lets you switch to DOS temporarily to run a program or DOS command without exiting Commute. When you're done, typing **EXIT** from the DOS prompt and pressing ENTER returns you to the Commute screen.

- The **E**xit option has one of two effects, depending on Commute's status. If Commute is already resident, **E**xit forces it back into the background and returns you to your underlying application, allowing you to bring up the Commute screen again at any time by pressing ALT-RIGHT SHIFT. However, if

Commute *isn't* already resident, **Exit** simply closes the program and clears it from memory, freeing up space for other programs.

- The **Unload** from Memory option both exits Commute and clears it from memory, freeing up space for other programs. Unlike **Exit**, **Unload** is available only when Commute is already resident.

To close the **File** menu, press ESC. You're returned to the Commute main screen.

Commute Parameters

You can specify certain options, called *parameters*, following Commute's program name. You can include any single parameter (for example, COMMUTE /R) or combine a number of parameters (for example, COMMUTE /RGL /BT=ON /DR=AB /PR=ON) to achieve the effect you want. Keep in mind that parameters require a *forward* slash (/, located on the bottom of the ? key) as opposed to the backslash (\) used to specify DOS directories.

Commute supports 33 parameters specific to the program. These fall into four categories—General, Memory-Resident, Communication Configuration, and Security—and are covered in the following four sections.

General Parameters

- **/?**   This "help" parameter lists and briefly describes each parameter specific to Commute. It should not be combined with any other parameter.

- **/VIDEO**   This "help" parameter lists and briefly describes the standard PC Tools video and mouse parameters. It should not be combined with any other parameters. For more information, see the "Video and Mouse Parameters" section in Appendix A, "PC Tools Installation and Configuration."

- *scriptname*   This parameter sets an Auto-Call script to run as soon as Commute is loaded. (For example, to run a script file named SUPPORT.CSF, type **COMMUTE SUPPORT**.) It should precede any other parameters.

- *listname*   This parameter sets Commute to call the specified name from your Private Call List. It should precede any other parameters except *scriptname*.

- *username*   This parameter sets Commute to call the specified user name when using a LAN connection. It should precede any other parameters except *scriptname*.

- **/8250**   This parameter eliminates problems when you're using Commute with a modem or direct cable connection and have a defective 8250 UART chip.

- **/AL=ON** or **OFF**   This parameter turns Commute activity recording on and off.

- **/CF**   This parameter sets Commute to go through the initial configuration process as if you were running the program for the first time.

- **/NA=*name***   This parameter sets your Commute user name.

Memory-Resident Parameters

- **/NE**   This parameter prevents Commute from using your system's expanded memory for buffers and swap files.

- **/NL**   This parameter specifies that no LAN is available and prevents the LAN driver from being loaded, saving about 4K of memory.

- **/NU**   This parameter prevents Commute from loading in the high memory blocks between 640K and 1MB, preserving this area for other programs.

- **/NX**   This parameter prevents Commute from using your system's extended memory for buffers and swap files.

- **/R** or **/RL**   These parameters set Commute to load into memory and then wait in the background for a caller to either take control of your PC or give control to your PC. The /R parameter accepts any caller, while the /RL parameter restricts accepted callers to those on your Call List.

- **/RG** or **/RGL**   This parameter sets Commute to load into memory and then wait in the background for a caller to take control of your PC. The /RG parameter accepts any caller, while the /RGL parameter restricts accepted callers to those on your Call List.

- **/RT**   This parameter sets Commute to load into memory and then wait in the background to take control of any PC that calls in.

- **/U**   This parameter unloads Commute from memory, preventing any further Commute connections with other PCs and freeing up room for other programs.

Communication Configuration Parameters

- **/BR=*nnnnnn***   This parameter sets the baud rate to use with Commute, where *nnnnnn* is 1200, 2400, 4800, 9600, 19200, 38400, 57600, or 115200.

- **/CP=***n*   This parameter sets the COM port to be used by Commute, where *n* is 1, 2, 3, or 4.

- **/CT=D** or **L** or **M**   This parameter specifies the type of connection you'll be using with Commute, where D represents a direct cable connection, M represents a modem connection, and L represents a LAN connection. (For example, if you're using a LAN connection, type **COMMUTE /CT=L**.)

- **/MA=***string*   This parameter sets the modem answer string. If the string includes a space, enclose the entire string in quotation marks (for example, "*string1 string2*").

- **/MD=***string*   This parameter sets the modem dial string.

- **/MH=***string*   This parameter sets the modem hangup string.

- **/MI=***string*   This parameter sets the modem initialization string.

Security Parameters

- **/BT=ON** or **OFF**   If set to ON, this parameter allows the controlling PC to reboot your PC; if set to OFF, it prevents remote rebooting.

- **/DPW=***password*   This parameter sets the default password to use with Commute. If *password* is left out (that is, if a blank space follows the = sign), password-protection is turned off.

- **/DR=A** or **B** or **AB** or **N**   This parameter sets which of your floppy disk drives a controlling PC can use, where A represents the A drive only, B represents the B drive only, AB represents both drives, and N represents neither drive.

- **/IA=***n*   This parameter sets how many minutes inactivity is allowed before Commute automatically disconnects a session, where *n* is any number from 0 to 60.

- **/L=A** or **M**   This parameter selects the Auto-Login (A) or Manual Login (M) security option.

- **/LK=ON** or **OFF**   If set to ON, this parameter allows the controlling PC to lock your keyboard; if set to OFF, it prevents keyboard locking.

- **/PR=ON** or **OFF**   If set to ON, this parameter allows the controlling PC to use your printer; if set to OFF, it prevents the other PC from accessing your printer.

Commute Command Reference

Much of Commute's power lies in its menu commands, which help you configure the program's settings and automate its operations. Like many PC Tools programs, Commute's first menu is Control and its last menu is Help. These menus are covered in this book's Introduction.

Commute also contains two other menus: File and Configure. The following sections cover the options in these menus. After the name of each option are the keystrokes that invoke it, a description of what the option does, and a reference to the section in this chapter that discusses the option in detail.

The File Menu

The File menu lets you set up directories of PCs you call frequently and that call you frequently, record and print information about your Commute sessions, ignore calls, temporarily exit to DOS, exit Commute, and unload Commute from memory. It contains the following eight options:

Private Call List (F, P)

Brings up directory of PCs you can call and take control of. Covered in "Using the File Menu."

Give Control List (F, G)

Brings up directory of callers who you'll allow to take control of your PC. Covered in "Using the File Menu."

Record Activity (F, R)

When on, records when each session begins and ends, who the session is with, and what files were transferred. Covered in "Using the File Menu."

Print Activity **L**og (F, L)

Prints or translates as a text file the record of your Commute sessions. Covered in "Using the File Menu."

Ignore All Calls (F, I)

Sets Commute to ignore all callers. Covered in "Using the File Menu."

Unload From Memory (F, U)

Exits Commute and unloads it from memory, freeing up room for other programs. Covered in "Using the File Menu."

DOS **S**hell (F, S)

Temporarily exits to DOS. Typing **EXIT** and pressing ENTER returns to Commute. Covered in "Using the File Menu."

E**x**it (F, X)

Exits the Commute screen without prompting for confirmation. If Commute was resident, it remains resident in the background. Covered in "Using the File Menu."

The Configure Menu

The **C**onfigure menu lets you specify the hotkey, modem, COM port, baud rate, connection, user name, security options, schedules, and Auto-Call scripts you use with Commute. In addition, it lets you save your settings for future sessions, or clear your settings to the program's initial defaults. It contains the following 11 options:

Hotkey (C, K)

Sets the keystroke to invoke Commute when it's memory resident. Covered in "Using the Configure Menu."

Modem List (C, M)

Specifies the model of modem you're using for Commute modem connections. Covered in "Using the Configure Menu."

COM Port (C, C)

Sets the COM port you're using with Commute for modem and cable connections. Covered in "Using the Configure Menu."

Baud Rate (C, B)

Sets the baud rate you're using with Commute for modem and cable connections. Covered in "Using the Configure Menu."

Connection **T**ype (C, T)

Specifies your connection for the session as **Modem, LAN,** or **D**irect (cable). Covered in "Using the Configure Menu."

Commute **U**ser Name (C, U)

Sets your Commute user name. Covered in "Using the Configure Menu."

Security (C, E)

Sets login, password, disconnect, and access restrictions when you give control of your PC to another PC. Covered in "Using the Configure Menu."

Schedule Calls (C, H)

Schedules Auto-Call scripts to run on specified days and times automatically. Covered in "Using the Configure Menu."

Auto-Call Scripts (C, A)

Brings up a list of your Auto-Call scripts, and lets you create, edit, rename, and delete scripts. Covered in "Using the Configure Menu."

Restore Defaults (C, R)

Restores **C**onfigure menu options to their initial default settings. Covered in "Using the Configure Menu."

Save Configuration (C, S)

Saves your **C**onfigure menu settings to disk for future sessions. Covered in "Using the Configure Menu."

Part *V*

Using PC Shell

Chapter *15*

PC Shell Overview

PC Shell is a powerful file and disk management program that's easy to learn and use. It lets you perform basic operations such as copying, moving, renaming, and deleting files; moving and renaming directories; and formatting, copying, and comparing disks.

It also lets you perform advanced operations such as searching for files based on their names or contents, displaying technical information about a file or disk, editing the sectors of a file or disk, and using DOS commands instead of menu commands.

In addition, PC Shell offers special features that go well beyond the abilities of typical file and disk managers. These include an application launcher, which lets you select a file and then automatically run the program that created it; file viewers, which show you data files in the formats of their applications without requiring you to load the applications; DeskConnect, which lets you transfer data between two computers connected by cable; and full support for network-compatible DOS functions on NOVELL and IBM PC LAN networks.

Despite its many powerful features, however, PC Shell is easy to use. It displays directories in a tree format that clearly illustrates how your disk is organized, and then shows you the files of any directory you select. It also lists its commands in menus you can operate with either the keyboard or a mouse. The menus save you from having to remember which commands are available and make it simple to choose the commands you want.

Perhaps best of all, PC Shell can be installed memory resident, taking up as little as 12K of conventional memory (or, if you're using a high memory manager, virtually 0K). When resident, it can be invoked at any time with a single keystroke. This means that if you're in the middle of an application and suddenly need to format a disk, or manipulate files, or use a DOS command, or even run an entirely different application, you can press the keystroke and bring up PC Shell to do the job. When you're finished and exit PC Shell, you're returned to precisely where you left off in the application.

This chapter covers running PC Shell, exploring PC Shell's screen elements, using the program's configuration options, and exiting the program. It then describes PC Shell parameters, PC Shell files, new PC Shell features in PC Tools 7, and all PC Shell menu commands.

After reading this chapter to get an overview of PC Shell, read Chapters 16, 17, and 18 for detailed information on its various features. Specifically:

- Chapter 16, "Managing Your Files," covers how to copy, move, rename, delete, compare, verify, find, examine, edit, and print files.

- Chapter 17, "Managing Your Directories and Disks," covers how to select, create, copy, move, rename, delete, examine, and print directories. It also explains how to format, copy, compare, verify, search, rename, examine, and park disks.

- Chapter 18, "Using Advanced PC Shell Features," covers how to run programs from PC Shell, transfer data between adjacent computers, edit sectors, and display system information.

Running PC Shell

Once you've copied PC Shell's files to your hard disk using Install (see Appendix A, "PC Tools Installation and Configuration"), you're ready to run the program.

PC Shell can be run as either a memory-resident or standalone program. Most people make PC Shell memory resident, but the standalone mode also has certain advantages. These two options are covered in the next two sections.

There are also a number of other options you can specify when starting up PC Shell. These are covered later in the section "PC Shell Parameters."

Running PC Shell Memory Resident

To run PC Shell as a memory-resident program, type **PCSHELL /R** from the DOS prompt and press ENTER. (Be sure to use a *forward* slash before the "R," not a backslash.) PC Shell loads itself as resident, taking up about 12K of conventional memory, and a message like this appears:

```
PCTOOLS PC Shell (TM)
Version 7
Copyright (c) 1985-1991
Central Point Software, Inc.
462 Kbytes free
Hotkey: <CTRL> <ESC>
```

You're then returned to the DOS prompt. PC Shell will now wait invisibly in the background while you work in other applications.

You can automate this step by entering the command into your AUTOEXEC.BAT file (including it after all PC Tools programs except the Desktop), or by having the Install program enter it for you. For more information, see Appendix A.

When you want to bring up PC Shell, press CTRL-ESC. PC Shell first saves your current application to disk (or, if available, to expanded memory, which greatly speeds the invoking process). PC Shell then loads its own files, taking up about 480K of conventional memory, and displays a screen like the one in Figure 15-1. The program is then ready for your use.

If using CTRL-ESC as the keystroke, or hotkey, to invoke PC Shell creates program conflicts in your system, you can define a different hotkey, using the /Fn parameter (see "PC Shell Parameters" later in this chapter) or the SWAPSH parameters (see the next section).

Alternative PC Shell Loading Options

In addition to the basic procedure just described, there are several other ways in which you can run PC Shell resident.

First, you can use the /RL (or /RLARGE) parameter, which loads *all* of PC shell resident, taking up about 480K of conventional memory. This doesn't leave much room for running other programs. However, if you tend to dedicate your system to

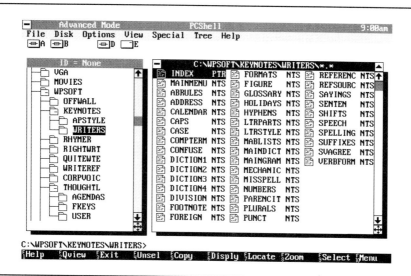

Figure 15-1. *The PC Shell screen*

PC Shell and a few other utilities that don't require much memory (such as the Desktop in its resident mode), it enables you to invoke PC Shell instantly from RAM.

The /RSMALL and /RMEDIUM parameters from PC Shell 6 are not supported in version 7.

Second, if you have enough extended memory available to create a RAM disk of 800K, you can use the /O*d* parameter to store PC Shell temporary files on the disk, using *d* to specify the letter of the drive. (For example, if your RAM drive's letter is E, use the command line **PCSHELL /R /OE**.) Like the /RL parameter, this makes PC Shell come up almost instantly when you invoke it. However, this method takes up only 12K of conventional memory, leaving you plenty of room for running other programs. (You can use this option with expanded memory, as well, but it usually isn't necessary because PC Shell's /R parameter is set to automatically take advantage of expanded memory.)

Third, you can use the new SWAPSH program to swap PC Shell to extended or expanded memory, or to disk. If you do so, PC Shell will take up no room at all in conventional memory, while the SWAPSH program will take up about 9K (a net savings of 3K). In addition, if you're using a memory manager such as DOS 5's EMM386, you can load SWAPSH in high memory, so that it takes up virtually 0K of conventional memory.

To use SWAPSH from the DOS prompt, type **SWAPSH** and press ENTER. This loads PC Shell automatically, taking up 9K instead of 12K of conventional memory. Also, if you have enough expanded or extended memory, it automatically swaps PC Shell there so the program can come up almost instantly when you invoke it.

A better alternative, however, is to use SWAPSH from your AUTOEXEC.BAT file. When you do so, you should include the following *two* command lines:

LH SWAPSH /N

PCSHELL /R

The LH option loads SWAPSH into high memory if you're using a memory manager, so that virtually no space is taken up in conventional memory. The /N parameter prevents PC Shell from being loaded immediately, which would interfere with batch file execution. The "PCSHELL /R" line then loads the program, at which point SWAPSH swaps it to your expanded or extended memory, or (if necessary) to disk.

In addition to memory savings, if you don't want to invoke PC Shell using CTRL-ESC for some reason, SWAPSH gives you the option of using virtually any ALT, CTRL, or SHIFT keystroke instead. Specifically, when loading SWAPSH you can include the parameters /A /K*xx* to specify an ALT keystroke, /C /K*xx* to specify a CTRL keystroke, /L /K*xx* to specify a left SHIFT keystroke, and /R /K*xx* to specify a right SHIFT keystroke, where *xx* is a two-character code representing the letter you want to use.

To see a complete list of letters and their corresponding codes, type **SWAPSH /?** from the DOS prompt and press ENTER twice. For example, to specify ALT-S as your invoking keystroke, use the parameters /A /K1F. In the AUTOEXEC.BAT example mentioned previously, the command lines would look like this:

LH SWAPSH /N /A /K1F

PCSHELL /R

If you want to hotkey out of PC Shell, however (as described in "Exiting PC Shell" later in this chapter), you still have to press CTRL-ESC.

You can alternatively choose a hotkey consisting of CTRL *and any function key from* F1 *to* F10 *(for example,* CTRL-F1*). This approach relies on a PC Shell parameter, and so will work even without SWAPSH. In addition, it allows you to both invoke and exit PC Shell using your designated hotkey. For more information, see the /Fn option in the "PC Shell Parameters" section later in this chapter.*

SWAPSH also supports a few other parameters, such as /U to unload the program, and /P*x* and /T*x* to set the size and transmission speed of the memory buffer used by the PC Shell text editor (see Chapter 16). For a list and description of these parameters, type **SWAPSH /?** from the DOS prompt and press ENTER.

Running PC Shell as a Standalone Program

To run PC Shell as a standalone program, type **PCSHELL** from the DOS prompt and press ENTER. PC Shell loads, taking up about 480K of conventional memory, and displays a screen like the one in Figure 15-1. The program is then ready for your use.

You can automate this step by entering the command into your AUTOEXEC.BAT file (including it after all PC Tools programs except the Desktop), or by having the Install program enter it for you. For more information, see Appendix A.

There are several advantages to running PC Shell as a standalone program. First, it can save you at least 12K in conventional memory when you're not using PC Shell. If you're tight on memory, this extra space can be used for running other memory-resident programs, such as the PC Tools Desktop, Backtalk, or CP Scheduler. The space can also be used to enlarge a RAM disk for speeding file access.

Second, it avoids slowing down other applications. When PC Shell is resident, it monitors your keystrokes while in the background to detect a CTRL-ESC keypress. If your computer is based on an older chip such as the 8088 or if it's running complex applications, PC Shell's activity could create slight decreases in speed. If you use PC Shell only occasionally, you may therefore prefer keeping it out of the background to ensure that it doesn't degrade the performance of other programs.

Third, it may be necessary to run PC Shell nonresident if it conflicts with another program you need to use. For example, Microsoft Windows disables the memory-resident version of PC Shell, so the only way to access the Desktop from Windows is to run it as a standalone program.

In general, however, the advantages of running PC Shell resident significantly outweigh the disadvantages. If you use the program regularly, it's recommended that you make it resident.

Exiting PC Shell

When you're done using PC Shell, you can exit it in several ways.

First, if you're running PC Shell memory resident, you can simply press CTRL-ESC again. This sends it back into the background while retaining its current screen and menu option settings.

Second, you can bring up its Close box by pressing ESC; or ALT-F, X; or ALT-F4; or ALT-SPACEBAR, C. You can also bring up the box by clicking on the File menu and selecting Exit, or by clicking on the Control menu and selecting Close, or simply by double-clicking on the Control menu. When you perform any of these actions, the following dialog box appears:

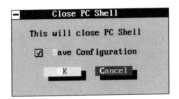

If you've changed your mind about exiting, press ESC or click Cancel. The box closes, and you're returned to the PC Shell screen.

Otherwise, decide whether you want to save your current screen and menu option settings to disk as new defaults. If you do, the Save Configuration option should have a checkmark to its left, while if you don't, no checkmark should appear. You can toggle the checkmark on and off by pressing S or clicking the option.

When you're done, press O or click OK. PC Shell exits and returns you to either the DOS prompt or your underlying application. If you loaded PC Shell memory resident, it's still resident. However, if you ran the program nonresident, it's automatically cleared from memory, freeing up space for other applications.

Unloading PC Shell

If you need to unload PC Shell from memory (for example, so you can run a large application that needs the extra memory PC Shell is using), you can do so in either of two ways.

First, you can type **KILL** from the DOS prompt and press ENTER. This unloads PC Shell from memory, and also unloads the Desktop Manager, Backtalk, Desk-Connect, Commute, and/or CP Scheduler if they were resident, freeing up the space these PC Tools programs were occupying.

Alternatively, you can bring up PC Shell's Special menu and select Remove PC Shell. This command clears PC Shell from memory without affecting any other resident PC Tools programs. However, it requires that you invoked PC Shell from DOS (as opposed to an application program) and that PC Shell was the last program you installed resident.

Exploring the PC Shell Screen

When you bring up PC Shell, the default screen in Figure 15-1 appears. This screen is split into six parts:

- The title and menu bars at the top, which let you access the eight PC Shell menus, and display the current user level and system time.

- The drive bar directly below the menu bar, which displays your available drives and highlights your currently selected drive.

- The Tree List at the left, which displays the directories of your selected drive.

- The File List at the right, which displays the files in your selected directory.

- The DOS command line below the Tree List and File List windows, which lets you run other programs and DOS commands.

- The message bar at the bottom, which displays function key definitions and information on PC Shell's activities.

The PC Shell Title and Menu Bars

At the top of the PC Shell screen is the title bar, which looks like this:

```
[-] Advanced Mode          PCShell                    9:00am
```

The bar contains the word "PCShell" in its center and the system time in its right corner. If your PC doesn't have a built-in clock, be sure to set the correct time at the DOS prompt before starting PC Shell so it can display the time accurately.

The bar also contains the words "Beginner Mode," "Intermediate Mode," or "Advanced Mode" in its left corner. This sets the number of options you'll see on the program's menus. While using this book, it's recommended you stay in Advanced mode, which displays *all* options. To do so, press ALT-O, U, A, O, ALT-O, A. (For more information, see "Setting Your User Level" later in this chapter.)

Finally, the title bar displays a dash in its leftmost corner, which represents the Control menu. As explained in this book's Introduction, the Control menu provides options for showing the version of the program you're using and for exiting the program. In addition, it provides options for changing the selected window's size and position. For more information, see "Using the Control Menu" later in this chapter.

Directly below the title bar is the menu bar, which displays the names of the seven additional menus available in PC Shell. Like other PC Tools programs, PC Shell activates the menu bar when you press ALT. However, unlike the other programs, PC Shell doesn't keep the menu bar active when you release ALT. Therefore, to display a PC Shell menu, you must keep ALT held down while you press the first letter of the menu. For example, instead of displaying the **File** menu by pressing ALT, F, you must press ALT-F.

To examine the PC Shell menus, follow these steps:

1. Press ALT-F or click File to display the **File** menu, which lets you perform such file operations as copying, moving, renaming, deleting, undeleting, editing, and printing.

2. Press RIGHT ARROW to display the **Disk** menu, which lets you perform such disk operations as formatting, copying, comparing, searching, and parking. It also lets you run the Directory Maintenance program, which is a powerful tool for managing your directories.

3. Press RIGHT ARROW again to display the **Options** menu, which lets you adjust such PC Shell elements as the file display, colors, menus, and function keys, and also lets you preserve all your new settings to disk.

4. Press RIGHT ARROW again to display the **View** menu, which lets you set which PC Shell windows are displayed and adjust how they're displayed.

5. Press RIGHT ARROW again to display the **S**pecial menu, which lets you examine system information; connect two computers; map files, disks, and your system's memory; and (if it's resident) unload PC Shell.

6. Press RIGHT ARROW again to display the **T**ree menu, which lets you expand and contract directories in the Tree List.

7. Press RIGHT ARROW again to display the **H**elp menu, which lists a number of topics you can read about online (including a **DOS** Advice option on how to handle disk-related problems).

8. Press ESC and ALT-SPACEBAR to display the Control menu, which lets you change the selected window's position and size.

9. Press ESC to close the menu. You're returned to the PC Shell screen.

Of these menus (see Figure 15-2), Control, **O**ptions, **V**iew, and **T**ree are covered in this chapter; **F**ile is covered in Chapter 16; **D**isk is covered in Chapter 17; and **S**pecial is covered in Chapter 18.

The PC Shell Drive Bar

Directly below the menu bar is the drive bar, which lists the drives available on your system and highlights the selected drive. To switch to a different drive using the keyboard, press TAB or SHIFT-TAB until the drive bar is activated (which is indicated by all the drive letters becoming highlighted), and then hold down CTRL and press the drive letter. Alternatively, simply click the drive letter in the bar using your mouse. In either case, PC Shell reads the data on your newly selected drive, and then displays its directories and root-level files in the Tree List and File List below the drive bar. These two windows are covered in the next section.

The PC Shell Tree List and File List

The Tree List is a window that displays the current drive's directories. It's called a tree because it represents your root directory (typically C:\) as having a trunk extending from it, and all your other directories as branching out from the trunk. To the right of the Tree List is the File List, which is a window that displays the files in the selected directory.

To move around in the Tree List, first activate it by pressing TAB or SHIFT-TAB until its title bar is highlighted, or simply by clicking anywhere in its window.

You can move along the Tree by directory using DOWN ARROW or UP ARROW, by 16 directories at a time using PGDN or PGUP, and to the bottom or top of the Tree using END or HOME. You can also scroll the Tree vertically using your mouse.

As you move to each directory, the directory's files are displayed in the File List. When you see the files you want to work with, press TAB or click the File List to activate the window.

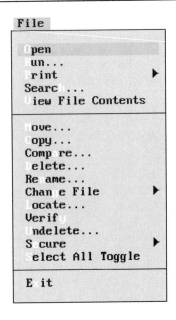

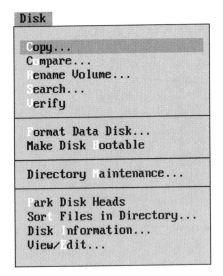

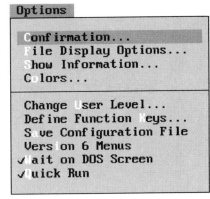

Figure 15-2.   *The PC Shell menus*

The File List typically displays three files per row and 16 rows per column, for a total of 48 files at a time. (You may see more or fewer files, depending on your particular display and configuration.) You can move by file using the arrow keys, by

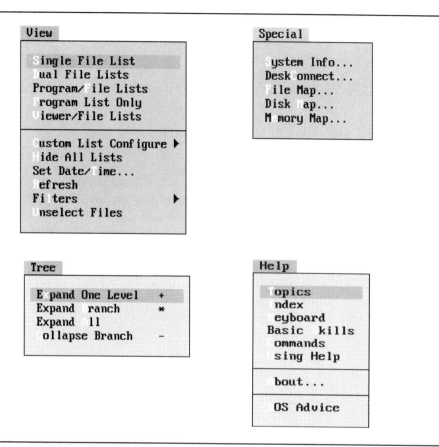

Figure 15-2.   *The PC Shell menus (continued)*

column using PGDN and PGUP, and to the last or first file using END or HOME. You can also scroll the list of files vertically using your mouse.

To get a feel for moving in the Tree List and File List, follow these steps:

1. Press TAB until you've activated the Tree List (indicated by its highlighted title bar).

2. Press HOME to move to the root directory.

3. Press DOWN ARROW to move to the next directory. Notice that the File List changes to display the new directory's files.

4. Press END to move to the last directory.

5. Press TAB to activate the File List. The highlighting shifts to *that* window's title bar.

6. Press END. You're moved to the last file.

7. Press HOME. You're returned to the first file.

Selecting and Unselecting Files

Before you use a PC Shell **F**ile command such as **C**opy or **D**elete, you must select the files in the File List that you want to work with.

Initially, whatever file the highlight cursor is on is considered to be selected. Therefore, if you want to work with a single file, simply move to it or click it with your right mouse button before invoking your command.

If you want to work with multiple files, the process is slightly more involved. First, decide on the order in which you want to work with the files (if any). Second, move to each file using the arrow keys and press ENTER, or click each file with your left mouse button. The file is highlighted to indicate that it's selected.

 In PC Shell 6, a number would appear next to each file indicating its order of selection. This feature has been abandoned in PC Tools 7. However, your order of selection still determines the order in which files are dealt with by a particular operation.

If the files you want to affect are adjacent to each other in the window, you can also select them as a group using your mouse. To do so, follow these steps:

1. Press your right mouse button and keep it pressed.

2. Position the highlight bar over the first file in the group.

3. Press your left mouse button and keep it pressed.

4. Drag the highlight bar over the rest of the files you want to select. The files are all highlighted.

5. Release both mouse buttons.

Once the files are selected, you can copy them, move them, print them, and so on. When you're done with your selected files, you can unselect them in several ways.

To unselect an individual file, move to the file and press ENTER, or click the file with your left mouse button. The file loses its highlighting.

To unselect *all* selected files, press F4 or click Unsel in the message bar, which removes the highlighting from all files. Alternatively, activate the Tree List and just move to a different directory, which automatically unselects all files.

To get a feel for selecting and unselecting files, follow these steps:

1. You should be on the first file in the File List. Press ENTER. The file is selected, and the status line at the bottom of the window now indicates the number and size of files selected.

2. Press ENTER twice more. The next two files are selected, as indicated by the status line.

3. Press UP ARROW three times. You're back on the first file.

4. Press ENTER. The file is unselected, and the status line reflects the change.

5. Press F4. The rest of the files are unselected, and the status line returns to reporting on *all* the files in the File List.

Selecting Files Using Wildcards   In addition to selecting files individually, you can select groups of files using wildcards. To do so, first press F9. The following File Select Filter dialog box appears:

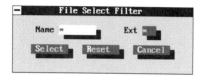

The box provides Name and Ext fields, which can hold text representing a filename and extension. They can also hold the DOS wildcards * (asterisk, to represent any combination of characters) and ? (question mark, to represent any single character). Initially, the fields both contain asterisks, representing all filenames and all extensions in the File List window.

To test out this selection method, follow these steps to select all files, files with TXT extensions, and files beginning with the letter "A":

1. As just mentioned, the Name and Ext fields currently specify files fitting the criteria *.*, or all files. Accept this criteria by pressing ALT-S or clicking Select. All the files in the File List are highlighted.

2. Press F4 to unselect all files.

3. Press F9 to bring up the dialog box again.

4. Press ENTER to accept the asterisk in the Name field.

5. Type **TXT** in the Ext field to specify all files with TXT extensions.

6. Press ENTER twice. Now only files with TXT extensions are highlighted.

7. Press F9 to bring up the dialog box again.

8. Type **A*** in the Name field to select all files starting with the letter "A."

9. Press ALT-S to execute the command. The TXT files from your previous selection are still highlighted, and in addition all files in the window that start with "A" are highlighted.

10. Press F4 to unselect all files again.

By combining the manual and wildcard methods of file selection, you can always select the files you want quickly and easily.

The DOS Command Line

Directly below the Tree and File Lists is the DOS command line. This line provides a DOS prompt from which you can run any DOS command or program. If you're familiar with DOS, you can perform certain operations (such as listing files using wildcards) more quickly by typing commands than by selecting PC Shell menu options.

Furthermore, if you keep PC Shell memory resident, you can invoke PC Shell from an application you're using and then use this command line to run an entirely different program. This is a powerful feature, as it lets you temporarily switch from any program to any other program. When you've finished using the second program and exit, the message "Press any key or a mouse button to re-enter PC Shell" appears. When you do so, you're returned to the PC Shell screen. If you then exit PC Shell, you're returned to the precise point where you left off in your first application. For more information on this feature, see "Running Programs" in Chapter 18.

If you want to use PC Shell *primarily* as a program switcher, you can suppress the display of everything but the DOS command line and the message bar below it (which is covered in the next section) by pressing ALT-V, H, or by clicking on the View menu and selecting Hide All Lists. This makes PC Shell relatively unobtrusive when you bring it up over your applications. You can still access the title and menu bars in this mode by holding down ALT. In addition, you can go back to displaying a standard PC Shell screen at any time by pressing F10.

On the other hand, if you don't anticipate using the DOS command line very often, you can suppress *its* display by pressing ALT-V, C, D, or by clicking on the View menu and selecting Custom List Configure and DOS Command Line. This makes the command line disappear, providing an extra display line for the Tree List and File List. You can still run programs, however, by pressing ALT-F, R, or by clicking on the File menu and selecting Run. This brings up a dialog box that performs the same function as the DOS command line, but that disappears from the screen as soon as you use it to run your program. In addition, you can bring back the DOS command line at any time by selecting View Custom List Configure DOS Command Line again.

The PC Shell Message Bar

The message bar displays information relevant to the PC Shell activity taking place. For example, if you're on a menu name, the bar provides a brief description of the menu's purpose, and if you're on a menu option, the bar tells you the option's function. You can then get more extensive information by pressing F1.

When no special activity is taking place, the message bar displays one-word descriptions of the operations assigned to the first ten function keys (F11 and F12 aren't supported). These will vary depending on the PC Shell screen you're using. For the default PC Shell screen, the operations are as follows:

Function Key	Action
F1 (Help)	Brings up context-sensitive help
F2 (Qview)	Selects File View File Contents
F3 (Exit)	Performs the same functions as ESC
F4 (Unsel)	Selects View Unselect Files
F5 (Copy)	Selects File Copy
F6 (Disply)	Selects Options File Display Options
F7 (Locate)	Selects File Locate
F8 (Zoom)	Toggles between expanding the current window to full-screen size and shrinking it to half size
F9 (Select)	Selects View Filters File Select
F10 (Menu)	Selects View Program List Only

Clicking on the function key description in the message bar has the same effect as pressing the function key.

Adjusting the PC Shell Display

The PC Shell View, Control, and Options menus provide you with a number of ways of adjusting the standard PC Shell screen. These include displaying two sets of List windows, hiding and displaying particular windows, placing a matted background behind the windows, resizing and moving windows, and sorting files and directories. These options are covered in the following sections.

Display changes are normally discarded when you end your session. If you want your changes to be retained for future sessions, press ALT-O, A, or click on the Options menu and select Save Configuration File. Alternatively, if you're ready to exit, simply make sure the **S**ave Configuration option has a checkmark next to it in the Close PC Shell dialog box. (For more information, see "Exiting PC Shell" earlier in this chapter.) In both cases, your changes are saved as new defaults in a configuration file named PCSHELL.CFG.

Opening, Hiding, and Combining Windows

PC Shell normally displays two windows, the Tree List and File List. However, it also has the ability to double that to four windows by adding a second pair of Tree and File Lists. This option is especially useful if you want to work with two different drives and/or directories at the same time while copying, moving, or comparing files.

Alternatively, PC Shell can display a View window that shows the contents of the currently selected file (see "Viewing Files" in Chapter 16), and a Program List window that makes popular applications on your hard disk easily available for selection (see "Running Programs" in Chapter 18). You can set PC Shell to display almost any combination of the Tree List window, File List window, View window, and Program List window; or to display *none* of them.

To access these window options, first press ALT-V or click on the View menu (shown in Figure 15-2). The menu's first option, **S**ingle File List, sets the default display of the Tree List and File List. This option can also be selected by pressing the DEL key.

The menu's second option, **D**ual File Lists, shrinks your original Tree and File List windows to half size, and then adds a second set of the windows. This option can also be selected by pressing the INS key.

The third and fifth options, Program/**F**ile Lists and Viewer/File Lists, split the screen into a Tree List window in the upper left, a File List window in the upper right, and, respectively, the Program List window or View window at the bottom.

On the other hand, the fourth option, **P**rogram List Only, displays nothing but the Program List. You can also toggle between that screen and a screen that shows the Tree and File Lists by pressing F10.

In addition, while the option doesn't appear on this menu, you can display nothing but the View window by pressing F2. You can also toggle between that screen and a screen that shows the Tree and File Lists by pressing F8.

To get a feel for these window display options, follow these steps:

1. With the **View** menu displayed, press F or click Program/File Lists. The Tree and File List windows shrink, and a window listing popular applications on your hard disk appears in the bottom half of the screen.

2. Press F10. The Tree and File List windows disappear, and the Program List changes to a more readable vertical orientation.

3. Press F10 again. You're switched back to the previous three-window display.

4. Press DEL. The Program List disappears, and you're returned to the default Tree List and File List display.

5. Press F2. The contents of the currently selected file are displayed in a View window that fills the screen.

6. Press F8. The View window shrinks to half size and shares the screen with the Tree List and File List.

7. Press DEL. The View window disappears, and you're returned to the default Tree List and File List display.

8. Press INS. The original Tree and File List windows shrink to half size, and a second set of Tree and File List windows is added to the screen. You can change to a different directory or drive in the second Tree List window without causing any display change in the first Tree List window, making it convenient to work with two directories or drives at the same time.

9. Press DEL. The second set of Tree and File List windows disappears, and you're returned to the default Tree List and File List display.

If you want even more control over the PC Shell windows, press ALT-V, C, or click on the View menu and select Custom List Configure. A submenu like this appears:

Notice that the first four options are Tree List, File List, **P**rogram List, and **V**iew Window. These commands let you toggle any window on (indicated by a checkmark) or off (indicated by the lack of a checkmark) by pressing its highlighted letter or clicking its name. Checkmarks currently appear next to the **T**ree List and **F**ile List options because these are the windows that are currently open. The only option the submenu doesn't allow is for both the Program List and View windows to be open at the same time; if you turn on one, the other is turned off automatically.

You can also use this submenu to turn off *all* the windows. However, as mentioned previously in "The DOS Command Line," it's faster to do this by pressing ALT-V, H, or by clicking on the View menu and selecting Hide All Lists. This provides an unobtrusive display when you're primarily using PC Shell as a program switcher. You can later return to a windowed display by pressing F10.

Another important option in the submenu is **W**indow Style. When set to CASCADED (which is the default), it allows you to resize and move your windows using either your mouse or the Control menu (see the next section). When set to TILE, however, it sets your windows directly next to each other (that is, without spaces between them) and doesn't allow you to resize or move them.

In addition, if you find yourself using the View window frequently, you may want to use the Viewer **C**onfig option. This sets the View window to be horizontal (which is the default) or vertical when it's displayed along with the Tree and File List windows. The vertical orientation is preferable for certain types of data, and also gives the View window a larger portion of the screen than the horizontal option.

The other two options in the submenu are **DOS Command Line**, which was covered previously in "The DOS Command Line" section, and Background **Mat**, which toggles between using a matted background behind the PC Shell windows (which is the default) and using the screen of your underlying application as the background.

In summary, PC Shell gives you enormous control over the "look" of your screen. This flexibility extends throughout the program and is one of its greatest strengths. You may seldom choose to use more than a fraction of these display options in your normal use of the program, but when you need them, they're there for your selection.

Using the Control Menu

As explained in this book's Introduction, every PC Tools 7 program has a Control menu in its upper-left corner, which you can display by pressing ALT-SPACEBAR or by clicking on its dash symbol. The Control menu always provides options for showing the version of the program you're using and for exiting the program. In certain applications, the menu also provides options for adjusting the currently active window. The menu's options (shown in Figure 15-2) are as follows:

- *Version*   This option displays the program's version number and a copyright notice.

- *Restore*   This option restores a maximized window to its previous size.

- *Move*   This option allows you to reposition the current window using the arrow keys.

- *Size*   This option allows you to resize the current window using the arrow keys.

- *Maximize*   This option expands the current window to fill the screen.

- *Close*   This option brings up a Close dialog box.

At times, a particular option won't be appropriate; for example, if the active window isn't maximized, the **Restore** option won't have any effect. In these cases, the pertinent Control menu option may be disabled, which is indicated by the absence of highlighting on the letter you normally use to select it.

The four window-related menu options—Maximize, **Restore**, Size, and Move— are covered in the following sections.

Maximizing and Restoring a Window

The default size of most PC Shell windows is significantly smaller than your screen so that other open windows can display on the screen simultaneously. If you want to see as much of a window as possible, however, you can expand, or *maximize,* it to fill the screen.

To maximize the active window using the keyboard, press ALT-SPACEBAR, X, or click on the Control menu and select Maximize. The window fills the space between the menu and message bars. To restore the window to its previous size, press ALT-SPACEBAR, R, or click on the Control menu and select Restore. The window shrinks back to its previous proportions.

You can also maximize the window by using your mouse. To do so, simply click on the triangular Maximize button in the window's upper-right corner. When you want to shrink the window back, just click on the button again, which has turned upside-down to indicate that it's become a Restore button.

Resizing a Window

You can expand or contract any window's size. This is useful if you have several windows open and you want to resize and reposition them for an optimal display.

To resize the active window using the keyboard, press ALT-SPACEBAR, S, or click on the Control menu and select Size. A small box appears telling you to "use cursor keys to adjust." Press the RIGHT ARROW and DOWN ARROW keys to expand the window, and the LEFT ARROW and UP ARROW keys to contract the window. When you're done, press ENTER. The message box disappears, and you're returned to the now-resized window.

You can alternatively resize the window with your mouse by clicking on the Resize box in the window's lower-right corner and dragging.

Moving a Window

You can move a window anywhere on the screen (as long as it stays between the menu and message bars). This is useful if you have several windows open and you want to position them so they're all visible.

To move the active window using the keyboard, press ALT-SPACEBAR, M, or click on the Control menu and select Move. A small box appears telling you to "use cursor keys to adjust." Press the arrow keys to move the window in the directions you want. When you're done, press ENTER. The message box disappears, and you're returned to the now-repositioned window.

You can also move the window using your mouse. To do so, position the mouse pointer over any portion of the window's title bar, click your mouse button, and drag in the desired direction. When you've placed the window where you want it, release the mouse button.

Adjusting the File List Display

The File List normally displays filenames based on their physical order on the disk. However, you can optionally reset this window to display files in a different order and/or to display file characteristics in addition to filenames. To do so, press ALT-O, F, or press F6, or click on the Options menu and select File Display Options. The following dialog box appears:

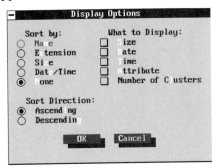

The right side of the box lists five file characteristics that you can display in addition to filenames. These display options are as follows:

- *Size*   This option displays each file's size in bytes.

- *Date*   This option displays the creation date of each file.

- *Time*   This option displays the creation time of each file.

- *Attribute*   This option displays each file's attributes. (For information about attributes, see "Editing File Attributes" in Chapter 16.)

- *Number of Clusters*   This option displays the number of clusters each file occupies. (For information about clusters, see "Understanding How Disks Are Organized" in Chapter 4, "Data Recovery Overview.")

To turn any option on or off, press its highlighted letter or click it. When an option is on, a checkmark appears to its left. You can turn on as few or as many options as you want.

The left side of the dialog box lists five file characteristics by which you can sort the File List display. These sort options are as follows:

- *Name*   This option sorts the File List display alphabetically by filename.

- *Extension*   This option sorts the File List display by extension. Also, within groups of files with the same extension, it sorts files alphabetically by filename.

- *Size*   This option sorts the File List display by each file's size in bytes.

- *Date/Time*   This option sorts the File List display chronologically by creation date and time.

- *None*   This option turns File List sorting off, allowing files to be displayed in their physical order on the disk.

You can select only one of these five sorting options; the default is **None**. You can additionally set the sorting order to be Ascending (lowest to highest; for example, 1, 2, 3) or Descending (highest to lowest; for example, 3, 2, 1).

When you're done selecting options, press O or click OK. The dialog box closes and your settings are applied to all File List displays. If you chose a sorting option, keep in mind that only the *display* of your files is being sorted, not their physical arrangement on your disk. Therefore, your files will still appear unsorted when you list them from DOS or an application. To physically sort files, see the next section.

If you have a mouse, you can always display a file's characteristics by positioning the mouse pointer over the filename in the File List and holding down the right mouse button. The bottom of the window shows the file's size, creation date and time, and attributes. In addition, you can display a selected file's characteristics by choosing the **Options Show Information** *command (see "Displaying Information About Selected Files" in Chapter 16).*

Physically Sorting Files and Directories

Files are normally arranged in an arbitrary order on your disk. As just explained in the previous section, you can set files to display in a particular order in the File List, but this won't change how they're displayed outside of PC Shell. In addition, display sorting has no effect on the Directory Tree. Therefore, PC Shell additionally provides a **Disk Sort** Files in Directory command, which *physically* sorts files by name, extension, size, creation date and time, or selection sequence, and in ascending (lowest to highest) order or descending (highest to lowest) order. Furthermore, if you select the root directory of the Tree List before invoking the command, you can physically sort the directories on your disk, making it much easier to navigate the Tree List.

To sort files or directories on your disk, follow these steps:

1. Select the Tree List using TAB or your mouse.

2. Use the arrow keys or your mouse to move to the directory you want to sort. (If you want to sort the Directory Tree itself, press HOME to select the root.)

3. If you want to sort files based on their selection order, activate the File List using TAB or your mouse, and select the files in the order you want.

4. Press ALT-D, T, or click on the Disk menu and select Sort Files in Directory. A Directory Sort dialog box appears with five sorting options and two ordering options.

5. Press 1 to sort alphabetically by filename (the default), 2 to sort by file type or by extension, 3 to sort by size in bytes, 4 to sort chronologically by creation date and time, or 5 to sort based on your file selection order. (If you're sorting directories, it's best to sort by filename.)

6. Press 6 to sort in ascending (1, 2, 3) order, or press 7 to sort in descending (3, 2, 1) order. The default is ascending. (If you sort by selection number, ascending is the only ordering option available.)

7. Press ENTER or click Sort. A second dialog box appears that offers the options of first viewing what the results of the sort will be (**View**), returning to the first dialog box to select different sorting options (**R**esort), canceling the operation and returning to the PC Shell screen (**C**ancel), or executing your specified sorting (**U**pdate).

8. Press U or click Update. Your sorting specifications are executed in memory (but not necessarily on the disk), and you're returned to the PC Shell screen.

9. Press ALT-V, R, or click on the View menu and select Refresh. If your sorting specifications weren't already executed on your disk, they are now, as indicated by your disk drive light flashing on. When the operation is completed, the Tree List and File List reflect your changes. You'll also see the new ordering when you examine your affected files or directories outside of PC Shell.

If you want to sort all your files and directories, use the Compress program. This utility provides numerous options for reorganizing your disk and optimizing it for maximum efficiency. For more information, see Chapter 9, "Speeding Your Disks Using Compress."

Adjusting PC Shell Configuration Options

The PC Shell **O**ptions menu provides you with a number of miscellaneous options for tailoring the program to your particular needs. These include setting your user level, redefining the function keys, setting how programs launched from PC Shell return upon exiting, and switching to PC Shell 6 menus. These options are covered in the following sections.

Configuration changes are normally discarded when you end your session. If you want your changes to be retained for future sessions, press ALT-O, A, or click on the Options menu and select Save Configuration File. Alternatively, if you're ready to exit, press ESC, turn on the **S**ave Configuration option, and press ENTER. In either case, your changes are saved to disk as new defaults.

Setting Your User Level

If you tend to use only the more elementary PC Shell commands and find the many other commands distracting, you can restrict the menus to display only basic or intermediate options. To do so, press ALT-O, U, or click on the Options menu and select Change User Level. The following dialog box appears:

To choose only the most basic commands, press B or click Beginner User Mode; to choose both basic commands and some commands of intermediate difficulty, press I or click Intermediate User Mode; to choose *all* available commands, press A or click Advanced User Mode. It's highly recommended that you stay in Advanced mode while you're working with this book to learn all the commands PC Shell has to offer. For a list of each menu command and its user level, see the "PC Shell Command Reference" section at the end of this chapter.

Once you've selected the option you want, press ENTER or click OK. The dialog box closes, and your new user level is displayed in the left corner of the title bar.

Toggling Program Screen Pausing

After a program you've run from PC Shell has finished executing, its last screen is normally paused and you're instructed to press a key or click your mouse to return to PC Shell. This allows you to read any message produced by an exiting program before it's replaced by the PC Shell display. If you want to set PC Shell to instead return automatically without pausing, press ALT-O, W, or click on the Options menu and select Wait on DOS Screen. The checkmark next to the option disappears to indicate it's been switched off. If you later want to turn the option on again (for example, to run a DIR or CHKDSK command), select **O**ptions **W**ait on DOS Screen again.

Redefining the Function Keys

If there's a command you use frequently, you can assign it to a function key to speed its selection. To do so, first press ALT-O, K, or click on the Options menu and select Define Function Keys. The following dialog box appears:

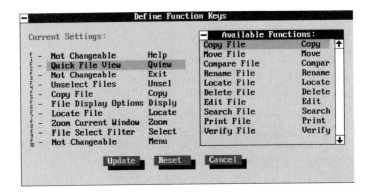

The left side of the box lists the ten function keys, their current definitions, and their message bar descriptions. To select a function key to change, move to it using DOWN ARROW or UP ARROW, or click on it. (The definitions of F1, F3, and F10 can't be changed, so you can't select them here.)

The right side of the box provides a list of all PC Shell menu commands (including submenu options). After selecting a function key, press ENTER or TAB, or use your mouse, to activate the command list. You can move by command using DOWN ARROW and UP ARROW, by ten commands at a time using PGDN and PGUP, and to the bottom or top using END or HOME. You can also scroll through the list vertically using your mouse. The commands are listed in their order of appearance on the menus.

When you see the command you want, move to it and press ENTER, or click it. The command is assigned to the function key you selected, as shown on the left side of the box. Also, the left side of the box is activated again, allowing you to select another function key to redefine.

When you're done redefining keys, press U or click Update to save your revisions. Alternatively, if you've changed your mind, press ESC twice or click Cancel twice to abort your current changes, or press R or click Reset to restore the default meanings of the function keys.

Setting the Quick Run Option

When PC Shell is running nonresident, it ordinarily doesn't free up any memory before running another program. This speeds running programs from PC Shell and returning to PC Shell when they've completed executing. On the other hand, if you want to run a large program, it may require extra memory to load.

You can toggle PC Shell's freeing up of memory by pressing ALT-O, Q, or by clicking on the Options menu and selecting Quick Run. When a checkmark appears next to the option, it means that PC Shell will launch programs without freeing up memory, thus making them "run quick"; when no checkmark appears, PC Shell is set to free up memory (allowing you to run large applications) and then reload itself from disk when an application finishes executing.

The **O**ptions **Q**uick Run command is only switchable when PC Shell is running nonresident. When PC Shell is resident, it automatically frees up memory before running another application, and so keeps the option turned off.

PC Shell Parameters

As explained earlier in this chapter, you can run PC Shell memory resident by including the /R parameter after the program name. You can also use a different single parameter (for example, PCSHELL C:) or combine a number of parameters (for example, PCSHELL /R /OE /F6) to achieve the effect you want. Keep in mind that parameters require a *forward* slash (/, located on the bottom of the ? key) as opposed to the backslash (\) used to specify DOS directories.

The ten parameters available for PC Shell are as follows:

- **/?**   This "help" parameter lists and briefly describes each of PC Shell's parameters.

- **/VIDEO**   This "help" parameter lists and briefly describes the standard PC Tools video and mouse parameters. It should not be combined with any other parameters. For more information, see the "Video and Mouse Parameters" section in Appendix A, "PC Tools Installation and Configuration."

- *d*:   This parameter is a letter and colon specifying the drive you want to work with. PC Shell will come up displaying the directories on this drive instead of the drive the PC Shell files are stored on. If you include it, it must be the first parameter after the program name (for example, PCSHELL C: /R is correct, but PCSHELL /R C: is wrong).

- **/A***nnn*   This parameter sets the amount of memory PC Shell takes up when you've invoked it from the background. For example, to install PC Shell to take up 500K when invoked, you could use the command PCSHELL /R /A500. This parameter is primarily useful when you want to copy floppy disks using a single drive, since it can give PC Shell more room for loading the disk data and so require less disk swapping. You should also use it if you get the message "Insufficient memory" while running PC Shell.

    If you combine this parameter with the /RL parameter (for example, by using the command PCSHELL /RL /A500), PC Shell will take up the amount of memory specified by the /A parameter even when resident in the background.

- **/CF=***filename*   PC Shell ordinarily saves its configuration settings (for example, which windows are open, what the current user level is, and so on) to the file PCSHELL.CFG. This parameter directs such settings to be saved to a different file, which you specify. For example, to save the data to a file named MYCONFIG, use the parameter /CF=MYCONFIG.

- **/DQ**   If you experience problems when hotkeying into PC Shell from the DOS prompt (as opposed to from an application), try using this parameter. To speed loading, PC Shell ordinarily skips saving the contents of conventional memory to disk or expanded memory when invoked at the DOS prompt. This parameter disables the quick-load-from-DOS feature so that the contents of conventional memory are saved to disk or expanded memory under all circumstances.

- **/F***n*   This parameter changes the keystroke that invokes (and hotkeys out of) PC Shell from CTRL-ESC to CTRL and any function key from F1 through F10. For example, to install PC Shell to be invoked with CTRL-F1, you could use the command PCSHELL/R/F1. This is useful if some other program in your system is already using CTRL-ESC.

- **/O***d*   When you press CTRL-ESC to swap PC Shell into or out of memory, it first saves the current memory contents into three files named PCSHELL.OVL, PCSHELL.IMG, and PCSHELL.THM. The files are ordinarily saved to the current disk drive or, if available, to expanded memory. The /O parameter followed by a drive letter directs the files to be saved to the specified drive instead. This allows you to direct saving to a RAM disk in extended memory to speed execution, to a physical drive to disable saving to expanded memory, and so on. If you use a RAM disk, it should provide about 800K to hold both PC Shell's files and the data of the application from which PC Shell was invoked.

- **/R**   This is the most commonly used Desktop parameter. It installs PC Shell as a memory-resident program while taking up 12K of conventional memory. You can instead use /RL; for more information, see "Alternative PC Shell Loading Options."

- **/RL**   This parameter fully installs PC Shell in conventional memory, taking up about 480K. For more information, see "Alternative PC Shell Loading Options."

PC Shell Files

When you use the Install program to copy PC Shell to your hard disk, a number of files are generated. You may need to understand what each file represents in case a file gets damaged or you have to eliminate nonessential files to save disk space. You may also simply be curious about what these files do. The following table lists each PC Shell file and briefly describes it. In addition, if you allowed Install to create SYSTEM and DATA subdirectories in your PCTOOLS directory, it tells you in which directory each file resides.

*The following "Directory" columns will only be accurate if the line **SET PCTOOLS=C:\PCTOOLS\DATA** has been included in your AUTOEXEC.BAT file. If this line is left out, PC Shell will store certain files intended for the DATA directory into either your PCTOOLS directory or whatever directory is current instead. This does no harm, but it can make locating your various files difficult. For more information, see Appendix A, "PC Tools Installation and Configuration."*

File	Directory	Description
CPSCOLOR.DAT	DATA	PC Tools color configuration file
CPSTOOLS.INI	DATA	Group names and file specifications file used by File Find and Undelete
DESKCON.EXE	PCTOOLS	DeskConnect memory-resident program to run on the PC running PC Shell
DESKSRV.EXE	PCTOOLS	DeskConnect program to run on the PC you're connecting to
DM.EXE	PCTOOLS	Directory Maintenance program, which performs such operations as copying, moving, and deleting entire directories
FD.EXE	SYSTEM	File Find subprogram for locating duplicate files
FF.EXE	PCTOOLS	File Find program, which locates files
PCAPPLIC.CFG	DATA	Configuration file defining applications to be stored in the Program List
PCCONFIG.EXE	DATA	Configuration program defining color schemes for all PC Tools programs
PCFORMAT.EXE	PCTOOLS	PC Format program, which formats disks
PCFORM.EXE	PCTOOLS	"Engine" for the PC Format program
PCSECURE.EXE	PCTOOLS	PC Secure program, which encrypts files
PCSHELL.EXE	PCTOOLS	PC Shell program
PCSHELL.OVL	SYSTEM	Overlay file that PC Shell swaps in and out of memory as needed
PCTOOLS.BAT	PCTOOLS	Batch file that runs PC Shell using the PCTOOLS.CFG configuration file so it comes up in the Program List screen
PCTOOLS.CFG	DATA	Configuration file for making PC Shell come up in the Program List screen
PCRUN.COM	SYSTEM	Utility that PC Shell uses to run programs

File	Directory	Description
SL.EXE	SYSTEM	System Information program, which provides comprehensive data about your PC system
UNDEL.EXE	PCTOOLS	Undelete program, which locates, displays, and recovers deleted files
VIEW.EXE	PCTOOLS	View program, which lets you view data files in their native formats
VIEW.LIB	SYSTEM	Library of data viewers
WIPE.EXE	PCTOOLS	Wipe program, which destroys files

In addition, PC Shell and its associated programs automatically create the following files once you begin using them:

File	Directory	Description
CPS*.TRE	DATA	Stores Tree List data for PC Shell and Directory Maintenance
PCSECURE.CFG	DATA	PC Secure configuration file
PCSHELL.CFG	DATA	Configuration file storing settings for PC Shell window and menu settings
PCSHELL.IMG	DATA	Saves RAM video image of underlying application when PC Shell is invoked in resident mode
PCSHELL.RMG	DATA	Saves PC Shell data to disk when another program is run from PC Shell
PCSHELL.THM	DATA	Saves current memory of non-PC Shell applications (them) in resident mode

New PC Shell Features in Version 7

If you're familiar with PC Shell 6, you'll find version 7 to be fairly similar. (In fact, if you turn on the **O**ptions Version 6 Menus switch, the programs will appear almost identical.) The biggest change is that a number of PC Shell 6 commands have been turned into standalone programs. When you select one of these commands, PC Shell now transfers control to the appropriate program, and then takes back control when the program finishes executing.

You can also run any of these programs directly from the DOS prompt, which is especially convenient if you don't tend to keep PC Shell resident. In addition, virtually all these programs provide significantly more features than their command counterparts in PC Shell 6.

The nine PC Tools programs that can be invoked from PC Shell's menus are as follows:

- *Directory Maintenance*   This program lets you perform such operations as copying, moving, renaming, and deleting whole directories. You can run it from PC Shell by selecting **D**isk **D**irectory **M**aintenance **F**ull DM Program (or just **D**isk **D**irectory **M**aintenance in PC Tools 7.0), or from the DOS prompt by typing **DM** and pressing ENTER. It's covered in "Managing Your Directories" in Chapter 17, "Managing Your Directories and Disks."

- *File Find*   This program lets you search for files across multiple directories, or even across multiple disks, based on their names, text contents, dates, sizes, and/or attributes. You can run it from PC Shell by pressing F7 or selecting **F**ile **L**ocate, or from the DOS prompt by typing **FF** and pressing ENTER. It's covered in "Finding Files Anywhere in Your System" in Chapter 16, "Managing Your Files."

- *PC Config*   This program sets the color schemes used by all PC Tools programs. You can run it from PC Shell by selecting **O**ptions **C**olors, or from the DOS prompt by typing **PCCONFIG** and pressing ENTER. It's covered in "Using PC Config" in Appendix A, "PC Tools Installation and Configuration."

- *PC Format*   This program formats disks using interactive screens. You can run it from PC Shell by selecting **D**isk **F**ormat Data Disk (which lets you select any formatting options) or **D**isk **M**ake Disk **B**ootable (which automatically copies system files after formatting so the disk can start up your PC), or from the DOS prompt by typing **PCFORMAT** and pressing ENTER. It's covered in "Formatting Floppy Disks" in Chapter 17, "Managing Your Directories and Disks," and in "Running Interactive PC Format" in Chapter 5, "Safeguarding Your Data."

- *PC Secure*   This program encrypts and decrypts files, or even whole directories, using DES encryption. It can encrypt quickly or by Department of Defense security standards. You can run its engine from PC Shell by using the **F**ile **S**ecure submenu, or from the DOS prompt by typing **PCSECURE** and pressing ENTER. It's covered in Chapter 11, "Encrypting Data Using PC Secure."

- *System Information*   This program provides comprehensive information about your PC system. You can run it from PC Shell by selecting **S**pecial **S**ystem Info, or from the DOS prompt by typing **SI** and pressing ENTER. It's covered in "Displaying System Information" in Chapter 18, "Using Advanced PC Shell Features."

- *Undelete*   This program lets you recover deleted files. You can run it from PC Shell by selecting **F**ile **U**ndelete, or from the DOS prompt by typing **UNDEL** and pressing ENTER. It's covered in "Recovering Deleted Files" in Chapter 6, "Recovering Deleted or Formatted Data."

- *View*   This program lets you view the contents of data files in their native formats. You can run it from PC Shell by pressing F2 or selecting **F**ile **V**iew

File Contents, or from the DOS prompt by typing **VIEW** and pressing ENTER. It's covered in "Viewing Files" in Chapter 16, "Managing Your Files."

- *Wipe*   This program can totally destroy a file by overwriting its data at the same time you're deleting it. It can also overwrite whole directories and disks, and do so following Department of Defense security standards or your own specifications. You can run it from PC Shell by selecting **F**ile **C**hange File **C**lear File, or from the DOS prompt by typing **WIPE** and pressing ENTER. It's covered in "Destroying Files" in Chapter 16, "Managing Your Files," and in "Destroying Data Using Wipe" in Chapter 11, "Encrypting Data Using PC Secure."

In addition, if you're using PC Tools 7.0, you can run the Desktop Manager's Notepads application to edit text files by selecting **F**ile **C**hange File **E**dit File, and to create Program List descriptions by selecting the **D**escription option in the Program List's edit mode. If you're using PC Tools 7.1, however, a File Editor unique to PC Shell is loaded instead of Notepads. For more information, see "Editing Text Files" in Chapter 16, "Managing Your Files," and "Examining and Editing Program List Entries" in Chapter 18, "Using Advanced PC Shell Features."

Some small changes have also been made to PC Shell itself. For example, if you're not on the DOS command line and you start typing, a Speed Search box appears that moves you to the directory in the Tree List beginning with the letters you've typed. This provides a quick way of switching to the directory you want. For more information, see "Selecting Directories" in Chapter 17.

Another Tree List enhancement is a new **T**ree menu, which lets you hide (collapse) or display (expand) the subdirectories in a selected directory, or display all subdirectories in all directories (which is the default). If you're using a color monitor, collapsed directories are indicated by plus signs in their folders, while expanded directories are indicated by minus signs in their folders. You can also collapse the selected directory by pressing – (the minus sign), expand it by one subdirectory level by pressing + (the plus sign), and expand all its subdirectories by pressing * (asterisk), or toggle the directory's status by clicking on its folder.

The File List has undergone one small change: it no longer displays numbers to indicate your order of selection. While this provides you with less information, it also keeps the window from looking cluttered. In addition, menu commands will still operate on files based on your selection order.

The Application List has been replaced with a Program List, which provides similar options for listing and running other programs. You can toggle between the Program List and standard PC Shell screen by pressing F10 (which no longer activates the menu bar). You can also make PC Shell come up in the Program List screen by running a batch file named PCTOOLS.BAT; to do so, simply type **PCTOOLS** from the DOS prompt and press ENTER.

Lastly, all the windows in PC Shell can now be resized and moved from a Windows-like Control menu in the left corner of PC Shell's new title bar. In addition, you can adjust any window using your mouse. However, the windows are only adjustable when the **View C**ustom List Configure **W**indow Style viewer switch is set to CASCADED (which is the default), as opposed to TILE.

PC Shell Command Reference

Most of PC Shell's power lies in its menu commands, which enable you to manage your files, directories, and disks, adjust PC Shell's display, and perform such operations as displaying system information and connecting two adjacent computers.

Like a number of PC Tools programs, PC Shell's first menu is Control and its last menu is Help. These menus are covered in this book's Introduction and in this chapter's "Using the Control Menu" section.

PC Shell also contains six additional menus: File, Disk, Options, View, Special, and Tree. The following sections list the name of each menu option, the keystrokes that invoke it, its user level, and a description of what it does. Each command also includes a reference to the section that discusses it in detail in this chapter; in Chapter 16, "Managing Your Files"; in Chapter 17, "Managing Your Directories and Disks"; or in Chapter 18, "Using Advanced PC Shell Features."

The File Menu

The **File** menu provides a multitude of options for manipulating files. The menu contains 10 commands in Beginner mode, 15 commands in Intermediate mode, and 17 commands in Advanced mode. The following lists all 17 commands and specifies each command's user level:

Open (ALT-F, O or CTRL-ENTER) (Beginner)

After you optionally specify any parameters and press ENTER, runs the selected program file or the program associated with the selected data file. Covered in "Running Programs" in Chapter 18.

Run (ALT-F, R or CTRL-ENTER) (Beginner)

Brings up a DOS command line for running a program or DOS command (like the DOS command line near the bottom of the screen). Covered in "Running Programs" in Chapter 18.

Print (ALT-F, P) (Intermediate)

Offers the options of Print **File** to print selected files as normal text or in hex/ASCII format (covered in "Printing Files" in Chapter 16) and Print File **List** to print information about all the files in the current directory (covered in "Displaying Information About Selected Files" in Chapter 16).

Search (ALT-F, H) (Advanced)

Searches for text in your selected files, your unselected files, or all files in the File List or Located Files window. Covered in "Finding Files by Content in the Current Window" in Chapter 16.

View File Contents (ALT-F, V or F2) (Beginner)

Brings up a full-screen window, that displays each selected file in the format of the application that created it (if a viewer file is associated with it) or in the default format. Covered in "Viewing Files" in Chapter 16.

Move (ALT-F, M) (Beginner)

Copies the selected files to a different drive and/or directory, and then deletes the original files. Covered in "Moving Files" in Chapter 16.

Copy (ALT-F, C or F5) (Beginner)

Copies the selected files to the specified disk and/or directory. Covered in "Copying Files" in Chapter 16.

Compare (ALT-F, A) (Beginner)

Compares the contents of the selected files against files from the specified drive and/or directory. Covered in "Comparing Files" in Chapter 16.

Delete (ALT-F, D) (Intermediate)

Deletes the selected files after prompting for confirmation. Covered in "Deleting Files" in Chapter 16.

Rename (ALT-F, N) (Beginner)

Renames the selected files individually, or renames them as a group via the DOS wildcards * and ?. Covered in "Renaming Files" in Chapter 16.

Change File (ALT-F, G) (Intermediate)

Displays the text editing option **E**dit File (covered in "Editing Text Files" in Chapter 16), and the three technical options **H**ex Edit File (covered in "Editing Sectors" in Chapter 18), **C**lear File (covered in "Destroying Files" in Chapter 16), and **A**ttribute Change (covered in "Editing File Attributes" in Chapter 16).

Locate (ALT-F, L or F7) (Beginner)

Searches for files across multiple directories, or even across multiple disks, based on their names, text contents, creation dates, sizes, and/or attributes. Covered in "Finding Files Anywhere in Your System" in Chapter 16.

Verif**y** (ALT-F, Y) (Intermediate)

Scans the selected files for defects and optionally marks bad sectors as unusable. Covered in "Verifying Files" in Chapter 16.

Undelete File (ALT-F, U) (Intermediate)

Runs the interactive Undelete program to locate, display, and recover deleted files. Covered in "Using Interactive Undelete" in Chapter 6, "Recovering Deleted or Formatted Data."

S**e**cure (ALT-F, E) (Advanced)

Displays the three encryption options **E**ncrypt File, **D**ecrypt File, and **S**ettings. Covered in Chapter 11, "Encrypting Data Using PC Secure."

Select All Toggle (ALT-F, S) (Beginner)

Toggles between selecting all files and unselecting all files in the File List.

E**x**it (ALT-F, X or F3) (Beginner)

Brings up the Exit dialog box. Pressing ENTER or O, or clicking Exit, then quits PC Shell. Covered in "Exiting PC Shell" in this chapter.

The Disk Menu

```
Disk
 opy...
C mpare...
 ename Volume...
 earch...
 erify

 ormat Data Disk...
Make Disk  ootable

Directory  aintenance...

 ark Disk Heads
Sor  Files in Directory...
Disk  nformation...
View/ dit...
```

The **Disk** menu provides options for manipulating directories, and for copying, verifying, searching, comparing, formatting, examining, editing, renaming, and parking disks. The menu contains five commands in Beginner mode, ten commands in Intermediate mode, and 12 commands in Advanced mode. The following lists all 12 commands and specifies each command's user level:

Copy (ALT-D, C) (Beginner)

Copies the contents of one floppy disk to another floppy disk of the same type. Covered in "Copying Floppy Disks" in Chapter 17.

Compare (ALT-D, O) (Beginner)

Compares the contents of one floppy disk to another floppy disk of the same type. Covered in "Comparing Floppy Disks" in Chapter 17.

Rename Volume (ALT-D, R) (Intermediate)

Displays the volume label of the current disk and lets you rename it. Covered in "Renaming Disks" in Chapter 17.

Search (ALT-D, S) (Intermediate)

Finds the sector and offset location of specified data on the current disk. You can then display the filename the data is in, edit the data, continue the search, or exit the search. Covered in "Searching Disks" in Chapter 17.

Verify (ALT-D, V) (Intermediate)

Checks that all areas of the current disk are readable, and optionally marks bad sectors as unusable. Covered in "Verifying Disks" in Chapter 17.

Format Data Disk (ALT-D, F) (Beginner)

Runs the interactive version of PC Format to format a disk. Covered in "Formatting Floppy Disks" in Chapter 17.

Make Disk **B**ootable (ALT-D, B) (Beginner)

Runs the interactive version of PC Format to format a floppy disk and also to copy DOS system files to the disk, which enable it to start up, or *boot,* your PC. Covered in "Formatting Floppy Disks" in Chapter 17.

Directory **M**aintenance (ALT-D, M) (Beginner)

Runs the Directory Maintenance program, which lets you perform such tasks as select, create, copy, move, rename, delete, and examine directories. Covered in "Managing Your Directories" in Chapter 17.

Park Disk Heads (ALT-D, P) (Intermediate)

Positions your hard disk's read/write heads over an unused portion of your hard disk to ensure they don't damage data when you turn off or move your computer. Covered in "Parking Disks" in Chapter 17.

Sor**t** Files in Directory (ALT-D, T) (Intermediate)

Sorts the display of files in the current directory by name, extension, size, date/time, or selection order, and in ascending (lowest to highest) or descending (highest to lowest) order. Covered in "Physically Sorting Files and Directories" in this chapter.

Disk **I**nformation (ALT-D, I) (Advanced)

Displays technical information about the current disk. Covered in "Displaying Disk Information" in Chapter 17.

View/**E**dit (ALT-D, E) (Advanced)

Brings up a hex editor for revising sectors on the current disk. Covered in "Editing Sectors" in Chapter 18.

The Options Menu

The **O**ptions menu provides options for toggling confirmation messages; sorting the File List display; showing file information; changing colors, function key definitions, and your user level; saving the current PC Shell settings as new defaults; switching to PC Shell 6 menus; toggling pausing after a launched program finishes executing; and toggling whether all memory is freed for running a program when PC Shell is nonresident. It contains the following ten commands:

Confirmation (ALT, C)

Lets you turn on or off the three options Confirm on **D**elete (for when you're deleting selected files; the default is *on*), Confirm on **R**eplace (for when you're replacing old files while copying or moving selected files; the default is *on*), and Confirm on **M**ouse Operations (for when you're copying or moving files using the mouse instead of menu commands; the default is *off*).

File Display Options (ALT-O, F or F6)

Sets the file characteristics to be displayed in the File List, the characteristic to sort the display by, and whether the sort will be in ascending (lowest to highest) or descending (highest to lowest) order. The default is filenames only and no sorting. Covered in "Adjusting the File List Display" in this chapter.

Show Information (ALT-O, S)

Displays technical information about the selected files. Covered in "Displaying Information About Selected Files" in Chapter 16.

Colors (ALT-O, O)

Runs the PC Config program to let you change the colors used for all PC Tools programs. Covered in Appendix A, "PC Tools Installation and Configuration."

Change **U**ser Level (ALT-O, U)

Selects a user level of **B**eginner, **I**ntermediate, or **A**dvanced to adjust the number of options displayed in the **F**ile, **D**isk, and **S**pecial menus. Covered in "Setting Your User Level" in this chapter.

Define Function **K**eys (ALT-O, K)

Assigns new meanings and message bar descriptions to the function keys you specify. Covered in "Redefining the Function Keys" in this chapter.

Save Configuration File (ALT-O, A)

Saves your current PC Shell settings as the new defaults. Covered in "Adjusting the PC Shell Display" and "Adjusting PC Shell Configuration Options" in this chapter.

Version 6 Menus (ALT-O, I)

Switches PC Shell to displaying the menus used in its previous version, PC Shell 6. Covered in "New PC Shell Features in Version 7" in this chapter.

Wait on DOS Screen (ALT-O, W)

Affects how PC Shell behaves after you've executed a DOS command. If the option's off, you're returned to the PC Shell screen automatically. If the option's on, you aren't returned until you've pressed a key or clicked your mouse button. The default is *on*. Covered in "Running Programs" in Chapter 18.

Quick Run (ALT-O, Q)

When off, frees almost all memory before running a program or DOS command by temporarily saving current PC Shell data to disk. This is useful when you want to run a program that requires a lot of memory, but slows exiting and returning to PC Shell. The default setting is *on*. This option only appears when PC Shell is running nonresident. Covered in "Setting the Quick Run Option" in this chapter.

The **V**iew Menu

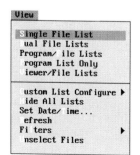

The View menu contains the following 11 commands for adjusting PC Shell windows, setting the date and time, refreshing the screen, specifying which files are selected and/or displayed in the File List, and unselecting all files:

Single File List (ALT-V, S or DEL)

Displays the default Tree List/File List screen. Covered in "Opening, Hiding, and Combining Windows" in this chapter.

Dual File Lists (ALT-V, D or INS)

Displays two sets of Tree List and File List windows, which is useful for such operations as copying, moving, or comparing files on two different drives and/or directories. Covered in "Opening, Hiding, and Combining Windows" in this chapter.

Program/**F**ile Lists (ALT-V, F)

Divides the screen between the Tree List and File List windows (at the top) and a Program List window (at the bottom). Covered in "Opening, Hiding, and Combining Windows" in this chapter.

Program List Only (ALT-V, P or F10)

Toggles the display between a Program List screen and the standard PC Shell screen. Covered in "Opening, Hiding, and Combining Windows" in this chapter and "Using the Program List" in Chapter 18.

Viewer/File Lists (ALT-V, V or F2, F8)

Divides the screen between the Tree List and File List windows (at the top) and a View window (at the bottom). Covered in "Opening, Hiding, and Combining Windows" in this chapter and "Viewing Files" in Chapter 16.

Custom List Configure (ALT-V, C)

Provides display commands for toggling on or off the **T**ree List, **F**ile List, **P**rogram List, **V**iew Window, Background **M**at, and **D**OS Command Line (the default being for all these elements to be on *except* the Program List and View window.) In addition, provides the option Viewer **C**onfig to let you set the View window to be horizontal or vertical (the default being horizontal, or HORZ). Lastly, provides the option **W**indow Style to set *all* the PC Shell windows to be tiled (that is, set adjacent to each other) or the default of cascaded (that is, initially set with spaces between them, and with the ability to move and overlap on top of each other). Covered in "Opening, Hiding, and Combining Windows" in this chapter.

Hide All Lists (ALT-V, H)

Toggles the display of all windows on or off. When all windows are off, only the DOS command line and message bar are visible (unless you press ALT, in which case the title bar and menu bar are also displayed). This can be useful if you wish to use

PC Shell primarily as an unobtrusive program switcher (see "Running Programs" in Chapter 18). Pressing F10 brings back the standard PC Shell screen. Covered in "The DOS Command Line" and "Opening, Hiding, and Combining Windows" in this chapter.

Set Date/Time (ALT-V, T)

Displays, and lets you change, the system date and time.

Refresh (ALT-V, R)

Rereads your drive to update the Tree List and File List, and implements a **Disk Sort Files in Directory** command. The latter is covered in "Physically Sorting Files and Directories" in this chapter.

Filters (ALT-V, L)

Provides the two options File **L**ist (which lets you restrict the File List to files matching your filename specifications) and File **S**elect (which lets you select files matching your filename specifications). Filters File **S**elect can also be invoked by pressing F9, and is covered in "Selecting Files Using Wildcards" in this chapter.

Unselect Files (ALT-V, U or F4)

Unselects all selected files in the File List. Covered in "Selecting and Unselecting Files" in this chapter.

The Special Menu

The **S**pecial menu provides options for displaying system information, connecting two PCs, mapping a file, mapping a disk, mapping memory, and (when it's resident) unloading PC Shell. The menu contains three commands in both Beginner and Intermediate modes, and six commands in Advanced mode. The following lists all six commands and specifies each command's user level:

System Info (ALT-S, S) (Beginner)

Runs the SI program, which provides comprehensive information about your computer system. Covered in "Displaying System Information" in Chapter 18.

DeskConnect (ALT-S, C) (Beginner)

Connects a computer running both PC Shell and the memory-resident program DESKCON with a second computer attached by serial cable and running the program DESKSRV. Covered in "Connecting Computers Using DeskConnect" in Chapter 18.

File Map (ALT-S, F) (Advanced)

Displays a map showing where each selected file is located on your disk. Covered in "Mapping Files" in Chapter 16.

Disk Map (ALT-S, M) (Advanced)

Displays a map of the current disk. Covered in "Mapping Disks" in Chapter 17.

Memory Map (ALT-S, E) (Advanced)

Lists the names and sizes of programs currently occupying your system's memory. Covered in "Displaying System Information" in Chapter 18.

Remove PC Shell (ALT-S, R) (Beginner)

Exits PC Shell and unloads it from memory, freeing up space for other programs. This command only appears when PC Shell is loaded memory resident. Covered in "Unloading PC Shell" in this chapter.

The Tree Menu

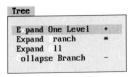

The Tree menu provides the following four options for expanding and collapsing directories on the Tree List:

Expand One Level (ALT-T, X or +)

If the selected directory on the Tree List isn't displaying all its subdirectories (indicated by its folder displaying a + on a graphics screen), displays all subdirectories one level down. Covered in "New PC Shell Features in Version 7" in this chapter.

Expand Branch (ALT-T, B or *)

Displays all of the subdirectories contained in the selected directory. Covered in "New PC Shell Features in Version 7" in this chapter.

Expand **All** (ALT-T, A)

Displays all subdirectories in the Tree List. Covered in "New PC Shell Features in Version 7" in this chapter.

Collapse Branch (ALT-T, C or –)

Hides the subdirectories in the selected directory. Covered in "New PC Shell Features in Version 7" in this chapter.

Chapter *16*

Managing Your Files

In Chapter 15, "PC Shell Overview," you learned how to run PC Shell, and use such screen elements as the Tree List, File List, and menu bar. In this chapter, you'll learn how to use these skills to manage your files.

The chapter first covers the preliminary steps for performing virtually *any* file operation. It then details how to copy, move, rename, and delete files. These four operations are the ones you'll perform most frequently, and they will form the core of your file management activities.

The chapter then explains how to compare files; verify that files are free of media defects; find files based on their names, contents, creation dates, and/or sizes; edit file attributes, creation dates, and creation times; display information about selected files; view files in their native formats; edit text files; and print files.

Preparing for a File Operation

Before you can perform a file operation using PC Shell, you must invoke PC Shell and select the files you want to work with. To do so, follow these steps:

1. If you aren't already in PC Shell, call it up now. If you've installed the program to be memory resident, press CTRL-ESC. Otherwise, type **PCSHELL** from the DOS prompt and press ENTER.

2. If you aren't already in Advanced mode (indicated in the upper-left corner of the title bar), press ALT-O, U, A, O to reset your user level. This lets you access all menu options.

3. If the files you want to affect aren't on the current drive, switch to a different drive by pressing TAB until you're at the drive bar, and then holding down CTRL and pressing the drive letter; or by simply clicking the letter in the drive bar. For example, to switch to drive C, press CTRL-C from the drive bar, or click on C in the drive bar.

4. If the Tree List isn't already activated, press TAB until it is, or click the Tree List window.

5. Use the arrow keys to move to the directory you want to work with, or click the directory.

6. Activate the File List by pressing TAB or clicking the File List window.

7. Select each file you want to affect by moving to it and pressing ENTER, or by clicking it. (Alternatively, select *all* files in the window by pressing F9, ALT-S.) These are your *source* files. If you're copying or moving them, the location you're directing them to is their *target* location.

You're now ready to proceed with a File menu operation. To continue, go to the section that covers the specific operation you're interested in.

Copying Files

One of PC Shell's most important options is to create duplicates of your files. Copying has several uses. First, it allows you to safeguard your data by creating backups of your original files. Second, it lets you share your data with others via floppy disks. Third, it lets you transfer files directly to an adjacent computer connected by PC Shell's DeskConnect feature (see "Connecting Computers Using DeskConnect" in Chapter 18, "Using Advanced PC Shell Features").

You can always copy files using the File Copy command. In addition, if you have a mouse, you can copy files by clicking and dragging.

Copying Files Using the Copy Command

To copy one or more files using the File Copy command, follow these steps:

1. Perform the steps in "Preparing for a File Operation" to select the files you want to copy.

2. Press ALT-F, C, or press F5, or click on the File menu and select Copy. A dialog box like this appears listing your available drives:

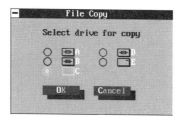

3. Press the letter of the drive to which you want to move your files and press ENTER, or click the drive and click OK. If the drive's disk has no directories other than the root directory (for example, if it's a blank floppy disk), go to step 5.

    Otherwise, you're prompted to select the directory you want to copy to.

4. Position the cursor on the directory in the Tree List you want to copy to and press ENTER, or click the directory.

5. If your target location doesn't contain any files with the same names as your selected files, then the selected files are copied, and you're returned to the PC Shell screen.

    Otherwise, a dialog box like this warns you that you're about to overwrite a file with the same name:

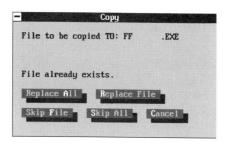

6. To copy all your selected files, replacing any files at the target location with the same name, press ENTER or click Replace All. Use this option with care, as there's no way to recover a replaced file.

    Alternatively, press R or click Replace File to copy only the current file; press F or click Skip File to skip copying the current file and proceed to the next one; press S or click Skip All to skip copying *any* files that would replace existing files; or press ESC or click Cancel to abort the rest of the copying operation altogether.

7. Repeat step 6 as many times as necessary. When you're done copying, you're returned to the PC Shell screen.

Copying Files Using Your Mouse

To copy files by clicking and dragging, follow these steps:

1. Perform the steps in "Preparing for a File Operation" to select the files you want to copy.

2. Position your mouse pointer over *any* of the selected files, hold down your left mouse button, and drag. A small box indicating the number of files you're copying moves along with your pointer as you drag.

3. Drag the box to the name of the directory in the Tree List you want to copy to. If you're using a Single File List display, the directory must be on the same drive you're copying from. If you're using a Dual Files List display, the directory can be from either Tree List.

4. Release the mouse button. If your target location doesn't contain any files with the same names as your selected files, then the selected files are copied and you're returned to the PC Shell screen.

    Otherwise, follow step 6 in the previous "Copying Files Using the Copy Command" section. When you're done copying, you're returned to the PC Shell screen.

Moving Files

If you want to reorganize files on your disk, you can copy the files to another location and then delete the originals. However, it's more efficient to perform both operations in one step by *moving* the files.

You can always move files using the **File Move** command. In addition, if you have a mouse, you can move files by clicking and dragging.

Moving Files Using the Move Command

To move one or more files using the **File Move** command, follow these steps:

1. Perform the steps in "Preparing for a File Operation" to select the files you want to move.

2. Press ALT-F, M, or click on the File menu and select Move. You're first prompted to confirm that you want to delete your selected files from their current locations.

3. Press ENTER or click OK. A dialog box appears listing your available drives.

4. Press the letter of the drive you want to move your files to and press ENTER, or click the drive and click OK. If the drive's disk has no directories other than the root directory (for example, if it's a blank floppy disk), go to step 6.

   Otherwise, you're prompted to select the directory you want to copy to.

5. Position the cursor on the directory in the Tree List you want to move the files to and press ENTER, or click the directory.

6. If your target location doesn't contain any files with the same names as your selected files, then the selected files are copied to the new location and deleted from the old one. You're then returned to the PC Shell screen.

   Otherwise, a dialog box warns you that you're about to overwrite a file with the same name.

7. To move all your selected files, replacing any files at the target location with the same name, press ENTER or click Replace All. Use this option with care, as there's no way to recover a replaced file.

   Alternatively, press R or click Replace File to move only the current file, press F or click Skip File to skip moving the current file and proceed to the next one, press S or click Skip All to skip moving *any* files that would replace existing files, or press ESC or click Cancel to abort the rest of the move operation altogether.

8. Repeat step 7 as many times as necessary. When you're done moving files, you're returned to the PC Shell screen.

Moving Files Using Your Mouse

To move files by clicking and dragging, follow these steps:

1. Perform the steps in "Preparing for a File Operation" to select the files you want to move.

2. While holding down CTRL, position your mouse pointer over *any* of the selected files, hold down your left mouse button, and drag. A small box indicating the number of files you're moving advances along with your pointer as you drag. At this point, you can release the CTRL key (but *not* the mouse button).

3. Drag the box to the name of the directory in the Tree List you want to move the files to. If you're using a Single File List display, the directory must be on the same drive as your source files. If you're using a Dual Files List display, the directory can be from either Tree List.

4. Release the mouse button. You're asked to confirm that you want to move the files.

5. Click OK. If your target location doesn't contain any files with the same names as your selected files, then the selected files are copied to the target location and deleted from the source location. You're then returned to the PC Shell screen.

Otherwise, follow step 7 in the previous "Moving Files Using the Move Command" section. When you're done moving files, you're returned to the PC Shell screen.

Renaming Files

Sometimes you'll want to change a file's name to make it better reflect its contents. You can rename files individually using the File Rename Single command. You can also change the names of an entire group of files simultaneously (for example, change all RPT extensions to TXT extensions) by using the File Rename Global command.

Renaming Files Individually

To rename one or more files individually, follow these steps:

1. Perform the steps in "Preparing for a File Operation" to select the files you want to rename.

2. Press ALT-F, N, or click on the File menu and select Rename. If you've selected one file, go to step 4.

3. If you've selected two or more files, a dialog box asks you to choose between the options Global and Single. Press S, O, or click Single and OK, to rename each file individually.

4. A dialog box appears displaying the file's current name and prompting you to enter a new one. If you've selected multiple files and want to skip renaming this current one, press ALT-N or click Next File to bring up the next one.

Otherwise, type a new name in the Name field to replace the current one. If your new name is shorter, press SPACEBAR or DEL to erase the extra characters. When you're done, press ENTER.

5. Type a new extension in the Ext field to replace the current one. If your new extension is shorter, press SPACEBAR or DEL to erase the extra characters.

6. Press ENTER twice or click Rename to accept the new name.

7. If your new filename already exists in the current directory, the message "Name duplicates existing file" appears. If this occurs, press ENTER or click OK, and then repeat steps 4 through 6 using a different filename.

8. If you selected only one file, the operation is completed, and you're returned to the PC Shell screen.

   Otherwise, the name of the next selected file is displayed. Repeat steps 4 through 7 until you've renamed all your selected files, or press ESC or click Cancel at any point to skip renaming the remaining files. When you're done renaming, you're returned to the PC Shell screen.

Renaming Multiple Files Simultaneously

To rename a group of files at the same time, follow these steps:

1. Perform the steps in "Preparing for a File Operation" to select two or more files you want to rename.

2. Press ALT-F, N, or click on the File menu and select Rename.

3. A dialog box asks you to choose between the options **G**lobal (which is the default) and **S**ingle. Press O or click OK to rename all the files as a group. The following dialog box appears:

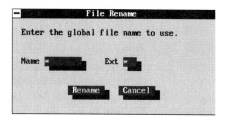

4. The box provides Name and Ext fields which can hold text for a filename, and also the DOS wildcards * (asterisk) to represent any combination of characters and ? (question mark) to represent any single character.

   For example, to give all selected files TXT extensions, accept the asterisk in the Name field by pressing ENTER, type **TXT** in the Ext field, and press ENTER twice. The front portion of each file's name is unchanged, but each file's extension is changed to TXT.

   As another example, to make all selected files start with the number 1, type **1*** in the Name field and press ENTER three times. The first character in each file's name is replaced with the number 1, while the rest of each file's name and extension is left unchanged.

5. During the process of renaming each file, if PC Shell finds that a new name is already being used by an existing file in the same directory, a "file cannot be renamed" error message appears. Press ENTER or click Skip to bypass renaming the file that caused the problem but allow the remaining files to be renamed, or press ESC or click Cancel to end the renaming operation.

   When the renaming process is completed, you're returned to the PC Shell screen.

Deleting Files

Obsolete files clutter your disk, making it difficult to locate important files and make room for new files. You should therefore regularly delete files that you no longer need.

At the same time, however, always be careful not to accidentally delete a file you still need. To safeguard against losing data this way, see "Monitoring Deleted Files" in Chapter 5, "Safeguarding Your Data."

Once you're sure one or more files are obsolete, follow these steps to delete them:

1. Perform the steps in "Preparing for a File Operation" to select the files you want to eliminate.

2. Press ALT-F, D, or click on the File menu and select Delete.

3. If you selected only one file, a dialog box lists the filename and prompts you to choose either **D**elete or **C**ancel. To change your mind and leave the file unchanged, press ESC or click Cancel. Otherwise, press ENTER or click Delete to erase the file. You're returned to the PC Shell screen and, if you selected Delete, the file is no longer listed in the File List.

4. If you selected two or more files, a dialog box like this appears:

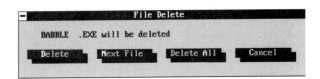

5. To delete the current file, press ENTER or click Delete. The file is eliminated, and the name of the next selected file is displayed.

   To skip deleting the current file, press N or click Next File. The file is unaffected, and the name of the next selected file is displayed.

To delete the current file and also all the selected files to follow it, press A or click Delete All. The current file and your subsequent selected files are eliminated, and you're returned to the PC Shell screen.

Lastly, to abort the delete operation at any point, press ESC or click Cancel. The current file and any subsequent selected files are left unchanged, and you're returned to the PC Shell screen. However, any files you've already deleted remain deleted.

If you delete a file accidentally using the File Delete command, try to recover it immediately *by using the File Undelete command. For more information, see Chapter 6, "Recovering Deleted or Formatted Data."*

Destroying Files

When you delete a file, the space it was occupying on the disk is marked as being available for new files, but its data is left unaffected. This is normally desirable, since it gives you a chance to recover files you've deleted accidentally. However, if you have high security needs, you may not want your deleted files to be recoverable. If this is the case, you can totally destroy a file by overwriting its data at the same time you're deleting it. This is also known as *wiping* or *clearing* a file.

To wipe one or more files, follow these steps:

1. Perform the steps in "Preparing for a File Operation" to select the files you want to destroy.

2. Press ALT-F, G, C, or click on the File menu and select Change File and Clear File. You're asked to wait while the standalone Wipe program (which is new to PC Tools 7) is loaded into memory. For more information on this utility, see "Destroying Data Using Wipe" in Chapter 11, "Encrypting Data Using PC Secure."

3. A dialog box warns you that wiping the current selected file will make it unrecoverable. If you've changed your mind and want to bypass the current file, press S or click Skip. The file is left unchanged, and the next selected file is listed.

   Otherwise, if you want to go ahead and destroy the current file, press W or click Wipe. The file is overwritten based on the current settings in the Wipe program.

4. Repeat step 3 until you've dealt with all your selected files. At that point a screen appears, summarizing the results of the wipe operation.

5. When you're done examining the screen, press ENTER or click OK. The Wipe program exits, and you're returned to the PC Shell screen.

You can wipe a group of files, or an entire directory, or even an entire disk, in just one step by running the Wipe program from the DOS prompt. For more information, see "Destroying Data Using Wipe" in Chapter 11.

Comparing Files

Sometimes you'll want to know if two files have the same contents. For example, you may need to verify that a backup file is an accurate copy of the original. You may also wish to check whether the contents of a current version of a file are different from an earlier version.

You can always compare files using the standard Single File List display. However, if the files you're comparing are on two different disks, you'll find it more convenient to compare them using the Dual Files List display. The following sections cover both methods.

Comparing Files Using the Single File List Display

To compare files using the standard Tree List and File List display, follow these steps:

1. Perform the steps in "Preparing for a File Operation" to select the first half of each pair of files you want to compare.

2. Press ALT-F, A, or click on the File menu and select Compare File. A dialog box appears listing your available drives.

3. Press the letter of the drive containing the files to which you want to compare your selected files and press ENTER, or click the drive and click OK. The following dialog box appears:

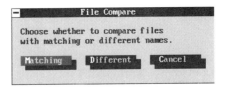

4. If the files you want to compare against have the same names as your selected files, press ENTER or click Matching. Otherwise, press D or click Different.

5. If the disk you selected has no directories other than the root directory (for example, if it's a one-directory floppy disk), go to step 6.

Otherwise, you're prompted to select the directory containing the files you want to compare. Position the cursor on the directory and press ENTER, or click the directory.

6. If you chose the **Different** option, skip to step 8.

 If you chose the **Matching** option, each of your selected files is automatically compared against its counterpart in the target location. If each set of files matches, a dialog box appears saying "Files are identical." When you press ENTER, the operation ends and you're returned to the PC Shell screen.

7. If a set of files doesn't match, a dialog box appears identifying the filename and how the files differ (for example, "Compare UNSUCCESSFUL, not the same size"). Note the filename, and then press ENTER or click OK to continue the operation.

 On the other hand, if a matching file isn't found, a dialog box identifying the selected file is displayed, and you're given the option of specifying the name of the file to compare it against. Either do so as prompted, or press ESC and ENTER to just skip the file and continue the operation.

 Continue this procedure until a dialog box displays the message "File compare finished," meaning that all your selected files have been processed, and then press ENTER or click OK to return to the PC Shell screen.

8. Because you chose to compare your selected files to files with different names, the compare operation can't proceed automatically. Instead, for each file, it prompts you for the name of the file to compare against. Type an appropriate name and extension into the Name and Ext fields, and then press ALT-O, M, or click OK and Compare, to execute the comparison.

 When the comparison is completed, a dialog box appears informing you of the result (for example, "Compare UNSUCCESSFUL, not the same size"). If necessary, mark down the result, and then press ENTER or click OK to continue the operation.

 Continue this procedure until a dialog box displays the message "File compare finished," meaning that all your selected files have been processed, and then press ENTER or click OK to return to the PC Shell screen.

Comparing Files Using the Dual Files List Display

To compare files using a Dual Files List display, follow these steps:

1. Perform the steps in "Preparing for a File Operation" to select the first half of each pair of files you want to compare.

2. If PC Shell isn't already set to a Dual Files List display, press INS. An extra set of Tree List and File List windows appears at the bottom of the screen.

3. If the second Tree List isn't already activated, select it by using TAB or by clicking its window.

4. Select the drive and directory containing the files to which you want to compare your selected files.

5. Return to your first Tree List by using SHIFT-TAB or by clicking its window.

6. Press ALT-F, A, or click on the File menu and select Compare File.

7. A dialog box asks you to choose the type of compare operation you want to perform. If the files you want to compare against have the same names as your selected files, press ENTER or click Matching. Otherwise, press D or click Different.

8. You're asked to confirm that you want to compare your selected files to the files in the directory of the second Tree List. Press ENTER or click OK to do so.

9. If you selected the Matching option, follow steps 6 and 7 of the previous section. If you selected the Different option, follow step 8 of the previous section. When all selected files have been compared, you're returned to the PC Shell screen.

10. If you want to go back to the standard Single File List display, press DEL.

Verifying Files

If you aren't sure whether your drive saved certain files properly, or if you suspect that the areas of the disk the files are on have become defective, you can check the files for readability. To do so, follow these steps:

1. Perform the steps in "Preparing for a File Operation" to select the files you want to check.

2. Press ALT-F, Y, or click on the File menu and select Verify.

3. A File Verify dialog box displays the name and sectors of each selected file as it's checked. If no errors are found in any file, the operation ends with a display of the last selected file and the message that it "verifies OK!" If this occurs, press ENTER to close the dialog box. You're returned to the PC Shell screen.

4. If a selected file is found to be defective, a dialog box tells you which sector on the disk was found to be unreadable, and offers to let you continue the verify process or view the defective area.

5. If you want to continue the verify process, press V or click Verify. If another defect is found, return to step 4. Otherwise, go to step 6.

   If you want to see which section of the file is defective (which is generally only useful for text files), press E or click View/Edit. A screen displaying sector data in both hexadecimal and ASCII appears. To understand and use this technical screen, see "Editing Sectors" in Chapter 18, "Using Advanced PC Shell Features." When you're done, press ESC to continue the verify process. If other defects are then found, return to step 3.

6. After all your selected files have been checked, if one or more files were found to be defective, a dialog box appears listing them. Note the filenames, and then press ENTER or click OK to return to the PC Shell screen.

If a defective file was found and you have a sound backup copy of it, it's recommended that you delete the file and then run DiskFix to mark the file's areas as unusable (see Chapter 7, "Repairing Disks Using DiskFix").

On the other hand, if you don't have a backup copy of the file, you may be able to recover most of its data by revising bytes on the defective sector and saving the file to disk again (see "Editing Sectors" in Chapter 18). You can then try to use printed versions of the file's contents and your recollections to fill in any missing data.

Finding Files

A hard disk typically holds hundreds of files. It's therefore easy to forget which directory contains a file, and even easier to forget which particular file contains the information you're looking for.

You can search for files in several ways. If the files are anywhere on your disk, or are even scattered across multiple disks, the File Locate command can find them based on their names, text contents, dates, sizes, and/or attributes. Alternatively, if the files are all in the File List, you can use the View Filters File List command to find the files based on their names, and the File Search command to find the files based on their text or hexadecimal contents.

Finding Files Anywhere in Your System

To search for files across multiple directories, or even across multiple disks, based on their names, text contents, dates, sizes, and/or attributes, follow these steps:

1. Perform steps 1 through 3 in "Preparing for a File Operation" to select the drive you want to search.

2. Press ALT-F, L, or press F7, or click on the File menu and select Locate. A powerful standalone program called File Find (which is new to PC Tools 7) is loaded into memory, and the screen in Figure 16-1 appears.

You're started in the File Specification field. You can use this field to restrict your search to particular filenames and/or directories. You can also use it to specify a different drive from your current one, or to specify multiple drives.

First, you can use the DOS wildcards * (asterisk) to represent any combination of characters and ? (question mark) to represent any single character. For example, to specify batch files, type ***.BAT**; to specify dBASE files, type ***.DBF**; and to specify all files beginning with REPORT, type **REPORT*.***.

You can also exclude files by preceding your specification with a dash. For example, -*.EXE excludes searching for EXE program files, and -M*.* excludes searching for any files beginning with the letter "M."

In addition, you can use the backslash key (\) to specify directories. For example, \PCTOOLS*.* specifies all files in the PCTOOLS directory, \PCTOOLS*.TXT specifies all files with TXT extensions in the PCTOOLS directory, and -\PCTOOLS\DATA*.CFG excludes all PC Tools configuration files.

Furthermore, you can precede your specification with a drive letter to search a drive other than your current one (which is indicated at the top of the window). For example, B:*.TXT specifies all TXT files on drive B, and C:\PCTOOLS*.* specifies all files in the PCTOOLS directory of drive C, regardless of what your current drive is.

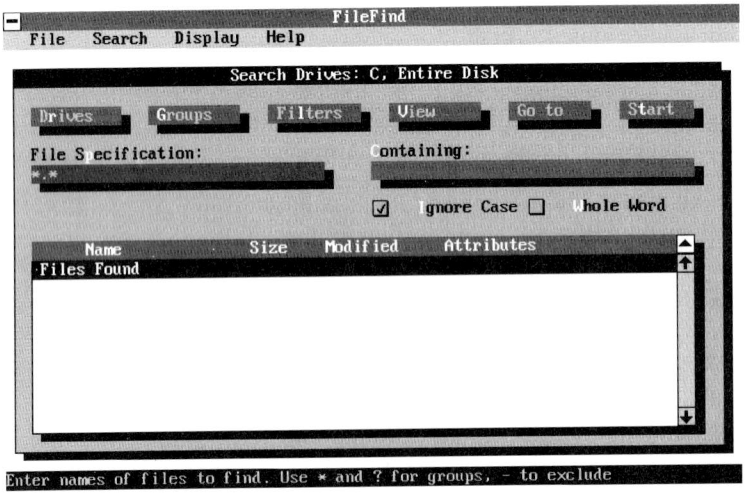

Figure 16-1.   The File Find screen

You can also fine-tune your criteria by entering multiple specifications, separated by spaces. The only limit on these criteria is that they don't exceed a total of 100 characters.

For example, the following three criteria specify all program files on your current drive:

*.EXE *.COM *.BAT

As another example, the following four criteria specify all dBASE files, Lotus 1-2-3 files, and TXT files on your current drive that are *not* in the PCTOOLS directory:

*.DBF *.WK? *.TXT -\PCTOOLS*.*

The list is processed from left to right. Therefore, the first three criteria specify DBF, WK?, and TXT files, while the last one excludes any such files in the PCTOOLS directory.

As a third example, the following three criteria specify searching three different drives in your system for dBASE files:

A:*.DBF B:*.DBF C:*.DBF

Such multiple criteria give you a great deal of control over which files are listed or searched.

Once you've entered your file specifications—or accepted the default specification of *.* to include all files on your current drive—press TAB or ALT- C, or click the Containing field. This moves you to a field where you can specify a text sequence, or *string*, up to 127 characters long to further narrow your search.

For example, you could type **Fourth Quarter** to restrict your search to files containing that phrase. The default is to search without paying attention to upper- and lowercase differences, so such instances as "FOURTH QUARTER," and "fourth quarter" would be considered valid matches. To restrict the search to matching the exact case specified, press ALT-I or click Ignore Case to turn that switch *off*.

The default is also to search without paying attention to whether the phrase is part of a larger phrase, so in the current example such instances as "Fourth Quarterly" and "1991Fourth Quarter" would be considered valid matches. To restrict the search to matching only occurrences that don't have other characters adjacent to them (other than spaces and punctuation marks), press ALT-W or click Whole Word to turn that switch *on*.

Lastly, you can restrict your search to files falling within a specified date range or size range, and/or to files with certain attributes. To do so, press ALT-L or click the Filters button near the top center of the window. The following dialog box appears:

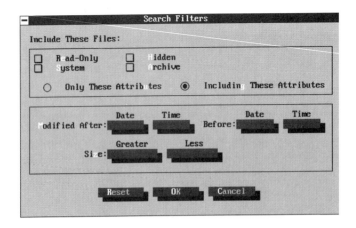

Fill in the appropriate information for whichever options you want to use, and then press ALT- O or click OK. (Alternatively, clear all the settings in the box and exit by pressing ALT-R, O, or clicking Reset and OK.)

Once you've entered your file specifications and/or text string and/or search filters, you're ready to initiate the locate operation. To do so, press ENTER or ALT-T, or click the Start button in the window's upper-right corner.

If you didn't specify a text string, the search is completed fairly quickly. If you did, however, the search may take several minutes, particularly if you didn't use your filename criteria to restrict it to a small range of files. You can interrupt the operation at any time by pressing ESC or ALT-T, or by clicking the Stop button in the upper-right corner. You can then press ESC or click Cancel to stay in the File Find screen and try again with different specifications.

Once the operation is completed, a dialog box appears saying "Search complete, Return to PCSHELL?" If you want to stay in the File Find screen, press ESC or click Cancel. You can then examine a list of the files found, broken down by directory, in the File List box in the bottom of the window. You can move in this List by file using DOWN ARROW and UP ARROW, by window using PGDN and PGUP, and to its bottom or top using END or HOME; or scroll its files vertically using your mouse. When you select the files you want, you can use File Find's own **File** menu to manipulate them. Finally, when you're done, you can optionally conduct an entirely new search operation.

Alternatively, press ENTER or click OK in response to the "Search complete" dialog box. The File Find program exits, but a Located Files window opens within PC Shell. You can then use any PC Shell command (other than File **Locate**) to manipulate the located files. For example, you can use the File Sear**ch** command (as explained shortly) to pick out files in the window containing a certain text or hexadecimal sequence; copy, rename, or delete selected files; edit or print selected files; and so on.

When you're done working with the Located Files window, press ESC or click on its Close box. You're returned to the standard PC Shell screen.

*File Find is a standalone program, so you can run it directly from the DOS prompt by typing **FF** and pressing ENTER. This is especially convenient if you don't tend to keep PC Shell resident.*

Using Search Groups

In the previous section, you entered your filename criteria into the File Specification field. You can alternatively select a predefined group of filename criteria, which is called a *Search Group*. This saves you the bother of having to type in filename criteria that you use frequently.

To display Search Groups while in the File Find screen, press ALT-G or click the Groups command button. A dialog box like this appears:

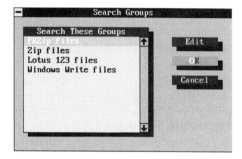

The box lists the Search Groups that were automatically entered by the Install program based on the applications it found on your hard disk during the installation process (see Appendix A). For example, if Install found Lotus 1-2-3 on your hard disk, the entry Lotus 123 Files is included in the box. This Search Group consists of such criteria as *.WK1 *.WKS to specify various versions of 1-2-3 files.

To enter a Search Group's criteria into the File Specification field, press TAB twice to select the List box, select the Group you want using the arrow keys or your mouse, and then press ENTER or click OK. The criteria are instantly typed into the field. You can then accept the criteria, edit them, or add to them for your particular search.

You can also revise, add, and delete search groups. To do so, press ALT-E or click Edit from the Search Groups dialog box. The following dialog box appears:

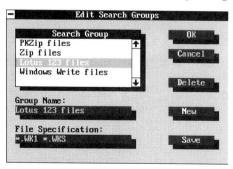

When you select a listed Search Group using the arrow keys or your mouse, its criteria appears in a File Specification field. You can move to this field using TAB or your mouse, and then revise the criteria to your liking.

Additionally, the selected Search Group's name appears in a Group Name field. If you move to this field and change the name, your File Specification revisions won't be applied to the current Search Group, but instead will be used to create an entirely *new* Search Group listed under the name you supplied.

When you're done making revisions to the selected Search Group, press ALT-S or click Save to register them. Otherwise, when you select a different Search Group, your changes will be discarded.

You can also use the New option to explicitly create a new Search Group, and the Delete option to eliminate the selected Search Group.

When you're done making all your changes, press ALT-O or click OK. Your Search Group revisions are saved to disk to preserve them for future sessions. The Edit Search Groups dialog box then closes, and you're returned to the Search Groups dialog box. You can then use a revised Search Group by selecting it, and pressing ALT-O or clicking OK; or you can just return to the File Find screen by pressing ESC or clicking Cancel.

Finding Files by Name in the File List

All searches for filenames can be conducted via the File Locate command. However, if you're only interested in finding files in the current directory, it's much faster to use the View Filters File List command. This option searches the File List based on a single file specification, and then sets the window to display only those files that matched the specification. When you later move to a different directory, the File List automatically returns to displaying all directory files.

To restrict the File List display to specified files, follow these steps:

1. Perform steps 1 through 5 in "Preparing for a File Operation" to select the directory you want to search.

2. Press ALT-V, L, L, or click on the View menu and select Filters and File List. The following dialog box appears:

The box provides Name and Ext fields, which can hold text representing a filename and extension. They can also hold the DOS wildcards * (asterisk) to represent any combination of characters and ? (question mark) to represent any single character. The fields initially contain asterisks, representing all filenames and all extensions in the File List window.

3. Type appropriate characters and/or wildcards in the Name field. (For example, to find files starting with the letter "A," type **A***.)

4. Press ENTER. You're moved to the Ext field.

5. Type appropriate characters and/or wildcards in the Ext field. (For example, to find any version of a Lotus 1-2-3 spreadsheet, type **WK?**).

6. Press ENTER twice or click Display to execute the search. After a moment, only those files matching your criteria are displayed in the File List. You can now work with these files using PC Shell commands.

7. If you want the File List to return to displaying all the files in the current directory, you can bring up the File List Filter dialog box again, press ALT-R or click Reset to set the Name and Ext fields back to asterisks again, and then press ALT-D or click Display.

   However, in most cases you'll probably find it simpler to just activate the Tree List and move to a different directory. This automatically resets the File List to display all directory files. You can then return to your original directory.

Finding Files by Content in the Current Window

Most searches for filenames can be conducted via the **File Locate** command. However, if you want to search files already in a Located Files window, or search only selected files or only unselected files within a window, or search for hexadecimal characters, you must use the **File Search** command instead. This option finds files in a File List or Located Files window based on the text or hexadecimal sequence you specify. It then either selects all files found; or pauses after each file and lets you continue searching for further occurrences, edit the file's sectors, select the file, or skip to the next file.

To use **File Search**, follow these steps:

1. Perform steps 1 through 5 in "Preparing for a File Operation" near the beginning of this chapter to select the directory you want to search. Alternatively, follow the steps in "Finding Files Anywhere in Your System" earlier in this chapter to display a Located Files window.

2. If you want to search only certain files in the window, select those files now.

3. Press ALT-F, H, or click on the File menu and select Search. The following dialog box appears:

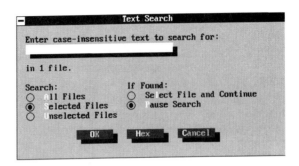

At the top of the box is a field that can hold up to 32 characters of the text string to search for. If you're conducting a text search, type your string in this field in either upper- or lowercase; the search doesn't pay attention to case differences.

4. If you're searching for a hexadecimal sequence instead (for example, if you're a programmer or if you're looking for formatting codes), press ALT-H or click Hex. The dialog box expands to allow you to type up to 64 digits of your hex string. Only valid hex digits (0 through 9 and A through F) are accepted. As you enter every two hex digits, a corresponding ASCII character is displayed below the field (see "Using the ASCII Table" in Chapter 28, "Using the Desktop Utilities").

5. If you want to search all files in the File List or Located Files window, press ALT-A or click All Files. If you want to restrict your search to unselected files in the window, press ALT-U or click Unselected Files. If you want to restrict your search to selected files in the window, accept the default of **Selected Files**. After you make your choice, the number of files included in the search is displayed in the line under your string.

6. If you want the search to proceed without interruption, press ALT-L or click Select File and Continue. After all your files are searched, the dialog box will close automatically, and the files that matched your specifications will be highlighted in the window.

Alternatively, accept the default option of **Pause Search** to pause after each file found. (If you've chosen the **Selected Files** option, you can only choose the **Pause Search** option, and vice versa.)

7. Press ALT-O or click OK to commence the search.

8. If no specified file matches your search string, a dialog box appears with the message "The search string was NOT found." To return to the File List or Located Files window, press ENTER or click Cancel.

9. If you chose the **S**elect File And Continue option, the search continues until all specified files are searched, and then automatically returns you to the File List or Located Files window. In addition, all specified files found to contain at least one instance of the string are selected in the window.

10. If you chose the **P**ause Search option, the search operation pauses every time a specified file is found to contain your search string and displays a dialog box identifying the file. The box also offers the options **S**elect, **N**ext File, **E**dit, and **C**ancel.

    If you want the file to be highlighted when the operation ends, press S or click Select. You can then press N or click Next File to continue the search operation. Alternatively, if you don't want the file highlighted, just press N or click Next File to continue.

    You can also choose the technical option of editing the file's sectors by pressing E or clicking Edit. A Sector Edit screen appears with the cursor at the beginning of your search string. To understand and use this screen, see "Editing Sectors" in Chapter 18. To exit the screen, press ESC.

    Lastly, you can abort the search at any time by pressing ESC or clicking Cancel. If you do, you're returned to your window, and any files you've previously set to be selected are highlighted.

*If while using **File Search** you see strange messages such as "Searching file 968 of 7," you're probably using PC Tools 7.0. To eliminate this and various other problems, contact Central Point Software about getting the more recent version 7.1. For more information, see this book's Introduction.*

Editing File Attributes

Files can have up to four special characteristics, or *attributes*: system, hidden, read-only, and archive.

System files are special DOS files such as IBMBIO.COM and IBMDOS.COM, or MSBIO.SYS and MSDOS.COM. They're used to load DOS when you start your computer.

Hidden files are files that don't display when you list filenames from DOS or an application. For example, system files are hidden to ensure they're not accidentally deleted. Hidden files are also sometimes generated as part of an application's copy protection scheme.

Read-only files are files that have been protected from being altered. In other words, you can read them, work with them, copy their data, and so on, but you can't replace them with an updated version. This option is often used on system files and network files.

Archive files are files that have been created or revised since the last time you backed up your hard disk. For more information, see "Backup Methods and Strategies" in Chapter 2, "Backing Up Your Hard Disk."

In addition, every file is stamped with the system time and date when it's created and every time it's revised.

To examine and edit a file's attributes, and its time and date, follow these steps:

1. Perform the steps in "Preparing for a File Operation" to select the files you want to examine and/or edit.

2. Press ALT-F, C, A, or click on the File menu and select Change File and Attribute Change. A File Attribute box appears that lists each selected file's name; attributes (with H for hidden, S for system, R for read-only, and A for archive); and creation time and date. It also lists each file's size (which can't be edited).

3. To toggle a file's attribute on or off, select the file using the arrow keys or your mouse, and then press the letter of the attribute. For example, to make a normal file read-only, move to the file and press R. To make the file revisable again, press R again.

 Never *change the attributes of system files or copy protected files. If you do, you may not be able to start your computer from your hard disk or run a particular application until you return the files to their previous states.*

4. To change a file's time or date, use the arrow keys or your mouse to move to the time or date, and then type new characters to replace the old ones.

    For times, use the format *HH:MM*a/p, where *HH* represents hours, *MM* represents minutes, "a" represents A.M., and "p" represents P.M.

    For dates, use the format *MM-DD-YY*, where *MM* represents months, *DD* represents days, and *YY* represents the last two digits of the year 19*YY*.

5. If you change your mind and want to exit *without* saving your changes, press ESC or click Cancel. However, if you want the files revised as specified, press ALT-U or click Update. In either case, the dialog box closes and you're returned to the PC Shell screen.

Displaying File Information

PC Shell provides several ways to display information about a file. For example, as explained in Chapter 15, you can set the File List to display each file's size, creation date, creation time, attributes, and/or number of clusters using the **O**ptions **F**ile Display Options command (see "Adjusting the File List Display" in Chapter 15).

In addition, you can display information about selected files using the **O**ptions **S**how Information command, and generate a map showing a file's location on your disk by selecting the **S**pecial **F**ile Map command. These topics are covered in the following sections.

Displaying Information About Selected Files

To display basic information about one or more files, follow these steps:

1. Perform the steps in "Preparing for a File Operation" to select the files you want to get information on.

2. Press ALT-O, S, or click on the Options menu and select Show Information. A dialog box like this appears:

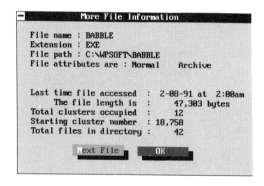

The box shows the following information:

- The file's name and extension
- The file's drive and directory
- The file's attributes
- The date and time when the file was last saved to disk
- The file's size in bytes
- The file's number of clusters (see Chapter 4)
- The ID number of the file's first cluster
- The total number of files in the current directory

When you're done examining the information, press ENTER. If you selected more than one file, information about the next file is displayed. After you go through all your selected files, you're returned to the PC Shell screen.

You can also print information about all the files currently displayed in the File List. To do so, make sure your printer is on and online, and then press ALT-F, P, L, or click on the File menu and select Print and Print File List. A printout is generated that shows the name of each file in the File List, as well as its size, number of clusters, creation date, creation time, and attributes. In addition, the end of the printout shows the total number and size of the files in the File List, the total number and size of files in the current directory, the total number and size of the files currently selected, and the amount of free space left on the current drive.

Mapping Files

To map files on your disk, follow these steps:

1. Perform the steps in "Preparing for a File Operation" to select the first file you want to map.

2. Press ALT-S, F, or click on the Special menu and select File Map. A map like the one in Figure 16-2 appears, showing the area of your disk that contains the selected file.

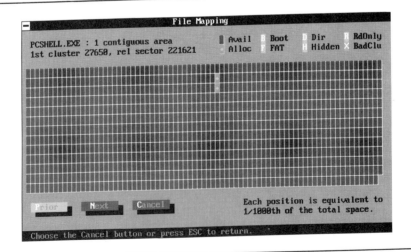

Figure 16-2.   *The File Mapping screen*

Each position on the map represents a cluster (see Chapter 4). As indicated by the legends above the map, each cluster is represented by one of the following symbols:

- *Avail*   This is a cluster that's available (that is, that's not being used by the current file). It's represented on the map by a dotted rectangle symbol.

- *Alloc*   This is a normal cluster that's allocated (that is, that's in use by the current file). It's represented on the map by a diamond symbol.

- *Boot*   This is a cluster storing the boot record, which is used to start up your computer. It's always at the beginning of a disk and is represented on the map by the letter "B".

- *FAT*   This is a cluster storing the File Allocation Table, or FAT, which contains the locations of the disk's files. It follows the boot record and is represented on the map by the letter "F".

- *Dir*   This is a cluster storing the root directory, which contains the names of the disk's files. It follows the FAT and is represented on the map by the letter "D".

- *Hidden*   This is a cluster in use by the current file which has a "hidden" attribute. It's represented on the map by the letter "H".

- *RdOnly*   This is a cluster in use by the current file which has a read-only attribute. It's represented on the map by the letter "R".

- *BadClu*   This is a defective, or "bad," cluster that's in use by the current file. It's represented on the map by the letter "X".

The proportions of the map are automatically scaled down to fit your screen. For example, the map of a 10MB disk might display a symbol for every 15 sectors, while the map of a 40MB disk might display a symbol for every 60 sectors. As a result, certain areas such as the boot record and FAT might not show up because they only take up a few sectors.

You can use the map to determine if a file's clusters are adjacent to each other, if the file contains any defective clusters, and so on. You can also read the file's beginning cluster and sector ID numbers in the upper-left corner of the window.

To map the file that follows the current one in the File List, press N or click Next. To map the file that precedes the current one in the File List, press P or click Prior. (The order of files here is determined entirely by the File List display, *not* by any files you've selected other than your first file.)

When you're done mapping files, press ESC or click Cancel. You're returned to the PC Shell screen.

Viewing Files

One of the most useful features in PC Shell is the ability to view files in the formats of the applications that created them. For example, you can display Lotus 1-2-3 files in their column and row format, dBASE files in their field and record format, and WordPerfect files in their document format, all from within PC Shell.

This feature is made possible by a group of *viewers* that are part of the PC Shell package. When you ask to view a selected file, PC Shell first analyzes the format of the file, and then uses the data in the appropriate viewer to display the file properly. This means that you can examine your data files from popular applications without having to waste time running each application. If you keep PC Shell memory resident, it also means that you can examine data files while you're running entirely unrelated applications.

To view a file, follow these steps:

1. Perform the steps in "Preparing for a File Operation" to select the files you want to view.

2. Press ALT-F, V, or press F2, or click on the File menu and select View File Contents. The data in the first file selected fills the screen. If a viewer for the file's data is available, the file is displayed in its native format. Otherwise, if the file contains text, it's displayed as either a text or ASCII file. Lastly, if no text is detected, the file is displayed in binary (appropriate for program EXE and COM files). The type of viewer being used, as well as the file's name, appears at the top of the window.

3. Scroll through the file using the arrow keys to move by lines and columns, PGDN and PGUP to move by screen, and END and HOME to move to the bottom and top; or by clicking the window's scroll bars with your mouse.

4. Notice that several new commands have appeared on the message bar. For example, press F2 (Info). A dialog box displays the type of viewer being used for the file, and the file's name, size, and creation date and time. Press ESC to close the Info box.

5. Press F6 (Viewer). A list of all 37 available viewers is displayed. Scroll through the list using the arrow keys or your mouse. If you think a listed viewer is more appropriate for your current file than the one PC Shell selected, you can switch to that viewer by moving to it and pressing ENTER, or by double-clicking it. Otherwise, just press ESC to close the list. (More information about available viewers appears in the next section.)

6. Press F5 (GoTo). A dialog box identifies the line and column you're on, and the number of lines and columns in the entire file. It also offers to let you jump to a specified line and column. For example, type **5** and then press ENTER twice. You're moved to line 5.

7. Press F7 (Search). A dialog box like this appears:

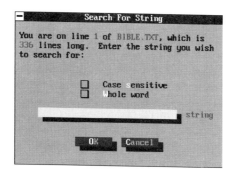

Like the previous dialog box, this tells you the number of the line you're on and the total number of lines in the file. In addition, it prompts you to enter a text string (which can be up to 30 characters long). Furthermore, it provides the options Case **S**ensitive (to make the search pay attention to upper- and lowercase), and **W**hole Word (to make the search ignore occurrences in which your string is part of a larger string).

8. Try out the Search feature by typing **A** and then pressing ENTER twice. The first occurrence of the letter "A" (in either upper- or lowercase) in the file is highlighted. Press SHIFT-F7. The next occurrence is found. If you continue pressing SHIFT-F7, you continue moving to the next occurrence until a "No further match found" message appears.

9. Press F10 (NxtFle). Your next selected file is displayed.

10. Press F9 (PrvFle). Your previous file is displayed.

11. Press F8 (Unzoom). The View window shrinks from its full-screen size to a window in the standard PC Shell screen, once again giving you access to the Tree List and File List.

12. Activate the File List window by pressing SHIFT-TAB or clicking the window.

13. Move to a different file using the arrow keys or your mouse. The View window changes to display the new file. Move to a few different files in the File List and continue watching how the View window changes.

You can optionally change the View window from its default horizontal orientation to vertical for a better view of certain types of data (see "Opening, Hiding, and Combining Windows" in Chapter 15). You can also resize and reposition the window using Control menu commands or your mouse (see "Using the Control Menu" in Chapter 19).

14. Press TAB or click the View window to activate it again.

15. Press F8 (Zoom). The View window expands back to full-screen size.

16. Press ESC. The View window closes, and you're returned to the standard PC Shell screen.

Because the View feature is so useful, it's been expanded to other programs in PC Tools 7. You can now also view files in CP Backup (see Chapter 1), the File Find program (see "Finding Files Anywhere in Your System" earlier in this chapter), and the Undelete program (see "Using Interactive Undelete" in Chapter 6).

In addition, the View feature is included as a standalone program that can be run separately from PC Shell. To invoke it from the DOS prompt, type **VIEW** (optionally following by a file specification, such as C:\DATA*.DBF or A:\RE-PORTS*.DOC) and press ENTER. The files from either the current directory or (if you included it) the command-line file specification are listed. You can then view any file by moving to it with the arrow keys and pressing ENTER, or by double-clicking on the file.

List of Viewers

As you saw in the previous section, PC Tools 7 provides viewers for 37 different types of data files. Five of these viewers—Text, ASCII, DCA Final Form, DCA Revisable Form, and Binary—are generic.

The Text viewer is used when a file's format isn't supported by any of the other viewers, and the file contains text. Such files are usually produced by word processors not in the viewer list, or by word processors saving in the generic ASCII format (such as the Desktop's Notepads application).

The ASCII viewer is almost identical to the Text viewer. The main difference is that the Text viewer will display graphics characters (for example ☺ ♥½√♠☻), while the ASCII viewer displays text exclusively.

The DCA Final Form and DCA Revisable Form viewers are for files in these particular formats only. DCA is a generic format that supports word processing codes such as underlining and boldface (unlike ASCII), and which can be translated to and from a number of other word processing formats.

Lastly, the Binary viewer is used for files that have unrecognized formats and that *don't* contain text, such as EXE and COM program files. It provides a technical display consisting of hexadecimal digits and ASCII characters.

The remaining 32 viewers are devoted to files produced by specific applications. The following table lists each of these viewers and identifies its software category.

Application	Category
Borland Quattro	Spreadsheet
Borland Quattro Pro	Spreadsheet

Application	Category
Borland Paradox	Database
dBASE II	Database
dBASE III	Database
DisplayWrite	Word processor
Lotus 1-2-3	Spreadsheet
Lotus 1-2-3 1.*x* and 2.*x*	Spreadsheet
Lotus 1-2-3 3.*x*	Spreadsheet
Lotus Symphony	Spreadsheet
Microrim R:BASE	Database
Microsoft Excel 1.*x* and 2.*x*	Spreadsheet
Microsoft Excel 3.*x*	Spreadsheet
Microsoft Windows Write	Word processor
Microsoft Word	Word processor
Microsoft Works Database	Database
Microsoft Works Spreadsheet	Spreadsheet
Microsoft Works WP	Word processor
Mosaic Twin	Spreadsheet
MultiMate	Word processor
PC Secure	DES Encryption (just identifies the file as being encrypted by PC Secure)
PCX	Graphics
WordPerfect 4.2	Word processor
WordPerfect 5.*x*	Word processor
WordStar 2000	Word processor
WordStar 5.5	Word processor
XyWrite/XyWrite Plus	Word processor
LZH Archive Catalog	Compressed file library
PAK Archive Catalog	Compressed file library
SEA Archive Catalog	Compressed file library
ZIP Archive Catalog	Compressed file library
ZOO Archive Catalog	Compressed file library

The data compression viewers only display information about what files are contained in the libraries, not the files' contents.

If you're familiar with PC Tools Deluxe 6, you may wonder why you don't see a slew of VWR files in your PC Tools 7 directory. The reason is that the viewers are no longer stored as separate files. Instead, they're now all kept in one large file named VIEW.LIB in the SYSTEM subdirectory.

Using Viewer Commands

As you saw previously, when a View window is active, PC Shell revises the message bar to provide certain commands relevant to the file being displayed. The following commands are provided for all files:

- *Info* (F2)   This command brings up a dialog box displaying the type of viewer being used for the file, and the file's name, size, and creation date and time. To close the dialog box, press ESC.

- *Launch* (F4)   This command temporarily exits PC Shell, runs the application associated with the viewed file, and loads the file into the application. When you exit the application, you're prompted to press any key to return to PC Shell. (For more information, see Chapter 18, "Using Advanced PC Shell Features.")

- *GoTo* (F5)   This command moves you to a specified line and/or column. To use it, press F5, type the number of the line you want to move to, press TAB, type the number of the column you want to move to, and press ENTER twice.

- *Viewer* (F6)   This command displays a list of all 37 available viewers. To apply a listed viewer to the current file, move to the viewer and press ENTER, or double-click on the viewer.

- *Search* (F7)   This command finds a specified text string up to 30 characters long. To use it, press F7, type your text, optionally turn on the Case **S**ensitive and/or **W**hole Word switches, and press ENTER twice. If the string isn't found, a message appears telling you so. Otherwise, the entire string is highlighted. To find the next occurrence, press SHIFT-F7.

- *Unzoom/Zoom* (F8)   This command toggles the View window between half-screen and full-screen size. To select it, press F8 or click on the window's Zoom arrow in its upper-right corner.

- *PrvFle* (F9)   If you explicitly selected files, this command displays the contents of the previous selected file. Otherwise, it displays the contents of the previous file in the File List. (When you're on the first of your selected files or first file in the File List, this command has no effect.)

- *NxtFle* (F10)   If you explicitly selected files, this command displays the contents of the next selected file. Otherwise, it displays the contents of the next file in the File List. (When you're on the last of your selected files or the last file in the File List, this command has no effect.)

In addition, certain commands are provided for specific types of files. Database files are provided with these five customized commands:

- *Info* (F2)   In addition to standard viewer and file information, this command displays the number of records and fields in the database file.

- *Fields* (SHIFT-F2)   This command displays the name, type, and length of each field in the database file.

- *GoTo* (F5)   This command moves the cursor to the specified data entry. To use it, press F5, type the number of the record and/or field you want, and press ENTER.

- *Tables* (SHIFT-F5)   This command is available only for R:BASE. It displays a list of tables and lets you select the one you want.

- *Record* (SHIFT-F9)   This command toggles the window between the default column-row display and a display that shows one record at a time.

Spreadsheet files are provided with these four customized commands:

- *Info* (F2)   In addition to standard viewer and file information, this command displays the number of rows and columns in the spreadsheet file.

- *Cells* (SHIFT-F2)   This command displays the letter, type, and width of each column that contains data in the spreadsheet file.

- *Sheet* (SHIFT-F3)   This command is available only for Lotus 1-2-3 3.x files. It lists a group of worksheets and lets you select the one you want.

- *Goto* (F5)   This command moves the cursor to the specified cell. To use it, press F5, type a row number and/or column number (column *letters* are *not* allowed), and press ENTER.

PCX graphics files are provided with these two customized commands:

- *Modes* (SHIFT-F3)   This command lists the different video modes available for displaying the graphic and lets you choose the one you want.

- *Graph* (F8)   This command toggles between showing the graphic (the default if your system can display the picture) and showing a text screen providing information on the graphic (the default if your system can't display the picture).

Lastly, text files (that is, files viewed with the text viewer) are provided with this one customized command:

- *Wrap* (SHIFT-F3)   This command toggles the window between wrapping the text to fit in the current window size (the default) and unwrapping each paragraph to scroll past the window until its ENTER code is encountered.

Editing Text Files

You'll usually want to create or edit a document using a full-featured word processor. However, if you only need to create a small file or make some simple revisions to an existing text file, you can use PC Shell's text editor instead.

To call up the text editor, follow these steps:

1. Perform the steps in "Preparing for a File Operation" earlier in this chapter to select the text files you want to edit. (If you want to create a document instead of edit one, it doesn't matter which file is selected.)

> Don't *select a word processing file that contains important formatting codes. If you do, you'll probably be able to load and edit the file, but when you save it in the text editor's default ASCII format you'll lose the formatting codes for such features as underlining and boldfacing, headers and footers, and so on.*

2. Press ALT-F, G, E, or click on the File menu and select Change File and Edit File. What you see next depends on the version of PC Tools you're using.

3. If you're using PC Tools 7.0, a dialog box appears that displays the name of the currently selected file. You can accept this name, or enter the name of a different text file in the directory, or enter the name of a file that *doesn't* exist in the directory (which will create an entirely new file). Once the name of the file you want to edit is set, press ALT-O or click OK.

   If you're using PC Tools 7.1, a dialog box appears that displays the name of the currently selected file. If you want to edit this file, press E or click Edit. If you want to create a new file instead, press R or click Create. (If you want to edit a different file, you must start over by pressing ESC, selecting the file you want in the File List, and then pressing ALT-F, G, E, E.)

If you're using PC Tools 7.0, a limited version of the Desktop Manager's Notepads application is now loaded with your file. Specifically, all commands but Exit are deactivated in the Desktop menu, all but the Save and Exit Without Saving commands are deactivated in the File menu, the spell-checking commands are deactivated in the Edit menu, and the Switch To command is deactivated in the Control menu. However, all the basic text creation and editing commands are still available. For information on how to use them, see Chapter 20, "Using Notepads." When you're done composing or editing your document, pressing ESC both saves it and closes it, returning you to the PC Shell screen.

If you're using PC Tools 7.1, however, the File Editor from PC Tools Deluxe 6 is now loaded with your selected file. (Among the reasons for this regressive change is that not everyone installs the Desktop along with PC Shell.) The rest of this section deals with this version of the text editor.

Examining the File Editor Screen

The File Editor screen is made up of several components. If you're revising an existing file, the top-left corner of the editing window displays the directory and name of the file. If you're creating a file, it doesn't have a name yet, so the top-left corner just displays the current directory.

The top-right corner of the window shows whether you're in Insert mode (indicated by the word "INSERT"), in which your typing pushes existing text to the right; or in Overtype mode (indicated by blank space), in which your typing overwrites existing text. You can switch between modes by pressing INS. The default is Insert mode.

The bottom of the window displays a ruler line. The line provides a guide to what column in the window the cursor is on and shows where the tab stops are set.

Finally, the last line of the screen displays ten File Editor commands. To select any command, press the function key to its left, or hold down ALT and press the command's highlighted letter, or click on the command. These commands are covered in the following sections.

Typing and Editing

The procedures for basic typing and editing in the File Editor are similar to those in Notepads. Therefore, to get a feel for the Editor, work through the "Basic Typing" and "Moving Around in Your Document" sections in Chapter 20. The only differences in the File Editor are that there's no Line Number Counter, you can't turn off word wrap, and you can't jump to a particular line.

The File Editor also lets you manipulate an entire section, or *block*, of text. To do so, you must first highlight the block using the Select command. You can then use the **C**ut command alone to delete the block, or the **C**ut and **P**aste commands to move the block, or the **C**opy and **P**aste commands to copy the block.

More specifically, you can define a block of text you want to affect by following these steps:

1. Position the cursor at one end of the block.

2. Press ALT-L or click on the Select command.

3. Move the cursor until all the text you want to mark is highlighted. (If you change your mind, unselect the block by pressing ALT-L again or by clicking Select again to remove the highlighting.)

Once the block is marked, you can delete it by pressing F7 or ALT-C, or by clicking on the Cut command. You can then optionally move it by positioning the cursor at another location in your document, and then pressing F9 or ALT-P, or clicking on the Paste command. You can also insert additional copies of the block in other locations by repositioning the cursor and pressing F9 again.

Alternatively, you can copy a text block by pressing F8 or ALT-O, or by clicking on the Copy command. This copies the block into a temporary storage area in memory while leaving the original text unaffected. You can then position the cursor at another location in your document, and insert your copy by pressing F9 or ALT-P, or clicking on the Paste command. You can also insert additional copies in other locations by repositioning the cursor and pressing F9 again.

You can also search for text by pressing F4 or ALT-E, or by clicking on the Search command; you can replace text by pressing F5 or ALT-R, or by clicking on the Replace command. Your text sequence can be up to 32 characters long. The search does *not* make a distinction between upper- and lowercase.

In addition, you can optionally display hidden ENTER codes as highlighted arrows by pressing F10 or ALT-H, or by clicking on the Show command. This makes it easier to delete ENTER codes, count blank lines, and so on. To hide the codes again, press F10 again.

Saving and Exiting

To preserve your work, it's recommended that you save your file to disk every 15 minutes or so. In addition, you should save your file before you exit it. To do so, first press F2 or ALT-S, or click on the Save command.

If the file already has a name, it's saved immediately to the current directory, while its previous version is renamed with a BAK extension. A dialog box then appears with the message "File saved successfully." When you press ENTER, you're returned to the editing screen.

On the other hand, if the file hasn't been assigned a name yet, you're prompted for one now. Type a name up to eight characters long, press ENTER, optionally type an extension up to three characters long, and press ENTER twice more. The file is preserved to disk in the current directory, and a dialog box appears with the message "File saved successfully." When you press ENTER, you're returned to the editing screen.

When you're finished revising your document, press ESC or F3 or ALT-X, or click on the Exit command. If you haven't made any changes to the file since the last time you saved it, the file closes. Otherwise, a dialog box appears prompting you to save your work before exiting. Press ENTER or click Save to preserve your changes; or press X or click Exit to abandon your changes; or press ESC or click Return to return to the editing screen.

After you exit your document, if you selected multiple files before calling up the File Editor, you're prompted to edit the next file. Otherwise, you're returned to the PC Shell screen.

Once you've finished editing your selected files, you may want to print them to paper. To do so, see the next section.

Printing Files

If you want to print a word processing file that contains formatting codes, you'll get the best results by printing it from the application that created it. However, if you just want to print an ASCII text file (such as the files normally created by the Desktop's Notepads application), or if you want to print out a nontext file in hexadecimal (which is useful for programmers), you can do so quickly and easily using PC Shell's **File Print Print File** command.

PC Shell can only print to the LPT1 port. However, unless you have more than one printer connected to your system, the chances are that your printer is cabled into LPT1.

To print your files, follow these steps:

1. Perform the steps in "Preparing for a File Operation" earlier in this chapter to select the files you want to print.

2. Press ALT-F, P, or click on the File menu and select Print File. A submenu appears listing two options: Print File, which prints the contents of your selected files, and Print File List, which prints information about all the files in the File List. For information on the latter, see the Tip in the "Displaying Information About Selected Files" section earlier in this chapter.

3. Press F or click Print File. The following dialog box appears:

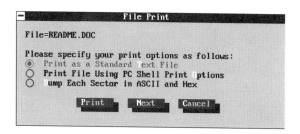

4. The name of your selected file appears in the upper-left corner of the box. If you decide you want to skip printing the file, press N or click Next. The file is bypassed, and your next selected file is listed.

5. If you want to print the listed text file and aren't interested in adjusting how it will appear on paper, make sure your printer is on and online, and then press T, P, or click Print as a Standard Text File and click Print. Your document is printed, and your next selected file is listed.

6. If you want to adjust how your text document will appear on paper, press O, P, or click Print File Using PC Shell Print Options and click Print. A dialog box appears that lets you specify the document's page length, line spacing, margins, and headers and footers. It also lets you turn on page numbering, set printing to pause after each page (which is useful for manual-feed printers), and set the last printed page to be ejected (or, for some printers, set an extra blank page to be ejected following printing). For detailed information about any particular option, move to the option and press F1.

   When you're done adjusting settings, make sure your printer is on and online, and then press P or click Print. Your document is printed, and your next selected file is listed.

7. If you want to print (or "dump") the listed file sector by sector in hexadecimal and ASCII, make sure your printer is on and online, and then press D, P, or click Dump Each Sector in ASCII and Hex and click Print. Your file is printed, and your next selected file is listed.

8. Repeat steps 4, 5, 6, and/or 7 until you've dealt with all your selected files. You're then returned to the PC Shell screen.

Chapter *17*

Managing Your Directories and Disks

In Chapter 16, "Managing Your Files," you learned how to use PC Shell to manage your files. In this chapter you'll learn how to use PC Shell to manage the other two data storage elements of your system: your directories and your disks.

This chapter first covers how to select, create, copy, move, rename, and delete directories; edit a directory's attributes; and display and print directory information. It then explains how to format, copy, compare, verify, search, rename, examine, and park disks.

Preparing for a Directory or Disk Operation

Before you can perform a directory or disk operation using PC Shell, you must invoke PC Shell and select the drive you want to work with. In addition, for a directory operation you must invoke the new Directory Maintenance program. To do so, follow these steps:

1. If you aren't already in PC Shell, call it up now. If you've installed the program to be memory resident, press CTRL-ESC. Otherwise, type **PCSHELL** from the DOS prompt and press ENTER.

2. If you aren't already in Advanced mode (indicated in the upper-left corner of the title bar), press ALT- O, U, A, O to reset your user level. This lets you access all menu options.

3. If you don't want to work with the current drive, switch to a different drive by pressing TAB until you're at the drive bar, and then holding down CTRL and pressing the drive letter; or by simply clicking the letter in the drive bar. For example, to switch to drive C, press CTRL-C from the drive bar, or click on C in the drive bar.

4. For the sections covering directory management, press ALT-D, M, F, or click on the Disk menu and select Directory Maintenance and Full DM Program. (If you're using PC Tools 7.0, just press ALT-D, M, or click on the Disk menu and select Directory Maintenance.) This runs the Directory Maintenance program, which is new to PC Tools 7. Directory Maintenance displays only the Tree List (as shown in Figure 17-1) and provides two menus, Volume and Directory, which contain directory commands exclusively (as shown in Figure 17-2).

*You can also run Directory Maintenance directly from the DOS prompt by typing **DM** (optionally followed by parameters) and pressing ENTER. For a list of available parameters, type **DM /?** at the DOS prompt and press ENTER.*

Managing Your Directories

A hard disk typically holds hundreds of files. If these files were all stored in the same directory, they'd appear as a confusing jumble of names and extensions. This would

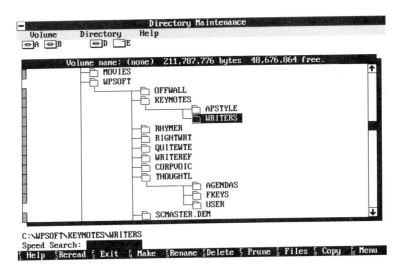

Figure 17-1.   *The Directory Maintenance screen*

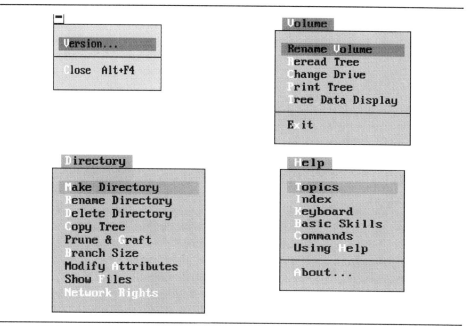

Figure 17-2. *The Directory Maintenance menus*

make it difficult to locate particular files, identify which files were associated with each other, and remember the functions of individual files.

It's therefore recommended that you make liberal use of directories to divide your data into small groups of related files. You can use these directories to organize the computer files on your disk just as you would use folders to organize paper files in a filing cabinet. Thoughtful use of directories will greatly enhance your ability to access specific data quickly and easily. The following sections explain how to select, create, move, rename, delete, and change the attributes of directories.

If PC Shell is memory resident, avoid changing a directory that's currently in use by any underlying application. Otherwise, errors may occur when you return to the application and it tries to continue reading and writing to a directory path that no longer exists.

If you're using PC Tools 7.0, the only tool provided for managing directories is the Directory Maintenance program, which is loaded when you select **Disk Directory Maintenance**.

If you're using PC Tools 7.1, however, selecting **Disk Directory Maintenance** displays a submenu with the commands **Add a Subdirectory, Rename a Subdirectory, Delete a Subdirectory, Prune and Graft, Modify Attributes,** and **Full DM Program**. The first five commands (which are lifted from PC Tools Deluxe 6) were primarily added in case you skipped installing the Directory Maintenance program (see the last portion of "Installing PC Tools on Your Hard Disk" in Appendix A, "PC Tools Installation and Configuration"). However, these submenu options generally aren't as easy to use or as powerful as their Directory Maintenance counterparts; for example, the **D**elete a Subdirectory command will only remove an *empty* directory, while the Directory Maintenance **D**elete Directory command will remove *any* directory, automatically deleting all files and subdirectories contained in the directory. The following sections cover both methods, but their emphasis is on Directory Maintenance, which is accessed by selecting **F**ull DM Program from the **D**isk Directory **M**aintenance submenu.

Selecting Directories

Like PC Shell, Directory Maintenance makes it extremely easy to select a different directory to work with. To do so, type the first letter of the directory's name. The Speed Search feature immediately moves you to the first directory on the Tree starting with that letter. If you proceed by typing the next letter, you're jumped to the directory closest to the top of the Tree that starts with the two letters you've specified. You can continue typing the name in this way until you're moved to the directory you want. This procedure is much faster than having to be prompted for a directory name and then being required to type out the entire name.

In addition, you can always scroll the Tree using the arrow keys to move by directory, PGDN and PGUP to move by screen, and END and HOME to move to the bottom and top of the Tree. Lastly, you can move by clicking on the vertical scroll bar with your mouse, and then clicking on the directory you want to work with.

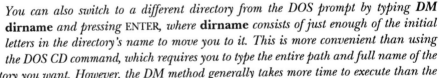

You can also switch to a different directory from the DOS prompt by typing **DM** **dirname** *and pressing* ENTER, *where* **dirname** *consists of just enough of the initial letters in the directory's name to move you to it. This is more convenient than using the DOS CD command, which requires you to type the entire path and full name of the directory you want. However, the DM method generally takes more time to execute than the CD command, because it must first search for appropriate directory names on your disk.*

Creating Directories

You can create an unlimited number of directories. A directory can be added directly to your disk's root, or it can be added as a subdirectory of an existing directory.

To create a directory using Directory Maintenance, follow these steps:

1. Perform the steps in "Preparing for a Directory or Disk Operation."

2. Select where on the Tree you want to add your directory. For example, if you want to add the directory to the root, press HOME. If you want to make it a

subdirectory of an existing directory, move to the existing directory using the arrow keys or your mouse, or by typing its name.

3. When you're done selecting the new directory's location, press ALT-D, M, or press F4, or click on the Directory menu and select Make Directory.

4. You're prompted for the new directory's name. Type the name, and then press ENTER twice or click OK.

   After a moment, your directory is created on your disk and displayed on the Tree. If you added the directory to the root, it appears near the top of the Tree. Otherwise, it appears as the first subdirectory of the existing directory you selected.

5. If you're done with Directory Maintenance, exit by pressing ESC. You're returned to the PC Shell screen.

6. If necessary, update any batch files affected by your change. For example, if you want to access files in your new directory from anywhere on your disk, add the directory's name to the PATH line in your AUTOEXEC.BAT file (see "Revising the PATH Statement" in Appendix A).

You can also create a directory from the DOS prompt by typing **MD** **pathname** *(where* **pathname** *is the path and name of the new directory) and pressing* ENTER.

Using the Add a Subdirectory Command

If you're using PC Tools 7.1 (as opposed to 7.0), you can also create a directory with PC Shell's **A**dd a Subdirectory command. To do so, follow these steps:

1. Perform steps 1 through 3 in "Preparing for a Directory or Disk Operation."

2. Press ALT-D, M, A, or click on the Disk menu and select Directory Maintenance and Add a Subdirectory.

3. Select where on the Tree you want to add your directory. For example, if you want to add the directory to the root, press HOME; if you want to make it a subdirectory of an existing directory, move to the existing directory using the arrow keys or your mouse. When you're ready, press ENTER.

4. You're prompted for the new directory's name. Type up to eight characters for the name, press ENTER, optionally type up to three letters for the extension, and press ENTER twice more. After a moment, your directory is created on your disk and displayed on the Tree. If you added the directory to the root, it appears at the bottom of the Tree. Otherwise, it appears as the last subdirectory of the existing directory you selected.

5. If necessary, update any batch files affected by your change. For example, if you want to access files in your new directory from anywhere on your disk, add the directory's name to the PATH line in your AUTOEXEC.BAT file (see "Revising the PATH Statement" in Appendix A).

Copying Directories

Just as you can create copies of your files using PC Shell's File menu, you can create copies of your directories using Directory Maintenance. Copying has several uses. For example, it allows you to safeguard the data in important directories by creating backups on a different drive or in a different Tree level on the same disk. Also, it lets you share the data in directories with others via floppy disks.

To copy a directory, follow these steps:

1. Perform the steps in "Preparing for a Directory or Disk Operation."

2. Select the directory you want to copy using the arrow keys or your mouse, or by typing its name.

3. Press ALT-D, C, or press F9, or click on the Directory menu and select Copy Tree. The directory and all its subdirectories are highlighted. In addition, a duplicate set of the directory and its subdirectories now appears directly below it on the Tree.

4. If you're copying the directory to another location on the same drive, go to step 5.

   If you're copying the directory to a different drive, click on the drive's letter in the upper-left corner of the screen, or hold down CTRL and press the drive's letter. The Tree of this second drive is displayed.

5. Position the selected directory to the location you want it copied to on the Tree. If you want to copy the directory to the root, press HOME. If you want to copy it to an existing directory, move to the existing directory by using the arrow keys or your mouse, or by typing its name. The selected directory moves on the Tree in response to your keypresses or mouse clicks.

6. When the selected directory is positioned properly, press ENTER or F9. You're asked to confirm the copy.

7. Press ENTER or click OK. The message "Copying directory" is displayed. After a moment, the directory and all its subdirectories are copied to the new location you specified, as shown in the Tree. If you copied the directory to the root, it appears near the top of the Tree. Otherwise, it appears as the first subdirectory of the directory you copied it to.

8. If you're done with Directory Maintenance, exit by pressing ESC. You're returned to the PC Shell screen.

*You can also copy a directory from the DOS prompt by typing **DM CO** pathname* **targetpath** *(where **pathname** is the current path and name of the directory and* **targetpath** *is the location you're copying it to) and pressing* ENTER.

Moving Directories

If you want to quickly rearrange large amounts of data on your disk, you can move an entire directory and all its subdirectories by using the Directory Maintenance Directory Prune & Graft command. *Prune* refers to the subdirectory "branches" being removed from the disk's directory tree, while *Graft* refers to the "branches" being attached to a different location on the directory tree.

To move a directory and its subdirectories using Directory Maintenance, follow these steps:

1. Perform the steps in "Preparing for a Directory or Disk Operation."

2. Select the directory you want to move using the arrow keys or your mouse, or by typing its name.

3. Press ALT-D, G, or press F7, or click on the Directory menu and select Prune & Graft.

4. If you're moving the directory to another location on the same drive, go to step 5.

   If you're moving the directory to a different drive, click on the drive's letter in the upper-left corner of the screen, or hold down CTRL and press the drive's letter. The Tree of this second drive is displayed.

5. Reposition the selected directory to its new location on the Tree. If you want to attach the directory to the root, press HOME. If you want to attach it to an existing directory, move to the existing directory using the arrow keys or your mouse, or by typing its name. The selected directory moves on the Tree in response to your keypresses or mouse clicks.

6. When the selected directory is positioned properly, press ENTER or F7. You're asked to confirm the move.

7. Press ENTER or click OK. The message "Grafting directory" is displayed. After a moment, the directory and all its subdirectories are moved to the new location you specified, as shown in the Tree. If you moved the directory to the root, it appears near the top of the Tree. Otherwise, it appears as the first subdirectory of the directory you moved it to.

8. If you're done with Directory Maintenance, exit by pressing ESC. You're returned to the PC Shell screen.

9. If necessary, update any batch files affected by your change. For example, if you want to access files in your repositioned directory from anywhere on your

disk, add the directory's new path to the PATH line in your AUTOEXEC.BAT
file (see "Revising the PATH Statement" in Appendix A).

You can also move a directory from the DOS prompt by typing **DM PG** **pathname**
targetpath *(where* **pathname** *is the current path and name of the directory and*
targetpath *is the location you're moving it to) and pressing* ENTER.

Using the Prune and Graft Command

If you're using PC Tools 7.1 (as opposed to 7.0), you can also move a directory using
PC Shell's **P**rune and Graft command (though only to another location on the *same*
drive). To do so, follow these steps:

1. Perform steps 1 through 3 in "Preparing for a Directory or Disk Operation."

2. Press ALT-D, M, P, or click on the Disk menu and select Directory Maintenance,
   and then Prune and Graft.

3. Select the directory that you want to move by using the arrow keys or your
   mouse. When you're ready, press ENTER once to indicate your selection, and
   then press ENTER a second time to confirm your selection.

4. Reposition the selected directory to its new location on the Tree. For example,
   if you want to attach the directory to the root, press HOME; if you want to
   attach it to an existing directory, move to the existing directory using the
   arrow keys or your mouse.

5. When you're ready, press ENTER once to indicate your selection, and then
   press ENTER a second time to confirm your selection. The message "Prune
   and Graft in progress" is displayed. After a moment, the directory and all its
   subdirectories are moved to the new location you specified, as shown in the
   Tree.

6. If necessary, update any batch files affected by your change. For example, if
   you want to access files in your repositioned directory from anywhere on your
   disk, add the directory's new path to the PATH line in your AUTOEXEC.BAT
   file (see "Revising the PATH Statement" in Appendix A).

Renaming Directories

Sometimes you'll want to change a directory's name to make it better reflect the
directory's contents. To rename a directory using Directory Maintenance, follow
these steps:

1. Perform the steps in "Preparing for a Directory or Disk Operation."

2. Select the directory that you want to rename by using the arrow keys or your mouse, or by typing its name.

3. Press ALT-D, R, or press F5, or click on the Directory menu and select Rename Directory. A dialog box displays the directory's current name and prompts you to enter a new one.

4. Type a new directory name, and press ENTER twice or click OK. After a moment, your directory is renamed on your disk, and its new name is displayed on the Tree.

5. If you're done with Directory Maintenance, exit by pressing ESC. You're returned to the PC Shell screen.

6. If necessary, update any batch files affected by your change. For example, if you want to access files in your renamed directory from anywhere on your disk, add the directory's new name to the PATH line in your AUTO-EXEC.BAT file (see "Revising the PATH Statement" in Appendix A).

You can also rename a directory from the DOS prompt by typing **DM RN** **pathname** **newname** *(where* **pathname** *is the path and current name of the directory and* **newname** *is the new name of the directory) and pressing ENTER.*

Using the Rename a Subdirectory Command

If you're using PC Tools 7.1 (as opposed to 7.0), you can also rename a directory using PC Shell's **R**ename a Subdirectory command. To do so, follow these steps:

1. Perform steps 1 through 3 in "Preparing for a Directory or Disk Operation."

2. Press ALT-D, M, R; or click on the Disk menu and select Directory Maintenance and Rename a Subdirectory.

3. Select the directory that you want to rename by using the arrow keys or your mouse. When you're ready, press ENTER.

4. You're prompted for a new directory name. Type up to eight characters for the name, press ENTER, optionally type up to three letters for the extension, and press ENTER twice more. After a moment, your directory is renamed on your disk, and its new name is displayed on the Tree.

5. If necessary, update any batch files affected by your change. For example, if you want to access files in your renamed directory from anywhere on your

disk, add the directory's new name to the PATH line in your AUTO-EXEC.BAT file (see "Revising the PATH Statement" in Appendix A).

Deleting Directories

Obsolete directories clutter your disk, making it difficult to locate important directories and make room for new directories. You should therefore regularly delete directories that you no longer need.

At the same time, however, always be careful not to accidentally delete a directory you still require. To safeguard against losing data this way, see "Monitoring Deleted Files" in Chapter 5, "Safeguarding Your Data."

Once you're sure a directory is obsolete, follow these steps to delete it using Directory Maintenance:

1. Perform the steps in "Preparing for a Directory or Disk Operation."

2. Select the directory that you want to delete by using the arrow keys or your mouse, or by typing its name.

3. Press ALT-D, D, or press F6, or click on the Directory menu and select Delete Directory. If the directory is empty (that is, contains no files or subdirectories), skip to step 5.

4. The following dialog box appears, warning you that the operation will delete *everything* within the directory (an improvement over PC Shell 6, which was only able to delete empty directories):

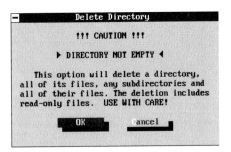

If you want to change your mind, press ESC or click Cancel to abort the operation. However, if you're certain that you want to eliminate the directory and all the data it contains, press O or click OK.

5. You're asked to confirm the deletion. Press ENTER or click OK to do so. In a few moments, the directory, its files, and all its subdirectories and all their

files, are deleted from your disk. Also, the directory and its subdirectories disappear from the Tree.

If you later decide you've erased some files accidentally, see "Undeleting Files" in Chapter 6, "Recovering Deleted or Formatted Data."

6. If you're done with Directory Maintenance, exit by pressing ESC. You're returned to the PC Shell screen.

7. If necessary, update any batch files affected by your change. For example, if you included the directory in the PATH line of your AUTOEXEC.BAT file, edit the line to remove the directory's name (see "Revising the PATH Statement" in Appendix A).

*You can also delete a directory from the DOS prompt by typing **DM DD** pathname (where **pathname** is the path and name of the directory) and pressing ENTER. However, this is a powerful command, so use it with care.*

Using the Delete a Subdirectory Command

If you're using PC Tools 7.1 (as opposed to 7.0), you can also remove a directory using PC Shell's **D**elete a Subdirectory command. However, this command will only affect *empty* directories, that is, directories without subdirectories or files (like the DOS RD command). To remove an empty directory, follow these steps:

1. Perform steps 1 through 3 in "Preparing for a Directory or Disk Operation."

2. Press ALT-D, M, D, or click on the Disk menu and select Directory Maintenance and Delete a Subdirectory.

3. Select the directory that you want to delete by using the arrow keys or your mouse. When you're ready, press ENTER to indicate your selection.

4. If the message "The directory is not empty" appears, it means that the selected directory contains subdirectories. In this case, press ENTER to return to the PC Shell screen, and then follow the steps in the previous tutorial to perform the deletion using Directory Maintenance.

    Otherwise, press ENTER to confirm the deletion.

5. If the message "The directory is not empty" appears, it means that the directory contains files. In this case, press ENTER to return to the PC Shell screen, and then follow the steps in the previous tutorial to perform the deletion using Directory Maintenance.

    Otherwise, the selected directory is removed from your disk, and its name disappears from the Tree.

6. If necessary, update any batch files affected by your change. For example, if you included the directory in the PATH line of your AUTOEXEC.BAT file, edit the line to remove the directory's name (see "Revising the PATH Statement" in Appendix A).

Editing Directory Attributes

Directory Maintenance lets you examine and set two special directory characteristics, or *attributes*: system and hidden.

System directories typically contain special files used to load DOS when you start your computer.

You should always be extremely careful about changing a system directory in any way. For example, when the Compress program reorganizes your hard disk, it doesn't move your system directories, because DOS expects certain system data to always be in the same disk location. If you turn off the system attribute of such a directory, its data will be repositioned the next time you run Compress, and as a result you may no longer be able to start up your PC from your hard disk.

Hidden directories don't display when you list directories from DOS or an application. They're usually generated as part of an application's copy protection scheme. They're also sometimes used for safeguarding data; for example, if you use Delete Sentry, PC Tools 7 creates a hidden SENTRY directory to store deleted files (see "Monitoring Deleted Files" in Chapter 5, "Safeguarding Your Data").

You should also exercise caution in turning off the attribute of a hidden directory. For example, if the directory belongs to a copy protected program, that program may cease to function after you switch off the directory's hidden attribute.

To examine and optionally revise the status of a directory's system and hidden attributes using Directory Maintenance, follow these steps:

1. Perform the steps in "Preparing for a Directory or Disk Operation."

2. Select the directory you want to work with by using the arrow keys or your mouse, or by typing its name.

3. Press ALT-D, A, or click on the Directory menu and select Modify Attributes. A dialog box displays the directory name, and the attributes **H**idden and **S**ystem.

4. To toggle an attribute on or off, press the first letter of the attribute or click it. When the attribute is on, a checkmark appears to its left. For most directories, both attributes will be off. (As just mentioned, be very wary about

turning a directory's attribute off unless you're *certain* the attribute isn't necessary.)

5. When you're done examining and/or setting attributes, press O or click OK. The dialog box closes, and any changes you made are applied to the directory.

6. If you're done with Directory Maintenance, exit by pressing ESC. You're returned to the PC Shell screen.

You can also change the attributes of a directory from the DOS prompt by typing (with **pathname** *representing the path and name of the directory)* **DM pathname MA S** *(which turns off the hidden attribute) or* **DM pathname MA H** *(which turns off the system attribute) and pressing ENTER.*

Using the Modify Attributes Command

If you're using PC Tools 7.1 (as opposed to 7.0), you can also examine and edit a directory's attributes by using PC Shell's Modify Attributes command. (In addition to system and hidden attributes, this command displays read-only and archive attributes. However, the latter don't have much relevance for directories, so you'll generally want to ignore them.) To use the command, follow these steps:

1. Perform steps 1 through 3 in "Preparing for a Directory or Disk Operation."

2. Press ALT-D, M, M, or click on the Disk menu and select Directory Maintenance and Modify Attributes.

3. Select the directory you want to work with by using the arrow keys or your mouse. When you're ready, press ENTER to indicate your selection. A dialog box appears that displays the directory name and the attributes **H**idden, **S**ystem, **R**ead Only, and **A**rchive.

4. To toggle an attribute on or off, press the first letter of the attribute or click it. When the attribute is on, a checkmark appears to its left. For most directories, all attributes will be off. As mentioned previously, be very wary about turning a directory's system or hidden attribute off unless you're *certain* that the attribute isn't necessary.

5. When you're done examining and/or setting attributes, press U or click Update. The dialog box closes, and any changes you made are applied to the directory.

Displaying Directory Information

When you're running Directory Maintenance, you can display information about a directory in a number of ways. Specifically:

- To display a box listing the directory's first-level files, select **Directory Show Files**.

- To display the total number and size of the directory's files, select **Directory Branch Size**.

- To display access rights on a network directory, select **Directory Network Rights**.

- To change the information displayed to the left of the Tree, select **Volume Tree Data Display**.

To get a feel for using these commands, follow these steps:

1. Perform the steps in "Preparing for a Directory or Disk Operation."

2. Select the directory you want to display information about by using the arrow keys or your mouse, or by typing its name.

3. To display the directory's first-level files, press ALT-D, F, or press F8, or click on the Directory menu and select Show Files. A dialog box lists the names of all the files in the first level of the directory (but not its subdirectories). In addition, the top of the box shows the total size of the first-level files. To close the box, press ESC.

4. To display the directory's total size, press ALT-D, B, or click on the Directory menu and select Branch Size. A dialog box like this appears:

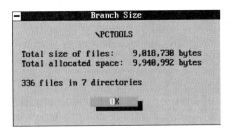

The box displays the total size of *all* the files in the directory, *including* its subdirectory files. The box also shows the amount of space allocated to the directory by DOS (which is usually slightly more space than the files take up), the total number of files, and the total number of directories (that is, the directory itself plus all of its subdirectories). To close the box, press ESC.

5. If you're on a network drive, display your access rights to the directory by pressing ALT-D, N, or by clicking on the Directory menu and selecting **Network Rights**. A dialog box displays such information on the directory as whether you can read its files and copy them to other locations (Read or Open), revise

its files (Write), create subdirectories and new files in it (Create), delete its empty subdirectories (Erase or Delete), rename and change the attributes of its files and/or subdirectories (Modify), and so on. For more information about network rights and their meanings, see your network manual or supervisor. To close the box, press ESC.

6. To change the information displayed to the left of the Tree, press ALT-V, T, or click on the Volume menu and select Tree Data Display. A dialog box like this appears:

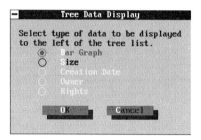

Initially, a bar graph appears to the left of each directory, showing each directory's relative size. If you prefer seeing their sizes represented by numbers, press S and ENTER, or click Size and OK. The display to the left now shows the amount of disk space each directory takes up (not including any space taken up by its subdirectories), rounded to the nearest 1K or 1MB.

7. Select Volume Tree Data Display again. If you're on a network drive, you can alternatively choose Creation Date to display the date each directory was created, Owner to display who created each directory, or Rights to display the rights you have for each directory. Select one of these options, or switch back to the default display by pressing B and ENTER, or by clicking Bar Graph and OK.

8. Lastly, if you want to print the Tree, press ALT-V, P, or click on the Volume menu and select Print Tree. A dialog box like this appears:

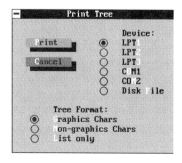

The Device options to the right let you select the port your printer is connected to. (Most printers are connected to LPT1, which is the default selection.) They also include the option Disk File, which instead of printing saves the information to a disk file named TREELIST.PRN in the directory where the DM.EXE program is installed (typically your PC Tools directory).

The box also offers three printing options: **Graphics Chars**, which prints a representation of the Tree using graphics characters; **Non-Graphics Chars**, which prints the Tree using various punctuation symbols (appropriate for printers that don't support graphics characters); and **List Only**, which prints a straightforward list of the directories on the drive.

After you've selected the options you want, make sure your printer is on and online, and then press P or click Print. After a moment, the requested data is printed.

9. If you're done with Directory Maintenance, exit by pressing ESC. You're returned to the PC Shell screen.

Managing Your Disks

You'll usually manage your data by working with files and directories. However, sometimes you'll need to work with a disk as a whole. The following sections explain how to use PC Shell's **D**isk menu to format, copy, compare, verify, search, rename, examine, and park disks.

Formatting Floppy Disks

As explained in Chapter 4, "Data Recovery Overview," most blank floppy disks are sold unformatted. This means that they initially have no information on them and so are unreadable to DOS. You must format a disk before you can use it.

You usually need to format a disk only once. However, you may occasionally reformat a disk to wipe out its contents, or to "rejuvenate" it if it has developed numerous defects.

In addition, you have the option of making the disk able to start up, or *boot,* your compute, by having system files that load DOS into your system on startup copied to the disk during the formatting process.

Once a disk is reformatted, its data can be difficult or impossible to recover, so always think twice before formatting a disk with files on it. For more information, see "Using PC Format" in Chapter 5, "Safeguarding Your Data."

To format a floppy disk from PC Shell, follow these steps:

1. Locate a floppy disk that's unformatted or that contains data you no longer need. Insert the disk into a drive.

2. If you want to format the disk to just hold data, press ALT-D, F, or click on the Disk menu and select Format Data Disk.

    Alternatively, if you want to format the disk and also make it able to start up your PC by placing system files on it (slightly reducing the amount of space available for other data), press ALT-D, B, or click on the Disk menu and select Make Disk Bootable.

3. The new interactive version of PC Format is loaded, and you're prompted to select the drive you want to format. Press the letter of your drive and press ENTER, or click the drive's icon and click OK.

4. To proceed, follow the screen prompts. For information about any option, see the "Running Interactive PC Format" section in Chapter 5.

5. When the format is completed, you're prompted to select a drive again. If you want to format another disk, do so and return to step 4.

    When you're done formatting, press ESC and ENTER, or click Exit and OK, to exit the program. You're returned to the PC Shell screen.

You can also run PC Format directly from the DOS prompt by typing **PCFORMAT** *(optionally followed by parameters) and pressing* ENTER. *For a list of available parameters, see "PC Format Parameters" in Chapter 5.*

Copying Floppy Disks

You'll sometimes find it useful to make duplicates of your floppy disks. This allows you to safeguard your data by creating backups of your original disks. In addition, it lets you share your data with others via the duplicate disks.

To copy a floppy disk from PC Shell, follow these steps:

1. Locate the disk you want to copy from. This is your *source* disk. If you have a write-protect tab, place it over the notch on the disk's upper-right side.

2. Locate the disk you want to copy to. This is your *target* disk. It should be blank or contain only obsolete data.

3. If you have two floppy drives of the same type (for example, drives that are both 360K, or both 1.2MB, or both 1.44MB), insert your source disk in one drive and your target disk in the other drive.

    If you have only one drive, or two drives of different types, insert your source disk into the single drive you'll be using.

4. Press ALT-D, C, or click on the Disk menu and select Copy. A dialog box prompts you to select your source floppy drive.

5. Press the letter of the drive containing your source disk and press ENTER, or click to the left of the drive letter and click OK.

6. A dialog box prompts you to select your target floppy drive. If you're using two drives, press the letter of the drive containing your target disk. Otherwise, press the letter of your single drive again. When you're done, press ENTER or click OK.

7. A dialog box prompts you to insert your source disk in your source drive. In addition, if you selected a different target drive, it prompts you to insert your target disk. Do so, and press ENTER or click OK. The copy operation begins.

A dialog box indicates the progress of the copy. First, the letter "R" is displayed for each area, or *track*, being read from the source disk. When PC Shell has read as much data as it can into memory, if you're using a single drive, you're prompted to replace the source disk with the target disk. If you're using two drives, the operation switches to the target disk automatically.

When the operation turns to the target disk, it first formats each track, as indicated by the letter "F." The data in memory is then written to each track, as indicated by the letter "W." If the source data is written to a track successfully, a dot is displayed, as in this example:

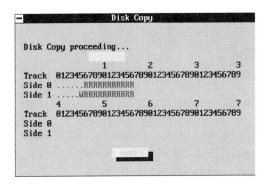

However, if a track is defective, an error message is displayed. Press R or click Retry to try to write to the track again. If several attempts prove unsuccessful, press ENTER to skip writing to the track. A letter "E" appears to remind you that data wasn't copied in that track.

If you're using two drives and no defective tracks are encountered, the entire copy process is automatic. When it's done, you're returned to the PC Shell screen.

If you're using one drive, you have to periodically swap the source and target disks, and then press ENTER or click OK. Do so as prompted, while being very careful not to mix up the two disks. When the copy is completed, you're returned to the PC Shell screen.

To quickly verify that the copy has been executed properly, use TAB to move to the drive bar, and then hold down CTRL and press the letter of the target drive to display the target disk's contents. You can also perform a more thorough check by using the **Disk Compare** command, as explained in the next section.

If you only have one drive for copying disks (or comparing them, as covered in the next section) and you frequently use PC Shell for this purpose, you may want to install PC Shell with the /RL parameter. This will provide the program with more memory for reading in your source disk's data and so minimize the number of times you have to swap disks. For more information, see "Running PC Shell Memory Resident" in Chapter 15.

Comparing Floppy Disks

Sometimes you'll want to know if the contents of two floppy disks are identical. For example, you may need to verify that a backup disk is an accurate copy of the original. You may also wish to check whether a current version of a disk differs from an earlier version.

To compare two floppy disks from PC Shell, follow these steps:

1. If you have two floppy drives of the same type (for example, drives that are both 360K, or both 1.2MB, or both 1.44MB), insert your two disks into the two drives.

    If you have only one drive, or two drives of different types, insert one of the two disks into the single drive you'll be using.

2. Press ALT-D, O, or click on the Disk menu and select Compare. A dialog box prompts you to select your first floppy drive.

3. Press the letter of the drive containing your first disk and press ENTER, or click to the left of the drive letter and click OK.

4. A dialog box prompts you to select your second floppy drive. If you're using two drives, press the letter of the drive containing your second disk. Otherwise, press the letter of your single drive again. When you're done, press ENTER or click OK.

5. A dialog box prompts you to insert your first disk in your first drive. In addition, if you selected a different second drive, it prompts you to insert your second disk. Do so, and press ENTER or click OK. The compare operation begins.

A dialog box indicates the progress of the comparison. First, the letter "R" is displayed for each area, or *track*, being read from the first disk. When PC Shell has read as much data as it can into memory, if you're using a single drive, you're prompted to replace the first disk with the second disk. If you're using two drives, the compare operation switches to the second disk automatically.

When the operation turns to the second disk, it reads each track and compares it to the data in memory, as indicated by the letter "C" displayed for each compared track. If the two sets of data match, a dot is displayed. However, if the sets of data don't match, a message like this appears:

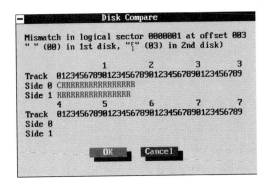

If this occurs, press ENTER or click OK. A letter "E" is displayed to remind you that the track didn't compare successfully, and the operation proceeds.

If you're using two drives and no unmatched tracks are encountered, the entire compare process is automatic. However, if you're using one drive, you have to periodically swap the first and second disks, and then press ENTER or click OK. Do so as prompted, while being careful not to mix up the two disks.

When the compare operation is completed, the message "Diskette compare complete" appears. Press ENTER or click Cancel. You're returned to the PC Shell screen.

Verifying Disks

If you suspect that areas on a hard or floppy disk have become unreadable, you can check the disk for defects. To do so, follow these steps:

1. Perform steps 1 through 3 in "Preparing for a Directory or Disk Operation."

2. Press ALT-D, V, or click on the Disk menu and select Verify. A dialog box prompts you to confirm the command.

3. Press ENTER or click Verify. Each 512-byte section, or *sector*, of the disk is checked for readability, as indicated by a dialog box like this showing the progress of the verification:

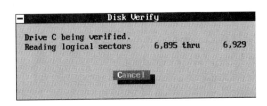

4. If a previously unmarked defective sector is found, an error message displays the number of the sector. You're then told whether the sector is part of the free space on the disk, part of the system area, or part of a file. If the sector is part of the disk's free space, it's marked as unusable to block new files from being saved to it. However, if the sector contains system or file data, it's left unmarked so that you can try to recover the data using another program. When you press ENTER or click OK, the verification process continues.

5. You can end the scan at any time by pressing ESC or clicking Cancel. If you do so, you're returned to the PC Shell screen.

   Otherwise, the scan continues until it's checked every sector on the disk. A dialog box then appears displaying the number of bytes marked bad, as in this example:

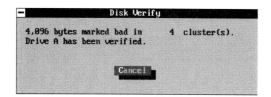

6. Press ENTER or click Cancel. You're returned to the PC Shell screen.

7. If the verification process found any defective sectors containing data, you should run DiskFix as soon as possible to salvage the data and effect any necessary repairs. For more information, see Chapter 7, "Repairing Disks Using DiskFix."

Searching Disks

A hard disk holds millions of characters of data. It's therefore easy to forget where on a disk a particular piece of data is located.

PC Shell lets you search for any short sequence, or *string*, of text or hexadecimal (base 16) characters using the **D**isk **S**earch Disk command. This will find your string anywhere on the disk, even if it's part of a deleted file.

To search a hard or floppy disk, follow these steps:

1. Perform steps 1 through 3 in "Preparing for a Directory or Disk Operation."

2. Press ALT-D, S, or click on the Disk menu and select Search. The following dialog box prompts you to type in your text string:

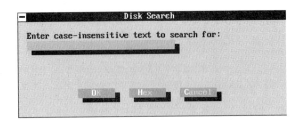

3. If you want to search for text, type up to 32 characters. Don't pay attention to upper- and lowercase differences, since the search ignores case distinctions.

4. If you're searching for a hexadecimal sequence instead (useful if you're a programmer or if you're looking for formatting codes), press ALT-H or click Hex. The dialog box expands to allow you to type up to 64 digits of your hex string. Only valid hex digits (0 through 9 and A through F) are accepted. As you enter every two hex digits, a corresponding ASCII character is displayed below the field (see "Using the ASCII Table" in Chapter 28, "Using the Desktop Utilities").

5. To accept your string, press ENTER twice or click OK. The search is initiated, and a dot moving in a black bar indicates that the search is progressing.

6. If an occurrence is found, a dialog box offers the options OK, Name, Edit, and Cancel. First, press N or click Name. A box displays the name of the file or disk area (for example, boot sector) containing the occurrence. Optionally write down any filename so that you can work with the file later using an application program or PC Shell's File menu commands (covered in Chapters 16 and 18). To close the box, press ENTER or click Cancel.

7. You can also choose the technical option of examining and editing the disk area by pressing E or clicking Edit. A Sector Edit screen appears, with the cursor at the beginning of your search string. To understand and use this screen, see "Editing Sectors" in Chapter 18. To exit the screen, press ESC.

8. When you're ready to proceed with the search, press O or click OK. The search will continue until the next occurrence is found. When this occurs, return to step 6.

9. If you want to exit the search at any point, press ESC or click Cancel. You're returned to the PC Shell screen.

   Otherwise, the search will continue until the entire disk has been checked. If any matches were previously found, you're automatically returned to the

PC Shell screen. However, if no occurrences were found, a dialog box appears with the message "The search string was NOT found." When you press ENTER or click Cancel, you're returned to the PC Shell screen.

Renaming Disks

When you format a disk, you have the opportunity to assign it a name, or *volume label*. This provides a quick way of identifying the contents of the disk. If you skipped this option when formatting the disk, or if you want to change the name you entered, follow these steps:

1. Perform steps 1 through 3 in "Preparing for a Directory or Disk Operation."

2. Press ALT-D, R, or click on the Disk menu and select Rename Disk. A dialog box prompts you to type in a new volume label.

3. Type in a name up to 11 characters long. If your new name is shorter than the current one, press SPACEBAR or DEL to erase the extra characters.

4. Press ENTER twice or click Rename. The new name is saved to your disk, and you're returned to the PC Shell screen. You can now see the new name displayed by the ID indicator at the top of the Tree List.

Examining Disks

PC Shell provides several ways to examine a floppy or hard disk. You can display basic information by selecting the **Disk Disk Information** command, and generate a map by selecting the **Special Disk Map** command. These topics are covered in the following sections.

You can also examine and edit a disk's sectors. For more information about this option, see "Editing Sectors" in Chapter 18.

Displaying Disk Information

To display basic information about the current floppy or hard disk, follow these steps:

1. Perform steps 1 through 3 in "Preparing for a Directory or Disk Operation."

2. Press ALT-D, I, or click on the Disk menu and select Disk Information. A dialog box like this appears:

```
┌─────────────────────────────────────────────────┐
│ ■            Disk Information                     │
├───────────────────────────────────────────────  │
│ Volume Label None                                 │
│     211,787,776 bytes of total disk space.        │
│      47,042,560 bytes available on volume.        │
│          81,920 bytes in        3 hidden files.   │
│     163,602,432 bytes in    5,203 user files.     │
│         774,144 bytes in      181 directories.    │
│               0 bytes in bad sectors.             │
│             512 bytes per sector.                 │
│               8 sectors per cluster.              │
│              35 sectors per track.                │
│          51,706 total clusters.                   │
│         414,085 total sectors.                    │
│          11,831 total tracks.                     │
│              12 sides.                            │
│             986 cylinders.                        │
│                                                   │
│                   ┌──────┐                        │
│                   │  OK  │                        │
│                   └──────┘                        │
└─────────────────────────────────────────────────┘
```

The box shows the following information:

- The disk's volume label, if any

- The total number of bytes the disk can hold

- The number of bytes of free space on the disk

- The number of bytes taken up on the disk by hidden files, normal files, directories, and bad (unusable) sectors

- The number of bytes per sector, which is typically 512

- The number of sectors per cluster, which is the smallest area used by DOS when saving files

- The number of sectors per track, which refers to the way DOS divides up a disk

- The total number of clusters, sectors, and tracks

- The number of sides provided by the disk's platters, which will be two for a floppy disk, and four or more for a hard disk

- The number of cylinders, which is the number of tracks on a single side of a disk platter

When you're done examining the disk information, press ENTER or click OK. You're returned to the PC Shell screen.

Mapping Disks

To display a map of the current floppy or hard disk, follow these steps:

1. Perform steps 1 through 3 in "Preparing for a Directory or Disk Operation."

2. Press ALT-S, M, or click on the Special menu and select Disk Map. A map like the one shown in Figure 17-3 appears. Each position on the map represents a cluster, which is a unit of measurement of disk space. As indicated by the legends above the map, each cluster is represented by one of the following symbols:

   - *Avail*   This is a cluster that's available (that is, that's not being used by the current file). It's represented on the map by a dotted rectangle symbol.

   - *Alloc*   This is a normal cluster that's allocated (that is, that's in use by the current file). It's represented on the map by a diamond symbol.

   - *Boot*   This is a cluster storing the boot record, which is used to start up your computer. It's always at the beginning of a disk and is represented on the map by the letter "B."

   - *FAT*   This is a cluster storing the File Allocation Table, or FAT, which contains the locations of the disk's files. It follows the boot record and is represented on the map by the letter "F."

   - *Dir*   This is a cluster storing the root directory, which contains the names of the disk's files. It follows the FAT and is represented on the map by the letter "D."

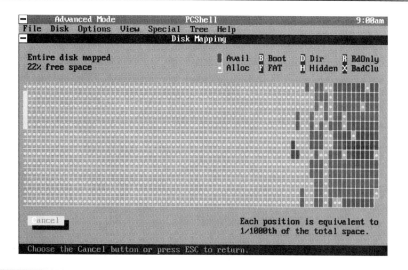

Figure 17-3.   *The Disk Mapping screen*

- *Hidden*   This is a cluster in use by the current file, which has a "hidden" attribute. It's represented on the map by the letter "H."

- *RdOnly*   This is a cluster in use by the current file, which has a read-only attribute. It's represented on the map by the letter "R."

- *BadClu*   This is a defective, or "bad", cluster that's in use by the current file. It's represented on the map by the letter "X."

If the disk is nearly full, the map will consist mostly of diamond symbols. If the disk is nearly empty, the map will consist mostly of dotted rectangles.

The proportions of the map are automatically scaled down to fit your screen. For example, the map of a 10MB disk might display a symbol for every 15 sectors, while the map of a 40MB disk might display a symbol for every 60 sectors. As a result, certain areas such as the boot record and FAT might not show up because they take up only a few sectors.

When you're done examining the map, press ENTER or click Cancel. You're returned to the PC Shell screen.

Parking Disks

To maintain your hard disk, it's recommended that you position, or *park*, all of its read/write heads over an unused portion of the disk right before turning off your computer. This is *especially* recommended if you're going to move the computer. For more information, and to learn how to park from the DOS prompt using the Park program, see "Parking Your Hard Disk" in Chapter 7, "Repairing Disks Using DiskFix."

If you want to park your hard disk from PC Shell, follow these steps:

1. Ready your computer for shutdown by saving your files and exiting any application programs you're running.

2. Perform the steps in "Preparing for a Directory or Disk Operation."

3. Press ALT-D, P, or click on the Disk menu and select Park Disk Heads. A dialog box like this prompts you to turn off your PC:

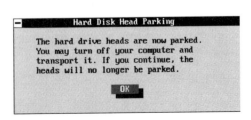

4. If you've changed your mind, press ENTER or click OK. You're returned to the PC Shell screen. You can now continue using your computer normally; the drive heads will automatically unpark.

Otherwise, turn your computer's power switch off. Your hard disk data is now protected from the rigors of being moved or your next system startup.

Chapter *18*

Using Advanced PC Shell Features

In Chapter 15, "PC Shell Overview," you learned how to run PC Shell, and how to use such screen elements as the Tree List, File List, and menu bar. In this chapter, you'll use these skills to access advanced PC Shell features. Specifically, you'll learn how to run programs from PC Shell, transfer data between adjacent computers, edit sectors, and display system information.

Preparing for an Advanced PC Shell Operation

Before you attempt to perform an advanced PC Shell operation, follow these steps:

1. If you aren't already in PC Shell, call it up now. If you've installed the program to be memory resident, press CTRL-ESC. Otherwise, type **PCSHELL** from the DOS prompt and press ENTER.

2. If you aren't already in Advanced mode (indicated in the upper-left corner of the title bar), press ALT- O, U, A, O to reset your user level. This lets you access all menu options.

3. If you don't want to work with the current drive, switch to a different drive by pressing TAB until you're at the drive bar, and then holding down CTRL and pressing the drive letter; or by simply clicking the letter in the drive bar. For example, to switch to drive C, press CTRL-C from the drive bar, or click on C in the drive bar.

4. If appropriate, select the directory you want to work with. First, if the Tree List isn't already activated, press TAB until it is, or click the Tree List window. Second, use the arrow keys to move to the directory you want to work with, or click the directory.

5. If appropriate, select the files you want to work with. First, activate the File List by pressing TAB or clicking the File List window. Second, select each file you want to affect by moving to it and pressing ENTER, or by clicking it. (To select all files in the window, press F9, ALT-S.)

Running Programs

One of the most useful features of the memory-resident version of PC Shell is its ability to let you switch from one program to another.

For example, you can start off by editing a report in WordPerfect, and then realize you need to change the data in a Lotus 1-2-3 spreadsheet. Instead of having to exit WordPerfect, you can simply press CTRL-ESC to invoke PC Shell, view various 1-2-3 files from the File List until you've found the one you want, and then press a keystroke to run 1-2-3 with that data file. PC Shell saves the current contents in memory to disk, clears virtually all of your system's memory for the second application, and then both runs 1-2-3 and makes the program load your selected data file automatically. When you're done revising your spreadsheet and exit 1-2-3, you're automatically returned to PC Shell. You can then press CTRL-ESC to send PC Shell back into the background, and return to the precise point where you left off in WordPerfect.

There are several ways you can run other programs from PC Shell. First, you can use TAB or your mouse to activate the DOS command line near the bottom of the screen, and then simply type the appropriate program name and press ENTER.

Alternatively, you can press ALT-F, R, or click on the File menu and select Run, to bring up a similar command line into which you can type the program name and press ENTER. This option is especially useful if you tend to keep the DOS command line turned off (via the View Custom List Configure DOS Command Line switch) to provide more room on the screen for your windows.

A slightly faster method is to use the File List to select the program you want to run (which must have an EXE, COM, or BAT extension), and then press either CTRL-ENTER or ALT-F, ENTER (which selects the File Open command). Alternatively, if you have a mouse, you can simply double-click on the file. In all of these cases, a dialog box like this appears to give you the opportunity to add command-line parameters:

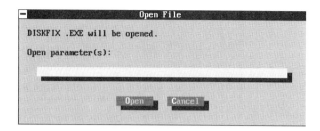

Type any desired parameters (such as the name of an appropriate data file), and then press ENTER twice to run the specified program.

In all these cases, when your program has finished executing, you're prompted to press any key or click your mouse to return to PC Shell. When you do so, you're returned to the PC Shell screen. You can then continue using internal PC Shell commands, run another program from PC Shell, or exit to your underlying application. If you do the latter, you're returned to precisely the point where you left off in the application.

You can optionally set PC Shell to not *have the last screen of an exiting program pause until you press a key or mouse button to return to PC Shell. To do so, press ALT- O, W, or click on the Options menu and select Wait on DOS Screen, to toggle the switch off. The advantage of this is it eliminates a step in returning to PC Shell. However, it also makes it difficult to read the information produced by commands and programs that display data and then exit automatically, such as the DOS DIR and CHKDSK commands, and PC Tools' MI program. To turn the pausing back on, select* **O***ptions* **W***ait on DOS Screen again.*

In addition to the methods for running programs already covered, you can run data files associated with applications entered into a menu called a *Program List*. The next few sections are devoted to this powerful option.

Using the Program List

You can display the Program List either from the DOS prompt by typing **PCTOOLS** and pressing ENTER, or from PC Shell by pressing F10 or selecting **View Program List Only**. When you do, a Main Menu box like this appears:

Even if you haven't used this feature before, you'll see at least a few programs listed as a result of the Install program previously scanning your hard disk for popular applications (see Appendix A, "PC Tools Installation and Configuration"). In addition to each program name, Install entered such information as which directory on your disk contains the program, any parameters the program requires, and the extensions of data files associated with the program (for example, *.DBF for dBASE files, *.WK3 for Lotus 1-2-3 3.*x* files, and so on).

Using this information, PC Shell can not only run programs you select, but can also run *data files* you select. In other words, if you select a data file in the File List associated with a program in the Program List and press CTRL-ENTER, or if you double-click on the data file, PC Shell will swap the current memory contents to disk, load the program associated with the file, and also use a command-line parameter to make the program automatically load the data file.

Similarly, you can select a data file associated with a program in the Program List, and then directly select the program from the List. Again, PC Shell swaps out memory, loads the program, and also includes a parameter to make the program load the data file on startup.

Alternatively, you can first view the data from a particular application by selecting an appropriate file in the File List and pressing F2 (as explained in "Viewing Files" in Chapter 16, "Managing Your Files"). Once the View window is open, you can press F8 to shrink it, and then move in the File List until you've located the file you want. If the file is associated with an application on the Program List, you can then both run the application and have the file loaded into the application automatically by simply pressing F4 from the View window.

Running applications this way can be significantly faster than running a program and then manually loading an initial file using the program's internal commands. Also, as with all other PC Shell "run" methods, when you exit the program, you're automatically returned to PC Shell, from where you can run more programs, perform system maintenance, or return to your underlying application.

To make full use of the Program List, you should customize it to reflect your particular use of programs and data files on your system. This topic is covered in the next section.

Revising the Program List

When you display the Program List, the following commands appear on the message bar:

Function Key	Action
F1 (Help)	Brings up context-sensitive help
F2 (Dscrpt)	Displays descriptions of menu entries
F3 (Exit)	Performs the same functions as ESC
F4 (New)	Adds a new menu entry
F5 (Edit)	Displays and lets you revise menu entries
F6 (Delete)	Deletes the current menu entry
F7 (Cut)	Deletes the current entry from the menu and inserts it into a temporary memory buffer for relocation
F8 (Copy)	Copies an entry into a temporary memory buffer without affecting the entry
F9 (Paste)	Inserts the contents of the memory buffer into the current menu location
F10 (Shell)	Switches between the Program List and PC Shell

Using these commands is covered in the following sections.

Examining and Editing Program List Entries

To examine or edit Program List entries, follow these steps:

1. Press F2. A description of the current menu entry appears.

2. Press DOWN ARROW or use your mouse to scroll through the menu and read the descriptions of the various applications listed. When you're done, press F2 to close the description window.

3. Move to an entry representing a program you're familiar with and press F5. A dialog box like this appears:

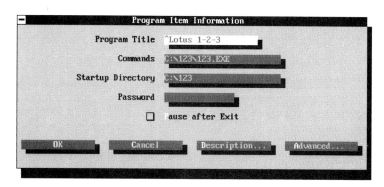

The box offers the following nine options:

- *Program Title*   This field specifies the name of the application as it appears on the menu. You can insert a ^ (carat) in front of the letter you want to use for selecting the option. If no ^ is included, you'll only be able to select the option by moving to it with the arrow keys and pressing ENTER, or by clicking it.

- *Commands*   This field specifies the command line used to run the program, including the appropriate path, program name, and parameters.

- *Startup Directory*   This field specifies the drive and directory you want to use as soon as the application is loaded (for example, the directory where you keep the application's data files).

- *Password*   This field specifies any password required to run the program.

- *Pause after Exit*   If on, this option pauses the last screen of an application that's exiting. This is useful for programs that supply important information after they finish executing. This option will override the setting of the **O**ptions **W**ait on DOS Screen switch (see "Toggling Program Screen Pausing" in Chapter 15, "PC Shell Overview").

- *Description*   This option loads the PC Shell text editor so that you can write a new description of the menu entry. The description is displayed after you press F2 and select the entry.

    Which text editor is loaded depends on the version of PC Tools you're using. If you're running PC Tools 7.0, a limited version of the Desktop Notepads application is loaded. However, if you're running PC Tools 7.1, the File Editor from PC Tools Deluxe 6 is loaded. For more information, see "Editing Text Files" in Chapter 16.

- *Advanced*   This option brings up another screen of options.

- *OK*   This option saves your changes and closes the dialog box.

- *Cancel*   This option abandons your changes and closes the dialog box.

To see the rest of the options, press ALT-A or click Advanced. A dialog box like this appears:

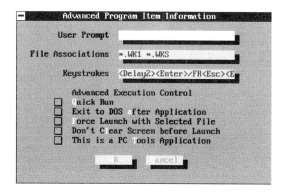

The box offers the following eight options:

- *User Prompt*   This option pauses the application just before it's about to be run and displays the text you enter into this field. This option is useful for applications requiring special instructions, such as a copy-protected program that needs a key disk to execute.

- *File Associations*   This field specifies the files associated with this application. For example, the file specifications for Lotus 1-2-3 could be ***.WK3 *.WK1 *.WKS** to specify all versions of 1-2-3 files.

- *Keystrokes*   This field enters keystrokes once the program is loaded as if you were typing the keys yourself. To enter a code for a noncharacter key, first press F7 and then the key. For example, to insert the code for ENTER, first press F7 and then ENTER.
      You can also press F8 to display a list of keyword codes. The most important is <Path>, which lets you load a selected file from within the application if the application doesn't accept filename parameters (see the Force Launch with Selected File option that follows shortly).

- *Quick Run*   When on, this option sets whether PC Shell clears as much conventional memory as possible before running the program. The default is *off*, meaning that PC Shell will clear memory. This delays the application loading, but it ensures that there's room in conventional memory to run the application.

- *Exit to DOS after Application*   When on, this option lets you exit to DOS instead of PC Shell after you're done with the application. Its default is *off*.

- *Force Launch with Selected File*   If on, this option sets the application to run with a selected file in the File List. Use this option if the program accepts a filename as a command-line parameter for loading the file. Otherwise, use the <Path> command and appropriate keystrokes in the Keystrokes field (covered previously in this list) to load the file using the application's internal commands.

- *Don't Clear Screen before Launch*   If on, this option prevents PC Shell from clearing the screen before running another program. This is useful on certain systems where clearing causes their screens to flash. Its default is *off*.

- *This is a PC Tools Application*   This option specifies that the current program is part of PC Tools 7. This helps PC Shell run the program quickly without causing any screen flicker.

You can revise any field by moving to it and editing the existing field data, using BACKSPACE and DEL to erase characters, and INS to switch between Insert mode and Overtype mode.

When you're done, press ALT-O or click OK to save your changes, or press ESC or click Cancel to abandon them. The dialog box closes, and you're returned to the PC Shell screen.

Adding Program List Entries

To add a Program List entry, follow these steps:

1. Move to the spot on the menu where you want to add the entry.

2. Press F4. You're prompted to select Item to add one program or **Group** to add several programs. A *group* on the menu is roughly equivalent to a directory on a disk, in that it lets you organize your programs into related units.

3. To create a single program entry, press ENTER or click OK. The Program Item Information dialog box you examined in the previous section opens. Fill in the appropriate data for your program in the first box and the **Advanced** box. When you're done, press ALT-O or click OK from the first box to save your changes and exit. Your entry is added to the menu.

4. To create a group folder entry, press G, O, or click Group and OK. You're prompted to enter a title for the group, and optionally a password and description. Enter at least a title, and then press ALT-O or click OK. The group folder is added to the menu. You can later add single program entries into this folder.

Copying, Moving, and Deleting Program List Entries

To rearrange Program List entries, follow these steps:

1. To copy an entry, select it and press F8, position the cursor to where you want the copy on the menu, and press F9. The copy is inserted at the cursor location.

You can then edit the copy to create a new entry, which is often faster and easier than creating a new entry from scratch.

2. To move an entry, select it and press F7, which makes the entry disappear. Next, position the cursor to where you want the entry repositioned, and then press F9. The entry is inserted at the new location. This procedure lets you quickly rearrange entries on the menu.

3. To delete an entry, select it and press F6. A dialog box asks you to confirm the deletion. Press ENTER or click Delete. The entry is eliminated.

Editing Sectors

Just as you can edit text files using the PC Shell text editor, you can edit *any* type of file using the Sector Editor. As explained in Chapter 4, "Data Recovery Overview," a disk is typically split up into 512-byte sections called sectors. The Sector Editor lets you move to any sector on the disk and revise the data it contains byte by byte. This is one of the most advanced features in PC Tools, and you normally won't need it unless you're a programmer. However, there may be occasions when this feature can help repair a defective sector.

The sector editing feature is a powerful one, but at the same time a potentially destructive one if you aren't sure of what you're doing. Use it to alter data only if you're absolutely certain you understand the effect your changes will have. Furthermore, be especially wary of editing sectors near critical disk areas such as the boot record, FAT, and root directory, because doing so may produce serious data losses on your disk. (If such an accident occurs, see Chapters 4, 6, and 7.)

There are a number of ways to bring up the Sector Editor:

- If you select **File Verify** and a defective sector in the file is found, select View/**E**dit so you can try to repair the sector (see "Verifying Files" in Chapter 16).

- If you select **File Search** and an occurrence of your text or hexadecimal string is found, select **E**dit to examine or edit the sector the string appears in (see "Finding Files by Content in the Current Window" in Chapter 16).

- If you select **Disk Search** and an occurrence of your text or hexadecimal string is found, select **E**dit to examine or edit the sector the string appears in (see "Searching Disks" in Chapter 17).

- If you want to edit particular files, select them and then select **File Change File Hex Edit File**. This brings up a screen called File Edit, which is virtually identical to the Sector Edit screen.

- If you want to explicitly edit particular sectors on the disk, select **Disk View/Edit**. This brings up a screen called Disk Edit, which is virtually identical to the Sector Edit and File Edit screens.

To get a feel for working with sectors, follow these steps:

1. Perform the steps in "Preparing for an Advanced PC Shell Operation" to select a couple of files to edit.

2. Press ALT-F, G, H, or click on the File menu and select Change File and Hex Edit File. A screen like the one shown in Figure 18-1 appears.

Examining the Sector Editing Screen

The sector editing screen is made up of several components. On the top line is the name of the file you're viewing; the number of the sector relative to the start of the file (for example, the first sector in the file is sector 0, the second is sector 1, and so on); the number of the sector's cluster (see Chapter 4); and the sector's number relative to the start of the disk, which is called its *absolute* number. These indicators track your position in the file as you move from sector to sector.

The bulk of the window is taken up by three columns. The first column contains the byte number, or *offset,* relative to the sector. For example, the first byte in a sector is byte 0, and the tenth byte in a sector is byte 9.

Next to the decimal offset number is the same number in hexadecimal, or base 16. For example, the second line in the column displays 16 decimal and 10 hex (1 ×

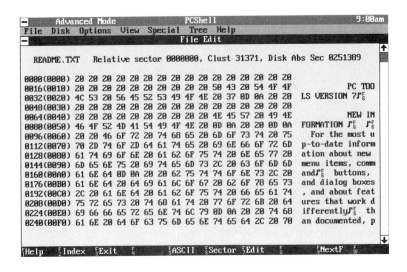

Figure 18-1. The sector editing screen

16), the next line displays 32 decimal and 20 hex (2 × 16), and so on. Hex is the number system of choice for displaying raw computer data, since it's a convenient-sized multiple of base 2, the number system that's the foundation of all PC operations.

The second column represents the bytes in the file in hex. Each byte is shown as a two-character hex value, and each row contains 16 bytes.

The third column contains the ASCII character corresponding to the value in each byte (see "Using the ASCII Table" in Chapter 28, "Using the Desktop Utilities"). This column is only half as wide as the second column because it takes two hex characters to represent one ASCII character. For example, hex 20 represents a blank space, hex 41 represents the capital letter A, hex 0D represents a carriage return, and so on.

Finally, the message bar displays the commands assigned to the function keys. These are explored in the next section.

Using Sector Editing Commands

The message bar contains four relevant commands: ASCII (F5), Sector (F6), Edit (F7), and, if you've selected more than one file, NextF (F9).

The ASCII option switches you to a screen that displays only the file's ASCII characters. To try it, press F5. If you're viewing a text file, your display now looks a lot more readable. If you're viewing a nontext file, the word "Hex" appears on the message bar, and whether your display is an improvement depends largely on the particular data in the file. You can view any part of the file in this way, but you can't edit in this mode. To return to the first screen, press F5 again.

To view different portions of the file in either mode, you can press PGDN and PGUP to move by screen, press END or HOME to move to the bottom or top of the file, and scroll the display vertically using your mouse. In addition, you can jump to a particular sector by pressing F6, typing a sector number relative to the start of the file, and pressing ENTER twice. For example, press F6, press END, type 5, and press ENTER twice. If your file has at least six sectors, you're moved to sector 5 in the file, as indicated by the "Relative sector" indicator at the top of the window. However, if the sector number is too high for the file, you're just left in your original screen.

To edit the file, press F7. A blinking rectangular cursor appears on the first byte in the hex column. To change a particular byte, you can simply move to the byte using the arrow keys and overwrite the existing hex characters with other characters. (However, as mentioned previously, be *very* careful to only make changes you're *certain* are appropriate.)

You can also move to the ASCII column by pressing F8, and then overwrite ASCII characters. Any change you make in one column is automatically reflected in the other. You can switch back to the hex column by pressing F8 again.

If you want to save the changes you've made, or just write the data back to the sector again (which can sometimes help recover data in a slightly defective sector), press F5. The change is saved, and you're returned to the first screen.

On the other hand, if you want to abandon the changes you've made, press ESC. A dialog box asks if you want to save your changes or cancel them. Press ESC or click Cancel. The bytes you've changed revert to their original values, and you're returned to the first screen.

When you're done with a file, press F9. The file closes, and the next selected file appears. When you've gone through all the selected files, pressing F9 returns you to the PC Shell screen.

Connecting Computers Using DeskConnect

If you have two computers on the same desk, or if you have a desktop computer and a laptop computer, you can use DeskConnect to make all their drives equally available on the PC Shell drive bar. This makes it very easy to copy, move, and compare files between the two machines.

 If you used the LapLink Quick Connect program in PC Shell 6, you'll be able to use DeskConnect just as easily, because it's only a slightly updated and renamed version of LQC. If you require a more powerful program, see Chapter 14, "Connecting Computers Using Commute."

To connect your two computers, each of them must have a serial port available, and you must have a special cable, called a *null modem*, that can plug into both serial ports. The cable must support at least lines 2 (transmit data line) and 3 (receive data line) to work with DeskConnect. In addition, if you want to be able to use Commute (covered in Chapter 14), the cable should *also* support lines 4 (request to send) and 5 (clear to send). You can buy a null modem from almost any PC hardware supplier at a price ranging from about $10 to about $40; just be sure to specify the data lines you want supported.

DeskConnect consists of two programs and a PC Shell command. The first program is DESKCON, which must be installed memory resident on the computer that will be running PC Shell. DESKCON takes up about 9K of conventional memory. If you ever want to remove it, you can type **DESKCON /U** at the DOS prompt and press ENTER to unload it alone, or type **KILL** at the DOS prompt and press ENTER to unload it and other PC Tools programs (such as PC Shell and the Desktop) from memory.

The second program is DESKSRV, which must be run on the computer you want to connect to. DESKSRV runs nonresident; when you exit it, it removes itself from memory automatically.

After both programs are installed, you can run PC Shell and select **S**pecial DeskConnect to connect the two machines. This is especially convenient if you frequently need to transfer files between a desktop and laptop PC.

To connect your first computer (the one you run PC Shell on) with a second computer, follow these steps:

1. Connect your null modem cable to a serial port on each of the two computers.

2. Run the DESKSRV program on the second computer. For example, if you have the program on a floppy disk in drive A, type **A:DESKSRV** and press ENTER. This sets the program to use COM port 1 and transmit at a speed of 115200 baud. (If you need to use different settings, see the next section, "DeskConnect Parameters.")

3. The DESKCON program must be loaded *before* PC Shell. If you installed both PC Shell and DESKCON in your AUTOEXEC.BAT file using the Install program (see Appendix A, "PC Tools Installation and Configuration"), then the programs have already been loaded in the proper order. In this case, skip to step 6.

   If you're running PC Shell but didn't load DESKCON first, you must exit PC Shell and, if it's resident, remove it from memory. For information on how to do so, see "Exiting PC Shell" in Chapter 15.

4. Load the DESKCON program on your first computer by typing **DESKCON** from the DOS prompt and pressing ENTER. This sets the program to use COM port 1 and transmit at a speed of 115200 baud. (If you need to use different settings, see "DeskConnect Parameters.")

5. Bring up PC Shell on your first computer (for example, by typing **PCSHELL /R** from the DOS prompt, pressing ENTER, and pressing CTRL-ESC).

6. Press ALT-S, C, or click on the Special menu and select DeskConnect. The machines are connected.

The drives of the second computer are now added to PC Shell's drive bar. For example, if the drive bar previously displayed drives A, B, and C, the second computer's drives would be displayed on the bar as D, E, and so on. You can therefore select a drive on the second machine as easily as you can on the first; as usual, just move to the drive bar using TAB, hold down CTRL, and press the drive letter; or simply click the letter in the drive bar.

You can now readily transfer and compare files between the two machines using commands in the **File** menu. For more information, see "Copying Files," "Moving Files," and "Comparing Files" in Chapter 16.

You can also continue to use all other PC Shell commands with your first machine, and many of the PC Shell commands with your second machine. However, you can't use a number of PC Shell's disk-related and directory-related commands in conjunction with the second machine, whose drives are treated as networked drives. This means, for example, that you must stick to the File **C**opy and File **M**ove commands to transfer files between the two systems.

When you're finished using the second computer, select **S**pecial Desk**C**onnect again. The second computer's drives disappear from the drive bar, and the machines are disconnected. Lastly, press ESC, Y on the second machine to quit the DESKSRV program.

DeskConnect Parameters

When you run the DESKCON and DESKSRV programs, you can specify certain options, called parameters, following the program name. You can include a single parameter (for example, DESKCON /B:2400) or several compatible parameters (for example, DESKCON /B:2400 /C:2) to achieve the effect you want. The parameters for DESKCON and DESKSRV are identical. Keep in mind that parameters preceded by a slash require a *forward* slash (/, located on the bottom of the ? key) as opposed to the backslash (\) used to specify DOS directories.

There are six parameters available for DESKCON and DESKSRV. They are as follows:

- **?** This "help" parameter lists and briefly describes every DESKCON or DESKSRV option. It will work both with and without a slash in front of it. It should not be combined with any other parameters.

- **/B:***nnnnnn* DESKCON and DESKSRV ordinarily transmit data at a speed, or *baud rate*, of 115200. This speed may be too high on some systems to work properly. If you encounter problems, try using this parameter and setting *nnnnnn* to a slower baud rate. The following rates are available, with the lower numbers being the slowest: 300, 600, 1200, 2400, 4800, 9600, 19200, 38400, 57600, and 115200. If you use this parameter, be sure to use it with *both* DESKCON and DESKSRV, or the two programs won't be able to communicate.

- **/C:***n* DESKCON and DESKSRV ordinarily use the serial port COM1 on their respective computers for transmitting and receiving data. If you attach your null modem cable to COM2, COM3, or COM4 on one or both of your computers, you must use this parameter to specify that port, with *n* representing the port number. For example, if you're using COM1 on your first computer and COM2 on the second computer, use the command **DESKSRV /C:2** to run DESKSRV on the second computer. For COM3 and COM4, you must also include the /I:*n* and /P:*nnn* parameters.

- **/I:***n* This parameter specifies the IRQ used by your serial port COM3 or COM4, where *n* represents an interrupt number from 2 to 15. For more information and to identify the number you need, see your computer, serial card, or modem hardware manual. You must also include the /C:*n* and /P:*nnn* parameters.

- **/P:nnn**   This parameter specifies the port address used by your serial port COM3 or COM4, where *nnn* represents the address. For more information and to identify the appropriate address, see your computer, serial card, or modem hardware manual. You must also include the /C:*n* and /I:*n* parameters.

- **/U**   This parameter unloads DESKCON from memory, but doesn't affect other PC Tools memory-resident programs (as opposed to typing **KILL** from the DOS prompt, which removes most PC Tools programs from memory).

Displaying System Information

To get comprehensive information about your system from PC Shell, press ALT-S, S, or click on the Special menu and select System Info. The System Information program (a standalone utility new to PC Tools 7) is loaded, and a screen like the one in Figure 18-2 appears. This initial screen provides basic information about the hardware in your system at the left, the relative performance of your system at the right, and your system's memory usage at the bottom.

You can also display a great deal more information using the menus at the top of the screen and the function key commands listed on the message bar. For example, if you press ALT-B, O, or click on the Benchmarks menu and select Overall Performance, such factors as your CPU and disk drive speed are evaluated, and then a chart appears

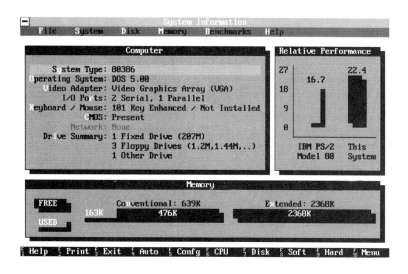

Figure 18-2.   *The System Information screen*

comparing your system against an IBM XT, an IBM AT, and an IBM PS/2 Model 80. To close the chart, press ESC.

As another example, press ALT-M, N, or click on the Memory menu and select Conventional. A map of your system's conventional memory appears. This screen is the same one displayed when you select the Special Memory Map command from PC Shell.

If you want to get a complete list of your system information without jumping around a lot of menus and screens, you can direct all the data to your printer or a disk file. To do so, follow these steps:

1. Press F2. A screen lists all the information SI can provide.

2. If there are options you aren't interested in, select them to turn their checkmarks off. When you're done, press P or click Print.

3. A dialog box appears that lets you direct your printing to a different port than LPT1 (which most printers are connected to). It also offers a Disk File option to direct the information to your disk instead of your printer. Select an appropriate option, or accept the default of LPT1.

4. If you chose the file option, press P or click Print. After a few moments, the information is saved to the file SI.RPT in your current directory. You can examine the file when you return to PC Shell by selecting it in the File List and pressing F2.

5. If you chose a printer port, make sure your printer is on and online, and then press P or click Print. The report is typically about ten pages long, so the printing will take a while. As the pages come out, look them over for information you didn't previously know about your system.

When you're done using the SI program, press ESC from the main screen. The program exits, and you're returned to the PC Shell screen.

 *You can also run the System Information program directly from the DOS prompt by typing **SI** and pressing ENTER.*

Mapping Your System's Memory Using MI

If you're not in PC Shell and you want a quick look at what programs are currently resident, use the MI utility. This small (8K) program quickly displays how your memory is being allocated and then exits automatically. To run it, simply type **MI** from the DOS prompt and press ENTER.

Part VI

Using the Desktop Manager

Chapter *19*

Desktop Manager
Overview

The PC Tools Desktop manages a collection of programs covering almost every major PC category. It includes such powerful applications as a word processor, a dBASE-compatible database, telecommunications programs for both modems and fax cards, simulations of Hewlett-Packard calculators, and a full-featured appointment scheduler.

The Desktop's programs all use a menu command structure that you can operate using either the keyboard or a mouse. Since the programs share a similar interface, once you've learned your way around one application, it's much easier to learn how to use any of the others.

In addition, you can keep up to 15 files open at the same time. The files can all be from the same application, or they can be from a mix of different Desktop applications in any combination. Each file is in a window that you can move and resize, or maximize to fill the screen.

You can also transfer data between your windows, because the Desktop includes an electronic Clipboard that cuts, copies, and pastes text across files.

Perhaps the most impressive aspect of the Desktop, however, is that despite its great power and versatility, you can install it as a memory-resident program that takes up a mere 25K of conventional memory (or, if you're using a high memory manager, virtually 0K). While it's resident in the background, you can access such Desktop features as the Clipboard for text transferal, an Autodialer for dialing phone numbers on the screen, macros for automating PC tasks, and pop-up alarms set in the Appointment Scheduler. You can also bring up the Desktop in the middle of any application and access all of its hundreds of features.

This chapter first explains the applications the Desktop provides. It then covers running the Desktop, using common Desktop elements, and understanding the Desktop files. Lastly, it describes the new Desktop features in PC Tools 7.

Desktop Applications Overview

The Desktop contains a wide variety of applications. The following lists each Desktop program, describes its main features, and identifies the chapter it's covered in.

- *Notepads*   This easy-to-use word processor lets you quickly create, edit, save, and print documents. It supports such standard features as word wrap, automatic indenting, keystroke movement shortcuts, and file merging. It also provides a 100,000-word spelling checker; the ability to copy, move, or delete blocks of text; the ability to find and replace text; a timed file saver; and header and footer options. Notepads is a fundamental part of the Desktop—it's used in conjunction with the Appointment Scheduler and Electronic Mail, and most of its features are duplicated in Outlines, the Clipboard, and the Macro Editor—so it's recommended that you become familiar with it. Notepads is covered in Chapter 20.

- *Outlines*   This application enables you to assign levels of importance to every section of your document. You can then quickly expand and collapse various sections in order to work with your document's overall structure and its minutiae at the same time. Outlines is covered in Chapter 21.

- *Clipboard*   This storage area holds text that you want to transfer from one location to another. The locations may be in the same Desktop file, in different Desktop files, in a Desktop file and a non-PC Tools application, or even in different non-PC Tools applications. The Clipboard's ability to transfer text within and across files makes it one of the most powerful and widely used features of the Desktop. The Clipboard is covered in Chapter 22.

- *Appointment Scheduler*   This application helps you organize your time. It contains a Calendar, a To-Do list, and a Daily Scheduler. The latter provides a variety of appointment options, such as letting you attach notes and pop-up alarms, graph appointments by week, search for appointments based on assorted criteria, and print out appointments in a variety of formats. In addition, it lets you schedule programs, batch files, and macros to run on your PC unattended. The Appointment Scheduler is covered in Chapter 23.

- *Calculators*   The four Desktop calculators simulate a standard Algebraic Calculator with editable "paper" tape; an HP-12C Financial Calculator that computes such values as interest rate, depreciation, and cash flow; an HP-16C Programmer's Calculator that converts between different number systems and performs sophisticated bit arithmetic; and an HP-11C Scientific Calculator that computes probability, statistical, and transcendental functions. The calculators are covered in Chapter 24.

- *Databases*   This database manager enables you to define and edit fields; add, edit, and delete records; sort, search, and select records; and create data forms and form letters. It reads and writes files in the popular dBASE format, so it's a convenient alternative to loading a full-featured dBASE-compatible program. Databases is covered in Chapter 25.

- *Autodialer*   This utility will dial any telephone number on your screen (or, in Databases, in the current record) via your modem. The Autodialer is covered in Chapter 25.

- *Modem Telecommunications*   This application works with your modem to transmit computer data over phone lines. It supports such basic features as a phone directory, and the ASCII and XMODEM protocols for transferring files. It also allows you to transfer files in the background, use scripts to automate your online sessions, and access database fields to transmit such information as electronic mail IDs. Modem Telecommunications is covered in Chapter 26.

- *Electronic Mail*   This application automates the procedures for receiving and sending electronic mail over the popular online services MCI Mail, CompuServe, and EasyLink. Electronic Mail is covered in Chapter 26.

- *Send a Fax/Check the Fax Log*   This application lets you exchange faxes with any modern (Group 3) fax machine or fax board. It requires a fax board that supports CAS, such as Intel's SatisFAXtion Board or Connection CoProcessor, or SpectraFAX's Personal Link. In addition to providing basic features, the program allows you to transfer faxes in the background and transmit computer files. On Novell networks, it also allows a fax board in any PC to be used by anyone on the network. Fax telecommunications is covered in Chapter 26.

- *Macro Editor*   This application lets you create small programs, called macros, that replay sequences of computer keystrokes. The macros can be created manually or by a keystroke recorder, and can be set to work within the Desktop only or across all your applications. The Macro Editor is covered in Chapter 27.

- *Utilities*   This heading covers three utilities that bring up an ASCII table, reassign Desktop hotkeys, and unload the Desktop from memory when it's memory resident. The Utilities are covered in Chapter 28.

Running the Desktop

Once you've copied the Desktop files to your hard disk using the Install program (see Appendix A, "PC Tools Installation and Configuration"), you're ready to run the Desktop and its applications.

You can run the Desktop as either a memory-resident or standalone program. Most people make the Desktop memory resident, but the standalone mode also has certain advantages. These two options are covered in the next two sections.

There are also a number of other options you can specify when starting up the Desktop. These are covered in the third section, "Desktop Parameters."

Running the Desktop Memory Resident

To install the Desktop as a memory-resident program, type **DESKTOP /R** from the DOS prompt and press ENTER. (Be sure to use a *forward* slash before the "R," not a backslash.) The Desktop loads itself as resident, taking up about 25K of conventional memory, and a message like the following appears:

```
PCTOOLS Desktop (tm)
      Version 7
Copyright (c) 1988-1991
Central Point Software, Inc.
463 Kbytes free, 15 windows
   Hotkey: <CTRL><SPACE>
```

You're then returned to the DOS prompt. The Desktop will wait invisibly in the background while you work in other applications.

You can automate this step by entering the command into your AUTOEXEC.BAT file (including it as the last *line), or by having the Install program enter it for you. For more information, see Appendix A.*

When you want to bring up the Desktop, simply press CTRL-SPACEBAR, which is one of four Desktop *hotkeys* that work across all applications. The Desktop first saves your current application to disk (or, if available, to expanded memory), and then loads its own files (taking up about 384K of conventional memory) and is ready for your use.

The screen of whatever application you were just in appears in the background. For example, if you invoked the Desktop after listing your files from DOS, you would see something like Figure 19-1, in which the Desktop's title bar, menu bar, and message bar are superimposed over the previous screen.

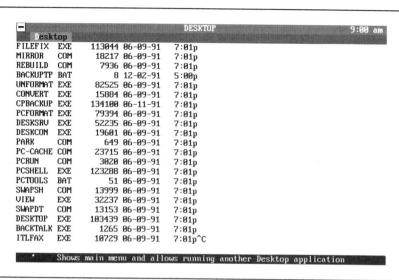

Figure 19-1.   *The Desktop running memory resident*

If you prefer to have the Desktop provide its own background, start the program from the DOS prompt by typing **DESKTOP /R /CS** *instead of* **DESKTOP /R**. *Whenever you invoke the Desktop, you'll get a calendar background like the one shown in Figure 19-2 for standalone mode.*

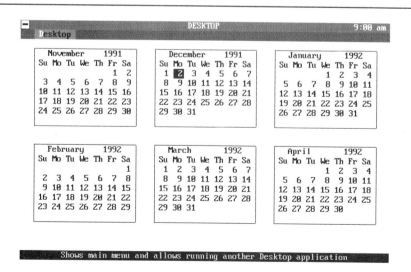

Figure 19-2.   *The Desktop running as a standalone program*

When you're done using the Desktop, press CTRL-SPACEBAR again, or double-click on the Control menu. If you have any windows open, the Desktop saves and closes their files, and in addition saves the window settings to a file named DESKTOP.DOV (*DOV* stands for *Disk Overlays*). It then shrinks back to 25K and loads your application back into conventional memory, returning you to precisely where you left off. When you invoke the Desktop again, it uses the file DESKTOP.DOV to restore your windows precisely as you left them.

Alternatively, you can save and close all your Desktop windows and exit by pressing ESC repeatedly; or by clicking on window Close boxes repeatedly; or by pressing ALT-D, X; or by clicking on the Desktop menu and selecting Exit. The Desktop will continue to be resident, but when you invoke it again, you'll just bring up its initial screen, not your previous windows.

Lastly, you can exit by first pressing ALT-F4; or by pressing ALT-SPACEBAR, C; or by clicking on the Control menu and selecting Close. This brings up a Close PC Tools Desktop dialog box with a Save Configuration option. If the option is checked (which is the default), it saves your window settings to DESKTOP.DOV before exiting; otherwise, it abandons the settings. Use the TAB and ENTER keys, or your mouse, to turn Save Configuration on or off, and then press X or click Exit to close the Desktop.

Even when the Desktop is in the background, it's still working. First, it's constantly tracking the system clock so that it can activate any alarms, programs, or macros you've set to go off using the Appointment Scheduler (see Chapter 23). Second, it's constantly tracking your typing so that it can invoke any active macro whose keystroke you press (see Chapter 27). Third, it's constantly checking for one of these four hotkeys: CTRL-DEL, which lets you copy part or all of the current text screen to the Clipboard (see Chapter 22); CTRL-INS, which pastes the current contents of the Clipboard at your cursor position (see Chapter 22); CTRL-O, which invokes the Autodialer for dialing a phone number on the screen (see Chapter 25); and CTRL-SPACEBAR, which brings up the Desktop itself. Keeping the Desktop memory resident therefore gives you access to it from any application with a single keystroke, as well as constant access to several of its most powerful features.

If you run Microsoft Windows, the memory-resident version of the Desktop is disabled until you exit Windows. However, you can run the Desktop from Windows as a standalone program, as explained shortly.

If you need to unload the Desktop from memory (for example, to run a large application that needs the extra 25K the Desktop's using), you can do so in either of two ways.

First, you can type **KILL** from the DOS prompt and press ENTER. This unloads the Desktop from memory, and also unloads Backtalk, PC Shell, DeskConnect, Commute, and CP Scheduler if they were resident, freeing up the space Desktop and any of the other PC Tools programs were occupying.

Alternatively, you can bring up the **D**esktop menu and select **U**tilities **U**nload PCTOOLS Desktop **U**nload. This command clears the Desktop without affecting other resident PC Tools programs. However, it requires that you invoked the Desktop from DOS (as opposed to an application program), and that the Desktop was the last program you installed resident. For more information, see Chapter 28, "Using the Desktop Utilities."

Alternative Desktop Loading Options

In addition to the basic procedure just described, there are several other ways you can run the Desktop resident.

First, if you have enough extended memory available to create a RAM drive of 800K, you can use the /O*d* parameter to store Desktop temporary files on the drive, using *d* to specify the drive letter. (For example, if your RAM drive's letter is E, use the command line **DESKTOP /R /OE**.) This makes the Desktop come up almost instantly when you invoke it. You can use this option with expanded memory, as well, but it usually isn't necessary because the Desktop's /R parameter is set to automatically take advantage of expanded memory.

Second, you can use the new SWAPDT program to swap the Desktop to extended or expanded memory, or to disk. If you do so, the Desktop will take up no room at all in conventional memory, while the SWAPDT program will take up about 9K (a net savings of 16K). In addition, if you're using a memory manager such as DOS 5's EMM386, you can load SWAPDT into high memory so that it takes up virtually 0K of conventional memory.

To use SWAPDT from the DOS prompt, type **SWAPDT** and press ENTER. This loads the Desktop automatically, taking up 9K instead of 25K of conventional memory. In addition, if you have enough expanded or extended memory, it automatically swaps the Desktop there so that the program can come up almost instantly when you invoke it.

A better alternative, however, is to use SWAPDT from your AUTOEXEC.BAT file. When you do so, you should include the following *two* command lines:

LH SWAPDT /N

DESKTOP /R

The LH option loads SWAPDT into high memory if you're running a high memory manager, so that virtually no space is taken up in conventional memory. The /N parameter prevents the Desktop from being loaded immediately, which would interfere with batch file execution. The DESKTOP /R line then loads the program resident, at which point SWAPDT swaps it to your expanded or extended memory, or (if necessary) to disk.

SWAPDT also supports a few other parameters, such as /U to unload the program, and /P*x* and /T*x* to set the size and transmission speed of the memory buffer used by the Clipboard (see Chapter 22). For a list and description of these parameters, type **SWAPDT /?** from the DOS prompt and press ENTER.

Running the Desktop as a Standalone Program

To install the Desktop as a standalone program, type **DESKTOP** from the DOS prompt and press ENTER. The Desktop fully loads itself, taking up about 384K of conventional memory, and is ready for your use. It initially displays a title bar, menu bar, and message bar against a calendar background, as shown in Figure 19-2. You can work in the Desktop as you would in any standalone integrated program.

You can automate this step by entering the command into your AUTOEXEC.BAT file. If you do, be sure to enter it as the last line in the file, because otherwise your batch execution will stall at this point and will not continue until you exit the Desktop.

There are three advantages to running the Desktop as a standalone program. First, it saves you 25K in conventional memory. This extra RAM can be used for running other memory-resident programs such as Data Monitor, PC Shell, or PC-Cache. The space can also be used to enlarge a RAM disk for speeding file access.

Second, it avoids slowing down other applications. As mentioned previously, when the Desktop is resident, it remains active even when in the background. While this is usually helpful, if your computer is based on an older chip such as the 8088, or if it's running complex applications, the Desktop's activities could create noticeable decreases in speed. In such cases, you may prefer keeping the Desktop out of the background to ensure it doesn't degrade the performance of your other programs.

Third, it may be necessary to run nonresident if the Desktop conflicts with another program you need to use. For example, Microsoft Windows disables the memory-resident version of the Desktop, so the only way to access the Desktop from Windows is to run it as a standalone program.

When you're done using the Desktop, press CTRL-SPACEBAR or double-click on the Control menu. If you have any windows open, the Desktop saves and closes their files, and in addition saves the window settings to a configuration file named DESKTOP.DOV. It then clears itself from memory, freeing up space for other applications. However, the next time you run the Desktop, it uses the file DESKTOP.DOV to restore your windows precisely as you left them.

Alternatively, you can save and close all your Desktop windows and exit by pressing ESC repeatedly; or by clicking on window Close boxes repeatedly; or by pressing ALT-D, X; or by clicking on the Desktop menu and selecting Exit. The Desktop clears itself from memory. Further, the next time you run it, you'll just bring up its initial screen, not your previous windows.

Lastly, you can exit by first pressing ALT-F4; or by pressing ALT-SPACEBAR, C; or by clicking on the Control menu and selecting Close. This brings up a Close PC Tools Desktop dialog box with a Save Configuration option. If the option is checked (which is the default), it saves your window settings to DESKTOP.DOV before exiting; otherwise, it abandons the settings. After you turn Save Configuration on or off, press X or click Exit to close the Desktop.

Desktop Parameters

As mentioned previously, you can run the Desktop as a memory-resident program from the DOS prompt by adding /R after the program name. Options such as /R are called *parameters.* You can include any single parameter (for example, DESKTOP /RA) or combine a number of parameters (for example, DESKTOP /R /CS /OE) to achieve the effect you want. Keep in mind that parameters require a *forward* slash (/, located on the bottom of the ? key) as opposed to the backslash (\) used to specify DOS directories.

The ten parameters specific to the Desktop are as follows:

- **/?** This "help" parameter lists and briefly describes all parameters specific to the Desktop. It should not be combined with any other parameters.

- **/VIDEO** This "help" parameter lists and briefly describes the standard PC Tools video and mouse parameters. It should not be combined with any other parameter. For more information, see the "Video and Mouse Parameters" section in Appendix A, "PC Tools Installation and Configuration."

- *path\filename* This parameter starts the Desktop in the application specified by the extension of *filename,* and then loads the specified file from the drive and directory *path* you specify. For example, DESKTOP C:\PCTOOLS-\DATA\REPORT.TXT would bring up the Desktop's Notepads window with the file REPORT.TXT in it.

- **/C3** or **C4=IRQ,***base port address* If you want the Autodialer and/or Telecommunications programs to use serial port COM3 or COM4 and you don't use a PS/2 computer, you must include this parameter to identify the IRQ and base port address. For example, to use serial port 3 your parameter might read /C3=4,3E8. For the values of IRQ and the base port address for your system, see your modem or fax board manual.

- **/CS** If you're including the /R or /RA parameter to run the Desktop memory resident, adding this parameter will make the Desktop use its calendar background when invoked instead of using the current application screen as the background.

- **/DQ** If you experience problems when hotkeying into the Desktop from the DOS prompt (as opposed to from an application), try using this parameter. To speed loading, the Desktop ordinarily skips saving the contents of conventional memory to disk or expanded memory when invoked at the DOS prompt. This parameter disables the quick-load-from-DOS feature so the contents of conventional memory are saved to disk or expanded memory under all circumstances.

- **/MM**   In both Desktop resident and standalone modes, if you press CTRL-SPACEBAR while Desktop windows are open, the window settings are recorded in a file named DESKTOP.DOV. The next time you bring up the Desktop, the DESKTOP.DOV file is used to restore all your windows precisely as you left them. This is normally desirable. However, if you want to run a particular application (for example, from PC Shell), it's preferable to start off with nothing open but the Desktop main menu. The parameter /MM accomplishes this by forcing the Desktop to ignore the DESKTOP.DOV file. You can use this option even when the Desktop is resident.

- **/O***d*   When you press CTRL-SPACEBAR to swap the Desktop into or out of memory, it first stores the current memory contents into three files named DESKTOP.OVL, DESKTOP.IMG, and DESKTOP.THM. The files are ordinarily saved to your current disk drive or, if available, to expanded memory. The /O parameter followed by a drive letter directs the files to be saved to the specified drive instead. This allows you to direct saving to a RAM disk to speed execution, to a physical drive to disable saving to expanded memory, and so on. If you're using a RAM disk, it must be able to hold at least 800K to store the Desktop files and at least 1.6MB to store both Desktop and PC Shell files.

- **/R**   This is the most commonly used Desktop parameter. It installs the Desktop as a memory-resident program.

- **/RA**   This parameter installs the Desktop as a memory-resident program and then brings up your most recently loaded Appointment Scheduler file. (If you don't have an Appointment Scheduler file with at least one appointment set, the Desktop main screen comes up instead.) If you install the Desktop from your AUTOEXEC.BAT file, this should be the last command in the file, since no other batch commands will be able to execute until you exit the Desktop.

Once the Desktop is installed as memory resident, you can both invoke it and open files from any Desktop applications simultaneously by using a macro. For more information, see the "Using <desk>" section in Chapter 27, "Using the Macro Editor."

Common Desktop Elements

The Desktop has certain elements that are available in virtually every application. These include the Desktop title bar, menu bar, and message bar; the Desktop and

Control menus; and the File Load dialog box. These elements are covered in the following sections.

For information on how to use menus and dialog boxes with either the keyboard or a mouse, see this book's Introduction.

The Desktop Title and Menu Bars

At the top of every Desktop screen is the Desktop title bar, which looks like this:

■	DESKTOP	9:00 am

The bar contains the word "DESKTOP" in its center and the system time in its right corner. If your PC doesn't have a built-in clock, be sure to set the correct date and time at the DOS prompt before starting the Desktop so that it can display this information accurately.

The title bar also displays a dash in its left corner, which represents the Control menu. As explained in this book's Introduction, the Control menu provides options for showing the version of the program you're using and for exiting the program. In most Desktop applications, this menu also provides options for changing the current window's size, position, and colors. For more information, see the "Using the Control Menu" section that follows shortly.

Directly below the Desktop title bar is the menu bar, which displays the names of the one to five additional menus available for the current application. The bar always begins with the **Desktop** main menu. For example, this is the menu bar for Notepads:

Desktop	File	Edit	Search	Controls

You can display a menu by first pressing ALT to activate the bar and then pressing the first letter of the menu's name. You can also hold down ALT and press the letter at the same time. In addition, you can click on the menu name with your mouse. For example, to display the **File** menu you can press ALT, F, or press ALT-F, or click on File. For more information on using menus, see this book's Introduction.

The Desktop Message Bar

On the bottom line of every Desktop application is a message bar. The bar displays information relevant to the Desktop activity taking place.

For example, if you're on a menu name, the message bar provides a brief description of the menu's purpose; and if you're on a menu or dialog box option, the bar tells you the option's function. (You can get more extensive information by pressing F1.) The bar also occasionally displays other pertinent information, such as error messages.

When no special activity is taking place, the message bar displays one-word descriptions of the operations assigned to the first ten function keys (F11 and F12 aren't supported.) The descriptions for function keys F4 through F8 vary with each Desktop application. However, keys F1, F2, F3, F9, and F10 always perform the following operations:

- F1 is the Help key. It displays information relevant to what you're currently doing.

- F2 is the Index key. It displays subject headings you can select for information on a variety of topics.

- F3 is the Exit key. Like the ESC key, it closes menus and dialog boxes, and saves and exits open files. Whenever a Desktop chapter instructs you to press ESC, you can press F3 instead.

- F9 is the Switch key. Like the Control menu's Switch To command, F9 lets you switch to a different open window. For more information, see "Opening Multiple Windows" and "Switching to Another Window" later in this chapter.

- F10 is the Menu key. Like the ALT key, it activates the menu bar. Whenever a Desktop chapter instructs you to press ALT, you can press F10 instead.

Clicking on the function key description in the message bar has the same effect as pressing the function key.

Using the Desktop Menu

The **Desktop** main menu is the gateway to all Desktop applications. As a result, Desktop is the first menu you see when you start the Desktop program. It's also the first menu in every Desktop application.

To bring up the **Desktop** menu, press ALT, D or click on Desktop. The following list of applications appears:

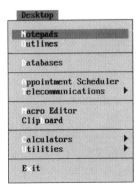

To select an application, press the application's first letter (with the exception of the Clip**b**oard, which requires that you press B), or move to it using the arrow keys and press ENTER, or click on it.

Three of the application headings on the menu lead to submenus. These are Telecommunications, Calculators, and Utilities, as indicated by the pointing triangles to their right. If you move to one of these headings using the arrow keys, its submenu appears to its right, as shown in Figure 19-3. If you then press ENTER, or if you press the heading's first letter, or if you click on it, you're moved into the submenu itself, where you can choose the application you want.

At the bottom of the menu is an E**x**it option. As mentioned previously, this option saves and closes all your open windows, and then exits the Desktop.

The menu will additionally list **PCSHELL** as an option (directly above E**x**it) if you've installed PC Shell to be memory resident, as shown in Figure 19-3. This is true regardless of whether the Desktop itself is resident. If you select it, PC Shell temporarily swaps the Desktop out of memory while it executes, and then loads it back when it exits, returning you to the precise point where you left off. For more information about PC Shell, see Chapter 15, "PC Shell Overview."

Opening Multiple Windows

In addition to opening your initial application window, the **D**esktop menu can open 14 additional windows, for a total of 15. These windows can all hold files from the same application or from a mix of different applications.

You can activate any window by pressing F9, or pressing ALT-SPACEBAR, W, or clicking on the Control menu and selecting Switch To (see "Switching to Another Window" later in this chapter). You can also copy or move data between windows with the Clipboard (see Chapter 22, "Using the Clipboard").

The idea of using more than one window at a time may seem a little strange at first, but it actually reflects how most people normally work. For example, while you're composing a report in a Notepads window, you may need to refer to data scattered in several other Notepads files. You may also want to work with an outline for the report in an Outlines window. In the meantime, you might get a phone call asking for some information in a database file, for which you'd open a Databases window. Your caller might then ask you to change an appointment to another time, for which you'd open an Appointment Scheduler window...and so on. Rather than impose artificial separations between its different files and applications, the Desktop's multiple windows feature accommodates the natural rhythm and flow of your working habits.

To use the feature is easy. After you open your first application window using the **D**esktop main menu, you can bring up the menu again at any time by pressing ALT, D, or by clicking on Desktop in the application's menu bar. You can then select the same application, or a different one, to open another window. This process can be repeated over and over again until a total of 15 files are open.

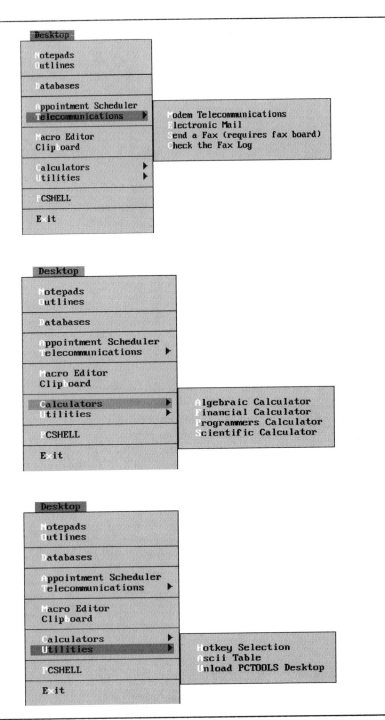

Figure 19-3.   *The Telecommunications, Calculators, and Utilities submenus*

Once you've opened 15 windows, trying to open another one produces the error message "Application stack full. Cannot add another window." If this occurs, first press ENTER to eliminate the message, and then activate and close a window you don't need open at the moment. You can then proceed to use the vacant slot for your new window.

As mentioned previously, you can save and close all your open windows simultaneously by bringing up the **D**esktop menu and selecting E**x**it. However, this option doesn't work when you have all 15 windows open. To get around this, simply press ESC to close one window, and then select the option.

Using the Control Menu

As explained in this book's Introduction, every PC Tools 7 program has a Control menu in its upper-left corner, which you can display by pressing ALT-SPACEBAR or by clicking on its dash symbol. The Control menu always provides options for showing the version of the program you're using and for exiting the program. In most Desktop applications, the menu also provides options for adjusting the current window, as shown here:

The options offered on this full version of the menu are as follows:

- *Version*   This option displays the Desktop version number and a copyright notice.

- *Restore*   This option restores a maximized window to its previous size.

- *Move*   This option allows you to reposition the current window using the arrow keys.

- *Size*   This option lets you resize the current window using the arrow keys.

- *Maximize*   This option expands the current window to fill the screen.

- *Application Colors*   This option lets you change the colors of the current window.

- *Close* This option brings up a Close PC Tools Desktop dialog box.
- *Switch To* This option lets you switch to a different open window.

The windows in certain Desktop applications either aren't resizable or aren't moveable, or both. In addition, the Switch To option won't work when you have only one window open. In these cases, the pertinent Control menu options are disabled, which is indicated by the absence of highlighting on the letters you'd normally use to select them.

The six menu options that adjust application windows—Maximize, Restore, Size, Move, Switch To, and Application Color—are covered in the following sections.

Maximizing and Restoring a Window

In most Desktop applications, the default window size is significantly smaller than your screen so that portions of other open windows can display on the screen simultaneously. If you want to see as much of a window as possible, however, you can expand, or *maximize*, it to fill the screen.

To maximize the current window using the keyboard, press ALT-SPACEBAR, X, or click on the Control menu and select Maximize. The window fills the space between the menu and message bars. To restore the window to its previous size, press ALT-SPACEBAR, R, or click on the Control menu and select Restore. The window shrinks back to its previous proportions.

You can also maximize the window using your mouse. To do so, simply click on the triangular Maximize button in the window's upper-right corner. When you want to shrink the window back, just click on the button again, which has turned upside-down to indicate that it's become a Restore button.

Resizing a Window

In most Desktop applications, you can expand or contract the window's size. This is useful if you have several windows open and you want to resize and reposition them so they're all visible.

To resize the current window using the keyboard, press ALT-SPACEBAR, S, or click on the Control menu and select Size. A small box appears telling you to "use cursor keys to adjust." Press the RIGHT ARROW and DOWN ARROW keys to expand the window, and the LEFT ARROW and UP ARROW keys to contract the window. When you're done, press ENTER. The message box disappears, and you're returned to the now-resized window.

You can also resize the window using your mouse. To do so, position the mouse pointer over the Resize box represented by the four arrowheads in the window's lower-right corner, click your mouse button, and drag in the direction you want to resize. When the window is the size you want, release the mouse button.

Moving a Window

In most Desktop applications, you can move a window anywhere on the portion of the screen between the menu and message bars. This is useful if you have several windows open and you want to position them so that they're all visible.

To move the current window using the keyboard, press ALT-SPACEBAR, M, or click on the Control menu and select Move. A small box appears telling you to "use cursor keys to adjust." Press the arrow keys to move the window in the directions you want. When you're done, press ENTER. The message box disappears, and you're returned to the now-positioned window.

You can also move the window using your mouse. To do so, position the mouse pointer over any portion of the window's title bar, click your mouse button, and drag in the desired direction. When you've placed the window where you want it, release the mouse button.

Switching to Another Window

As explained in "Opening Multiple Windows" earlier in this chapter, you can keep up to 15 windows open at the same time. You can also quickly switch from the window you're in to any other open window.

If any portion of the window you want to move to is visible on screen, you can simply click on the window to activate it.

Otherwise, press F9, or press ALT-SPACEBAR, W, or click on the Close menu and select Switch To. If you have two windows open, you'll automatically be switched from the current window to the other window.

However, if you have three or more windows open, a Change Active Window dialog box like this appears to list all your open windows:

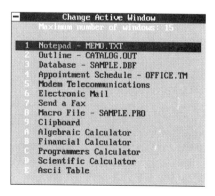

The windows are numbered from 1 through 9, and then from A through F. To switch to a listed window, press the number or letter to its left, or click on it, or move to it using the arrow keys and press ENTER.

Changing Window Colors

To change the current window's colors, press ALT-SPACEBAR, A, or click on the Control menu and select Application Colors. A dialog box appears that lists the elements whose colors you can change on the left and the colors you can select from on the right. The elements listed will vary from application to application, but the color choices will remain consistent across applications.

Before you modify any colors, it's recommended that you write down the current color settings so you can return to them if you're later unhappy with your changes. Once you've done so, select the element you want to change, and then use the UP ARROW and DOWN ARROW keys to try different colors. As you move, the selected element changes to your selected color.

When you're satisfied with a choice, simply select a different element and repeat the process. When you've made all your color changes, press ESC. The dialog box closes, and you're returned to your now-recolored window. Your color settings for the window will be saved to disk the next time you save the file.

You can also define your color settings as defaults for *all* new windows in the application. To do so, see the next section.

Applying Window Settings to New Files

Any display changes you make to a file's window are saved when you close the file and retained in future Desktop sessions with the file. Ordinarily, all other files and windows are unaffected.

However, when you're using the Notepads, Outlines, Databases, or Macro Editor application, you have the option of applying a display change you've made in the current window to *all* new windows created by the particular application. To do so, simply press ALT, C, S, or click on the Controls menu and select Save Setup. This defines your current Control and Controls menu settings as the application's new default settings. Using this command and the Control menu, you can therefore create new default window sizes, positions, and colors for these Desktop applications.

Using the File Load Dialog Box

The File Load dialog box is used throughout the Desktop to list files, create new files, open existing files, and delete files. It's the first element you see after selecting the Appointment Scheduler, Databases, Macro Editor, Notepads, or Outlines applications. It's also available through the File Load command within these applications and Modem Telecommunications.

To bring up the File Load box, follow these steps:

1. First, call up the Desktop Manager. If you've installed the Desktop to be memory resident, press CTRL-SPACEBAR. Otherwise, type **DESKTOP** from the DOS prompt and press ENTER.

2. Press ENTER to select the Notepads application. A File Load dialog box like this appears:

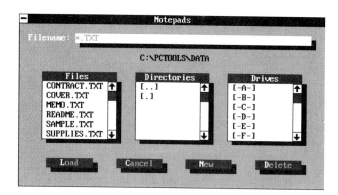

At the top of the box is the Filename field. You can type the drive, directory, and name of the file you want here, and then press ENTER to load it.

Alternatively, you can type the wildcard * and an extension, and then press ENTER, to list files from a particular application. For example, since you selected Notepads, the Filename default is *.TXT, which lists all files in the current directory with Notepads TXT extensions. The applications supporting the File Load dialog box and what you should type to display their files are as follows:

Application	Data File Extension
Appointment Scheduler	*.TM
Databases (database files)	*.DBF
Databases (form files)	*.FOR
Databases (record files)	*.REC
Macro Editor	*.PRO
Modem Telecommunications	*.TEL
Notepads	*.TXT
Outlines	*.OUT

If you don't specify an extension when typing a filename, the extension of the application you've selected is automatically appended to the name. If you don't want this to occur, type a period at the end of the name. For example, in Notepads the name "MEMO" would become MEMO.TXT, but the name "MEMO." would remain MEMO (that is, remain without an extension).

Centered below the Filename option is a line showing the current drive and directory path. This line is for display only; it can't be edited. Its contents change when you type a different path in the Filename field and press ENTER, or when you choose a new selection from the boxes beneath it labeled Directories and Drives.

Using TAB or your mouse, you can move to the Files, Directories, and Drives boxes, which respectively display your specified files, and your available directories and drives, in alphabetical order. Each box shows up to six selections initially. You can scroll through the items one at a time using DOWN ARROW and UP ARROW, scroll by six items at a time using PGDN and PGUP, and jump to the bottom or top of each list using END or HOME. You can also click on a box's vertical scroll bar.

When you see a listed item you want to select, move to it and press ENTER, or double-click on it. If the item is a drive or directory, you're switched to it, while if the item is a file, the file is loaded. These boxes therefore provide you with an alternative to typing in a path and filename in the Filename field.

At the bottom of the File Load box are four command options: Load, Cancel, New, and Delete.

The Load option loads your specified file. To use it, type or select the file you want, and then press ALT-L or click Load. The dialog box closes, and a window opens that displays the file.

The Cancel option simply closes the dialog box without performing any action. To select it, press ESC or click Cancel.

The New option creates new files or replaces existing files with blank ones. To use it, type the new file's name in the Filename field or specify the existing file, and then press ALT-N or click New. If the file doesn't already exist, the dialog box closes and a blank window with the file's name appears. However, if the file *does* exist, a warning message appears, because proceeding will destroy the contents of the existing file. If you want to abort the operation, press ESC or click Cancel to exit the dialog box. However, if you want to continue, press ENTER or click OK; the contents of the file are erased, the dialog box closes, and a blank window with the file's name appears.

You can also quickly open a "scratch" file by entering nothing into the Filename field and just pressing ALT-N. The File Load box automatically uses the filename WORK followed by the extension of the application you've selected.

Lastly, the Delete option erases a file. To use it, specify the existing file you want to eliminate, and then press ALT-D or click Delete. A warning message appears, asking for confirmation. If you want to abort the operation, press ESC or click Cancel. Otherwise, press ENTER or click OK to execute the deletion. In either case, you're returned to the File Load dialog box.

Be sure to use the Delete option with care, as there is no way to retrieve a deleted file through the Desktop. If you delete a file accidentally, see Chapter 6, "Recovering Deleted or Formatted Data."

If you press TAB to move to the Files box and then try to delete the topmost file, you may not be able to because that file's name isn't entered immediately into the Filename field. If you experience this problem, try pressing DOWN ARROW and then UP ARROW (which will usually get the file's name into the field), and then try deleting again.

Desktop Files

When you used the Install program to copy the Desktop to your hard disk, a number of files were generated. You may need to understand what each file represents in case one gets damaged or you have to eliminate nonessential files to save disk space. You may also simply be curious about what these dozens of files do. The following table lists each Desktop file in alphabetical order and briefly describes it. In addition, if you allowed Install to create SYSTEM and DATA subdirectories in your PCTOOLS directory, it tells you in which directory each file resides.

The following "Directory" columns will only be accurate if the line **SET PCTOOLS=C:\PCTOOLS\DATA** *has been included in your AUTOEXEC.BAT file. If this line is left out, the Desktop will store certain files intended for the DATA directory into either your PCTOOLS directory or whatever directory is current instead. This does no harm, but it can make locating your various files difficult. For more information, see Appendix A, "PC Tools Installation and Configuration."*

File	Directory	Description
BACKTALK.EXE	PCTOOLS	Background Modem Telecommunications
CIS.SCR	DATA	Script for logging onto CompuServe
CPS.SCR	DATA	Script for logging onto the Central Point BBS
CPSPRINT.DAT	DATA	Printer configuration data
DESKTOP.DOV	DATA	All Desktop application overlay files
DESKTOP.EXE	PCTOOLS	Main Desktop program
DESKTOP.HLP	SYSTEM	Online help (accessed by F1 and F2)
DESKTOP.MSG	SYSTEM	Desktop message bar help messages
DICT.SPL	DATA	Spelling checker dictionary
EMAIL.TM	DATA	Electronic Mail scheduling data
EPSON.PRO	DATA	Printer macros for Epson FX-80
ESL.SCR	DATA	Script for logging onto EasyLink
FAX7.CFG	DATA	Fax configuration data
HPLJF.PRO	DATA	Printer macros for HP LaserJet
ITLFAX.EXE	PCTOOLS	Link to CAS-compatible fax board
KILL.EXE	PCTOOLS	Unloads Desktop from DOS
LETTER.FOR	DATA	Sample Databases form letter
MCI.SCR	DATA	Script for logging onto MCI Mail
PANA.PRO	DATA	Sample macros for Panasonic printers

File	Directory	Description
PCTOOLS.PCX	DATA	Graphical logo for fax COVER.TXT page
PHONE.TEL	DATA	Modem Telecommunications directory
PROPTR.PRO	DATA	Printer macros for IBM ProPrinter
READCIS.SCR	DATA	Script for picking up CompuServe messages
READESL.SCR	DATA	Script for picking up EasyLink messages
READMCI.SCR	DATA	Script for picking up MCI Mail messages
SAMPLE.DBF	DATA	Sample Databases database file
SAMPLE.FAX	DATA	Sample fax file
SAMPLE.FOR	DATA	Sample Databases form file
SAMPLE.MAI	DATA	Sample electronic mail
SAMPLE.OUT	DATA	Sample Outlines file
SAMPLE.PRO	DATA	Miscellaneous sample macros
SAMPLE.TLX	DATA	Sample telex
SAMPLE.TM	DATA	Sample Appointment Scheduler file
SAMPLE.TXT	DATA	Sample Notepads file
SENDCIS.SCR	DATA	Script for sending CompuServe messages
SENDESL.SCR	DATA	Script for sending EasyLink messages
SENDMCI.SCR	DATA	Script for sending MCI Mail messages
TELECOM.DBF	DATA	Sample Databases/Telecommunications file

In addition, the Desktop automatically creates the following files once you begin using it:

File	Directory	Description
*.FOR	DATA	Generated by Databases files
*.REC	DATA	Generated by Databases files
CALC.TMP	DATA	Algebraic Calculator data
COVER.TXT	DATA	Text for fax cover page
DESK.OVL	SYSTEM	Desktop application overlays
DESKTOP.CFG	DATA	Desktop configuration data
DESKTOP.IMG	DATA	Saves RAM video image in resident mode

File	Directory	Description
DESKTOP.THM	DATA	Stores current data of non-Desktop applications (them) after the Desktop has been invoked in resident mode
EMAIL.CFG	DATA	Electronic Mail configuration data
EMLREAD.ERR	DATA	Electronic Mail download error messages
EMLREAD.ERS	DATA	Electronic Mail download error messages
EMLSEND.ERR	DATA	Electronic Mail upload error messages
EMLSEND.ERS	DATA	Electronic Mail upload error messages
FAX.PHO	DATA	Fax directory
FINCALC.TMP	DATA	Financial Calculator data
HEXCALC.TMP	DATA	Programmer's Calculator data
LEARN.PRO	DATA	Stores macros created in Learn mode
TALK.CFG	DATA	Stores Telecommunications configuration
TALKONLN.CFG	DATA	Stores Telecommunications online screen
TRANSFER.LOG	DATA	Background Modem Telecommunications log
SCICALC.TMP	DATA	Scientific Calculator data

New Desktop Features in Version 7

If you're familiar with PC Tools Deluxe 6, you'll find that the Desktop has been significantly improved as a result of some changes to existing features and a number of new features. These changes are covered in the following sections. Also, they're marked throughout subsequent chapters by the "7" icon to the left of this paragraph.

System-Wide Changes

The most noticeable change in the Desktop is that it's a lot more attractive. While its basic design has remained unchanged, the Desktop now makes much better use of color, and its windows, menus, and dialog boxes all have a more streamlined and consistent look.

Another visual improvement is the Desktop background. Instead of a plain shaded background, the Desktop now has a handsome and useful calendar background, which displays the dates for the previous month, the current month, and the following four months. Also, the Desktop menu no longer automatically pops down when you start the program, so that you're provided with an unobstructed view of the calendar before you begin selecting applications.

In addition, the Desktop has some new elements that make it even more similar to a Microsoft Windows program. Specifically, its top line is now a title bar with a Control menu in its left corner. This Control menu has assumed the options previously assigned to the Window menu (see "Using the Control Menu" earlier in this chapter), and so the Window menu has been eliminated. Also, the Control menu has added the Microsoft Windows-like keystroke CTRL-ESC as another way of switching between windows (though this keystroke will bring up PC Shell instead if PC Shell is resident).

The menu bar, which used to be combined with the title bar on the top line, has now been split out into a separate line directly below the title bar. As a result, when you look at the menu bar in any Desktop application, keep in mind that there's always one more menu available than that bar displays, which is the Control menu in the upper-left corner.

The options on the main **Desktop** menu are fundamentally the same. However, the fax options no longer appear in the Telecommunications submenu unless the Desktop detects a CAS-compatible fax board and fax software installed in your system (see Chapter 26). Also, the System Menu/Window Colors option has been eliminated from the Utilities option, because all PC Tools system-wide changes are now made through the PC Config program (see Appendix A).

The message bar at the bottom of the screen is also fundamentally the same *if* you use PC Tools in text mode. However, if you use it in graphics mode (by selecting that option through the PC Config program), new graphic symbols are used to represent the function keys, as shown here:

```
 Help   Index   Exit   Load   Email   Find   Again   Spell  Switch   Menu
```

In addition, if you press F1 to expand on a message bar description, you'll find that the context-sensitive online help in the Desktop has been enormously improved. The explanations displayed are now much more informative about the specific feature you were examining when you invoked Help.

One other system-wide Desktop element that's changed is the File Load dialog box, which has been expanded to include a Drives box and Directories box in addition to a Files box. As a result, you can now select and load a file using your mouse exclusively. For more information, see "Using the File Load Dialog Box" earlier in this chapter.

Another new feature is the *filename* parameter, which forces the Desktop to start up in the application specified by the extension of the filename you specify and then load the file automatically. For more information, see "Desktop Parameters" earlier in this chapter.

Lastly, the Desktop now takes up only 25K in conventional memory instead of 40K. If you run the Desktop resident, this means you now have an extra 15K available for loading other memory-resident programs or running large applications. In addition, a new program called SWAPDT can reduce the amount of conventional memory the Desktop takes up when resident to virtually *0K*! For more information, see "Running the Desktop Memory Resident" and "Alternative Desktop Loading Options" earlier in this chapter.

New Options

A new application has been added to the Desktop's already large inventory of programs. This is Electronic Mail, which now appears in the **Desktop** menu's Telecommunications submenu. Electronic Mail automates the procedures for sending, receiving, and organizing your online messages on the popular services MCI Mail, CompuServe, and EasyLink. Also, in conjunction with this feature, both Notepads and Outlines contain two new commands: **C**ontrols **E**lectronic Mail Page Layout for formatting an online message, and **F**ile **S**end Electronic Mail for transmitting an online message. For more information, see "Using Electronic Mail" in Chapter 26, "Using Telecommunications."

In addition, several new options have been added to the Appointment Scheduler, the Hewlett-Packard calculator simulations, the database manager, and Fax Telecommunications; and a significant change has been made to Notepads. These subjects are covered in the following sections.

New Options in the Appointment Scheduler

The Appointment Scheduler now lets you choose from among five different screen layout designs via the command **C**ontrols **S**chedule Layouts. This allows you to emphasize the components of the Scheduler that are most important to you.

In addition, function key F4 now toggles the display of the Daily Scheduler on and off, F6 toggles the Calendar display, and F7 toggles the To-Do List display. Furthermore, F5 toggles the display of the initial appointments you have scheduled for the week, and F8 toggles the display of a set of bar graphs representing your appointments for the week.

Also, a new **L**ayout option has been added to the **F**ile **P**rint command. If you select it, you're presented with a wide range of print formatting choices (including US Legal, Half-Page, and Pocket), eight different layout styles, and a Mirror Image option that in effect doubles the number of layout styles available.

Lastly, the Daily Scheduler now provides a "group scheduling" option that allows network users to share an Appointment Scheduler file devoted to the group's meetings. Each member of the group can check the schedule to make sure it accommodates his or her own and, if the person has write privileges, can enter new appointments for the group and/or revise existing appointments to eliminate conflicts. This procedure can greatly ease the process of coordinating meeting times between a number of busy people.

For more information about these new features, see Chapter 23, "Using the Appointment Scheduler."

New Options in Calculators

The appearance of the Hewlett-Packard calculator simulations has been significantly streamlined. First, they now display in normal windows (looking much more like real calculators), as opposed to full screens. As a result, while they still can't be resized, they can now be repositioned if you need to make portions of other windows more visible.

Second, only one function per key is displayed at any time. When you press F7, all the keys instantly change to display their "f" functions, and when you press F8, they all change to display their "g" functions. After you've selected the function you want (or pressed a key that isn't listed, such as SPACEBAR), the keys go back to displaying their default functions. This approach gives the calculators a much less cluttered look than the previous method of always displaying all three functions for each key.

A side benefit of this approach is that the keypads of the Financial and Scientific Calculators now take up a lot less room, providing extra display space to the left. You can use this space to constantly display the stack registers, or the data registers, or (in the case of the Financial Calculator) the financial registers. You also have the option of displaying no registers, in which case the space is left blank except for a copyright notice.

For more information on the Desktop's HP Calculators, see Chapter 24, "Using the Calculators."

New Options in Databases

Databases now displays the alphabet at the top of each database window, and provides a File Modify Data switch that lets you specify whether you only want to view records or also to modify them. When the switch is off, pressing any letter on your keyboard or clicking any letter in the alphabet display instantly moves you to the first record in your sorted field that begins with the letter. This provides you with a Rolodex-like method for moving around your records. For more information, see Chapter 25, "Using the Database Manager."

New Options in Fax Telecommunications

In addition to the Personal Link from SpectraFAX Corp. and the Connection CoProcessor from Intel PCEO, Fax Telecommunications now supports the SatisFAXtion Board, which is Intel's updated version of its Connection CoProcessor.

For more information about faxing, see "Using Fax Telecommunications" in Chapter 26, "Using Telecommunications."

New Formatting Default for Notepads

There's one application change in PC Tools 7 that's especially worth noting: Notepads now automatically saves its files in ASCII (a universal format understood by virtually all PC programs) instead of the PCTOOLS Desktop format (which retains Desktop formatting information, such as margins, headers and footers, and window position).

This modification makes it convenient to use Notepads for such purposes as electronic mail. However, since Notepads is used by a number of applications, the change can also lead to unexpected results. For example, if you create a form in Databases and neglect to explicitly save it in the PCTOOLS Desktop format, your layout settings will be lost and the form probably won't work. You should therefore remember to select the PCTOOLS Desktop format the first time you save a file with Desktop formatting information. (After the first time, you can save and exit the file by simply pressing ESC, because it will retain your selected format as its new default.) For more information, see "Saving Your Document" in Chapter 20, "Using Notepads."

Chapter *20*

Using Notepads

Notepads is an easy-to-use word processor that lets you quickly create, edit, save, and print documents.

Like any word processor, Notepads has several advantages over a typewriter. First, it lets you type in a continuous flow, so you don't have to press a carriage return at the end of every line or change paper at the end of every page. Second, it allows you to move around in your document easily and make frequent editing changes. Third, it prints your document for you as often as you wish. In addition, Notepads includes such special features as a 100,000-word spelling checker; access to an electronic storage area for deleting, moving, and copying text; a timed file saver; and such layout options as headers and footers.

A Notepads file can hold approximately 60,000 characters, or about 40 double-spaced pages. Therefore, Notepads is best for the production of short and medium-sized documents such as memos, letters, and reports. If you make the Desktop memory resident, Notepads is also an ideal tool for jotting down notes while you're in the middle of running a non-word processing program.

This chapter first covers basic Notepads tasks, such as typing and simple editing, moving around in your document, navigating the menus, saving your document, and printing. It then covers advanced Notepads features such as deleting, moving, and copying text; combining files; finding and replacing text; spell-checking; and document formatting.

Basic Features

This section covers the fundamental aspects of Notepads you need to know to make the program perform useful work. After finishing this section, you'll be able to create, edit, save, and print documents easily.

Getting Started

Before you can do anything in Notepads, you have to bring up the application screen. Follow these steps to run the Desktop, select Notepads, and open a document file:

1. First, call up the Desktop Manager. If you've installed the Desktop to be memory resident, press CTRL-SPACEBAR. Otherwise, type **DESKTOP** from the DOS prompt and press ENTER.

2. Press ENTER or click on Desktop to display the main menu.

3. Press ENTER or click Notepads to select the application. The File Load dialog box appears.

4. Type **MEMO** to create a text file named MEMO.TXT. (If you don't specify an extension, Notepads automatically appends TXT to your filename.)

5. Press ALT-N, or press ENTER twice, or click New. A blank document window appears, as shown in Figure 20-1.

The window includes such usual elements as scroll bars, and Close and Zoom boxes. In addition, it contains the following special indicators:

- *Line Number Counter*   This indicator is displayed in the upper-left corner of the window. It tracks the line your cursor is on. You start on line 1.

- *Column Number Counter*   This indicator is displayed directly to the right of the Line Number Counter. It tracks the column your cursor is on. You start on column 1.

- *Mode Indicator*   This indicator displays "INS" in the upper-right corner of the window if *Insert mode* is on (meaning that your typing will push subsequent text to the left), or it displays nothing if *Overtype mode* is on (meaning that your typing will overwrite existing text). You start in Insert mode.

- *Filename*   This indicator is centered in the window's title bar. It displays the name of the file you're working on (in this case, MEMO.TXT).

- *Tab ruler*   This indicator is on the window's second line. It shows where the document's tab stops are currently set; the default is a tab every five columns. Unlike the other indicators, the ruler can be turned off with the **C**ontrols **T**ab Ruler Display command.

At the top of the screen are the six menus available in Notepads (and, in the right corner, the system time). You'll examine these menus later in the chapter.

At the bottom of the screen is the message bar. When a Notepads activity is taking place, the bar displays appropriate definitions or instructions. Otherwise, it displays the following commands assigned to the function keys:

Function Key	Action
F1 (Help)	Brings up context-sensitive help
F2 (Index)	Brings up the online help index
F3 (Exit)	Performs the same functions as ESC
F4 (Load)	Selects **F**ile **L**oad
F5 (Email)	Selects **F**ile **S**end **E**lectronic Mail
F6 (Find)	Selects **S**earch **R**eplace
F7 (Again)	Selects **S**earch **F**ind **A**gain
F8 (Spell)	Selects **E**dit **S**pellcheck **F**ile
F9 (Switch)	Activates a different open window
F10 (Menu)	Performs the same functions as ALT

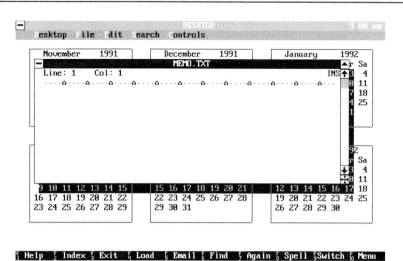

Figure 20-1.   *The Notepads screen*

Basic Typing

Once you've opened a Notepads file, you can begin creating your document. Typing in Notepads is similar to using a typewriter; the letter and number keys, SHIFT and CAPS LOCK keys, and SPACEBAR all perform in the ways you expect. There is one important difference, however. On a typewriter, when you get near the right margin, you press the carriage return to move to the beginning of the next line. In Notepads, when you near the right margin, the word you're typing is moved *automatically* to the beginning of the next line. This feature, called *word wrap,* lets you type in a steady flow. It's only when you want to end a line that doesn't reach to the right margin, create a blank line, or end an entire paragraph that you need to press ENTER (which is the PC equivalent of the carriage return). For example, follow these steps to create the header and text for a short memo:

1. For the first line, type **TO: Wayne Jordan**.

   If you make a mistake, simply erase it using BACKSPACE and then type the correct text.

   Notice that the *cursor* (the blinking underline that shows where you are on the screen) moves as you type.

2. This line doesn't reach to the right margin, so press ENTER to end it and move to the beginning of the next line.

   Notice that the Line Number Counter tracks your cursor position; it currently shows that you're on line 2 and column 1.

3. For the second line, type **FROM: Susan Allen** and press ENTER.

4. For the third line, type **RE: Video 'N Things Inventory** and press ENTER.

5. Press ENTER again to create a blank line.

6. Type the following paragraph. This time, don't press ENTER at the ends of lines; just type continuously.

   We're continuing to experience great demand for movies starring computers. Please order another 50 videos in this category immediately. Concentrate on getting copies of Colossus: The Forbin Project, 2001: A Space Odyssey, and The Computer Wore Tennis Shoes.

   Notice that when a word reached the end of a line, it automatically wrapped to the beginning of the next line. Your window now looks similar to this:

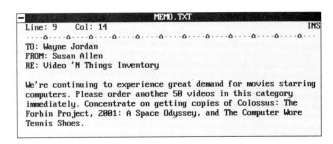

(Words may have wrapped differently on your screen as a result of different display hardware or a different window size.)

7. Press ENTER to end the paragraph.

Basic Editing

One of the most important features of Notepads is its ability to let you easily move to and change anything in your document.

If you don't see the text you want to edit, you can move down and up a window at a time by using PGDN and PGUP. Once your text is in sight, you can go to it by moving down and up a line at a time with DOWN ARROW and UP ARROW, to the end and beginning of a line with END and HOME, and right and left a character at a time with RIGHT ARROW and LEFT ARROW.

Once you've properly positioned the cursor, you can delete the character the cursor is under by pressing DEL, or delete the character to the left of the cursor by pressing BACKSPACE.

You can also add new text by simply typing as usual. That's because Notepads starts off in Insert mode, as shown by "INS" appearing in the Mode Indicator. When Insert is on, whatever you type pushes existing text over to the right. If you press INS, you switch the program into Overtype mode, as shown by "INS" disappearing from the Mode Indicator. When Overtype is on, whatever you type erases and replaces existing text. You can switch back to Insert mode by pressing INS again.

To get a feel for these editing techniques, follow these steps to make some changes in your memo:

1. Change "Susan" to "Suzanne." First, press PGUP twice to move to the beginning of the document.

2. Press HOME to move to the beginning of line 1.

3. Press DOWN ARROW to move to line 2.

4. Press RIGHT ARROW eight times to move to the small "s" in "Susan."

5. Notice that the Mode Indicator displays "INS," showing you're in Insert mode. Type **z**. The letter is inserted, pushing subsequent text to the right.

6. Press DEL. The "s" over the cursor is deleted.

7. Press RIGHT ARROW twice to move past the "n."

8. Type **ne**. Again, your text is inserted, pushing subsequent text to the right.

9. Now change "Allen" to "Allan." First, press RIGHT ARROW four times to move under the "e."

10. Press INS to switch to Overtype mode. The Mode Indicator is now blank.

11. Type **a**. This time, your new text overwrites the previous text.

12. Press INS again. The Mode Indicator shows you're back in Insert mode.

 Word wrap can be turned off by pressing ALT, C, W, *or by clicking on the Controls menu and selecting Wordwrap. This option is useful if you want to type past the right margin. Selecting Controls Wordwrap again turns word wrap back on.*

Moving Around in Your Document

You can get to any spot in your document eventually by using PGUP, PGDN, HOME, END, and the arrow keys. However, to help make your editing faster and more fluid, Notepads also provides a number of shortcut keystrokes for moving the cursor. For example, you can move forward or backward a word at a time in the document by pressing CTRL-RIGHT ARROW or CTRL-LEFT ARROW; to the bottom or top of the window by pressing END, END or HOME, HOME; and to the end or beginning of the entire document by pressing CTRL-END or CTRL-HOME. You can also move to a specific line by pressing ALT, E, G (which invokes the **Edit G**oto command), typing the line number, and pressing ALT-O. A complete list of movement shortcuts appears in Table 20-1.

Keystroke	Action
CTRL-RIGHT ARROW	Move forward by word
CTRL-LEFT ARROW	Move backward by word
END	Move to end of line
HOME	Move to beginning of line
END, END	Move to end of window
HOME, HOME	Move to beginning of window
PGDN	Move down one window
PGUP	Move up one window
CTRL-PGDN	Scroll document down one line independent of the cursor
CTRL-PGUP	Scroll document up one line independent of the cursor
CTRL-END	Move to end of document
CTRL-HOME	Move to beginning of document
ALT, E, G (**Edit G**oto)	Move to specified line
ALT, S, F (**Search F**ind)	Move to specified text string

Table 20-1. *Notepads Keystroke Movement Shortcuts*

To get a feel for the different ways you can move around a document, follow these steps:

1. If you completed the previous exercise, you're currently on line 2. Press END to move to the end of the line.

2. Press HOME to move to the beginning of the line.

3. Press END, END to move to the bottom of the window.

4. Press HOME, HOME to move to the top of the window.

5. Press CTRL-RIGHT ARROW five times to move forward five words. You should be at the beginning of "Allan."

6. Press CTRL-LEFT ARROW five times to move backward five words. You should be at the end of "TO:".

7. Press CTRL-END to move to the bottom of the memo.

8. Press CTRL-HOME to move to the top of the memo.

9. Jump to line 8. First, press ALT, E, G. The Go To dialog box appears, as shown here:

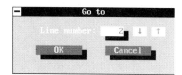

10. Type **8** and press ALT-O. The cursor jumps to the beginning of line 8, as indicated by the Line Number Counter.

Of course, if you have a mouse you can also move quickly around your document by using the vertical and horizontal scroll bars.

The Go To dialog box retains the last number you entered. You can therefore "Go To" a line, move to another spot in your document, and then return to the original line at any time by pressing ALT, E, *G and* ALT-O.

Navigating the Notepads Menus

Most of Notepads' power lies in its menu options (shown in Figure 20-2). Like all Desktop applications, Notepads' first two menus are Control and Desktop.

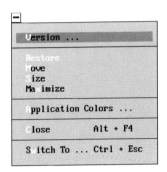

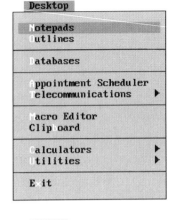

```
┌─┐
│─│
└─────────────────────────┐
│  Version ...            │
├─────────────────────────┤
│  Restore                │
│  Move                   │
│  Size                   │
│  Maximize               │
├─────────────────────────┤
│  Application Colors ... │
├─────────────────────────┤
│  Close          Alt + F4│
├─────────────────────────┤
│  Switch To ... Ctrl + Esc│
└─────────────────────────┘
```

```
Desktop
┌──────────────────────────┐
│  Notepads                │
│  Outlines                │
├──────────────────────────┤
│  Databases               │
├──────────────────────────┤
│  Appointment Scheduler   │
│  Telecommunications    ▶ │
├──────────────────────────┤
│  Macro Editor            │
│  Clipboard               │
├──────────────────────────┤
│  Calculators           ▶ │
│  Utilities             ▶ │
├──────────────────────────┤
│  Exit                    │
└──────────────────────────┘
```

```
File
┌──────────────────────────┐
│  Load ...                │
│  Save ...                │
├──────────────────────────┤
│  Send Electronic Mail ...│
│  Print ...               │
├──────────────────────────┤
│  Autosave ...            │
├──────────────────────────┤
│  Exit Without Saving     │
└──────────────────────────┘
```

```
Edit
┌──────────────────────────┐
│  Cut to Clipboard        │
│  Copy to Clipboard       │
│  Paste from Clipboard    │
├──────────────────────────┤
│  Mark Block              │
│  Unmark Block            │
├──────────────────────────┤
│  Delete All Text ...     │
│  Insert File ...         │
│  Goto ...                │
├──────────────────────────┤
│  Spellcheck Word ...     │
│  Spellcheck Screen ...   │
│  Spellcheck File ...     │
└──────────────────────────┘
```

```
Search
┌──────────────────┐
│  Find ...        │
│  Find Again      │
├──────────────────┤
│  Replace ...     │
└──────────────────┘
```

```
Controls
┌──────────────────────────────────┐
│  Page Layout ...                 │
│  Electronic Mail Page Layout ... │
│  Header/Footer ...               │
├──────────────────────────────────┤
│  Tab Ruler Edit                  │
├──────────────────────────────────┤
│  Save Setup                      │
├──────────────────────────────────┤
│ ✓ Tab Ruler Display              │
│   Overtype Mode                  │
│   Control Char Display           │
│ ✓ Wordwrap                       │
│ ✓ Auto Indent                    │
└──────────────────────────────────┘
```

Figure 20-2.   The Notepads menus

Notepads also contains four additional menus: File, Edit, Search, and Controls. To examine these menus, follow these steps:

1. Press ALT, F or click on File to display the File menu, which lets you load, save, print, transmit, and exit your document.

2. Press RIGHT ARROW to display the Edit menu, which lets you move, copy, and delete text; spell-check text; move the cursor to a specified line; and combine documents.

3. Press RIGHT ARROW again to display the Search menu, which lets you find and replace text.

4. Press RIGHT ARROW again to display the Controls menu, which lets you control page layout, Insert/Overtype mode, word wrap, tab stops, automatic indentation, and the display of the Tab Ruler and control characters.

5. Press RIGHT ARROW again to wrap around to the Desktop menu, which lets you have up to 15 Desktop files open simultaneously.

6. Press ESC and ALT-SPACEBAR to display the Control menu, which lets you change the current window's colors, position, and size.

7. Press ESC to close the menu and return to your memo.

A definition of each menu option appears at the end of this chapter.

Saving Your Document

When you're editing a document, your changes exist only in your computer's memory, which loses all its contents when you turn your PC off. To preserve your work, your document must therefore be saved to disk.

Notepads provides three ways to save: the File Save command, which lets you save at any time and adjust saving options; the File Autosave command, which lets you specify that saving should occur automatically at periodic intervals; and pressing ESC or clicking on the Close box, which first saves the document and then closes it.

File Save

This command can be used to save at any time. Follow these steps to save under the current filename and the current saving options:

1. Press ALT, F, S, or click on the File menu and select Save. The following Save File To Disk dialog box appears:

2. Press ALT-S or click Save. After a moment, your disk is accessed, the file is saved, and you're returned to your document.

You can also adjust the filename, backup, and file format options before saving:

- *Filename*   This field lets you specify the drive, directory, and /or name of the document. Keep in mind that Notepads automatically appends TXT to filenames without extensions. To prevent this, include a period at the end of the name (for example, type the name "REPORT." instead of "REPORT"). Also, if you want to separate words in a filename, use the underscore (for example, FOR_FRED.TXT or 1_ON_1.TXT).

- *Make backup file*   When you save a new version of a document, the previous version is ordinarily renamed with a BAK extension. If you turn this option off, the previous version will simply be erased.

- *PCTOOLS Desktop/ASCII*   A document is ordinarily saved in ASCII format. This is a generic format that can be understood by almost any PC program, but that doesn't retain special Control and Controls menu formatting information such as tab stops, margins, headers and footers, and window position. You can instead choose to save in PCTOOLS Desktop format, which preserves all your formatting settings.

After setting the appropriate options, press ALT-S or click Save, and the document is saved. Also, the **File Save** setting changes you've made will be retained for the document.

Having ASCII be the default format is new to PC Tools 7. Since Notepads is used by a number of applications, this change can lead to unexpected results. For example, if you create a form in Databases (see Chapter 25) and neglect to explicitly save it in the PCTOOLS Desktop format, your layout settings will be lost and the form probably won't work. If you intend on using Desktop formatting features frequently, you may therefore prefer having PCTOOLS Desktop as the default. To do this, simply save a file in that format, and then press ALT, C, S. All the settings in your current window are preserved as defaults for all new Notepads windows.

File Autosave

It's a good idea to save periodically, so if your PC's plug accidentally gets pulled out or some other mishap occurs, you won't lose hours of work. File Autosave can do this periodic saving for you automatically. To use the command, press ALT, F, A, or click on the File menu and select Autosave. The Automatic File Save dialog box appears, as shown here:

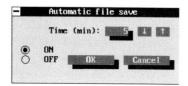

For the Time field, you can enter any number of minutes from 0 to 99999 (0 being the equivalent of turning autosaving off). The default is 5 minutes. However, you may find such a short interval annoying, since your typing is interrupted each time your document is saved. For most people, 15 minutes is probably a good compromise.

You can also turn autosave off by selecting the OFF option. This method retains your Time setting, so you don't have to remember and reenter the number each time that you want to turn autosaving back on.

When you're done adjusting settings, exit the dialog box and return to your document by pressing ALT-O or clicking OK. The changes you've made will affect *all* your Notepads documents, not just your current one. In addition, they'll affect all files in the other three Desktop applications that contain a **File Autosave** command: Outlines, the Appointment Scheduler, and the Macro Editor.

Saving When Exiting

When you're ready to exit your document, press ESC or click on the Close box. Notepads automatically saves your document and then closes it.

If you *don't* want to save upon exiting, see the following section.

Abandoning Your Document

Usually, you'll want to save your work. However, there will be times when you'll prefer to abandon your document and start over. There are three commands that let you do this: the **File Exit** Without Saving command, the **Edit Delete** All Text command, and the **File Load** command.

File Exit Without Saving

This command lets you exit your document without saving it to disk. This is especially useful if you've made editing changes to an existing document and then decide you prefer your original, since it allows you to exit and leave the original unchanged.

To use this option, press ALT, F, X, or click on the File menu and select Exit Without Saving. The current document is instantly erased from memory, its window is closed, and nothing is saved to disk.

The command takes effect immediately and is irreversible, so be sure you want to lose your editing changes before invoking it.

Edit Delete All Text

This command erases all the text in your document. It's useful when you've begun creating a document, and then decide you're better off abandoning your work and starting from scratch.

To use this option, press ALT, E, D, or click on the File menu and select Delete All Text. Your PC beeps and this warning box appears:

If you aren't absolutely certain you want to lose your text, press C or click Cancel. Otherwise, confirm by pressing ENTER or O, or clicking OK. The text is instantly erased from memory, but the file itself remains open, ready for the entry of new text.

File Load

This command replaces the document in the current window with another document. It's appropriate when you want to abandon your current document but keep its window open for a different file.

To use this option, press ALT, F, L, or press F4, or click on the File menu and select Load. The File Load dialog box appears. Type or select the name of the file you want to edit, and then press ALT-L or click LOAD. Your previous document is replaced by the file you specified.

Printing Your Document

After you're done editing your document and saving it to disk, you're ready to print it on paper. Follow these steps to print under the default options:

1. Press ALT, F, P, or click on the File menu and select Print. The Print dialog box appears, as shown here:

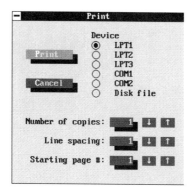

2. Make sure your printer is on and online, and then press P or click Print. After a moment, your document is printed.

You can also adjust the following options before printing:

- *Device*   This option allows you to redirect printing to a different printer port (which is useful, for example, if you have more than one printer). It also allows you to redirect printing to a disk file, which includes appropriate printer codes and can be printed at any time directly from the DOS prompt. Print files have PRT extensions.

- *Number of copies*   This field sets the number of copies of the document to be printed. You can enter any number from 1 to 99999. The default is *1*.

- *Line spacing*   This field sets the spacing between lines of text. The default is *1*, or single spacing. (In PC Tools 6, this command was accessed through the **C**ontrols **P**age Layout dialog box.)

- *Starting page #*   This field sets the page number to start with when numbering pages. The default is *1*. This setting has no practical effect unless you insert a # code in a header or footer, as described in the "Controls Header/Footer" section later in this chapter. (In PC Tools 6, this command was accessed through the **C**ontrols **P**age Layout dialog box.)

When all your options are properly set, make sure your printer is on and online, and then press ALT-P or click PRINT.

*If your pages don't come out the way you expected, or if you simply want to make them more professional looking, format your document with **Controls** menu options before printing. For details, see "Setting Tab Stops and Indents" and "Laying Out the Page" in the following "Advanced Features" section.*

Notepads doesn't directly provide such formatting features as underlining, boldface, italics, and font changes. However, you can send the appropriate codes for these features to your printer by using macros. PC Tools 7 already includes macros for such popular printers as the Epson FX-80 and the Hewlett-Packard LaserJet. You can also create your own macros. For more information, see Chapter 27, "Using the Macro Editor."

Advanced Features

This section covers the more complex menu options. You can use Notepads without taking advantage of these commands, but your work will go a lot faster and easier *with* them. After finishing this section, you'll be able to move and copy text, find and replace text, spell-check your document, format your document for printing, and transmit your file as electronic mail.

Deleting, Moving, and Copying

You can delete, move, or copy a continuous section of text by using the **E**dit menu options **M**ark Block, **C**ut to Clipboard, **C**opy to Clipboard, and **P**aste from Clipboard. These commands are powerful tools for rearranging and reusing your words. The process for employing them may seem a little involved, but in practice it's quick and straightforward (as is demonstrated at the end of this section). Once you get used to them, you'll probably find yourself taking advantage of these options frequently.

Before you begin, you need to understand three terms: marked block, the Clipboard, and pasting.

- A *block* is any continuous section of text that you want to delete, move, or copy. You define the text you want to work with by highlighting, or *marking*, it using a menu command, the SHIFT key, or your mouse.

- The *Clipboard* is a temporary storage area in memory that is maintained by the PC Tools Desktop. Because the Clipboard is independent of any file, it provides a medium for moving text from one spot in a document to another spot, or from one document to an entirely different document. (This should not be confused with the Windows Clipboard, which is a similar but separate memory area maintained by Microsoft Windows.) For more information, see Chapter 22, "Using the Clipboard."

- *Pasting* refers to copying the contents of the Clipboard into a file at the cursor position. In Notepads, pasting is done with the **E**dit **P**aste From Clipboard command.

Marking a Block of Text

To work with a block of text, you first must mark it. The block is automatically unmarked after being deleted, moved, or copied.

You can mark any amount of text. However, if you want to do anything with a block other than delete it, don't mark more than 4000 characters, or about three pages of double-spaced text, since that's the maximum amount the Clipboard can hold.

There are three ways of marking a block: the menu, SHIFT, and mouse methods.

The Edit Menu Method   To mark a block with the **E**dit menu, follow these steps:

1. Position the cursor at one end of the block.

2. Press ALT, E, M, or click on the Edit menu and select Mark Block.

3. Move the cursor until all the text you want to mark is highlighted.

4. If you change your mind, unmark the block by pressing ESC or by selecting the **E**dit **U**nmark Block command.

The SHIFT Method   To mark a block with the SHIFT key, follow these steps:

1. Position the cursor at one end of the block.

2. Press SHIFT and keep it held down.

3. Move the cursor until all the text you want to mark is highlighted.

4. If you change your mind, unmark the block by pressing ESC.

The SHIFT *method works best if you have a keyboard with an alternative keypad dedicated to moving the cursor (as opposed to the primary keypad that can also produce numbers). If you lack this second keypad, you may find pressing your arrow keys with* SHIFT *creates numbers instead of highlighting. In this case, press the* NUM LOCK *key directly before and directly after each* SHIFT *block operation; or simply ignore this method in favor of the menu and mouse methods.*

The Mouse Method   To mark a block with your mouse, follow these steps:

1. Click at one end of the block.

2. Press your left mouse button and keep it held down.

3. Drag the mouse until all the text you want to mark is highlighted.

4. If you change your mind, unmark the block by pressing ESC, or by simply clicking anywhere while the left mouse button is *not* pressed.

Deleting or Moving a Marked Block

Deleting a block erases it from the document. Moving a block erases it from its current location and places it in another location. To perform either operation, first mark the block you want to affect and then follow these steps:

1. Press ALT, E, T, or press SHIFT-DEL, or click on the File menu and select Cut To Clipboard. The block is removed from the document and stored in the Clipboard. If all you want to do is delete, you're done. If you want to move the block, continue with steps 2 through 4.

2. Position the cursor where you want to place the block. This can be in another spot in the current document, in a different Notepads document, or in the file of an entirely different Desktop application.

3. Press ALT, E, P, or press SHIFT-INS, or click on the Edit menu and select Paste from Clipboard. The block is inserted.

4. The block still remains in the Clipboard, so you can perform steps 2 and 3 repeatedly, making multiple insertions in multiple locations.

Copying a Marked Block

Copying a block leaves the original block unchanged and inserts a copy of it in another location. To perform the operation, first mark the block you want to affect and then follow these steps:

1. Press ALT, E, C, or click on the File menu and select Copy to Clipboard. The original text is unaffected, but a copy of the text is placed in the Clipboard.

2. Position the cursor where you want to place the block. This can be in another spot in the current document, in a different Notepads document, or in the file of an entirely different Desktop application.

3. Press ALT, E, P, or press SHIFT-INS, or click on the Edit menu and select Paste from Clipboard. The block is inserted.

4. The block still remains in the Clipboard, so you can perform steps 2 and 3 repeatedly, making multiple insertions in multiple locations.

Tutorial: Moving a Line in the Memo

The preceding instructions may sound a bit complicated, but they're actually easy to use in practice. In the "Basic Typing" section earlier in this chapter, you created a short memo. If it isn't already on screen, bring it up now, and follow these steps to move the memo's second line to the top and bottom of the document:

1. Press CTRL-HOME to move to the top of the memo.

2. Press DOWN ARROW to move to line 2.

3. Hold down SHIFT and press DOWN ARROW to mark line 2. (If necessary, press NUM LOCK before and after marking.) Your window should look similar to this:

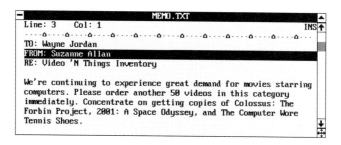

4. Press SHIFT-DEL to cut line 2. The line is deleted from the memo and placed in the Clipboard.

5. Press UP ARROW to move to the top of the memo again.

6. Press SHIFT-INS to paste the line to a new location. The text is inserted, as shown here:

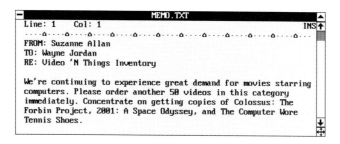

7. Press CTRL-END to move to the bottom of the memo.

8. Press SHIFT-INS to paste another copy of the line. The text is inserted.

It's as simple as that.

You can display and edit whatever text is currently in the Clipboard by pressing ALT, D, B. *To hide the Clipboard again, press* ESC.

If you make the Desktop memory resident, you can transfer text between Desktop files and non-PC Tools applications. For more information, see Chapter 22, "Using the Clipboard."

Combining Files

The previous section explained how you can copy text from one document to another with the Clipboard. However, if you want to copy *all* the text from a document, use the **Edit Insert File** command instead. This command generally requires fewer steps than copying and pasting. Also, the Clipboard restricts blocks to 4000 characters, while the only size limit with **Edit Insert File** is that the two documents together cannot exceed 60,000 characters, the maximum size of a Notepads file.

This command can be especially useful when you're creating boilerplate documents such as contracts. If you save each frequently used paragraph as a separate file with a brief name (for example, P1, P2, P3,...) and keep a printed list of the contents of each file, you can quickly construct documents by inserting appropriate paragraphs.

To use **Edit Insert File**, simply position the cursor where you want to insert the other file's contents; press ALT, E, I, or click on the Edit menu and select Insert File; type or select the name of the file you want to insert; and press ALT-L or click LOAD.

For example, follow these steps to insert a copy of another file into your memo:

1. Press CTRL-HOME to move to the top of the memo.

2. Press ALT, E, I, or click on the Edit menu and select Insert File.

3. Type **SAMPLE.TXT** to select the sample file that came with PC Tools. (If SAMPLE.TXT isn't in your directory, select another file.)

4. Press ALT-L or click Load. A copy of the contents of SAMPLE.TXT is inserted at the cursor position. At the same time, SAMPLE.TXT itself is unaffected.

5. Press PGDN to view the new, compound file you've created.

6. Be careful not to confuse this command with File Load, which *replaces* one file with another. For example, invoke the File Load command now by pressing F4, typing **MEMO.TXT**, and pressing ALT-L. The compound file is erased and replaced by your original memo.

Finding and Replacing

The **Search** menu contains three options: **F**ind, which moves the cursor to the first occurrence of the text sequence, or string, that you specify; Find **A**gain, which moves the cursor to the next occurrence of the current text string; and **R**eplace, which finds a specified text string and replaces it with a different text string. All three commands are useful and powerful.

Search Find and Search Find Again

There are numerous uses for the Find commands. Among them are checking how often a particular word or phrase appears in your document; moving instantly to any section of your document that contains a few words you can recall; and marking spots with unique strings (for example, 1**, 2**, 3**,...) you can quickly return to from any location in your document.

To use **S**earch **F**ind, first position the cursor above the text you want to search (for example, to search the entire document, press CTRL-HOME). To initiate the command, press ALT, S, F, or click on the Search menu and select Find. The following Find dialog box appears:

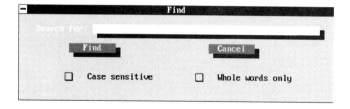

The box offers these options:

- *Search for*   This field holds the text you want to find (up to 48 characters).

- *Case sensitive*   If this option is on, it limits the search to text with the same upper- and lowercase letters as the search string. The default setting is *off*.

- *Whole words only*   If this option is on, it excludes the search from matching text that's part of a larger text string (for example, if the search string is "too", such matches as "tool" and "toot" will be ignored). The default setting is *off*.

After setting your search requirements, press ALT-F or click Find. The cursor jumps to the first occurrence of the string below your cursor position, and you're returned to the normal editing screen.

If you now want to find the *next* occurrence of the string, simply press F7, or press ALT, S, A, or click on the Search menu and select Find Again. The cursor instantly jumps to the next occurrence. You can continue pressing F7 until you've found *all* occurrences of the string, at which point a beep sounds to indicate that you've completed your search.

Search Replace

There are also numerous uses for the **R**eplace command. Among them are replacing abbreviated words in your document with their full versions (allowing you to do less initial typing) and making instant corrections of a word or phrase that turns out to have been consistently misspelled.

*Because this command can make extensive changes in your text instantly, it's a good idea to first preserve the current version of your document with the **File Save** command. That way, if it turns out you don't like the results of the replace operation, you'll have the option of returning to your original document and trying again.*

To use **S**earch **R**eplace, first position the cursor above the text you want to replace (for example, to make replacements throughout the document, press CTRL-HOME). To initiate the command, press ALT, S, R, or press F6, or click on the Search menu and select Replace. The following Find and Replace dialog box appears:

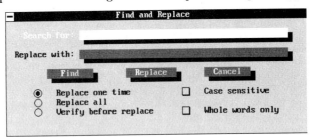

The box offers the following options:

- *Search for*   This field holds the text you want to replace (up to 48 characters).

- *Replace with*   This field holds your replacement text (up to 48 characters).

- *Replace one time*   If on, this option sets the operation to replace only the next occurrence. This is the default over the following two options.

- *Replace all*   If on, this option sets the operation to *automatically* replace *every* occurrence in the document. This is a powerful option, so use it with care.

- *Verify before replace*   If on, this option sets the operation to request verification before making each replacement.

- *Case sensitive*   If on, this option limits the search to text with the same upper- and lowercase letters as the search string. The default setting is *off*.

- *Whole words only*   If on, this option excludes the search from matching text that is part of a larger text string (for example, if the search string is "too", such matches as "tool" and "toot" will be ignored). The default setting is *off*.

- *Find*   This command moves the cursor to the next occurrence of the search string without replacing.

- *Replace*   This command executes the replace operation.

- *Cancel*   This command ends the replace operation, closes the dialog box, and returns you to the document. Pressing ESC has the same effect.

After setting your replace options, execute the operation you've specified by pressing ALT-R or clicking Replace. What happens next depends on which option you've selected.

Replace One Time   With this option selected, the first occurrence is replaced and the dialog box remains open. To replace each subsequent occurrence, select Replace again. You can continue until there are no more occurrences, at which point a beep sounds, the dialog box closes, and the cursor is left on the last replacement. Alternatively, you can interrupt replacement at any time and return to the document by pressing ALT-C or ESC, or by clicking Cancel. You can also resume at any time by pressing F6 again; all your settings will be retained.

Replace All   With this option selected, all the occurrences of the search string are instantly replaced. The dialog box then closes, and the cursor is left at the bottom of the file.

Because this option is virtually instantaneous and can alter the entire document, use it with care. As mentioned earlier, it's a good idea to save your document before selecting this option to protect against unanticipated results.

Verify Before Replace   With this option selected, the cursor moves to the first occurrence, and the dialog box is replaced by instructions at the bottom of the screen directing you to:

- Press ENTER to make the replacement and proceed to the next occurrence.

- Press SPACEBAR to skip making the replacement and proceed to the next occurrence.

- Press ESC to skip making the replacement and abort the replacement operation.

If you continue pressing ENTER and /or SPACEBAR until there are no more occurrences, the screen instructions clear and the cursor is left at the bottom of the file.

Tutorial: Searching and Replacing in the Memo

Follow these steps to find and replace text in your memo:

1. Use the **Find** option to manually change 50 to 100. First, press CTRL-HOME to move to the top of the document.

2. Press ALT, S, F. The Find dialog box appears.

3. Type **50** for the text you want to find.

4. Press ALT-F. The cursor jumps to the first (and in this case, only) occurrence of the text.

5. Press DEL to delete the 5.

6. If you aren't in Insert mode, press INS; then type **10** to complete the change.

7. Now perform an automatic replacement, changing "Computer" to "PC". First, press F6 (Find and Replace).

8. From the Search For field, type **Computer** and press ENTER. You're moved to the Replace With field.

9. Type **PC** for the replacement text.

10. Press TAB four times to move to the replacement options.

11. Press DOWN ARROW until you've selected the Replace All option.

12. Press ALT-R. The replacement is made instantly, changing the last movie to "The PC Wore Tennis Shoes".

Spell-Checking

Notepads provides an electronic spelling checker, which can quickly check the text in your document against its 100,000-word dictionary. If a word doesn't match, it offers suggestions from the dictionary that are its best guesses on which word you really meant. You have the option of selecting one of the suggestions, editing the word yourself, accepting the word as it is and moving on, or accepting the word and also permanently adding it to the dictionary.

You can check the spelling of a word, a screen, or the entire document. To spell-check a word, first position the cursor anywhere on the word; then press ALT, E, W, or click on the Edit menu and select Spellcheck Word. To spell-check a screen, first position the text you want to check so that it's displayed on the screen; then press ALT, E, S, or click on the Edit menu and select Spellcheck Screen. To check the entire file, no preparation is necessary, because checking advances from the top of the file to the bottom regardless of cursor position; simply press ALT, E, F, or press F8, or click on the Edit menu and select Spellcheck File.

After you've selected a spell-checking option, a "Please Wait" message is displayed as each word is checked against the built-in dictionary. If all the specified words are found in the dictionary, the message disappears and you're returned to your document.

If a word isn't matched, a Word Misspelled dialog box like this appears:

The box offers the following options:

- *Ignore*   Selecting this option leaves the word unchanged and advances the checking to the next word.

- *Correct*   Selecting this option brings up the Word Correction dialog box, which displays the word in question and a list of suggested replacements from the dictionary. If you see a suggestion that's appropriate, select it; otherwise, move to the misspelled word using TAB or your mouse, and then edit it so that it's correct. When you're done, press ALT-A or click Accept. The incorrect word in the document is replaced by the new one, and the checker advances to the next word.

- *Add*   Selecting this option permanently adds the word to the dictionary and advances the checking to the next word.

An added word can't be deleted later, so use the Add option rarely and with care.

- *Quit*   Selecting this option aborts the checking operation and returns you to your document. Pressing ESC has the same effect.

Continue selecting one of the appropriate options until all the words have been checked. The "Please Wait" message then disappears, and you're returned to the document.

If there are a number of words you use frequently that aren't in the Notepads dictionary (for example, jargon specific to your particular profession), you can quickly add the words by typing them into a file, spell-checking the file, and selecting the Add option for each word. However, as previously noted, be careful about which words you include, because there's no way to remove a word from the dictionary.

Controlling Ruler and Code Displays

There are two sets of display elements within the Notepads screen that you can control: the line/column counters and tab ruler (which are usually displayed) and the control codes (which are usually hidden).

The line/column counters and tab ruler normally occupy the first two lines of the window, indicating the position of the cursor and the current tab stops. You can suppress their display by pressing ALT, C, T, or by clicking on the Controls menu and selecting Tab Ruler Display. The indicators disappear, and your text moves up to fill every line in the window. To make the counters and ruler reappear, simply select **C**ontrols **T**ab Ruler Display again.

The symbols representing ENTER codes, TAB codes, and spaces are usually hidden. To make them visible, press ALT, C, C, or click on the Controls menu and select Control Char Display. ENTER codes will now appear on the screen as arrows pointing left, TAB codes will appear as arrows pointing right, and spaces will be displayed as dots, as shown here:

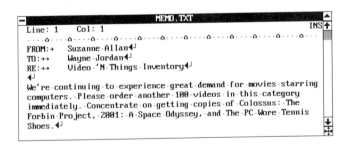

Displaying these codes clarifies where they exist in the document, and makes it easier to move or delete them. In addition, the dots are helpful if you need to tell whether there are one or two spaces between each sentence of a document. However, many people find the symbols distracting. To turn them off, simply select **C**ontrols **C**ontrol Char Display again.

Setting Tab Stops and Indents

You can set tab stops anywhere on the ruler line, either manually or automatically. You can also set automatic indentation to take place along tab stops.

Controls Tab Ruler Edit

To adjust your document's tab stops, first make sure the ruler line is displayed (see the previous section). Next, press ALT, C, R, or click on the Controls menu and select Tab Ruler Edit. The cursor is placed on the ruler line, and the message "Editing Tab Ruler" is displayed.

To change tab stops manually, position the cursor at the appropriate spots on the ruler line, and use INS to insert tab stops and DEL to delete tab stops. You can move along the ruler line by column using RIGHT ARROW and LEFT ARROW, move directly to current tab stops using TAB and SHIFT-TAB, and move to the ends of the ruler line using END and HOME.

To automatically reset tab stops, type any number between 3 and 29. All previous tab stops are cleared and new ones, evenly spaced by the number you've typed, are inserted. (The default spacing between tab stops is 5.)

When you're done revising the tab stops, press ESC to return to the normal editing window. The changes you've made will affect only your current document.

Controls Auto Indent

Automatic indentation causes every line you type to take on the indentation of the line above it. This is useful when you want to set off a portion of text from the body of your document (for example, a quotation in the middle of a report) without having to insert a tab in front of each line. The default for **Auto** Indent is *on*.

To turn automatic indentation off, press ALT, C, A, or click on the Controls menu and select Auto Indent. To turn it back on, select **C**ontrols **A**uto Indent again.

Laying Out the Page

To make your document more professional-looking, you can adjust its page layout settings before printing. There are two commands that affect page layout: **C**ontrols **P**age Layout and **C**ontrols **H**eader/Footer.

Controls Page Layout

This command controls such page elements as margins, paper size, line spacing, and page numbering. To use it, press ALT, C, P, or click on the Controls menu and select Page Layout. This Page Layout dialog box appears:

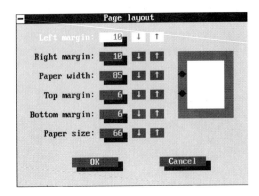

The box offers these options:

- *Left margin*   This field sets the distance from the left edge of the page where text should begin. The default is *10 columns.*

- *Right margin*   This field sets the minimum distance between the ends of text lines and the right edge of the page. The default is *10 columns.*

- *Paper width*   This field defines the width of the page being used. The default is *85 columns.*

- *Top margin*   This field sets the distance from the top edge of the page where text should begin. The default is *6 lines,* which on most printers is equivalent to 1 inch.

- *Bottom margin*   This field sets the minimum distance between the last text line on the page and the bottom edge of the page. The default is *6 lines,* which on most printers is equivalent to 1 inch.

- *Paper size*   This field sets the length of the page being used. The default is *66 lines,* which corresponds to a standard 11-inch page (assuming that your printer, like most, is set to 6 lines per inch). To print on 14-inch legal paper, set this field to 84 lines instead.

It may be that your printer already adds default margins to your printouts. If it does, you should adjust appropriate settings to compensate. For example, many laser printers automatically add top and bottom margins; to compensate, try changing the top and bottom margin settings to 2, and the paper size setting to 60.

After revising the layout settings, press ALT-O or click OK to close the dialog box and return to your document. The settings will remain in effect for your document until you change them again.

Controls Header/Footer

This command allows you to print the same lines of text at the top and/or bottom of every page. It's typically used for placing such information as the page number, the document title, and the author credit on every page of a document.

To use this option, press ALT, C, H, or click on the Controls menu and select Header/Footer. This Page Header & Footer dialog box appears:

The box offers the following options:

- *Header*   This field holds up to 50 characters of text to appear at the top of every page. The text can include a page number code, which is represented by the # symbol. The default is *no header*.

- *Footer*   This field holds up to 50 characters of text to appear at the bottom of every page. This text can also include a page number code represented by the # symbol. The default is a *footer page number*.

Since you can mix the page number symbol with text, you can enhance the number by typing, for example, **Page #, - # -,** or **(#)**.

All your text should be entered flush left; it will automatically be centered between your left and right margins (as set in the Page Layout dialog box) when the document is printed.

When you're done entering your header or footer, press ALT-O or click OK. The dialog box closes, and you're returned to your document. Your header or footer won't appear on screen, but *will* appear when your document is printed. Your settings will be retained for your document until you revise them again.

Sending Electronic Mail

It used to be that the final steps in getting a document read were to print it out on paper and mail it. In recent years, however, electronic mail services have made it possible to transmit documents directly from your PC. As a result, PC Tools 7 has added a number of commands to facilitate the sending of electronic mail through the Desktop's Notepads, Outlines, and Telecommunications applications. For details, see "Using Electronic Mail" in Chapter 26, "Using Telecommunications."

Once the Desktop's Electronic Mail application has been set up properly, you can follow these steps to send a Notepads file as an online message:

1. Enter the address headers appropriate for your online service (if they aren't already there), fill in the header information, and type your message.

2. Set your document's margins by pressing ALT, C, E, or by clicking on the Controls menu and selecting Electronic Mail Page Layout. The dialog box that appears is the same as the one covered in the previous "Controls Page Layout" section, except that its default margins are more appropriate for electronic mail than for printing. When you're done, press ALT-O or click OK.

3. Press ALT, F, E, or press F5, or click on the File menu and select Send Electronic Mail. The following dialog box appears:

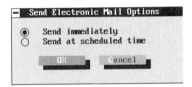

4. If you want your document transmitted immediately, select the Send Immediately option. Otherwise, select the Send at Scheduled Time option to have the file stored in the OUTBOX directory set up on your hard disk to await the next time you've scheduled electronic mail transmission to take place.

5. Press ALT-O or click OK. Your selection is executed.

Notepads Command Reference

Most of Notepads' power lies in its menu commands, which control how your words are edited, formatted, saved, and printed. Like all Desktop applications, Notepads' first two menus are Control and Desktop. These menus are covered in Chapter 19, "Desktop Manager Overview."

Notepads also contains four additional menus: File, Edit, Search, and Controls. The following section covers the options in these menus. After the name of each option are the keystrokes that invoke it, a description of what the option does, and a reference to the section in this chapter that discusses the option in detail.

The File Menu

The **File** menu performs such operations as loading, saving, transmitting, and printing a document. It contains the following six options:

Load (ALT, F, L or F4)

Replaces the document in the current window with another document. Covered in "Abandoning Your Document."

Save (ALT, F, S)

Saves your document to disk. Covered in "Saving Your Document."

Send **E**lectronic Mail (ALT, F, E or F5)

Transmits your document to an electronic mailbox via modem. Covered in "Sending Electronic Mail."

Print (ALT, F, P)

Prints your Notepads file. Covered in "Printing Your Document."

Autosave (ALT, F, A)

Automatically saves your document to disk at specified intervals. Covered in "Saving Your Document."

E**x**it Without Saving (ALT, F, X)

Closes your document window without saving your document. Covered in "Abandoning Your Document."

The Edit Menu

```
┌─ Edit ──────────────┐
│ Cu  to Clipboard    │
│  opy to Clipboard   │
│  aste from Clipboard│
│                     │
│  ark Block          │
│  nmark Block        │
│                     │
│  elete All Text ... │
│  nsert File ...     │
│  oto ...            │
│                     │
│ Spellcheck  ord ... │
│ Spellcheck  creen ..│
│ Spellcheck  ile ... │
└─────────────────────┘
```

The **Edit** menu performs such operations as moving, copying, and deleting text; spell-checking text; moving the cursor to a specified line; and combining documents. It contains the following 11 options:

Cut to Clipboard (ALT, E, T or SHIFT-DEL)

Deletes marked text and places it into the Clipboard. Used to delete or move text. Covered in "Deleting, Moving, and Copying."

Copy to Clipboard (ALT, E, C)

Places a copy of marked text into the Clipboard without affecting the original text. Used to copy text. Covered in the section "Deleting, Moving, and Copying."

Paste from Clipboard (ALT, E, P or SHIFT-INS)

Inserts text from the Clipboard into your document at the cursor position. Covered in "Deleting, Moving, and Copying."

Mark Block (ALT, E, M)

Marks a section, or block, of text to be cut or copied into the Clipboard. Covered in "Deleting, Moving, and Copying."

Unmark Block (ALT, E, U or ESC)

Unmarks a text block. Covered in "Deleting, Moving, and Copying."

Delete All Text (ALT, E, D)

Removes all the text in your document. Covered in "Abandoning Your Document."

Insert File (ALT, E, I)

Copies the text from a document on disk into your current document. Covered in "Combining Files."

Goto (ALT, E, G)

Moves the cursor to the specified line number. Covered in "Moving Around in Your Document."

Spellcheck **W**ord (ALT, E, W)

Checks the spelling of the word the cursor is on. Covered in the section "Spell-Checking."

Spellcheck **S**creen (ALT, E, S)

Checks the spelling of the text on the screen. Covered in "Spell-Checking."

Spellcheck **F**ile (ALT, E, F or F8)

Checks the spelling of all the text in the document. Covered in "Spell-Checking."

The Search Menu

The **S**earch menu contains the following three options for finding and replacing text:

Find (ALT, S, F)

Moves the cursor to the first occurrence of the specified text string. Covered in "Finding and Replacing."

Find **A**gain (ALT, S, A or F7)

Moves the cursor to the next occurrence of the current text string. Covered in "Finding and Replacing."

Replace (ALT, S, R or F6)

Replaces a specified text string with a different specified string. Covered in "Finding and Replacing."

The Controls Menu

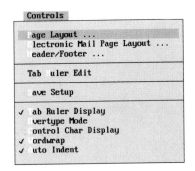

The **C**ontrols menu offers layout and display choices. It contains the following ten options:

Page Layout (ALT, C, P)

Sets margins, paper width, and paper size. Covered in "Laying Out the Page."

Electronic Mail Page Layout (ALT, C, E)

Sets margins for electronic mail. Covered in "Sending Electronic Mail."

Header/Footer (ALT, C, H)

Sets specified text to print on the top and bottom of every page. Covered in "Laying Out the Page."

Tab **R**uler Edit (ALT, C, R)

Sets and deletes tab settings on the ruler line. Covered in "Setting Tab Stops and Indents."

Save Setup (ALT, C, S)

Saves current **C**ontrols menu settings—and current window size, position, and color settings—to be used as defaults for new documents.

Tab Ruler Display (ALT, C, T)

Turns ruler line display on or off. Covered in "Controlling Ruler and Code Displays."

Overtype Mode (ALT, C, O or INS)

Toggles between Insert mode and Overtype mode. Covered in "Basic Editing."

Control Character Display (ALT, C, C)

Turns the display of codes and spaces on and off. Covered in "Controlling Ruler and Code Displays."

Wordwrap (ALT, C, W)

Sets words being typed past the right window margin to either wrap to the beginning of the next line or scroll past the margin. Covered in "Basic Typing."

Auto Indent (ALT, C, A)

Makes a line of text with no tabs take on the indentation of the previous line. Covered in "Setting Tab Stops and Indents."

Chapter *21*

Using the Outliner

Sometimes a document contains so many details that it's hard to keep track of its overall structure; in other words, "you can't see the forest for the trees." This situation is especially difficult when you're trying to organize a project that demands that you keep both the little details and the "big picture" in sight at the same time.

The Outlines application provides an elegant solution to this problem. It requires you to assign levels of importance, or *headlines,* to the different sections of your document via indentation. The most important, or *level 1,* headline you don't indent at all; the second-most important, or *level 2,* headline you indent with one tab; the third-most important, or *level 3,* headline you indent with two tabs; and so on. (Indented headlines are also referred to as *subheads,* since they're subsections of the headlines one or more levels above them.) With this arrangement, you can enter as many low-level details as you want, as long as they're properly indented.

Once you've created your document, Outlines lets you instantly collapse your text so that you see only your level 1 headlines, or only the subheads under a specified headline, or only the headlines above a specified level. This flexible and rapid control of the levels of information displayed lets you work with a document's overall structure and its minutiae at the same time.

An additional advantage of Outlines is that it lets you treat a headline and all its subheads as a single unit. For example, if you've collapsed subheads under a headline and then you move that headline, the subheads are automatically moved along with it. This makes reorganizing your document especially quick and easy.

Also, when you print your document, only the headlines you're displaying on screen will appear on paper. This screen-to-paper correspondence means that you can easily produce printouts, suppressing different sections of information for different audiences.

The Outliner Versus Notepads

In most respects, Outlines is identical to Notepads, the Desktop application covered in Chapter 20. Outlines contains the same screen elements (Line and Column Number Counters, tab ruler, and so on), supports the same cursor movement keystrokes (CTRL-RIGHT ARROW to move forward by word, CTRL-END to move to the bottom of the document, and so on), and uses the same file formats for saving documents (PCTOOLS Desktop and ASCII). Outlines also contains all six Notepads menus: Control, Desktop, File, Edit, Search, and Controls (see Figure 21-1).

However, the two applications differ in several important ways. First, to get any benefit out of Outlines, you must structure your document by levels of importance. To facilitate this structuring, Outlines always keeps the Controls menu's Wordwrap feature turned *off*, so that you must press ENTER at the end of *every line*. Since the default for Controls Auto Indent is *on*, this has the effect of making every line automatically take on the indentation level of the line above it. An additional difference is that Outlines has a seventh menu, called Headlines, which contains options for collapsing, expanding, and changing the level of headlines in various ways. This menu doesn't exist in Notepads.

This chapter doesn't cover the many features that Outlines and Notepads have in common. It's therefore recommended that you read Chapter 20, "Using Notepads," before continuing. The rest of this chapter assumes that you're familiar with Notepads and concentrates on the areas that make Outlines unique. Specifically, it covers creating an outline in the appropriate format, basic editing of the outline, and using the various commands in the Headlines menu to manipulate the outline's text.

Getting Started

Before you can do anything in Outlines, you have to bring up its application screen. Follow these steps to open an outline file:

1. Call up the Desktop Manager. If you've installed the Desktop to be memory resident, press CTRL-SPACEBAR. Otherwise, type **DESKTOP** from the DOS prompt and press ENTER.

2. Press ENTER or click on Desktop to display the main menu.

3. Press O or click Outlines to select the application.

4. Type **CATALOG** to create a file named CATALOG.OUT. (If you don't specify an extension, Outlines automatically appends OUT to your filename.)

5. Press ALT-N, or press ENTER twice, or click New. The blank document window shown in Figure 20-2 appears.

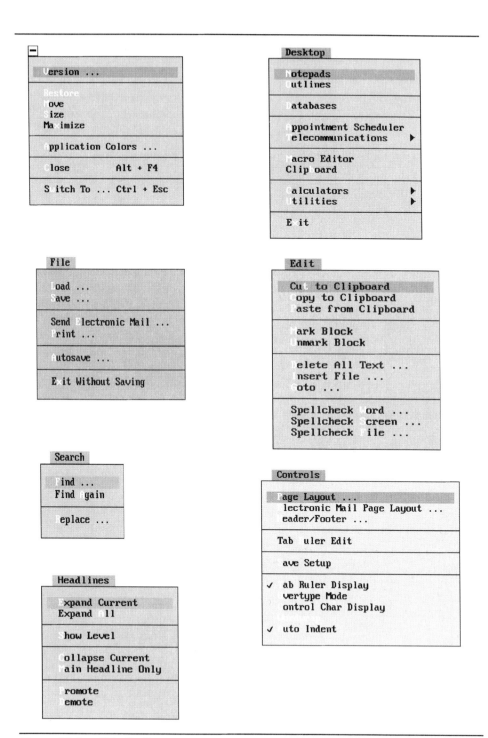

Figure 21-1.   *The Outlines menus*

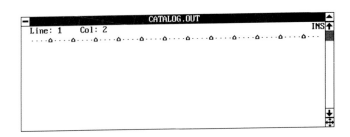

Figure 21-2.   *The Outlines screen*

There are only a few differences between this window and the Notepads window. First, the menu bar includes the **Headlines** menu, which isn't available in Notepads. Second, the filename in the title bar has the extension OUT, as opposed to TXT. Lastly, the window's cursor starts in column 2 rather than in column 1. In Outlines, column 1 is reserved for special markers that indicate when headlines have hidden subheads. These markers are covered later in this chapter.

Typing the Outline

Typing in Outlines differs from typing in Notepads in the following three ways:

- You establish levels of importance by indenting with tabs.

- You must press ENTER at the end of *every* line, not just the ends of paragraphs and short lines.

- A line automatically takes on the indentation of the previous line. (You can change a line's automatic indentation by inserting or deleting tabs.)

These rules don't prevent Outlines from providing great flexibility. For example, a headline can be of any length, not just a single line. Also, headlines with different levels can be mixed in any combination.

To illustrate, follow these steps to create a rough outline for videocassette categories in a video store catalog, using various combinations of level 1, level 2, and level 3 headlines:

1. For the first level 1 headline, type **Feature Films**. (If you make a mistake, erase it using BACKSPACE and then type the correct text.)

2. Press ENTER to end the line and move to the next line.

3. Press TAB to begin a level 2 subhead for the Feature Films category.

4. Type **Drama** for the subhead.

5. Press ENTER. Notice that the indentation is retained.

6. Type **Comedy** and press ENTER. Again, the indentation is retained.

7. Press TAB to begin a subhead for the Comedy category.

8. Type **Musicals** and press ENTER. The level 3 headline is accepted and its indentation is retained.

9. Type **Cartoons** and press ENTER. This completes the Feature Films category, as shown here:

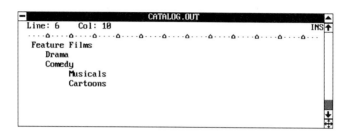

You're now ready to enter a new level 1 headline.

10. Press BACKSPACE twice. The two TAB codes in front of the cursor are deleted, promoting whatever you type to level 1.

11. Type **Music Videos** and press ENTER. There won't be any subheads for this headline, so the next entry will also be at level 1.

12. Type **Documentaries** and press ENTER for this new main headline.

13. Press TAB to begin a level 2 subhead.

14. Instead of entering a single line, this time type the following entire paragraph. Be sure to press ENTER at the end of *every line* in the paragraph *except* the last line:

> **We don't have any titles in this category yet. However, we're in the process of acquiring a sizable collection of topnotch theatrical and TV documentaries. Check the next catalog for a detailed list.**

As before, each line took on the indentation of the previous line, as shown by the following:

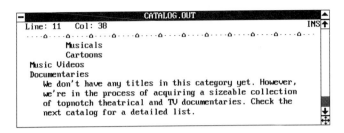

15. Save your work by pressing first ALT, F, S and then ALT-S.

You've successfully created an outline with different level 1, level 2, and level 3 headlines, including a multiple-line subhead. Because of the flexibility provided in headline combinations and length, there are no limits to the kinds of outlines you can create.

You can also easily make changes in your outline, as shown in the next section.

Basic Editing of the Outline

Editing an outline is largely a matter of adding and deleting TAB codes. To get a feel for it, follow these steps to revise the video catalog:

1. Press CTRL-HOME to move to the top of the outline.

2. If "INS" isn't displayed in the upper-right corner of the window, press INS to switch to Insert mode.

3. While it isn't mandatory, it's often useful to display TAB codes while editing so you can see exactly what you're changing. To do this, press ALT, C, C, or click on the Controls menu and select Control Char Display. After a moment, all the document's TAB codes are displayed as arrows pointing right. Also, ENTER codes are displayed as bent arrows pointing left and spaces are displayed as dots, making your outline look like this:

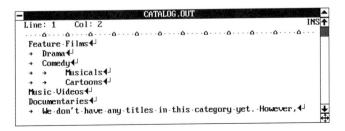

4. Now add a level 2 subhead under "Feature Films." First, press END to move to the end of the headline.

5. Press ENTER to create a new line.

6. Press TAB and type **Action**. You've successfully added the subhead.

7. Now try promoting the "Musicals" subhead from level 3 to level 2. First, press DOWN ARROW three times to move to the line.

8. Press BACKSPACE. A TAB code is deleted, promoting "Musicals" to level 2.

9. Now promote the "Cartoons" subhead from level 3 to level 1. First, press DOWN ARROW to move to the line.

10. Press BACKSPACE to delete the first TAB code.

11. Press DEL to delete the second TAB code. "Cartoons" is now a level 1 headline.

12. Add two subheads under "Cartoons." First, press END, ENTER, and TAB to start a level 2 subhead.

13. Type **Disney** and press ENTER.

14. Type **Warner Brothers**. You've successfully added the two subheads.

15. Hide the TAB codes by pressing ALT, C, C again. The TAB, ENTER, and space symbols disappear, making your outline look like this:

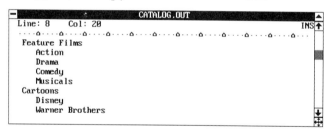

16. Save your work by pressing ALT, F, S and ALT-S.

So far, you've learned how to create and edit a properly formatted outline. The next section shows how to take advantage of your setup work by using the menu commands unique to Outlines.

Using the Headlines Menu

Most of Outlines's power lies in its Headlines menu, which contains five options for collapsing and expanding headlines, and two options for adjusting headline levels. The names, invoking keystrokes, and descriptions of the seven options are as follows:

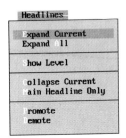

Expand Current (ALT, H, E)

Displays the subheads of the headline the cursor is on.

Expand All (ALT, H, A)

Displays everything in the outline.

Show Level (ALT, H, S)

Displays headlines at or above the level of the headline the cursor is on.

Collapse Current (ALT, H, C)

Hides the subheads of the headline the cursor is on.

Main Headline Only (ALT, H, M)

Hides all subheads; that is, displays level 1 headlines exclusively.

Promote (ALT, H, P)

Raises the headline the cursor is on and its subheads to the next highest levels.

Demote (ALT, H, D)

Lowers the headline the cursor is on and its subheads to the next lowest levels.

In the following sections, you'll use these options to adjust your catalog outline.

Expanding and Collapsing Headlines

As mentioned previously, being able to rapidly control the levels of information displayed in your document allows you to work with both its small details and primary elements at the same time. For example, you can view the lowest-level headlines in the catalog outline, and then switch to displaying level 1 headlines exclusively to regain a sense of the overall structure. You can also expand and collapse selected headlines without affecting the rest of the outline.

To demonstrate, follow these steps to collapse and expand headlines:

1. Press CTRL-HOME to move to the top of the outline. Currently, all the headlines are displayed.

2. Press ALT, H, M, or click on the Headlines menu and select Main Headline Only. The outline instantly collapses to display level 1 headlines exclusively, as shown here:

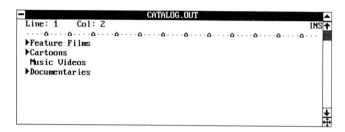

3. Notice that column 1 (unused until now) contains triangles pointing right. A triangle indicates that the headline it's in front of has hidden subheads. "Music Videos" is the only headline without a triangle because it's the only headline without subheads.

4. Press ALT, H, E, or click on the Headlines menu and select Expand Current. The subheads of "Feature Films" (the headline the cursor is on) are displayed again, and the triangle in front of "Feature Films" disappears. However, the rest of the outline is unaffected, so your window looks like this:

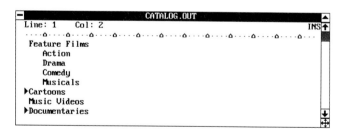

5. Press ALT, H, A, or click on the Headlines menu and select Expand All. All the text in the outline is displayed again. Press PGDN to confirm that all the headlines have expanded, and then press CTRL-HOME to return to the top of the outline.

6. Press ALT, H, C, or click on the Headlines menu and select Collapse Current. The subheads of "Feature Films" (the headline the cursor is on) are hidden

again; and the triangle in front of "Feature Films" reappears. However, the rest of the outline is unaffected, so your window looks like this:

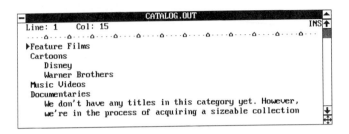

Promoting and Demoting Headlines

In the "Basic Editing of the Outline" section, you revised headline levels by inserting and deleting tabs. This method is fine for single headlines, but becomes tedious when you need to alter entire groups of them. Therefore, the Headlines menu provides two commands, **P**romote and **D**emote, that affect not only a headline but also all of its subheads. For example, using the **D**emote command on a level 1 headline with level 2 subheads will both shift the headline to level 2 *and* shift the subheads to level 3.

To demonstrate, follow these steps to use the **D**emote command to reorganize your catalog outline:

1. Create a new level 1 headline named "Short Films," and place "Cartoons" and "Music Videos" under it. First, press RIGHT ARROW, ENTER, and UP ARROW to create a blank line. (Ordinarily, you would simply press ENTER to create a blank line. However, when you're at the end of a collapsed headline, pressing ENTER may disrupt hidden codes between the current headline and its subheads.)

2. Type **Short Films** for the new level 1 headline.

3. Press RIGHT ARROW to move to "Cartoons."

4. Press ALT, H, D, or click on the Headlines menu and select Demote. "Cartoons" (the headline the cursor is on) is demoted from level 1 to level 2. At the same time, its subheads "Disney" and "Warner Brothers" are demoted from level 2 to level 3.

5. Press DOWN ARROW three times to move to "Music Videos."

6. Again, press ALT, H, D, or click on the Headlines menu and select Demote. "Music Videos" is demoted from level 1 to level 2. In this case, nothing else

is affected since the headline has no subheads, and your outline looks like this:

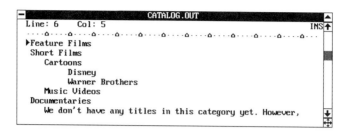

Expanding and Collapsing by Level

Previously, you collapsed and expanded the entire outline and specified headlines. You can also collapse and expand based on a specified *level*. For example, follow these steps to first display headlines at level 2 or above, and then at level 1:

1. You're currently on "Music Videos," a level 2 headline. Press ALT, H, S, or click on the Headlines menu and select Show Level. All level 1 and level 2 headlines are displayed, including the subheads previously hidden under "Feature Films." At the same time, the level 3 headlines under "Cartoons" are now hidden.

2. Press DOWN ARROW to move to the level 1 headline "Documentaries."

3. Again, press ALT, H, S, or click on the Headlines menu and select Show Level. Since the current headline is at level 1, the outline now collapses to display only level 1 headlines.

Treating Headline Groups as Blocks

As explained previously, the **Promote** and **Demote** commands treat a headline and its subheads as a single unit. If you collapse a group of subheads into their headline, you can also delete, move, or copy them as a single unit simply by treating the headline as a text block. This procedure makes it extremely easy to reorganize your document. For example, follow these steps to move a headline and subhead simultaneously, and then print the results:

1. The paragraph subhead of "Documentaries" is currently collapsed under the headline. Press ALT, E, M, DOWN ARROW to mark "Documentaries" as a block.

2. Press ALT, E, T to cut the block. Both the headline and its hidden subhead are deleted.

3. Press UP ARROW to move to "Short Films."

4. Press ALT, E, P to insert the "Documentaries" category in between the "Feature Films" and "Short Films" categories.

5. Press ALT, H, E, or click on the Headlines menu and select Expand Current. The subhead under "Documentaries" expands, confirming that it was moved along with the level 1 headline, and your outline looks like this:

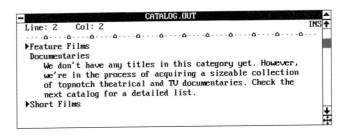

6. Save your work by pressing ALT, F, S and ALT-S.

7. Print the outline by making sure your printer is on and online, and then pressing ALT-F, P, P. Notice that the printout shows exclusively what you're displaying on screen. This correspondence between the screen display and printout makes it easy to provide others with only the portions of your document that you want them to see.

In this section, you used the Headlines menu to collapse and expand your entire outline, specified headlines, and specified levels. You also learned how to promote and demote a headline and all its subheads simultaneously; treat a headline with collapsed subheads as a text block that can be deleted, moved, or copied; and create printouts of whatever display version of your outline you desire. These features make Outlines an excellent tool for organizing your thoughts and your documents.

Chapter 22

Using the Clipboard

The Clipboard is a temporary storage area for text you want to transfer from one location to another. The text may be up to 4000 characters, or about three double-spaced pages. The locations may be in the same Desktop file, in different Desktop files, in a Desktop file and a non-PC Tools application, or even in different non-PC Tools applications.

The Clipboard's ability to transfer text within and across files makes it one of the most powerful and widely used features of the Desktop. For example, it enables you to

- Reorganize a document by moving text around, as opposed to having to erase the text and then retype it.

- Copy text similar to what you want to say and edit it, as opposed to typing new text from scratch.

- Automate your writing by placing into the Clipboard a long name or phrase that you plan to use repeatedly, and then copying the text to wherever you need it.

- Rapidly transfer text from one file to another, instead of having to isolate the text in its own file, save it, and load it into the destination file.

- Transfer text within a non-PC Tools application that doesn't support copy operations.

- Capture the screens of non-PC Tools applications, which can be useful for creating presentation and PC training materials.

This chapter explains how to perform all these operations. After covering Clipboard basics, it details how to transfer text among Desktop files, copy from and to underlying applications, and work directly with the Clipboard.

The Desktop Clipboard should not be confused with the Clipboard in Microsoft Windows. The latter, while performing similar functions, is an entirely separate memory area that's linked exclusively to Windows.

Clipboard Basics

Using the Clipboard is relatively quick and easy. To move or copy text involves four basic steps:

1. Mark the section of text, or *block*, that you want to transfer.

2. Place a copy of the block in the Clipboard, using a keystroke or a menu command.

3. Move to the location where you want to insert, or *paste*, the Clipboard's contents.

4. Paste the block, using a keystroke or a menu command.

The Clipboard will retain your block until you place a new block into it. Therefore, you can execute steps 3 and 4 repeatedly, pasting your text multiple times in multiple locations.

You may have noticed that none of the steps requires *displaying* the Clipboard. Most of the time, you'll probably use the Clipboard only as an invisible storage area. However, you also have the option of bringing up the Clipboard like any other Desktop file and directly editing its contents.

The procedures for the steps just covered vary depending on whether you're transferring text within or outside of the Desktop. The next section discusses the steps for moving or copying blocks within Desktop applications.

Transferring Text Within the Desktop

You can move and copy text among three Desktop applications: Notepads, Outlines, and the Macro Editor. Each of these programs has an **Edit** menu with the following Clipboard-related options:

Mark Block (ALT, E, M)

This option marks the section of text you want to delete, move, or copy.

Unmark Block (ALT, E, U or ESC)

This option unmarks the current block.

Cut to Clipboard (ALT, E, T or SHIFT-DEL)

This option deletes a block and places it into the Clipboard. It's used to delete or move text.

Copy to Clipboard (ALT, E, C)

This option places a copy of a block into the Clipboard without affecting the original text. It's used to copy text.

Paste from Clipboard (ALT, E, P or SHIFT-INS)

This option inserts the Clipboard's contents into the location you specify, starting at the cursor position.

For example, to transfer text within the same Desktop file using these commands, you could perform the following steps:

1. Highlight the text using the **Edit M**ark Block command.

2. Select **Edit C**ut to Clipboard to move it or **E**dit **C**opy to Clipboard to copy it.

3. Go to the spot where you want the text inserted.

4. Select **Edit P**aste From Clipboard.

For more details on using these commands (as well as their keystroke and mouse alternatives), read the "Deleting, Moving, and Copying" section of Chapter 20, "Using Notepads." While the section is directed at Notepads, it's equally applicable to Outlines and the Macro Editor.

Transferring text between different Desktop files is fundamentally the same as transferring within the same file. To do so, follow these steps:

1. Go to the Notepads, Outlines, or Macro Editor file that contains the text to be transferred.

2. Move the cursor or mouse pointer to one end of the text.

3. Press ALT, E, M followed by any combination of cursor movement keystrokes, or hold down your mouse button and drag, until you reach the other end of the text. Your block is now marked.

4. Press ALT, E, C to *copy* the text or ALT, E, T to *move* the text. In either case, a copy of the block is placed in the Clipboard.

5. Use the **Desktop** menu to open, or F9 to switch to, the Notepads, Outlines, or Macro Editor file into which you want to insert the text.

6. Move to the spot in the second file where you want the text placed.

7. Press ALT, E, P. The Clipboard's contents are inserted, starting at your cursor position.

You can also access the Clipboard from the Algebraic Calculator. This application contains the **O**ptions menu command Copy to Clipboard, which copies the contents of the calculator's electronic "tape" to the Clipboard. For more information, see Chapter 24, "Using the Calculators."

When pasting, the Clipboard sometimes transmits its text faster than certain PCs can handle, resulting in beeping and lost data. If you encounter this problem, see "Using the Copy/Paste Menu" later in this chapter.

Transferring Text Outside the Desktop

When the Desktop is memory resident, the Clipboard can act as a gateway between the Desktop and a non-PC Tools program, or even between different non-PC Tools programs.

Copying text with the Clipboard is generally faster than having to isolate the text in its own file, save it, and then load it into the destination file. Furthermore, using the Clipboard can often bypass any filename and file format incompatibilities between the Desktop and non-PC Tools programs. In addition, certain data, such as application screens, *can't* be saved through their own programs and so must be captured with the Clipboard.

You can copy text from an underlying (that is, non-PC Tools) application to the Clipboard by using CTRL-DEL, and from the Clipboard to an underlying application by using CTRL-INS. The following sections detail the steps involved.

You can use keystrokes other than CTRL-DEL and CTRL-INS to copy and paste by changing the Utilities Hotkey Selection table. For details, see Chapter 28, "Using the Desktop Utilities."

Copying from an Underlying Application

Being able to copy data from non-PC Tools programs to the Desktop has a number of uses. For example, it lets you place reference information from a standalone application into a Desktop file that you can pop up at any time. It also allows you to integrate data from several incompatible programs—say, a spreadsheet, a database, and a word processor—into a single Desktop file.

To copy from an underlying application to the Clipboard, follow these steps:

1. Install the Desktop so that it's memory resident.

2. Bring up the application screen you want to copy from.

3. Press CTRL-DEL. After a moment, a nonblinking rectangular cursor appears in the center of the screen.

4. Use the arrow keys or your mouse to position the cursor at one end of the area you want to copy.

5. Press ENTER, or click your mouse button and keep it pressed, to mark the beginning of the block.

6. Use the arrow keys to move the cursor, or drag your mouse, until the entire portion of the screen you want to copy is highlighted.

7. Press ENTER, or release your mouse button, to mark the end of the block. The highlighting disappears, and the block is copied into the Clipboard.

Copying to an Underlying Application

Being able to send data from the Desktop to non-PC Tools programs also has a number of uses. For example, it lets you quickly consolidate text previously jotted down within various Notepads files into a standalone word processor. It also enables you to place the electronic "tape" from the Desktop's Algebraic Calculator into a spreadsheet or some other number-crunching program.

To copy from the Desktop to an underlying program, follow these steps:

1. Install the Desktop so that it's memory resident.

2. Place the text you want to copy into the Clipboard, either by cutting or copying (as discussed earlier in this chapter) or by typing in the text directly (as discussed later in this chapter).

3. If you're currently in the Desktop, press CTRL-SPACEBAR to exit it.

4. If the application screen you want isn't already displayed, bring it up now.

5. Move the application's cursor to the spot where you want the text placed.

6. Press CTRL-INS. The Clipboard's contents are inserted, starting at the cursor position.

7. The text still remains in the Clipboard, so you can perform steps 4 through 6 repeatedly, making multiple insertions in multiple locations.

 There's a small chance that incompatibilities will exist between the Clipboard and a particular underlying application. Therefore, it's best to do a careful trial run when pasting to any non-PC Tools program for the first time.

Copying Both to and from Underlying Applications

Since the Clipboard can copy from an underlying application and paste to an underlying application, it can be used to transfer text from one underlying application to another. This is useful for such activities as copying text within an application that doesn't have a copy command, copying between applications that don't share common file formats, and simply getting text across applications quickly and easily.

To copy from one non-PC Tools program to another, follow these steps:

1. Install the Desktop so that it's memory resident.

2. Bring up the application screen you want to copy *from.*

3. Press CTRL-DEL.

4. Use the arrow keys or your mouse to position the rectangular cursor at one end of the area you want to copy.

5. Press ENTER, or click your mouse button and keep it pressed, to mark the beginning of the block.

6. Use the arrow keys to move the cursor, or drag your mouse, until the entire portion of the screen you want to copy is highlighted.

7. Press ENTER, or release your mouse button, to copy the block.

8. Bring up the application screen you want to copy *to.*

9. Move the application's cursor to the spot where you want the text placed.

10. Press CTRL-INS. The Clipboard's contents are inserted, starting at the cursor position.

11. The text still remains in the Clipboard, so you can perform steps 8 through 10 repeatedly, making multiple insertions in multiple locations.

Working Directly with the Clipboard

So far in this chapter, you've moved and copied text without ever seeing the Clipboard. You also have the option of bringing up the Clipboard like any other Desktop file. This is useful if you want to check what's currently in the Clipboard, edit the Clipboard's contents, clear the Clipboard and type in new text, or insert text from a file on disk.

To display the Clipboard, first bring up the Desktop, and then press ALT, D, B, or click on the Desktop menu and select Clipboard. The Clipboard window shown in Figure 22-1 appears. If you cut or copied a block earlier, that text is now displayed; otherwise, the window is blank.

The Clipboard Versus Notepads

Aside from "Clipboard" appearing in its title bar, the Clipboard window looks identical to Notepads, the Desktop application covered in Chapter 20. In fact, with respect to basic text creation and editing, the two applications are virtually identical. For example, the Clipboard contains the same window elements (Line and Column Number Counters, tab ruler, and so on), supports the same cursor movements (CTRL-RIGHT ARROW to move forward by word, CTRL-END to move to the bottom of

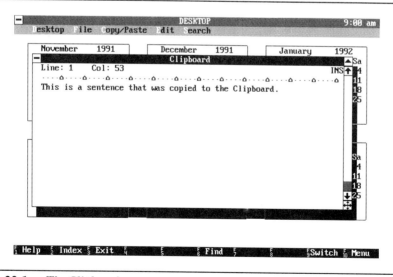

Figure 22-1. *The Clipboard screen*

the document, and so on), and has many of the same menu options. Therefore, for information about creating and editing text in the Clipboard, read the "Basic Typing," "Basic Editing," and "Moving Around in Your Document" sections of Chapter 20, "Using Notepads."

At the same time, there are fundamental differences between the two applications. For example, you can create an unlimited number of Notepads files, but there's only one Clipboard, which is created automatically by the Desktop. Also, while you can open, close, and save Notepads files, the Clipboard is always open, and it can't save its contents to disk (except indirectly, by copying its contents to an application file that can be saved). A Notepads file's capacity is also much greater, holding up to 60,000 characters as opposed to the Clipboard's 4000-character limit. Also, the Clipboard lacks the document-formatting commands that are present in Notepads, as the Clipboard's main function is temporary text storage, not document generation.

The Clipboard Message Bar

At the bottom of the screen is the message bar. When a Clipboard activity is taking place, the bar displays appropriate definitions or instructions. Otherwise, it displays the following commands assigned to the function keys:

Function Key	Action
F1 (Help)	Brings up context-sensitive help
F2 (Index)	Brings up the online help index
F3 (Exit)	Performs the same functions as ESC
F4	Undefined
F5	Undefined
F6 (Find)	Selects Search Find
F7	Undefined
F8	Undefined
F9 (Switch)	Activates a different open window
F10 (Menu)	Performs the same functions as ALT

Navigating the Clipboard Menus

At the top of the screen are the six menus available when you're displaying the Clipboard (and, in the right corner, the system time). Follow these steps to examine the menus:

1. Press ALT, F or click on File to display the File menu, which lets you print the Clipboard's contents.

2. Press RIGHT ARROW to display the Copy/Paste menu, which lets you copy to or from an underlying application, and adjust the Clipboard's pasting speed.

3. Press RIGHT ARROW again to display the Edit menu, which lets you mark, unmark, and delete blocks; clear the Clipboard; copy a file into the Clipboard; and move the cursor to a specified line.

4. Press RIGHT ARROW again to display the Search menu, which lets you find and replace text.

5. Press RIGHT ARROW again to wrap around to the Desktop menu, which lets you have up to 15 Desktop files open simultaneously.

6. Press ESC and ALT-SPACEBAR to display the Control menu, which lets you change the Clipboard's colors, position, and size.

7. Press ESC to close the menu and return to the Clipboard.

Of these menus (shown in Figure 22-2), Control and Desktop are in every Desktop application, and File, Edit, and Search are similar to their counterparts in Notepads. The one menu unique to the Clipboard is Copy/Paste.

Using the Copy/Paste Menu

The Copy/Paste menu contains commands for exchanging data with underlying programs and for controlling the speed of character transmission when pasting.

The first two options are Paste from Clipboard and Copy to Clipboard. These commands simply provide menu alternatives to pressing CTRL-INS when copying to underlying applications and CTRL-DEL when copying from underlying applications (as described in "Transferring Text Outside the Desktop" earlier in this chapter). However, these menu commands require more keystrokes than their hotkey counterparts, and they will *not* work if the Desktop is installed with the /CS option, so it's generally easier to just use the hotkeys.

The menu's third option is Set Playback Delay. This command is useful if your computer sometimes beeps and loses data when you paste. Such results indicate that the Clipboard is pasting text faster than your computer can handle (or, in technical terms, is overloading your keyboard buffer). To eliminate such problems, follow these steps:

1. Press ALT, C, S, or click on the Copy/Paste menu and select Set Playback Delay. The following Macro/Clipboard Playback Delay dialog box appears:

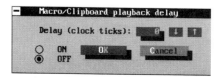

2. Enter the number of clock ticks (each 1/18th of a second) by which to delay the pasting speed. Generally, a number from 1 to 5 will be appropriate. If you enter too high a number, text will be pasted very slowly. A few minutes of experimentation will probably yield the ideal delay value for your system. The default is *0*, or no delay, sending a character every 1/18th of a second.

3. Press TAB and UP ARROW to select the ON option (if it isn't already selected). The default is *OFF*, meaning no delay.

4. Press ALT-O or click OK.

The Macro/Clipboard Playback Delay dialog box is also available through the Macro Editor command **C**ontrols **P**layback Delay, since a macro can encounter the

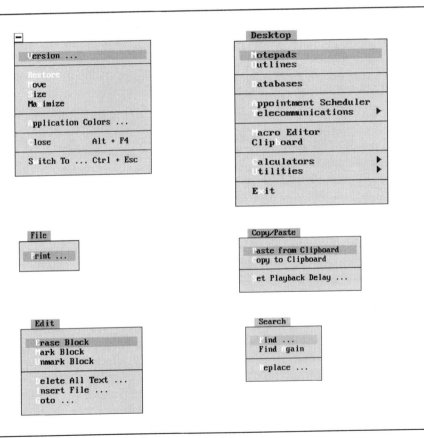

Figure 22-2. *The Clipboard menus*

same speed problems in transmitting keystrokes. Any change from the Clipboard in the dialog box carries over to the Macro Editor, and vice versa.

Clipboard Command Reference

The Clipboard is usually used as an invisible storage area, so you'll seldom access its window or menus. However, if you ever need to directly manipulate the Clipboard's contents, its six menus provide a number of commands for doing so.

Like all Desktop applications, the Clipboard's first two menus are Control and Desktop. These menus are covered in Chapter 19, "Desktop Manager Overview."

The Clipboard's four other menus are **File**, **Copy/Paste**, **Edit**, and **Search**. This section covers the options in these menus. The name of each option is followed by the keystrokes that invoke it, a description of what the option does, and a reference to the section in either this chapter or in Chapter 20 that discusses the option in detail.

The File Menu

Because the Clipboard is a temporary storage area, typical **File** menu options such as **Load**, **Save**, and **Exit Without Saving** don't apply to it. Therefore, this menu contains only the following option for printing:

Print (ALT, F, P)

Prints the current contents of the Clipboard. Covered in "Printing Your Document" in Chapter 20.

The Copy/Paste Menu

The **Copy/Paste** menu enables you to copy to and from underlying applications and to control the speed of character transmission when pasting. It contains the following three options:

Paste from Clipboard (ALT, C, P or CTRL-INS)

Copies the Clipboard's contents to the underlying application, starting at the application's cursor position. Covered in "Copying to an Underlying Application" and "Using the Copy/Paste Menu" in this chapter.

Copy to Clipboard (ALT, C, C or CTRL-DEL)

Copies the specified portion of the screen of the underlying application to the Clipboard. Covered in "Copying from an Underlying Application" and "Using the Copy/Paste Menu" in this chapter.

Set Playback Delay (ALT, C, S)

Controls the speed at which the Clipboard pastes its contents. Covered in "Using the Copy/Paste Menu" in this chapter.

The Edit Menu

The Edit menu performs such operations as marking, unmarking, and deleting blocks; clearing the Clipboard; reading file contents into the Clipboard from disk; and moving the cursor to a specified line. It contains the following six options:

Erase Block (ALT, E, E or SHIFT-DEL)

Deletes a block marked in the Clipboard. (In Notepads, Outlines, and the Macro Editor, the equivalent command is **C**ut to Clipboard, which deletes a marked block and copies it to the Clipboard. Such a command in the Clipboard itself would be circular.) Use this option with care, as there's no way to retrieve a deleted Clipboard block.

Mark Block (ALT, E, M)

Marks a block in the Clipboard. Blocks are usually marked for cutting or copying to the Clipboard, but in this case the operation's only use is to define a block for erasing from the Clipboard (see the previous option). Marking blocks is covered in "Deleting, Moving, and Copying" in Chapter 20.

Unmark Block (ALT, E, U or ESC)

Unmarks a block. Covered in "Deleting, Moving, and Copying" in Chapter 20.

Delete All Text (ALT, E, D)

Erases all current text, in this case clearing the Clipboard of its contents. Use with caution; there's no way to retrieve deleted text. Covered in "Abandoning Your Document" in Chapter 20.

Insert File (ALT, E, I)

Copies the text from a file on disk into the Clipboard starting at the cursor position. Covered in "Combining Files" in Chapter 20.

Goto (ALT, E, G)

Moves the cursor to the specified line number. Covered in "Moving Around in Your Document" in Chapter 20.

The Search Menu

The **S**earch menu contains the following three options for finding and replacing text:

Find (ALT, S, F)

Moves the cursor to the first occurrence of the specified text string. Covered in "Finding and Replacing" in Chapter 20.

Find **A**gain (ALT, S, A)

Moves the cursor to the next occurrence of the current text string. Covered in "Finding and Replacing" in Chapter 20.

Replace (ALT, S, R or F6)

Replaces a specified text string with a different specified string. Covered in "Finding and Replacing" in Chapter 20.

Chapter **23**

Using the Appointment Scheduler

Earlier in this book, you learned how to use PC Tools to manage your hard disk and your files. In this chapter, you'll learn how to use PC Tools to manage your personal activities. The Desktop program that handles this job is the Appointment Scheduler, which is made up of three distinct components:

- The Calendar, which displays the dates of whatever month and year you specify.

- The To-Do List, which lets you itemize the tasks you want to get done within a specified period of time.

- The Daily Scheduler, which lets you record your appointments. This feature-rich application also lets you do such things as set alarms to go off, notes to pop up, and programs to execute at specified times.

Examining the Appointment Scheduler

The simplest way to understand how the Appointment Scheduler is set up is to examine its screen. Therefore, follow these steps to bring up the application:

1. First, if your system isn't set to the current date and time, set it now by using the DATE and TIME commands from DOS (see your DOS manual) or PC Shell's View Date/Time command (see Chapter 15, "PC Shell Overview").

2. Call up the Desktop Manager. If you've installed the Desktop to be memory resident, press CTRL-SPACEBAR. Otherwise, type **DESKTOP** from the DOS prompt and press ENTER.

3. Press ENTER or click Desktop to display the main menu.

4. Press A or click Appointment Scheduler to select the application.

5. Type **OFFICE** to create a time management file named OFFICE.TM. (If you don't specify an extension, TM is automatically appended to your filename.)

6. Press ALT-N or press ENTER twice, or click New. The Appointment Scheduler screen appears.

In PC Tools 7, the Scheduler's default is to devote the top half of its screen to the Calendar. When first learning the program, however, you may find it easier to work with the layout from PC Tools Deluxe 6, which gives more emphasis to the Daily Scheduler component. To switch layouts, press ALT, C, S, or click on the Controls menu and select Schedule Layouts, which is a new command in PC Tools 7. A dialog box like this appears:

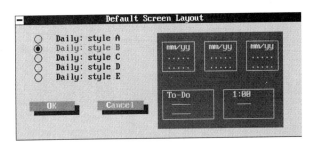

Notice that the left side of the box displays your current layout design. To see other layout schemes, press DOWN ARROW repeatedly. Each layout tends to emphasize one particular aspect of the Scheduler over another (for example, by eliminating the Calendar to expand the To-Do List and Daily Scheduler, or by eliminating the To-Do List in favor of the Daily Scheduler). Examine all five of the layouts, and then press HOME to select the top Daily: style A option. This is the layout that you'll be using to perform the exercises in this chapter. To accept your selection, press ALT-O or click OK. You're returned to the Scheduler screen, which now looks like Figure 23-1.

The screen is split into three distinct areas:

- The Calendar, displayed in the upper-left corner, initially shows the dates of the current month and year, and highlights the current day.

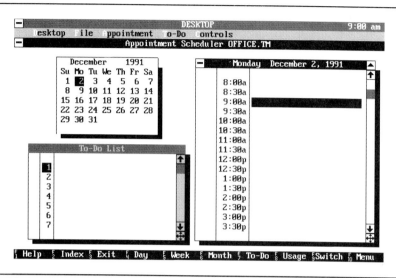

Figure 23-1. *The Style A Appointment Scheduler screen*

- The To-Do List, displayed in the lower-left corner, is initially blank except for a highlighted line numbered 1 for your first entry.

- The Daily Scheduler, displayed in the right side of the window, initially lists the times from 8:00 A.M. to 5:00 P.M. in 30-minute intervals. The listed time directly following the current time will usually be highlighted.

You can move from one area of the window to another by pressing TAB or SHIFT-TAB, or by clicking on the area you want to activate.

The Appointment Scheduler Message Bar

At the bottom of the screen is the message bar. When an Appointment Scheduler activity is taking place, the bar displays appropriate definitions or instructions. Otherwise, it displays the following commands assigned to the function keys:

Function Key	Action
F1 (Help)	Brings up context-sensitive help
F2 (Index)	Brings up the online help index
F3 (Exit)	Performs the same functions as ESC
F4 (Day)	Toggles the display of the Daily Scheduler
F5 (Week)	Toggles the display of the Weekly Appointment Display box
F6 (Month)	Toggles the display of the Calendar

Function Key	Action
F7 (To-Do)	Toggles the display of the To-Do List
F8 (Usage)	Toggles the display of the Time Usage Graph box
F9 (Switch)	Activates a different open window
F10 (Menu)	Performs the same functions as ALT

Notice that function keys F4, F6, and F7 can suppress the display of the standard areas of the Scheduler screen. For example, if you aren't working with the To-Do List, you can press F7 to hide it. This clears your screen of unnecessary distractions and provides more space for your other windows. To bring the To-Do List back, simply press F7 again.

Function keys F5 and F8, on the other hand, display elements that aren't part of the standard Scheduler screen. Pressing F5 brings up a box that shows the initial appointments you have scheduled for Monday through Saturday of the current week (a feature new to PC Tools 7). Similarly, pressing F8 brings up a set of bar graphs representing your appointments for Sunday through Saturday of the current week. These graphs illustrate how you divide your time, point out any scheduling conflicts, and allow you to easily compare one day's schedule with another. With both the F5 and F8 displays, you can select other weeks by pressing PGDN and PGUP, or by scrolling vertically with your mouse. You can also return to the current week at any point by pressing HOME. When you're done examining the display, press the function key that called it up (that is, F5 or F8) to hide it again.

Navigating the Appointment Scheduler Menus

At the top of the screen are the six menus available in the Appointment Scheduler (and, in the right corner, the system time). Follow these steps to examine the menus:

1. Press ALT, F or click on File to display the **File** menu, which lets you load, save, print, network, and exit your Scheduler file.

2. Press RIGHT ARROW to display the **Appointment** menu, which lets you create, delete, edit, find, and attach notes to appointments in the Daily Scheduler.

3. Press RIGHT ARROW again to display the **To-Do** menu, which lets you create, delete, and attach notes to items in the To-Do List.

4. Press RIGHT ARROW again to display the **Controls** menu, which lets you change Daily Scheduler defaults such as the range of times displayed, revise how the elements of the Scheduler screen are laid out, set the Daily Scheduler to keep track of specified holidays, and delete all appointments before a specified date.

5. Press RIGHT ARROW again to wrap around to the **Desktop** menu, which lets you open up to 15 Desktop files.

6. Press ESC and ALT-SPACEBAR to display the Control menu, which lets you change the current window's colors and position. (Unlike some other Desktop windows, the Scheduler's window is *not* resizeable.)

7. Press ESC to close the menu and return to the Appointment Scheduler.

Of these menus (see Figure 23-2), Control and **D**esktop are in every Desktop application, and **F**ile is similar to its counterpart in Notepads. However, the **T**o-Do, **A**ppointment, and **C**ontrols menu options are unique to the Scheduler.

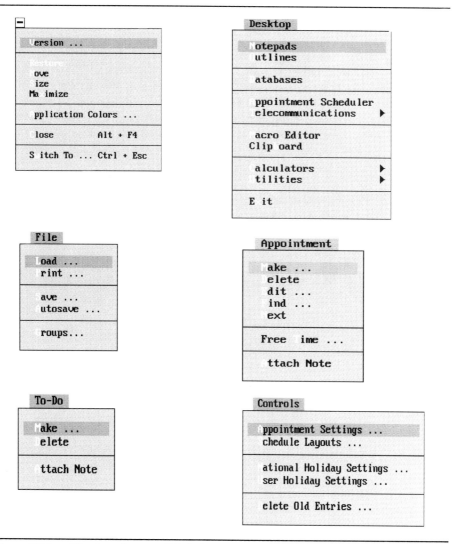

Figure 23-2.   The Appointment Scheduler menus

This chapter will cover the use of the Calendar, entering and editing items in the To-Do List, and entering and editing appointments in the Daily Scheduler. It will also cover advanced Daily Scheduler features; scheduling for programs, batch files, and macros; and using the Daily Scheduler on a network.

Using the Calendar

Even if you aren't interested in keeping to-do lists or schedules, you'll find the Calendar useful. When the Desktop is memory resident, you can always pop up the Calendar to remind yourself of the current date, to check what day a particular date falls on, or for any of the other reasons you'd normally use a calendar. Unlike a paper calendar, however, this electronic one doesn't take up any valuable space on your desk. Also, it can never be misplaced; as long as your computer is on, it's only a few keystrokes away.

Another important advantage of the Calendar is that it spans a time period much longer than the standard 12 or 16 months. In fact, it ranges from January 1 of year 1 to December 31 of year 32,767. Although you'll probably never need to reference dates that are centuries and millennia from now, you probably *will* sometimes want to check dates from last year, or five years ago, or 10 years in the future. The Calendar makes it easy.

You can move by day using RIGHT ARROW and LEFT ARROW, by week using DOWN ARROW and UP ARROW, by month using PGDN and PGUP, and by year using CTRL-PGDN and CTRL-PGUP. As an alternative, you can select any displayed date by clicking on it, and move by month by clicking on the arrows in the Calendar's upper-right corner. You can also return directly to the current date by pressing HOME.

To demonstrate, follow these steps to navigate through some Calendar dates:

1. Select the Calendar by pressing TAB until a Close box and scroll arrows appear on either side of its month/year heading, or simply click on it.

2. Press DOWN ARROW and/or RIGHT ARROW until the cursor is on the last day of the current month.

3. Press RIGHT ARROW. You're moved to the first day of the next month.

4. Press PGDN three times. You're still on the first day, but you've moved forward three months.

5. Press CTRL-PDGN. You're still on the first day of the same month, but you've moved forward one year.

6. Press CTRL-PGUP three times. You're moved back three years.

7. Press HOME. You're returned to the current date, month, and year.

In addition to being a reference tool, the Calendar sets the dates used by the To-Do List and the Daily Scheduler. These components of the Appointment Scheduler are covered in the following sections.

Using the To-Do List

There are always a number of things you need to take care of. Some of the matters are urgent and have to be dealt with before the day is over (for example, a timely office report), others are less pressing but still need to be addressed within a certain period of time (for example, monthly bills), and others can wait indefinitely until you're ready to tackle them (for example, an enticing new novel by a favorite author).

You may be keeping such to-do lists in your head right now. If you're comfortable with this system and don't find yourself letting significant items slip through the cracks, you probably have little use for written lists. On the other hand, if you find it a nuisance to have to constantly remember all the things that need to be done and the priority of these things at any given moment, or if you sometimes forget to attend to important tasks, or even if you just have trouble following up on all the things you want to do, then you might try maintaining a written list.

If you use your computer with any frequency, you're better off keeping an *electronic* list because of the ease with which you can add, edit, delete, and rearrange items. If flexibility is paramount, you may simply want to maintain your list in a word processor such as Notepads. However, if you'd prefer to be supported by list management features (for example, having items automatically ordered by priority and displayed exclusively within specified date ranges), try using the Scheduler's To-Do List and see if it helps you make better use of your time.

Entering To-Do Items

It's easy to enter an item into the To-Do List. The List (which can hold up to 80 items) automatically highlights the next available line, so you can just type a short description of your task and press ENTER. This brings up the following New To-Do Entry dialog box:

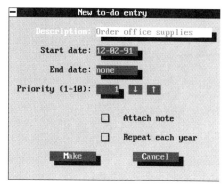

The box offers the following options:

- *Description*   This field holds your brief item description (up to 24 characters). The text can be typed directly in the To-Do List or entered here after you bring up the dialog box.

- *Start date*   This field sets the date to start displaying the item. The default is the *Calendar date.*

- *End date*   This field sets the last date to display the item. The default is *none.*

- *Priority (1-10)*   This number determines the item's display order in the List, with 1 being most important and 10 least important. The default is *1.*

- *Attach note*   When turned on, this option brings up a Notepads document into which you can type additional information about the item. The default is *off.*

- *Repeat each year*   When turned on, this option displays the item each year for the specified dates. This is useful for keeping track of birthdays, anniversaries, and other annual events. The default is *off.*

- *Make*   This option saves your settings and closes the dialog box.

- *Cancel*   This option abandons your settings and closes the dialog box.

To create a To-Do item, set these options appropriately, and then press ALT-M or click Make.

If Attach Note is *off,* your settings are saved, and the item is placed into the List in Priority order.

If Attach Note is *on,* your settings are saved, and then a Notepads file opens. You can type any additional information you want about the item, and then press ESC or click on the window's Close box to save and close the document. The item is then placed into the List in Priority order.

For example, follow these steps to enter an annual checkup as a medium-priority, recurring item:

1. Make sure the Calendar is set to today's date. Once it is, select the To-Do List by pressing TAB until its heading is highlighted, or by clicking on it.

2. Enter a reminder to go to your doctor for an annual checkup. First, type **Annual checkup** and press ENTER. The New To-Do Entry dialog box appears.

3. Press ENTER once to accept your description, and press ENTER again to accept today as the date to begin displaying this item. You're moved to the End Date field.

4. Type a date two weeks from today as the last day to display this item, and then press ENTER. You're moved to the Priority (1-10) field.

5. Type **3** and press ENTER for the priority, since the checkup is important but doesn't need to be done immediately.

6. Press TAB to skip past the Attach Note option, indicating that no additional information is required for this entry.

7. Press ENTER to turn on the Repeat Each Year option, which will display this item each year during the two-week period you've set.

8. Press ENTER to accept your settings. Your settings are saved, and you're returned to the Scheduler screen. Also, the List now contains a new highlighted line, ready for a second entry.

9. Even while you're in the To-Do List, you can change dates on the Calendar using RIGHT ARROW and LEFT ARROW. For example, press LEFT ARROW to move to yesterday's date (as indicated on both the Calendar and the title bar of the Appointment Scheduler). Your item disappears from the list because you've preceded the date at which it's set to begin displaying.

10. Press RIGHT ARROW twice. Your item reappears because you've returned to the two-week range in which it's set to display.

Editing and Deleting To-Do Items

It's as easy to edit or delete an item in the To-Do List as it is to create it.

First, move to the item you want to affect. You can do this using DOWN ARROW and UP ARROW to move by an item at a time, PGDN and PGUP to move by a screen (seven items) at a time, and HOME and END to move to the top and bottom of the entire list. You can also scroll vertically through the list using your mouse.

Once you've selected the item you want, press ENTER. The following dialog box appears, asking you to choose between the options of **D**elete, **E**dit, **A**lter Note, and **C**ancel:

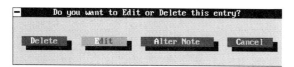

To remove the item from the List (for example, after you've accomplished the task it represents), press D or click Delete. Both the item and any attached note are erased, and all subsequent items are renumbered automatically. Be sure to use this option with care, as there's no way to retrieve a deleted item.

To adjust the item's description or settings, press ENTER or E, or click Edit. The New To-Do Entry dialog box appears. Change the appropriate options, and then press ALT-M or click Make.

To display or edit the note attached to the item, press A or click Alter Note. The appropriate Notepads document appears, ready for viewing and/or revision. When you're done with the file, save and close it by pressing ESC or by clicking on its Close box.

Lastly, to change your mind and exit the dialog box, press ESC or C, or click Cancel. The item is unaffected.

To demonstrate, follow these steps to attach a note to your annual checkup item:

1. If you aren't already on the To-Do List, select it by pressing TAB until its heading is highlighted, or by clicking on it.

2. Press UP ARROW. You're moved back to the first item on the list, which is your "Annual Checkup" entry.

3. Press ENTER to bring up the Edit/Delete dialog box.

4. Press A or click Alter Note. A Notepads document named OFFICE.001 appears. Also, the date, priority, and original description of the item are automatically entered on the window's first line.

5. Press DOWN ARROW and ENTER to move to line 3.

6. Type **Call Dr. Phinebone at 555-1666 to make the appointment.**

7. Press ESC to save and close the note. After a moment you're returned to the Scheduler screen. Also, an "N" now appears to the left of your item to indicate that it has a note attached.

Using the Daily Scheduler

In the previous section you learned how to use the To-Do List to record activities you typically want to accomplish within a period of days or weeks. You can also narrow in on your activities by assigning them to a specific day, start time, and end time with the Daily Scheduler.

You may not need to use a scheduler. For example, if you maintain a fairly consistent routine or, at the other extreme, tend to put off plans until the last minute, you'll probably find logging your appointments more trouble than it's worth.

Also, even if you do need to record your engagements, you may not have sufficient access to your PC Tools files over the course of a business day to make depending on an electronic scheduler practical. If you don't use your PC on a daily basis, or if you travel a lot without a laptop computer, you're probably better off continuing to keep your scheduling on paper.

However, if you *do* make a number of appointments, and you tend to be near your PC for at least several hours a day, and you keep the Desktop memory resident, then you may find the Daily Scheduler to be a great organizational aid.

In addition to running your own activities, you can use the Scheduler to manage your *computer's* activities. That's because it enables you to schedule programs, batch files, and macros to run at specified times when you're away from your PC. The Daily Scheduler makes it easy to take advantage of this very powerful feature.

Finally, PC Tools 7 has added a *group* feature, which lets network users all use the same scheduling file. This can greatly aid you and your colleagues in coordinating your joint schedules.

The following sections will first cover the Appointment Scheduler's basic and advanced features, and then its program-scheduling and group features.

Entering Appointments

Entering an appointment is similar to entering an item into the To-Do List. After you select the appropriate day on the Calendar and then select the Daily Scheduler, you can move to the time your appointment begins (using DOWN ARROW and UP ARROW to move by line, PGDN and PGUP to move by screen, END and HOME to go to the bottom and top of the schedule, or your mouse to scroll vertically). Type a short description of your appointment, and press ENTER. This brings up the following Make Appointment dialog box:

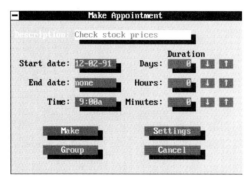

The box offers the following options:

- *Description*   This field holds your brief appointment description (up to 24 characters). You can enter the text directly on the schedule line, or you can enter it here after you bring up the dialog box.

- *Start date*   This field sets the date to start displaying the appointment. The default is the *Calendar date.*

- *End date*   This field sets the last date to display the item. The default is *none,* which repeats the appointment indefinitely (within the confines of the When option selected).

- *Time*   This field sets the time when the appointment begins. The default is *the time selected* when you opened the Make Appointment dialog box.

- *Duration*   This option sets the length of the appointment in days, hours, and/or minutes. The default is *0* days, hours, and minutes.

- *Make*   This option saves your settings and closes the dialog box.

- *Cancel*   This option cancels your changes and closes the dialog box.

- *Group*   This option lets you add the appointment to an existing group schedule on your network. For more information, see "Scheduling Groups on a Network" later in this chapter.

- *Settings*   This option brings up the following dialog box with additional settings:

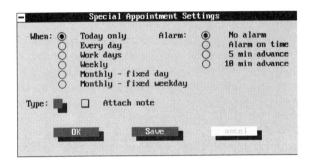

This Special Appointment Settings dialog box offers the following extra options:

- *When*   This option determines whether the appointment is set for Today Only (that is, nonrepeating), Every Day, Work Days, Weekly, Monthly–Fixed day, or Monthly–Fixed Weekday. The default is *Today only*.

- *Alarm*   This option sounds a beep and brings up a dialog box to remind you of the appointment. It can be set to No alarm, Alarm on time (which beeps at the time of the appointment), 5 Min advance (which beeps five minutes before the appointment), or 10 min advance (which beeps 10 minutes before the appointment). The default is *No alarm*.

- *Type*   This field sets an ID character to classify the appointment. (For example, you might categorize each of your clients with a unique one-letter or one-digit code.) This helps you narrow searches when using the **A**ppointment **F**ind command, as explained later in this chapter. The default is *a space*.

- *Attach note*   When turned on, this option brings up a Notepads document into which you can type additional information about the appointment. The default is *off*.

- *OK*   This option accepts your settings and returns you to the Make Appointment dialog box.

- *Save*   This option is identical to the **OK** option.

- *Cancel*   This option cancels your settings and returns you to the Make Appointment dialog box.

To create an appointment, adjust the appropriate options in the Special Appointment Settings and Make Appointment dialog boxes, and then press ALT-M or click Make.

If Attach Note is off, your settings are saved, and the appointment is entered into the schedule.

If Attach Note is on, your settings are saved and then a Notepads file opens. You can type any additional information you want about the appointment, and then press ESC or click on the window's Close box to save and close the document. The appointment is then entered into the schedule.

If you've set an alarm, at the appropriate time your computer beeps and the following Alarm dialog box pops up on your screen:

You can press ENTER or click OK to turn the alarm off; or press S or click Snooze to close the box, but make it and the beep recur in five minutes.

An alarm will only go off if the Desktop is running and/or memory resident at the appropriate time, and the particular TM file it's in is active (that is, was the last file loaded in the Appointment Scheduler). Furthermore, certain programs may prevent the alarm from going off until you exit them. It's therefore a good idea to test out which of your programs the alarm works with before you start relying on it.

To practice entering appointments, follow these steps to record a weekly sales meeting:

1. Make sure the Calendar is set to today's date; then select the Daily Scheduler by pressing TAB until its date heading is highlighted, or by clicking on it.

2. Your appointment is a weekly meeting with your salespeople which runs from 10:00 A.M. to 11:00 A.M. Move to the listed time 10:00a.

3. For the description of the appointment, type **Weekly sales meeting** and press ENTER. The Make Appointment dialog box appears.

4. Press TAB five times to accept the default settings for Start Date, End Date, Time, and Days. You're at the Hours field.

5. Press UP ARROW or type **1** to set the appointment's duration to one hour.

6. Press ALT-S or click Settings. The Special Appointment Settings dialog box appears.

7. Press DOWN ARROW three times to select the Weekly option, which sets the appointment to display on this day every week. Press TAB to move to the Alarm option.

8. Press DOWN ARROW twice to select 5 Min Advance, which sets the beep to sound and the Alarm dialog box to pop up five minutes before the meeting is scheduled to take place. Press TAB to move to the Type option.

9. Type **S** to enter a code identifying the appointment as sales-related.

10. Press ALT-O or click OK to skip attaching a note and to accept your other settings. You're returned to the Make Appointment dialog box.

11. Press ALT-M or click Make to enter your appointment. Your settings are saved, and you're returned to the Scheduler screen. The description of the appointment now appears to the right of the 10:00a listed time. Also, a musical symbol appears to the left of the time to indicate that an alarm has been set, and a line runs from 10:00a to 11:00a to show that the appointment is set to last for one hour, as in the following:

If you're running on a monochrome or LCD system, the line indicating the interval of an appointment might not be displayed.

12. Even while you're in the Daily Scheduler, you can change dates on the Calendar with RIGHT ARROW and LEFT ARROW. For example, press RIGHT ARROW to select the next day. Your appointment disappears because it isn't scheduled for tomorrow.

13. Press RIGHT ARROW another six times. Your appointment reappears because it's set to take place every week.

14. Press HOME to return to today's date.

Editing and Deleting Appointments

The procedures for revising an appointment are similar to those for the To-Do List. First, you select any time within the range of the appointment you want to affect and press ENTER. This causes the Edit/Delete dialog box to appear, which asks you to choose between the options of **D**elete, **E**dit, **A**lter Note, and **C**ancel.

To remove the appointment from the schedule (for example, after it's taken place or has been canceled), press D or click Delete. If the appointment is set for Today Only, both it and any attached note are immediately erased. If the appointment is recurring, the following dialog box appears:

Press T or click Today to erase only today's instance of the appointment; or press A or click All! to erase *all* instances of the appointment, as well as any attached note. Use this option with care, as there's no way to retrieve a deleted appointment.

To adjust the appointment's description or settings, press ENTER or E, or click Edit. The Make Appointment dialog box appears. Change the appropriate options, and then press ALT-M or click Make.

To display or edit the note attached to the appointment, press A or click Alter Note. The appropriate Notepads document appears, ready for viewing and/or revision. When you're finished with the file, save and close it by pressing ESC or clicking on the window's Close box.

Lastly, to change your mind and exit the dialog box, press ESC or C, or click Cancel. The appointment is unaffected.

To get a feel for editing appointments, follow these steps to reschedule your sales meeting and add a note to it:

1. If you aren't already in the Daily Scheduler, select it by pressing TAB until its date heading is highlighted, or by clicking on it.

2. Select 10:00a and press ENTER. The Edit/Delete dialog box appears.

3. Press ENTER or click Edit. The Make Appointment dialog box appears.

4. Press TAB three times to move to the Time option.

5. Type **11:00a** to schedule the meeting for an hour later.

6. Press ALT-S or click Settings to bring up the Special Appointment Settings box.

7. Press TAB three times to move to the Attach Note option, and then press ENTER. A mark appears to indicate that the option's been turned on, and you're moved to the **OK** option.

8. Press ENTER and then ALT-M to accept your new settings. Because you attached a note, a Notepads document named OFFICE.002 (or OFFICE with some other number extension) now appears. The date, time, and original description of your appointment are entered automatically on the first line.

9. Press DOWN ARROW and ENTER to move to line 3, and then type the following:

   Talk about concentrating on marketing this coming quarter. Drum in our new research findings that improved marketing can lead to 70% higher sales.

   When you're done, your note looks like this:

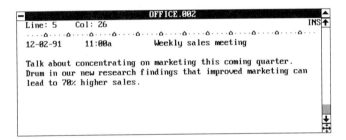

10. Press ESC to save and close the note. After a moment, you're returned to the Scheduler screen, which (if your system can display the extension line to the left) shows your appointment shifted from 10:00a through 11:00a to 11:00a through 12:00p. Also, an "N" appears to the left of the appointment's starting time to show that a note has been attached.

Deleting Multiple Appointments

An appointment isn't deleted automatically; even after its end date has passed, the appointment continues to take up disk space until it's explicitly removed. As the previous section explained, you can delete a single appointment at a time. However, to clear out a number of old appointments, it's more efficient to press ALT, C, D, or click on the Controls menu and select Delete Old Entries. When you do so, the following dialog box appears:

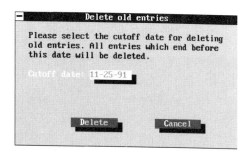

Type a cutoff date for deleting appointments, and press ALT-D or select Delete. All appointments that end *before* the specified date are instantly removed. However, recurring appointments that extend to or past the date, and one-time appointments on or past the date, are unaffected.

Use this option with care, as there's no way to retrieve deleted appointments.

Printing Appointments

When you're away from your PC, it can be convenient to have a printed copy of your schedule to refer to. To print your appointments, follow these steps:

1. Press ALT, F, P, or click on the File menu and select Print. The following Print dialog box appears:

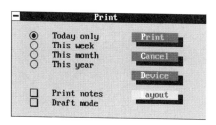

2. Use the arrow keys or your mouse to select the option of printing your appointments for Today Only, This Week, This Month, or This Year.

3. If you want your attached notes included in the printout, select the Print Notes option.

4. If you want to print quickly but at a lower resolution, select Draft Mode. (This option won't work with all printers.)

5. To configure the program for your particular printer and printer port, or to print to a disk file, press D or click Device. For more information on this option, see the "Printing Your Document" section in Chapter 20, "Using Notepads."

6. To adjust the layout of your printout, press L or click Layout. The following Schedule Printout Options dialog box, which is new to PC Tools 7, appears:

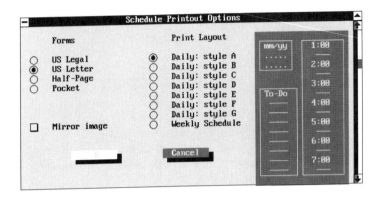

7. Use the arrow keys or your mouse to select a printing size of US Legal (8 1/2- by 14-inch), US Letter (8 1/2- by 11-inch, which is the default), Half-Page (8 1/2- by 5 1/2-inch), or Pocket (3 3/4- by 6 3/4-inch). (The latter two options will print in the upper-left corner of 8 1/2- by 11-inch sheets of paper, which you can then cut to the proper size.)

8. Press TAB twice to move to the Print Layout options, and then use DOWN ARROW to examine each layout style; or use your mouse to click on each listed style. (Note that these *print* styles are totally separate from the *display* style you chose previously with the **Controls Schedule Layouts** command.) Continue moving from layout to layout until you've found the one you want.

9. If you want to use the reverse of a selected layout, press SHIFT-TAB and ENTER, or use your mouse, to select the Mirror Image option.

10. When you're done choosing settings, press O or click OK. You're returned to the Print box.

11. Make sure your printer is on and online, and then press P or click Print. After a moment, printing begins.

Advanced Daily Scheduler Features

In addition to letting you create, edit, delete, and print appointments, the Daily Scheduler provides a number of advanced options. The **Appointment** menu contains commands for finding the next appointment, searching for specified appointments, and finding free time between appointments; the **Controls** menu contains commands for changing time defaults and holiday settings. The following sections will cover these options.

Finding Appointments

If you want to find your *next* appointment in the day's schedule, press ALT, A, N, or click on the Appointment menu and select Next. The highlight cursor moves to the next appointment in the day directly following the current time. If there *aren't* any more appointments for the day, the cursor moves instead to the listed time directly following the current time.

If you want to find a *specific* appointment, first set the Calendar to the date from which you want to begin searching, because you can only find appointments that follow the Calendar date and current time. Next, press ALT, A, F, or click on the Appointment menu and select Find. The following dialog box appears:

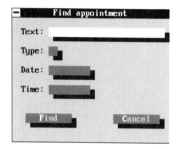

The box offers these options:

- *Text*   This field matches appointment descriptions that contain the specified text string. (There's no distinction made between upper- and lowercase text.)

- *Type*   This field matches appointments that have the same specified ID character.

- *Date*   This field matches appointments that take place during the specified date.

- *Time*   This field matches appointments that take place during the specified time.

If an option is left blank, it automatically matches anything. For example, if you enter nothing into the dialog box, it will match *every* appointment. Along the same lines, you can narrow your search by entering more information. For example, entering **lunch** in the Text field will find all lunch appointments, while adding **12:00p** in the Time field will exclusively find lunch appointments that take place during noon.

Once you've set the appropriate options, initiate the search by pressing ALT-F or clicking Find. If a match is found, the highlight cursor moves to the appointment and the dialog box remains open, ready for another search. You can continue by selecting **F**ind again, or you can end the operation by pressing ESC or clicking Cancel.

If no match is found during a search, a beep sounds and the dialog box closes, ending the operation.

Finding Time Between Appointments

Once your schedule starts filling up, it may not be easy to find the next period of time you have available to fit in a new appointment. However, you can have the Scheduler do this for you by pressing ALT, A, T, or by clicking on the Appointment menu and selecting Free Time. This brings up the following dialog box:

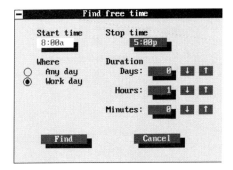

The box offers these options:

- *Start time*   This field sets the time from which to start the search. The default is the *earliest time*.

- *Stop time*   This field sets the time not to search past. The default is the *latest time*.

- *Where*   This option lets you search any day or restrict the search to a work day. The default is *Work day*.

- *Duration*   This option sets the amount of free time to find, specified in number of days, hours, and/or minutes. The default is *one hour*.

Once you've set the proper options, initiate the search by pressing ALT-F or clicking Find. If an appropriate free period is found, the highlight cursor moves to the time at which the period begins, and the operation ends.

If no appropriate free period is found within a year from the starting date, a beep sounds and a message box informs you that the search was "unable to find specified free time." Press ENTER or click OK, and the operation ends with the cursor position unchanged.

Changing Daily Scheduler Defaults

When you create an Appointment Scheduler file, the Daily Scheduler's times run from 8:00 A.M. to 5:00 P.M. in 30-minute intervals, dates appear in *MM-DD-YY* format, and work days are assumed to be Monday through Friday. You can change any or all of these defaults. To do so, press ALT, C, A, or click on the Controls menu and select Appointment Settings. The following dialog box appears:

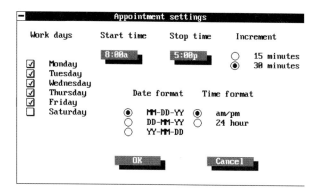

The box offers these options:

- *Work days*   This option defines the days you work, affecting appointments you've set to display exclusively on work days. The default is *Monday through Friday*. (A nonwork day is indicated in the Daily Scheduler by an asterisk [*] to the left of the date heading.)

- *Start time*   This field sets the time from which the schedule begins. The default is *8:00 am*.

- *Stop time*   This field sets the time at which the schedule ends. The default is *5:00 pm*.

- *Increment*   This option sets the interval between listed times as either 15 minutes or 30 minutes. The default is *30 minutes*.

- *Date format*   This option sets the format in which appointment dates must be entered and will be displayed. With *MM* representing up to two month digits, *DD* up to two day digits, and *YY* the last one or two digits of the year 19*YY*, the available formats are *MM-DD-YY* (U.S. standard), *DD-MM-YY* (European standard), and *YY-MM-DD* (military standard). The default is *MM-DD-YY*.

- *Time format*   This option sets the format in which appointment times must be entered and will be displayed. The available formats are am/pm (used by most people) and 24 hour (also known as military time, running from 0:00 to 24:00). The default is *am/pm*.

After adjusting the appropriate options, press ALT-O or click OK. Your new settings take effect immediately in the current file. However, they don't affect any other Appointment Scheduler files.

Changing Holiday Settings

As explained previously, your appointments can repeat indefinitely. However, you probably don't want them to display on holidays. The Daily Scheduler can track up to 19 holidays on which it doesn't schedule repeating appointments (*except* for those set to repeat every day).

To view the default holidays, press ALT, C, N, or click on the Controls menu and select National Holiday Settings. A dialog box appears, which displays ten national holidays, such as New Year's Day and Columbus Day. Initially, all the holidays are selected. To allow your appointments to display on a particular holiday, move to the holiday using TAB and press ENTER, or click on its checkmark, to remove the check to its left. When you're done, press ALT-O or click OK.

You can also define your own special days, such as other holidays, birthdays, and anniversaries, to be tracked against repeating appointments. To do so, press ALT, C, U, or click on the Controls menu and select User Holiday Settings. A dialog box appears with nine empty fields into which you can enter appropriate dates. When you're done with the box, press ALT-O or click OK.

Scheduling Programs, Batch Files, Macros, and Notes

The Daily Schedule's main function is to record your appointments. However, you can also use it to *control your computer* by scheduling programs, batch files, or macros to run at specified times. The procedure for using this sophisticated feature is easy: you simply enter ¦ (the broken vertical bar above the backslash) and the name of the program (including its EXE or COM extension), batch file (including its BAT extension), or macro (enclosed in <angle brackets>) as an appointment title.

 If the program or batch file you're scheduling won't always be in your current directory or path, specify its directory name in the appointment description.

For example, follow these instructions to schedule a batch file named BACK-UPTP.BAT. This file backs up files to tape and will run every day at 5:00 P.M.

1. Make sure the Calendar is set to today's date; then select the Daily Scheduler by pressing TAB until its date heading is highlighted, or by clicking on it.

2. Move to the listed time 5:00p and press ENTER. The Make Appointment dialog box appears.

3. Type **¦BACKUPTP.BAT** for the description.

4. The date and time fields are already set correctly, and the Duration fields don't apply here, so press ALT-S or click Settings.

5. Press DOWN ARROW to select Every Day, and then press TAB to move to the Alarm option.

6. Press DOWN ARROW to select the Alarm on Time option.

7. Press ALT-O to accept your Special settings, and then press ALT-M to save your settings. You're returned to the Scheduler screen.

That's all there is to scheduling programs. (Of course, you also need some expertise in creating batch files or macros that correctly run your computer without you, but that's another issue. For details on the latter, see Chapter 27, "Using the Macro Editor.")

You can also make the Scheduler ask for confirmation before executing by placing text in front of the vertical bar. For example, if you want to be prompted before running the BACKUPTP batch file, you can enter an appointment title such as **Backup now?¦BACKUPTP.BAT**. When the scheduled time arrives, the following dialog box pops up:

If you press S or click Snooze, the box closes but will pop up again in five minutes; if you press ESC or click Cancel, the box closes until its next scheduled time arrives. However, if you press ENTER or click OK, the requested program, batch file, or macro commences execution.

In addition to scheduling programs using the Appointment Scheduler, you can set scheduling from directly within certain programs, which is a new feature in PC Tools 7. Specifically, you can generate a CPBACKUP.TM file from CP Backup (see "Scheduling Backups" in Chapter 2), a COMMUTE.TM file from Commute (see "Scheduling Commute" in Chapter 14), and an EMAIL.TM file from the Desktop's Electronic Mail application (see "Scheduling Electronic Mail" in Chapter 26). The Appointment Scheduler will run the programs specified in these files just as it will any programs specified in its own active TM file (though in the case of a scheduling conflict, it will give its own file top priority).

Finally, you can schedule a note instead of a program. To do so, just enter the name of a text file instead of a program in the appointment description. At the scheduled time, the file will be opened as a Notepads document. This is handy if, for example, you want to be reminded of a meeting and to review your notes on it before the meeting starts.

 Like the alarm, a program or note can only go off on schedule if the Desktop is running and/or memory resident and the appropriate TM file is active (that is, was the last file loaded in the Appointment Scheduler). Also, certain applications may prevent a scheduled program or note from going off until you've exited them. It's therefore a good idea to test out which of your applications this feature works with before you start relying on it.

Alternative Program Scheduling Utilities

 In addition to the Desktop's Appointment Scheduler, PC Tools 7 includes a new memory-resident program called CP Scheduler. This utility will execute any program scheduling specified by the CPBACKUP.TM file generated by CP Backup and/or the COMMUTE.TM file generated by Commute. To load it, simply type **CPSCHED** from the DOS prompt and press ENTER. You can later unload it (and a number of other PC Tools programs, such as Commute and PC Shell) by typing **KILL** from the DOS prompt and pressing ENTER.

CP Scheduler is quite limited; it will *not* run any Desktop-related scheduling, and it doesn't contain any features for setting scheduling itself. If you're not using the Desktop, this utility can save you some memory, because it takes up less that 5K. In most cases, though, it's best to keep the Desktop resident (which, as explained in Chapter 19, can take up anywhere from 25K to virtually 0K of conventional memory), if only so you can also execute scheduling from Electronic Mail and from the Appointment Scheduler itself.

On the other hand, if you're running Microsoft Windows 3, the Desktop Scheduler is disabled until you return to DOS. In its place, you should use the new CP Scheduler for Windows program, which is much more capable than its DOS counterpart. Specifically, CP Scheduler will execute the CPBACKUP.TM file shared by the DOS and Windows versions of CP Backup, the COMMUTE.TM file generated by Commute, the EMAIL.TM file generated by Desktop Electronic Mail, and the currently active Appointment Scheduler file. In addition, it lets you schedule DiskFix to regularly check your disks for defects, and provides dialog boxes that let you adjust all your other scheduling settings. If you allowed it to, the Install program (see Appendix A) inserted a command line in your WIN.INI file to load this utility automatically whenever you run Windows. For more information, see "Using CP Scheduler for Windows" in Chapter 29, "Windows Utilities Overview."

Scheduling Groups on a Network

 If your PC is connected to a network, you and other network users who need to get together regularly can form a *group* that shares an Appointment Scheduler file devoted to the group's meetings. Each member of the group can then check the schedule to make sure it accommodates his or her own schedule. If the person has write privileges, he or she can enter new appointments for the group and/or revise existing appointments to eliminate conflicts. This procedure (which is new to PC Tools 7) can greatly ease the process of coordinating meeting times between a number of busy people.

To form a group, first choose a name for it (for example, OURGANG) and have your network administrator create a directory devoted to it (for example, H:\GROUPS\RASCALS). Each person wishing to join should then follow these steps:

1. Press ALT, F, G, or click on the File menu and select Groups. The following dialog box appears:

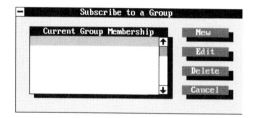

2. Press N or click New. You're prompted for the group name and path name.

3. Type the name of the group you want to join and press ENTER, type the name of the full directory path on the network the group files are stored in and press ENTER, and press ENTER again to save your settings. You're now a member of the group you specified. You can repeat steps 1 through 3 to join as many other existing groups as you like.

If you have write privileges in your group, you can make a group appointment in almost the same way that you would an individual appointment. The only difference is that after completing your settings in the Make Appointment box, you must press ALT-G or click Group (as opposed to selecting **M**ake). All the groups you belong to are listed, and you're asked to select the one this appointment was made for. Use the arrow keys or your mouse to move to the appropriate group, and then press ALT-M or click Make. The appointment is saved, and each of your fellow group members will be notified of it the next time he or she opens the Appointment Scheduler.

If your group ever changes its name or directory path, each member simply has to select the **F**ile **G**roups command, select the listed group that needs to be changed, select the **E**dit option, revise the group information, and select **OK**.

Finally, if you ever want to leave a group (because, for example, you've been transferred to a different division in your company), just select the **F**ile **G**roups command, select the listed group that needs to be changed, and select the **Delete** option. However, use this option with care, since the command deletes your group information without any prompting to verify that you've selected the correct command.

Appointment Scheduler Command Reference

You can perform basic Appointment Scheduler activities without ever accessing its menus. However, there are a number of advanced features you can exploit by using menu commands.

Like all Desktop applications, the Appointment Scheduler's first two menus are Control and Desktop. These menus are covered in Chapter 19, "Desktop Manager Overview."

The Appointment Scheduler also contains four additional menus: **File**, **Appointment**, **To-Do**, and **Controls**. This section covers the options in these menus. After the name of each option are the keystrokes that invoke it, a description of what the option does, and a reference to the section in either this chapter or Chapter 20 that discusses the option in detail.

The File Menu

The File menu performs such operations as loading, saving, and printing files. It contains the following five options:

Load (ALT, F, L)

Clears the file in the current window from memory and then loads it with the specified file. Covered in "Abandoning Your Document" in Chapter 20.

Print (ALT, F, P)

Prints specified appointments or To-Do List items via a variety of layout options. Covered in "Printing Appointments."

Save (ALT, F, S)

Saves your file to disk. After you optionally edit the filename and set the format to save in, press ALT-S or click Save. General information about saving files is covered in "Saving Your Document" in Chapter 20.

Autosave (ALT, F, A)

Automatically saves your file to disk at specified intervals. Covered in "Saving Your Document" in Chapter 20.

Groups (ALT, F, G)

Lets you join group appointment files on your network. Covered in "Scheduling Groups on a Network."

The Appointment Menu

Previously, you learned how to create, delete, and edit appointments by selecting them and pressing ENTER. The Appointment menu contains four commands that duplicate these functions. In addition, the menu contains the advanced commands covered previously for finding the next appointment, searching for specified appointments, and finding free time between appointments. The menu's seven options are as follows:

Make (ALT, A, M)

Brings up the Make Appointment dialog box for the time selected. Details on the box's options are covered in "Entering Appointments."

Delete (ALT, A, D)

Deletes the selected appointment from the schedule. Unlike the Edit/Delete dialog box, this option prompts for confirmation before deleting any appointment (not just recurring ones). The Edit/Delete dialog box is covered in "Editing and Deleting Appointments."

Edit (ALT, A, E)

Brings up the Make Appointment dialog box of the selected appointment and lets you alter its settings. Details on setting and revising the dialog box are covered in "Entering Appointments" and "Editing and Deleting Appointments."

Find (ALT, A, F)

Searches for appointments matching specified criteria. Covered in "Finding Appointments."

Next (ALT, A, N)

Searches for the next appointment of the day. Covered in "Finding Appointments."

Free Time (ALT, A, T)

Searches for your next period of unscheduled time. Covered in "Finding Time Between Appointments."

Attach Note (ALT, A, A)

If the selected appointment doesn't have a Notepads file attached, attaches an appropriate file and opens it so that you can enter additional information. If the selected appointment already has a note attached, displays the note and gives you the opportunity to edit it. Attaching and editing notes are covered in "Entering Appointments" and "Editing and Deleting Appointments."

The To-Do Menu

Previously, you learned how to create, delete, and edit To-Do List items by selecting them and pressing ENTER. The **To-Do** menu contains the following three commands that duplicate these functions:

Make (ALT, T, M)

Brings up the New To-Do Entry dialog box for the next available line in the To-Do List. Details on the box's options are covered in "Entering To-Do Items."

Delete (ALT, T, D)

Removes the selected item from the To-Do List. All subsequent items are automatically renumbered. Like the Edit/Delete dialog box, this command does *not* prompt for verification before deleting an item. Use this option with care, as there's no way to retrieve a deleted item. The Edit/Delete dialog box is covered in "Editing and Deleting To-Do Items."

Attach Note (ALT, T, A)

If the selected item doesn't have a Notepads file attached, attaches an appropriate file and opens it so that you can enter additional information. If the selected item already has a note attached, displays the note and gives you the opportunity to edit it. Attaching and editing notes are covered in "Entering To-Do Items" and "Editing and Deleting To-Do Items."

The Controls Menu

The Controls menu enables you to change Daily Scheduler defaults such as the times displayed, time and date formats, and which holidays to skip appointments. You can also use this menu to revise how the Scheduler screen is laid out and to delete all appointments before a specified date. The menu's five options are as follows:

Appointment Settings (ALT, C, A)

Lets you change Daily Scheduler defaults such as the times displayed, the time intervals that separate them, and time and date formats. Covered in "Changing Daily Scheduler Defaults."

Schedule Layouts (ALT, C, S)

Lets you choose among five different layout designs for the Scheduler screen. Covered in "Examining the Appointment Scheduler."

National Holiday Settings (ALT, C, N)

Lets you set the holidays on which repeating appointments will and will not be displayed. Covered in "Changing Holiday Settings."

User Holiday Settings (ALT, C, U)

Lets you define your own special dates on which repeating appointments will *not* be displayed. Covered in "Changing Holiday Settings."

Delete Old Entries (ALT, C, D)

Clears out all appointments that end before a specified date. Covered in "Deleting Multiple Appointments."

Chapter 24

Using the Calculators

A PC is fundamentally a computing machine. However, when you need to perform even a simple computation, you may find yourself turning from your powerful computer to a handheld calculator. There are two reasons for this. First, most PC programs that perform computations are difficult to learn and use. Second, these programs generally require you to devote your PC to them while they're running, so they aren't much help while you're in the middle of using an application such as a word processor or database manager.

The Desktop solves both these problems with its four calculator simulations. Because they imitate handheld calculators people are already familiar with, they're easy to learn and use. Also, if the Desktop is memory resident, they can be popped up in whatever application you're currently running. The four Desktop calculators are as follows:

- A standard algebraic calculator that performs simple math computations.

- A Hewlett-Packard HP-12C financial calculator that computes such values as interest rate, depreciation, and cash flow.

- A Hewlett-Packard HP-16C programmer's calculator that converts between different number systems and provides numerous bit arithmetic functions.

- A Hewlett-Packard HP-11C scientific calculator that computes probability, statistical, and transcendental function problems.

This chapter will cover using the Algebraic Calculator; fundamental concepts of the HP calculators (including key functions, data registers, stacks, and reverse Polish notation); the basic characteristics of each of the three HP calculators; and the numerous functions provided by each of the HP calculator keypads.

Using the Algebraic Calculator

The Algebraic Calculator is a standard calculator that performs addition, subtraction, multiplication, and division. It comes with a simulated paper tape that stores up to 1000 lines of your entries and results.

To bring up the calculator, follow these steps:

1. First, call up the Desktop Manager. If you've installed the Desktop to be memory resident, press CTRL-SPACEBAR. Otherwise, type **DESKTOP** from the DOS prompt and press ENTER.

2. Press ENTER or click on Desktop to display the main menu.

3. Press C or click on Calculators. The following list of calculators appears:

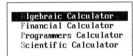

4. Press ENTER or A, or click Algebraic Calculator. The calculator screen in Figure 24-1 appears.

The Algebraic Calculator Window

The calculator's window consists of three parts: the display, the simulated paper tape, and the keypad.

The display is at the bottom left of the window. It's the line on which you make your entries and see your results.

Directly above the display is the simulated paper tape (referred to from now on as simply "tape"), which records everything that appears in the display.

On the right side of the window is the calculator's keypad, which you use to enter numbers and operators. You can select the following keys on the pad either by pressing their keyboard equivalents or by clicking them with your mouse:

- The numbers 0 through 9
- . for setting a decimal point
- + for addition
- – for subtraction
- * for multiplication
- ÷ for division (press /, the forward slash key)
- % for percentage
- = to display the result (press = or ENTER)
- CLR for clearing your current entry (press C or F4)
- M+ to add your current entry to the *data register,* which is a temporary storage area in memory that holds a single number (press M, +)
- M– to subtract your current entry from the data register's contents (press M, -)
- MRCL to recall the data register's contents (press M, R)
- MCLR to clear the data register (press M, C)

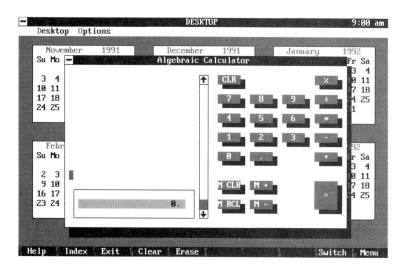

Figure 24-1.   *The Algebraic Calculator screen*

The Algebraic Calculator Message Bar and Menus

At the bottom of the screen is the message bar. When a calculator activity is taking place, the bar displays appropriate definitions or instructions. Otherwise, it displays the commands assigned to the function keys. The only functions unique to the Algebraic Calculator are F4 (Clear), which clears the display, and F5 (Erase), which clears the tape.

At the top of the screen are the three menus available in the Algebraic Calculator (including, in the upper-left corner, the dash representing the Control menu). Of these menus, which are shown in Figure 24-2, Control and **Desktop** are in every Desktop application, and are covered in Chapter 19, "Desktop Manager Overview."

The last menu is **O**ptions, which you can display by pressing ALT, O or by clicking on Options. This menu contains commands for clearing the display (the same as F4), clearing the tape (the same as F5), copying the last 100 lines of the tape to the Clipboard, printing the tape, and toggling the display of the keypad on or off. Each of these options will be covered in the following sections. To close the menu, press ESC.

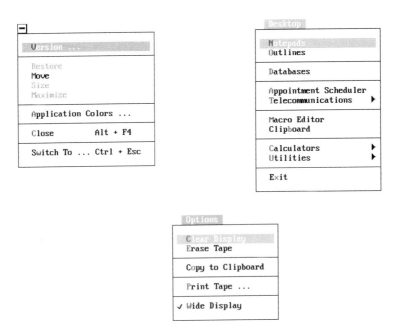

Figure 24-2.   *The Algebraic Calculator menus*

Making Calculations

To make a calculation using the Algebraic Calculator, simply type a number, an appropriate operator (such as + or –), and another number. You can then display the result by pressing ENTER or = to end the computation (for example, **1 + 2 =**), or by entering another operator to continue the computation (for example, **1 + 2 +**).

You can also place the number in the display into the data register, which saves time if you use the same number repeatedly.

For example, follow these steps to perform the calculation (123 + 456 – 78.9) / 5, save the result in the data register, and multiply the register's contents by 60 and by 60 percent:

1. To add 123 and 456, first enter **123** by pressing the number keys above the letter keys, or by turning on NUM LOCK and using the numeric keypad, or by clicking the appropriate numbers on the calculator's keypad. As you type, the digits appear in the calculator's display.

   If you make a mistake, use BACKSPACE to correct single digits, or press F4 or C to clear the whole entry and start over.

2. Press +. The display remains unchanged, but the tape records your entry.

3. Type **456**. The previous number is replaced.

4. Press = or ENTER to get the result. The total, 579, appears in the display. It also appears on the tape with a "T" to its right, which marks it as the result of a completed calculation, as shown here:

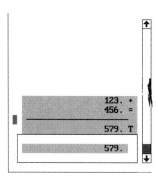

5. Type **–78.9** to subtract 78.9.

6. Press / (forward slash) to get an interim result, 500.1, and to continue the calculation.

7. Type **5** and press ENTER to divide by 5. The final result, 100.02, appears.

8. Store the current number into the data register by pressing M, +, or by clicking M+ on the calculator's keypad. An "M" appears to the left of the tape to show that the register now contains a value.

9. Multiply 100.02 by 60 by typing * (the sign for multiplication), **60**, and pressing = or ENTER. The result 6,001.2 appears (including a comma for readability).

10. Recall the value in the data register by pressing M, R, or by clicking MRCL on the calculator keypad. The number 100.02 reappears in the display.

11. Type ***60%** to find 60 percent of 100.02. The result, 60.012, appears.

12. Clear the data register by pressing M, C, or by clicking MCLR on the calculator's keypad. The "M" to the left of the tape disappears, and the tape and display now look like this:

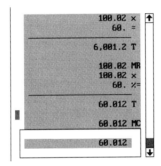

Working with the Algebraic Calculator Tape

The tape that records your entries and results can be scrolled, edited, copied to the Clipboard, printed to paper, and erased with a keystroke. The following sections detail these features.

Editing the Tape

While the tape typically shows only its last 12 lines, it stores up to 1000 lines. With NUM LOCK off, you can move to the top and bottom of the tape using HOME and END, up and down 12 entries using PGUP and PGDN, and from entry to entry using UP ARROW and DOWN ARROW. You can also scroll through the tape using your mouse.

When you're on a tape entry, the number also appears in the display, giving you the opportunity to replace it by typing a new number. All numbers on the tape dependent on the value you changed are recalculated appropriately.

For example, follow these steps to move around the tape and then change 123 to .123:

1. If NUM LOCK is on and you don't have a separate cursor keypad, press NUM LOCK to turn it off and enable the arrow keypad.

2. Press HOME to move to the top of the tape. If you began the previous tutorial with a blank tape, you're now on 123, the first number you entered.

3. Press DOWN ARROW a few times. Notice that you can move only to numbers you entered, not results entered by the calculator itself.

4. Press HOME (or, if your tape doesn't begin with the 123 entry, the arrow keys) to move to 123 again. Replace the whole number with a fraction by typing **.123**.

5. Press DOWN ARROW three times. Notice that the values dependent on the number have changed accordingly.

6. Press DOWN ARROW one more time. Notice the value recorded as being placed into the data register remains 100.02, as shown here:

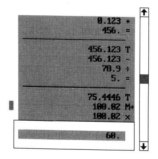

The register operation is considered the beginning of a new, independent calculation and so is unaffected by previous changes.

7. Press END to return to the bottom of the tape.

Copying the Tape

You can copy the last 100 lines of the tape to the Clipboard, which is the Desktop's gateway between applications. From the Clipboard, you can copy the data into a Desktop program such as Notepads (say, to create a report or an expense account); or into a non-PC Tools program, such as an electronic spreadsheet, to further manipulate the numbers.

To copy the tape, press ALT, O, O, or click on the Options menu and select Copy to Clipboard. The last 100 lines are instantly placed into the Clipboard, while the tape itself is unaffected.

To verify the copy, you can display the Clipboard by pressing ALT, D, B, and then move to the top of the text by pressing CTRL-HOME. To close the Clipboard, press ESC.

For more information about copying between applications, see Chapter 22, "Using the Clipboard."

Printing the Tape

If you want to look at your calculations away from your PC or show them to someone else, you can print the tape to paper. To do so, follow these steps:

1. Press ALT, O, P, or click on the Options menu and select Print Tape. The Print dialog box appears.

2. If appropriate, change the settings for Device, Number of Copies, Line Spacing, and/or Starting Page #. For information on these options, see the "Printing Your Document" section of Chapter 20, "Using Notepads."

3. Make sure your printer is on and online, and then press P or click Print. After a moment, the tape is printed.

Clearing the Tape

You never have to clear the tape to make room for more data. That's because once its 1000 lines are filled, its oldest data is automatically erased and subsequent data bumped up as new numbers are entered. However, it's easier to move around and edit the tape when it contains less data, so you may prefer to clear it occasionally before beginning a new series of computations.

To delete the tape's data, press ALT, O, E, or press F5, or click on the Options menu and select Erase Tape. Everything on the tape is instantly removed, leaving only a zero in the display. However, *use this option with care*, as there's no way to retrieve the lost data.

Controlling the Algebraic Calculator's Display

The Algebraic Calculator has several display elements that you can control. These are the number of decimal places shown, commas, and the calculator's keypad.

Setting Decimal Places

The Algebraic Calculator ordinarily displays only as many digits past the decimal point as necessary (up to 13) to represent a number. However, you have the option of making all numbers display with the same number of decimal places by pressing D followed by a digit from 0 to 9.

Changing the way numbers are displayed on screen has absolutely no effect on the way they're stored and calculated internally.

For example, follow these steps to enter some numbers, set them to display with different decimal places, and then return to the default display:

1. Type **100.100** and press ENTER. Notice that the extra zeros at the end of the number are discarded.

2. Type **/3** and press ENTER to divide by three. The result, 33.3666666666666, is carried to 13 decimal places in the display and then truncated.

3. Type **+.03** and press ENTER to add .03.

4. Press D, 9. The numbers that had fewer than nine decimal places are padded with zeros on their right, while the numbers that had more than nine decimal places are rounded, as shown here:

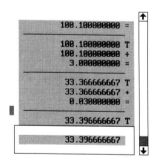

5. Press D, 2. The numbers contract to two decimal places and are rounded accordingly; for example, 33.3966666666666 is displayed as 33.40.

6. Press D, 0. The numbers are rounded to no decimal places; for example, .03 is now displayed as 0.

7. Press D, . (that is, D and a period). The calculator returns to its default state of showing as many decimal places as appropriate for each number.

Setting Commas

The Algebraic Calculator normally inserts commas in large numbers to make them more readable. However, you can turn this feature off by simply pressing , (that is, the comma key). To turn it on again, just press , again.

Setting Window Width

Ordinarily, the Algebraic Calculator window consists of the display and tape on the left and the keypad on the right. However, if you'd like more room on the screen for other windows, you can suppress the keypad portion of the window by pressing ALT, O, W, or by clicking on the Options menu and selecting Wide Display. The keypad disappears, reducing the calculator's width by 50 percent. To bring the keypad back, select Options Wide Display again to toggle the option back on.

Saving and Exiting the Algebraic Calculator

Once you're done using the Algebraic Calculator, you can save it and exit by pressing ESC or clicking on the window's Close box. The contents of the tape, as well as all your display settings, are automatically saved for future sessions (in a file named CALC.TMP), and the calculator closes.

HP Calculators Overview

In addition to the Algebraic Calculator, the Desktop provides simulations of the Hewlett-Packard HP-12C financial calculator, HP-16C programmer's calculator, and HP-11C scientific calculator. While these three calculators are used for different purposes, they all share some common characteristics, such as the way they represent HP keypads, their use of data registers and stacks, and their use of reverse Polish notation.

Understanding the HP Calculator Keys

Like the Algebraic Calculator, each of the Desktop HP calculators includes a representation of a keypad. However, the HP keypads are considerably more complicated. To begin exploring the differences, follow these steps to bring up the Financial Calculator:

1. Press ALT-D to bring up the Desktop menu.

2. Press C or click Calculators.

3. Press F or click Financial Calculator. The screen in Figure 24-3 appears.

The first thing you probably notice is that the HP keypad has many more keys than the Algebraic Calculator. Also, in place of an electronic tape at the left, windows for Stack Registers and Last X Register appear. These windows will be explained later in the "Understanding the Stack" section.

Another difference is that the HP keys have no natural correspondence to anything on your keyboard. As a result, PC keys are somewhat arbitrarily assigned to them. The letter or symbol you press to activate a particular calculator key appears on the screen to the left of the key. (For example, the top row of keys in the Financial Calculator are assigned to the PC keys Q, A, C, [, and].)

An additional difference is that the HP calculator keys generally perform two or even three distinct functions. In PC Tools Deluxe 6, a key's first function is represented by a mnemonic label in its center, the second by a label at its top, and the third by a label at its bottom. This displays all functions simultaneously, but it gives the HP keypads a cluttered look. Therefore, in PC Tools 7 the keypads have been redesigned to display only one set of functions at a time.

The keys start off displaying the first, or default, set of functions. If you press F7 (which represents the gold "f" key on handheld HP calculators), the labels on all the keys change to the second set of functions. Similarly, if you press F8 (which represents the blue "g" key on handheld HP calculators), the labels on all the keys change to the third set of functions. After you press the appropriate PC key to select the function you want, the labels on all the keys automatically change back to the default set of functions.

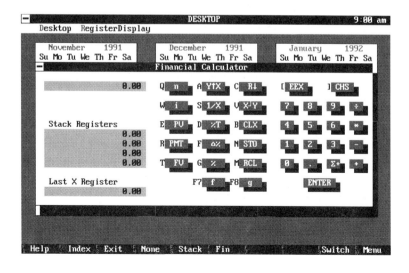

Figure 24-3.   *The Financial Calculator screen*

For example, the default function for the first key in the Financial Calculator is "n," which you select by pressing the letter Q. If you want the AMORT function instead, you first press F7, which displays the second set of functions, and then press Q. Similarly, if you want the 12x function instead, you first press F8, which displays the third set of functions, and then press Q.

You can also use your mouse to click the appropriate keys. For example, for the first key in the Financial Calculator, you can select the "n" function by just clicking the key, the AMORT function by clicking the "f" key that appears at the bottom of the screen and then AMORT, and the 12x function by clicking the "g" key that appears at the bottom of the screen and then 12x.

If you press a number on the numeric keypad, be sure that NUM LOCK *is on so the key registers as a number and not a movement key. This is an especially easy mistake to make after pressing* F7 *or* F8, *since these keys change the labels on the onscreen numeric keypad from numbers to function names.*

Understanding the HP Data Registers

Just as the Algebraic Calculator has one data register into which you can store a single value, the HP calculators have numerous data registers into which you can store multiple values. Specifically, the Programmer's Calculator has ten data registers (labeled R0 through R9), and the Financial and Scientific Calculators each have 20 data registers (labeled R0 through R9 and R.0 through R.9).

You can view the contents of the first set of ten data registers by pressing ALT, R, D; you can view the second set of ten (if supported) by pressing ALT, R, R. This is a major advantage of the Desktop over handheld calculators, which aren't equipped to display registers.

For example, press ALT, R, D now. The following display of the Financial Calculator's first ten data registers pops up:

```
R0          0.00
R1          0.00
R2          0.00
R3          0.00
R4          0.00
R5          0.00
R6          0.00
R7          0.00
R8          0.00
R9          0.00
```

On the display's left side are registers R0 through R9 (referred to in calculations as 0 through 9), and on the right are its current contents. All the registers start off containing zero.

Now press ALT, R, R. The registers R.0 through R.9 are displayed (referred to in calculations as .0 through .9). Again, the register contents appear to the right and initially are all zero.

You can put numbers into the registers using the STO key, which in the Financial Calculator is assigned to N on your keyboard. For example, follow these steps to put 200 into registers R2 and R.9:

1. Press ALT, R, D, or click the RegisterDisplay menu and select Data Registers R0 - R9, to display the first set of data registers.

2. Type **200**. The number appears in the display in the upper-left corner. (The Financial Calculator default is to display two decimal places, so the result is shown as 200.00.)

3. Press N, 2 to store the current number in register R2. The value 200 appears to the right of R2 in the register window.

4. Press ALT, R, R, or click the RegisterDisplay menu and select Data Registers R.0 - R.9, to display the second set of data registers.

5. Press N, ., 9 (that is, N, a period, and 9) to store the current number in register R.9. The value 200 appears to the right of R.9 in the register window.

Similarly, you can recall a register's contents using the RCL function, which in the Financial Calculator is assigned to M on your keyboard. For example, follow these steps to enter another number, and then recall the contents of registers R1 and R2:

1. Press ALT, R, D to bring up the first set of data registers again.

2. Type **400**. The number replaces the previous value of 200 in the display.

3. Press M, 1 to recall the contents of R1. The number in the display is replaced by 0.

4. Press M, 2 to recall the contents of R2. The 0 in the display is replaced by 200.

Understanding the Stack

Just as you can use the data registers to temporarily store numbers you want to work with, the HP calculators use *stack registers* to temporarily store the numbers entered during calculations. The *stack* consists of four linked registers that may be thought of as being "stacked" on top of each other. They're named, from bottom to top, X, Y, Z, and T (for top of stack).

Register X is especially important because your entries are initially placed into it and your calculation results end up in it. In fact, register X always contains the value in the upper-left corner display, which may be thought of as a window on the register. (The one qualifier is that decimal place settings may round off a number in the display, while they have absolutely no effect on the way the number is stored and calculated internally.)

There's also a fifth stack register, named *Last X,* which holds the previous value in register X resulting from an arithmetic operation. Last X is basically a backup register that lets you recover from entry errors during calculations.

The HP calculators' default is to display the stack. However, if you've switched to a different set of registers (such as, in this case, the data registers), you can switch back to the stack by pressing ALT, R, S, or pressing F5, or clicking on the RegisterDisplay menu and selecting the Stack Registers option. To demonstrate, press F5 now. The following two stack windows appear:

```
Stack Registers
              200.00
              400.00
                0.00
              200.00

Last X Register
                0.00
```

The window labeled Stack Registers shows registers X, Y, Z, and T, which contain the values used in your previous operations. Below is the window labeled Last X Register, which is positioned as if ready to take the next arithmetic value that "falls out of" X.

Currently, T contains 200, the first value you entered; Z contains 400, which was your second entry; Y contains 0, which was your third entry via the RCL command; and X contains 200, which was your fourth and most recent entry. In other words, each of your display entries started in X and was then bumped up the stack. This illustrates one of the four ways the stack handles numbers. The complete list of rules is as follows:

- When you type a number into the display, the value goes into register X, and the other values in the stack are bumped up one level. In other words, X's previous value moves to Y, Y's moves to Z, Z's moves to T, and T's is bumped out of the stack (that is, erased).

- When you press ENTER, something slightly different happens: the number in the display is placed in both the X *and* Y registers. At the same time, Y's previous value is bumped up to Z and Z's is bumped up to T.

- When you type in a number directly *after* pressing ENTER, the number is placed into register X, and the other registers are *unaffected.*

- When you type in an operator (such as + or –), the values in registers X and Y are acted on in accordance with the operator and the result is left in X. The value in Z is then bumped *down* to Y, and T's value is copied to Z.

These four rules encompass all the workings of the stack. While they may seem abstract at the moment, their significance is brought down to earth in the next section, which explains how to enter calculations.

At the time of this writing, the Programmer's and Scientific Calculators conform precisely to the stack rules just listed, but the Financial Calculator does not; *instead, it uses a different but similar set of rules that achieve the same result. As long as you don't study the stack every step of the way while using the Financial Calculator, you won't even notice the differences (for example, the operation rules in the next section apply to all three calculators equally). However, if you're specifically interested in studying HP stack operations, concentrate on the other two calculators until the Financial Calculator is reprogrammed to strictly conform with them.*

Understanding Reverse Polish Notation

In the Algebraic Calculator, you add 1 and 2 by typing **1+2** and pressing ENTER. This method of entry is called *infix notation.*

In the HP calculators, however, you add 1 and 2 by typing **1**, pressing ENTER, and then typing **2+**. In other words, you first enter the numbers to be operated on, then the operator. This method is called *reverse Polish notation* (after its Polish inventor, J. Lukasieqicz). It may seem unintuitive at first, but it works extremely well in conjunction with the stack. The advantage of reverse Polish notation is that it never forces you to write down intermediate results; those results are instead stored automatically by the stack as you generate them. This makes it an ideal method for tackling complex computations.

To get a feel for calculating the HP way, follow these steps to open the Scientific Calculator, and then find the result of (20+7)/(11–8) while keeping an eye on the stack:

1. Press ALT, D, C, S to open the Scientific Calculator. A window appears that's similar to the Financial Calculator but provides different keypad functions (as shown in Figure 24-4).

2. If the stack isn't already displayed, press F5.

3. Type **20**. Notice that 20 is entered into both the top display and the X register at the bottom of the stack.

4. Press ENTER. The current number, 20, is now copied into the Y register. (Also, the number is padded with four zeros on its right, because this calculator's default is four decimal places.)

5. Type **7** for the second operand. The number is entered into the X register, while the other registers remain unchanged.

6. Press +. The numbers in X and Y are added and the result, 27, appears in the display. In the stack, X contains 27, while the contents of all the other registers are bumped down.

7. Type **11** and press ENTER. X and Y now contain 11, while the intermediate result of 27 is bumped up and out of the way until needed.

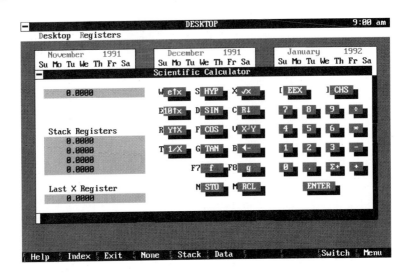

Figure 24-4.   The Scientific Calculator screen

8. Type **8** for the second operand. X contains 8, while the other registers are unchanged.

9. Press –. The number in X is subtracted from the number in Y and the result, 3, appears in the display. In the stack, X contains 3, while the contents of the other registers are bumped down so that Y now contains your first result, 27.

10. Press /. The number in Y is divided by the number in X, and the final result, 9, appears in the display.

Notice that the stack automatically stored the intermediate result of 27 until you needed it. In a conventional calculator, you must record the intermediate result before proceeding with the calculation. While in this example the saved effort is a small one, the stack's efficiency grows more pronounced with more complex calculations.

When you're finished experimenting with the calculators you have open, close them one by one by pressing ESC a few times.

HP Calculator Books

In this overview, you learned how to select HP key functions, view and use data registers, view and understand the stack, and enter calculations using reverse Polish notation. With these fundamental skills under your belt, you're ready to learn the specific features of the HP-12C financial calculator, HP-16C programmer's calculator and/or HP-11C scientific calculator. The following sections briefly describe the characteristics of each calculator and its functions. However, none of this material is intended as anything approaching a comprehensive treatment. To get full use out of a particular Desktop HP calculator simulation, it's recommended that you read a manual and/or instructional book on its handheld counterpart. These are some especially useful ones:

- *Hewlett-Packard HP-12C Owner's Handbook and Problem-Solving Guide* (from EduCALC, part number 718).

- *Hewlett-Packard HP-16C Owner's Handbook and Problem-Solving Guide* (from EduCALC, part number 720).

- *Hewlett-Packard HP-11C Owner's Handbook and Problem-Solving Guide* (from EduCALC, part number 717).

If you don't mind tiny print, you'll probably find these handbooks serve well as both reference manuals and instructional guides. They can be ordered from the national mail-order vendor EduCALC at (800) 677-7001.

If you're interested in a more accessible instructional approach, you might also want to try *An Easy Course in Using the HP-12C*, which you can order from either EduCALC (part number 260), or direct from the publisher, Grapevine Publications, at (800) 338-4331. This book utilizes friendly instructions, big print, and whimsical drawings to guide you through using the financial calculator.

Using the Financial Calculator

As mentioned previously, the Financial Calculator is a simulation of the HP-12C. It's a valuable tool for computing such business values as interest, cash flow, depreciation, appreciation, and mortgages.

You've already used this calculator in the previous section. Bring it up again by pressing ALT-D, C, F. The screen in Figure 24-3 appears again.

At the bottom of the screen is the message bar, which reminds you that pressing F5 displays the stack. In addition, the bar displays a "Fin" description for F6. This is for yet another set of registers in the calculators called the *financial registers*. To view them, press F6 now. A display like this appears:

```
Number of Months
                    0.00
Interest Rate
                    0.00
Present Value
                    0.00
Payment
                    0.00
Future Value
                    0.00
```

The five registers are as follows:

- *Number of Months*   Number of identical sequential time periods, entered or computed by function n.

- *Interest Rate*   Interest rate accruing over every n periods, entered or computed by function i.

- *Present Value*   Entered or computed by function PV.

- *Payment*   Entered or computed by function PMT.

- *Future Value*   Entered or computed by function FV.

These registers are used to solve five-key problems. By entering appropriate data in any four of the registers, you can find the value of the fifth.

The calculator additionally contains *statistical storage registers* for solving statistical problems. However, you can't display these registers. Data is entered into them directly from the calculator during statistical computations.

Lastly, if there are times when you don't want to look at *any* registers, select the remaining display option on the message bar, None, by pressing F4. A copyright message replaces the register display.

At the top of the screen are three menus of the Financial Calculator (and, in the right corner, the system time). The Control and **D**esktop menus are in all Desktop applications, and information about them appears in Chapter 19. However, **R**egisterDisplay is devoted to calculator-related options.

To examine the last menu, press ALT, R or click RegisterDisplay. You now see options that duplicate the function key commands for suppressing a register display, displaying the stack, and displaying the financial registers. In addition, the bottom of the menu contains the two options you used earlier in this chapter to display the calculator's two sets of data registers. To close the menu, press ESC.

In the upper-left corner of the screen is the display window, which is where you enter numbers and see the results of your computations. You can set the number of decimal places displayed by pressing F7 and then a digit from zero to nine (or a period for scientific notation). The default is two decimal places. Decimal place settings do *not* affect how numbers are stored internally; the Financial Calculator uses 12 digits of precision for all calculations.

The heart of the calculator is its keypad, which fills most of the window. The numerous functions these calculator keys provide are listed and defined in Table 24-1.

In Table 24-1, the display number is the number in register X. However, keep in mind that a number may be rounded in the display due to decimal place settings, while the number stored internally in register X is never affected by such settings unless explicitly rounded by the RND function.

Function	Keystrokes	Action
n	Q	Stores or computes the number of identical sequential time periods in financial calculations. See also i, PMT, PV, and FV.
i	W	Stores or computes the interest rate accruing over every n period in financial calculations. See also n, PMT, PV, and FV.
PV	E	Stores or computes the present value (the initial cash flow) in financial calculations. See also n, i, PMT, and FV.
PMT	R	Stores or computes the payment amount in financial calculations. See also n, i, PV, and FV.
FV	T	Stores or computes the future value (final cash flow) in financial calculations. See also n, i, PMT, and PV.
Y↑X	A	Raises the number in register Y to the power of the display number.
1/X	S	Finds the reciprocal of the display number by dividing it into 1.
%T	D	Finds what percentage the display number is of the total value in register Y.
Δ%	F	Finds the percent difference between the display number and the number in register Y.
%	G	Finds the display number percent of the number in register Y.
f	F7	Activates the function at the top of the next key selected.
R↓	C	Rolls the stack down by one register.
X↔Y	V	Swaps the X and Y registers' contents.
CLX	B	Clears register X.
STO	N	Stores the display number into a specified data register.
RCL	M	Recalls a specified data register's contents to the display.

Table 24-1. *The Financial Calculator Functions*

Function	Keystrokes	Action
g	F8	Activates the function at the bottom of the next key selected.
EEX	[	Makes the next number entered an exponent of the display number.
CHS	]	Changes the sign of the display number.
7	7	Enters the number 7.
4	4	Enters the number 4.
1	1	Enters the number 1.
0	0	Enters the number 0.
8	8	Enters the number 8.
5	5	Enters the number 5.
2	2	Enters the number 2.
.	.	Sets the decimal place.
9	9	Enters the number 9.
6	6	Enters the number 6.
3	3	Enters the number 3.
Σ+	&	Collects data from registers X and Y into the statistics registers.
÷	/	Divides.
*	*	Multiplies.
−	−	Subtracts.
+	+	Adds.
ENTER	ENTER	Copies the number in register X into register Y and disables stack-lift for the next entry.
AMORT	F7, Q	Amortizes x number of periods using the display number and values stored in registers i, PMT, and PV; updates the values in registers n and PV.
INT	F7, W	Finds simple interest, storing the 360-day interest in register X and the 365-day interest in register Z. (This function has no relation to the INT function invoked by F8, G.)
NPV	F7, E	Finds the net present value.

Table 24-1.   *The Financial Calculator Functions (continued)*

Function	Keystrokes	Action
RND	F7, R	Rounds the mantissa of the internally stored 12-digit number in register X to match the display.
IRR	F7, T	Finds the internal rate of return.
PRICE	F7, A	Finds a bond's price for a specified YTM.
YTM	F7, S	Finds a bond's yield to maturity for a specified PRICE.
SL	F7, D	Finds the straight line depreciation.
SOYD	F7, F	Finds the sum-of-the-year's-digits depreciation.
DB	F7, G	Finds the declining balance depreciation.
FIN	F7, V	Clears the financial registers.
REG	F7, B	Clears all registers (the stack, data, financial, and statistical registers).
Σ	F7, SHIFT-X	Clears the statistical storage registers and the stack registers.
12x	F8, Q	Multiplies the display value by 12 and stores the result in both register X and register n. See also 12÷.
12÷	F8, W	Divides the display value by 12 and stores the result in both register X and register i. See also 12X.
CFo	F8, E	Used at the beginning of a discounted cash flow problem; stores the display number in Ro and 0 in n, and sets No to 1. See also CFj.
CFj	F8, R	Used for all cash flows except the beginning cash flow in a discounted cash flow problem; stores the display number in Rj, adds 1 to n, and sets Nj to 1. See also CFo.
Nj	F8, T	Sets the number of periods CFo or CFj amounts apply to.
√x	F8, A	Finds the square root of the display number.
EXP	F8, S	Raises e (2.718281828) to the power of the display number to find the number's natural antilogarithm.

Table 24-1.   *The Financial Calculator Functions (continued)*

Function	Keystrokes	Action
LN	F8, D	Finds the natural logarithm of the display number, that is, its logarithm to the base *e*.
FRC	F8, F	Discards the display number's digits to the left of the decimal point, leaving a fraction.
INT	F8, G	Discards the display number's digits to the right of the decimal point, leaving an integer. (This function has no relation to the INT function invoked by F7, i.)
ΔDY	F8, [	Finds the number of days between the date in register Y and the display date.
DAT	F8,]	Given "display number" days past the date in register Y, finds the end date, and also the day (with 1 representing Monday and 7 representing Sunday).
BEG	F8, 7	Sets the annuity mode for payments due at the beginning of the payment period. Used for compound interest calculations. See also END.
DMY	F8, 4	Sets the calendar date format to Day-Month-Year (dd.mmyyyy). For example, after selection May 14, 1958 should be entered as 14.051958. See also MDY.
x,r	F8, 1	Finds a linear projection for x based on the rate of change of y.
x	F8, 0	Averages the x and y values in the statistics registers after you've used the + function.
END	F8, 8	Sets annuity mode for payments due at the end of the payment period. Used for compound interest calculations. See also BEG.
MDY	F8, 5	Sets calendar date format to Month-Day-Year (mm.ddyyyy). For example, after selection May 14, 1958 should be entered as 5.141958. This format is the default. See also DMY.
y,r	F8, 2	Finds a linear projection for y based on the rate of change of x.
s	F8, .	Finds the standard deviation of the x and y values in the statistical storage registers after you've used the Σ+ function.

Table 24-1.   *The Financial Calculator Functions (continued)*

Function	Keystrokes	Action
xw	F8, 6	Finds the weighted average of the x and y values in the statistics registers after you've used the Σ+ function.
n!	F8, 3	Finds the factorial of the display number.
Σ–	F8, &	Subtracts data from the statistics registers to correct data collection errors.
no symbol	F8, ENTER	Copies the contents of the Last X register to the display.

Table 24-1.   *The Financial Calculator Functions (continued)*

To get a feel for how to use the calculator keys to quickly compute simple interest, five-key problems, and statistical problems, go through the following exercises.

Calculating Simple Interest

To compute simple interest, first store the principal amount in register Present Value, the yearly interest rate in register Interest Rate, and the number of days the interest is accruing in register Number of Months. To then get the result, press F7, W to select the INT function. (Be sure not to confuse the interest function with the integer function, also labeled INT.) The 360-day interest is returned in register X and the 365-day interest is returned in register Z.

For example, assume you want to borrow $100,000 to start a small video rental business. Follow these steps to find the interest on the loan at 13 percent interest over 30 days:

1. Press F6 to display the financial registers.

2. Press F7, B to clear the financial registers. They should now all contain the value 0.

3. Type **100000** and press E to store the principal amount in the Present Value register.

4. Type **13** and press W to store the yearly interest rate in the Interest Rate register.

5. Type **30** and press Q to store the number of days the interest is accruing in the Number of Months register.

6. Press F7, W to select the INT function. The result, –1,083.33, appears for 360-day interest. The amount is negative because you're paying it, not receiving it.

7. Press C, C to roll down the contents of register Z into register X. You now see the result, –1,068.49, for 365-day interest.

Calculating Five-Key Problems

To solve five-key problems, first enter appropriate data into four of the five financial registers, and then select the function representing the fifth register to calculate the solution. Make sure that the values in registers Number of Months, Interest Rate, and Payment always refer to the same Defined Interest Period.

For example, assume you want to borrow $10,000 to buy a state-of-the-art home entertainment system. The current interest rate is 12.5 percent A.P.R. (Annual Percentage Rate), and you want a 24-month loan with regular payments at the end of each month, that completely pays off the loan in the two-year period. Follow these steps to find your monthly payment:

1. Press F6 and F7, B to display and clear the financial registers. They should now all contain the value 0.

2. Press F8, 7 to bring up the "beg" annunciator below the display window. (If you press the 7 on the numeric keypad, be sure that NUM LOCK is on so that the key registers as 7 and not HOME.) This sets Begin mode for payments made at the *beginning* of each period.

3. Press F8, 8 to switch to End mode. The annunciator disappears. Stay in End mode, since in this problem the payments will be made at the *end* of every month.

4. Type **10000** and press E to store the loan you're receiving in the Present Value register.

5. Type **24** and press Q to store the number of monthly payments in the Number of Months register.

6. The values in Payment, Number of Months, and Interest Rate must all refer to the same time period. Since in this case Payment and Number of Months are monthly, you must convert the A.P.R. to a monthly D.I.R. (Defined Interest Rate). To do so, type **12.5**, and then press F8, W to divide the rate by 12. The result, 1.04, is automatically copied to the Interest Rate register.

7. The only number left to enter is Future Value, which in this case represents the amount remaining after the 24th payment. Since in this problem the goal is to pay back, or amortize, the loan by the 24th payment, the 0 currently in

the register is appropriate. (If you did not clear the register in step 1, simply type **0** and press T to clear it now.)

8. Press R to select the Payment function. The message "Calculating" appears briefly in the display window, and then the answer, –473.07, comes up. As in the previous problem, the result is negative because you're paying it, not receiving it.

Now assume you can spare only $350 a month to pay off your $10,000 loan. Follow these steps to find out what the remaining balance, or balloon payment, will be after 24 months:

1. Type **350** for the new payment amount.

2. Since this is money you're paying out, change the positive value to negative by pressing] to select the CHS function.

3. Press R to store the –350 in the Payment register.

4. The other financial registers still contain your entries from the previous problem, so simply press T to select the Future Value function. The answer, –3,336.16, is displayed.

Calculating Statistical Problems

To perform statistical analysis on a set of data points, enter each data point into register X—and if two variables are involved, also register Y—and press & to select the ¨+ function, which accumulates the data in the statistical registers. If you make an entry error, reproduce the error and press F8, & instead of &. This will undo your mistake.

For example, assume a business had the following quarterly profits in the past two years:

Last Year	This Year
12,000	20,000
10,000	24,000
15,000	30,000
21,000	34,000

Follow these steps to accumulate the data for last year using register X and this year using register Y, and then find the average quarterly profit for each year:

1. Press F5 to display the stack.

2. Press F7, X to clear both the stack and the statistical registers R1 through R6.

3. Type **20,000** and press ENTER to place this year's first quarter profits in Y.

It isn't necessary to include commas in your numeric entries. However, you may sometimes find that it makes entering long numbers less confusing. The HP calculators totally ignore any commas you type.

4. Type **12,000** to place last year's first quarter profits in X.

5. Press & to store your first set of values in the statistics registers. A 1 is displayed to indicate your first set of data points.

6. Type **24,000**, press ENTER, type **10,000**, and press &. A 2 is displayed for your second set of data points.

7. Type **30,000**, press ENTER, type **15,000**, and press &. A 3 is displayed for your third set of data points.

8. Type **34,000**, press ENTER, type **21,000**, and press &. A 4 is displayed for your fourth set of data points.

9. Press F8, 0 to find the average quarterly profits for each year. Last year's average, 14,500, appears.

10. Press V to swap the contents of the X and Y registers. This year's average, 27,000, is now displayed.

11. You can now continue performing calculations on the data you've entered using only a couple of keystrokes. For example, press F8, 6 to compute the weighted average, press F8, . (F8 and a period) to compute the standard deviation, and so on. For more information on these and related functions, see Table 24-1.

Saving and Exiting the Financial Calculator

Once you're done using the Financial Calculator, you can save it and exit by pressing ESC or clicking on the window's Close box. The contents of the registers, as well as your display settings, are automatically saved for future sessions (in a file named FINCALC.TMP), and the calculator closes.

Using the Programmer's Calculator

As mentioned previously, the Programmer's Calculator is a simulation of the HP-16C. It's a superb tool for anyone working with hexadecimal (base 16, typically abbreviated as *hex*), octal (base 8), and/or binary (base 2) numbers. The calculator automatically converts between these number systems and decimal (base 10), and can perform computations in any of the four number systems. In addition, it provides numerous functions for shifting, rotating, masking, ANDing, ORing, and otherwise manipulating bits.

To examine the Programmer's Calculator, press ALT, D, C, P, or click on the Desktop menu and select Calculators and Programmers Calculator. The screen in Figure 24-5 appears.

At the bottom of the screen is the message bar, which tells you that pressing F4 displays the stack and pressing F6 displays the data registers.

At the top of the screen are three menus of the Programmer's Calculator (and, in the right corner, the system time). The Control and **D**esktop menus are in all Desktop applications, and information about them appears in Chapter 19; **R**egisterDisplay contains two redundant calculator options. To view the latter, press ALT, R or click on the menu. You now see the options, which simply duplicate the function key commands for displaying the stack and displaying the data registers. To close the menu, press ESC.

The heart of the calculator is its window, which consists of two parts. Its lower portion, which makes up the bulk of the window, is a calculator keypad especially suited for programmers. The numerous functions these keys provide are listed and defined in Table 24-2.

In Table 24-2, unless otherwise stated, all results are returned in register X.

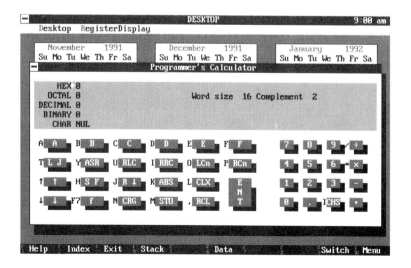

Figure 24-5. *The Programmer's Calculator screen*

Function	Keystrokes	Action
A	A	Enters a hexadecimal A.
B	B	Enters a hexadecimal B.
C	C	Enters a hexadecimal C.
D	D	Enters a hexadecimal D.
E	E	Enters a hexadecimal E.
F	F	Enters a hexadecimal F.
LJ	T	Left justifies the bit pattern in register X within its word size. The result is returned in register Y, while the number of bit shifts that took place is returned in X.
ASR	Y	Shifts the word in register X one bit to the right. The rightmost bit drops off into the carry bit and whatever number was there previously is inserted in the leftmost position (retaining the number's sign).
RLC	U	Rotates the word in register X one bit to the left through the carry bit.
RRC	I	Rotates the word in register X one bit to the right through the carry bit.
LCn	O	Rotates left the word in register Y through the carry bit the number of times specified in register X.
RCn	P	Rotates right the word in register Y through the carry bit the number of times specified in register X.
↑	UP ARROW	Like ↓, sets numbers to display and calculations to take place in the number base the triangle cursor points to. Options are hex, octal, decimal, binary, and char (which displays the corresponding ASCII code or IBM graphics character for the number's last two hex digits).
SF	H	Sets the flag.
R↓	J	Rotates the stack contents down once.
ABS	K	Finds the absolute value of the number in register X.
CLX	L	Clears register X.

Table 24-2. *The Programmer's Calculator Functions*

Function	Keystrokes	Action
↓	DOWN ARROW	Like ↑, sets numbers to display and calculations to take place in the number base the triangle cursor points to. Options are hex, octal, decimal, binary, and char (which displays the corresponding ASCII code or IBM graphics character for the number's last two hex digits).
f	F7	Activates the function at the top of the next key selected.
CRG	N	Clears the data registers.
STO	M	Stores the number in register X into a specified data register (type the register number after selecting the function).
RCL	,	Recalls a specified data register's contents into register X.
ENT	ENTER	Copies the number in register X into register Y and disables stack-lift for the next entry.
7	7	Enters the number 7.
8	8	Enters the number 8.
9	9	Enters the number 9.
÷	/	Divides.
4	4	Enters the number 4.
5	5	Enters the number 5.
6	6	Enters the number 6.
x	* or X	Multiplies.
1	1	Enters the number 1.
2	2	Enters the number 2.
3	3	Enters the number 3.
−	−	Subtracts.
0	0	Enters 0.
.	.	Sets the decimal place.
CHS	]	Changes the sign of the number in register X.
+	+	Adds.

Table 24-2.   *The Programmer's Calculator Functions (continued)*

Function	Keystrokes	Action
SL	F7, A	Shifts the word in register X one bit to the left. The leftmost bit drops off into the carry bit and a 0 is inserted in the rightmost position.
SR	F7, B	Shifts the word in register X one bit to the right. The rightmost bit drops off into the carry bit and a 0 is inserted in the leftmost position.
RL	F7, C	Rotates the bits in register X one bit to the left.
RR	F7, D	Rotates the bits in register X one bit to the right.
RLn	F7, E	Rotates left the word in register Y the number of times specified in register X.
RRn	F7, F	Rotates right the word in register Y the number of times specified in register X.
#B	F7, T	Counts the number of bits in the number in register X.
DBR	F7, Y	Divides a double word, with its high bits in the Y register and its low bits in Z, by the single word in register X. The remainder is returned to X and the quotient is lost. (See also function DB÷.)
DB÷	F7, U	Divides a double word, with its high bits in the Y register and its low bits in Z, by the single word in register X. The quotient is returned to X and the remainder is lost. (See also function DBR.)
DBX	F7, I	Multiplies the single words in registers X and Y and returns a double-word result, with X holding the most significant bits and Y the least significant bits.
√x	F7, O	Finds the square root of the number in register X.
1/X	F7, P	Finds the reciprocal of the number in register X.
RST	F7, UP ARROW	Restores the calculator's startup state, clearing registers and resetting defaults.
CF	F7, H	Clears the flag.
R↑	F7, J	Rotates the stack contents up once.
X'Y	F7, K	Swaps the X and Y registers' contents.
BSP	F7, L or BACKSPACE	During entry of a number, erases the last digit; after entry, clears the number.
CPX	F7, N	Cancels the F prefix of a partially entered command.

Table 24-2.   *The Programmer's Calculator Functions (continued)*

Function	Keystrokes	Action
WSZ	F7, M	Sets word size.
PRC	F7, ,	Sets the number of decimal places displayed based on the number in register X.
LST	F7, ENTER	Copies the contents of the Last X register to register X.
MKL	F7, 7	Creates left-justified mask of 1s in the current word size. The number of 1s in the mask is based on the number in register X. (Turn leading zero control on before using this function.)
MKR	F7, 8	Creates right-justified mask of 1s in the current word size. The number of 1s in the mask is based on the number in register X. (Turn leading zero control on before using this function.)
RMD	F7, 9	Divides the number in register Y by the number in register X and returns the remainder in register X.
XOR	F7, /	Compares the single words in registers X and Y and enters a 1 bit in the result only where the corresponding bits are different from each other.
SB	F7, 4	Sets the bit of a number in register Y to 1. The bit to set is specified by the number in register X.
CB	F7, 5	Clears a bit of a number in register Y to 0. The bit to clear is specified by the number in register X.
ZER	F7, 6	Inserts leading zeros in the binary, octal and hex versions of the number in register X. Selecting the function again eliminates the leading zeros.
AND	F7, *	Compares the single words in registers X and Y and enters a 1 bit in the result only where both corresponding bits are 1.
1s	F7, 1	Sets 1's complement mode.
2s	F7, 2	Sets 2's complement mode.
UNS	F7, 3	Sets unsigned mode.
NOT	F7, –	Reverses all bits in the number in register X.
OR	F7, +	Compares the single words in registers X and Y and enters a 0 bit in the result only where both corresponding bits are 0.

Table 24-2. *The Programmer's Calculator Functions (continued)*

The other part of the window is its upper quarter. It's here that you enter and view numbers. It's also here that you select the number system you want to use for entering and computing, as well as for displaying the numbers in the data and stack registers. Your options are hex, octal, decimal, binary, and char (which displays the corresponding ASCII code or IBM graphic character for a number's last two hex digits). However, regardless of your choice, the currently displayed value is automatically shown in *all* the number systems in the window's upper-left corner.

Follow these steps to get a feel for selecting number systems, entering numbers, and viewing the effects of your actions on the registers:

1. Press DOWN ARROW until the triangle-shaped cursor is at the DECIMAL option, or just click the option.

2. Type **22**. The following conversions automatically appear:

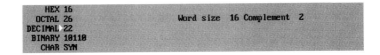

```
    HEX 16
  OCTAL 26
DECIMAL▶22                Word size  16 Complement  2
 BINARY 10110
   CHAR SYN
```

3. Press DOWN ARROW to select the BINARY option.

4. Type **11010**. Again, appropriate conversions are automatically displayed.

5. Press F4 to display the stack. The register contents are represented in binary, as shown here:

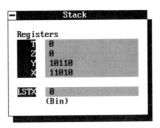

```
┌─────────────────────────┐
│ ─        Stack          │
├─────────────────────────┤
│ Registers               │
│    T    0               │
│    Z    0               │
│    Y    10110           │
│    X    11010           │
│                         │
│   LSTX  0               │
│         (Bin)           │
└─────────────────────────┘
```

Unlike the Financial and Scientific calculators, the Programmer's Calculator can't display the stack while you enter data, so press ESC to close the display.

6. Press UP ARROW three times to select HEX.

7. Press F4 to display the stack again. The register contents are now represented in hex. Press ESC.

8. Press UP ARROW to wrap around to the CHAR option.

9. Type **M, 0** to use the STO function to copy the current number to data register R0.

10. Press F6 to display the ten data registers. The register contents of 1A hex and 0 are represented in ASCII codes.

11. Press ESC to close the data register display.

Differences with the HP-16C

The Programmer's Calculator simulates many aspects of the HP-16C, but not all of them. The principle differences in the Desktop version are as follows:

- The HP-16C's programming capabilities aren't supported.

- Because there's no programming, significantly fewer functions need to be represented. Therefore, there's no "g" key in the Desktop keypad.

- Scientific notation is not supported.

- Floating-point precision is set by entering the number of decimal places desired and then selecting the PRC function, as opposed to the HP-16C method. (You can also initiate floating point automatically by just entering a decimal fraction.)

Saving and Exiting the Programmer's Calculator

Once you're done using the Programmer's Calculator, you can save it and exit by pressing ESC or clicking on the window's Close box. The contents of the registers, as well as your display settings, are automatically saved for future sessions (in a file named HEXCALC.TMP), and the calculator closes.

Using the Scientific Calculator

As mentioned previously, the Scientific Calculator is a simulation of the HP-11C. It's a powerful tool for working out complex arithmetic, probability and statistics, and transcendental function problems. However, the Desktop version does *not* support the HP-11C's programming capabilities.

To take a closer look at the Scientific Calculator, press ALT, D, C, S, or click on the Desktop menu and select Calculators and Scientific Calculator. Once again, the screen in Figure 24-4 appears.

At the bottom of the screen is the message bar, which tells you that pressing F5 displays the stack, pressing F6 displays the first set of data registers, and pressing F4 suppresses any register display.

At the top of the screen are the three menus of the Financial Calculator (and, in the right corner, the system time). The Control and Desktop menus are in all Desktop applications, and information about them appears in Chapter 19. However, RegisterDisplay is devoted to calculator-related options. To examine it, press ALT, R or click on the menu.

You now see options that duplicate the function key commands for suppressing a register display, displaying the stack, and displaying the first set of ten data registers. In addition, the last option displays the second set of ten data registers. To close the menu, press ESC.

The calculator additionally contains statistical storage registers for solving statistical problems. However, you can't display these registers. Data is entered into them directly from the calculator during appropriate computations.

At the upper-right of the screen is the display window, which is where you enter numbers and see the results of your computations. You can set the number of decimal places displayed by pressing F7, 7 to select the FIX function and then pressing a digit from zero to nine; the default is four. You can also set decimal places in a scientific notation format by pressing F7, 8 to select the SCI function, and then pressing a digit from zero to six; or set the display to engineering notation by pressing F7, 9 to select the ENG function. Regardless of your display settings, the Scientific Calculator represents each number internally as a ten-digit mantissa and a two-digit exponent of 10.

The heart of the calculator is its keypad, which fills most of the window. The numerous functions these calculator keys provide are listed and defined in Table 24-3.

In Table 24-3, the display number is the number in register X. However, keep in mind that a number may be rounded in the display due to decimal place settings, while the number stored internally in register X is never affected by such settings unless explicitly rounded by the RND function.

Function	Keystrokes	Action
e↑x	W	Raises e (2.718281828) to the power of the display number to find the number's natural antilogarithm.
10↑x	E	Raises 10 to the power of the display number to find the number's common antilogarithm.
Y↑X	R	Raises register Y's contents to the power of the display number.

Table 24-3.   The Scientific Calculator Functions

Function	Keystrokes	Action
1/X	T	Finds the reciprocal of the display number by dividing it into 1.
HYP	S	Finds the hyperbolic sine, cosine, or tangent of the display number using SIN, COS, and TAN, respectively.
SIN	D	Finds the sine of the display number.
COS	F	Finds the cosine of the display number.
TAN	G	Finds the tangent of the display number.
f	F7	Activates the function at the top of the next key selected.
STO	N	Stores the display number into a specified data register.
√x	X	Finds the square root of the display number.
R↓	C	Rolls the stack down by one register.
x↔y	V	Swaps the X and Y registers' contents.
←	B or BACKSPACE	During entry of the display number, erases the last digit; after entry, clears the display number.
g	F8	Activates the function at the bottom of the next key selected.
RCL	M	Recalls a specified data register's contents to the display.
EEX	[	Makes the next number entered an exponent of the display number.
CHS	]	Changes the sign of the display number.
7	7	Enters the number 7.
4	4	Enters the number 4.
1	1	Enters the number 1.
0	0	Enters the number 0.
8	8	Enters the number 8.
5	5	Enters the number 5.
2	2	Enters the number 2.
.	.	Sets the decimal place.
9	9	Enters the number 9.

Table 24-3.   *The Scientific Calculator Functions (continued)*

Function	Keystrokes	Action
6	6	Enters the number 6.
3	3	Enters the number 3.
Σ+	&	Collects data from registers X and Y into the statistics registers R0-R5. See also Σ-.
÷	/	Divides.
*	*	Multiplies.
−	−	Subtracts.
+	+	Adds.
ENTER	ENTER	Copies the number in register X into register Y and disables stack-lift for the next entry.
FRAC	F7, N	Discards the display number's digits to the left of the decimal point, leaving a fraction.
Σ	F7, X	Clears the statistics registers and all stack registers except the Last X register.
REG	F7, V	Clears all data registers.
PREFX	F7, B	Cancels the F or G prefix of a partially entered command.
<-R	F7, [	Converts the numbers in registers X and Y representing polar coordinates (magnitude r, angle $\emptyset$) to rectangular coordinates (x,y). See also <-P.
Pi	F7,]	Enters pi carried to up to nine decimal places (3.141592654).
FIX	F7, 7	Sets the number of decimal places displayed (press a number from 0 to 9 after selecting the function).
Pyx	F7, 1	Finds the number of permutations of y taken x at a time without repetitions.
x!	F7, 0	Finds the factorial of the display number.
SCI	F7, 8	Sets the display to scientific notation.
HMS	F7, 2	Converts the display number from a decimal hours (or degrees) format to hours (or degrees), minutes, seconds, decimal seconds format. See also H.

Table 24-3. *The Scientific Calculator Functions (continued)*

Function	Keystrokes	Action
y,r	F7, .	Finds the linear estimate and correlation coefficient after you've used the Σ+ function to accumulate statistics.
ENG	F7, 9	Sets the display to engineering notation.
RAD	F7, 3	Converts the display number from decimal degrees to radians. See also DG.
L.R	F7, &	Finds the linear regression, with the slope in register Y and intercept in register X, after you've used the Σ+ function to accumulate the statistics of a series of two or more data pairs.
ENTER	F7, ENTER	Copies the number in register X into register Y and disables stack-lift for the next entry.
LN	F8, W	Finds the natural logarithm of the display number, that is, its logarithm to the base e.
LOG	F8, E	Finds the common logarithm of the display number, that is, its logarithm to the base 10.
%	F8, R	Finds the display number percent of the number in register Y.
Δ%	F8, T	Finds the percent difference between the display number and the number in register Y.
AHYP	F8, S	Finds the inverse hyperbolic sine, cosine, or tangent of the display number using SIN, COS, and TAN, respectively.
ASIN	F8, D	Finds the arcsine of the display number.
ACOS	F8, F	Finds the arccosine of the display number.
ATAN	F8, G	Finds the arctangent of the display number.
INT	F8, N	Discards the display number's digits to the right of the decimal point, leaving an integer.
x°	F8, X	Finds the square of the display number.
R↑	F8, C	Rolls the stack up by one register.
RND	F8, V	Rounds the actual display number (not just its display on screen) to the number of digits specified by the current FIX, SCI, or ENG setting.
CLX	F8, B	Clears the display number (register X).

Table 24-3. *The Scientific Calculator Functions (continued)*

Function	Keystrokes	Action
<-P	F8, [	Converts the numbers in registers X and Y representing rectangular coordinates (x,y) to polar coordinates (magnitude r, angle $\varnothing$). See also <-R.
ABS	F8,]	Finds the absolute value of the display number.
DEG	F8, 7	Sets the display to degrees (for trigonometric functions). See also RAD and GRD.
Cyx	F8, 1	Finds the number of combinations of y taken x at a time without repetitions.
x	F8, 0	Averages the x and y values in registers R1 and R3 after you've used the Σ+ function.
RAD	F8, 8	Sets the display to radians (for trigonometric functions). See also DEG and GRD.
H	F8, 2	Converts the display number from hours (or degrees), minutes, seconds, decimal seconds format to decimal hours (or degrees) format. See also HMS.
s	F8, .	Finds the standard deviation of the x and y values in the statistics registers after you've used the Σ+ function to accumulate statistics.
GRD	F8, 9	Sets the display to grads (for trigonometric functions). See also DEG and RAD.
DG	F8, 3	Converts the display number from radians to decimal degrees. See also RAD.
Σ-	F8, &	Subtracts data from the statistics registers to correct data collection. See also Σ+.
ENTER	F8, ENTER	Copies the contents of the Last X register to the display.

Table 24-3. *The Scientific Calculator Functions (continued)*

Saving and Exiting the Scientific Calculator

Once you're done using the Scientific Calculator, you can save it and exit by pressing ESC or clicking on the window's Close box. The contents of the registers, as well as your display settings, are automatically saved for future sessions (in a file named SCICALC.TMP), and the calculator closes.

Chapter *25*

Using the Database Manager

The Desktop database manager, *Databases,* is surprisingly powerful for a pop-up application. It enables you to create and edit database structures; add, edit, and delete data; sort, search, and select data; create data forms and form letters; and even dial a selected telephone number with your modem.

Another important aspect of Databases is that it reads and writes files in the popular dBASE format. This means you can use it to access the vast number of existing dBASE files, and to exchange data with most database users and programs. It also means that Databases provides a very convenient alternative to loading a full-featured dBASE-compatible program every time you want to work with some data.

Additionally, like any Desktop application, Databases lets you open up to 15 windows containing database or other Desktop files. This is a feature that many standalone database programs lack, so if you have a special need for it, you may actually find Databases to be your database manager of choice. (For more information, see "Opening Multiple Windows" in Chapter 19, "Desktop Manager Overview.")

This chapter first explains database concepts and terms, and details Databases' technical specifications. It then covers such database basics as defining fields, entering records, moving around and editing records, sorting records, searching and selecting records, hiding and deleting records, and printing. Lastly, it covers such advanced topics as editing field definitions, using and creating forms, creating form letters, transferring and appending records, using the Autodialer, and working on a network.

Understanding Database Concepts and Terms

Before using a database manager, you should understand what a database is, what it's used for, and how it's structured. The next two sections cover these topics.

If you're already familiar with such terms as fields and records, you may want to skip ahead to the "Examining Database Files" section.

Understanding Database Uses

A *database* is a collection of related information, or data. The data is typically organized in a format that allows it to be stored, retrieved, and manipulated easily. Some everyday examples of a database are a telephone book, a library card catalog, and a list of the movies in your videotape collection.

You can maintain a database manually with index cards, filing cabinets, or some other nonelectronic system. However, if you have a lot of data, or if you want to deal with data quickly and flexibly, it's more efficient to keep them in a computer database manager such as Databases.

For example, if created properly, a Databases file tracking your videotape collection could quickly find you all the movies with the word "Alien" in the title, or all movies that were made in 1976, or all movies that shared some other common detail. In addition, it could swiftly sort your entire movie list alphabetically by title, or chronologically by release date, or by some other appropriate criteria. Furthermore, it would make it easy for you to enter, edit, and delete movie entries.

Another advantage of a database is that it's flexible enough to handle a number of different types of information. Typical office uses of databases include managing such varied data as inventory, billing, accounts receivable, and personnel files.

What gives a database this flexibility, as well as a certain amount of rigidity, is its structure. This topic is covered in the next section.

Understanding the Database Structure

You can think of a database as being divided into columns and rows. For example, typical entries in an address database might be displayed as follows:

FIRST_NAME	LAST_NAME	ADDRESS
Norma	Baker	32-36 Wildwood Lane
Issur	Danielovitch	2155 Argo Street
W.C.	Dunkenfield	800 Murdock Avenue
Frances	Gumm	1 Moonshadow Place
Betty	Perske	1940 Winsor Plaza
Bernie	Schwartz	222 Kingsbridge Road

Notice that the data is grouped into three columns. The first column is devoted to first names, the second holds only last names, and the third exclusively contains addresses. In Databases, these columns are called *fields.* As these examples indicate, a field is devoted to one particular kind of data, such as first names, ZIP codes, telephone numbers, ID codes, salaries, birthdays, and so on.

The data is also grouped into a number of rows. For example, the first row contains Norma Baker's first name, last name, and address. While these are different types of data, they're all *conceptually* related because they all concern the same person, Norma Baker. Similarly, the fourth row contains information revolving around Frances Gumm, and the sixth row holds information about Bernie Schwartz. In Databases, these rows are called *records.* As these examples indicate, a record contains a group of data items related to a particular person, place, or thing.

To create a database, you first define its structure by naming and setting the characteristics of each of its fields. Once these field definitions are completed and saved, you can enter your data into them, typically a record at a time. When your data entry is completed, both the field definitions and the data records are saved in the same file. This file has a DBF extension and is dBASE-compatible.

The best way to clarify these concepts is to look at an actual file. The steps for doing this are covered in the next section.

Examining Database Files

Databases enables you to open an existing database with only a few keystrokes. Once the file is open, you can display records one record at a time (which is especially convenient when you need to enter new records), or you can view multiple records organized in columns and rows. The latter format is called *browse mode,* because it lets you browse through many records at a time. You can switch between these two display formats with the **File B**rowse command. The bulk of this chapter will use browse mode, which is the default.

In both display formats, you can move forward and backward by field using TAB and SHIFT-TAB, to the next and previous records using F6 and F5, to the end and beginning of a record using END and HOME, and to both the beginning and end of the database using F4. In addition, PC Tools 7 gives you the new ability of jumping to a record in a field sorted alphabetically by simply pressing the first letter of the record.

The Desktop comes packaged with a sample address file named SAMPLE.DBF. To get a better feel for how databases are structured, follow these steps to examine SAMPLE.DBF:

1. First, call up the Desktop Manager. If you've installed the Desktop to be memory resident, press CTRL-SPACEBAR. Otherwise, type **DESKTOP** from the DOS prompt and press ENTER.

2. Press ENTER or click on Desktop to display the main menu.

3. Press D or click on Databases to select the application. The File Load dialog box appears.

4. Type **SAMPLE** and press ENTER. A database window like this appears:

If your window isn't in the same column-row format, press ALT, F, B. You should see a sample file demonstrating how to store an address book. It includes fields for company names, last and first names, phone numbers, addresses, and comments. It currently holds three records devoted to fictional characters such as Roger Rabbit. Only three fields are initially visible: COMPANY, LAST_NAME, and FIRST_NAME.

5. Press TAB five times. The SALUT (for salutations), PHONE, and ADDRESS fields scroll into view, as well as part of the CITY field.

6. Press TAB again. The CITY field comes fully into view, as well as the STATE field (which holds two-letter state abbreviations), and part of the ZIP field.

7. Press TAB three more times. The fields for ZIP (which holds ZIP codes) and COMMENTS (which holds brief notes) fully scroll into view.

8. Press TAB again. Nothing happens, meaning that COMMENTS is the last field in the database.

9. Press SHIFT-TAB three times. You're moved back three fields.

10. Press HOME. You're returned to the first field.

11. Press B. You're moved to the record beginning with the letter B, as indicated by the Rolodex-style lettering at the top of the window. (This Rolodex feature only works when the **F**ile **M**odify **D**ata switch is *off*. Therefore, if pressing B didn't move you to another record, first press ESC to cancel your typing, then press ALT, F, M to turn off the switch, and then try again.)

12. The third line of the window shows you're on record 3 of 4. Press F6 to move down a record. The Record indicator now shows you're on record 4.

13. Press F4. You're moved to the top of the database.

14. Press F4 again. You're moved back to the bottom, as indicated by the Record indicator.

15. Press ESC to close the file. You're returned to the Desktop screen.

Understanding Databases' Limits

A database file can be fairly small, like the one you've just examined, or large enough to encompass scores of fields and thousands of records. However, there are certain limits on Databases you should keep in mind. Specifically:

- It can't support a database structure larger than 128 fields.

- It can't support a field larger than 70 characters.

- It can't support a record totaling more than 4000 characters.

- While it supports most dBASE data types, Databases does *not* support memo fields.

- It can't support a database with more than 10,000 records.

If you load or copy records from a database that exceeds these limits to a Databases file, Databases will read in as much data as possible and ignore the rest. For example, if a field has more than 70 characters, Databases will copy only the first 70; if a database has more than 10,000 records, Databases will load in only the first 10,000; and if a database has memo fields, Databases will ignore those particular fields.

Databases' 10,000-record capacity isn't absolute; it's proportionally diminished when you use a large field for sorting (see "Sorting the Database"). However, you can sometimes "trick" Databases into letting you add more records by exiting it and then starting it again. You can also use the Edit Delete and Edit Pack Database commands to make more room by deleting obsolete records (see "Deleting Records"). Finally, you can opt to sort on a smaller field.

Understanding Databases' REC and FOR Files

As mentioned previously, a database's field definitions and its records are saved together in a dBASE-compatible file with a DBF extension (for example, CLIENTS .DBF).

In addition, Databases supports two supplementary file types which are similar to, but *not* compatible with, dBASE NDX and FMT files.

The first has the same name as the database file but the extension REC, for record (for example, CLIENTS.REC). It maintains record display information, such as the order in which sorted records appear and which records are set to be hidden from view. REC files are created and managed directly by Databases, so you never have to access them yourself.

The second type has the extension FOR, for form. This file is a Notepads document that contains a mix of descriptive text and areas for displaying field data. A form can display the database one record at a time, as opposed to the column-row format you've seen until now.

Databases automatically creates a default form with the same name as the database (for example, CLIENTS.FOR). In addition, you can create your own custom forms (for example, CLIENTS2.FOR) to enhance the data's display clarity, and so help cut down on data entry and interpretation errors. For more information, see "Using Forms" later in this chapter.

You now have a grasp of the underlying concepts of Databases. The rest of this chapter will be devoted to understanding and using Databases features.

Creating a Database

Previously, you examined existing database files. In this section, you'll learn how to create a database yourself. This is an important skill, because it allows you to make customized databases that are tailored to your unique needs. For this example, you'll create a movie database for a videotape rental catalog.

Examining the Field Editor

To begin creating your database, follow these steps to open a new file and bring up a dialog box for defining fields:

1. You should be at the main Desktop screen. Press D,D to select Databases. The File Load dialog box appears.

2. Type **MOVIES** to create a database file named MOVIES.DBF. (If you don't specify an extension, DBF is automatically appended to your filename.)

3. Press ALT-N, or press ENTER twice, or click New. The following Field Editor dialog box appears for creating the database structure:

On the left side of the box are four options: Field Name, Field Type, Size, and Decimal.

The Field Name option sets the name of the field you're creating. This name must begin with a letter, must have a length of one to ten characters, and cannot contain any spaces (although you can separate words with an underscore). It doesn't matter whether you enter the name in upper- or lowercase, as it's automatically set to all uppercase when it's added to the database structure.

The four Field Type selections define the type of data the field will hold. Related to them are the Size option, which defines how large the field will be, and (for numeric data only) the Decimal option, which sets the number of decimal places.

If you're using PC Tools 7.0, the Decimal option might not accept a value of 0, preventing you from defining a numeric field to contain whole numbers. This problem, along with a number of other problems, has been fixed in version 7.1. For more information, see the "PC Tools 7.0 versus 7.1" section in this book's Introduction.

The field types and their corresponding size limits are as follows:

- *Character*   This data type is for letters, certain symbols (specifically, _, #, $, *, &, and ASCII graphics characters), and static numbers (that is, numbers you would not perform calculations on, such as telephone numbers and ZIP codes). Its field size can be up to 70 characters. Its default size is *1* and its default value is *a space*.

- *Numeric*   This data type is for dynamic numbers—that is, numbers you can perform calculations on, such as inventory counts or salaries. (Databases can't perform calculations, but you can always transfer numeric fields into a more powerful dBASE-compatible program that *does* support calculations.) Its field size can be up to 19 characters, which includes an optional plus or minus sign, an optional decimal point, and optional decimal places. Its default size is *1* with no decimal place, and its default value is *0*.

- *Logical*   This data type is for information that can be represented as "Y" for "Yes" and "N" for "No," or "T" for "True" and "F" for "False." This option is useful for tracking conditions with only two possibilities, such as whether or not a client has paid a bill, or whether a test question has been marked true or false. It's always set to a size of *1* and has a default value of *F*.

- *Date*   This data type is for dates in *MM/DD/YY* (month/day/year) format, with 19 assumed as the first two digits of the year. It's always set to a size of *8* and has a default value of *no date*.

On the right side of the dialog box are six additional options: Add, Delete, Next, Prev, Save, and Cancel.

- **A**dd enters the current field definition into the database structure, and **D**elete removes the current field definition from the database structure. Both options then move you to the next field.

- **N**ext and **P**rev simply move you to the next or previous field.

- **S**ave saves all your field definitions and changes, exits the dialog box, and moves you to the database records.

- **C**ancel abandons all your new field definitions and changes, and closes the dialog box. Pressing ESC has the same effect.

While in most parts of the Desktop pressing ESC saves your work and then closes it, in the Field Editor pressing ESC abandons your work, losing all your new field definitions and changes. Furthermore, it does so without providing any warning. Therefore, when you're ready to save and exit your field definitions and changes, be sure to select the Save option by pressing ALT-S or clicking Save with your mouse.

Defining Fields

You're now ready to create the structure of your movie database, which will contain four fields. The first field will hold each movie's title, the second its release date, the third its running time in minutes, and the fourth a "Y" or "N," indicating whether the movie is currently available on videotape.

First, follow these steps to define the movie title field:

1. Type **TITLE** for the Field Name and press ENTER. You're moved to the Character option.

2. Movie titles consist of characters, so press ENTER to accept the Character data type. You're moved to the Size option.

3. The longest movie title used in this chapter is 31 characters, so type **31** and press ENTER. You're moved to the Decimal option.

4. Decimal size doesn't apply to character fields, so press ENTER to skip this option. You're moved to the Add option.

5. Press ENTER to add this first field to the database structure. You're moved to the second field, as shown by the Field Number counter changing from 1 to 2.

Next, follow these steps to define the release date field:

1. Type **RELEASED** for the Field Name and press ENTER. You're moved to the Character option.

2. Press UP ARROW and ENTER to select the Date data type. You're moved to the Size option.

3. Date fields are automatically set to a size of 8, so press ALT-A to skip the Size and Decimal options and just add this second field to the database structure. You're moved to the third field.

4. Press ALT-P or click Prev to move back to the RELEASED field. Notice the Size option indicates that as soon as the field was added, its size was automatically set to 8.

5. Press ALT-N or click Next to return to the next open field.

Now follow these steps to define the running time field:

1. Type **MINUTES** for the Field Name and press ENTER. You're moved to the Character option.

2. Minutes are numbers you can perform calculations on, so press DOWN ARROW and ENTER to choose the Numeric data type. You're moved to the Size option.

3. No movie is likely to run longer than 999 minutes, so type **5** and press ENTER to set the field to hold up to three whole-number digits, a decimal point, and a decimal digit. You're moved to the Decimal option.

4. Allow a single decimal place by typing **1** and pressing ENTER. You're moved to the **Add** option.

5. Press ENTER to add this third field to the database structure. You're moved to the fourth field.

Lastly, follow these steps to define the videotape availability field:

1. Type **AVAILABLE** for the Field Name and press ENTER. You're moved to the Character option.

2. This field will hold only "Y" and "N," so press DOWN ARROW twice and press ENTER to choose the Logical data type.

3. Logical fields are automatically set to a size of 1, so press ALT-A to skip the Size and Decimal options and just add this fourth field to the database structure. You're moved to the fifth field.

You've now completed entering your field definitions. The next step is to save them. To do so, press ALT-S or click Save. After a moment, the definitions are saved to disk and the database screen in Figure 25-1 appears. (If your window isn't in column-row format, press ALT, F, B.) It's in this screen that you'll be performing most of your database activities.

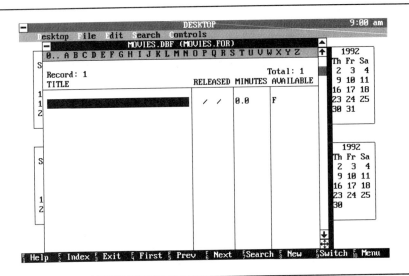

Figure 25-1. The MOVIES database screen

The Databases Message Bar

At the bottom of the screen is the message bar. When a Databases activity is taking place, the bar displays appropriate definitions or instructions. Otherwise, it displays the following commands assigned to the function keys:

Function Key	Action
F1 (Help)	Brings up context-sensitive help
F2 (Index)	Brings up the online help index
F3 (Exit)	Performs the same functions as ESC
F4 (First)	Moves you to the first or last record
F5 (Prev)	Moves you to the previous record
F6 (Next)	Moves you to the next record
F7 (Search)	Selects Search Find Text in Sort Field
F8 (New)	Selects Edit Add New Record
F9 (Switch)	Activates a different open window
F10 (Menu)	Performs the same functions as ALT

Navigating the Databases Menus

At the top of the screen are the six menus available in Databases (and, in the right corner, the system time). Follow these steps to examine the menus:

1. Press ALT, F or click on File to display the File menu, which lets you load a form, print selected records, copy records to and from other databases, switch

between displaying records in column-row and form formats, and toggle on or off the ability to modify the data you're browsing.

2. Press RIGHT ARROW to display the Edit menu, which lets you add, delete, undelete, hide, and permanently remove records; select certain records or all records; sort records based on a particular field; and edit a database's field definitions.

3. Press RIGHT ARROW again to display the Search menu, which lets you search for text in all fields, search for text only in the sort field, or go to a specified record number.

4. Press RIGHT ARROW again to display the Controls menu, which lets you control the page layout for printing, adjust Autodial settings, use the Autodialer to call the phone number in the current record, and save your Control and Controls menu settings as new defaults.

5. Press RIGHT ARROW again to wrap around to the Desktop menu, which lets you have up to 15 Desktop files open simultaneously.

6. Press ESC and ALT-SPACEBAR to display the Control menu, which lets you change the current window's colors, position, and size.

7. Press ESC to close the menu and return to the database.

Of these menus (see Figure 25-2), the options in Control and **Desktop** are in every Desktop application, and are covered in Chapter 19, "Desktop Manager Overview." However, virtually all the options in File, Edit, Search, and Controls are unique to Databases. These options are covered in the following sections, and are also listed and described in the "Databases Command Reference" section at the end of this chapter.

Entering Records

You've finished defining and saving your fields, and you've examined the Databases screen. You're now ready to enter data.

The database must always contain at least one record. Therefore, as shown previously in Figure 25-1, the first record has been automatically inserted, with default values of 0 for the Numeric field and F for the Logical field. You can replace these values with your own by simply writing over them. Once you're done with the first record, you can add more records by pressing F8 or by selecting the Edit Add New Record command.

Databases automatically orders, or *sorts*, your records as you enter them. This sorting is based on the data in a particular field. If you don't specify a *sort field*, Databases defaults to using the first field.

To get a feel for the process, enter some Disney movies into your database. First, follow these steps to enter "Snow White and the 7 Dwarfs":

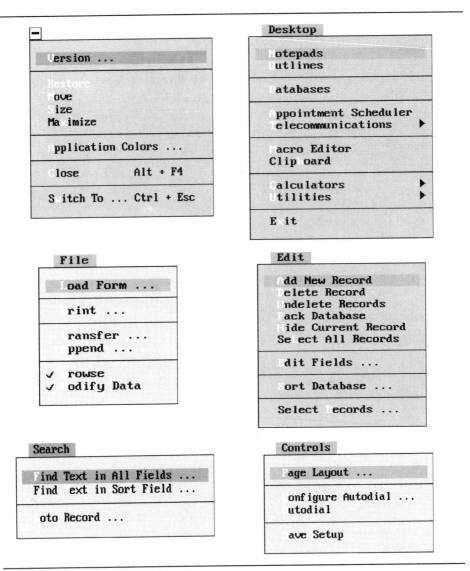

Figure 25-2.   The Databases menus

1. Press ALT, F, or click on the File menu, to check the status of the Modify Data switch. If there's currently no checkmark by the option, press M or click the option to turn it on. (Otherwise, just press ESC to close the menu.) You can now enter data instead of just viewing it.

2. For the title, type **Snow White and the 7 Dwarfs**. If you make a typing mistake, use BACKSPACE or DEL to erase the error, and then type in the correct text.

You can also clear *all* your text as you're entering it by pressing ESC, and then type the title again from scratch.

3. When you're done entering the title, press ENTER. You're moved to the RELEASED field.

4. For the release date, type **02/04/38** and press ENTER. You're moved to the MINUTES field.

5. For the running time, type **83**, press SPACEBAR to erase the extra zero, and press ENTER. You're moved to the AVAILABLE field.

6. For videotape availability, type **N** for No. You've now completed the first record.

Next, follow these steps to enter "Fantasia":

1. Press F8 to add a new record. Databases initially adds new records to the front of the database, so the "Snow White" record is pushed down into the number 2 position.

2. For the title, type **Fantasia** and press ENTER. Databases now automatically checks the alphabetical order of this entry against other entries in the TITLE field. Since "Fantasia" is alphabetically ahead of "Snow White," its record remains in the top position.

3. For the release date, type **11/13/40** and press ENTER.

4. For the running time, type **120** and press ENTER.

5. For videotape availability, type **N** for No. You've completed this record.

Now follow these steps to enter "Pinocchio":

1. Press F8 to add a third record. A new record is again inserted at the front of the database, and the Fantasia and Snow White records are pushed down.

2. For the title, type **Pinocchio** and press ENTER. Databases again checks the alphabetical order of your new entry against the other TITLE field entries. Since "Pinocchio" follows "Fantasia" alphabetically, its record is moved to the number 2 position, and Fantasia temporarily scrolls out of view as it returns to the top position.

3. For the release date, type **02/23/40** and press ENTER.

4. For the running time, type **88**, press SPACEBAR to erase the extra zero, and press ENTER.

5. For videotape availability, type **Y** for Yes. You've completed this record.

Use the procedures just covered to enter the following additional seven records. Keep in mind that each new record will be sorted alphabetically after you type its TITLE data and press ENTER.

TITLE	RELEASED	MINUTES	AVAILABLE
Dumbo	10/23/41	64	Y
Bambi	08/13/42	69	Y
Cinderella	02/15/50	74	Y
Alice in Wonderland	07/28/51	75	Y
Peter Pan	02/05/53	77	N
Lady and the Tramp	06/16/55	75	Y
One Hundred and One Dalmatians	01/25/61	79	N

When you're done, press F4 to move to the top record. Your database should look like this:

```
┌─────────────────────────────────────────────────────────────┐
│ ─           MOVIES.DBF (MOVIES.FOR)                        ▲ │
│ 0.. -A- B C D E F G H I J K L M N O P Q R S T U V W X Y Z ↑ │
│                                                              │
│ Record: 1                                    Total: 10       │
│ TITLE                           RELEASED MINUTES AVAILABLE   │
│ ┌──────────────────────────────┬────────┬──────┬─────────┐  │
│ │ Alice in Wonderland          │07/28/51│ 75.0 │Y        │  │
│ │ Bambi                        │08/13/42│ 69.0 │Y        │  │
│ │ Cinderella                   │02/15/50│ 74.0 │Y        │  │
│ │ Dumbo                        │10/23/41│ 64.0 │Y        │  │
│ │ Fantasia                     │11/13/40│120.0 │N        │  │
│ │ Lady and the Tramp           │06/16/55│ 75.0 │Y        │  │
│ │ One Hundred and One Dalmations│01/25/61│ 79.0 │N        │  │
│ │ Peter Pan                    │02/05/33│ 77.0 │N        │  │
│ │ Pinocchio                    │02/23/40│ 88.0 │Y        │  │
│ │ Snow White and the 7 Dwarfs  │02/04/38│ 83.0 │N        │  │
│ └──────────────────────────────┴────────┴──────┴─────────┘  │
└─────────────────────────────────────────────────────────────┘
```

You now know how to open a new Databases file, define its fields, and enter records into it to create a new database. The next section covers how to manipulate your existing records.

Manipulating Database Records

In addition to storing data, a database must allow you to quickly and easily retrieve and manipulate data. Databases therefore provides a number of commands for navigating, editing, sorting, searching, selecting, hiding, and deleting database records. Once you're done, Databases will print the resulting records to paper. The following sections detail these features.

Navigating and Editing Records

One of the advantages of Databases is the ease with which you can move around its records. If you have a mouse, you can scroll through the database vertically. In addition, Databases provides a number of movement shortcut keystrokes.

As mentioned earlier in "Examining Database Files," you can move forward and backward by field using TAB and SHIFT-TAB, to the next and previous record using F6 and F5, to the end and beginning of a record using END and HOME, and to both the beginning and end of the database using F4.

Keystroke	Action
TAB	Move to the next field
SHIFT-TAB	Move to the previous field
CTRL-END	In browse mode, move to the last record; in a form, move to the end of the form
CTRL-HOME	In browse mode, move to the first record; in a form, move to the start of the form
PGDN	Move down by window
PGUP	Move up by window
CTRL-PGDN	Scroll down one line (independent of the cursor)
CTRL-PGUP	Scroll up one line (independent of the cursor)
F6	Move to the next record
F5	Move to the previous record
F4	Move to the first record; if already at the first record, move to the last record
ALT, S, G (**S**earch **G**oto Record)	Move to the specified record number
ALT, S, F (**S**earch **F**ind Text in All Fields)	Move to the specified text string
ALT, S, T (**S**earch **F**ind **T**ext in Sort Field)	Move to the specified text string in the sort field

When Modify Data is ON

letter	Overwrite current data
RIGHT ARROW	Move forward by character
LEFT ARROW	Move backward by character
CTRL-RIGHT ARROW	Move forward by word
CTRL-LEFT ARROW	Move backward by word

Table 25-1.   Databases Keystroke Movement Shortcuts

Keystroke	Action
END	Move to the end of the field; if already at the end, same as END, END
HOME	Move to the start of the field; if already at the start, same as HOME, HOME
END, END	Move to the end of the record; if already at the end, same as END, END, END
HOME, HOME	Move to the start of the record; if already at the start, same as HOME, HOME, HOME
END, END, END	In browse mode, move to the end of the database
HOME, HOME, HOME	In browse mode, move to the start of the database

When Modify Data is OFF

letter	Move to the first record in the sort field that starts with the letter
RIGHT ARROW	Move to the next field, like TAB
LEFT ARROW	Move to the previous field, like SHIFT-TAB
END	Move to the end of the record
HOME	Move to the start of the record
END, END	Move to the end of the database
HOME, HOME	Move to the start of the database

Table 25-1.   Databases Keystroke Movement Shortcuts (continued)

Databases also offers such additional shortcuts as moving to a specified record number using the **Search Goto Record** command, and (when the **File Modify Data** switch is on) moving forward and backward by word using CTRL-RIGHT ARROW and CTRL-LEFT ARROW. A complete list of movement shortcut keystrokes appears in Table 25-1.

Once you've moved to the field entry you want to affect, first make sure the **File Modify Data** switch, which is a new option in PC Tools 7, is *on.* This allows you to revise the data you're viewing. To check the switch's status, press ALT, F, and then see if a checkmark appears next to the last option, **Modify Data.** If it does, simply press ESC to close the menu. Otherwise, press M to turn the switch on.

You can replace data by simply overwriting it, or insert new data by pressing INS to type in Insert mode. You can also delete characters using BACKSPACE and DEL. If you change your mind before leaving the field, you can cancel your revisions by pressing ESC.

For example, follow these steps to move to record 10 and change "7" to "Seven":

1. Press ALT, F or click on the File menu. If no checkmark appears next to Modify Data, press M; otherwise, just press ESC.

2. You should be on the first record of your MOVIES database. Press F4. You're moved to the first field of the last record.

3. Press CTRL - RIGHT ARROW four times to move to the 7.

4. Type **S**. The 7 is overwritten.

5. Press INS to turn on Insert mode. "INS" appears in the upper center of the window to show that whatever you type will now push existing text to the right instead of erasing it.

6. Type **even** and press ENTER. The change is completed and saved.

Now follow these steps to move to record 7 and change "One Hundred and One" to "101":

1. Press F5 three times to move to record 7.

2. Press SHIFT-TAB to move to the first field.

3. Press HOME to move to the beginning of the record.

4. Press INS to return to Overtype mode. The centered "INS" near the top of the window disappears.

5. Type **101**. The digits overwrite the word "One."

6. Hold down DEL until the next three words are erased. (If you press DEL too long, you can press ESC to recover the old title and then repeat steps 5 and 6.)

7. Press ENTER to save the change. Notice that the record is instantly repositioned as the first record. Databases considers numbers to be "alphabetically" higher than letters, so starting the title with a number put it at the top of the field's sort order.

Lastly, follow these steps to move to record 8 and change its AVAILABLE field from "N" to "Y":

1. To jump directly to the record, press ALT, S, G, or click on the Search menu and select Goto Record. The following dialog box appears:

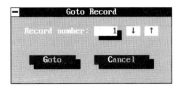

2. Type **8**, and then press ENTER twice or click Goto. You've moved to the second field of record 8.

3. Press TAB twice to move to the fourth field.

4. Type **Y** and press ENTER. The change is made and saved.

5. Press F4 to return to the top of the database. Your database now looks like this:

```
┌─────────────────────────────────────────────────────────┐
│ ▬            MOVIES.DBF (MOVIES.FOR)                   ▲  │
│            0  -1- 2 3 4 5 6 7 8 9  ..Z                 ♦  │
│ ┌─────────────────────────────────────────────────────┐ │
│ Record: 1                              Total: 10         │
│ TITLE                        RELEASED MINUTES AVAILABLE  │
│                                                          │
│ 101 Dalmations              01/25/61  79.0  N            │
│ Alice in Wonderland         07/28/51  75.0  Y            │
│ Bambi                       08/13/42  69.0  Y            │
│ Cinderella                  02/15/50  74.0  Y            │
│ Dumbo                       10/23/41  64.0  Y            │
│ Fantasia                    11/13/40 120.0  N            │
│ Lady and the Tramp          06/16/55  75.0  Y            │
│ Peter Pan                   02/05/33  77.0  Y            │
│ Pinocchio                   02/23/40  88.0  Y            │
│ Snow White and the Seven Dwarfs 02/04/38 83.0 N          │
└─────────────────────────────────────────────────────────┘
```

In addition to changing the database by editing records, you can change it by assigning it a different sort field. How to do this is covered in the next section.

Sorting Records

One of the most powerful features of Databases is its ability to quickly sort all database records from lowest to highest based on the data in a specific field.

So far, the movie database has been sorted alphabetically by movie title. It can just as easily be sorted chronologically by date, numerically by minutes, or logically by "N" and "Y" entries.

To choose a different sort field, press ALT, E, S, or click on the Edit menu and select Sort Database. A dialog box like this appears:

Near the top of the box are Field Number and Field Name indicators, which display the field currently selected. Below the indicators are four options: **Next,**

which selects the next record; **P**rev, which selects the previous record; **S**ort, which executes a sort using the selected field; and **C**ancel, which aborts the operation. Follow these steps to sort the movies based on each of the other three fields:

1. The Sort Field Select dialog box should still be open. Press ENTER or click Next to select the second field, RELEASED.

2. Press S or click Sort to execute the sort operation. The dialog box closes, and the records are rearranged from earliest to latest release date. Your database now looks like this:

```
┌─────────────────────────────────────────────────────────┬──┐
│ ▬          MOVIES.DBF (MOVIES.FOR)                        │▲ │
├───────────────────0─-1-─2 3 4 5 6 7 8 9 ..Z──────────────┼──┤
│                                                           │↑ │
│  Record: 1                                   Total: 10    │  │
│  TITLE                            RELEASED MINUTES AVAILABLE │
│ ┌──────────────────────────────┬────────┬─────┬─────────┐│  │
│ │Peter Pan                     │02/05/33│ 77.0│Y        ││  │
│ │Snow White and the Seven Dwarfs│02/04/38│ 83.0│N        ││  │
│ │Pinocchio                     │02/23/40│ 88.0│Y        ││  │
│ │Fantasia                      │11/13/40│120.0│N        ││  │
│ │Dumbo                         │10/23/41│ 64.0│Y        ││  │
│ │Bambi                         │08/13/42│ 69.0│Y        ││  │
│ │Cinderella                    │02/15/50│ 74.0│Y        ││  │
│ │Alice in Wonderland           │07/28/51│ 75.0│Y        ││  │
│ │Lady and the Tramp            │06/16/55│ 75.0│Y        ││↓ │
│ │101 Dalmations                │01/25/61│ 79.0│N        ││↔ │
│ └──────────────────────────────┴────────┴─────┴─────────┘│⊹ │
└─────────────────────────────────────────────────────────┴──┘
```

3. Bring up the dialog box again by selecting **E**dit **S**ort Database. The box confirms that the current sort field is field 2.

4. Press ENTER or click Next to select the third field, MINUTES.

5. Press S or click Sort. The dialog box closes, and the records are rearranged from shortest to longest running time.

6. Bring up the dialog box again by selecting **E**dit **S**ort Database. The box confirms that the current sort field is field 3.

7. Press ENTER or click Next to select the fourth field, AVAILABLE.

8. Press S or click Sort. The dialog box closes, and the records are rearranged alphabetically by "N" and "Y" entries, which represent availability on videotape.

  Notice that there are duplicate entries in the current sort field. It would be useful if Databases allowed you to designate a secondary sort field to permit further ordering under these circumstances. However, this feature isn't currently available in the Desktop. If you need to sort by more than one field, you should save your database file, exit the Desktop, and then order the file with a more powerful dBASE-compatible program.

9. Bring up the dialog box one more time by selecting **E**dit **S**ort Database. The box confirms that the current sort field is field 4.

10. Press P three times or click Prev three times to select the first field, TITLE, again.

11. Press S or click Sort. The dialog box closes, and the records are returned to their original alphabetical order.

You should note that the term "sorting" in most dBASE-compatible programs refers to physically ordering records in the database DBF file. However, this type of ordering is *not* supported in the Desktop. The sorting you've just been performing is instead equivalent to *indexing* in other dBASE programs. In other words, rather than adjusting the database records, you've been adjusting the pointers to each record, which are kept in the database's corresponding REC file (see "Understanding REC and FOR Files" earlier in this chapter). This method is generally much faster than physically ordering records.

This distinction can be ignored while you remain in the Desktop. If you access database files from another program, though, your sorting information won't be available because REC files are not dBASE-compatible. You can, however, always order the database again using the other program's indexing or sorting commands.

In addition to sorting records, you can search for records that contain particular data. How to do this is explained in the next section.

Searching Records

Just as you can search for text in a word processor such as Notepads, you can search for text in your database records. This is useful, for example, if you want to move to a record quickly but remember only one detail about it, or if you want to see how many records contain a certain piece of information.

The search does not distinguish between upper- and lowercase. Also, it doesn't distinguish between data types; for example, if you're searching for a number, it will find occurrences of that number regardless of whether it's in a character, numeric, or date field.

*The search feature acts as if the digits 19 are a part of the year portion of each date. Therefore, if you search for 1, 9, or 19, you'll match all dates in addition to nondate fields containing the digits. At the same time, this means you can enter **1990** to search for such dates as 12/03/90, as opposed to entering **90** and potentially matching nondate fields containing 90.*

You can choose to search all fields, or you can search in the sort field exclusively. To search all fields, press ALT, S, F, or click on the Search menu and select Find Text in All Fields. Alternatively, to search only in the sort field, press ALT, S, T, or press

F7, or click on the Search menu and select Find Text in Sort Field. In either case, a dialog box like this appears:

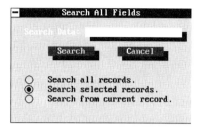

Near the top of the box is the Search Data option, which holds up to 20 characters of your search text (also called a *search string*). Directly below are the **S**earch option, which executes the operation, and the **C**ancel option, which aborts the operation.

Near the bottom of the box are the following three options, which determine how your search is conducted:

- *Search all records*   This option begins the search from the first record. It includes all records in the database or in the sort field, depending on the command you chose.

- *Search selected records*   This option begins the search from the first record. However, it excludes hidden and deleted records (which are covered in the next sections).

- *Search from current record*   This option begins the search from the current record. If the previous option chosen was Search All Records, it includes all records; if the previous option chosen was Search Selected Records, it excludes hidden and deleted records.

To close the box, press ESC or click Cancel.

To get a feel for database searching, follow these steps to find all movies with titles ending in the letter "A":

1. Press F7 to bring up the Search Sort Field dialog box.

2. Type **A** and a space. This will match all words in the TITLE field ending with "A" or "a."

3. Accept the default option of Search Selected Records and initiate the search by pressing ALT-S. You're moved to the first occurrence, which is "Cinderella" in record 4.

4. The dialog box has closed, so bring it up again by pressing F7. The Search from Current Record option is now selected. Accept it and press ALT-S to find the next occurrence. You're moved to "Fantasia" in record 6.

5. Press F7 and ALT-S again to find the next occurrence. In this case, there isn't one, so a dialog box appears telling you that no further match was found.

6. Press ENTER or click OK. The dialog box closes, and you're left on the last match found, the TITLE field of record 6.

Now try searching for dates by following these steps to find all movies released in 1940:

1. Press ALT, S, F to bring up the Search All Fields dialog box.

2. Type **1940**. This will match all dates in the RELEASE field (that is, the current sort field) for the year 1940.

3. Again, accept the default Search option by pressing ALT-S. You're moved to the first occurrence, which is 11/13/40 in record 6.

4. Press ALT-S, F, ALT-S to find the next occurrence. You're moved to 02/23/40 in record 9.

5. Press ALT-S, F, ALT-S to find the next occurrence. There are no more dates from 1940, so a dialog box again appears telling you that no other match could be found.

6. Press ENTER or click OK. The dialog box closes, and you're left on the last match found in record 9.

7. Press F4 to return to the top of the database.

Selecting Records

The Find Text commands covered in the previous section are useful for simple matching tasks. However, if you need access to a wider range of search criteria, or if you want to match a number of records simultaneously, or if you want to display only those records that match your criteria, you should use the **Edit Select Records** command instead. This option offers several powerful matching features.

First, it lets you use the ? *wildcard* symbol in your search string to represent any single character. For example, the search string COM?UTE? would match such words as "COMPUTER," "COMMUTER," and "COMPUTES."

Second, it lets you specify a *range* of text matches using the operator .. (two periods). For example, the search string "A..G" would match words beginning with the letter A, B, C, D, E, F, or G. Similarly, the string "AA..ATT" would match such words as "AARDVARK," "ARGUE," and "ATTACK."

You can also use .. to specify an *open range*. For example, "..T" matches data beginning with a character less than or equal to "T" (such as "100," "BAKER," "SISTERS," and "TELLER"); and "T.." matches data beginning with a character higher than or equal to "T" (such as "TELLER," "UNION," "ZERO," and "{NULL}").

Databases rates characters as higher or lower than others based on their ASCII codes. Therefore, to determine a character's relative order, bring up the ASCII table by pressing ALT, D, U, A, *and then search the table by pressing* DOWN ARROW *until you find the character you want. When you're done, close the table by pressing* ESC. *(For more information, see Chapter 28, "Using the Desktop Utilities.")*

In addition to these features for broadening a search, Select **R**ecords makes it possible to narrow a search by letting you set as many as eight different criteria simultaneously. For example, in an address database you could search the STATE field for all occurrences of "CA" *and* the LAST_NAME field for names in the range of "B..D". The result of the search would yield people living in California whose last names begin with B, C, or D.

Once a search is completed, only those records that have met your criteria are displayed. The rest of the records are hidden from view (until you bring them back using the **E**dit Select All Records command). This allows you to work with and print exclusively the data you want.

Despite all these features, however, Select **R**ecords lacks some of the advantages of the **S**earch menu commands. First, Select **R**ecords will check only the beginning of a field for a match, while the **S**earch commands will check the entire field. Second, Select **R**ecords will search only the fields you specify, while the Find Text in All Fields command will automatically search every field in the database. Third, using Select **R**ecords requires more work than the **S**earch commands because it forces you to type field names. Therefore, you won't want to use Select **R**ecords for *every* search activity, but you'll find it very useful for conducting complex and/or multiple field searches.

To get a feel for selecting records, follow these steps to display movies available on videotape and then narrow the search to titles in the "B" through "L" range:

1. Press ALT, E, R, or click on the Edit menu and click Select Records. The following dialog box appears:

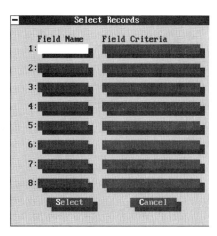

2. Type **AVAILABLE** and press ENTER to specify the field name you want to search. You're moved to the Field Criteria option.

3. Type **Y** to select only movies available on videotape.

4. Press ALT-S to execute the operation. The seven records that fit the criteria are selected, and the other three records are hidden. You could now work with the selected records or print them.

5. Display all database records again by pressing ALT, E, L, or by clicking on the Edit menu and clicking Select All Records.

6. Bring up the dialog box again by choosing **E**dit Select **R**ecords. Your previous entries still occupy the first option line.

7. Press TAB twice to move to the second Field Name option.

8. Type **TITLE** and press ENTER to also search in that field. You're moved to the second Field Criteria option.

9. Type **B..L** to narrow the search to titles beginning with the letters "B" through "L."

10. Press ALT-S or click Select to execute the operation. Now only the following four records are selected:

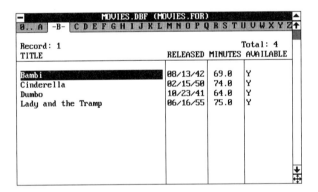

Of the other six records, three failed to meet the first criteria and three failed to meet the second criteria. If this was a large database, you might want to narrow the search even further by adding additional criteria.

11. Display all database records again by choosing **E**dit Select All Records.

Hiding and Deleting Records

In addition to hiding records that don't meet specified criteria, you can hide or delete individual records. If you know precisely which records you don't want to work with, it's sometimes easier to manually hide them than to create Select **R**ecords search criteria to eliminate them from the display.

To hide a record, simply move to it and select the **E**dit **H**ide Current Record command. For example, follow these steps to hide records 2 and 4:

1. You should currently be on record 1. Press F6 in order to move to record 2.

2. Press ALT, E, H, or click on the Edit menu and select Hide Current Record. The record disappears.

3. Press F6 twice to move to record 4.

4. Select **E**dit **H**ide Current Record again. This record also disappears.

5. Display all database records again by pressing ALT, E, L, or by clicking on the Edit menu and clicking Select All Records. The two hidden records reappear.

6. Press F4 to move back to record 1.

You can also choose to delete a record by moving to it and selecting the **E**dit **D**elete Record command. In Databases, deleting a record does *not* immediately remove it from the database. Instead, it *hides* it and also *marks* it for removal. You can later bring all deleted records back by selecting the **E**dit **U**ndelete Records command. Alternatively, you can *permanently remove* them by selecting the **E**dit **P**ack Database command. However, use this latter option with care, as there's no way to retrieve records after database packing.

*The **E**dit menu's **U**ndelete Records and **P**ack Database commands affect only deleted records, not hidden ones. Similarly, the **E**dit menu's Select All Records command affects only* hidden *records, not deleted ones.*

To demonstrate, follow these steps to delete records 2 and 4, then restore them, and then permanently remove record 4:

1. You should currently be on record 1. Press F6 to move to record 2.

2. Press ALT, E, D, or click on the Edit menu and select Delete Record. The record is both hidden and marked for removal.

3. Press F6 twice to move to record 4.

4. Select **Edit Delete** Record again. This record is also hidden and marked for removal.

5. Return all deleted records to normal status by pressing ALT, E, U, or by clicking on the Edit menu and choosing Undelete Records. The two hidden records reappear.

6. You're still on record 4. Select **Edit Delete** Record. The record is again hidden and marked.

7. Permanently remove all deleted records from the database by pressing ALT, E, P, or by clicking on the Edit menu and selecting Pack Database. The following message asking for confirmation appears:

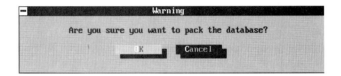

8. Press ENTER or click OK to verify you want to eliminate the records. The message "Please wait, the database is being packed" appears, and then the Cinderella record is erased, freeing up disk space.

One major reason for hiding or temporarily deleting records is to get irrelevant information out of the way before the database is printed. The procedures for printing are covered next.

Printing Records

One of the main strengths of an electronic database is its ability to quickly retrieve and print records. The methods for retrieving records were covered in the previous sections. Printing involves two commands: **Controls Page** Layout and **File Print**.

Controls Page Layout sets your printing margins and paper size. This command is identical to its counterpart in Notepads, so for more information see "Controls Page Layout" in Chapter 20, "Using Notepads." For best results, adjust all layout options appropriately before printing.

When you're done selecting the records you want to display and adjusting layout options, you're ready to use the **File Print** command. Follow these steps to do so using the default options:

1. Press ALT, F, P, or click on the File menu and select Print. If you're in browse mode, skip to step 5.

2. If you're using a form (see "Using Forms" later in this chapter), the following dialog box appears:

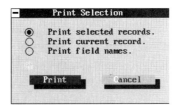

3. Choose Print Selected Records (the default); Print Current Record, which prints only the record currently displayed; or Print Field Names, which instead of records prints a list of the database field names.

4. Press P or click Print.

5. The Print dialog box appears. If necessary, select an appropriate printer port, and adjust the Number of Copies, Line Spacing, and Starting Page # options. (For more information about these options, see "Printing Your Document" in Chapter 20, "Using Notepads.") When you're ready, make sure your printer is on and online, and then press ALT-P or click Print. After a moment, the records you currently set to display are printed.

Advanced Databases Features

So far, this chapter has covered the basic commands for creating and working with databases. Databases also provides a number of advanced features to help you work more easily and efficiently. The following sections cover these features, which enable you to edit field definitions, use and create forms, create form letters, transfer and append records, electronically dial a record's telephone number, and work with database files on a network.

Editing Field Definitions

In earlier sections, you learned how to create a database by defining its fields. You aren't stuck with these initial field definitions, however. You can change any element of your database structure at any time.

To do so, press ALT, E, E, or click on the Edit menu and select Edit Fields. The same Field Editor dialog box you used earlier to define your structure appears. You can now use the **Next** and **Prev** commands to move to the fields you want to affect, and then edit data types or sizes. After making any field change, be sure to press ALT-A or click Add to register the change.

In addition, you can rename, delete, and add fields:

- To rename a field, simply move to its name and type a new name to replace the old one. Alternatively, you can use BACKSPACE and DEL to edit the existing name. When you're done, press ALT-A or click Add.

- To delete a field (including all its data), first move to the field, and then press ALT-D or click Delete. The field name disappears, and the field reverts to the Databases defaults. However, the field won't actually be deleted until you save your changes, so you can optionally change your mind by pressing ESC or clicking Cancel. Be sure to *use the Delete option with care,* as there's no way to retrieve a deleted field's data.

- To add a new field, first press ALT-N or click Next to move past all existing fields to the next empty field, and then enter the new field's name and settings. When you're done, press ALT-A or click Add.

When you've finished making *all* your changes, press ALT-S or click Save to save them to disk. The dialog box closes, and you're returned to the database.

If you revise the database structure by renaming, adding, or deleting a field, your default form (see the next section) must be updated for you to see the changes on your screen. This is true even if you're in browse mode. Furthermore, if you're using a custom form when the change is made, this active form must be updated as well.

In most cases, Databases will automatically update both your default form and active form for you. However, if you make several major changes in the Field Editor at once (for example, renaming a field and then adding a field), Databases may only update your display for the first change (for example, for the name change but not the added field). The other changes will also be implemented, but you'll need to manually change your forms to see them.

To avoid confusion, it's therefore recommended that you make all major changes in the Field Editor *one at a time.* For example, to rename a field and add another field, first bring up the Field Editor and rename the field, then save your change, then bring up the Field Editor a second time to add the other field, and then save this second change. Following this procedure should ensure that all your field definition changes show up on your screen. (Any nonactive custom form will have to be updated manually, though, regardless of how you save your changes.)

Because altering a database's structure can cause major changes in the file, it's highly recommended that you make a backup copy of your database before using the Field Editor. This will ensure that, if anything goes wrong, you still have your original file to go back to.

To briefly demonstrate how field editing works, follow these steps to expand the size of the TITLE field:

1. If the Field Editor dialog box isn't already open, press ALT, E, E, or click on the Edit menu and select Edit Fields. You're on the Field Name option of the first field.

2. Press TAB twice to move to the Size option.

3. Type **35** to replace the current size of 31.

4. Press ALT-A or click Add to enter the revised field definition to the database.

5. Press ALT-S or click Save to conclude the editing session and save your change. The TITLE field is now four characters longer, forcing the AVAILABLE field name to partially scroll off the window.

Using Forms

So far, you've been looking at the MOVIES database in the column-row browse mode format. As mentioned previously, Databases also lets you view one record at a time through a form. Databases automatically creates a default form with the name of your database and the extension FOR. In addition, you can create your own custom forms to enhance your data's display clarity, and so help cut down on data entry and interpretation errors.

You can switch between browse mode and the current form by using the File **Browse** command. The same procedures for moving around and editing records in browse mode work in the form. For example, while keeping an eye on the Record indicator near the top of the window, follow these steps to switch to the MOVIES default form and move around the database:

1. Press ALT, F, B, or click on the File menu and select Browse. The following screen appears:

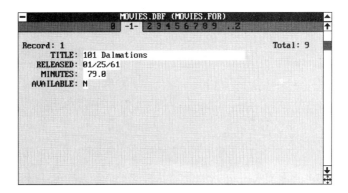

The Databases window will now display only one record at a time. This gives the window room to display many more fields per record simultaneously.

2. Press END. You're moved to the end of the field.

3. Press TAB. You're moved to the next field.

4. Press END, END. You're moved to the end of the record.

5. Press F6. You're moved to the next record.

6. Press F4 twice. You're moved to the last record.

7. Press F5. You're moved to the previous record.

8. Press F4 again. You're returned to the first record.

Now follow these steps to edit records 1 and 9 through the form:

1. Press ALT, F to see if the **File Modify Data** switch is on. If a checkmark doesn't appear by the option, press M; otherwise, press ESC.

2. You're currently on the title of the first record. Change "101" back to "One Hundred and One." First, press INS to switch to Insert mode. "INS" appears in the upper center of the window.

3. Type **One Hundred and One**. The previous text is pushed to the right.

4. Press DEL three times to erase "101."

5. Press ENTER to save the revision. The Record indicator shows the record is now demoted from its top spot to position 6. This is because the database is still being sorted by the TITLE field, and your edit changed the record's title to a lower alphabetical order.

6. Press F6 three times to move to record 9.

7. Change "Seven" to "7." First, press CTRL-RIGHT ARROW four times to move to "Seven."

8. Press INS to return to Overtype mode.

9. Type **7** to overwrite the "S."

10. Press DEL four times to erase the rest of the word.

11. Press ENTER to save your change.

If you don't care for the default form created by Databases, you can create your own forms. The steps for doing so are detailed next.

Creating Forms

A form is just a Notepads document. You can therefore create your own customized forms by opening a Notepads file, naming it with a FOR extension, entering descriptive text for each field, and entering the appropriate field names within square brackets. You can then load such forms using the **File Load Form** command.

Creating a form allows you to arrange the way your fields appear both onscreen and (when you're printing) on paper. It also allows you to use more descriptive labels for fields than their up-to-ten-letter names. Furthermore, creating a form enables you to enter additional text, such as a heading for the form.

For example, follow these steps to create a custom form for the MOVIES database:

1. Bring up Notepads by pressing ALT, D, N, or by clicking on the Desktop menu and selecting Notepads. The File Load dialog box appears.

2. Type **MOVIES2.FOR** to create a form file with a slightly different name than the current default form.

3. Press ALT-N, or press ENTER twice, or click New. A blank text file appears.

4. Press ALT, C or click on the Controls menu. If there's a checkmark by the **A**uto Indent option, press A or click the option to turn it off.

5. Press TAB five times and type **MOVIES DATABASE** to create a heading for the form.

6. Press ENTER three times to create some blank lines.

7. Press TAB, type **Movie Title:**, and type two spaces to label the first field.

8. Type **[TITLE]** to set the display location for the first field's data, and then press ENTER twice.

9. Press TAB, type **Release Date:**, and type two spaces to label the second field.

10. Type **[RELEASED]** to set the display location for the second field's data, and then press ENTER twice.

11. Press TAB, type **Running Time in Minutes:**, and type two spaces to label the third field.

12. Type **[MINUTES]** to set the display location for the third field's data, and then press ENTER twice.

13. Press TAB, type **Available on Videocassette?:**, and type two spaces to label the fourth field.

14. Type **[AVAILABLE]** to set the display location for the fourth field's data.

15. Press ALT, F, S to open the Save File to Disk dialog box.

16. Press SHIFT-TAB and UP ARROW, or click to the left of the PCTOOLS Desktop option, to select the format that preserves your layout settings. When you're done, press ALT-S or click Save. The file is saved.

In PC Tools 7, the default format for Notepads is ASCII, which fails to retain most Desktop formatting information. Therefore, it's important to explicitly save your form using the PCTOOLS Desktop option instead, following the procedures in steps 15 and 16.

17. Press ESC to close the window. You're returned to Databases.

18. Press ALT, F, L, or click on the File menu and select Load Form. A Load Form dialog box like this appears:

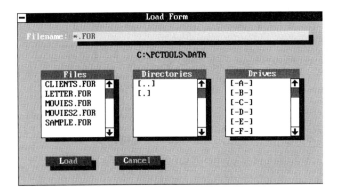

19. Type **MOVIES2** and press ENTER. You're switched from the default form to your customized form.

20. If your form isn't at full size, press ALT-SPACEBAR, X, or click on the window's triangular Maximize button in its upper-right corner. You should see the screen shown in Figure 25-3.

21. Press F4. You're moved to the first record.

22. Press F6. You're moved to the next record. Your form functions in the same way as the default form, but it's clearer and more attractive.

In addition to displaying records, you can use your custom forms to *print* records. This is particularly useful for generating form letters, as explained in the next section.

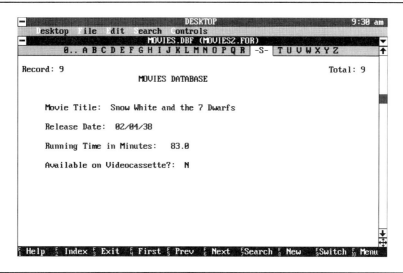

Figure 25-3. *A MOVIES database custom form*

Creating Form Letters

Letters that consist of the same text with different people's names and addresses plugged into appropriate spots are known as *form letters.* Such documents are usually generated by the merging of two files:

- A word processing file that contains the necessary text, together with designated locations for names and addresses.

- A database file that contains thousands of different names and addresses.

This is the same strategy employed by Databases with its forms. The forms are word processing (Notepads) files that contain a mix of text and designated locations for field data. Databases uses the template set by the form to funnel through field data for display and printing. Therefore, the same procedure for creating forms can be used to create form letters.

To create a form letter to work with a database address file such as SAMPLE.DBF, you could design something like the form in Figure 25-4. When you loaded the form, it would generate a display like the sample in Figure 25-5. This could then be printed with the **File Print** command (see "Printing Records" earlier in this chapter).

There are also more creative ways you can use form letters. Because of the tight integration between the Desktop's word processor and database applications, it's easy to experiment with different approaches until you find the form letter that best suits your needs.

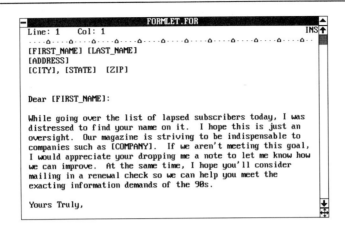

Figure 25-4. *A Databases template for a form letter*

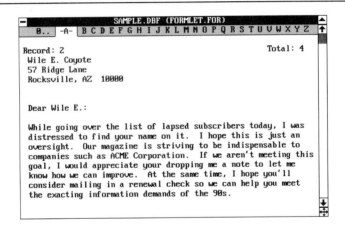

Figure 25-5. *A sample letter resulting from the template*

Appending and Transferring Records

Databases has two commands for copying records from one database to another. The File Append command copies *all* records *to* the current database from another database, while the File Transfer command copies *selected* records *from* the current database to another database.

To append records, follow these steps:

1. Open the database you want to append records to (in other words, your target file).

2. Press ALT, F, A, or click on the File menu and select Append. A list of existing database files appears.

3. Type in or select the name of the database you want to append from (in other words, your source file) and press ENTER. The operation commences.

To transfer records, follow these steps:

1. Open the database you want to transfer records from (in other words, your source file).

2. Press ALT, F, T, or click on the File menu and select Transfer. A list of existing database files appears.

3. Type in or select the name of the database you want to transfer to (in other words, your target file) and press ENTER. The operation commences.

In both appending and transferring operations, if your source file contains fields that your target file doesn't, the data in those fields will just be ignored. However, if your target file contains fields that your source doesn't, you'll be prompted to enter a default value for each such field.

When the operation is completed, all the source file records are copied to the end of the target file, and these new records automatically appear in sorted order along with the old records.

There's nothing in these procedures to screen out duplicate records from being copied. However, you can manually locate and remove duplicates after the copy takes place using the Edit Sort Database, Delete Record, and Pack Database commands (see "Manipulating Database Records" earlier in this chapter).

Using the Autodialer

If you tend to store telephone numbers on disk and you have a modem, you can turn your PC into an automatic dialing machine with the Desktop's Autodialer. This utility first searches for a number with three or more consecutive digits. The number can contain spaces, dashes, parentheses, hyphens, and the letter "x" for "extension." (It can also contain a "P" or "T" to specify pulse or tone dialing, a comma to pause two seconds before dialing continues, "@" or uppercase "W" to wait for a dial tone, and uppercase "K" to delay dialing until you select **R**esume Dialing from an Autodial Pause dialog box.)

In Databases, the Autodialer will search for this number exclusively in the selected record. Outside Databases, the Autodialer will search for the number anywhere on the screen.

PC Tools: The Complete Reference, Second Edition

When the Autodialer calls the number, first wait until you hear ringing, and then pick up the phone and press ESC to disengage the modem. You can then begin talking.

Configuring the Autodialer

Before using the Autodialer the first time, you have to adjust its settings for your phone line, modem, and telephone numbers. To do so, bring up any Databases file and press ALT, C, C, or click on the Controls menu and select Configure Autodial. The following dialog box appears:

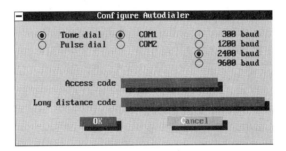

The box offers five items to adjust. First, select either Tone Dial or Pulse Dial, depending on your phone line. Second, select the COM port your modem is connected to. (If you're not sure, it's probably COM1.) Third, select the transmission speed, or *baud rate,* of your particular modem; the higher numbers represent faster speeds. Lastly, enter any Access Code and/or Long Distance Code numbers your phone system requires for you to get an outside line or to dial long distance. If you don't need such prefix digits, or if you include these prefixes within your individual phone numbers, leave these options blank.

When you're done adjusting your Configure Autodialer settings, save them and close the dialog box by pressing ALT-O or clicking OK. Your settings will remain in effect until you change them again.

If you've set a long distance prefix in the Autodialer and then later select a seven-digit phone number within Databases, the Autodialer is smart enough to suspect the number is local and provides the following prompt:

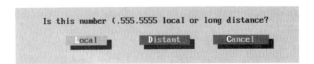

When this occurs, select **Local** to skip using the long distance prefix or **Distant** to include it.

Using the Autodialer in Databases

To invoke the Autodialer within Databases, press ALT, C, A, or click on the Controls menu and select Autodial. The Autodialer begins its search with the first character field of the current record (numeric and date fields are ignored).

As soon as the Autodialer finds a suitable number, it begins dialing it. Therefore, if you want to use this utility, you must define your telephone number field ahead of any other character field with data that the program would mistake for phone numbers (such as ZIP codes or addresses).

Once dialing begins, the following dialog box appears:

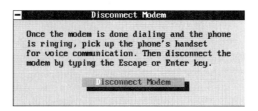

When you hear ringing, pick up the phone, and press ENTER or ESC, or click Disconnect Modem, to disengage your modem. You can then begin talking.

Using the Autodialer Outside Databases

If you're outside Databases, invoke the Autodialer by pressing the hotkey CTRL-O. The Autodialer begins its search with the top of your screen. When it finds a suitable number, the following dialog box appears:

To dial the current number, press ENTER or click Dial. To have the Autodialer search for the next telephone number on the screen, press N or click Next. To cancel the operation, press ESC or click Cancel.

Once dialing begins, the Disconnect Modem dialog box appears. When you hear ringing, pick up the phone, and press ENTER or ESC, or click Disconnect Modem, to disengage your modem. You can then begin talking.

Using Databases on a Network

Databases provides network support, so multiple network users can read the same database simultaneously. In addition, users with write privileges can revise any database. However, file-locking is supported, which means only *one* person can *write* to a database at a time. This ensures that database changes aren't accidentally lost in between file saves. Therefore, if you try to write to a file that's in the midst of being revised, you'll get a message explaining that you can't because the database is currently being written to by someone else.

Databases Command Reference

Most of Databases' power lies in its menu commands, which control how records are created, displayed, and printed. Like all Desktop applications, Databases' first two menus are Control and **Desktop**. These menus are covered in Chapter 19, "Desktop Manager Overview."

Databases also contains four additional menus: **File, Edit, Search,** and **Controls.** The following sections cover the options in these menus. After the name of each option are the keystrokes that invoke it, a description of what the option does, and a reference to the section in this chapter that discusses the option in detail.

The File Menu

The File menu performs such operations as loading forms, printing, copying records, switching between browse and form display modes, and switching between viewing and editing modes. It contains the following six options:

Load Form (ALT, F, L)

Loads a specified database form for displaying or printing records. Covered in "Creating Forms."

Print (ALT, F, P)

Prints specified records or the database field names. Covered in "Printing Records."

Transfer (ALT, F, T)

Copies selected records from the current database to a specified database. Covered in "Appending and Transferring Records."

Append (ALT, F, A)

Copies all records from a specified database to the current database. Covered in "Appending and Transferring Records."

Browse (ALT, F, B)

Switches between displaying multiple records in column-row format (or *browse* mode) and displaying one record at a time using a form. Covered in "Using Forms."

Modify Data (ALT, F, M)

Switches between letting you both view and modify records, or only view them. (When this option is off, you can move to a record in the sorted field by pressing its first letter.) Covered in "Navigating and Editing Records."

The Edit Menu

The **E**dit menu contains the following nine options for adding records, hiding and unhiding records, deleting and undeleting records, packing records, sorting and selecting records, and editing field definitions:

```
Edit
 dd New Record
 elete Record
 ndelete Records
 ack Database
 ide Current Record
Se ect All Records
 dit Fields ...
 ort Database ...
Select  ecords ...
```

Add New Record (ALT, E, A or F8)

Inserts a new record with default values. Covered in "Entering Records."

Delete Record (ALT, E, D)

Hides the current record *and* marks it for permanent removal. Covered in "Hiding and Deleting Records."

Undelete Records (ALT, E, U)

Restores all deleted records to normal status. Covered in "Hiding and Deleting Records."

Pack Database (ALT, E, P)

Permanently removes all deleted records from the database. Use with care, since there's no way to retrieve deleted records after packing. Covered in "Hiding and Deleting Records."

Hide Current Record (ALT, E, H)

Hides the current record. Covered in "Hiding and Deleting Records."

Select All Records (ALT, E, L)

Makes all hidden records display again. Covered in "Hiding and Deleting Records."

Edit Fields (ALT, E, E)

Lets you add and delete fields, and change field names, data types, and sizes. Covered in "Editing Field Definitions."

Sort Database (ALT, E, S)

Sorts database records from lowest to highest based on a specified field. Covered in "Sorting Records."

Select **R**ecords (ALT, E, R)

Hides all records not meeting specified criteria. Covered in "Selecting Records."

The Search Menu

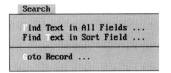

The **S**earch menu contains the following three options for finding specified records:

Find Text in All Fields (ALT, S, F)

Moves the cursor to the specified text string, which may be located in any field. Covered in "Searching Records."

Find **T**ext in Sort Field (ALT, S, T or F7)

Moves the cursor to the specified text string in the sort field. Covered in "Searching Records."

Goto Record (ALT, S, G)

Moves the cursor to the specified record number. Covered in "Navigating and Editing Records."

The Controls Menu

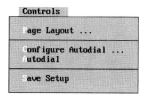

The **C**ontrols menu lets you adjust how your records are printed, configure settings for the Autodialer, use the Autodialer to dial a phone number, and save your current Control and **C**ontrols menu settings as defaults. The menu's four options are as follows:

Page Layout (ALT, C, P)

Sets printing margins and paper size. Covered in "Printing Records."

Configure Autodial (ALT, C, C)

Sets such Autodial options as tone versus pulse dialing, number of COM port, modem baud rate, and digit prefix codes. Covered in "Using the Autodialer."

Autodial (ALT, C, A)

Dials the telephone number in the current record. Covered in "Using the Autodialer."

Save Setup (ALT, C, S)

Saves the current Control and **C**ontrols menu settings to be used as defaults for new database files.

Chapter **26**

Using Telecommunications

The telephone line has traditionally been used for voice communications—that is, for speaking with people. However, because digital signals can be converted to audio tones, you can also use it for data communications—that is, for transferring data between machines.

Using a *modem,* which is a device that can transmit any kind of computer data over phone lines, and a program such as Modem Telecommunications, you have the ability to tap into a vast electronic universe of information. From the comfort of your home or office, you can dial into online libraries to search through encyclopedias, law books, and medical journals; news services to learn of the latest world events, stock prices, and sports scores; and electronic mail and bulletin boards to conveniently and affordably communicate with your fellow computer users around the world.

At the same time, using a *fax* (facsimile) board, which is a device that transmits text and graphics over phone lines, and a fax telecommunications program, you can join the enormous worldwide community of fax machine users. Without leaving your PC, you can receive documents from and send documents to any fax machine or other fax board.

This chapter first explains how to use the Modem Telecommunications program. Specifically, it covers configuring the program for your system; entering, editing, and deleting directory entries; saving and loading directories; dialing another computer system; sending and receiving files; using scripts; telecommunicating in the background; and accessing database files.

The chapter then describes how to use Electronic Mail, which is a new application in PC Tools 7 that automates the procedures for sending, receiving, and organizing online messages. The Electronic Mail sections describe how to configure the program, select an online service, create and send online messages, receive and read online messages, and schedule the automatic pickup and transmission of messages.

Lastly, the chapter details how to use the Desktop's two Fax Telecommunications programs. Specifically, it covers configuring the programs for your system; creating, editing, and sending a fax; and checking the Fax Log.

Using Modem Telecommunications

The Modem Telecommunications program provides such basic features as a phone directory that automatically dials the entry you select, and also offers you the option of entering a different phone number on the fly; an optional text buffer for storing everything that appears on your screen during an online session; and the ASCII and XMODEM transfer conventions, or *protocols*, for sending and receiving files.

The program also provides a number of advanced features, including the ability to transfer files in the background while you're doing work in other applications; the ability to write telecommunication programs, or *scripts*, to automate your online sessions; and the ability to access data directly from database fields.

Also, because Modem Telecommunications is part of the Desktop, you can use other Desktop applications in conjunction with it. For example, if you need to create or edit a message during an online session, you can do so using Notepads (see Chapter 20, "Using Notepads") rather than having to rely on the (often primitive) text editor of a computer service. Furthermore, if PC Shell is memory resident (see Chapter 15, "PC Shell Overview"), you can also readily view and manipulate your files during the online session.

In addition, if the Desktop is memory resident, you can invoke Modem Telecommunications from a non-PC Tools program. This is especially convenient if you tend to transmit files as soon as you're done creating them with your standalone word processor, spreadsheet, or other application.

To bring up Modem Telecommunications, follow these steps:

1. Call up the Desktop Manager. If you've installed the Desktop to be memory resident, press CTRL-SPACEBAR. Otherwise, type **DESKTOP** from the DOS prompt and press ENTER.

2. Press D or click on Desktop to display the main menu.

3. Press T or click Telecommunications. The following submenu appears:

```
 odem Telecommunications
 lectronic Mail
 end a Fax (requires fax board)
 heck the Fax Log
```

 If you haven't installed a fax board and the appropriate fax software to work with PC Tools, the two fax options don't appear on the submenu. For more information, see "Using Fax Telecommunications" later in this chapter.

4. Press M or ENTER; or click Modem Telecommunications. A screen like the one in Figure 26-1 appears. This is the *directory screen,* in which you adjust various telecommunications settings. When you're actually telecommunicating, a different *online screen* is displayed, as you'll see later in the chapter.

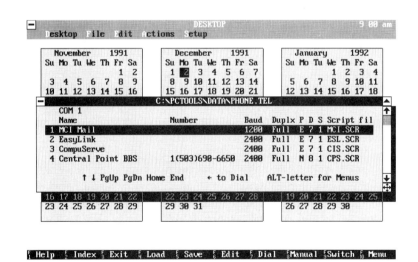

Figure 26-1. The Modem Telecommunications directory screen

Exploring the Directory Screen

In the center of the screen is the directory window, which holds the names, telephone numbers, and telecommunications settings of various computer systems you can dial into. A directory can hold up to 60 entries. If you need more space, you can create additional directory files, and then switch from one directory to another with a few keystrokes, as you'll see later.

The Desktop comes packaged with a directory named PHONE.TEL. If you haven't created other directories, PHONE.TEL is the file you're currently displaying, as indicated by its name in the window's title bar. (If another directory is displayed, switch to PHONE.TEL by pressing F4, selecting PHONE.TEL from the File List box, and pressing ENTER.)

This directory initially contains entries for four online services: MCI Mail, EasyLink, CompuServe, and the Central Point bulletin board service or *BBS*.

MCI Mail is a popular electronic mail center, serving over 400,000 subscribers. It allows you to create a letter in your word processor and then send the file to its destination within minutes. The letter can be electronically mailed to one person or to hundreds of people simultaneously. Like paper mail, the letter can be read at the convenience of each of its recipients, and each of the recipients' replies can be read at *your* convenience. Unlike the phone company and most online services, MCI Mail doesn't charge you based on the number of minutes you use it. Instead, like the post office, it charges you based only on the amount of mail you send out. MCI Mail also offers a number of other services, including fax and telex transmissions. If you're interested in more information, call (800) 444-6245.

EasyLink is an electronic mail center from AT&T that provides many of the same services as MCI Mail. In addition, because EasyLink was owned by Western Union until AT&T purchased it in January 1991, the service provides such Western Union specialties as mailgrams and telegrams. For more information, call (800) 832-7057.

CompuServe is one of the most popular online services in the world, serving over 800,000 subscribers. It offers an enormous variety of resources, including discussion forums on hundreds of topics, technical support sections hosted by major PC companies, areas for live online chatting with other subscribers, electronic shopping malls, indexes to material ranging from computer magazines to episodes of *Nightline,* sections for free and "try-before-you-buy" shareware programs that you can copy (or *download*) to disk, and (of course) electronic mail. CompuServe charges a base rate for the time you're on the system plus additional charges for various special features. If you're interested in more information, call (800) 848-8199.

The Central Point BBS is a service created specifically for users of PC Tools and other Central Point products. It provides a technical support team to answer your technical questions, a software area where you can download PC Tools utilities and information, and various bulletins about new Central Point activities. The BBS is free to Central Point customers. However, keep in mind that the phone company will bill you for whatever long distance charges you run up while using the system.

There are other useful services that also merit inclusion in the directory. However, discussing them is beyond the scope of this book. If you're interested in extensive coverage of the world of telecommunications, *Dvorak's Guide to PC Telecommunications* (Dvorak and Anis: Osborne/McGraw-Hill, 1990) is recommended.

The Directory Message Bar

At the bottom of the directory screen is the message bar. When a Modem Telecommunications directory activity is taking place, the bar displays appropriate definitions or instructions. Otherwise, it displays the following commands assigned to the function keys:

Function Key	Action
F1 (Help)	Brings up context-sensitive help
F2 (Index)	Brings up the online help index
F3 (Exit)	Performs the same functions as ESC
F4 (Load)	Selects File **L**oad
F5 (Save)	Selects File **S**ave
F6 (Edit)	Selects Edit **E**dit Entry
F7 (Dial)	Selects Actions **D**ial
F8 (Manual)	Selects Actions **M**anual
F9 (Switch)	Activates a different open window
F10 (Menu)	Performs the same functions as ALT

Navigating the Directory Menus

At the top of the directory screen are the six menus available for the Modem Telecommunications directory (and, in the right corner, the system time). Follow these steps to examine the menus:

1. Press ALT, F or click on File to display the **F**ile menu, which lets you save the current directory file and load a different directory file.

2. Press RIGHT ARROW to display the **E**dit menu, which lets you create, edit, and remove directory entries.

3. Press RIGHT ARROW again to display the **A**ctions menu, which lets you dial a selected phone number, dial a phone number you type in manually, and terminate your call.

4. Press RIGHT ARROW again to display the **S**etup menu, which lets you configure the program for your system, and toggle on or off two lines of status and help information at the bottom of the online screen.

5. Press RIGHT ARROW again to wrap around to the **D**esktop menu, which lets you have up to 15 Desktop files open simultaneously. However, it does *not* let

you have more than one Modem Telecommunications directory open at the same time.

6. Press ESC and ALT-SPACEBAR to display the Control menu, which lets you change the directory window's colors, position, and size.

7. Press ESC to close the menu and return to the directory window.

Of these menus (see Figure 26-2), the options in Control and **Desktop** are in every Desktop application, but virtually all the options in **File**, **Edit**, **Actions**, and **Setup** are unique to Telecommunications. In the following sections, you'll learn how to use these options to configure Modem Telecommunications for your system;

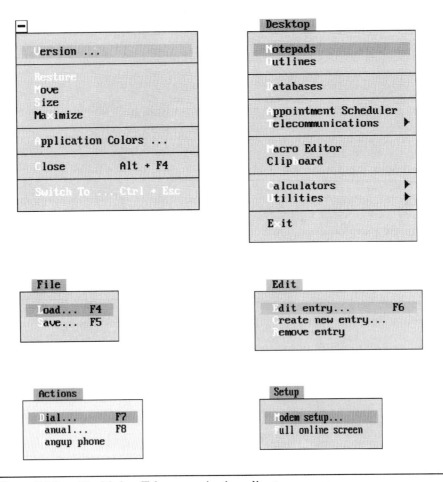

Figure 26-2. The Modem Telecommunications directory menus

create, edit, and delete directory entries; save, create, and load different directories; and call a selected computer system in a directory.

Configuring Modem Telecommunications for Your System

Before you can use Modem Telecommunications, you have to configure it for your particular modem, PC, and phone line. To do so, press ALT, S, M, or click on the Setup menu and select Modem Setup. This dialog box appears:

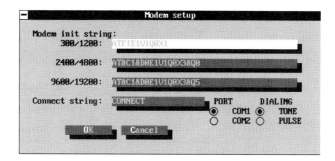

The box offers the following options:

- *Modem init string*   This option sets the startup modem code sequence, or *initialization string,* the program sends your modem when you dial an entry. If your modem is Hayes compatible (as are the vast majority of PC modems), you can skip this option. Otherwise, follow the instructions in your modem's manual to change the initialization strings appropriately.

- *Connect string*   This field sets the character sequence, or *string,* the program expects your modem to send once a connection is established. If you're using a Hayes compatible modem, accept the default string *CONNECT.* Otherwise, enter the string suggested by your modem manual.

- *Port*   This option specifies which communications, or COM, port in your computer your modem is attached to. This is usually COM1 or COM2.
    If you have a PS/2, or if you started the Desktop using the parameters /C3 or /C4 followed by *=IRQ,base port address* (for example, /C3=4,3E8), you can also use port COM3 or COM4. See your modem manual to find the appropriate values for IRQ and the base port address.

- *Dialing*   This option specifies whether you're using a pulse or tone phone line. The default is *TONE.*

When you're done adjusting options, press ALT-O or click OK to save your settings. The dialog box closes, and your COM port selection is displayed in the upper-left corner of the directory window. Modem Telecommunications is now set to work with your particular computer system. The next step is to enter the online services you're interested in.

Creating Directory Entries

As mentioned earlier, the directory holds the names, telephone numbers, and telecommunications settings of online services you can call. To create a new entry in the directory, press ALT, E, C, or click on the Edit menu and select Create New Entry. This Edit Phone Directory dialog box appears:

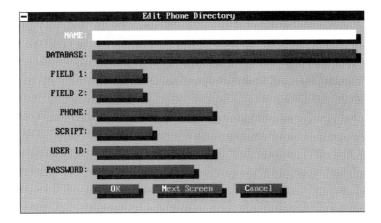

The box offers the following options:

- *NAME*   This field specifies the name of the online service (for example, MCI Mail). It can hold up to 56 characters, but only the first 24 characters will be displayed in the directory window.

- *DATABASE*   This optional field specifies the drive, directory, and file-name of a database whose fields you want to access (for example, C:\PCTOOLS\TELECOM.DBF). It can hold up to 56 characters. For more information on this and the following two options, see "Using Database Files" later in this chapter.

- *FIELD 1*   This optional field specifies the first database field whose data you want to access (for example, NAME).

- *FIELD 2*   This optional field specifies the second database field whose data you want to access (for example, MCI_ID).

- *PHONE*   This field specifies the telephone number of the online service. The number should include any appropriate access digits to get an outside line and long distance digits to dial long distance. For the sake of readability, separate the digits using spaces, parentheses, and dashes (for example, 1 (800) 555-5555). The field can hold up to 25 characters.

- *SCRIPT*   This optional field specifies the filename of any associated script (for example, MCI.SCR is the MCI Mail script file). For more information, see "Using Scripts" later in this chapter.

- *USER ID*   This optional field specifies the identification code by which you're known to the online service (for example, Rick). It can hold up to 25 characters and distinguishes between upper- and lowercase.

- *PASSWORD*   This optional field specifies the password you provide to access the online service (for example, Casablanca). It can hold up to 21 characters, and distinguishes between upper- and lowercase. Be sure to memorize your password; after you save your settings, the password is hidden to guard against its being seen by someone else.

When you're done adjusting the settings in the box, press ALT-N or click Next Screen. This second dialog box now appears:

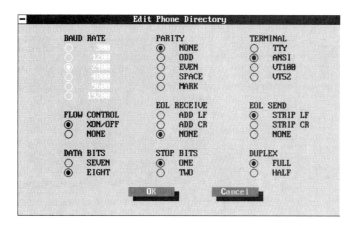

The box offers the following options:

- *BAUD RATE*   This option sets your transmission speed. You should choose the highest speed that both your modem *and* the computer system you're calling supports. The choices are 300, 1200, 2400, 4800, 9600, and 19200, with the higher numbers representing the faster speeds. The most common speeds are 2400 and 9600, and the default is *2400.*

- *PARITY*   This option sets the parity bit, which helps detect data errors. If this setting isn't compatible with the online service you're calling, you'll get meaningless character sequences on your screen. The choices are NONE, ODD, EVEN, SPACE, and MARK. The most common settings are NONE and EVEN, and the default is *NONE*.

- *TERMINAL*   This option sets the program's *terminal emulation*, meaning the group of codes the program will use to display characters and graphics onscreen. The choices are TTY, which emulates a plain teletype display; ANSI, which can display graphics and color on PCs that support such options and have the ANSI.SYS driver installed in CONFIG.SYS (see Appendix A, "PC Tools Installation and Configuration"); VT100, which emulates the DEC VT100 terminal; and VT52, which emulates the DEC VT52 terminal. The default is *ANSI*.

- *FLOW CONTROL*   This option sets the state of the XON/XOFF protocol, which helps ensure against data loss during ASCII file transfers. The default is *XON/XOFF*, meaning the option is on.

- *EOL RECEIVE/EOL SEND*   When set appropriately, these two "end of line" options ensure that every line of text ends with both a line feed, or LF, code to move the cursor down to the next line, and a carriage return, or CR, code to move the cursor to the beginning of the line. Specifically, if the online service sends only one of these two codes, set EOL RECEIVE to add the missing code when receiving text; and if the service expects to receive only one of these two codes, set EOL SEND to strip the unwanted code before sending text. The EOL RECEIVE choices are ADD LF, ADD CR, and NONE (meaning add no codes), and the default is *NONE*. The EOL SEND choices are STRIP LF, STRIP CR, and NONE (meaning strip no codes), and the default is *STRIP LF*.

- *DATA BITS*   This option sets the number of data bits, which helps detect data errors and must be compatible with the online service you're calling. The choices are SEVEN and EIGHT, and the default is *EIGHT*.

- *STOP BITS*   This option sets the stop bits protocol, which also helps detect data errors and must be compatible with the online service you're calling. The choices are ONE and TWO, and the default is *ONE*.

- *DUPLEX*   This option sets the protocol for properly displaying your typing on your screen. If you can't see what you're typing, select HALF; if you see two characters for each character you type, select FULL. Most online services are full duplex, so the default is *FULL*.

When you're done adjusting options, press ALT-O or click OK to save your settings. The dialog box closes, and your settings are entered into the next available line of the directory.

At first glance, creating an entry may look like a complicated operation. In reality, however, it's a relatively quick and easy procedure as long as you know the settings used by the computer system you're calling. To demonstrate, follow these steps to create an entry for the Central Point BBS that's customized to your particular computer system:

1. Press ALT, E, C, or click on the Edit menu and select Create New Entry. The Edit Phone Directory dialog box appears.

2. Type **Central Point BBS** and press ENTER to specify the service's name. You're moved to the DATABASE field.

3. You won't be using a database with this BBS, so skip the next three options by pressing ENTER three more times. You're moved to the PHONE field.

4. Type any appropriate outside line and/or long distance digits. For example, if you get long distance by dialing 1, type **1**.

5. Type **(503) 690-6650** and press ENTER to complete the telephone number. (The parentheses, space, and dash are optional; they just make the phone number more readable.) You're moved to the SCRIPT field.

6. Type **CPS.SCR**, which is the filename of the script packaged with PC Tools to automate calling the BBS, and press ENTER. You're moved to the USER ID field.

7. Unless you've called the BBS before, you haven't established an ID or password with it yet. Therefore, skip the next two options for now and bring up the second dialog box by pressing ALT-N. You're moved to the BAUD RATE option.

8. The Central Point BBS can support modem speeds of 1200 and 2400. If your modem can support 2400 baud, press ENTER to accept the default. Otherwise, press UP ARROW and ENTER to choose 1200 instead. You're moved to the PARITY option.

9. The default parity setting of NONE is appropriate for the Central Point BBS, so press ENTER again to move to the TERMINAL option.

10. If your PC can display graphics and you have ANSI.SYS installed, press ENTER to accept the ANSI default for the screen display. Otherwise, press UP ARROW and ENTER to choose the all-text TTY screen display; or, if you're working with DEC machines, choose the VT100 or VT52 emulation. You're moved to the FLOW CONTROL option.

11. The defaults for the last six options (XON/XOFF for FLOW CONTROL, NONE for EOL RECEIVE, STRIP LF for EOL SEND, EIGHT for DATA BITS, ONE for STOP BITS, and FULL for DUPLEX) are all appropriate for the Central Point BBS. Therefore, press ALT- O or click OK to save them and all

your other settings. The dialog box closes, and your entry is added to the end of the directory.

Notice that almost all your dialog box settings are displayed on your entry's line, as reflected by the headings near the top of the directory window. First are the Name, Number, Baud, and Duplx (duplex) settings. Following them are the P (parity), D (data bits), and S (stop bits) settings. At the end of the line is the filename you entered for the BBS script.

While your settings are now entered into the directory, you're not stuck with them. You can easily revise or delete entries, as explained in the next section.

Editing and Deleting Directory Entries

You can always revise an entry in your directory by simply moving to it and then bringing up its Edit Phone Directory dialog box.

There are a variety of ways to move to the entry. As the bottom line of the directory window indicates, you can use UP ARROW and DOWN ARROW to move by single entry, PGUP and PGDN to move by screen (five entries), and HOME and END to move to the top and bottom of the directory. You can also scroll the directory vertically with your mouse and then click on the entry you want.

Once the entry is selected, press ALT, E, E, or press F6, or click on the Edit menu and select Edit Entry. The Edit Phone Directory dialog box containing the entry's settings appears. Adjust the options that need to be changed, and then save the new settings by pressing ALT-O or clicking OK.

For example, follow these steps to edit the Central Point BBS entry you just created:

1. If you aren't already on the entry, press END to select it.

2. Press F6. The Edit Phone Directory dialog box appears with your settings from the previous exercise. You're in the NAME field.

3. Type **PC Tools BBS** to replace "Central Point BBS."

4. Press TAB four times to move to the PHONE field, and press HOME to move to the beginning of the field.

5. Edit the characters around the area code to change (503) to 503-. You can't switch to overtype mode in this dialog box, so just use the arrow keys, DEL, and BACKSPACE. When you're done, press TAB to move to the SCRIPT field.

6. The CPS.SCR script won't do anything useful until you have a user ID and password, so press SPACEBAR to eliminate the script for now.

7. Press ALT-O or click OK to save your revised settings. The dialog box closes, and the revised entry appears in the directory, reflecting your changes in the Name, Number, and Script fields.

While you can change every setting in an entry, sometimes it's easier just to eliminate the entry from the directory altogether. For example, if an online service goes out of business, you should delete its obsolete listing. Also, if you want to rearrange the order in which entries appear in the directory, you need to go through a series of deleting, creating, and editing commands.

To remove an entry, move to it and press ALT, E, R, or click on the Edit menu and select Remove Entry. The entry is erased, and any subsequent entries are renumbered and moved up to fill its place. *Use this option with care,* as there's no way to retrieve a deleted entry.

Saving the Directory

While you're creating, editing, and deleting entries, your changes exist only in your computer's memory. To preserve your work, your directory must be saved to disk. Modem Telecommunications provides two ways to do this.

If you want to save and remain in the directory, press ALT, F, S, or press F5, or click on the File menu and select Save. A Save File to Disk dialog box appears. When you press ALT-S or click Save, the directory is saved, and you're returned to its screen.

On the other hand, if you want to save and exit, you can simply press ESC or click on the window's Close box. Your directory is automatically saved and then closed.

Creating and Switching Between Multiple Directories

If you're an occasional modem user, you'll probably find one directory sufficient. However, if you need to keep track of more than 60 online services, or if you want to store each category of entries in its own file, you'll require additional directories. You can create and switch between multiple directories using the File Load command.

To demonstrate, follow these steps to create a new directory named PHONE2.TEL and then switch back to PHONE.TEL:

1. Press F5 and ALT-S to save the contents of your current directory.

2. Press ALT, F, L, or press F4, or click on the File menu and select Load. The File Load dialog box appears.

3. Type **PHONE2** to create a directory file named PHONE2.TEL. (If you don't specify an extension, TEL is automatically appended to your filename.)

4. Press ALT-N, or press ENTER twice, or click New. A new, empty directory window appears. You can enter additional online services in this directory using the **E**dit **C**reate New Entry command.

5. Press F5 and ALT-S to save the PHONE2 directory.

6. Press F4. The File Load dialog box appears again.

7. Type **PHONE** and press ENTER. The PHONE2.TEL directory is closed and the PHONE.TEL directory is opened again.

Setting the Online Screen Display

As mentioned earlier, Modem Telecommunications has two screens. Until now, you've been working in the directory screen. When you connect with an online service, however, you're switched to the online screen. You have the option of using the full 24 lines of this screen for your session, or of devoting the bottom two lines of the screen for status information and function key definitions.

To toggle between these two choices, first press ALT, S or click on the Setup menu. The option **F**ull Online Screen appears. The default is for the option to be off (that is, for status information to be displayed), as indicated by the lack of a checkmark to its left. If you want a full screen instead, press F or click the option to switch it on.

Understanding the Three Methods of Dialing

Modem Telecommunications provides three different ways of dialing an online service: automatic dialing, dialing an entry with an "open" phone number, and manual dialing.

Automatic dialing, which is the method you'll usually use, simply refers to the program dialing the telephone number in an entry for you. To use this method, just select the entry you want and press ENTER. (You can also use the redundant command Actions **D**ial, or press F7.) The call is made using all of the entry's settings.

Automatic dialing should always be your first choice when an online service already appears in the directory. However, there may be times when a service is *not* listed, and you need to call it only once or are just in too much of a hurry to create an entry for it. In such cases, you can select an existing entry with the appropriate connect settings and then type in a phone number on the fly. There are two ways to do this.

If you've previously prepared an entry that contains all your usual settings *except* for a telephone number, select that entry and press ENTER. You're prompted for the number to call. Type the phone number, and then press ENTER twice. The call is made using your supplied number and the entry's telecommunications settings.

If you haven't prepared a generic entry, then move to *any* entry with the appropriate telecommunication settings and press F8 (which selects the Actions **M**anual command). This switches you to the *online screen*. While no prompt appears telling you so, you should now type the command that makes your modem get a dial tone (for Hayes compatible modems, type **ATDT**) followed by the telephone number you want to call, and then press ENTER. (For example, to call 555-5555 using a Hayes compatible modem, type **ATDT555-5555** and press ENTER.) The call is made using your supplied number and the entry's telecommunications settings.

Calling the Central Point BBS

You've now configured Modem Telecommunications for your computer system, created a customized entry for a computer service, adjusted the online screen display, and learned about the different methods of dialing. It's time you made an actual call. Therefore, follow these steps to make a few final adjustments to your system and then dial into the Central Point BBS:

1. If you have an external modem, turn it on and make sure that it's cabled into the appropriate COM port. Alternatively, if you have an internal modem that needs to be turned on, switch it on now.

2. If you have call waiting, disable it by dialing ***70** on your phone or using whatever other method is appropriate for your region. Otherwise, a call coming in may disrupt your telecommunications session.

3. Plug your phone line into your modem.

4. Press END to select the PC Tools BBS entry you created earlier.

5. Press ENTER to automatically dial the service.

If your modem's sound is turned on, you should hear a dial tone, then the sounds of electronic dialing, then ringing, and then the high-pitched tone of a modem answering on the other end. After a few moments, you're connected to the Central Point BBS, and you're switched to the Modem Telecommunications online screen.

You're now ready to interact with the system. Keep in mind that the way the BBS operates may have changed since this chapter was written. Where it has, deviate from the following instructions. At the same time, though, pay attention to the general principles they represent, which apply to almost any telecommunications session:

1. You're first asked if your system supports ANSI graphics. If you selected ANSI when you created your BBS entry, type **Y** and press ENTER. Otherwise, type **N** and press ENTER.

2. A welcoming message appears, and you're asked for your user ID. Type **NEW** and press ENTER to identify yourself as new to the system.

3. You're asked to enter the number of characters your computer can display across the screen. If you have a typical PC system, type **80** and press ENTER.

4. You're asked to enter your name, address, and telephone number so you can be registered on the system. Enter the information as you're prompted for it.

5. You're asked to identify your computer system. Type **1** for the "IBM PC or compatible" selection and press ENTER.

6. You're asked to choose a user ID. This is the abbreviated name by which you'll be known publicly on the system; for example, it's the name that will appear on your messages and to which people can address electronic mail. Type a name from three to nine letters long that you can easily remember, and then press ENTER.

7. You're asked to verify your user ID. If you're comfortable with what you've entered, type **Y** and press ENTER. Otherwise, type **N** and press ENTER, and repeat steps 6 and 7.

8. You're asked to enter a password to uniquely identify yourself in future calls to the system. Type a password that will be hard for other people to guess but easy for you to remember, and then press ENTER.

9. Record your user ID and password in a secure place, and then press ENTER to proceed.

10. The system now displays its main menu. You can select any menu option by typing the number to its left and pressing ENTER. Explore the system by selecting various options.

11. When you're done exploring, keep an eye on the top of the screen and press ALT. A menu bar now appears on the second line of the screen. This provides commands for capturing or sending messages and files. It also lets you access the **Desktop** menu, giving you the opportunity to open a Notepads window to compose a message, run PC Shell (if resident) to manipulate files, and so on. These menus will be explored shortly. In the meantime, press ESC to suppress the menu bar and regain an extra display line.

12. Temporarily switch back to the directory screen by pressing ESC. You now have access to your directory commands again. However, you're still connected to the BBS. To switch back, press ENTER.

13. When you're done interacting with the BBS, exit it by returning to the main menu, typing **X** and pressing ENTER to log off, and typing **Y** and pressing ENTER to verify that you want to terminate the session. The BBS sends a goodbye message and hangs up, leaving you in the online screen.

Now that your telecommunications session is over, you can examine the online screen, which consists of three parts: the 22-line middle section that just displayed your session, the message bar and status information at the bottom, and the menu bar at the top (which isn't currently visible). The latter two portions of the screen are discussed in the following sections.

The Online Message Bar

On the bottom of the online screen is the message bar. When a Modem Telecommunications online activity is taking place, the bar displays appropriate definitions or instructions. Otherwise, it displays the following commands assigned to the function keys:

Function Key	Action
F1 (Help)	Brings up context-sensitive help
F2 (Index)	Brings up the online help index
F3 (Exit)	Performs the same functions as ESC
F4 (ASCII)	Selects **S**end ASCII
F5 (XModem)	Selects **S**end XMODEM
F6 (ASCII)	Selects **R**eceive ASCII
F7 (XModem)	Selects **R**eceive XMODEM
F8 (Hangup)	Selects Actions Hangup Phone
F9 (Switch)	Activates a different open window
F10 (Menu)	Performs the same functions as ALT

Directly above the message bar is an information line, which displays your telecommunications status. The first section of the line identifies your connection status. If it mistakenly says "Connected" right now, it's because the program gets confused when you don't use the Action Hangup Phone command to "officially" disconnect. You'll use this command later, right before making another call.

The rest of the line displays Send and Receive labels for function keys F4 through F7; your baud rate; your parity, data bit, and stop bit settings; your duplex setting; and your terminal emulation setting.

Navigating the Online Menus

As you saw earlier, the PC Tools 7 version of the online screen normally suppresses the menu bar so that you have an extra display line available. However, you can bring up the menu bar at any time by pressing ALT. To explore the menus, follow these steps:

1. Press ALT. The menu bar appears on the second line of the screen.

2. Press A or click on Actions to display the Actions menu, which lets you disconnect a call and end an ASCII file transfer.

3. Press RIGHT ARROW to display the **R**eceive menu, which lets you receive files using the ASCII and XMODEM protocols.

4. Press RIGHT ARROW again to display the **Send** menu, which lets you send files using the ASCII and XMODEM protocols.

5. Press RIGHT ARROW again to wrap around to the **Desktop** menu, which lets you have up to 15 Desktop files open simultaneously (but *not* more than one online screen at a time).

6. Press ESC and ALT-SPACEBAR to display the Control menu, which lets you change the screen's colors.

7. Press ESC to close the menu and return to the online screen.

Of these menus (see Figure 26-3), **Desktop** is identical to its counterpart in the directory screen; and Control is identical, except that its window manipulation commands are disabled (because the screen isn't moveable or resizable). However,

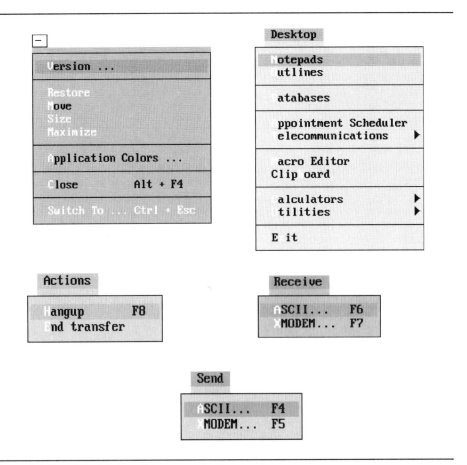

Figure 26-3. *The Modem Telecommunications online menus*

the **A**ctions, **R**eceive, and **S**end menus contain entirely different options from their
directory counterparts. These options will be explored in the following sections.

The ALT-ESC Indicator

At the top of the screen and to the left of the system time is an ALT-ESC status
indicator. This changes the online screen's key definitions, primarily for the sake of
VT100 and VT52 terminal emulations. The default is for ALT-ESC to be *on* for the
DEC emulations and *off* for TTY and ANSI emulations. You can toggle its status by
pressing ALT-ESC. The effects of its two states are summarized in Table 26-1.

Receiving and Sending Files

As you've just seen, most online commands revolve around sending and receiving
files. Modem Telecommunications supports two protocols for these operations:
ASCII and XMODEM.

ASCII is used for the transmission of text. Its main advantage is that it can save,
or *capture,* whatever text is sent to your screen. This means that you can capture an
entire telecommunications session by simply opening an ASCII file when the session
begins and closing the file when the session ends. ASCII is also useful because it lets
you see text as it's being transmitted. However, ASCII does no error-checking, so
it's unreliable on phone lines with significant electronic noise or static.

Keystroke	Action with ALT-ESC On	Action with ALT-ESC Off
ESC	Sends ESC code to modem	Switches to directory screen
SHIFT-ESC	Switches to directory screen	Sends ESC code to modem
F1 through F10	Sends ESC sequences to modem	Usual defined function
SHIFT-F1 through SHIFT-F10	Usual defined function	Sends ESC sequences to modem

Additionally, the following keys correspond to VT100 and VT52 keys when ALT-ESC *is on:*

PC Key	VT100/VT52 Key
F1	PF1
F2	PF2
F3	PF3
F4	PF4
CTRL-END	BREAK

Table 26-1. *Keystroke Actions Under* ALT-ESC *Modes*

XMODEM is used for the transmission of any kind of computer file. Because programs and many data files won't work after the introduction of even a tiny mistake, XMODEM does a great deal of error-checking to ensure that the files it transmits are exact duplicates of the originals. However, XMODEM can't capture text scrolling on your screen, and it doesn't display what it's transmitting.

There are several ways to invoke each protocol:

- To use ASCII to *receive* files from another computer system, press ALT, R, A, or press F6, or click on the Receive menu and select ASCII.

- To use XMODEM to *receive* files from another computer system, press ALT, R, X, or press F7, or click on the Receive menu and select XMODEM.

- To use ASCII to *send* files to another computer system, press ALT, S, A, or press F4, or click on the Send menu and select ASCII.

- To use XMODEM to *send* files to another computer system, press ALT, S, X, or press F5, or click on the Send menu and select XMODEM.

To get a feel for using these options, follow these steps to call the Central Point BBS again, capture a portion of your session to disk, and then download a file using XMODEM:

1. As before, make sure your modem is turned on, disable call waiting, and make sure your phone line is plugged into the modem.

2. "Officially" hang up from your last session by pressing F8 (**Actions Hangup**). The message bar displays the message "Disconnecting," and you're returned to the directory screen.

3. You're still on the PC Tools BBS entry. Press ENTER to automatically dial the service again. After a few moments, you're connected.

4. The system prompts you about using ANSI. Before answering, press F6 to open a file to capture your session. The Save File to Disk dialog box appears.

5. Type **SESSION.TXT** to name the file, and then press ENTER twice. The file is opened in your current directory, and you're returned to the session. The message bar will now display the number of lines of text your file receives, and also inform you that pressing ESC will save and close the file.

6. Answer the ANSI question appropriately and press ENTER.

7. You're asked for your user ID. Type the ID you established in the previous session and press ENTER.

8. You're asked for your password. Type the password you established in the previous session and press ENTER. The system now recognizes you, skips past all its previous questions, and moves you directly to its main menu.

9. Select the Download Files, CPS Anti-Virus Signature files, and Download Latest Signatures options to download the most recent version of the SIGNATUR.CPS file. (For more information about this file, see Chapter 13, "Detecting Viruses Using VDefend".) A description of the file and a list of available protocols are displayed.

10. You're going to use XMODEM to receive this file. However, you must first terminate your ASCII capture, because the two protocols won't work simultaneously. Therefore, press ESC. The text capture file is saved and closed, and the message bar returns to displaying function key definitions.

11. Select the XMODEM-CRC option, which is the standard version of XMODEM. The BBS tells you that it's ready to begin.

12. Press F7 to initiate an XMODEM download operation. The Save File to Disk dialog box appears again.

13. Type **SIGNATUR.CPS**, and then press ENTER twice. A Receive box appears that tracks the number of seconds elapsed, the number of bytes transferred, and the number of file blocks (a convention used by XMODEM) received. It also informs you of any transmission errors.

14. When the transfer is complete, the message bar tells you to "Press any key to continue." Press ENTER. You're returned to where you left off in the session.

15. Type **X** and press ENTER to exit each submenu until you're back at the main menu.

16. Type **X** and press ENTER, and then type **Y** and press ENTER to terminate the session. As before, the BBS sends a goodbye message and hangs up, leaving you in the online screen.

17. Press ALT-D and ENTER to select Notepads.

18. Type **SESSION** and press ENTER to bring up your capture file.

19. Press ALT-SPACEBAR, X to expand the window to fill the screen, and then scroll through the file using PGDN or your mouse. Notice that your entire telecommunications session was captured up to the point where you pressed ESC.

20. Press ESC to close the file and return to the online screen, and then press F8 to return to the directory screen.

21. Your telecommunications session is now completed. However, after you exit the Desktop, you may want to copy the SIGNATUR.CPS file you downloaded into your PC Tools main directory or SYSTEM directory so that VDefend, CP Backup, and DiskFix can work with the most current virus data available.

Using Scripts

Once you get used to an online service, you'll probably develop a routine for using it. For example, you might consistently provide your ID and password, check for electronic mail, download messages from a particular discussion area, and log off. Such a repetitive series of actions can be simulated in a *script*, which is a computer program made up of telecommunications commands. Scripts save you time and tedium, because they perform all your repetitive actions for you. They're especially useful if you schedule them to go off when you're not around (see the "Scheduling Programs, Batch Files, Macros, and Notes" section of Chapter 23, "Using the Appointment Scheduler"), or if you run them in the background (see "Using Modem Telecommunications in the Background," later in this chapter). Scripts are text files, so you can create and edit them using Notepads or any other word processor that saves in the ASCII file format.

To use a script in conjunction with a directory entry, enter the script's drive, directory, and name into the SCRIPT field of the entry's Edit Phone Directory dialog box (as covered previously in "Creating Directory Entries"). The script will then automatically take effect every time you dial the entry.

This section lists and describes available script commands. However, a discussion of the language and of programming concepts is beyond the scope of this book. If you're interested in writing scripts, use Notepads to study the four scripts packaged with the Desktop: MCI.SCR (for using MCI Mail), ESL.SCR (for using EasyLink), CIS.SCR (for using CompuServe), and CPS.SCR (for using the Central Point BBS). These files will give you a solid feel for how scripts are done and a jumping-off point for creating your own.

The following lists the Modem Telecommunications script commands in alphabetical order. For the sake of readability, the commands are printed in uppercase and their parameters are printed in lowercase (in italic text), but no case distinctions are made by the script language itself. Also, the script language supports three variables: v1, v2, and v3. A command with a *variable* parameter is referring to one of these variables unless otherwise stated.

*

Sets a line off as a comment instead of an executable command. Use * to copiously document your program so you can figure out what it does six months after you've written it.

BACKTALK

Runs the rest of the script commands in the background. The program Backtalk must be memory resident for this command to work. Keep in mind that user input commands, and the PRINT and ECHO commands, must appear before this command to have any effect.

DATABASE *variable*

Works in conjunction with the DATABASE and FIELD entries in the Edit Phone Directory dialog box to send the contents of up to two specified fields to the other computer system. The contents of the first field are stored in v1 and the second in v2.

DOWNLOAD *protocol* "*filename*"
DOWNLOAD *protocol variable*

Receives a file from the other computer system using the specified ASCII or XMODEM *protocol.* If *filename* already exists, it will first be deleted. This command must be preceded by commands preparing the other system to upload a file using the same protocol.

ECHO

Toggles the display of text from the other computer system on and off.

ECHO OFF

Turns the display of text from the other computer system off.

ECHO ON

Turns the display of text from the other computer system on.

GOTO *label*

Redirects program execution to the specified *label.*

HANGUP

Disconnects. Will abort a file transfer.

IF *variable* [=¦<>¦CONTAINS] *string* GOTO *label*

Redirects program execution based on the outcome of a test using such operators as =, <, >, and CONTAINS.

INPUT *variable*

Receives a text string up to 80 characters long (ended by a carriage return or line feed) from the keyboard and stores it in *variable*.

LABEL

See :LABEL.

:LABEL

Labels an area in the script to which program execution can be redirected using the GOTO command.

PAUSE
PAUSE *number*

Pauses execution for *number* seconds. If no parameter is specified, pauses execution for one second.

PRINT *variable*
PRINT *"string"*

Displays the value of *variable* or *string*. Following the command with a semicolon prevents sending a carriage return at the end of the line.

RECEIVE *variable*

Receives a text string up to 80 characters long (ended by a carriage return or line feed) from the other computer system and stores it in *variable*. If nothing is received within ten seconds, *variable* is set to null.

SEND *variable*
SEND *"string"*
SEND *user ID*
SEND *password*

Sends the parameter to the other computer system. *String* can include ^ to send control characters (for example, ^C for CTRL-C). Following the command with a semicolon prevents sending a carriage return at the end of the line.

TROFF

Short for Trace Off, this is a debugging command that resumes the normal program execution slowed down by the TRON command.

TRON

Short for Trace On, this is a debugging command that executes the script one command at a time as you press SPACEBAR. Pressing ESC cancels execution entirely. This command is ignored during background execution.

UPLOAD *protocol "filename"*
UPLOAD *protocol variable*

Sends a file to the other computer system using the specified ASCII or XMODEM *protocol*. If *filename* doesn't exist, the operation is aborted and program execution continues. This command must be preceded by commands preparing the other system to receive a file using the same protocol.

WAITFOR *"string"*

Halts script execution until *string* is received from the other computer system. No distinction is made between upper- and lowercase.

Using Modem Telecommunications in the Background

If you have a long file to send or receive, you shouldn't be forced to stare at your screen while the process is taking place. Modem Telecommunications therefore allows you to set such operations to occur invisibly in the background while you do work in some other application.

For this feature to take effect, the program Backtalk must be loaded resident, taking up about 64K of conventional memory, before you run the Desktop. In addition, the Desktop must also be loaded resident (that is, using the /R parameter, as explained in Chapter 19, "Desktop Manager Overview").

If you want to use Backtalk frequently, you should install it in your AUTO-EXEC.BAT file. You can do this using the Install program (see Appendix A), or you can do this manually by inserting a line such as

    BACKTALK /*port*

in your AUTOEXEC.BAT file, where *port* specifies the COM port you want the background operation to use. If the port is COM1 or COM2, simply include the number (for example, BACKTALK /1 for COM1). If the port is COM3 or COM4, however, also include the IRQ and base port address (for example, BACKTALK /3=4,3E8 for a system whose COM port 3 uses IRQ 4 and base port address 3E8).

To invoke background telecommunications, start a file transfer and then press ALT-B. The transfer continues, but you're returned to your underlying application (for example, the Desktop main screen or a standalone program). You can then perform other work, using any application except Modem Telecommunications and using any port except the COM port the transfer is taking place on. A "B" in the upper-right corner of your screen blinks to remind you that the file transfer is still occurring. When the transfer is complete, your PC beeps and the "B" disappears.

Background communications automatically keeps a record of any errors that occur during XMODEM transfers in a file named TRANSFER.LOG. Therefore, you should use Notepads to check TRANSFER.LOG after a transfer to make sure the transmission was successful.

You can also invoke background communications using the BACKTALK command in a script (see the previous "Using Scripts" section). To get a feel for how to do this, use Notepads to bring up the CIS.SCR script, use Search Find to locate sections that include the BACKTALK command, and then study those sections.

Using Database Files

A relatively unique feature of Modem Communications is the ability to access the data in database fields. This is done through a script that displays a specified database, prompts you to select records, and then sends data from the specified fields of those records.

Before the call is made, the database file, and the names of the one or two fields you want to use, must be specified in the DATABASE, FIELD 1, and FIELD 2 options of the Edit Phone Directory dialog box (as explained previously in "Creating Directory Entries").

For example, if you often have electronic mail you need to send to various people, you can use Databases to enter their names and electronic mailbox numbers in the TELECOM.DBF file packaged with PC Tools (see Chapter 25, "Using the Database Manager"). You can then write a script that calls a computer service, displays TELECOM.DBF so you can select the names of the people you want to send the message to, and then sends their corresponding mailbox numbers to the service along with your message. To get a feel for how to do this, use Notepads to bring up the CIS.SCR script, use Search Find to locate sections that include the DATABASE command, and then study those sections.

Using Electronic Mail

In addition to the general features provided by Modem Telecommunications, PC Tools 7 has added a customized communications center called Electronic Mail for sending, receiving, and managing your online messages. Electronic Mail is tailored to work exclusively with three popular services: MCI Mail, CompuServe, and EasyLink. Information about these services appears in "Exploring the Directory Screen" earlier in this chapter.

Electronic Mail doesn't do anything that you can't do yourself manually using Modem Telecommunications. However, like the scripts discussed previously, it automates your online activities. For example, it performs all the steps necessary to log onto your selected service, send and receive your messages, and log off. This saves you the tedium of dealing with a variety of online screens, and of having to remember and type long strings of online commands.

Furthermore, Electronic Mail makes it easy to stay organized by placing your incoming messages into an INBOX directory and your outgoing messages (if not sent immediately) into an OUTBOX directory. It even preserves the messages you've sent in a SENT directory. These three directories are normally created and placed within your PC Tools directory during the installation process (see Appendix A). You can alternatively create different directories (see "Creating Directories" in Chapter 17), and then set Electronic Mail to use those directories instead.

In addition, Electronic Mail can download and upload your messages at specified regular intervals (for example, every hour). This process can take place entirely in the background, allowing you to work undisturbed in other applications until you're ready to examine your mail.

To access Electronic Mail, follow these steps:

1. Call up the Desktop Manager. If you've installed the Desktop to be memory resident, press CTRL-SPACEBAR. Otherwise, type **DESKTOP** from the DOS prompt and press ENTER.

2. Press D or click Desktop to display the main menu.

3. Press T or click Telecommunications. The Telecommunications submenu appears.

4. Press E or click Electronic Mail. A screen like the one in Figure 26-4 appears.

In the center of the screen is a window showing the contents of your INBOX directory, which is where your incoming messages are stored. Since you haven't set up Electronic Mail yet, your inbox is currently empty.

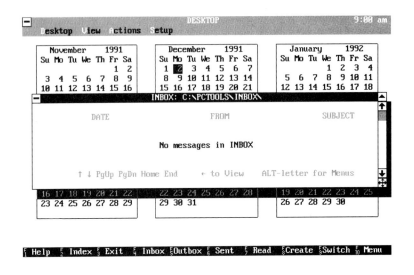

Figure 26-4. *The Electronic Mail screen*

The screen also has a message bar at the bottom and a menu bar at the top. These elements are covered in the following sections.

The Electronic Mail Message Bar

At the bottom of the screen is the message bar. When an Electronic Mail activity is taking place, the message bar displays appropriate definitions or instructions. Otherwise, it displays the following commands assigned to the function keys:

Function Key	Action
F1 (Help)	Brings up context-sensitive help
F2 (Index)	Brings up the online help index
F3 (Exit)	Performs the same functions as ESC
F4 (Inbox)	Selects **View Inbox**
F5 (Outbox)	Selects **View Outbox**
F6 (Sent)	Selects **View Sent**
F7 (Read)	Selects **Actions Read** Mail Now
F8 (Create)	Selects **Actions Create** Mail Message
F9 (Switch)	Activates a different open window
F10 (Menu)	Performs the same functions as ALT

Navigating the Electronic Mail Menus

At the top of the screen are the five menus available for Electronic Mail (and, in the right corner, the system time). Follow these steps to examine the menus:

1. Press ALT, V or click on View to display the View menu, which lets you see the contents of your INBOX, OUTBOX, or SENT directory.

2. Press RIGHT ARROW to display the Actions menu, which lets you read or delete the currently selected message, download your mail from your online service, or create a message.

3. Press RIGHT ARROW again to display the Setup menu, which lets you select an online service and configure settings; set schedules for sending and receiving mail; and specify the directories to act as your inbox, outbox, and sent box.

4. Press RIGHT ARROW again to wrap around to the Desktop menu, which lets you have up to 15 Desktop files open simultaneously. However, it does *not* let you have more than one Electronic Mail window open at the same time.

5. Press ESC and ALT-SPACEBAR to display the Control menu, which lets you change the Electronic Mail window's colors, position, and size.

6. Press ESC to close the menu and return to the directory window.

Of these menus (see Figure 26-5), the options in Control and Desktop are in every Desktop application, but the options in View, Actions, and Setup are unique to Electronic Mail. In the following sections, you'll learn how to use these options to configure Electronic Mail and then manage your messages.

Configuring Electronic Mail

Before you can use Electronic Mail, you have to select an online service and configure the program to access it. To do so, follow these steps:

1. Press ALT, S, M, or click on the Setup menu and select Mail Service. The following dialog box appears:

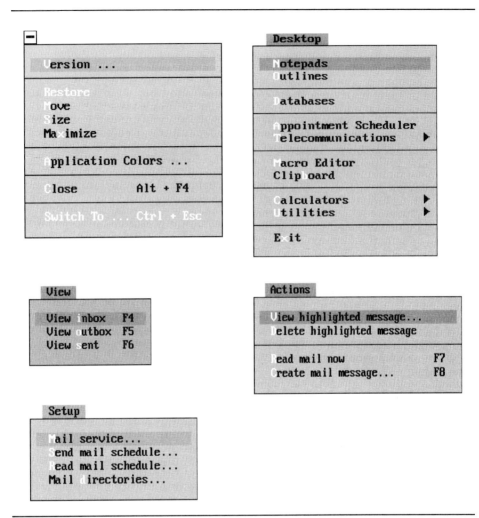

Figure 26-5. *The Electronic Mail menus*

2. Use UP ARROW or your mouse to select an online service you're currently using.

3. If you've already configured this service in Modem Telecommunications by revising its Edit Phone Directory dialog box (see "Editing and Deleting Directory Entries" earlier in this chapter), Electronic Mail can automatically get the rest of the information it needs from PHONE.TEL. If this is the case, press O or click OK. After a few moments of disk activity, the automatic configuration is completed, and you're returned to the standard Electronic Mail screen.

Otherwise, press N or click Configure. A dialog box like this appears:

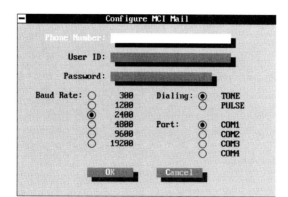

The box offers the following options:

- *Phone Number*   This field specifies the telephone number of the online service. The number should include any appropriate access digits to get an outside line and long distance digits to dial long distance. For the sake of readability, separate the digits using spaces, parentheses, and dashes (for example, 1 (800) 555-5555). The field can hold up to 25 characters.

- *User ID*   This field specifies the identification code by which you're known to the online service (for example, Rick). It can hold up to 25 characters, and distinguishes between upper- and lowercase.

- *Password*   This field specifies the password you provide to access the online service (for example, Casablanca). It can hold up to 21 characters, and distinguishes between upper- and lowercase. Be sure to memorize your password; after you save your settings, the password is hidden to guard against its being seen by someone else.

- *Baud Rate*   This option sets your transmission speed. You should choose the highest speed that both your modem *and* the computer system you're calling supports. The choices are 300, 1200, 2400, 4800, 9600, and 19200, with the higher numbers representing the faster speeds. The most common speeds are 2400 and 9600, and the default is *2400.*

- *Dialing*   This option specifies whether you're using a pulse or tone phone line. The default is *TONE.*

- *Port*   This option specifies which communications, or COM, port in your computer your modem is attached to. This is usually COM1 or COM2.
    If you have a PS/2, or if you started the Desktop using the parameters /C3 or /C4 followed by =*IRQ, base port address* (for example, /C3=4,3E8), you can

also use port COM3 or COM4. See your modem manual to find the appropriate values for IRQ and the base port address.

You don't have to specify any additional settings, as you did in Modem Communications, because Electronic Mail will take any other required information from the entry for your selected service in the PHONE.TEL directory. However, you must appropriately set every option that *is* listed to ensure that Electronic Mail works properly. When you're done, press ALT-O or click OK. The dialog box closes, your settings are saved to disk, and you're returned to the standard Electronic Mail screen.

You can now optionally return to step 1 to configure settings for a second online service you're using. You can also optionally go through the procedure a third time if you intend to use all three supported services.

Once you're done configuring, you can specify the service you want to work with at any time by selecting **S**etup **M**ail Service, the desired service from the dialog box, and **OK**. This allows you to quickly switch between different services and to access them all using the same menu commands.

Lastly, if you aren't happy with the current directories serving as your inbox, outbox, and sent box, press ALT, S, D, or click on the Setup menu and select Mail Directories. A dialog box appears that lists the paths for your three electronic mailboxes. Revise any or all of the paths as desired, and then press ALT-O or click OK.

Creating and Sending Electronic Mail

All the steps for creating and sending an online message can be handled exclusively through the Electronic Mail application. Alternatively, you can compose messages in your favorite word processor, and then simply save them to the OUTBOX directory for automatic transmission at a scheduled time. This section covers both methods.

To both create and send a message through Electronic Mail, follow these steps:

1. If the online service you want isn't already selected, press ALT, S, M, select the service, and press O.

2. Press ALT, A, C, or press F8, or click on the Actions menu and select Create Mail Message. A Notepads window opens with a filename such as MCI00001.EML or CIS00001.EML. The first part of the name identifies the service the document is intended for, the second part numbers it in sequence with your existing messages, and the extension identifies it as Electronic Mail.

   The message automatically begins with the appropriate headings for your selected service. For example, for MCI Mail the headings are TO:, CC:, and SUBJECT:, and for CompuServe the headings are TO:, FROM:, and SUBJECT:.

3. For each heading, type the appropriate information, and then press DOWN ARROW (*not* ENTER) to move to the next heading. After the last heading, DOWN ARROW moves you to the start of a blank line.

4. Type your message normally, allowing your lines to word wrap when they reach the window's right margin. (If you need information about writing in Notepads, see Chapter 20, "Using Notepads.")

5. Electronic Mail does *not* transmit your message "as is." Instead, it first formats the document using the margin settings in the Electronic Mail Page Layout box. Therefore, when you've finished your message, press ALT, C, E, or click on the Controls menu and select Electronic Mail Page Layout, and adjust the displayed settings appropriately for your particular message. For example, if your message is short, you may want to enter 1 for the top and bottom margins (as opposed to the default of 6), and set the paper size setting to a number smaller than its default of 66. Otherwise, your message will be padded with many extra blank lines. When you're done, press ALT-O or click OK.

6. Electronic Mail includes whatever header or footer is currently set up in Notepads. Since the Notepads default is to include a centered page number footer, this means your message will ordinarily include a page number. If you find this undesirable, press ALT, C, H; press TAB to move to the Footer option; press BACKSPACE to delete the # symbol (which is Notepads' page number code); and press ENTER twice.

7. Press ALT, F, E, or press F5, or click on the File menu and select Send Electronic Mail. The following dialog box appears:

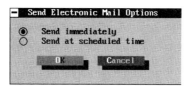

8. If you want your document transmitted immediately, make sure your modem is on and your phone line is connected, and press O or click OK. The Notepads window closes, the PHONE.TEL window opens, your service is dialed, and a special script logs on, sends your message, and logs off. To continue, go to step 9.

   Otherwise, press DOWN ARROW to select the Send at Scheduled Time option, and press O or click OK. The Notepads window closes, and the file is saved to your OUTBOX directory to await the next time you've scheduled electronic mail transmission to take place (see "Scheduling Electronic Mail" later in this chapter).

9. You're now returned to the Electronic Mail screen. If you have any more messages to create, simply return to step 1 and repeat the process you've just executed.

 You can also send messages from Outlines, since this Desktop application also includes a File Send Electronic Mail command.

If you don't like the way Electronic Mail formats Notepads messages as paper documents, you can alternatively create messages using *any* word processor and simply save the files to the OUTBOX directory. The files will be transmitted the next time you've scheduled electronic mail transmission to take place.

If you go this route, make sure each of your message files adheres to the following rules:

- The appropriate headings for your online service appear at the top of the document, with a line devoted to each heading. For example, MCI Mail requires the first three lines be devoted to the headings TO:, CC:, and SUBJECT:, and CompuServe requires the lines contain the headings TO:, FROM:, and SUBJECT:. Each heading should be followed by a TAB code and then the appropriate information for your particular message.

- The document's margins are set for your online service. Generally, a left margin of 0 and right margin of 65 are appropriate.

- The file's name ends with a PRT extension (for example, JOBOFFER.PRT or CONTRACT.PRT).

- The file is saved in ASCII format (an option provided by virtually all word processors).

- For some services, it may also be necessary to end each line with an ENTER code. Certain word processors can automatically insert these ENTER codes for you when saving in ASCII format.

Again, once you've completed each message, save it to your OUTBOX directory. You can repeat the process as many times as you like, since there's no limit to the number of files OUTBOX can hold. The files will all be transmitted "as is" (that is, without additional formatting) the next time you're scheduled to send online mail, as explained in "Scheduling Electronic Mail" later in this chapter.

Receiving, Reading, and Deleting Electronic Mail

To pick up and read messages from your online service, follow these steps:

1. If the online service you want isn't already selected, press ALT, S, M, select the service, and press O.

2. Make sure your modem is on and your phone line is connected.

3. Press ALT, A, R, or press F7, or click on the Actions menu and select Read Mail Now. The PHONE.TEL window opens, your service is dialed, and a special script logs on, downloads your messages, and logs off. You're then returned to the Electronic Mail screen, and any mail you've received appears in your INBOX window.

4. Highlight a message using the arrow keys or your mouse, and then press ALT, A, V, or click on the Actions menu and select View Highlighted Message. A Notepads window opens that contains the message. You can now read it.

5. If you want to reply to the message, press F9 to switch back to the Electronic Mail window, and then follow the steps in the previous "Creating and Sending Electronic Mail" section. You can use F9 to switch between the two Notepads screens if you need to refer to the original message while composing your reply.

6. When you're done with the message you received, press ESC to close the Notepads window. You're returned to the Electronic Mail screen.

7. If you're done with the message but want to save it, wait until you've exited the Desktop, and then move it to another directory for safekeeping using DOS or PC Shell commands (see "Moving Files" in Chapter 16, "Managing Your Files").

   Alternatively, if you're sure you no longer need the message, delete it by pressing ALT, A, D, or by clicking on the Actions menu and selecting Delete Highlighted Message. The file is instantly erased.

8. Repeat steps 4 through 7 for each of the remaining messages in the INBOX window until you've gone through all your mail.

9. Optionally check the messages in your OUTBOX directory by pressing F5 and/or in your SENT directory by pressing F6. After reading through these files and deleting any that are obsolete, return to the INBOX directory by pressing F4.

Scheduling Electronic Mail

If you always keep the Desktop resident, your modem on, and a phone line plugged into the modem, you can set Electronic Mail to pick up and send out your messages at regular intervals. This is especially convenient if you also keep the Backtalk program resident, because Backtalk allows the entire process to take place invisibly while you work in other applications. (For more information, see "Using Modem Telecommunications in the Background" earlier in this chapter.)

To schedule Electronic Mail to pick up your messages, follow these steps:

1. Press ALT, S, R, or click on the Setup menu and select Read Mail Schedule. A dialog box like this appears:

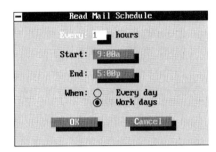

2. Type the interval in hours Electronic Mail should wait before dialing into your online service for your messages. The default is *1* hour. (If you decide you want to turn this scheduling feature *off,* type **0** and go to step 6.) When you're done, press ENTER.

3. Type the time that Electronic Mail should begin checking for your messages. The default is *9:00a.* When you're done, press ENTER.

4. Type the time that Electronic Mail should stop checking for your messages. The default is *5:00p.* When you're done, press ENTER.

5. Use the arrow keys or your mouse to select whether Electronic Mail should check for your messages every day or only on work days. ("Work days" means Monday through Friday *unless* you've redefined the term in the Appointment Scheduler's Appointment Settings dialog box. For more information, see "Changing Daily Scheduler Defaults" in Chapter 23, "Using the Appointment Scheduler.") The default is *Work days.*

6. Press ALT-O or click OK. Your settings are saved to a file named EMAIL.TM, which the Desktop's Appointment Scheduler will use to run an appropriate Electronic Mail script file at the times you've selected. The dialog box then closes, and you're returned to the Electronic Mail screen.

You can also schedule how often Electronic Mail sends whatever messages are in your OUTBOX directory. To do so, first press ALT, S, S, or click on the Setup menu and select Send Mail Schedule. You can now proceed to follow steps 2 through

6 again; just keep in mind that this time you're setting the schedule for message transmission rather than message pickup. The EMAIL.TM file will store your message transmission schedule along with your message pickup schedule.

Using Fax Telecommunications

The Desktop provides two fax applications that let you send faxes to and receive faxes from any modern (that is, Group 3) fax machine or fax board.

To use the programs, you need a fax board that supports a set of rules called the *Communicating Applications Specification,* or *CAS.* Such boards include Personal Link from SpectraFAX Corp. at (813) 643-5060; the SatisFAXtion Board from Intel PCEO at (800) 538-3373; and the Connection CoProcessor, which is an earlier version of Intel's current SatisFAXtion Board. If you aren't sure if your board supports CAS, ask the manufacturer.

Fax Telecommunications offers several special features, such as the ability to transfer faxes in the background while you're doing work in other applications (via the Backtalk program), and the ability to transfer computer files the way a modem does. If you're on a NOVELL network, the program also allows a fax board in any PC to be used by anyone on the network.

 There are two fax applications: Send a Fax and Check the Fax Log. Both of these programs are accessed through the **Desktop** menu's Telecommunications submenu. However, in PC Tools 7 these two options don't appear in the submenu until the Desktop detects an installed fax board, fax software, and the PC Tools ITLFAX program. Therefore, before bringing up the Desktop, follow these steps:

1. Install your fax board and its software following the directions of the board's manual.

2. If you haven't already installed the ITLFAX program to be loaded resident, do so now. To begin, go to the DOS prompt and switch to your PC Tools directory; for example, if the directory is named PCTOOLS, type **CD\PCTOOLS** and press ENTER.

3. Type **INSTALL** from the DOS prompt and press ENTER. The Install configuration menu appears.

4. Press D or click Desktop Manager.

5. Press F, O, or click Load Fax Support and OK.

6. Press ENTER or click OK to skip past the warning about already installing fax software.

7. Specify the directory you want to use for storing faxes, or accept the default of \PCTFAX, and then press ENTER or click OK.

8. Press L or click Fax Board is in Local Computer, or press R or click Fax Board is in Remote Network Workstation; and then press ENTER or click OK.

9. Press X or click Exit. A Close dialog box appears.

10. Make sure that Save Configuration has a checkmark next to it, and then press ENTER or click OK.

11. Press ESC or click Cancel to skip searching your disks for PC Shell's program list. You're returned to the DOS prompt.

12. When you're ready to restart your PC and have your configuration changes take effect, press CTRL-ALT-DEL from the DOS prompt. Your PC reboots and loads ITLFAX memory resident along with your fax software.

Once you've installed your fax board, fax software, and ITLFAX, you're ready to begin examining the fax applications. To do so, follow these steps:

1. Call up the Desktop Manager. If you've installed the Desktop to be memory resident, press CTRL-SPACEBAR. Otherwise, type **DESKTOP** from the DOS prompt and press ENTER.

2. Press ENTER or click Desktop to display the main menu.

3. Press T or click Telecommunications. The submenu should now include the two fax applications, as shown here:

```
 odem Telecommunications
  lectronic Mail
  end a Fax (requires fax board)
  heck the Fax Log
```

4. Press S or click Send a Fax. A screen like the one in Figure 26-6 appears. This is the fax directory screen, in which you adjust various fax settings and send faxes.

The Send a Fax Directory Window

In the center of the screen is the fax directory window, which holds fax entries. Specifically, it displays the name of the person or company the fax is directed to; the telephone number of the fax machine; the type of transmission, which is FAX for a normal transmission and File for a modem-like transfer of computer files; and a descriptive comment.

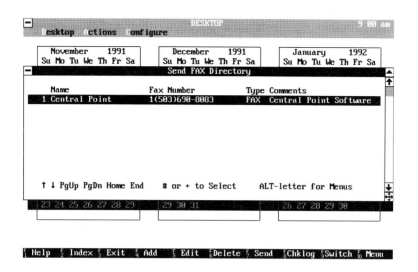

Figure 26-6.   *The Send a Fax screen*

The current directory is the only one Send a Fax supports. However, the directory can hold up to 99 entries, which is large enough for typical use. To get you started, the fax number of Central Point, the publisher of PC Tools, has been inserted as the first entry.

The Send a Fax Message Bar

At the bottom of the directory screen is the message bar. When a Send a Fax activity is taking place, the bar displays appropriate definitions or instructions. Otherwise, it displays the following commands assigned to the function keys:

Function Key	Action
F1 (Help)	Brings up context-sensitive help
F2 (Index)	Brings up the online help index
F3 (Exit)	Performs the same functions as ESC
F4 (Add)	Selects Actions **A**dd a New Entry
F5 (Edit)	Selects Actions **E**dit the Current Entry
F6 (Delete)	Selects Actions **D**elete the Current Entry
F7 (Send)	Selects Actions **S**end Files to Selected Entry
F8 (Chklog)	Selects Actions **C**heck Fax Log
F9 (Switch)	Activates a different open window
F10 (Menu)	Performs the same functions as ALT

Navigating the Send a Fax Menus

At the top of the screen are the four menus available in Send a Fax (and, in the right corner, the system time). Follow these steps to examine the menus:

1. Press ALT, A or click on Actions to display the **Actions** menu, which lets you add, edit, delete, and send faxes, and also lets you check the Fax Log.

2. Press RIGHT ARROW to display the **Configure** menu, which lets you adjust the formatting of your faxes.

3. Press RIGHT ARROW again to wrap around to the **Desktop** menu, which lets you have up to 15 Desktop files open simultaneously. However, it does *not* let you have more than one Send a Fax window open at the same time.

4. Press ESC and ALT-SPACEBAR to display the Control menu, which lets you change the current window's colors, position, and size.

5. Press ESC to close the menu and return to the fax directory.

Of these menus (see Figure 26-7), the options in Control and **Desktop** are in every Desktop application, but virtually all the options in **Actions** and **Configure** are unique to Send a Fax. These options will be covered in the following sections.

Configuring Send a Fax

Before using the Send a Fax application, you have to adjust its settings for your system. To do so, follow these steps:

1. You should still be in the Send a Fax main screen. Press ALT, C, F, or click on the Configure menu and select Fax Drive. The directory you selected with the Install program to hold your fax files appears. You have the option of changing this directory at any time. However, if you do so, you must *also* change the ITLFAX command line in your AUTOEXEC.BAT file (either manually or by reinstalling ITLFAX with the Install program). For now, accept the current directory by pressing ESC.

2. Press ALT, C, P, or click on the Configure menu and select Page Length. This option sets the length of your fax pages in inches. Enter any number from 1 to 99, or accept the default of *11 inches* (the length of a standard page). When you're done, press ALT-O or click OK.

3. Press ALT, C, C, or click on the Configure menu and select Cover Page. If this option is *on*, which is the default, you'll be prompted about including a cover page every time you send a fax. Press ENTER if you want to toggle the option off. When you're done, press ALT-O or click OK.

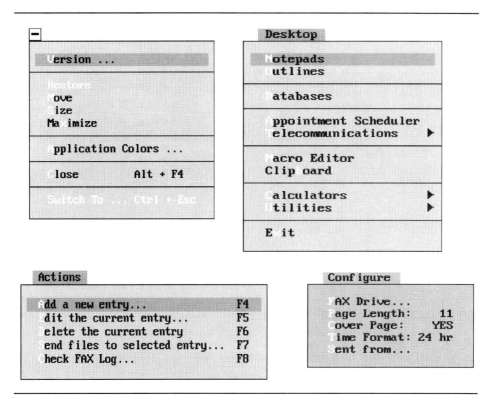

Figure 26-7.   *The Send a Fax menus*

4. Press ALT, C, T, or click on the Configure menu and select Time Format. This option sets the format in which times will be entered and displayed. Accept the default format *24 hr*, or press DOWN ARROW and ENTER to select the 12-hour format Am/Pm. When you're done, press ALT-O or click OK.

5. Press ALT, C, S, or click on the Configure menu and select Sent From. This option records your name as you want it to appear on the faxes you send. Type your name, and then press ALT-O or click OK.

Send a Fax automatically includes the following information at the top of every fax page you send: the name of the recipient, your name, the date and time the fax was sent, and the page number.

Creating and Sending a Fax

You've examined the Send a Fax screen and configured the program to your system. You're now ready to create and send faxes.

To create a fax, press ALT, A, A, or click on the Actions menu and select Add a New Entry. The following Fax Details dialog box appears:

```
┌─[−]──────────────────── FAX Details ───────────────────────┐
│  Date: 07/13/91              To: [_____]  │
│                                                             │
│  Time: 09:34          FAX Number: [_____]     │
│                                                             │
│  From: [_____]  Comments: [_____]   │
│         ⦿  Normal Resolution                                │
│         ○  Fine Resolution                                  │
│         ○  FAX Board To FAX Board                           │
│                                                             │
│  [ Select Files and Send ]  [ Make a new File and Send ]  [ Cancel ]  │
└─────────────────────────────────────────────────────────────┘
```

The box offers the following options:

- *Date*   This field sets the date your fax is sent. The default is *the system date* (which should be the current date). Change this field if you want to send your fax on a future date or if your system date is incorrect.

- *Time*   This field sets the time your fax is sent. The default is *the system time* (which should be the current time). Change this field if you want to send your fax at a later time (for example, when phone rates are lower) or if your system date is incorrect.

- *From*   This field identifies who the fax is coming from. The default is the name you entered using the **C**onfigure **S**ent From command, which is typically your own name. The field can hold up to 24 characters.

- *To*   This field identifies who the fax is going to. The field can hold up to 24 characters.

- *Fax Number*   This field sets the fax number to dial. The number should include any appropriate access digits to get an outside line and long distance digits to dial long distance. For the sake of readability, you should separate digits using spaces, parentheses, and/or dashes (for example, 1 (800) 555-5555). The field can hold up to 24 characters.

- *Comments*   This field lets you include a short note about the fax to display in the fax directory listing. The field can hold up to 24 characters.

- *Normal Resolution*   This option sets a faster transmission speed with lower quality reproduction. It's recommended for text but not graphics. The next two options are alternatives to this option, which is the default.

- *Fine Resolution*   This option sets a slower transmission speed with higher quality reproduction. It's recommended for graphics or for text you want reproduced crisply.

- *Fax Board to Fax Board*   This option allows your fax board to act like a modem by transmitting computer files of any kind to another CAS-compatible fax board.

When you're done adjusting options, choose **S**elect Files and Send to select up to 20 existing text files and send their contents; **M**ake a New File and Send to create a Notepads file, type a message into it, and then send the message; or **C**ancel to abort the operation. With the first two choices, your fax information is also entered into the fax directory for future use.

To send existing files, follow these steps:

1. Press ALT-S, or click Select Files and Send. A Files To Select dialog box like this appears:

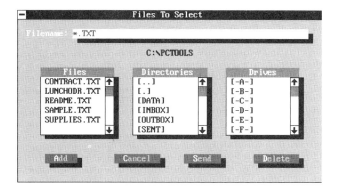

2. Specify a text file you want to send by typing its name in the Filename field or selecting it in the Files box, and then pressing ALT-A or clicking Add. The filename is recorded in a Files to Send box (which isn't currently visible).

3. Repeat step 2 until you've added all the files you want or have reached the Send a Fax limit of 20 files.

4. Press ALT-S or click Send. The Files to Send box now appears and lists the files you added in the order you added them.

5. If you've changed your mind about your file selections, press C or click Choose Different Files. Your selections are cleared, and you're returned to the Files to Select dialog box. To create a new file list, return to step 2.

6. When you're satisfied with the files listed, press S or click Send. If the Configure Cover Page option is off, go to step 8.

   Otherwise, you're asked if you want a cover page. If you don't, press N or select No Cover Page This Time, and then go to step 8.

7. If you *do* want a cover page, press ENTER or click OK. The box closes, and the Notepads file COVER.TXT opens. (If the file doesn't already exist, press ENTER an additional time to open it.) Type a cover message, and then save and close the file by pressing ESC.

8. The message "Your request has been routed to your fax card" is displayed, and the files you selected (plus any cover page you created) are sent. Press ENTER or click OK. You're returned to the fax directory window.

Alternatively, to create a new file and send it from the Fax Details dialog box, follow these steps:

1. Press ALT-M, or click Make a New File and Send. You're prompted for a Notepads filename.

2. Type a standard filename (for example, FAX1, CONTRACT, or SUPPLIES.PCS), and then press ENTER twice. The file opens.

3. Type your message, and then save and close the file by pressing ESC. If the Configure Cover Page option is off, go to step 5.

4. You're asked if you want a cover page. If you don't, press N or select No Cover Page This Time, and then go to step 5.

   Otherwise, press ENTER or click OK. A Notepads file named COVER.TXT opens. (If the file doesn't already exist, press ENTER an additional time to open it.) Type a cover message, and then save and close the file by pressing ESC.

5. The message "Your request has been routed to your fax card" is displayed, and the file you created (plus any cover page you created) are sent. Press ENTER or click OK. You're returned to the fax directory window.

Lastly, if you just want to abort the operation in the Fax Details dialog box, press ESC or click Cancel. The box closes without saving your changes.

Editing and Sending a Fax

As mentioned in the previous section, after you've created a fax using the Fax Details dialog box, its settings are entered into the fax directory. You can edit and/or reuse these settings to send the fax again.

First, highlight the entry you want to work with. As the bottom line of the window indicates, you can use UP ARROW and DOWN ARROW to move by single entry, PGUP and PGDN to move by window, and HOME and END to move to the top and bottom of the fax directory. You can also scroll the fax directory vertically with your mouse and then click the entry you want. Lastly, you can type the number to the left of the entry.

Once you've selected the entry, you can simply press ENTER to bring up its Fax Details dialog box. You can also do this by pressing F5; or F7; or ALT, A, E; or ALT, A, S. You can also click on the Actions menu and select either Edit the Current Entry or Send Files to Selected Entry. The only difference between all these methods is which option in the Fax Details dialog box is initially selected.

Once the Fax Details dialog box is open, make whatever option adjustments are necessary, and then press ALT-S, or click Select Files and Send. The Files to Send box appears and lists the same files you selected previously for the entry. To complete the operation, follow steps 5 through 8 in the tutorial on sending existing files in the previous "Creating and Sending a Fax" section.

Deleting a Fax

To delete a fax entry from the directory, simply move to the entry and press ALT, A, D, or press F6, or click on the Actions menu and select Delete The Current Entry. The entry is instantly removed.

Use this option with care, as there's no way to retrieve a deleted entry.

Checking the Fax Log

The Fax Log keeps track of the faxes you're sending and receiving. You can check it both from within the Send a Fax screen and from the **Desktop** menu.

To check it from within the Send a Fax screen, press ALT, A, C, or press F8, or click on the Actions menu and select Check Fax Log.

To check it from the **Desktop** menu, press ALT, D, T, C, or click on the Desktop menu and select Telecommunications and Check the Fax Log.

In either case, a window like this appears listing any faxes you've received:

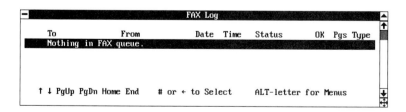

Also, the message bar changes to display the following Fax Log function key definitions:

Function Key	Action
F1 (Help)	Brings up context-sensitive help
F2 (Index)	Brings up the online help index
F3 (Exit)	Performs the same functions as ESC
F4	Undefined
F5 (Delete)	Selects Actions Delete the Selected Entry
F6 (Search)	Selects Actions Search
F7	Undefined
F8	Undefined
F9 (Switch)	Activates a different open window
F10 (Menu)	Performs the same functions as ALT

In addition, the Fax Log Actions menu offers the options Delete The Selected Entry, which removes the selected entry from the Log, and Search, which lets you search for Log entries using a text sequence up to 11 characters long.

Lastly, the Fax Log Configure menu offers two options. The first is Fax Drive, which sets the directory where your faxes are stored. Using it automatically changes the directory displayed with the Send a Fax Configure FAX Drive command, and vice versa. However, as mentioned previously in the "Configuring Send a Fax" section, you must also change the ITLFAX command line in your AUTOEXEC.BAT file (either manually or by reinstalling ITLFAX with the Install program).

The second Configure menu command is AutoUpdate, which sets how often the Log is updated for new faxes. The default period is *60* seconds, but you can change that to any update interval from 0 (which turns the updating off) to 9999 seconds by typing the appropriate number, and then pressing ENTER twice or clicking OK.

To exit the Fax Log, press ESC. The window closes, and you're returned to where you left off in your previous Desktop application (or, if you weren't in an application, to the Desktop main screen).

Telecommunications Command Reference

Most of the power of Modem Telecommunications, Electronic Mail, Send a Fax, and the Fax Log lie in their menu commands, which let you configure the programs to your computer system, manipulate directory entries or files, and send and receive data.

Like all Desktop applications, the Telecommunications programs' first two menus are Control and Desktop. These menus are covered in Chapter 19, "Desktop Manager Overview." The programs also provide the following additional menus:

- Modem Telecommunications' directory screen contains the four menus File, Edit, Actions, and Setup; and Modem Telecommunications' online screen contains the three menus Actions, Receive and Send.

- Electronic Mail contains the three menus View, Actions, and Setup.

- Send a Fax contains the two menus **Actions** and **Configure**.

- The Fax Log contains the two menus **Actions** and **Configure**.

The following sections cover the options in all of these menus. After the name of each option are the keystrokes that invoke it, a description of what the option does, and a reference to the section in this chapter that discusses the option in detail.

The File Menu (Modem Telecommunications Directory)

The File menu contains the following two options for saving, creating, and switching between directories:

Load (ALT, F, L or F4)

Closes the current directory without saving it and loads the specified directory in its place. Covered in "Creating and Switching Between Multiple Directories."

Save (ALT, F, S or F5)

Saves the current directory to disk. Covered in "Saving the Directory."

The Edit Menu (Modem Telecommunications Directory)

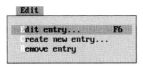
The Edit menu contains the following three options for creating, editing, and deleting directory entries:

Edit Entry (ALT, E, E or F6)

Brings up the Edit Phone Directory dialog box for the selected entry. Covered in "Editing and Deleting Directory Entries."

Create New Entry (ALT, E, C)

Creates a new directory entry. Covered in "Creating Directory Entries."

Remove Entry (ALT, E, R)

Deletes the selected directory. Covered in "Editing and Deleting Directory Entries."

The Actions Menu (Modem Telecommunications Directory)

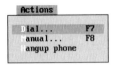

In the directory screen, the Actions menu contains the following three options for dialing automatically, dialing manually, and disconnecting:

Dial (ALT, A, D or F7)

Dials the telephone number in the selected entry. Covered in "Understanding the Three Methods of Dialing."

Manual (ALT, A, M or F8)

Provides a dialog box in which you can enter a phone number to dial the selected entry. Covered in "Understanding the Three Methods of Dialing."

Hangup Phone (ALT, A, H)

Disconnects; same as its counterpart in the online Actions menu.

The Setup Menu (Modem Telecommunications Directory)

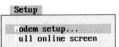

The Setup menu contains the following two options for configuring the program to your system and setting the information display for the online screen:

Modem Setup (ALT, S, M)

Sets the modem initialization strings, the modem connect string, the COM port to use, and tone or pulse dialing. Covered in "Configuring Modem Telecommunications for Your System."

Full Online Screen (ALT, S, F)

Toggles the online screen between displaying status and help information on its bottom two lines, and providing a full 24 lines for displaying online sessions. Covered in "Setting the Online Screen Display."

The Actions Menu (Modem Telecommunications Online)

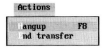

In the online screen, the Actions menu contains the following two options for disconnecting and for ending an ASCII file transfer:

Hangup Phone (ALT, A, H or F8)

Disconnects; same as its counterpart in the directory Actions menu. Covered in "Receiving and Sending Files."

End Transfer (ALT, A, E)

When an ASCII transfer is taking place (for example, when you've opened a file to capture the text of an online session), ends the transfer, and saves and closes the file. Pressing ESC has the same effect.

The Receive Menu (Modem Telecommunications Online)

The Receive menu contains the following two options for receiving data:

ASCII (ALT, R, A or F6)

Downloads text using the ASCII protocol. Covered in "Receiving and Sending Files."

XMODEM (ALT, R, X or F7)

Downloads computer files using the XMODEM protocol. Covered in "Receiving and Sending Files."

The Send Menu (Modem Telecommunications Online)

The Send menu contains the following two options for sending data:

ASCII (ALT, S, A or F4)

Uploads text using the ASCII protocol. Covered in "Receiving and Sending Files."

XMODEM (ALT, S, X or F5)

Uploads computer files using the XMODEM protocol. Covered in "Receiving and Sending Files."

The View Menu (Electronic Mail)

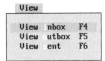

The **View** menu contains the following three options for switching between your INBOX, OUTBOX, and SENT directories:

View **I**nbox (ALT, V, I or F4)

Displays the messages in your inbox. Covered in "Receiving, Reading, and Deleting Electronic Mail."

View **O**utbox (ALT, V, O or F5)

Displays the messages in your outbox. Covered in "Receiving, Reading, and Deleting Electronic Mail."

View **S**ent (ALT, V, S or F6)

Displays the messages in your sent box. Covered in "Receiving, Reading, and Deleting Electronic Mail."

The Actions Menu (Electronic Mail)

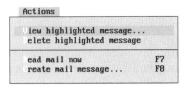

In Electronic Mail, the **Actions** menu contains the following four options for reading your messages, deleting messages, downloading your messages, and creating and transmitting a message:

View Highlighted Message (ALT, A, V)

Displays the contents of the selected message. Covered in "Receiving, Reading, and Deleting Electronic Mail."

Delete Highlighted Message (ALT, A, D)

Erases the selected message. Covered in "Receiving, Reading, and Deleting Electronic Mail."

Read Mail Now (ALT, A, R or F7)

Logs onto your selected online service, picks up your mail, logs off, and deposits the mail in your inbox. Covered in "Receiving, Reading, and Deleting Electronic Mail."

Create Mail Message (ALT, A, C or F8)

Helps automate the process of creating and sending an online message over your selected service. Covered in "Creating and Sending Electronic Mail."

The Setup Menu (Electronic Mail)

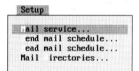

In Electronic Mail, the **S**etup menu contains the following four options for configuring and selecting your online service, setting schedules for sending and receiving your online messages, and changing your "box" directories:

Mail Service (ALT, S, M)

Configures Electronic Mail for your online services, and then lets you select which of the three available services to use at any time. Covered in "Configuring Electronic Mail."

Send Mail Schedule (ALT, S, S)

Sets how often Electronic Mail automatically transmits whatever messages are in your OUTBOX directory. Covered in "Scheduling Electronic Mail."

Read Mail Schedule (ALT, S, R)

Sets how often Electronic Mail automatically picks up your online messages and places them in your INBOX directory. Covered in "Scheduling Electronic Mail."

Mail **D**irectories (ALT, S, D)

Specifies the directories to be used as your inbox, outbox, and sent box. Covered in "Configuring Electronic Mail."

The Actions Menu (Send a Fax)

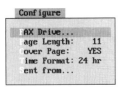

```
Actions
  dd a new entry...         F4
  dit the current entry...  F5
  elete the current entry   F6
  end files to selected entry... F7
  heck FAX Log...           F8
```

In the fax screen, the **Actions** menu contains the following five options for adding, editing, deleting, and sending faxes, and for checking the Fax Log:

Add a New Entry (ALT, A, A or F4)

Creates a new fax and sends it. Covered in "Creating and Sending a Fax."

Edit the Current Entry (ALT, A, E or F5)

Lets you edit the Fax Details dialog box of the selected fax and send the fax. Covered in "Editing and Sending a Fax."

Delete the Current Entry (ALT, A, D or F6)

Deletes the selected entry from the fax directory. Covered in "Deleting a Fax."

Send Files to Selected Entry (ALT, A, S or F7)

Lets you edit the Fax Details dialog box of the selected fax and send the fax. Covered in "Editing and Sending a Fax."

Check FAX Log (ALT, A, C or F8)

Displays the Fax Log. Covered in "Checking the Fax Log."

The Configure Menu (Send a Fax)

```
Configure
  AX Drive...
  age Length:    11
  over Page:    YES
  ime Format: 24 hr
  ent from...
```

In the fax screen, the **Configure** menu contains the following five options for setting up your fax format:

FAX Drive (ALT, C, F)

Sets the disk directory in which the program temporarily stores fax files. Covered in "Configuring Send a Fax."

Page Length (ALT, C, P)

Sets the standard fax page length. The default is *11 inches*. Covered in "Configuring Send a Fax."

Cover Page (ALT, C, C)

Sets whether you'll be prompted to add a cover page for every fax transmission. The default is *YES*. Covered in "Configuring Send a Fax."

Time Format (ALT, C, T)

Sets the format that time is entered and displayed in to 24 hr or Am/Pm. The default is *24 hr*. Covered in "Configuring Send a Fax."

Sent From (ALT, C, S)

Sets your name, which is printed at the top of every fax page. Covered in "Configuring Send a Fax."

The Actions Menu (Check the Fax Log)

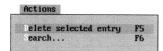

In the Fax Log, the **A**ctions menu contains the following two options for deleting faxes and searching through faxes:

Delete the Selected Entry (ALT, A, D or F5)

Removes the selected entry from the Fax Log. Covered in "Checking the Fax Log."

Search (ALT, A, S or F6)

Finds specified Fax Log entries. Covered in "Checking the Fax Log."

The Configure Menu (Check the Fax Log)

In the Fax Log, the **C**onfigure menu contains the following two options for setting the directory where faxes are held and the automatic update interval:

FAX Drive (ALT, C, F)

Sets the disk directory in which the program temporarily stores fax files. Covered in "Checking the Fax Log."

AutoUpdate (ALT, C, A)

Sets, in seconds, how often the Fax Log window will be updated. Covered in "Checking the Fax Log."

Chapter 27

Using the Macro Editor

When you work in an application, you typically use certain keystroke sequences over and over. The Desktop lets you create small programs, called *macros*, that automate such repetitive sequences. Just as a player piano can record each press of a piano key and then play the keyboard presses back for you, a macro can record your computer keystrokes and then play them back on your PC.

Macros provide several benefits. First, they eliminate tedium because they automate repetitive work. Second, they save time, because they execute your keystrokes at computer speed. Third, they guarantee precision, because they always play back your keystrokes exactly as you first entered them.

You can create macros to perform such operations as typing out frequently used phrases in your documents, calling up commands requiring numerous keystroke selections, starting an application and opening its files simultaneously, inserting the current date and time, formatting text to print in special styles such as boldface or italics, and redefining the keyboard to suit your tastes (for example, defining SHIFT-. to produce a period instead of the > symbol).

This chapter first outlines how macros are implemented in the Desktop. It then covers the Macro Editor screen; creating macros using Learn mode; adjusting the macro speed; examining, editing, clearing, and activating macros; creating macros manually; documenting macros; handling macro conflicts; chaining macros; using printer macros; and special macro commands.

Macro Overview

The fundamental concepts behind macros are the same in all programs, but the precise methods for their creation and use differ across applications. If you're already familiar with macros, the following two sections will give you a quick overview of the unique way macros are implemented in the Desktop.

If you're not familiar with macros, you may want to skip these sections for now, since they assume knowledge of macro basics. Most of the topics in the first section are covered in greater depth in appropriate sections throughout the chapter.

Macro Specifications

If the Desktop is memory resident, you can set it to record your keystrokes as you type them so that, in effect, it writes your macros for you. These macros are initially stored in memory, but when you hotkey into the Desktop, they're copied to a file named LEARN.PRO.

However, if the Desktop isn't memory resident, or if you want to use special macro commands, you must write your macros manually in Macro Editor files. Macros are entered as text, with special keystrokes enclosed by angle brackets (for example, ALT-F, P, ENTER is represented by the text <altf>p<enter>). This all-text format allows macros to be easily created, documented, and edited.

You can enter as many macros as you want in a Macro Editor file. When you then activate the file, you activate *all* the macros within it.

You can set a file to be active within the Desktop only, outside the Desktop only, or everywhere on your PC. The file remains active through subsequent Desktop sessions until you explicitly deactivate it.

In addition, you can set as many Macro Editor files to be active simultaneously as you want. This means that you can keep different categories of macros in different files, and activate and deactivate these groups of macros as your needs change.

The only constraint on the number of macros active at one time is the 7K macro memory buffer. The Desktop loads your active macros (keystroke sequences and all) into this buffer, so the total amount of space these macros take up must be under approximately 7000 characters. However, macros tend to be fairly short, so under normal circumstances you'll probably never come close to hitting this 7K boundary.

ProKey Compatibility

The Macro Editor's format is compatible with ProKey version 4, a standalone macro utility that also works across PC applications. It's because of this compatibility that the Macro Editor's default file extension is PRO. You can load a ProKey file's contents directly into a Macro Editor file and (generally) use it as is.

However, there are two important differences between the programs. First, the Macro Editor operates differently when dealing with macros that use the same invoking keystroke. For more information, see "Handling Macro Conflicts" later in this chapter.

Second, while ProKey can assign a macro to any keystroke, the Macro Editor supports only standard IBM BIOS code keystrokes. For a complete list of which invoking keystrokes are supported by the Macro Editor, see Table 27-1. Keep in

Key	SHIFT	ALT	CTRL
F1	SHIFT-F1	ALT-F1	CTRL-F1
F2	SHIFT-F2	ALT-F2	CTRL-F2
F3	SHIFT-F3	ALT-F3	CTRL-F3
F4	SHIFT-F4	ALT-F4	CTRL-F4
F5	SHIFT-F5	ALT-F5	CTRL-F5
F6	SHIFT-F6	ALT-F6	CTRL-F6
F7	SHIFT-F7	ALT-F7	CTRL-F7
F8	SHIFT-F8	ALT-F8	CTRL-F8
F9	SHIFT-F9	ALT-F9	CTRL-F9
F10	SHIFT-F10	ALT-10	CTRL-F10
A	A	ALT-A	CTRL-A
B	B	ALT-B	CTRL-B
C	C	ALT-C	
D	D	ALT-D	CTRL-D
E	E	ALT-E	CTRL-E
F	F	ALT-F	CTRL-F
G	G	ALT-G	CTRL-G
H	H	ALT-H	CTRL-H
I	I	ALT-I	CTRL-I
J	J	ALT-J	CTRL-J
K	K	ALT-K	CTRL-K
L	L	ALT-L	CTRL-L
M	M	ALT-M	CTRL-M
N	N	ALT-N	CTRL-N
O	O	ALT-O	CTRL-O
P	P	ALT-P	CTRL-P
Q	Q	ALT-Q	
R	R	ALT-R	CTRL-R
S	S	ALT-S	
T	T	ALT-T	CTRL-T
U	U	ALT-U	CTRL-U
V	V	ALT-V	CTRL-V
W	W	ALT-W	CTRL-W
X	X	ALT-X	CTRL-X
Y	Y	ALT-Y	CTRL-Y
Z	Z	ALT-Z	CTRL-Z
1	!	ALT-1	
2	@	ALT-2	CTRL-2
3	#	ALT-3	

Table 27-1. *Supported Keystrokes for Invoking a Macro*

Key	SHIFT	ALT	CTRL
4	$	ALT-4	
5	%	ALT-5	
6	^	ALT-6	CTRL-6
7	&	ALT-7	
8	*	ALT-8	
9	(	ALT-9	
0	)	ALT-0	
-	_	\<enddef>	\<vfld>
=	+	\<begdef>	
[	{		CTRL-[
]	}		\<ffld>
;	:		
'	"		
\	|		CTRL-\
,	<		
.	>		
/	?		
ESC			
TAB	SHIFT-TAB		
BACKSPACE			CTRL-BACKSPACE
ENTER			CTRL-ENTER
*			CTRL-PRTSC
HOME			CTRL-HOME
UP ARROW			
PGUP			CTRL-PGUP
RIGHT ARROW			CTRL-RIGHT ARROW
LEFT ARROW			CTRL-LEFT ARROW
END			CTRL-END
DOWN ARROW			
PGDN			CTRL-PGDN
INS			
DEL			
Keypad 1			
Keypad 2			
Keypad 3			
Keypad 4			
Keypad 5			
Keypad 6			
Keypad 7			
Keypad 8			
Keypad 9			
Keypad 0			
Keypad +			
Keypad -			

Table 27-1.   *Supported Keystrokes for Invoking a Macro (continued)*

mind that you can't use keystrokes defined as hotkeys; for example, CTRL-O is the default hotkey for the Autodialer.

Examining the Macro Editor

Macros are created with the Desktop's Macro Editor application. To create a macro file, follow these steps:

1. Call up the Desktop Manager. If you've installed the Desktop to be memory resident, press CTRL-SPACEBAR. Otherwise, type **DESKTOP** from the DOS prompt and press ENTER.

2. Press ENTER or click Desktop to display the main menu.

3. Press M or click Macro Editor to select the application. The File Load dialog box appears.

4. Type **TEMP** (for temporary) to create a macro file named TEMP.PRO. (If you don't specify an extension, PRO is automatically appended to your filename.)

5. Press ALT-N, or press ENTER twice, or click New. The Macro Editor screen appears, as shown in Figure 27-1.

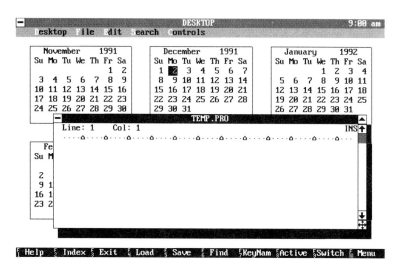

Figure 27-1.   *The Macro Editor screen*

The Macro Editor Versus Notepads

Aside from "Macro Editor" appearing in its top border, the Macro Editor window looks similar to Notepads, the Desktop application covered in Chapter 20. In fact, with respect to basic text creation and manipulation, the two applications are identical. For example, the Macro Editor contains the same window elements (such as the Line and Column Number Counters and the Tab Ruler), provides the same cursor movement shortcuts (such as CTRL-RIGHT ARROW to move forward by word and CTRL-END to move to the bottom of the document), supports the same file formats (PCTOOLS Desktop and ASCII), and has many of the same menu commands. Therefore, for information about creating and manipulating text in the Macro Editor, it's recommended that you read the "Basic Typing," "Basic Editing," "Moving Around in Your Document," "Saving Your Document," "Deleting, Moving, and Copying," "Combining Files," and "Finding and Replacing" sections of Chapter 20, "Using Notepads."

At the same time, the purposes of the two applications are fundamentally different. While Notepads is intended to generate documents, the Macro Editor's function is to generate executable macro instructions. Therefore, in place of the print, spell-checking, and document formatting commands in Notepads, the Macro Editor contains commands to control macro execution.

One other notable difference is that macros can operate virtually anywhere *except* in the Macro Editor itself. Therefore, even if a macro invokes commands common to both Notepads and the Macro Editor, it can run in the former but not the latter.

The Macro Editor Message Bar

At the bottom of the Macro Editor screen is the message bar. When a Macro Editor activity is taking place, the bar displays appropriate definitions or instructions. Otherwise, it displays the following commands assigned to the function keys:

Function Key	Action
F1 (Help)	Brings up context-sensitive help
F2 (Index)	Brings up the online help index
F3 (Exit)	Performs the same functions as ESC
F4 (Load)	Selects File **L**oad
F5 (Save)	Selects File **S**ave
F6 (Find)	Selects Search **R**eplace
F7 (KeyNam)	Inserts the macro code of the next key pressed
F8 (Active)	Selects File **M**acro Activation
F9 (Switch)	Activates a different open window
F10 (Menu)	Performs the same functions as ALT

Navigating the Macro Editor Menus

At the top of the screen are the six menus available in the Macro Editor (and, in the right corner, the system time). Follow these steps to examine the menus:

1. Press ALT, F or click File to display the **File** menu, which lets you load, save, and activate macros.

2. Press RIGHT ARROW to display the **Edit** menu, which lets you move, copy, and delete text; combine files; and move the cursor to a specified line.

3. Press RIGHT ARROW again to display the **Search** menu, which lets you find and replace text.

4. Press RIGHT ARROW again to display the **Controls** menu, which lets you deactivate all macros, set a delay interval between macro keystrokes, toggle the macro recorder on and off, and save your Control menu settings as new defaults.

5. Press RIGHT ARROW again to wrap around to the **Desktop** menu, which lets you have up to 15 Desktop files open simultaneously.

6. Press ESC and ALT-SPACEBAR to display the Control menu, which lets you change the current window's colors, position, and size.

7. Press ESC to close the menu and return to the Macro Editor window.

Of these menus (shown in Figure 27-2), Control and **Desktop** are in every Desktop application, and File, **Edit** and **Search** are similar to their counterparts in Notepads. However, the File menu's **Macro Activation** command, and the Controls menu's **Deactivate All Macros**, **Playback Delay**, and **Learn Mode** commands are unique to the Macro Editor. These macro options will be covered in the following sections.

Creating Macros Using Learn Mode

You can create macros automatically by recording them in Learn mode, or you can create them manually using the Macro Editor. This section covers recording in Learn mode. (For information on the manual method, see "Working in the Macro Editor" later in this chapter.)

As mentioned at the beginning of this chapter, the Desktop can record each of your computer keystrokes and then play them back on your PC. To prepare for this operation, you must perform the following steps:

• Decide what kind of macro you want to create.

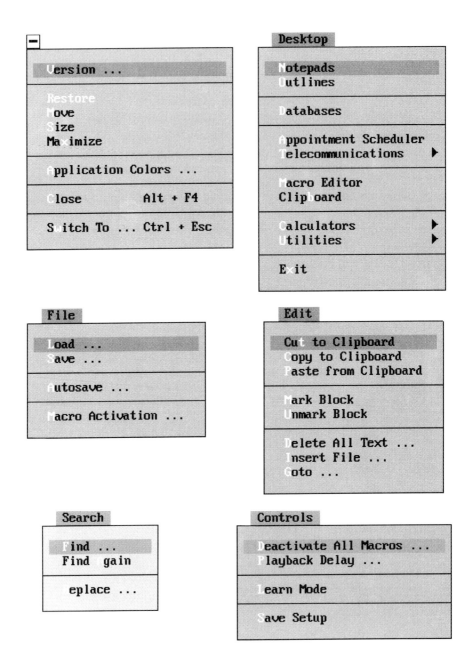

Figure 27-2. *The Macro Editor menus*

- Make the Desktop memory resident.

- Turn on the Macro Editor's Controls Learn Mode option.

- Move to the program for which you're creating the macro (or a program similar to it) to ensure that you press the correct keystrokes.

When you're ready to begin recording, press ALT-+ (that is, ALT and the plus sign near the top of your keyboard), and then the keystroke to which you're assigning the macro. All your subsequent keystrokes will be preserved. When you're done, end the recording by pressing ALT-- (that is, ALT and the minus sign near the top of your keyboard). You can then test the macro by simply pressing the keystroke you've assigned it.

Any operation that you perform frequently is a good candidate for a macro. For example, you may often list your files from the DOS prompt by typing **DIR** and pressing ENTER. You can assign this four-keystroke sequence to the single keystroke CTRL-D (for DIR).

Since you're already in the Macro Editor, first follow these steps to turn on Learn mode:

1. Press ALT, C or click on the Controls menu to display the Learn Mode option.

2. If there's a checkmark next to Learn Mode, the option is already on, so just press ESC to close the menu. Otherwise, press L or click the option to turn it on. It will remain on for subsequent Desktop sessions until you explicitly change it.

Next, follow these steps to exit to DOS and (if necessary) make the Desktop memory resident:

1. Press ALT, D, X to close the Macro Editor file and exit the Desktop.

2. If you're not in DOS, exit the current application to go to the DOS prompt.

3. If the Desktop isn't already memory resident, type **DESKTOP /R** and press ENTER. The Desktop is loaded, but you're still at the DOS prompt.

Finally, follow these steps to create and then test your macro:

1. Press ALT-+ to start recording a macro. (Be sure to press the plus sign near the top of your keyboard, not the plus sign on the numeric keypad.) The cursor changes to a blinking rectangle. Your subsequent keystrokes will now be recorded, so be careful to follow the rest of the instructions without deviation.

2. Press CTRL-D to assign the macro to this keystroke. Everything you type from now until you press ALT-- will be recorded as part of the macro keystroke sequence.

3. Type **DIR** and press ENTER. A list of the current directory's files scrolls on your screen.

4. Press ALT--to end the recording. (Be sure to press the minus sign near the top of your keyboard, not the minus sign on the numeric keypad.) The cursor changes back to its original shape, indicating that you're finished creating your macro.

You may find that sometimes the cursor doesn't return to its original form properly (for example, it may display on the line above instead of the current line). This doesn't impair the cursor's functioning, but it's disconcerting. To return the cursor to normal, try hotkeying in and out of the Desktop. If that doesn't work, run the DOS program MODE by typing from the DOS prompt **MODE MONO** *for a monochrome system or* **MODE CO80** *for a color system, and then pressing ENTER.*

5. Press CTRL-D to test the macro. The Macro Editor immediately transmits the characters DIR and the ENTER code, and your files are displayed again.

If you experience problems such as beeping when replaying your macro, see the next section, "Adjusting Macro Transmission Speed."

You can create Learn mode macros within the Desktop as well as outside of it. For example, you may often type your name and address in Notepads documents. To assign this procedure to the keystroke CTRL-A (for address), follow these steps:

1. Press CTRL-SPACEBAR to bring up the Desktop.

2. Press ENTER twice to select the Notepads application.

3. Press ALT-N (and, if necessary, ENTER) to open a temporary Notepads window.

4. Press ALT-+ to start the macro. As before, the cursor changes to a blinking rectangle. Your subsequent keystrokes will be recorded, so be careful to follow the rest of the instructions without deviation.

5. Press CTRL-A to assign your macro to the keystroke.

6. Type your name and press ENTER.

7. If appropriate, type your company name and press ENTER.

8. Type your street address on one or two lines, pressing ENTER after each line.

9. Type your city, state, and zip code, and press ENTER.

10. Press ENTER twice more to create some blank lines after your address.

11. Press ALT--to end the recording. The cursor changes back to its original shape, indicating that you're finished creating your macro.

12. Press CTRL-A to test the macro. Starting at the cursor position, the Macro Editor replays your keystrokes, typing out your full name and address again.

13. Press ALT, F, X to close the Notepads window without saving it.

Adjusting Macro Transmission Speed

You may find that your computer beeps and loses data while a macro is running. If this occurs, it's probably because the macro is transmitting its keystroke sequence faster than your computer can handle. (More technically, it's overloading your keyboard buffer.) The **C**ontrols **P**layback Delay command addresses this problem by letting you slow the macro transmission speed. To use it, follow these steps:

1. Press ALT-D, M, ALT-N (and, if necessary, ENTER) to open a temporary Macro Editor window.

2. Press ALT, C, P, or click on the Controls menu and select Playback Delay. The following Macro/Clipboard Playback Delay dialog box appears:

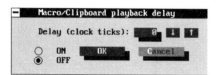

3. Enter the number of clock ticks (each 1/18th of a second) by which to delay the transmission speed. Generally, a number from 1 to 5 will be appropriate. If you enter too high a number, keystrokes will be transmitted very slowly. A few minutes of experimentation should yield the ideal delay value for your system. The default is *0*, or no delay, transmitting a keystroke every 1/18th of a second.

4. Select the ON option (if it isn't already selected). The default is *off*, meaning no delay.

5. Press ALT-O or click OK.

6. Press ESC to close the macro window.

This dialog box is also available through the Clipboard's **C**opy/Paste menu command **S**et Playback Delay, since when the Clipboard pastes characters it can encounter the same speed problems. Any change made from the Macro Editor in this box carries over to the Clipboard, and vice versa.

Working in the Macro Editor

So far, you've created macros by recording your keystrokes outside the Macro Editor. In this section, you'll manipulate and create macros within the Macro Editor. Specifically, you'll learn how to examine, edit, clear, activate, manually create, and document your macros.

Examining a Macro

When you create macros in Learn mode, they're stored in a 7000-character memory storage area called the *macro buffer*. When you bring up the Desktop, these macros are automatically copied to a file named LEARN.PRO. If the file doesn't already exist, the Desktop will first create LEARN.PRO; if the file does exist, the Desktop will add the macros to the end of the file.

For example, in the previous section you created a DOS macro and then brought up the Desktop. As a result, you now have a LEARN.PRO file that contains the macro. (Your second macro isn't in the file yet, though, because you haven't exited and re-entered the Desktop since creating it.) To examine the DOS macro, follow these steps:

1. Press ALT, D, M, or click on the Desktop menu and select Macro Editor.

2. Press TAB and use DOWN ARROW, or use your mouse, to scroll through the Files box until you see LEARN.PRO listed.

3. Select LEARN.PRO and press ENTER to open the file.

4. Press CTRL-END to move to the end of the file. You should see the text representation of your DOS macro. If LEARN.PRO didn't exist before you began this chapter, your DOS macro is the only macro in the file. Otherwise, it's the last macro in the file.

Your DOS macro should look like this:

<begdef><ctrld>DIR<enter><enddef>

If your macro is longer, it's because you pressed additional keys while creating it. For example, if you corrected any typing errors using BACKSPACE, both the errors and the BACKSPACE presses (represented as <bks> codes) were recorded as part of the keystroke sequence.

It's easy to correct mistakes in the macro, though, because macros consist exclusively of normal text. Even codes such as <begdef> and <enter> are just letters enclosed by < (the left angle bracket at the top of the comma key) and > (the right angle bracket at the top of the period key). In fact, the angle brackets provide the only way the Macro Editor can distinguish special keystrokes (such as ENTER) from words (such as "ENTER").

The text format of macros means that you can edit them in virtually the same way you would any other text. It also means that you can write macros manually from within the Macro Editor, which is sometimes more efficient than generating them automatically via Learn mode.

To write or edit macros, you must first understand how they're constructed. Macros are made up of four parts: the begin code, the invoking keystroke, the keystroke sequence, and the end code.

The Begin Code

The first part of a macro is its begin code, which is represented by <begdef> (begin macro definition).

When Learn mode is on and you're outside of the Macro Editor, pressing ALT-+ generates <begdef> invisibly in the macro buffer at the same time it turns keystroke recording on.

When you're in the Macro Editor, Learn mode has no effect, so pressing ALT-+ simply enters the characters <begdef> into the current file. This provides a quick alternative to typing the characters yourself.

The Invoking Keystroke

The second part of a macro is the invoking keystroke. In your DOS macro, the invoking keystroke is CTRL-D, and it's represented by the code <ctrld>. Other examples of keystroke codes are <alta> for ALT-A, <shiftf8> for SHIFT-F8, <pgdn> for PGDN, and <ctrlrgt> for CTRL-RIGHT ARROW.

When you're recording macros using Learn mode, pressing a keystroke automatically generates the appropriate code in the macro buffer. When you're within the Macro Editor, however, first press F7 and then the keystroke to insert the appropriate code into your file. For example, pressing F7, ENTER inserts the characters <enter> into the current file, pressing F7, CTRL-D inserts <ctrld>, and so on.

Preceding a keystroke with F7 is actually not necessary unless the keystroke has special meaning in the Desktop (for example, ENTER, F1, or ALT-D, as opposed to SHIFT-F1 or CTRL-D). However, keeping track of which keystrokes affect the Desktop and which don't while you're trying to enter your macro can become very distracting. Since pressing F7 first always *works, it's therefore recommended that you use F7 to insert* any *special keystroke in your macro file.*

When you select an invoking keystroke, you should try to avoid conflicts with the programs the macro will work with. For example, when creating macros for the Desktop, you should generally avoid hotkeys and ALT combinations as invoking keystrokes because they'll conflict with Desktop functions. At the same time, these keystrokes may be fine for macros that you use outside of the Desktop. For more information on this subject, see "Handling Macro Conflicts" later in this chapter.

In addition, while you can use most keyboard combinations for invoking macros, there are certain ones that the Macro Editor doesn't support. For a complete list of which invoking keystrokes are supported by the Macro Editor, see Table 27-1.

The Keystroke Sequence

The third part of a macro is the sequence of keystrokes it must duplicate. In your DOS macro, the keystroke sequence consists of the text DIR (or dir if you typed in lowercase) followed by an ENTER code.

A sequence can be as short as one keystroke or long enough to fill the 7000-character macro buffer. It can include virtually any keystroke, including many not supported as invoking keystrokes (but *not* any of the four Desktop hotkeys). It can also include the invoking keystroke of another macro (see "Chaining Macros" later in this chapter) and special macro commands (see "Using Macro Commands" later in this chapter).

The End Code

The last part of a macro is its end code, which is represented by <enddef> (end macro definition).

When Learn mode is on and you're outside of the Macro Editor, pressing ALT- - generates <enddef> invisibly in the macro buffer at the same time it turns keystroke recording off.

When you're in the Macro Editor, Learn mode has no effect, so pressing ALT- - simply enters the characters <enddef> into the current file. This provides a quick alternative to typing the characters yourself.

Editing, Clearing, and Activating Macros

Now that you understand how your DOS macro is constructed, you can proceed to edit it.

First, if the macro contains any errors and <bks> codes, delete them using BACKSPACE or DEL. (For more information, see the "Basic Editing" section of Chapter 20, "Using Notepads.") When you're done, your macro should look like this:

<begdef><ctrld>DIR<enter><enddef>

You can also bring in and edit your Notepads address macro. To do so, follow these steps:

1. Press CTRL-SPACEBAR to hotkey out of the Desktop. You're back in DOS.

2. Press CTRL-SPACEBAR to bring the Desktop up again. You're back in the LEARN.PRO window. Notice that your reentry into the Desktop has caused the Notepads macro to be copied from the macro buffer to the end of your file.

3. Delete any errors and <bks> codes using BACKSPACE or DEL. When you're done, the macro should consist of nothing but its begin code, its invoking keystroke <ctrla>, your name and address with <enter> codes following each line, and the macro's end code.

You can do more than just correct errors, though. You can also revise macros to enhance their operation. For example, in the case of your DOS macro, you may not have liked how quickly the files scrolled by on your screen. To fix this, you can pause each screen of the file display by adding the parameter /P to the DIR command.

In Learn mode, you'd have to redo your entire macro to make this one change. Using the Macro Editor, however, you can make the change in just two steps:

1. Using the arrow keys or your mouse, move the cursor directly past the "R" in "DIR."

2. Type **/P**. The characters are inserted into the macro.

As another example, in your Notepads macro you may prefer invoking the macro using a function key combination such as CTRL-F1. Again, in Learn mode you'd have to redo your entire macro to make the change. Manually, however, you can do it in three steps:

1. Using the arrow keys or your mouse, move the cursor directly past the "a" in "<ctrla>."

2. Press BACKSPACE. The "a" is deleted.

3. Type **F1** (that is, type **F** and **1**). The characters are inserted, changing the invoking keystroke to <ctrlF1>.

While you've made changes in your PRO file, your revised macros haven't automatically replaced your old ones in the macro buffer. You must therefore force the replacements to be made by clearing the macro buffer of its current contents and activating the LEARN.PRO file.

First, follow these steps to clear the buffer:

1. Press ALT, C, D, or click on the Controls menu and select Deactivate All Macros. The following warning box appears:

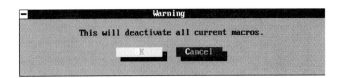

2. Press ENTER or click OK. The macro buffer's contents are cleared and any active Macro Editor files are deactivated.

Next, follow these steps to activate LEARN.PRO:

1. Press ALT, F, M, or press F8, or click on the File menu and select Macro Activation. The following dialog box appears:

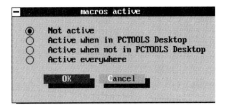

The box offers four options: Not Active, which is the default; Active when in PCTOOLS Desktop, which makes the file's macros active within the Desktop only; Active when not in PCTOOLS Desktop, which makes the file's macros active outside the Desktop only; and Active Everywhere, which makes the file's macros active both within and outside of the Desktop.

2. Your first macro works outside the Desktop and your second one works within it, so press UP ARROW, or click Active Everywhere, to move to that option.

3. Press ENTER twice, or click OK, to turn the Active Everywhere option on and close the dialog box.

The LEARN.PRO file is now activated. This means that all its macros have been copied into the macro buffer. It also means that the buffer will track changes in the file from now on.

The file will remain active for this and future Desktop sessions until you explicitly deactivate it by using the Controls Deactivate All Macros command; or by selecting

the **F**ile **M**acro Activation Not Active option; or by deleting the Desktop file
MACROS.DOV, which stores your Macro Editor settings.

You're now set to test your editing changes. To do so, follow these steps:

1. Press CTRL-SPACEBAR to hotkey out of the Desktop. You're back in DOS.

2. Press CTRL-D. Your DOS macro lists the first 23 files in your directory, but now pauses the display until you're ready to read the next screenful of files.

3. Press SPACEBAR. The next screenful of files appears.

4. Continue pressing SPACEBAR until you've listed all the files in the directory. You've demonstrated that your DOS macro change was successful.

5. Press CTRL-SPACEBAR to reenter the Desktop.

6. Press ALT-D, N, ALT-N (and, if necessary, ENTER) to bring up a temporary Notepads window again.

7. Press CTRL-A, which was your previous keystroke for invoking the address macro. Instead of running the macro, the keystroke now just inserts an ASCII graphics character. (For information on ASCII characters, see Chapter 28, "Using the Desktop Utilities.") Press BACKSPACE to delete the character.

8. Press CTRL-F1. The keystroke you reassigned to the macro now types your name and address. You've demonstrated that your Notepads macro change was successful, as well.

9. Press F9 to switch back to the LEARN.PRO file.

Creating Macros Manually

In the previous section, you edited macros to alter their operation. Using the same techniques, you can write a new macro directly in the Macro Editor.

For example, it's important that you save your files to disk frequently to ensure that you don't lose any of your work. In most Desktop applications, the keystrokes to do this are ALT-F, S, ALT-S. Follow these steps to write a new macro that assigns this sequence to SHIFT-F1:

1. Press CTRL-END and ENTER to move to the end of the LEARN.PRO file.

2. Press ALT-+ to mark the start of the macro. The begin code <begdef> is entered.

3. Press F7 to indicate that you want a keystroke code inserted.

4. Press SHIFT-F1 for the invoking keystroke. The code <shiftf1> is entered.

5. Press F7, ALT-F to insert the first keystroke of the macro sequence. The code <altf> is entered.

6. Type **S** for the next key in the sequence.

7. Press F7, ALT-S to insert the last keystroke in the sequence. The code <alts> is entered.

8. Press ALT- – to mark the end of the macro. The end code <enddef> is entered.

Now follow these steps to test your macro:

1. Press F9 to switch to the Notepads window.

2. Press SHIFT-F1. The File menu and then the Save File to Disk dialog box come up almost too quickly to be seen, and then the file is saved.

3. To verify the save procedure is taking place, keep an eye on your disk drive light and press SHIFT-F1 again. Notice that the light comes on, indicating that the drive's been accessed.

4. Press F9 to switch back to the LEARN.PRO file.

You've now demonstrated that macros you write manually perform just as well as macros you create automatically in Learn mode. You should use the manual method when the Desktop isn't memory resident, when you want to include special macro commands (see "Using Macro Commands" later in this chapter), or when it's simply quicker and more straightforward to type your macro directly into a Macro Editor file.

Documenting Macros

While a macro function may seem crystal clear to you the day you've created it, it may mystify you when it's faded from your memory six months later. It's therefore important that in addition to writing the macro itself, you also write a description of it.

The Macro Editor pays attention only to text appearing between the <begdef> and <enddef> codes. Therefore, you can include explanations anywhere in the file as long as you keep them outside of these codes. It's recommended that you place an explanation *above* each macro.

For example, follow these steps to document the three macros you've created in LEARN.PRO:

1. Press CTRL-HOME to move to the top of the file.

2. Press ENTER to create a blank line, and then UP ARROW to move back up to line 1.

3. Type **DOS: List files, pausing after each screen.** to describe the first macro's intended environment and function.

4. Press HOME, press DOWN ARROW twice, press ENTER twice, and press UP ARROW to position the cursor for your second description.

5. Type **Word Processor: Type name and address.** to describe the second macro's intended environment and function.

6. Press HOME, press DOWN ARROW three times, and press ENTER to position the cursor for your third description.

7. Type **Notepads, Outlines, Appointment Scheduler, Telecommunications: Save the current file to disk.** to describe the third macro's intended environments and function.

8. Press CTRL-HOME to move to the top of the file again. Your macros are now sufficiently documented to remind you of their function long after you created them.

Handling Macro Conflicts

You can have as many macros as you want in an active Macro Editor file, as long as they all fit into the macro buffer's 7000-character limit. Similarly, you can keep as many Macro Editor files active as you want, as long as all their macros together fit into the 7K buffer.

Because the Desktop allows such a large number and wide variety of macros to be active, it's likely that you'll run across situations in which a macro's invoking keystroke conflicts with either the current application or another macro. The Desktop doesn't provide any explanatory message when this occurs. Therefore, you need to understand how the Desktop handles conflicts, and how to analyze and resolve conflicts.

Understanding Macro Conflict Rules

There are two basic rules to remember about macro conflicts.

First, if two or more macros use the same keystroke in the same active file, the Desktop will use the macro closest to the top of the file and ignore the other ones.

For example, if macros 1, 2, and 3 appear in an active file in that order and use the same invoking keystroke, macro 1 will be active, while macros 2 and 3 will be ignored. If macro 1 is later moved below the other two macros in the file, macro 2 will become active, while macros 3 and 1 will be ignored.

Second, if macros using the same keystroke appear in two or more active files, the Desktop will use the macro in the file activated first and ignore the other ones.

For example, if you activate files A, B, and C in that order, the macros in file A will always override conflicting macros in B and C, and B will always override conflicting macros in C. Also, if A is deactivated, any macros previously ignored in

B will become active, and any macros previously ignored in C will become active as long as they don't conflict with B.

These rules cover virtually all conflicts between Desktop macros. However, you'll also experience conflicts between your macros and the applications you're using them in. Unfortunately, there are no straightforward rules for these situations, since each application behaves differently. A rule of thumb for playing it safe is to avoid using invoking keystrokes that even come close to keystrokes an application appears to reserve for itself.

For example, the Desktop itself doesn't respond consistently to conflicts; specifically, it usually allows a macro to override a keystroke's definition, but under some circumstances will just ignore the macro instead. Therefore, for macros designed to work within the Desktop, it's safest to avoid the following types of invoking keystrokes:

- ALT combinations such as ALT-D and ALT-SPACEBAR, which conflict with keystrokes that display Desktop menus.

- Function keys F1 through F10, to which the Desktop often assigns special meanings. (However, CTRL and SHIFT combinations such as CTRL-F1 or SHIFT-F1 are safe, because the Desktop never uses them.)

- The four Desktop hotkeys, which bring up the Desktop, paste text from the Clipboard, cut text to the Clipboard, and invoke the Autodialer. Initially, these are assigned to CTRL-SPACEBAR, SHIFT-INS, SHIFT-DEL, and CTRL-O, respectively. The first three keystrokes aren't even supported as invoking macros, so there's no danger of conflict with them; but CTRL-O *is* supported, so you must remember to avoid it.

In addition, if you reassign a hotkey to a supported keystroke (see Chapter 28, "Using the Desktop Utilities"), you must remember to avoid using that keystroke in your macros. At the same time, if you reassign the Autodialer to another keystroke, keep in mind that this frees up CTRL-O for macro use.

Analyzing and Resolving Macro Conflicts

As mentioned earlier, the Desktop doesn't warn you when macro conflicts occur. Therefore, you have to spot and analyze such conflicts yourself.

When you press the keystroke of an active macro and nothing happens, or something entirely different from the macro's keystroke sequence is generated, explore the possibilities step by step.

First, check Table 27-1 to make sure the keystroke is supported by the Macro Editor. If it isn't listed as an acceptable invoking keystroke, the problem is that you can't use the keystroke for *any* macro. In such cases, just edit your macro to change the keystroke.

If your keystroke is supported, next determine if there's a problem with the macro itself. To do so, edit the macro to temporarily change its invoking keystroke to one you're *certain* will provide no conflicts, and then test the macro again. If it reacts the same as before, the problem is probably with your macro definition. In this case, study the macro keystroke by keystroke, or try to create the macro again using Learn mode, until you eliminate the problem. (You can also try rebooting to determine if the problem was caused by some quirk in memory created by the interaction of different programs.)

However, if your macro behaves normally after you've changed its invoking keystroke, the problem is probably the result of a conflict. You should next determine the source of the conflict.

To begin, use the **S**earch **F**ind command to search through the file for another macro using the invoking keystroke. If you locate such a macro and it's higher up in the file than the original macro, you've discovered the difficulty. You can now decide which of the two macros will use the keystroke.

If your search doesn't yield a conflict, next determine if the problem is a macro in another file. To do so, first edit the macro to return its original invoking keystroke. Second, select the **C**ontrols **D**eactivate All Macros command to deactivate all macro files and clear the macro buffer. Third, activate the file your macro is in using the **F**ile **M**acro Activation command. Lastly, test the macro again. If it now works properly, the conflict was caused by a macro in another file. In this case, use the **S**earch Find **A**gain command to search through each macro file until you find the other macro. You can then decide which of the two macros to assign the keystroke.

On the other hand, if your macro still doesn't work properly, you probably have a conflict with the application itself. You'll either have to give up using the keystroke or (if possible) alter the application to make it free up the keystroke for your use.

Suppressing a Macro

If a keystroke is used by an application but is also appropriate for a macro you've created, you may decide to override the function that the application has assigned to the keystroke and use it for the macro. To give you flexibility in these situations, the Desktop allows you to access the keystroke's original function when you need it. To do so, just press ' (the back quote character at the bottom of the tilde key) before the keystroke. This suppresses your macro from being invoked and allows the application's meaning for the keystroke to come through instead.

For example, if you assigned a DOS macro to F3, it would override the key's usual function of typing out your last DOS command. If you wanted to suppress your macro definition, you'd simply press ' first, and then press F3 to get your last DOS command typed out.

Advanced Macro Features

So far, you've learned how to create macros that replay a sequence of keystrokes. You can also create macros that invoke other macros; format your text with printing codes; or use special commands to insert the date and time, call up the Desktop, pause execution, or accept input. These topics are covered in this section.

Chaining Macros

Since a macro can execute any keystroke and is also invoked by a keystroke, it follows that one macro can invoke another one. For example, part of the keystroke sequence of macro A can be the invoking keystroke of macro B. When you invoke A, it executes normally until reaching B, and then transfers execution to B. When macro B finishes executing, it returns control to macro A.

To add another wrinkle, before returning control to A, macro B can invoke macro C, macro C can invoke macro D, and so on.

Alternatively, a macro can invoke multiple other macros directly. For example, macro A can invoke macro B, then resume execution and invoke C, then resume execution and invoke B again, then resume execution and invoke D, and so on.

This ability to chain macros is quite useful, because it enables you to take advantage of what you've already created. For example, your save file macro could be used as a first step for a printing macro, as a last step for a data creation macro, as a middle step for an exit macro, and so on.

To get a feel for chaining macros, follow these steps to include your file save macro in your address macro:

1. Use the arrow keys or your mouse to move to the last line of your address macro.

2. Press END to move to the end of the line.

3. Press LEFT ARROW eight times to move to the beginning of the <enddef> code.

4. Press F7, SHIFT-F1 to insert the invoking keystroke of the file save macro as the last part of your address macro.

5. Press F9 to switch to your Notepads window. (If the window isn't still open, press ALT-D, N, ALT-N, ENTER.)

6. While keeping an eye on your disk drive light, press CTRL-F1. Your name and address are typed out as usual, and then the current file is saved, preserving the text on disk.

It's also worth noting that in addition to referring to other macros, a macro can refer to itself! This is useful when you want to repeat a keystroke sequence over and over again. To stop a repeating macro, just press ESC.

For example, follow these steps to create and test a macro that repeats a character pattern:

1. Press F9 to return to LEARN.PRO.

2. Press CTRL-END and ENTER to move to the bottom of the file.

3. Press ALT-+.

4. Press F7, CTRL-R to assign the repeating macro to CTRL-R.

5. Type *.*.*.*.*.*.*.*.*.*. to create a simple pattern consisting of ten pairs of asterisks and periods.

6. Press F7, ENTER to insert an ENTER code.

7. Press F7, CTRL-R to make the macro repeat.

8. Press ALT- -.

9. Press F9 to switch to the Notepads window.

10. Press CTRL-R. Your pattern is repeated endlessly.

11. Press ESC to stop the macro.

Formatting Text Using Printer Macros

The Desktop applications Notepads, Outlines, and Databases are centered around manipulating and printing text. However, they don't contain any commands for formatting text using boldface, underlining, italics, and other printer effects. You can get around this limitation by inserting formatting codes with printer macros.

The Desktop comes packaged with four printer macro files that use ESC codes compatible with the Hewlett-Packard LaserJet (HPLJF.PRO), the Epson FX-80 (EPSON.PRO), the IBM ProPrinter (PROPTR.PRO), and Panasonic printers (PANA.PRO). To activate one of these printer files, follow these steps:

1. Press ALT, D, M, or click on the Desktop menu and select Macro Editor. The File Load dialog box appears.

2. If you aren't already set to the directory that contains your PC Tools data files, switch to it now using the Drives and Directories boxes. The Files box should now list the HPLJF.PRO, EPSON.PRO, PROPTR.PRO, and PANA.PRO files.

3. Use TAB and DOWN ARROW, or use your mouse, to select the macro file most compatible with your printer. (If you aren't sure which file is most appropriate, select EPSON.PRO for an impact printer or HPLJF.PRO for an inkjet or laser printer.)

4. Press ENTER to open the file.

5. Press PGDN a few times to scroll through the file's macros. Notice that each macro first types out a description of what the macro does (for example, ¦ BOLD ON ¦ for turning boldfacing on, ¦ UND ON ¦ for turning underlining on), and then inserts a sequence of ESC codes to control your printer (for example, setting your printer to boldface or underline subsequent text). Also notice that the invoking keystroke for ¦ BOLD ON ¦ is CTRL-B, for ¦ BOLD OFF ¦ is CTRL-H, for ¦ UND ON ¦ is CTRL-U, and for ¦ UND OFF ¦ is CTRL-Y.

6. Press F8 to bring up the Macros Active dialog box.

7. Press DOWN ARROW and O to make the file active only in the Desktop. The dialog box closes, and the printer macros are activated.

8. Press ESC to close the file.

Now try out the boldface and underline macros in a Notepads window by following these steps:

1. You should be in your temporary Notepads window. Press ALT, E, D, ENTER to clear its contents.

2. Type **This is a line of unformatted text.** and press ENTER.

3. Press CTRL-B. The description "¦ BOLD ON ¦" (or something similar, depending on the macro file you've activated) is inserted. This description will display on your screen, but it won't appear on your printouts.

   At the same time, the ESC sequence for turning boldfacing on is inserted. These codes don't display on your screen, but they'll affect the way your text is printed.

4. Type **This is a line of boldfaced text.**, press CTRL-H to turn boldfacing off, and press ENTER.

5. Press CTRL-U to turn underlining on. The comment "¦ UND ON ¦" (or something similar, depending on the macro file you've activated) and a corresponding ESC sequence are inserted.

6. Type **This is a line of underlined text.**, press CTRL-Y to turn underlining off, and press ENTER.

7. Press CTRL-B, CTRL-U to turn both boldfacing and underlining on.

8. Type **This line is both boldfaced and underlined.**, press CTRL-H, CTRL-Y to turn both boldfacing and underlining off, and press ENTER. Your file should now look like this:

9. Press SHIFT-F1 to invoke your file save macro. The file is saved to disk.

10. Turn your printer on and online, and then press ALT, F, P, P. After a few moments, you should get a printout that looks similar to this:

This is a line of unformatted text.
This is a line of boldfaced text.
<u>This is a line of underlined text.</u>
<u>This line is both boldfaced and underlined.</u>

Notice that the formatting descriptions were suppressed, but their ESC sequences performed the formatting you wanted.

11. Exit your sample files by pressing ESC to close your Notepads window; pressing ALT-C, ENTER, ENTER to deactivate all your current macros; and pressing ESC to close the LEARN.PRO file.

If your printer isn't fully supported by one of the four files supplied with the Desktop, you can create a customized printer file. To do so, revise one of the supplied files, replacing its ESC sequences with the appropriate sequences specified in your printer manual. When you're done, save the file under a different name (for example, MYPRINTR.PRO) and activate it for use with your documents.

When you use any printer macros, it's a good idea to keep a printed list of their invoking keystrokes and their effects. The list will serve as a quick reference on how to invoke your various formatting codes. In addition, it will provide a reminder of which keystrokes are no longer available to you for use with other Desktop macros (as discussed in "Handling Macro Conflicts" earlier in this chapter).

Using Macro Commands

So far, the macros you've created have performed their functions using keyboard keystrokes. Macros can additionally include special commands that aren't available through the keyboard.

Specifically, the Desktop supports the following six commands for use with macros created in the Macro Editor:

- *<date>*   This command inserts the system date.
- *<time>*   This command inserts the system time.
- *<desk>*   This command brings up the Desktop when the Desktop is memory resident.
- *<cmd>d*   This command pauses macro execution for the amount of time specified.
- *<ffld>*   This command pauses macro execution until you input a fixed number of characters.
- *<vfld>*   This command pauses macro execution until you input a variable number of characters and press ENTER.

These commands are detailed in the following four sections.

Using <date> and <time>

You can make a macro generate the system date or time by including the commands <date> or <time>.

The date is displayed in the format *MM-DD-YY*, with *MM* representing two month digits, *DD* two day digits, and *YY* the last two digits of the year 19*YY*.

The time is displayed in the format *HH-MM*am or *HH-MM*pm, with *HH* representing up to two hour digits and *MM* two minute digits.

For example, if your PC's clock was set to December 2, 1991 at 8:15 A.M., the macro

<begdef><ctrld><date>, <time><enddef>

would generate the following text:

12-02-91, 8:15am

Using <desk>

When the Desktop is memory resident, you can bring it up by pressing the hotkey CTRL-SPACEBAR. However, if you also want operations performed directly after the

Desktop is invoked (for example, automatically opening your most-used application files), you have to bring up the Desktop using a macro.

The Macro Editor doesn't support hotkeys such as CTRL-SPACEBAR (see "Understanding Macro Conflict Rules" earlier in this chapter), but it *does* support the substitute command <desk>. You can use this feature to create macros that set up your Desktop environment in different ways for different tasks.

For example, the following macro assigns ALT-F10 to bring up the Desktop, open an existing Notepads file named MEMO.TXT, and open an existing Appointment Scheduler file named OFFICE.TM:

<begdef><altF10><desk><altd><enter>MEMO.TXT<enter>

<altd>aOFFICE.TM<enter><enddef>

Using <cmd>d

You can pause a macro's execution by as little as a tenth of a second and as much as 256 hours using the <cmd>d command. The command has the format

<cmd>d*HH:MM:SS.T*<enter>

with *HH:MM:SS.T* being the amount of time to pause. Specifically, *HH* represents the number of hours, *MM* the number of minutes, *SS* the number of seconds, and *.T* the number of tenths of a second.

For example, the following macro will pause for 3.5 seconds:

<begdef><ctrlg>Get ready...<cmd>d3.5<enter>Go!<enddef>

As another example, the following macro will pause for 1 hour, 5 minutes, and 30 seconds:

<begdef><ctrll>I'm out to lunch...<cmd>d1:5:30<enter>

<enter>...Now I'm back in the office.<enddef>

You can also delay a macro's execution until a specific day and time. For information on this, see the "Scheduling Programs, Batch Files, Macros, and Notes" section of Chapter 23, "Using the Appointment Scheduler."

Using <ffld> and <vfld>

So far, you've created macros that are self-contained and always perform the same operation. You can also create macros that interact with you and vary their operation based on your input.

To make a macro interactive, use either the <ffld> (fixed length field) command, which pauses the macro so you can input a fixed number of characters; or the <vfld> (variable length field) command, which pauses the macro so you can input a variable number of characters. You can generate <ffld> by pressing CTRL-] (CTRL and the right square bracket) and <vfld> by pressing CTRL- - (CTRL and the minus sign at the top of the keyboard).

The <ffld> command has the format

<ffld>n<ffld>

where "n" is a placeholder specifying the number of characters to be input. For example, to specify four characters, you'd type **nnnn**. The placeholder can be *any* character, so you could also type ####, **1234**, **$.$$**, and so on.

For example, you previously created a DOS macro to list your files. The following macro will type out "DIR/P" and a space, and then pause to let you input the letter of a disk drive. As soon as you enter the letter, the macro will continue executing and list the files from the drive you specified.

<begdef><ctrlf>DIR/P <ffld>d<ffld>:<enter><enddef>

The <vfld> command has the format

<vfld>*<vfld>

where "*" is a placeholder representing a variable number of characters. The placeholder can be *any* character (although the asterisk is an appropriate choice because of its usual function as a DOS wildcard).

For example, you might want your DOS macro to let you specify a directory path, wildcards, and/or other DIR parameters. The following macro will type out "DIR/P" and a space, and then pause to let you input one or more parameters of any length.

<begdef><ctrlf>DIR/P <vfld>*<vfld><enter><enddef>

Once you do so *and* press ENTER, the macro will continue executing, listing files based on your input.

The <ffld> and <vfld> commands don't support keys such as BACKSPACE *for correcting typing errors in your input field. Therefore, be careful to type accurately when running these macros.*

Macro Editor Command Reference

The Macro Editor offers most of the text editing commands in Notepads. In addition, it provides several commands for controlling macro execution.

Like all Desktop applications, the Macro Editor's first two menus are Control and Desktop. These menus are covered in Chapter 19, "Desktop Manager Overview."

The Macro Editor's four other menus are File, Edit, Search, and Controls. The following sections cover the options in these menus. After the name of each option are the keystrokes that invoke it, a description of what the option does, and a reference to the section in either this chapter or Chapter 20 that discusses the option in detail.

The File Menu

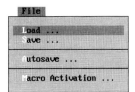

The File menu performs such operations as loading, saving, and activating macro files. It contains the following four options:

Load (ALT, F, L or F4)

Replaces the document in the current window with another document. Covered in "Abandoning Your Document" in Chapter 20.

Save (ALT, F, S or F5)

Saves your document to disk. Covered in "Saving Your Document" in Chapter 20.

Autosave (ALT, F, A)

Automatically saves your document to disk at specified intervals. Covered in "Saving Your Document" in Chapter 20.

Macro Activation (ALT, F, M or F8)

Sets a macro to be active only in the Desktop, outside the Desktop, or everywhere; or deactivates the macro. Covered in "Editing, Clearing, and Activating Macros."

The Edit Menu

The Edit menu performs such operations as moving, copying, and deleting text; moving the cursor to a specified line; and combining documents. It contains the following eight options:

Cut to Clipboard (ALT, E, T or SHIFT-DEL)

Deletes marked text and places it into the Clipboard. Used to delete or move text. Covered in "Deleting, Moving, and Copying" in Chapter 20.

Copy to Clipboard (ALT, E, C)

Places a copy of marked text into the Clipboard without affecting the original text. Used to copy text. Covered in "Deleting, Moving, and Copying" in Chapter 20.

Paste from Clipboard (ALT, E, P or SHIFT-INS)

Inserts text from the Clipboard into your document at the cursor position. Covered in "Deleting, Moving, and Copying" in Chapter 20.

Mark Block (ALT, E, M)

Marks a section, or "block," of text to be cut or copied into the Clipboard. Covered in "Deleting, Moving, and Copying" in Chapter 19.

Unmark Block (ALT, E, U or ESC)

Unmarks a text block. Covered in "Deleting, Moving, and Copying" in Chapter 20.

Delete All Text (ALT, E, D)

Removes all the text in your document. Covered in "Abandoning Your Document" in Chapter 20.

Insert File (ALT, E, I)

Copies the text from a document on disk into your current document. Covered in "Combining Files" in Chapter 20.

Goto (ALT, E, G)

Moves the cursor to the specified line number. Covered in "Moving Around in Your Document" in Chapter 20.

The Search Menu

The **S**earch menu contains the following three options for finding and replacing text:

Find (ALT, S, F)

Moves the cursor to the first occurrence of the specified text string. Covered in "Finding and Replacing" in Chapter 20.

Find **A**gain (ALT, S, A)

Moves the cursor to the next occurrence of the current text string. Covered in "Finding and Replacing" in Chapter 20.

Replace (ALT, S, R or F6)

Replaces a specified text string with a different specified string. Covered in "Finding and Replacing" in Chapter 20.

The Controls Menu

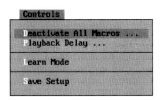

The **C**ontrols menu performs such operations as clearing active macros, delaying macro transmission, setting Learn mode, and saving menu settings. It contains the following four options:

Deactivate All Macros (ALT, C, D)

Deactivates all active Macro Editor files and clears the macro buffer. Covered in "Editing, Clearing, and Activating Macros."

Playback Delay (ALT, C, P)

Controls the speed at which macros transmit keystrokes. Covered in "Adjusting Macro Transmission Speed."

Learn Mode (ALT, C, L)

Toggles Learn mode on and off. When Learn mode is on, you can create macros by recording your keystrokes. Covered in "Creating Macros Using Learn Mode."

Save Setup (ALT, C, S)

Saves the current window size, position, and color settings to be used as defaults for new macro files.

Chapter **28**

Using the Desktop Utilities

There are three miscellaneous tasks that don't conceptually fit in with any of the Desktop's major applications: reassigning hotkeys, displaying ASCII codes, and unloading the Desktop from memory. Therefore, these jobs are handled by three small programs bundled under the heading of Utilities.

To display the Desktop utilities, follow these steps:

1. First, call up the Desktop Manager. If you've installed the Desktop to be memory resident, press CTRL-SPACEBAR. Otherwise, type **DESKTOP** from the DOS prompt and press ENTER.

2. Press ENTER or click on Desktop to display the main menu.

3. Press U or click Utilities. The following list of utilities appears:

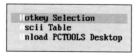

```
 otkey Selection
 scii Table
 nload PCTOOLS Desktop
```

These options are covered individually in the following sections.

The Utilities programs contain no menus aside from the Control and Desktop menus available throughout the Desktop. For information on these two menus, see Chapter 19, "Desktop Manager Overview."

Reassigning Hotkeys

A *hotkey* invokes a function that operates throughout the Desktop or, if the Desktop is memory resident, throughout your entire system. Because hotkeys range across many applications, conflicts can arise in which both an application and a hotkey use the same keystroke. To eliminate this problem, you can reassign a hotkey to a different keystroke using the Hotkey Selection option.

To do this, press ALT-D, U, H, or click on the Desktop menu and select Utilities and Hotkey Selection. A window like this appears:

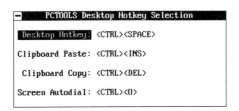

The window displays the following four system-wide Desktop functions:

- *Desktop Hotkey*   This function brings up the Desktop itself when the Desktop is memory resident. (For more information, see Chapter 19, "Desktop Manager Overview.") Its default keystroke is CTRL-SPACEBAR, which is displayed in the window as <CTRL><SPACE>.

- *Clipboard Paste*   This function pastes the contents of the Clipboard, starting at the cursor position. (For more information, see Chapter 22, "Using the Clipboard.") Its default keystroke is CTRL-INS, which is displayed in the window as <CTRL><INS>.

- *Clipboard Copy*   This function enables you to copy text from your current screen or an underlying application into the Clipboard. (For more information, see Chapter 22, "Using the Clipboard.") Its default keystroke is CTRL-DEL, which is displayed in the window as <CTRL><DEL>.

- *Screen Autodial*   This function lets you dial a telephone number on your screen. (For more information, see Chapter 25, "Using the Database Manager.") Its default keystroke is CTRL-O, which is displayed in the window as <CTRL><O>.

To change a function's hotkey, simply select the function and press a different keystroke. For example, follow these steps to experiment with selecting different keystrokes for invoking the Desktop:

1. You're currently on the Desktop Hotkey function. Press CTRL-D. The window now displays the keystroke assignment <CTRL><D>.

2. Press SHIFT-F8. The window displays <SHIFT><F8>.

3. Press CTRL-TAB. The window displays <CTRL><TAB>.

4. You can also select ALT-key combinations, although they can be a little trickier because ALT may activate the menu bar, confusing the Desktop. To get around this, simply remember to hold down ALT first and then, without releasing it, press the second key. For example, keep ALT held down and press F10. The window displays <ALT><F10>.

5. Press CTRL-SPACEBAR. The default hotkey <CTRL><SPACE> is restored.

To get some more practice, follow these steps to change the hotkey for Screen Autodial to CTRL-A and then test the change:

1. Press UP ARROW to wrap around to the Screen Autodial function.

2. Press CTRL-A. The function is now reassigned to the keystroke <CTRL><A>.

3. Press ESC to accept your change. (If nothing happens, press ESC again.) The window is saved and closed.

4. To test your change, press ALT-D, N, ALT-N (and, if necessary, ENTER) to open a new Notepads window.

5. Press ALT-SPACEBAR, X to maximize the window (blocking out any numbers in the background), and then type **555-5555** to put a telephone number on the screen.

6. Press CTRL-O. While this keystroke would previously have invoked the Autodialer, it's now undefined and so just produces a beep from your PC.

7. Press CTRL-A. Your new keystroke successfully invokes the Autodialer.

8. Press ESC to close the Autodialer and ALT-F, X to abandon the file.

9. Press ALT-D, U, H to bring up the Hotkey Selection window again.

10. Press UP ARROW and CTRL-O to restore the Screen Autodial hotkey default.

11. Press ESC to save your change and exit.

Using the ASCII Table

A simple but extremely useful Utilities option is the pop-up ASCII table. *ASCII* stands for American Standard Code for Information Exchange, and it's the universal format for representing characters on PCs. For example, the letter "A" is ASCII 65, the letter "a" is ASCII 97, the digit 1 is ASCII 49, and the punctuation mark ? is

ASCII 63. This numeric coding provides a standard that different PC applications can use to transfer data between them. This is why, for example, Notepads provides the option to save files in an ASCII format in addition to its own proprietary format.

The ASCII table isn't of interest only to programmers, however. There are also a couple of general-purpose reasons for popping up the table.

First, the order in which data are sorted is determined by their ASCII codes. Therefore, if you're using a program such as Databases, you need to study the ASCII table to determine, for example, if "Z" will come before "a" (it will) and if 1 will come before ! (it won't).

Second, the ASCII table helps you access special characters. In addition to the letters, numbers, and symbols on your keyboard, the table includes such characters as musical notes, fractions, accented letters, line and box drawing characters, and mathematical symbols. The table holds 256 characters altogether.

In many programs (including such Desktop applications as Notepads, Outlines, the Clipboard, and Databases), you can "type" a character that isn't on your keyboard by holding down ALT, typing its ASCII code on your numeric keypad, and then releasing ALT. You can also "type" some characters by holding down CTRL and pressing a keyboard key. However, you first have to study the table to see which special characters are available and what their corresponding numbers or CTRL codes are.

While you can get special characters to display on your screen, they'll print out only if they're supported by your particular printer.

In the Desktop, the ASCII table is split among nine windows. To display the first window, press ALT-D, U, A, or click on the Desktop menu and select Utilities and Ascii Table. The first window in Figure 28-1 appears. It's divided into the following five columns:

- *HEX*   This column contains the character's numeric code in hexadecimal (base 16).

- *(Unlabeled)*   This column contains the character itself.

If PC Tools has been configured to use its special graphics characters, those characters will appear in the ASCII windows in place of standard characters; for example, hex positions 3 through 6, 10 through 12, and BA through BC will contain the function key graphics characters displayed in the message bar.

- *DEC*   This column contains the character's numeric code in decimal (base 10).

- *CTL*   This column contains the key you can press together with CTRL to produce the character (that is, when you're in an application such as Notepads

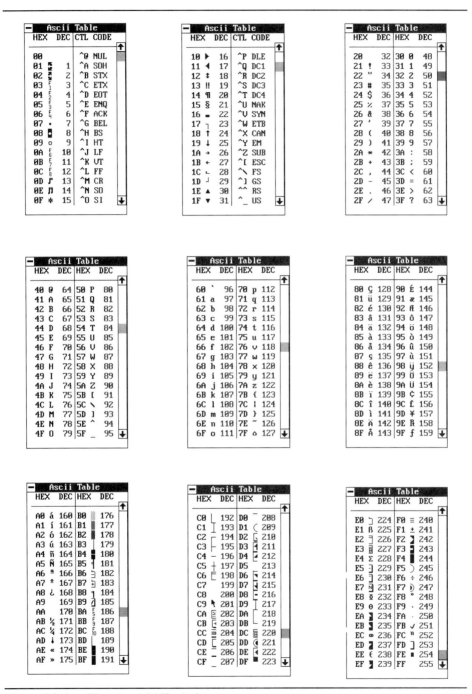

Figure 28-1.   *The nine ASCII windows*

that supports CTRL characters). It applies only to the first 32 ASCII characters and so appears in only the first two windows.

- *CODE*   This column contains an alternate, non-character meaning for the numeric code. (For example, ASCII 7 can represent either a dot character or a bell sound on the PC's speaker.) It applies only to the first 32 ASCII characters and so appears in only the first two windows.

There are a variety of ways to move around the nine ASCII windows. You can move a window at a time by pressing UP ARROW or DOWN ARROW, or PGUP or PGDN; or by clicking on either end of the arrows on the vertical scroll bar. You can also move to the first or last window by pressing HOME or END. Lastly, you can jump to the window containing a particular character by typing the character or (if applicable) its CTRL code.

To get a feel for moving around the table, follow these steps:

1. Press DOWN ARROW twice to move to the third window. Notice that the CTL and CODE columns are no longer included.

2. Press END. You're moved to the last window. Notice that the last character's number is 255 decimal.

3. Press t. You're moved to the window containing the uncapitalized letter "t" (116 decimal).

4. Press T. You're moved to the window containing the capitalized letter "T" (84 decimal).

5. Press CTRL-T. You're moved to the window containing the corresponding CTRL code (20 decimal, a paragraph marker character).

6. Press ESC to close the ASCII table.

Now follow these steps to practice entering ASCII characters into a Notepads file:

1. Press ALT-D, N, ALT-N to open a new Notepads file.

2. Press CTRL-T. A paragraph marker appears.

3. Press CTRL-N. A musical note appears.

4. Hold down ALT, type **84** on your numeric keypad, and then release ALT. A capital "T" appears.

5. Hold down ALT, type **171** on your numeric keypad, and then release ALT. A fraction appears.

6. Hold down ALT, type **130** on your numeric keypad, and then release ALT. An accented "e" appears.

7. Hold down ALT, type **251** on your numeric keypad, and then release ALT. A square root/checkmark symbol appears.

8. You now have a solid feel for entering ASCII characters, so press ALT-F, X to exit the file without saving it.

Unloading the Desktop

If the Desktop is memory resident, you can clear it from memory using the **U**nload PCTOOLS Desktop option. This command will automatically save and close all open files, and then flush the Desktop from memory to make room for other applications. Unlike typing **KILL** at the DOS prompt, this method affects only the Desktop, not any other PC Tools program (such as Backtalk, PC Shell, DeskConnect, Commute, or CP Scheduler) that may also be resident.

To unload the Desktop using the Utilities option, follow these steps:

1. Close any underlying applications so that when you exit the Desktop, you end up in DOS.

2. Unload any memory-resident programs you loaded *after* the Desktop.

3. Press ALT-D, U, U, or click on the Desktop menu and select Utilities and Unload PCTOOLS Desktop. The following dialog box appears, which in effect warns you to follow steps 1 and 2:

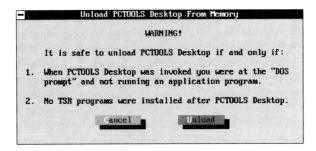

4. Press U or click Unload. The Desktop saves and closes any open files, closes itself, and is removed from memory.

Part VII

Using the Windows Utilities

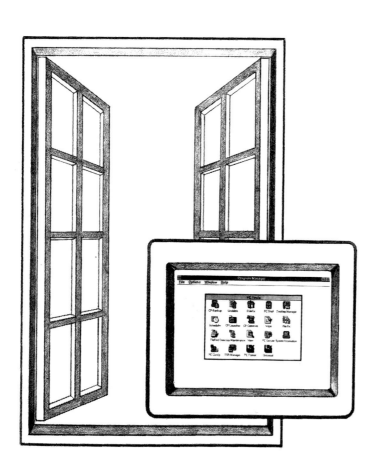

Chapter 29

Windows Utilities Overview

 One of the biggest changes in PC Tools 7 is its explicit support for Microsoft Windows 3. While most PC Tools 7 programs are still DOS-based, they now have the "look and feel" of Windows programs, and they're now configured to be run under Windows during the installation process. In addition, several PC Tools 7 programs are designed to work exclusively under Windows.

Supported Programs

PC Tools 7 includes the following five programs that work exclusively under Microsoft Windows 3:

- *CP Launcher*   This program lets you launch programs from any application menu, saving you the bother of having to first return to the Program Manager window. It's covered in Chapter 30, "Using CP Launcher for Windows."

- *CP Backup for Windows*   This program lets you back up and restore your hard disk data under Windows. It's very similar to CP Backup for DOS, but takes special advantage of Windows' graphics and multitasking capabilities. It's covered in Chapter 31, "Using CP Backup for Windows."

- *CP Undelete for Windows*   This program lets you restore deleted files under Windows. This program is necessary because the DOS version of Undelete contains a number of commands that conflict with Windows. It's covered in Chapter 32, "Using Undelete for Windows."

- *CP Scheduler for Windows*   This program executes scheduled events you've set from CP Backup, Commute, and the Desktop Manager's Appointment Scheduler and Electronic Mail applications. This program is necessary because both the resident version of the Desktop Manager's Appointment Scheduler (see Chapter 23, "Using the Appointment Scheduler") and the DOS version of CP Scheduler (see "Scheduling Backups" in Chapter 2, "Backing Up Your Hard Disk") are disabled under Windows. It's covered in the "Using CP Scheduler for Windows" section at the end of this chapter.

- *TSR Manager*   This program provides a "gateway" between certain PC Tools DOS programs and Windows. First, it allows messages to come through into Windows from the PC Tools memory-resident programs Commute, Data Monitor, and VDefend (as well as the VSafe program from the Central Point Anti-Virus package). Second, it allows you to run Commute, adjust the settings of Data Monitor, and turn VDefend off and on. If none of these programs are installed resident before you run Windows, however, TSR Manager won't run, and instead will just display the message "No DOS TSRs loaded, cannot load."

In addition, most DOS-based PC Tools 7 programs will work under Microsoft Windows 3. In fact, these programs have been designed to provide a Windows "look and feel" via their full mouse support, and their Windows-style menus and dialog boxes. If you're in Real or Standard mode, you can run the DOS-based programs in full screens. If you're in 386 Enhanced mode, you also have the option of running these programs in their own windows (as will be covered shortly).

To facilitate the running of DOS-based PC Tools programs, the Install program (see Appendix A, "PC Tools Installation and Configuration") performed several actions when you installed PC Tools on your hard disk. First, it created a PC Tools program group like this in your Windows directory:

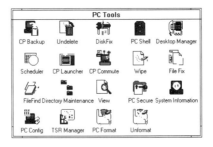

If you chose to install *all* of PC Tools, this window contains icons for the following DOS programs:

- *Commute*   This program lets you take control of a second PC via cable, modem, or LAN. For more information, see Chapter 14, "Connecting Computers Using Commute," and also the "Tips" section later in this chapter.

- *Desktop Manager*   This program provides over a dozen applications, including a word processor, an outliner, a dBASE-compatible database, modem and fax telecommunications software, Hewlett-Packard-compatible calculators, and an Appointment Scheduler. For more information, see Chapters 19 through 28, and also the "Tips" section later in this chapter.

- *Directory Maintenance*   This program lets you switch to, create, copy, move, rename, delete, examine, and print directories. For more information, see Chapter 17, "Managing Your Directories and Disks."

- *DiskFix*   This program analyzes and repairs disk defects. For more information, see Chapter 7, "Repairing Disks Using DiskFix," and also the "Tips for Running DOS-Based PC Tools Programs" section later in this chapter.

- *File Find*   This program locates files across multiple directories and drives based on their names, text contents, dates, sizes, and/or attributes. For more information, see "Finding Files Anywhere in Your System" in Chapter 16, "Managing Your Files."

- *File Fix*   This program analyzes and repairs defects in dBASE, Lotus 1-2-3, and Symphony data files. For more information, see Chapter 8, "Repairing dBASE and 1-2-3 Files Using File Fix."

- *PC Config*   This program lets you change the colors used by PC Tools programs. For more information, see "Using PC Config" in Appendix A, "PC Tools Installation and Configuration."

- *PC Format*   This program formats disks nondestructively, so its effects can optionally be undone and the data it's operated on recovered. For more information, see "Using PC Format" in Chapter 5, "Safeguarding Your Data."

- *PC Secure*   This security-oriented program encrypts files so they can't be read without a password. For more information, see Chapter 11, "Encrypting Data Using PC Secure," and also the "Tips for Running DOS-Based PC Tools Programs" section later in this chapter.

- *PC Shell*   This program provides scores of file, directory, and disk management commands. For more information, see Chapters 15, 16, 17, and 18, and also the "Tips for Running DOS-Based PC Tools Programs" section later in this chapter.

- *System Information*   This program provides comprehensive data about your computer system. For more information, see "Displaying System Information" in Chapter 18, "Using Advanced PC Shell Features."

- *Unformat*   This program recovers data on an accidentally formatted disk. For more information, see "Recovering Formatted Disks" in Chapter 6, "Recovering Deleted or Formatted Data."

- *View*   This program lets you view data files in their native formats. For more information, see "Viewing Files" in Chapter 16, "Managing Your Files."

- *Wipe*   This security-oriented program overwrites files as it deletes them to ensure they can't be reconstructed. For more information, see "Destroying Data Using Wipe" in Chapter 11, "Encrypting Data Using PC Secure."

In addition to the utilities represented in the PC Tools program group, Windows works with the following memory-resident PC Tools utilities if you load them from DOS *before* you run Windows (for example, by including their command lines in your AUTOEXEC.BAT file before your WIN command line):

- *Data Monitor*   Under Windows, this program helps ensure that deleted files are recoverable, encrypts and decrypts files in a specified directory on the fly, and write-protects selected drives. For more information, see "Monitoring Deleted Files" in Chapter 5, "Safeguarding Your Data"; "Using Directory Lock" and "Using Write Protection" in Chapter 12, "Shielding Data Using Data Monitor"; and the "Tips for Running DOS-Based PC Tools Programs" section later in this chapter.

- *PC-Cache*   This program keeps data you use frequently in memory, which your PC can access very quickly, as opposed to leaving the data on your hard disk, which takes a relatively long time to access. For more information, see Chapter 10, "Speeding Data Access Using PC-Cache," and also the "Tips for Running DOS-Based PC Tools Programs" section later in this chapter.

- *VDefend*   This security-oriented program constantly checks your system's memory for signs of known viruses. For more information, see Chapter 13, "Detecting Viruses Using VDefend," and also the "Tips for Running DOS-Based PC Tools Programs" section later in this chapter.

Install also performs several other actions to ensure that DOS-based PC Tools programs work under Windows. Specifically:

- It creates a Program Information File, or *PIF,* for each PC Tools program just mentioned. The default settings in the PIFs are Display Usage: **Full** Screen (as opposed to **Windowed**, which would set them to run in individual windows); Execution: **Exclusive** (as opposed to **Background**, which would set them to run in the background); and Display Options: Video Memory - **Text** and Monitor Ports - **Text** (as opposed to Low Graphics or High Graphics). At the same time, however, any graphics options you set in PC Config (such as Graphics Mouse, or **28** Lines, **43** Lines, or **50** Lines for the display) are still used.

The PIFs are all stored in your Windows directory. You can optionally revise them at any time using the Windows PIF Editor in your Accessories group window. For example, if you're using a 386 or 486 PC, you may want to edit the PIFs to set all programs to run in individual windows.

- It revises the Windows SYSTEM.INI file to allow CP Backup to work in 386 Enhanced mode. It also inserts new keyboard and mouse driver data in SYSTEM.INI to allow another PC running Commute to control your PC when you're running Windows. Your old file is renamed SYSTEM.SAV.

- It modifies the Windows WIN.INI file to automatically load TSR Manager and (optionally) CP Launcher and/or CP Scheduler for Windows every time you start up Windows. Your old file is renamed WIN.SAV.

- It adds a CPSDOS.GRP "group" line to your PROGMAN.INI file and renames your old file PROGMAN.SAV.

- It copies nine miscellaneous additional files (CPSDOS.GRP, CPSICONS .DLL, VDMAD.386, VFD.386, WNDOSLIB.DLL, WNDRTREE.DLL, WNGRAPHC.DLL, WNHK.DLL, and WNTSR.DLL) to your Windows directory, and two keyboard and mouse driver files (COMMKBD.DRV and COMMOU.DRV) to your Windows SYSTEM subdirectory.

Tips for Running DOS-Based PC Tools Programs

There are a few things that are useful to keep in mind when you're running DOS-based PC Tools 7 programs under Windows. The following sections first cover some general tips, and then offer advice on running Commute, Compress, Data Monitor, Desktop Manager, DiskFix, PC-Cache, PC Secure, PC Shell, and VDefend.

General Tips

As mentioned previously, if you're using a 386 or 486 PC, you'll probably find it more convenient to run all your programs in individual windows. To do so, revise each PC Tools PIF stored in your Windows directory to set Display Usage to **W**indowed instead of **F**ull Screen.

As also mentioned previously, if you want to use Data Monitor, PC-Cache, or VDefend under Windows, be sure to load these memory-resident programs from DOS *before* you run Windows (for example, by including their command lines in your AUTOEXEC.BAT file before your WIN command line).

Lastly, if your PC has a PS/2-style mouse port and you run a PC Tools program after exiting Windows, you may find that your mouse suddenly isn't working properly. If this occurs, run PC Config by typing **PCCONFIG** from the DOS prompt and pressing ENTER; select the **M**ouse option; select the Fast Mouse **R**eset option to turn it off (making the checkmark next to the option disappear); and then select **O**K, E**x**it, and **O**K. (Alternatively, run your PC Tools programs using the parameter /PS2 on the command line.) This will probably eliminate the problem.

Commute Tips

You can use Commute to control a PC running Windows, but doing so is a real exercise in patience. The process is quite slow, largely because each Windows screen requires a great deal of graphics information to be transmitted. If you possibly can, it's recommended that you run the PC in DOS mode.

However, if you must run under Windows, don't wait for each full graphics screen to be redrawn. Instead, just type your next few commands; your keystrokes will be preserved in a type-ahead memory buffer. Also, if the screen is taking a great deal of time to reflect your changes, try adjusting the video refresh rate using the Commute Session Manager's **A**dvanced Options Screen **O**ptions Screen Refresh Rate command.

Compress Tips

Compress should *never* be run under an environment such as Windows. That's because Compress totally reorganizes how your data is stored on your hard disk, while Windows is expecting to find its temporary files and all open files in specific locations on the hard disk. Using these two programs together would therefore result in potentially serious conflicts and data losses. As a result, if you attempt to run Compress from Windows, a dialog box appears with the message "Compress cannot be run within a multitasking environment." Therefore, wait until you exit Windows, and then run Compress from the DOS prompt.

Data Monitor Tips

Data Monitor's **D**elete Protection, **D**irectory Lock, and **W**rite Protection options are fully supported under Windows. However, the Disk **L**ight and **S**creen Blanker options (both of which are display dependent) are disabled.

Desktop Manager Tips

The memory-resident version of the Desktop is disabled when you're in Windows. Therefore, even if you have the Desktop loaded in memory, you must select the Desktop icon from the PC Tools program group to run it under Windows, and it will run in nonresident mode.

Also, while you can still use such features as macros and the Autodialer within the Desktop screen or window itself, these features are *not* supported outside of the

Desktop under Windows. One consequence of this is that any macros you've scheduled through the Appointment Scheduler will not execute while you're in Windows. On the other hand, any notes you've scheduled will still pop up, but via the Windows Notepad application instead of the Desktop's Notepads program.

DiskFix Tips

You can use the **R**epair a Disk option under Windows to check a disk for a variety of defects. However, if a problem is found, you *cannot* effect any repairs. Instead, you must exit Windows and run DiskFix from the DOS prompt to execute repair operations.

In addition, you can select **C**onfigure Options to configure DiskFix, and **A**dvice to get disk repair advice. However, you *can't* use the DiskFix **S**urface Scan, Re**v**italize a Disk, and **U**ndo a DiskFix Repair options; if you select any of them, a dialog box appears with the message "This operation cannot be done while running Windows."

If you use CP Scheduler for Windows, the Scheduler's default is to run DiskFix to check your hard disk or disks every hour between 9:15 A.M. and 5:15 P.M. on work days. You can change these settings by bringing up the Scheduler and clicking on its DiskFix button. For more information, see "Using CP Scheduler for Windows" later in this chapter.

PC-Cache Tips

The most important thing to keep in mind about PC-Cache is that you must *not* run it and another cache—such as the SmartDrive program packaged with Windows—at the same time. Having two caches in memory could lead to serious conflicts and data losses.

There are also a few things to note about PC-Cache parameters. First, the /WRITE=ON switch in PC-Cache is disabled under Windows. If you adjust PC-Cache parameters from a DOS prompt under Windows, it's important that you do *not* use either the /WRITE=ON or /WRITE=OFF parameters. You can turn the /WRITE=ON switch back on (if you prefer the extra speed it brings over the risk of losing data during a power loss) only after you *exit* Windows.

Second, if you set PC-Cache to use more than 300K of expanded memory, it normally will turn itself off while you're running Windows. If you want to prevent this from happening, add the /V1 parameter to the PC-Cache command line, which allows PC-Cache to continue using its large expanded memory cache under Windows.

Lastly, if your cache takes up a substantial amount of your available extended or expanded memory, you may want to include the /WIN parameter. This sets PC-Cache to automatically shrink itself to about half its specified size whenever Windows is run, which provides more memory for Windows itself to give over to your applications. Otherwise, if Windows runs out of memory, it will swap the applications out to disk, thus impairing rather than enhancing your system's performance.

PC Secure Tips

PC Secure is fully functional under Windows. However, because Windows can run several programs at the same time, you should be especially careful not to encrypt any file that's currently in use by either Windows or some open application.

PC Shell Tips

The memory-resident version of PC Shell is disabled when you're in Windows. Therefore, even if you have PC Shell loaded in memory, you must select the PC Shell icon from the PC Tools program group to run it under Windows, and it will run in nonresident mode.

VDefend Tips

If VDefend is interfering with your intentional efforts to low-level format a disk, or if it's mistaking a harmless program you're running as an infected one, you can turn VDefend off by using the TSR Manager.

Using CP Scheduler for Windows

CP Scheduler for Windows constantly checks your system clock until the time arrives for a scheduled event (such as running CP Backup using preset specifications for backing up your hard disk). It then displays a prompt telling you it's about to execute the scheduled event. If you don't select Cancel in 30 seconds, and you're running in Real or Standard mode, it interrupts the current application, executes whatever is scheduled, and then returns control to the original application. However, if you're in 386 Enhanced mode, it executes the event in the background (that is, without interrupting any application) while displaying a minimized icon to indicate what's occurring.

The Scheduler's actions are based on schedules you've created from the Desktop's Appointment Scheduler and Electronic Mail applications, from Commute, from both the DOS and Windows versions of CP Backup (which share the same scheduling file), and CP Scheduler's own DiskFix button (which lets you periodically check your drives for defects).

It doesn't matter whether you schedule events from Windows or from DOS, because all these programs save their scheduling information to the same individual TM files in both environments. Specifically, both the DOS and Windows versions of CP Backup use the file CPBACKUP.TM, Commute uses the file COMMUTE.TM, Desktop Electronic Mail uses the file EMAIL.TM, and the Desktop Appointment Scheduler uses whatever TM file was most recently loaded into it. CP Scheduler for Windows acts exclusively on the information in these TM files and its own DiskFix settings.

As mentioned previously, if you allowed it to during the installation process, the Install program modified your WIN.INI file to load CP Scheduler for Windows automatically whenever you start up Windows. You can also set Install to do this at any time by following these steps:

1. Insert your original Disk 1 installation disk in a floppy drive, switch to that drive from the DOS prompt, type **INSTALL**, and press ENTER.

2. Go through the initial installation prompts, pressing ENTER or clicking OK to get past each screen, until you're asked if you want to save your existing configuration. At that point, press N, O, or click Do Not Save Existing Configuration Files and OK.

3. You're asked to specify the path of your Windows directory. Enter the name of your Windows directory or (if it's accurate) accept the default of \WIN-DOWS. When you're done, press ENTER twice or click OK.

4. You're asked which portions of PC Tools you want to install. Press S, O, or click Install Selected PC Tools Applications and OK; and then press G, O, or click Nothing and OK. This tells the program to skip installing any files.

5. You're asked if you want to create a Recovery disk. Press S or click Skip to get to the next screen.

6. You're now asked if you want to set **CP** Launcher and CP **S**cheduler to be loaded automatically every time Windows is run. Initially, both options are checked. To turn an option off, press its highlighted letter or click the program name. When you've adjusted the load settings appropriately, press O or click OK. Your WIN.INI file is revised based on your settings, while your old file is renamed WIN.SAV.

7. At the next screen, press X or click Exit to bring up the Close dialog box, and then press ENTER or click OK. The Install program exits, and you're returned to the DOS prompt.

Install also always sets your WIN.INI file to automatically load the TSR Manager when you run Windows. It does this without prompting for permission because the TSR Manager provides the only way for the DOS memory-resident programs Commute, Data Monitor, VDefend, and VSafe (from the Central Point Anti-Virus package) to communicate with you under Windows. However, as mentioned previously, if none of these programs are installed resident before you run Windows, TSR Manager won't load.

You'll usually want to keep the Scheduler minimized, so that it stays active but out of the way. However, if you want to examine currently scheduled events or adjust Scheduler settings, double-click on the minimized icon. The following window appears:

You can select the Backup, Commute, or Email button to revise the current schedule for the application, or to just disable the schedule for that application. You can also select the DiskFix button to schedule DiskFix to periodically check your drives for defects. (The default is to have DiskFix check your hard disk drives every hour during business hours.)

In addition, you can select the Options menu to make the Scheduler's minimized icon totally invisible while remaining active (the default is for Show Icon to be *on*), turn off prompting before a scheduled event is launched (the default is for Prompt Before Event to be *on*), and disable the current schedule created by the Desktop's Appointment Scheduler (the default is for Enable Desktop Events to be *on*). Regarding the latter, as mentioned previously, any macros you've scheduled through the Appointment Scheduler will not execute while you're in Windows; while any notes you've scheduled will still pop up, but via the Windows Notepad application instead of the Desktop's Notepads program.

For more information about scheduling programs, see "Scheduling Programs, Batch Files, Macros, and Notes" in Chapter 23, "Using the Appointment Scheduler."

Chapter **30**

Using CP Launcher
for Windows

In the previous chapter, you learned about various features that make it easy to run PC Tools programs under Windows. The new CP Launcher for Windows utility goes a step further by making it easy to run *any* program under Windows. Specifically, it lets you:

- Run programs from the Control menu of any *application window* (that is, a window containing an open file or application), as opposed to having to first return to the Program Manager window and select its **File Run** command.

- Browse through your available directories and files from the Control menu of any application window and then double-click on the file you want to run, as opposed to having to remember and type the exact program name.

- Create a list of frequently run programs that you can select from the Control menu of any application window, as opposed to having to locate each program within its particular program group or directory.

- Quickly exit Windows (without saving your current settings) from the Control menu of any application window, as opposed to having to exit from the Program Manager.

You can load CP Launcher by double-clicking its icon in the PC Tools program group. When you do, the upper-left dash that represents the Control menu on all application windows turns red on color systems and a different shade of gray on monochrome systems to indicate the Launcher is active. If you click on such a

Control menu button, you'll see CP Launcher added as the bottom option. If you then press L or click CP Launcher, this second menu appears:

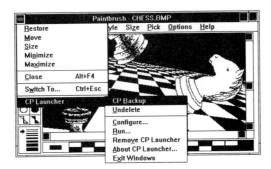

The options in this CP Launcher menu are covered in the following sections.

Using the Program List

At the top of the CP Launcher menu is a list of programs, called a *Program List*, that you can add to and revise. Once you've set it up, you can use this List to quickly select and run programs. The two applications initially listed are typically **CP Backup** and **Undelete**.

To revise the List, press C or click the Configure option. This dialog box appears:

The box offers the following options:

- *Current menu items* This box lists names representing programs in your list. Each name can be up to 25 characters long and can include spaces. The name can also include an ampersand (&) before a letter to make that letter underlined in the Program List, allowing you to select the program by pressing the letter.

- *Menu item*   This field lets you revise the name representing a program already on the List, or create a name for a program you want to add to the List.

- *Launch command*   This field contains a program's command line. It should specify the drive and directory of the program (unless the directory is already covered in your PATH statement) and the name of the program itself (*including* its EXE, COM, or BAT extension). In addition, the line can include parameters, such as the name of a data file to be loaded along with the program.

   You can alternatively specify the path and name of a Windows application *data file* you use frequently, which will load both the application and the data file. This works because Windows typically provides links between its programs and the files they produce. (For information on how file associations are set up in Windows, see a book about Windows.)

- *Initial directory (optional)*   This field specifies the directory that should be switched to as soon as the program is loaded. You can use it to automatically switch you to the directory containing the data files associated with the program you're running.

- *Browse*   If you select this option by pressing ALT-B or clicking Browse, the following dialog box appears:

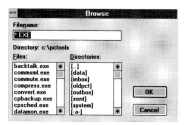

   This box lets you look through the directories and files on your current disk until you find the program you want. You can then double-click on the file to insert its path and filename into the Launch field, which ensures that it's entered into the field with the correct spelling and syntax. In addition, it inserts the program's name (*without* its extension) into the Menu Item field, and the program's directory path into the Initial Directory field.

- *New*   This option clears all fields so you can enter appropriate data for a new program you're adding to the List.

- *Save*   This option saves your changes and leaves the dialog box open (as opposed to **OK**, which saves your changes and *closes* the box).

- *Delete*   This option deletes the currently selected menu item. It's useful if an entry has become obsolete.

- *Control-menu box*   This option lets you adjust the appearance of application window Control menu buttons. The default Central Point Launcher selection sets the Control buttons to be red or a different shade of gray to indicate CP Launcher is loaded. Alternatively, you can choose the Normal selection to leave the appearance of the Control buttons unchanged. In the latter case, CP Launcher will still be available as the bottom option when you open an application window's Control menu; there just won't be any visual reminder that CP Launcher is loaded when the menu is closed.

- *OK*   This option saves your changes and closes the dialog box (as opposed to **Save**, which saves your changes but leaves the box open).

- *Cancel*   This option abandons your changes and closes the dialog box.

To get a feel for how to use these Configure options, follow these steps to add a new menu item:

1. Click on any application window's Control menu button. If CP Launcher is loaded, it appears as the last menu option.

2. Press L or click CP Launcher. The utility's menu appears.

3. Press C or click Configure. The Configure Central Point Launcher dialog box appears.

4. Press ALT-N or click New. All fields are cleared to provide space for a new program entry.

5. Press ALT-B or click Browse. A list of your files and directories appears.

6. Use TAB and the arrow keys, or use your mouse, to scroll through the Directories box until you locate the directory you want. When you do, highlight the directory and press ENTER, or double-click on it. The Files box now displays the directory's contents.

7. Use TAB and the arrow keys, or use your mouse, to scroll through the Files box until you locate the file you want. When you do, highlight the file and press ENTER, or double-click on it. The file information is inserted into the **Menu Item**, **Launch Command**, and **Initial Directory** fields.

8. Make any desired changes to the file information. For example, you can insert an ampersand (&) in the **Menu Item** name to make the item selectable by letter. You can also add parameters to the end of the **Launch Command** line, and specify a different **Initial Directory**.

9. When you're done, press ALT- S or click Save. Your changes are saved, and the dialog box remains open.

10. Optionally, repeat steps 4 through 9 to add more menu items. When you're totally done, press ALT- O or click OK to close the dialog box.

11. Select your new menu items at any time from the CP Launcher menu to quickly and easily run the applications they represent.

Running Programs Using CP Launcher

There are two ways to run programs from the CP Launcher menu. First, as just explained, you can double-click on one of the items on the Program List at the top of the menu. This is the easiest way to launch applications and data files you use frequently.

However, if the program you want isn't listed, you can instead press R or click the menu's Run option. This brings up the following dialog box:

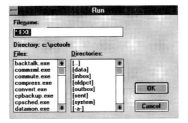

This box lets you look through the directories and files on your current disk until you find the program or data file you want. You can then double-click on the file to run it.

Alternatively, you can click on the file once to insert its name into the Filename field; or just type the information directly in the field. You can then optionally add any parameters to the end of the command line. When you're done, press ENTER or click OK to run the program.

Loading and Unloading CP Launcher

As mentioned previously, you can load CP Launcher by simply double-clicking on its icon in the PC Tools program group. However, you'll probably find it more convenient to have the program loaded for you automatically every time you start Windows.

If you permitted it, the Install program modified your WIN.INI file during the installation process to load CP Scheduler automatically (as explained in Appendix

A, "PC Tools Installation and Configuration"). You can also set Install to do this at any time by following these steps:

1. Insert your original Disk 1 installation disk in a floppy drive, switch to that drive from the DOS prompt, type **INSTALL**, and press ENTER.

2. Go through the initial installation prompts, pressing ENTER or clicking OK to get past each screen, until you're asked if you want to save your existing configuration. At that point, press N, O, or click Do Not Save Existing Configuration Files and OK.

3. You're asked to specify the path of your Windows directory. Enter the name of your Windows directory or (if it's accurate) accept the default of \WIN-DOWS. When you're done, press ENTER twice or click OK.

4. You're asked which portions of PC Tools you want to install. Press S, O, or click Install Selected PC Tools Applications and OK; and then press G, O, or click Nothing and OK. This tells the program to skip installing any files.

5. You're asked if you want to create a Recovery disk. Press S or click Skip to get to the next screen.

6. You're now asked if you want to set **CP L**auncher and **CP S**cheduler to be loaded automatically every time Windows is run. Initially, both options are checked. To turn an option off, press its highlighted letter or click the program name. When you've adjusted the load settings appropriately, press O or click OK. Your WIN.INI file is revised based on your settings, while your old file is renamed WIN.SAV.

7. At the next screen, press X or click Exit to bring up the Close dialog box, and then press ENTER or click OK. The Install program exits, and you're returned to the DOS prompt.

You can also unload CP Launcher from memory at any time. To do so, follow these steps:

1. Click on any application window's Control menu button and select the bottom CP Launcher option. The CP Launcher menu appears.

2. Press V or click the Remove CP Launcher option. A dialog box prompts you to confirm you want to remove the utility from all application window Control menus.

3. Press ENTER or click OK. The dialog box closes, and CP Launcher is cleared from memory.

CP Launcher will remain unloaded for the rest of your session. However, if you've set it to load automatically, it will *reload* the next time you start Windows. If you want to keep the utility permanently out of memory, repeat the steps just covered for using Install to load it, but select the **CP** Launcher option in step 6 to *remove* the checkmark next to it.

Getting Help on CP Launcher

You can get help on CP Launcher at any time by moving to one of its options and pressing the F1 key. In addition, you can get help by selecting the **A**bout CP Launcher option from the utility's menu and then selecting the **H**elp button.

Using CP Launcher to Exit Windows

If you want to exit Windows quickly, follow these steps:

1. Click on any application window's Control menu button and select the bottom CP Launcher option. The CP Launcher menu appears.

2. Press X or click Exit Windows to select the last option. The following dialog box offers to exit Windows without saving your current screen settings:

3. If you want to change your mind, press ESC or click Cancel. The dialog box closes, and you're returned to the application window you selected.

    Otherwise, press ENTER or click OK. The dialog box closes, and you're prompted to save any revised data in your application windows. After you respond to the prompts, Windows exits and returns you to DOS.

Chapter *31*

Using CP Backup for Windows

CP Backup is a program that copies, or *backs up,* the data on your hard disk to another media for safekeeping. PC Tools 7 provides both a DOS and a Windows version of this program. The DOS version is fully covered in Chapter 1, "CP Backup Overview"; Chapter 2, "Backing Up Your Hard Disk"; and Chapter 3, "Comparing and Restoring Backup Files." This chapter covers the differences between that program and the Windows version.

You can run the DOS version of CP Backup from either DOS or Windows. In fact, if you're in Real mode, you *must* use the DOS version, and it's this version that comes up when you double-click on the CP Backup icon in the PC Tools program group.

If you're running Windows in Standard or 386 Enhanced mode, however, double-clicking on the CP Backup icon brings up the CP Backup for Windows program instead. In most respects, this version is virtually identical to the DOS version. For example, it uses very similar screens, supports almost all the same keystrokes and mouse clicks to activate commands, and produces backup files that are interchangeable with the files from the DOS version. However, there are a few notable differences.

First, the Windows version provides a more attractive display because it can take advantage of Windows' graphics capabilities (as shown in Figure 31-1 and Figure 31-2). For example, its command buttons are much larger and look much more like real buttons, making it easy (and even fun) to select them.

Second, the Windows version has the ability to run in the background while you continue to use other programs, taking advantage of Windows' multitasking capabilities. Therefore, once you begin a backup to tape or some other media that doesn't

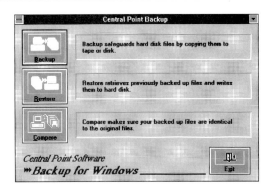

Figure 31-1. *The CP Backup for Windows main menu*

require your attention, you can minimize the CP Backup window and proceed to work in other applications as the backup continues.

Furthermore, if you've scheduled a backup to take place (see "Using CP Scheduler for Windows" in Chapter 29) and you're in 386 Enhanced mode, the backup will *automatically* execute in the background, with only a minimized CP Backup icon to remind you of what's occurring. This powerful combination of scheduling and background execution eliminates virtually all the inconvenience typically associated with making backups.

Another important difference is that the Windows version supports only Express mode, not Tree List mode. As a result, when you select the Configure User Level command in the Windows version, no Express Mode option is provided in the Select User Level box. (Instead, you're offered the option Use Password, which lets you "lock in" the user level for anyone without the password you specify.)

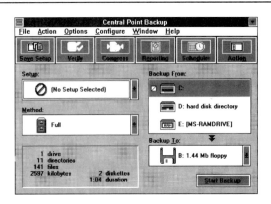

Figure 31-2. *The CP Backup for Windows Backup screen*

On the other hand, you can open multiple Tree List windows. To do so, simply double-click on each drive in the Backup From, Restore To, or Compare To box whose directory Tree you want to display. You can close all these windows simultaneously by clicking on the **Window** menu (which is unique to the Windows version) and selecting Close All. You can also reopen or switch to any Tree window by selecting it from a list that appears at the bottom of the **Window** menu.

Besides the **Window** menu, there are a few small differences in the menus the two versions have in common. Specifically, the Windows version's File menu offers the additional option **Pri**nter Setup (because it can draw on Windows' own printer support); its **O**ptions menu lacks the **T**ime Display option (because it uses Windows' own clock, so there's no chance of the backup timer creating a conflict and so no need to provide an option for turning it off); its **A**ction Backup menu lacks the commands Backup **F**rom and **C**hoose Directories (although these commands are available on the Express screen); and its Restore and Compare **A**ction menus provide two additional history commands, **L**oad History and **R**etrieve History.

The Windows version also provides two additional menus when you're displaying a Tree List: **F**ile and **T**ree. The **F**ile menu offers the options **S**elect All (which selects all files *except* those specifically excluded by Include/Exclude settings), **D**eselect All (which unselects all files), and **I**nvert Selections (which, as its name implies, selects your unselected files and unselects your selected files).

The **T**ree menu offers the options Expand **O**ne Level (which displays an extra subdirectory level for all directories), Expand **B**ranch (which displays all subdirectories in the selected directory), Expand **A**ll (which displays all subdirectories in all directories), Collapse **B**ranch (which hides all subdirectories in the selected directory), Collapse All (which hides all subdirectories in all directories, and which is the default), and Close **W**indow (which closes the current Tree window). You can also expand and collapse directories by clicking on their + and – icons, which respectively indicate whether a directory is collapsed or expanded.

Selecting options using the keyboard is also slightly different. In the DOS version, you can select options in such areas as the main menu and the command buttons by just pressing the appropriate highlighted letter. In the Windows version, you often must press ALT in conjunction with the highlighted letter.

Lastly, while the DOS version stores its configuration information in the file CPBACKUP.CFG, the Windows version stores its data in the file WNBACKUP.INI. Therefore, you must configure each program separately, and any change you make to one will *not* be made automatically in the other.

On the other hand, both programs use the same CPBACKUP.TM file to store scheduling information. As a result, any scheduling you create in one version will also affect the other version.

As mentioned at the beginning of this chapter, complete information on using CP Backup appears in Chapters 1, 2, and 3. While these chapters concentrate on CP Backup for DOS, virtually all their information applies equally to CP Backup for Windows, aside from the exceptions noted in this chapter.

Chapter 32

Using Undelete for Windows

If you've accidentally deleted files, you can typically recover most or all of them using the Undelete program.

PC Tools 7 provides both a DOS and a Windows version of Undelete. The DOS version is fully covered in the "Recovering Deleted Files" section of Chapter 6, "Recovering Deleted or Formatted Data." This chapter covers the differences between that version and the Windows version.

If you've just accidentally deleted one or more files from your hard disk and you're not using the Delete Sentry method of protection, don't do anything that could write to the hard disk. For example, if you're in DOS, now is not *the time to run Microsoft Windows, because Windows writes temporary files to your disk on startup. Instead, turn to the "Preparing for Hard Disk Recovery" section near the beginning of Chapter 6, and then follow its instructions for using the DOS version of Undelete.*

The DOS version of Undelete is appropriate for recovering files when you're in DOS, but you should *never* use it when running Windows. That's because certain DOS Undelete commands have the ability to reorganize how data is stored on your hard disk, while Windows expects to find its temporary files and certain other data in specific locations on the hard disk. Using the more advanced Undelete commands under Windows could therefore result in potentially serious conflicts and data losses. As a result, if you attempt to run the DOS Undelete program from Windows, you get the message "Undelete for DOS may not be run under Windows. Please use Undelete for Windows."

To run Undelete for Windows, double-click on the Undelete icon in the PC Tools program group. This brings up a version of Undelete that's missing the following commands from the DOS version:

- **F**ile **V**iew File, which displays the contents of deleted files in their native formats. (This feature doesn't actually conflict with Windows; it simply relies on a DOS-based program that hasn't yet been implemented for Windows.)

- **F**ile **A**dvanced Undelete **M**anual Undelete, which lets you reconstruct a file cluster by cluster.

- **F**ile **A**dvanced Undelete **C**reate a File, which lets you create a file cluster by cluster.

- **F**ile **A**dvanced Undelete **A**ppend to Existing File, which lets you add clusters to an existing file.

- **F**ile **A**dvanced Undelete **R**ename Existing File, which lets you rename an existing file with the same name as a deleted one you want to recover. (The Windows version will let you rename the deleted file instead.)

- *All* the **D**isk menu commands, which locate deleted Lotus 1-2-3, dBASE, and/or text files; deleted files containing a specified text sequence; and deleted files belonging to deleted directories.

- **O**ptions **S**how Existing Files, which displays existing files as well as deleted ones.

- **O**ptions **U**se Mirror File, which sets Undelete to use the information in the disk's Mirror file instead of DOS to recover unprotected files.

In addition, the Windows version does not use a Tree List, but instead displays only the deleted files, as shown in Figure 32-1.

Therefore, if you need to use any of the more advanced undelete commands, or if you prefer working with a directory tree, exit Windows and then run the Undelete for DOS program.

At the same time, the Windows version of Undelete has a few commands the DOS version doesn't. For example, its File menu includes the command Change **D**rive/Directory to display deleted files on a different drive or directory, and the commands Print **L**ist and Printer **S**etup to print a list of the deleted files in the selected directory. Also, the **O**ptions menu includes the command **C**onfigure Delete Protection, which lets you select a different protection option in the Data Monitor command line in your AUTOEXEC.BAT file (see "Monitoring Deleted Files" in Chapter 5, "Safeguarding Your Data").

Also, the Windows version provides buttons for the commands **U**ndelete, **D**rive/Dir, **F**ind, **S**ort By, **P**rint, and **I**nfo, as shown in Figure 32-1. These buttons make it easy to execute Undelete operations using only a few mouse clicks.

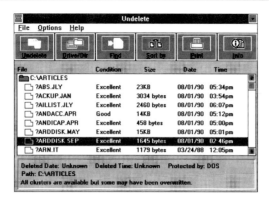

Figure 32-1.   *The Undelete for Windows screen*

As mentioned at the beginning of this chapter, complete information on how to undelete files appears in "Recovering Deleted Files" in Chapter 6. The sections on starting Undelete, using command line Undelete, and using Undelete parameters don't apply to Undelete for Windows. However, the rest of the chapter's information applies to both the DOS and Windows versions of Undelete, aside from the exceptions noted in this chapter.

Part *VIII*

Appendixes

Appendix *A*

PC Tools Installation and Configuration

PC Tools 7 can be used on any IBM PC-compatible computer with at least 512K of conventional memory (although 640K is recommended), a floppy disk drive, and a hard disk running DOS 3.2 or higher.

Before you can use PC Tools, you must install its files on your hard disk. This is necessary because most PC Tools files are initially compressed so they can fit on as few floppy disks as possible. This saves you from having to handle a large number of disks, but it also means you can't run files directly from the floppies.

There's one component of PC Tools that isn't compressed: the data recovery utilities. That's because if an accident occurs on your hard disk, installing files on it may destroy any chance you have of retrieving your lost data. PC Tools therefore allows you to run the programs Undelete, Unformat, Rebuild, DiskFix, and File Fix directly from the original floppy disks. For more information, see Chapter 6, "Recovering Deleted or Formatted Data"; Chapter 7, "Repairing Disks Using DiskFix"; and Chapter 8, "Repairing dBASE and 1-2-3 Files Using File Fix."

You can install PC Tools 7 using a program named, appropriately, Install. This copies and decompresses the PC Tools files you select. In addition, it presents you with a number of options for configuring PC Tools in your system. You can always change your configuration choices later by running Install again and selecting different choices.

Before you begin the installation process, it's recommended that you at least skim the following sections on configuring your AUTOEXEC.BAT and CON-

713

FIG.SYS files. These will help you understand what Install is doing when you direct it to configure your system. In addition, they tell you how to avoid conflicts with DOS 5, direct PC Tools to save files it generates to a particular directory, configure a monochrome display running off a color graphics card, and deal with an "Out of environment space" message.

Revising AUTOEXEC.BAT

When you turn on your computer and it reads your hard disk, the following operations are performed:

- The commands in the CONFIG.SYS file in the hard disk's root are executed. The significance of this file will be covered shortly.

- DOS (short for Disk Operating System) is loaded into memory. This software provides your PC with the foundation for running all other programs, operating your disk drives, and performing other fundamental operations.

- The commands in the AUTOEXEC.BAT file in your hard disk's root are executed.

AUTOEXEC.BAT is just a text file. However, every line it contains is executed as if you typed it manually from the DOS prompt. For example, the following AUTOEXEC.BAT file switches to a directory named PCTOOLS, and then loads the PC Shell and Desktop Manager programs as memory resident:

```
CD\PCTOOLS
PCSHELL /R
DESKTOP /R
```

AUTOEXEC.BAT therefore allows you to automate setting up your system by running appropriate DOS commands and loading various programs.

You can create and revise the AUTOEXEC.BAT file with any word processor that saves in the ASCII file format, such as the Notepads application in the Desktop Manager.

You can also direct Install to create or revise the AUTOEXEC.BAT file for you by selecting configuration options that insert or remove command lines from the file. For example, if you instruct the program to install PC Shell as memory resident, the line

```
PCSHELL /R
```

is automatically inserted into your AUTOEXEC.BAT file.

Revising the PATH Statement

A DOS command commonly used in an AUTOEXEC.BAT file is the PATH statement, which specifies directories DOS should search if it can't find your program in the current directory.

For example, if you're at the DOS prompt, type **PCSHELL**, and press ENTER, DOS will search the current directory for a program named PCSHELL. If it doesn't find one, it will then search each directory entered in your PATH statement for the PCSHELL program. If it finds the program in one of these directories, it proceeds to run it. Otherwise, it displays a "Bad command or file name" message.

A typical PATH statement looks like this:

PATH=C:\;C:\PCTOOLS;C:\DOS;

This tells DOS that if it can't find a program in the current directory, it should next search the root of your C drive, a directory named PCTOOLS on your C drive, and a directory named DOS on your C drive.

You can create and revise the PATH statement in your AUTOEXEC.BAT file just as you can any other text in the file. However, be sure to keep the PATH above any lines in the file that run programs outside the current directory.

If you allow Install to configure your system, it will automatically create or revise the PATH statement in your AUTOEXEC.BAT file to include the name of your PC Tools directory. This allows you to run PC Tools programs from anywhere on your disk.

This book assumes that your PATH statement includes your PC Tools directory. As a result, the book's tutorials don't direct you to switch to the directory before running a PC Tools program, since this step is unnecessary when your PATH is set properly.

Lastly, if you're using DOS 5, it's recommended that you make sure your PC Tools directory is placed *before* your DOS directory in your AUTOEXEC.BAT file's PATH statement. This will help avoid any conflicts between PC Tools 7.*x* programs and the PC Tools programs included in DOS 5. (For more information, see the Tip near the beginning of Chapter 4, "Data Recovery Overview.") If you're installing PC Tools 7.1 and you allow Install to configure your system, this will be done for you automatically. However, if you're installing PC Tools 7.0, or if you don't allow Install to configure your system, you must revise AUTOEXEC.BAT manually to place your PC Tools directory first in your PATH line.

Using the SET Command

Another DOS command commonly used in an AUTOEXEC.BAT file is SET, which can adjust certain program settings. For example, without the SET command, PC Tools saves the data and configuration files it generates to the same directory you're running its programs from (typically, a directory on drive C named PCTOOLS), which mixes your program and data files together. Install therefore inserts a SET command like the following to direct generated files to a subdirectory named DATA instead:

    SET PCTOOLS=C:\PCTOOLS\DATA

You can also redirect temporary files created by the CP Backup program (covered in Chapters 1, 2, and 3) from the current drive and directory to a different drive. To do so, use the command

    SET CPTMP=*d*:\

where *d* is the letter of the other drive. This gives you the opportunity to direct the files to a RAM disk in memory to speed execution.

In addition to redirecting files, you can use the SET command to adjust your display. Specifically, if you're using a monochrome monitor and a color graphics card, your display may appear fuzzy or have unreadable shades of gray. To prevent this problem, insert the following line into your AUTOEXEC.BAT file:

    SET PCTV=/BW

This suppresses all PC Tools programs from using color, ensuring that your monochrome display is clear and crisp.

There are also a couple of network-related SET commands for PC Tools, but these are primarily of interest to network supervisors. For more information, see Appendix B, "Installing and Using PC Tools on a Network."

Revising CONFIG.SYS

When you turn on your computer, the first file it looks for is CONFIG.SYS in your hard disk's root. Like AUTOEXEC.BAT, CONFIG.SYS is just a text file. However, the lines it contains are executed to set up special device drivers (such as mouse drivers and partition table handlers), allocate memory space in DOS, and adjust other system options.

For example, a typical CONFIG.SYS file might contain the following lines:

    DEVICE=MOUSE.SYS
    BUFFERS=30
    FILES=40

In this example, the file first specifies the devices you have installed—in this case, a mouse. Whether you need to include any such information depends on the types of equipment you're using in your particular system.

The second line sets aside areas in memory called *buffers,* which store frequently used data. Buffers cut down on the number of times your system has to access your disk drives for data, thus speeding up your PC's operation. You should normally specify at least 30 buffers. If you use a cache program, however (see Chapter 10, "Speeding Data Access Using PC-Cache"), you can often lower the number of buffers to 20 or less, saving some memory.

The third line in the example sets the number of files that can be open at one time. If you allow Install to configure your system, it will revise your CON-FIG.SYS file to specify at least 30 files. If you don't allow Install to configure your system, it's recommended that you edit the CONFIG.SYS file yourself to specify *40* files, which will typically allow your system to handle any software you're likely to run.

Setting Your Environment Space

System information such as PATH and SET commands (as well as PROMPT and COMSPEC commands, which are beyond the scope of this book) are stored in a special area in memory called the *environment.* The default amount of space allocated to the environment is 128 bytes for DOS 3.2, 160 bytes for DOS 3.3 through DOS 4, and 256 bytes for DOS 5. Therefore, this is a small area, and it can get filled up pretty easily. Even if Install does nothing but add the name of your PC Tools directory to your PATH statement, it may push your environment data past the default limit, resulting in the error message "Out of environment space."

If this occurs, you can expand your environment by including a SHELL command at the top of your CONFIG.SYS file. For example, if you start up your computer from the root of drive C, the following command inserted at the beginning of CONFIG.SYS will increase your environment space area to 512 bytes:

SHELL=C:\COMMAND.COM /P /E:512

Be sure not to include any spaces at either side of the equal sign, to include a space between the options following the equal sign, and not to mix up the backslash (\) and slash (/) characters.

For more information about the SHELL command, or about any of the other aspects of DOS that have been touched on here, see your DOS manual or a book about DOS.

Installing PC Tools on Your Hard Disk

To install PC Tools, follow these steps:

1. At your hard disk's DOS prompt, type **DIR** and press ENTER to determine the amount of free space on the disk. A complete PC Tools installation requires about 8MB. You can also perform a partial installation, as explained in step 12. If necessary, delete nonessential files from your hard disk to create enough room for the PC Tools files you want to copy.

2. Insert the PC Tools floppy labeled Disk 1 into drive A. (If you use a different drive, substitute its letter for "A" in steps 3 and 4.)

3. If you aren't using a standard monochrome or graphics system, or if you anticipate having problems using your mouse, type **A:INSTALL /VIDEO** from the DOS prompt and press ENTER. This displays a list of command line options, or *parameters*, that adjust how the Install program appears on your particular system and works with your mouse. (For more complete explanations of these options, see the "Video and Mouse Parameters" section at the end of this chapter.) For example, if you're using a liquid crystal display computer such as a laptop, type **A:INSTALL /LCD** in step 4; if you're using a monochrome monitor and color graphics card, type **A:INSTALL /BW** in step 4. If your system is typical, however, you can ignore these parameters.

4. Type **A:INSTALL** (followed by any necessary parameters) and press ENTER. A screen appears identifying the program. Press ENTER or click OK.

5. If you're using a graphics card, a screen appears that lets you adjust the way the Install display looks on your system. If this occurs, make any necessary adjustments, and then press ENTER or click OK.

6. A message appears warning you to abort the installation process if you need to recover deleted or damaged data from your hard disk. That's because when you copy PC Tools (or anything else) to your hard disk, you risk overwriting the data you want to restore. In such a case, exit the Install program by pressing ESC and ENTER, and then go to Chapter 6, "Recovering Deleted or Formatted Data."

   However, if you don't currently need to recover data from your hard disk, press ENTER or click OK to continue the installation process.

7. If you're connected to a network, you're prompted to choose between the options Install on a Personal Computer, Install on a Network Server, and Customize for this Network Workstation. If you're installing PC Tools for use on your own computer exclusively, press C or click Install on a Personal Computer, and then proceed to step 8.

   Otherwise, if you're a network supervisor who wants to install PC Tools on the server or customize a workstation to work with the copy of PC Tools already installed on the server, see Appendix B, "Installing and Using PC Tools on a Network."

8. You're prompted to specify the drive and directory that will hold your PC Tools programs. Most people accept the default of C:\PCTOOLS, which directs PC Tools programs to be copied to a directory named PCTOOLS on drive C. If you want to change this, however, revise the drive and directory path appropriately.

When the path line is set correctly, press ENTER or click OK to accept it and continue.

9. If your specified directory doesn't exist, you're asked to confirm that you want Install to create the directory for you. If this occurs, press ENTER or click Yes, and then press ENTER or click OK to again accept the path line.

10. If Microsoft Windows is detected on your system, you're prompted to specify the drive and directory to hold your PC Tools Windows files. It's recommended that you accept the suggestion of saving to your Windows directory. Otherwise, revise the drive and directory path appropriately. When you're ready, press ENTER or click OK.

If your specified directory doesn't exist, confirm you want Install to create it for you by pressing ENTER or clicking Yes, and then pressing ENTER or clicking OK to again accept the path line.

11. The messages "Analyzing your hard disk" and "Writing help files to your hard disk" appear as Install copies files that provide general online help. You're then prompted to allow Install to create two subdirectories, DATA and SYSTEM, within your main PC Tools directory. This provides some organization for the hundreds of files Install will soon copy to your hard disk. For a directory diagram and further explanation, press F1, and then press ESC to return to the prompt.

It's recommended that you *accept* the subdirectory option by pressing ENTER or clicking OK. However, if you prefer to have all the different types of files grouped together in the PC Tools directory, press ALT-S or click Skip.

12. The following screen appears offering installation options:

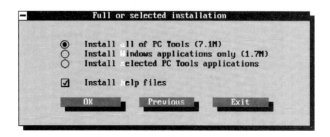

The first option sets Install to copy all PC Tools files to your hard disk, taking up about 6.5MB (on a system without Microsoft Windows) or about 8MB (on a system with Windows). To toggle the option off and on, press A or click the option.

The second option sets Install to copy only PC Tools Microsoft Windows files to your hard disk, taking up about 1.5MB. This option is only available if you already have Windows installed on your system. To toggle it on and off, press W or click the option.

The third option (which is the default) sets Install to copy only the categories of PC Tools programs that you select. This is useful if your hard disk space is limited, or if there are certain types of PC Tools utilities you don't expect to use. To toggle the option on and off, press S or click the option.

You can only select one of the first three options. You can then optionally adjust the last option, which sets Install to copy accompanying help files for each program installed. The default is for this last option to be *on,* and it's *highly* recommended that you accept this setting unless you're very short of disk space. To toggle the option off and on, press H or click the option.

13. When you're done choosing your installation options, press ENTER or click OK. If you chose to install either all PC Tools files or only Windows files, you're prompted to confirm that you're ready to begin the copying process. Press ENTER or click OK, and then go to the following "Copying PC Tools Files" section.

 Otherwise, if you chose to install selected files, the screen in Figure A-1 appears. This screen lists the following eight categories of programs you can install, all of which are initially selected:

- *PC Shell*   This program is an extremely powerful but easy-to-use file and disk manager. (For more information, see Chapter 15, "PC Shell Overview.") To toggle its selection off or on, press S or click the option.

 Selecting PC Shell also copies a few associated programs, such as File Find, PC Format, and View, but does *not* copy other related programs, such as Directory Maintenance, PC Secure, System Information, Undelete, and Wipe. Therefore, to be able to access the latter programs from PC Shell's menus, you must also select the **Data Recovery, Data Protection/Security,** and Performance/System categories.

- *Desktop Manager*   This program provides a collection of nearly a dozen full-featured applications, including a word processor, a dBASE-compatible database, telecommunications programs for both modems and fax cards, simulations of Hewlett-Packard calculators, and an appointment scheduler. (For more information, see Chapter 19, "Desktop Manager Overview.") To toggle its selection off or on, press K or click the option.

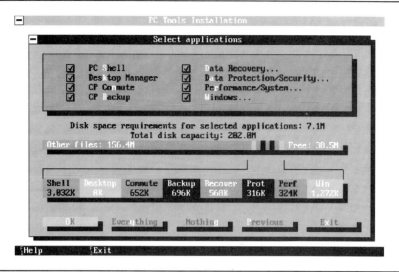

Figure A-1.   *The Install Select Applications screen*

- *CP Commute*   This program allows one computer to take control of a second computer when both systems are running Commute and are connected by modems, a null modem cable, or a LAN. (For more information, see Chapter 14, "Connecting Computers Using Commute.") To toggle its selection off or on, press M or click the option.

- *CP Backup*   This program backs up and restores the data on your hard disk, and offers dozens of useful features such as explicit tape drive support, scheduling, data viewers, and virus detection. (For more information, see Chapter 1, "CP Backup Overview.") To toggle its selection off or on, press B or click the option.

- ***Data Recovery***   This category represents the data recovery programs Undelete, Unformat, Rebuild, DiskFix, and File Fix. (For more information, see Chapter 4, "Data Recovery Overview.") To toggle its selection off or on, press D or click the option.

- *Data Protection/Security*   This category represents the data safeguarding and security programs Mirror, Data Monitor, PC Format, PC Secure, Wipe, and VDefend. (For more information, see Chapter 5, "Safeguarding Your Data," Chapter 11, "Encrypting Data Using PC Secure," and Chapter 13, "Detecting Viruses Using VDefend.") To toggle its selection off or on, press A or click the option.

- *Performance/System*   This category represents the system enhancement and maintenance programs Compress, PC-Cache, View, Directory Maintenance, and System Information. (For more information, see

Chapter 9, "Speeding Your Disks Using Compress"; Chapter 10, "Speeding Data Access Using PC-Cache"; the "Viewing Files" section in Chapter 16, "Managing Your Files"; the "Managing Your Directories" section in Chapter 17, "Managing Your Directories and Disks"; and the "Displaying System Information" section in Chapter 18, "Using Advanced PC Shell Features.") To toggle its selection off or on, press R or click the option.

- *Windows*   This category represents the Windows utilities CP Launcher for Windows, CP Backup for Windows, Undelete for Windows, CP Scheduler for Windows, and TSR Manager, as well as PIF files for most DOS-based PC Tools programs. (For more information, see Chapter 29, "Windows Utilities Overview.") To toggle its selection off or on, press W or click the option. (If you don't already have Windows installed on your system, this option is unavailable.)

When you turn a category off, it disappears from the "disk space" bar in the lower portion of the screen to clearly indicate your selection. If you turn the category back on, it reappears on the bar. When a category is displayed, the bar also shows the amount of space its associated files will take up on your hard disk.

You can turn all the categories *on* by pressing Y or clicking Everything, or turn them all *off* by pressing G or clicking Nothing. The latter option is useful if you've already installed PC Tools 7 and now only want to change a particular configuration option.

When you've placed a checkmark next to all the PC Tools categories you want copied to your hard disk, press O or click OK to accept your selections, and then press ENTER or click OK to begin the copying process. To proceed, read the next section.

Copying PC Tools Files

After you've worked through the initial installation screens, Install starts copying PC Tools files to the directory you specified on your hard disk. The files copied include the Install program, which allows you to modify your installation choices later on; PC Config, which lets you adjust PC Tools display, keyboard, and mouse settings; and the text file README.TXT, which contains last-minute news about the program that didn't make it into the documentation.

When the files from the first disk are copied, you're prompted to insert a different numbered disk, and then press ENTER or click OK. Follow the screen instructions as prompted. Depending on how much of PC Tools you chose to install and the speed of your system, the process will take anywhere from 5 minutes to 20 minutes. A "Percent Completed" bar near the bottom of the screen tracks your progress as you proceed with the copying process.

When the copying is completed, you're asked if you want to create a Recovery Disk, which is a floppy disk that stores your critical system information and PC Tools data restoration programs, and can later be used to help you recover lost files or system data. It's *highly* recommended that you take the few minutes necessary to create this disk. To do so, press ENTER or click OK, and then work through the next section, "Creating a Recovery Disk."

Otherwise, press S or click Skip, and then continue to the section "Configuring Windows Programs." You can then optionally create a Recovery Disk at some later time by following the instructions in Chapter 5, "Safeguarding Your Data."

Creating a Recovery Disk

If you've chosen to let Install create a Recovery Disk, follow these steps:

1. You're prompted to select the drive that contains your AUTOEXEC.BAT file and is used to start up, or boot, your system. Press the letter of the appropriate drive and press ENTER, or click on the drive's icon and click OK. The following dialog box appears:

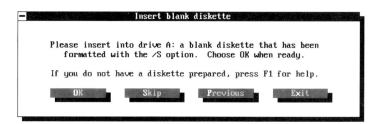

2. Locate a blank floppy disk that's the proper size for your A drive and that's been formatted with the /S option (which makes the disk able to start up your PC). If you don't have such a formatted disk available, use any blank floppy that's compatible with your A drive and then see step 3.

    Put a label on the floppy and write "PC Tools Recovery Disk" on it (or use the label supplied in your PC Tools package), and write the current date on the label. When you're done, insert the disk into your A drive.

3. If your floppy hasn't been formatted with the /S option, press F1 and follow the onscreen instructions.

4. Press ENTER or click OK. Install now writes to the floppy the files CON-FIG.SYS, REBUILD.COM, MI.COM, UNFORMAT.EXE, SYS.COM, and the

file PARTNSAV.FIL (which contains your partition table and CMOS data). A message then tells you the Recovery Disk has been successfully created.

5. If your hard disk requires a device driver, wait until you've completed the installation process, and then use the DOS COPY command or PC Shell's File Copy option (see Chapter 16, "Managing Your Files") to transfer the driver to the Recovery Disk. Also, edit the floppy's CONFIG.SYS file to specify the driver; or, if you aren't sure how to do so, just copy the hard disk's CONFIG.SYS file to the floppy. If you need more information about hard disk device drivers, contact your hard disk vendor or manufacturer.

   When you're done with your Recovery Disk, put it in a safe place. If you later have some sort of data accident, see Chapter 5 for more information on what data the Recovery Disk contains, and Chapter 6 for instructions on how to use that data to restore what was lost.

6. Press ENTER or click OK, and then proceed to the next section to continue with the installation process.

Configuring Windows Programs

If you have Microsoft Windows installed on your system, and you chose to install either all PC Tools files or selected files that included the Windows category, you're now offered the option of setting CP Launcher and/or CP Scheduler for Windows to be loaded automatically every time Windows is run. As explained in Chapters 29 and 30, CP Launcher lets you run programs and exit Windows without having to access the Program Manager window, while CP Scheduler lets you schedule programs to run at specified times. The default is to have both programs load automatically, as indicated by the checkmarks next to both program names.

To turn the CP Launcher checkmark off or on, press C or click the option; to turn the CP Scheduler checkmark off or on, press S or click the option. When you've adjusted the automatic load settings appropriately, press O or click OK. Your WIN.INI file is revised based on your settings, while your old file is renamed WIN.SAV.

Configuring PC Format

If you chose to install all PC Tools files, or if you chose selected files and included the Data Protection/Security category, you're now asked if you want to use PC Format instead of DOS FORMAT. PC Format is much less destructive to data (as explained in "Using PC Format" in Chapter 5), so it's *highly* recommended that you accept this option by pressing ENTER or clicking OK. If you do so, your DOS FORMAT.COM program is renamed FORMAT!.COM to ensure you don't run it accidentally, and a FORMAT.BAT batch file is created in your PC Tools directory that simply runs PC Format in case you, out of habit, type **FORMAT** from the DOS prompt and press ENTER.

Otherwise, if you don't want PC Format configured for some reason, press S or click Skip. This still allows you to run PC Format, but doesn't provide protection against using DOS FORMAT accidentally. You can, however, always manually perform the renaming and batch file procedures just described, or rerun the Install program at some later time to perform them for you.

Configuring Undelete

If you're running DOS 5, and you chose to install either all PC Tools files or selected files that included the Data Recovery category, you're now asked if you want to use the PC Tools 7 Undelete program instead of the DOS 5 Undelete utility. The latter is a version of Undelete from PC Tools Deluxe 6, and it's not nearly as powerful or versatile as the PC Tools 7 version (as explained in "Recovering Deleted Files" in Chapter 6). Therefore, it's *highly* recommended that you accept this option by pressing ENTER or clicking OK. If you do so, your DOS 5 UNDELETE.EXE program is renamed UNDELET!.EXE to ensure you don't run it accidentally.

Otherwise, if you don't want Undelete configured for some reason, press S or click Skip. This still allows you to run the PC Tools 7 Undelete program (which is named UNDEL.EXE), but doesn't provide protection against your running the DOS 5 version (which is named UNDELETE.EXE) accidentally. You can, however, always manually perform the renaming procedure just described, or rerun the Install program at some later time to perform it for you.

If you're installing PC Tools 7.0, the Undelete configuration screen just described doesn't appear. Instead, Install renames the UNDELETE.EXE in your DOS directory automatically without asking for confirmation.

Converting Setup Files

If you chose to install all PC Tools files, or if you chose selected files and included the CP Backup category, you're now asked if you want Install to search for any setup files on your hard disk generated by Norton Backup or Fastback Plus and convert them into setup files compatible with CP Backup. If you do, press ENTER or click OK, and then follow the screen prompts. Your original setup files will remain unchanged, but their CP Backup versions will be copied to your PC Tools DATA subdirectory (or your PC Tools directory if you chose not to create subdirectories).

Otherwise, press S or click Skip to just continue with the installation process. You can always convert setup files at a later time using the Convert program (see "New Hardware and Software Support" in Chapter 1, "CP Backup Overview").

Configuring PC Tools

At this point, the Install program has copied the PC Tools files you've requested to your hard disk. However, it has *not* made any modifications to your AUTO-EXEC.BAT or CONFIG.SYS files. Therefore, you're now asked if you want to configure PC Tools by having Install set specified programs to automatically load memory resident every time you start up your PC.

If you don't (which isn't recommended), press S or click Skip, confirm your decision by pressing ENTER or clicking Yes, and exit Install by pressing ENTER or clicking Exit. You're returned to the DOS prompt. However, you can return to this configuration step of the installation process at any time by simply typing **INSTALL** from the DOS prompt and pressing ENTER. Meanwhile, keep in mind that until you do so, such important revisions to AUTOEXEC.BAT as adding a SET PCTOOLS line and adding your PC Tools directory to the PATH statement won't be implemented unless you perform them manually.

If you edit your AUTOEXEC.BAT file manually, it's recommended that you arrange commands in the following order to avoid program conflicts: DOS commands, VDefend, Mirror, mouse drivers, network drivers, print spoolers, ITLFAX, PC-Cache, Data Monitor, Commute, Backtalk, DeskConnect, macro programs, other non-PC Tools programs, PC Shell, and Desktop.

On the other hand, if you *do* want to configure PC Tools (which is recommended), press ENTER or click OK. After a few moments, the Configuration screen in Figure A-2 appears. This screen offers the program options PC **S**hell, **D**esktop Manager, Commute, **M**irror, **V**Defend, Data Mo**n**itor, **PC**-Cache, and **S**cheduler.

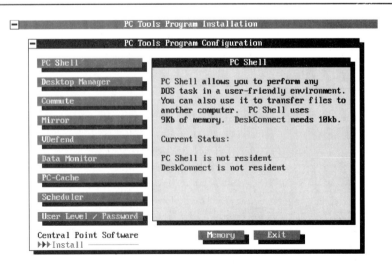

Figure A-2.   The PC Tools Program Configuration screen

You can select any option by pressing its highlighted letter or clicking the program name. When you do, a dialog box appears offering to insert a command line in your AUTOEXEC.BAT file that will always load the program memory resident. (The two exceptions are **VDefend**, which provides the *additional* choice of having Install insert the command line in your CONFIG.SYS file, and Mirror, which doesn't load memory resident, but instead actually executes from AUTO-EXEC.BAT, taking only a few moments to back up critical system data on your hard disk.)

Certain programs allow you to select additional options. For example, PC **S**hell provides an **A**pplications option that searches your hard disk and compiles a Program List of applications it's able to associate with particular data files (see "Running Programs" in Chapter 18). As another example, selecting Data Monitor gives you the ability to adjust virtually every setting in the program.

If you aren't sure what an option does, you can press F1 to get a brief online description of it. You can also get a more in-depth explanation by checking the appropriate chapter in this book. Specifically:

- For PC **S**hell, see Chapter 15, "PC Shell Overview," and the sections "Running Programs" and "Connecting Computers Using DeskConnect" in Chapter 18, "Using Advanced PC Shell Features."

- For **D**esktop Manager, see Chapter 19, "Desktop Manager Overview," and the sections "Using Modem Telecommunications in the Background" and "Using Fax Telecommunications" in Chapter 26, "Using Telecommunications."

- For **C**ommute, see Chapter 14, "Connecting Computers Using Commute."

- For **M**irror, see "Using Mirror" in Chapter 5, "Safeguarding Your Data." (Unlike all the other options, the default setting for this option is *on.*)

- For **V**Defend, see Chapter 13, "Detecting Viruses Using VDefend."

- For **D**ata Monitor, see "Monitoring Deleted Files" in Chapter 5, "Safeguarding Your Data," and see Chapter 12, "Shielding Data Using Data Monitor."

- For **P**C-Cache, see Chapter 10, "Speeding Data Access Using PC-Cache."

- For **S**cheduler, see "Scheduling Backups" in Chapter 2, "Backing Up Your Hard Disk."

In addition to the program options, the Configuration screen provides the choice User Level/Password. This sets the number of options displayed on the program menus of the programs CP Backup and PC Shell. The three possible levels are **B**eginner (few options), **I**ntermediate (mid-range of options), or **A**dvanced (all options). Furthermore, you can enter a password to "lock in" the selected level, which is useful if you're a PC supervisor who wants to restrict access to certain features.

The Configuration screen also provides a **Memory** option. If you select it, it provides a chart showing how much of your conventional memory will be filled by the program loading selections you've made.

When you're done selecting options, press X or click Exit from the Configuration screen. The following Close dialog box appears:

If you want to see the changes that Install plans on making to your AUTO-EXEC.BAT and CONFIG.SYS files, press V or click View Configuration. First your AUTOEXEC.BAT file is displayed, with any new or changed lines highlighted. You activate the text window by pressing SHIFT-TAB or clicking on the window, and then scroll through it using the arrow keys or the window's vertical scroll bar. You can also select Delete **Line** to delete the line the highlight cursor is on, **Discard** to abandon all changes to the file, **Save** to save the file as is (in which case your old file is renamed AUTOEXEC.SAV), **Save** As to save this revised file under a different name (leaving your current AUTOEXEC.BAT file unaffected), or **Cancel** to simply return to the Close box while retaining the changes Install plans to make.

If you select any option but **Cancel**, you're then shown your CONFIG.SYS file *if* Install plans to make any changes to it. Otherwise, the Close box exits.

If you *don't* want to select the **View Configuration** option, just make sure the **Save** Configuration option has a checkmark next to it, and then exit the Close box by pressing ENTER or clicking OK.

Next, a dialog box asks if you want Install to search for applications to be added to the PC Shell Program List. This option is identical to the PC **Shell Applications** option mentioned previously. If you haven't already used it, optionally press S or click Search to add to the Program List. Otherwise, press ESC or click Cancel.

Lastly, a dialog box tells you that any changes made to your AUTOEXEC.BAT and/or CONFIG.SYS files won't take effect until you restart your computer. First, remove any installation disks still in your system and put them in a safe place. If you then want your configuration choices to take effect right away (which is recommended), press ENTER or click Reboot to restart your PC. Otherwise, press D or click DOS to simply return to the DOS prompt. In either case, the installation process ends, and your selection is implemented.

*If you ever want to revise your configuration, simply type **INSTALL** from the DOS prompt and press ENTER. The Configuration screen appears again, giving you the opportunity to make as many changes to your PC Tools setup as you want. In addition, it gives you the opportunity to have Install update your PC Shell Program List, which is useful if you've added new applications to your hard disk.*

Using PC Config

In addition to configuring individual program options, you can adjust display, mouse, and keyboard options for *all* PC Tools programs. To do so, type **PCCONFIG** from the DOS prompt and press ENTER. The following main menu appears:

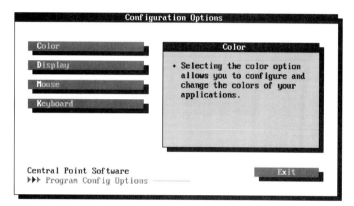

The menu provides the four options Color, Display, Mouse, and Keyboard. These are covered in the following four sections.

You can also set display and mouse options for individual programs using command line parameters. For more information, see the "Video and Mouse Parameters" section at the end of this chapter.

Changing Colors

If you press C or click Color, a Color Options screen like the one shown in Figure A-3 appears. The screen provides options on the left and shows the results of your different choices on the right.

First, select the **S**cheme option to try out different preset color combinations, or *schemes.* If you like the way the different colors in a scheme look together, accept the scheme without change. Otherwise, customize the scheme you've chosen by selecting a particular screen element using the **E**lement option, and then a different color using the **C**olor option.

Alternatively, select a screen category using the **C**ategory option, click on the element you want to change in the display on the right, and then select the color you want from the **C**olor list (which drops down automatically).

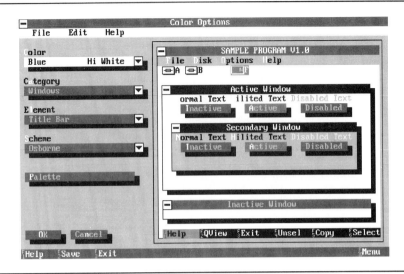

Figure A-3.   *The PC Config Color Options screen*

When you're done, press O or click OK to accept your selections and return to the main menu.

Changing Display Settings

If you press D or click Display, a Display Options dialog box like this appears:

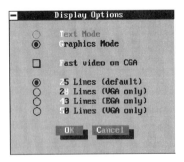

If you have a VGA or EGA display, you can set PC Tools programs to use the attractive graphic fonts designed for version 7 by selecting the **G**raphics Mode option. However, if you don't have a VGA or EGA display, or if you need to print or capture PC Tools screens and are experiencing problems in graphics mode, select the **T**ext Mode option instead.

If you have a CGA display, you can turn on the Fast Video on CGA option to scroll your screens more quickly. However, if you experience too much screen flickering, or "snow," turn the option off.

Lastly, if you have a VGA display, you can choose to see 28 or 50 lines per screen instead of 25; if you have an EGA display, you can choose to see 43 lines per screen instead of 25.

When you've finished making your display selections, press O or click OK to accept them. You're returned to the main menu.

Changing Mouse Settings

If you press M or click Mouse, a Mouse Options dialog box like this appears:

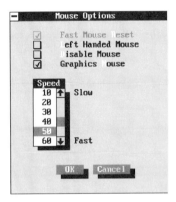

The box provides the following five options:

- *Fast Mouse Reset*   If you're experiencing mouse problems, turning this option off will probably solve them, *particularly* if your mouse is connected to a PS/2 mouse port and the problems arise after you exit Microsoft Windows.

- *Left Handed Mouse*   This option switches the functions of the left and right mouse buttons, which can be useful if you're left-handed.

- *Disable Mouse*   This option disables mouse support, which is useful if you're experiencing mouse problems and turning off the Fast Mouse Reset option didn't help. Such problems are usually due to an old mouse driver, so in these cases contact your mouse manufacturer to get the latest version of its mouse software (after confirming that it works with PC Tools 7).

- *Graphics Mouse*   This option displays the mouse pointer as an arrow instead of a solid block on VGA and EGA displays.

- *Speed*   This option lets you set how quickly your mouse pointer moves across the screen. If you choose too high a speed, you'll have trouble controlling the positioning of the mouse pointer, while if you choose too low a speed, you'll become distracted by the amount of time it takes for the pointer to move. You should therefore optimally select the fastest speed that provides you fine control of your mouse.

When you're done selecting your mouse options, press O or click OK to accept them. You're returned to the main menu.

Changing Keyboard Settings

If you press K or click Keyboard, a Keyboard Options dialog box like this appears:

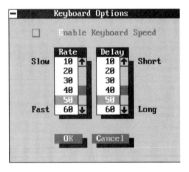

The box offers the options Rate, which sets how quickly a keystroke is repeated when you hold down the key, and Delay, which sets how long you need to hold down a key before it begins repeating. To put your settings into effect, select the **Enable Keyboard Speed** option to turn it on, and press O or click OK. You're returned to the main menu.

Video and Mouse Parameters

When you start a PC Tools program from the DOS prompt or modify its AUTOEXEC.BAT line, you can specify certain options, called *parameters,* following the program name. You can include any single parameter (for example, DESKTOP /BW) or combine a number of parameters (for example, DESKTOP /28 /IN /LE) to achieve the effect you want. Keep in mind that parameters require a *forward* slash (/) as opposed to the backslash (\) used to specify DOS directories.

The following is a list of the 15 video and mouse parameters available for virtually any PC Tools program:

- **/25**   This parameter sets the program to display 25 lines per screen (which is the default).

- **/28**   This parameter sets the program to display 28 lines per screen on a VGA display.

- **/43**   This parameter sets the program to display 43 lines per screen on either a VGA or EGA display.

- **/50**   This parameter sets the program to display 50 lines per screen on a VGA display.

- **/BF**   This parameter (which is short for BIOS font) can fix display problems you might experience with PC Tools 7 graphics characters on a VGA or EGA display.

- **/BW**   If you use a color graphics card with a monochrome monitor, this "black and white" parameter can clear up a display that appears fuzzy or has unreadable shades of gray.

- **/FF**   This parameter will speed up screen scrolling on a CGA display. (However, if you find it creates too much screen flickering, or "snow," stop using it.)

- **/IM**   This parameter disables mouse support. It's useful if you're having problems using your mouse and including the /PS2 parameter didn't help. Such problems are usually due to an old mouse driver, so in these cases contact your mouse manufacturer to get the latest version of its mouse software (after confirming that it works with PC Tools 7).

- **/IN**   This parameter sets your program to use the default PC Tools color scheme instead of the one you selected using PC Config (covered in the previous section).

- **/LCD**   This parameter provides a crisper image on liquid crystal display PCs, such as laptops.

- **/LE**   This parameter switches the functions of the left and right mouse buttons, which can be useful if you're left-handed.

- **/MONO**   This parameter may provide a crisper image on an IBM monochrome display.

- **/NF**   This parameter turns off the special PC Tools 7 graphics characters designed for VGA and EGA displays.

- **/NGM**   This parameter changes your mouse pointer from an arrow icon to a solid block on a VGA or EGA display.

- **/PS2**   This parameter will usually fix a mouse problem you're experiencing. It's especially effective if your mouse is connected to a PS/2 mouse port and you've just exited Microsoft Windows.

*You can display this list at any time from the DOS prompt by typing the name of a PC Tools program followed by the parameter /VIDEO (for example, **DESKTOP/VIDEO**), and then pressing* ENTER.

Appendix **B**

Installing and Using PC Tools on a Network

PC Tools 7 can be used on a NOVELL network running NOVELL Advanced NetWare 286 2.12 or higher, or NOVELL NetWare 386. It can also be used on an IBM Token Ring network running IBM PC Local Area Network Program 1.02 or higher.

If you're a network supervisor and want to install PC Tools on your server to make it available to multiple workstations, follow the directions provided here. They tell you how to copy PC Tools files to the server, and how to configure each workstation appropriately.

Once PC Tools has been installed and configured, see the "Unsupported Operations" section in this appendix for a list of PC Tools programs and commands that can't be used on networked drives, and the "Network Features" section in this appendix for a list of PC Tools features specific to networks.

 A network license or site license, or multiple copies of the software, should be purchased before PC Tools is installed on a network.

Installing PC Tools on the Server

To install PC Tools on your network's server, follow these steps:

1. Follow steps 1 through 6 in the "Installing PC Tools on Your Hard Disk" section in Appendix A.

2. When the Select Workstation dialog box appears, press S or click the Install on a Network Server option.

3. When you're prompted for the drive and directory to which you want to copy the PC Tools files, type the drive letter of the server, a colon, and the path of the directory. For example, to store the files on drive H in subdirectory \HOME\PCTOOLS, type **H:\HOME\PCTOOLS**. When you're done, press ENTER or click OK.

4. Follow steps 9 through 13 in the "Installing PC Tools on Your Hard Disk" section in Appendix A to initiate the copying process, and then insert each installation disk following the screen prompts.

5. At the end of the copying process, you are *not* given the opportunity to create a Recovery Disk or configure PC Tools, because these operations must be performed later at individual workstations. Therefore, when the copying is completed, exit Install. You're returned to the operating system.

6. Assign all users read and open privileges for the server's PC Tools directory. For NOVELL NetWare 286, assign the privileges Read From File, Open Existing Files, and Search For Files. For NOVELL NetWare 386, assign the privileges Read and File Scan.

   When you're done, continue by reading the next section, "Configuring PC Tools."

Configuring PC Tools

After you've copied PC Tools files to a standalone PC, Install provides the option of configuring the system. However, Install does *not* provide this option after you've copied PC Tools files to a server. Therefore, in this case you must perform the configuration steps manually. Specifically, you should do the following:

- Set up access to the server's PC Tools directory and establish an individual directory for each workstation.

- Revise the CONFIG.SYS file on each workstation appropriately.

- Run Install on each workstation to select appropriate configuration options.

- Run PC Config to adjust display, mouse, and keyboard settings.

These procedures are covered in the following sections.

Setting Up PC Tools Directories

For PC Tools to work on the network properly, you must make the server's PC Tools directory available to each workstation. You must also assign each workstation a unique directory for storing its individual PC Tools-generated files, such as configuration (CFG) files, temporary (TMP) files, overlay (DOV, THM, IMG, and RMG) files, and data files. How you perform these configuration tasks depends on the type of network you're using.

Configuring on an IBM Token Ring Network

If you're using an IBM Token Ring network, perform the following steps for each workstation:

1. Insert the pathname of the server directory containing the PC Tools files at the front of the PATH statement in the workstation's AUTOEXEC.BAT file. This allows the workstation to access PC Tools from anywhere in its system.

2. Create a directory with write privileges on the workstation for storing PC Tools-generated files specific to the workstation (for example, \PCTOOLS\DATA).

3. Insert the following line in the workstation's AUTOEXEC.BAT file to direct its PC Tools files to the appropriate directory:

       SET PCTOOLS=*d:\directory*

   For the *d* parameter, use the letter of the workstation's drive, and for the *directory* parameter, use the name of the directory you've created on the workstation to store its PC Tools-generated files (for example, SET PCTOOLS=C:\PCTOOLS\DATA). Be sure not to insert any spaces directly in front of or anywhere past the equal sign.

Repeat steps 1 through 3 for each workstation on the network that's going to run PC Tools.

Configuring on a NOVELL Network

If you're using a NOVELL network, you can follow the instructions in the previous section for an IBM Token Ring network. However, it's more efficient if you take advantage of the special features provided by NOVELL. To do so, follow these steps:

1. Map a search path for the server's PC Tools directory.

2. Create a directory with write privileges on each workstation for storing PC Tools-generated files specific to the workstation (for example, \PCTOOLS\DATA).

3. Create a HOME directory on the server (if it doesn't already exist) and a directory for each user branching from the HOME directory.

4. Insert a command like the following into the NOVELL System Login script on the server:

   DOS SET PCTOOLS="H:\\HOME\\%LOGIN_NAME"

The directory below HOME should have the same name as the user's login name, and the user should have full write privileges.

Don't insert any spaces directly in front of or anywhere past the equal sign. Also, use uppercase for all the text past the equal sign.

Configuring CONFIG.SYS

For PC Tools to work properly, the following CONFIG.SYS minimum settings are recommended:

    BUFFERS=30
    FILES=40

However, the number of buffers can be lowered if the workstation is using a cache program.

In addition, if a mouse is installed in a workstation to be used with PC Tools, any necessary mouse driver specification must be included in CONFIG.SYS.

Lastly, if after revising the workstation's AUTOEXEC.BAT file an "Out of environment space" message comes up, insert a line like this in CONFIG.SYS to expand the environment to a larger size (in this case, 512 bytes):

    SHELL=C:\COMMAND.COM /P /E:512

Configuring PC Tools Programs for Each Workstation

You're now ready to configure individual PC Tools programs for each workstation. To do so, rerun Install on each workstation from the installation disks, go through the initial screens until the Select Workstation dialog box appears, and select the Customize for this Network Workstation option.

You can then select any Install option other than actually copying files to the workstation. For example, you can perform the steps for creating a Recovery Disk, adjusting automatic load settings for CP Launcher and CP Scheduler for Windows, configuring PC Format and Undelete, and converting existing Norton Backup and Fastback Plus setup files. In addition, you can use the PC Tools Program Configuration screen to insert AUTOEXEC.BAT commands for loading selected memory-resident programs on startup, search the workstation's hard disk for applications to add to its PC Shell Program List, and set the Desktop's Fax Telecommunications option to work with a fax board that's in a networked PC. For more information on these procedures, see Appendix A.

Configuring Display, Mouse, and Keyboard Settings

Lastly, after you're done using Install to configure individual programs, you can adjust the workstation settings for *all* PC Tools programs by running PC Config. This utility lets you adjust PC Tools color, video display, mouse, and keyboard settings for the workstation. For more information, see "Using PC Config" in Appendix A.

Unsupported Operations

All PC Tools programs are fully supported for use on individual workstations. However, certain disk-related PC Tools programs won't work with networked drives. Specifically, the data safeguarding and recovery programs PC Format, Unformat, Rebuild, DiskFix, and File Fix (see Chapters 4 through 8), and the speedup utilities Compress and PC-Cache (see Chapters 9 and 10), will not function at all when directed at networked drives.

In addition, the Data Monitor Delete Tracker option (see "Monitoring Deleted Files" in Chapter 5) can't be used to protect deleted files on a networked drive. Along the same lines, Undelete (see "Recovering Deleted Files" in Chapter 6) will only display and can only recover files on a networked drive that were protected by the Data Monitor Delete Sentry option.

Another safeguarding program with a few restrictions is CP Backup, which can't back up NOVELL network bindery files or any files that are open during the backup. It's therefore best to schedule the program to back up after office hours, when no one is using the system.

Also, the following ten disk-related commands in PC Shell (see Chapters 15 through 18) won't work when directed at a networked drive:

- **D**isk **D**isk Information, which displays byte, sector, and cluster information about a disk.

- **D**isk **F**ormat Data Disk, which formats a disk via PC Format.

- **D**isk Make Disk **B**ootable, which formats and copies system files to a disk via PC Format.

- **D**isk **R**ename Volume, which changes a disk's volume label.

- **D**isk **S**earch, which finds the sector and offset location of specified data on a disk.

- Disk **S**ort Files in Directory, which physically sorts the files in the current directory.

- **D**isk **V**erify, which checks that all sectors on a disk are readable.

- **D**isk **V**iew/**E**dit, which lets you edit a disk's sectors.

- **S**pecial Disk **M**ap, which displays a cluster map of a disk.

- **S**pecial File Map, which displays a cluster map of the selected file on the current disk.

Lastly, the PC Shell File **U**ndelete command runs the Undelete program, and so will only recover files protected by Delete Sentry.

Network Features

There are a number of special features that PC Tools offers on networks. Many of these are provided by the Desktop Manager (see Chapter 19, "Desktop Manager Overview"). Specifically:

- If you're using a NOVELL network, the Desktop allows a CAS-compatible fax board in any workstation to be accessed by any other workstation. For more information, see "Using Fax Telecommunications" in Chapter 26, "Using Telecommunications."

- The Desktop's dBASE-compatible Databases application supports file-locking on networks. As a result, multiple people can read a database at a time, but only one person can write to the database at a time. This ensures that database changes aren't accidentally lost in between file saves. For more information, see Chapter 25, "Using the Database Manager."

- The Desktop's Appointment Scheduler application now supports group scheduling, which allows a number of people on a network to share a scheduler file devoted to the group's meetings. For more information, see "Scheduling Groups on a Network" in Chapter 23, "Using the Appointment Scheduler."

Other PC Tools programs also offer strong network support. For example:

- CP Backup (see Chapters 1 through 3) is ideal for backing up large networked drives because of its speed, efficient data compression, explicit tape drive support, and scheduling features.

- Commute (see Chapter 14) allows one network user to take control of another user's PC. This is an extremely convenient feature for a PC supervisor who must support multiple workstations.

- Data Monitor (see Chapters 5 and 12) protects deleted files via its Delete Sentry option, and can also protect data via its Write Protect and Directory Lock options. In addition, its Disk Light option (which displays a drive letter on screen whenever a drive is accessed) is especially useful for networked drives, which can't physically display drive lights on workstations.

- Directory Maintenance (see Chapter 17) provides the new option of moving (or "pruning and grafting") entire directories on a networked drive. In addition, it can display a selected directory's network rights, or be set to constantly display the creation date, owner, or rights for all directories on the Directory Tree. The only restriction in the program is that it doesn't let you change the attributes of a directory on a networked drive.

- File Find (see Chapter 16) can search networked drives as easily as workstation drives. In addition, on NOVELL networks it can search based on NOVELL file attributes, and it displays the NOVELL attributes of located files.

- PC Shell (as well as CP Backup) allows you to select a networked drive from the drive bar just as easily as you can select a workstation drive. However, the Tree List will only show directories for which a workstation has at least read privileges. This prevents scores of irrelevant server directories from cluttering up the Tree List display. For more information, see Chapters 1 and 15.

- Lastly, System Information (see Chapter 18) can, in addition to all the other data it provides, display information about network users, volumes, and groups.

Appendix **C**

PC Tools Menu Commands

This appendix lists the commands for the major PC Tools 7 DOS programs with pull-down menus. The programs covered are Commute, Compress, CP Backup, the Desktop Manager applications, Directory Maintenance, PC Secure, PC Shell, and Undelete.

The programs are listed in alphabetical order. However, the menus and commands in each program are listed in their order of appearance on the screen. The Control and **Help** menus (if any) are not included, since their options tend to be the same across programs; for information on these, see this book's Introduction.

The left-hand column lists each command's name and the keystrokes that invoke it. If the command is associated with a particular user level, a (B) for Beginner, (I) for Intermediate, or (A) for Advanced is also listed.

The right-hand column briefly describes the function of each command. For more information, see the chapter that covers the command.

Commute

The File Menu

Private Call List F, P	Brings up a directory of PCs you can call and take control of.
Give Control List F, G	Brings up a directory of callers who you'll allow to take control of your PC.

Record Activity F, R	When on, records when each session begins and ends, who the session is with, and what files were transferred.
Print Activity Log F, L	Prints or translates as a text file the record of your Commute sessions.
Ignore All Calls F, I	Sets Commute to ignore all callers.
Unload From Memory F, U	Exits Commute and unloads it from memory, freeing up room for other programs.
DOS Shell F, S	Temporarily exits to DOS. Typing **EXIT** and pressing ENTER returns to Commute.
Exit F, X	Exits Commute without prompting for confirmation.

The Configure Menu

Hotkey C, K	Sets the keystroke to invoke Commute when it's memory resident.
Modem List C, M	Specifies the model of modem you're using for Commute modem connections.
COM Port C, C	Sets the COM port you're using with Commute for modem and cable connections.
Baud Rate C, B	Sets the baud rate you're using with Commute for modem and cable connections.
Connection Type C, T	Specifies your connection for the session as **Modem**, **LAN**, or **Direct** (cable).
Commute User Name C, U	Sets your Commute user name.
Security C, E	Sets log-in, password, disconnect, and access restrictions when you give control of your PC to another PC.
Schedule Calls C, H	Schedules Auto-Call scripts to run on specified days and times automatically.
Auto-Call Scripts C, A	Brings up a list of your Auto-Call scripts, and lets you create, edit, rename, and delete scripts.
Restore Defaults C, R	Restores Configure menu options to their default settings.
Save Configuration C, S	Saves your Configure menu settings to disk for future sessions.

Compress

The Compress Menu

Begin Compress
C, B or F4

Initiates the defragmentation process.

Choose Drive
C, C

Lets you select a different drive to map, analyze, and defragment.

Exit Compress
C, X

Quits Compress.

The Analysis Menu

Disk Statistics
A, D or F5

Provides an analysis of the selected disk's cluster use and fragmentation.

File Fragmentation Analysis; A, F

Provides an analysis of the cluster size and fragmentation of each file on the disk.

Show Files in Each Map Block; A, S

Displays cluster numbers, filenames, and fragmentation status of areas on disk map.

The Options Menu

Compression Technique O, C or F6

Sets which disk reorganization method Compress uses.

Ordering Methods
O, O or F7

Sets order in which directories and files are moved during defragmentation.

Directory Order
O, D or F8

Sets which directories are moved closest to the front of the disk.

Files to Place First
O, F

Sets which files are moved closest to the front of the disk (following directories).

Unmovable Files
O, U

Forces Compress to leave specified files in place during defragmentation.

File **S**ort Options
O, S or F9

Sorts files in each directory by date, name, extension, or size.

Print Report
O, P

Prints a report on the results of the defragmentation.

CP Backup

The File Menu

Load Setup F, L	Loads a setup file to reset CP Backup to your previous option and file selections.
Save Setup F, S	Saves your current option settings and file selections to the currently active setup file.
Save Setup **As** F, A	Saves your current option settings and file selections to a new setup file that you name.
Save as **Default** F, D	Saves your current option settings and file selections as new CP Backup defaults.
Print History F, P	Lets you print backup report information from the selected history file.
Exit F, X or F3	Brings up the Close dialog box. Pressing ENTER or O, or clicking OK, then quits CP Backup.

The Action Menu

Start Backup/ Restore/Compare A, S or F5/F6/F9	Starts a backup, restore, or compare operation (depending on the screen you're in).
Backup **From** A, F	Lets you select the drives to back up from. This option appears only in the Backup screen.
Restore/Compare **To** F, T	Selects the drives to restore to or compare. Appears only in the Restore and Compare screens.
Choose Directories A, H	Reads in directories from the selected drive (Backup) or history file (Restore/Compare).
Schedule Backups A, D	Lets you schedule backups. This option appears only in the Backup screen.
Search History Files A, A	Searches through history files for specified backup files. In Restore and Compare only.
Backup/ **Restore/Compare** A, B/A, R/A, C	Switches to the selected screen. The screen you're currently in is the only one *not* listed.

The Options Menu

Backup Method O, B (I)	Selects the backup method (**Full, Incremental, Differential, Full** Copy, **Separate Incremental**).
Reporting O, R (B)	Directs a backup report to be printed or saved as a text file.

Compress O, C (A)	Sets the degree of data compression during backup versus the speed of backup.
Verify O, V (A)	If on, verifies each track during backup to ensure it's been copied accurately.
Media Format O, F (A)	Sets whether to use **DOS** Standard or CPS **F**loppy format, and CPS **T**ape or **Q**IC Compatible format.
Format Always O, M (A)	If on, formats every disk or tape during backup, even if already formatted.
Error Correction O, E (A)	If on, saves extra data on each disk or tape to safeguard against future media defects.
Virus Detection O, U (A)	Toggles on or off automatic scanning of your files for viruses before they're backed up.
Save History O, H (A)	If on, saves a copy of the backup history file to your hard disk in addition to your backup set.
Overwrite Warning O, O (I)	If on, alerts you when you're about to overwrite data during a backup or restore.
Time Display O, T (A)	If on, displays status line clock that times the backup process; conflicts with some networks.
Selection Options O, S (I)	Leads to the four file selection options **S**ubdirectory Inclusion, **I**nclude/**E**xclude Files, **A**ttribute Exclusions, and **D**ate Range Selection.
Display Options O, D (I)	Leads to the options Sort **O**ptions and **L**ong Format (sets 1 file or 3 files per row).

The Configure Menu

Choose Drive And Media C, M or F7	Defines the media you're using for backup.
Define Equipment C, E or F8	Defines the drives you're using for backup.
Backup Speed C, B	Sets backup speed to High Speed (DMA), Medium Speed (non-DMA), or Low Speed/DOS Compatible.
User Level C, U	Sets the user level to Beginner, Intermediate, or Advanced; and turns Express mode on or off.

Desktop: Appointment Scheduler

The File Menu

Load ALT, F, L	Clears the file in the current window from memory and then loads the specified file.
Print ALT, F, P	Lets you print the current file using a broad range of layout options.
Save ALT, F, S	Saves the current file to disk after letting you optionally change its name and format.
Autosave ALT, F, A	Automatically saves the current file to disk at specified intervals.
Groups ALT, F, G	Lets you join group appointment files on your network.

The Appointment Menu

Make ALT, A, M	Brings up the Make Appointment dialog box for the time selected.
Delete ALT, A, D	Deletes the selected appointment from the schedule (after prompting for confirmation).
Edit ALT, A, E	Brings up the Make Appointment dialog box of the selected appointment for viewing and editing.
Find ALT, A, F	Searches for appointments matching specified criteria.
Next ALT, A, N	Searches for the next appointment of the day.
Free Time ALT, A, T	Searches for your next period of unscheduled time.
Attach Note ALT, A, A	Attaches a Notepads file to the selected appointment (or displays already existing note).

The To-Do Menu

Make ALT, T, M	Brings up the New To-Do Entry dialog box for the next available line in the To-Do List.
Delete ALT, T, D	Removes the selected item from the To-Do List. Doesn't prompt for confirmation before deleting.

| Attach Note
ALT, T, A | Attaches a Notepads file to the selected To-Do list item (or displays already existing note). |

The Controls Menu

Appointment Settings ALT, C, A	Changes Daily Scheduler defaults such as times displayed, time intervals, and time format.
Schedule Layouts ALT, C, S	Lets you choose among five different layout designs for the Scheduler screen.
National Holiday Settings ALT, C, N	Sets national holidays to be skipped by repeating appointments.
User Holiday Settings ALT, C, U	Sets personal special days to be skipped by repeating appointments.
Delete Old Entries ALT, C, D	Clears out old appointments ending before a specified date.

Desktop: Calculators

The Algebraic Calculator Options Menu

Clear Display ALT, O, C or F4	Clears the current number in the display.
Erase Tape ALT, O, E or F5	Clears the electronic "paper" tape.
Copy to Clipboard ALT, O, O	Copies the contents of the tape to the Clipboard.
Print Tape ALT, O, P	Prints the contents of the tape.
Wide Display ALT, O, W	If off, suppresses the keypad display.

The Financial Calculator RegisterDisplay Menu

| No Registers Displayed
ALT, R, N or F4 | Replaces the display of registers with a copyright notice. |
| Stack Registers
ALT, R, S or F5 | Displays the stack. |

Financial Registers ALT, R, F or F6	Displays the financial registers.
Data Registers R0-R9 ALT, R, D	Displays data registers R0 through R9.
Data Registers R.0-R.9 ALT, R, R	Displays data registers R.0 through R.9.

The Programmer's Calculator RegisterDisplay Menu

Stack Registers ALT, R, S or F4	Displays the stack.
Data Registers ALT, R, D or F6	Displays the data registers.

The Scientific Calculator RegisterDisplay Menu

No Registers ALT, R, N or F4	Replaces the display of registers with a copyright notice.
Stack Registers ALT, R, S or F5	Displays the stack.
Data Registers R0-R9 ALT, R, D or F6	Displays data registers R0 through R9.
Data Registers R.0-R.9 ALT, R, R	Displays data registers R.0 through R.9.

Desktop: Clipboard

The File Menu

Print ALT, F, P	Prints the current contents of the Clipboard.

The Copy/Paste Menu

Paste from Clipboard ALT, C, P or CTRL-INS	Copies the Clipboard's contents to the underlying application.
Copy to Clipboard ALT, C, C or CTRL-DEL	Copies the screen of the underlying application to the Clipboard.

Set Playback Delay
ALT, C, S

Controls the speed at which the Clipboard pastes
its contents.

The Edit Menu

Erase Block
ALT, E, E or SHIFT-DEL

Deletes a block marked in the Clipboard.

Mark Block
ALT, E, M

Marks a block in the Clipboard.

Unmark Block
ALT, E, U or ESC

Unmarks a block.

Delete All Text
ALT, E, D

Clears the Clipboard of its contents.

Insert File
ALT, E, I

Inserts all of a file's contents into the Clipboard.

Goto
ALT, E, G

Moves the cursor to the specified line number.

The Search Menu

Find
ALT, S, F

Lets you specify a text sequence and move the
cursor to the first occurrence of it.

Find Again
ALT, S, A

Moves the cursor to the next occurrence of your
text sequence.

Replace
ALT, S, R or F6

Replaces a text sequence with a different sequence.

Desktop: Databases

The File Menu

Load Form
ALT, F, L

Loads a specified database form for displaying or
printing records.

Print
ALT, F, P

Prints specified records or the current database's
field names.

Transfer
ALT, F, T

Copies selected records from the current database
to a specified database.

Append ALT, F, A	Copies all records from a specified database to the current database.
Browse ALT, F, B	Toggles between displaying multiple records in column-row format and one record at a time.
Modify Data ALT, F, M	Switches between letting you both view and modify records, or only view them.

The Edit Menu

Add New Record ALT, E, A or F8	Inserts a new record with default values.
Delete Record ALT, E, D	Hides the current record and marks it for permanent removal.
Undelete Records ALT, E, U	Unhides and unmarks all deleted records, restoring them to normal status.
Pack Database ALT, E, P	Permanently removes all deleted records from the current database. Use with care.
Hide Current Record ALT, E, H	Hides the current record.
Select All Records ALT, E, L	Makes all hidden records display again.
Edit Fields ALT, E, E	Lets you add and delete fields, and change field names, data types, and sizes.
Sort Database ALT, E, S	Sorts database records in ascending order based on a specified field.
Select Records ALT, E, R	Hides all records not meeting specified criteria.

The Search Menu

Find Text in All Fields ALT, S, F	Moves the cursor to the specified text sequence.
Find Text in Sort Field ALT, S, T or F7	Moves the cursor to the specified text sequence in the sort field.
Goto Record ALT, S, G	Moves the cursor to the specified record number.

The Controls Menu

Page Layout
ALT, C, P

Sets margins, paper size, line spacing, and page numbering.

Configure Autodial
ALT, C, C

Sets such Autodial options as COM port, baud rate, and digit prefix codes.

Autodial
ALT, C, A

Dials the telephone number in the current record.

Save Setup
ALT, C, S

Saves the current Control and **C**ontrols menu settings.

Desktop: Macro Editor

The File Menu

Load
ALT, F, L or F4

Clears the file in the current window from memory and then loads the specified file.

Save
ALT, F, S or F5

Saves your macro file to disk.

Autosave
ALT, F, A

Saves your macro file to disk at specified intervals.

Macro Activation
ALT, F, M or F8

Activates the current macro file within the Desktop only, outside it only, or everywhere.

The Edit Menu

Cut to Clipboard
ALT, E, T or SHIFT-DEL

Deletes or moves text via the Clipboard.

Copy to Clipboard
ALT, E, C

Copies text via the Clipboard.

Paste from Clipboard
ALT, E, P or SHIFT-INS

Inserts text from the Clipboard.

Mark Block
ALT, E, M

Marks a section of text to be cut or copied.

Unmark Block
ALT, E, U or ESC

Unmarks a text block.

Delete All Text
ALT, E, D

Clears all the text in the current window from memory.

Insert File ALT, E, I	Inserts the text from a file on disk into the current window, starting at the cursor position.
Goto ALT, E, G	Moves the cursor to the specified line number.

The Search Menu

Find ALT, S, F	Lets you specify a text sequence and move the cursor to the first occurrence of it.
Find **A**gain ALT, S, A	Moves the cursor to the next occurrence of your text sequence.
Replace ALT, S, R or F6	Replaces a text sequence with a different sequence.

The Controls Menu

Deactivate All Macros ALT, C, D	Deactivates all Macro Editor files and clears the buffer.
Playback Delay ALT, C, P	Controls the speed at which macros transmit keystrokes.
Learn Mode ALT, C, L	Toggles keystroke recording on and off.
Save Setup ALT, C, S	Saves current Control menu settings.

Desktop: Notepads

The File Menu

Load ALT, F, L or F4	Clears the file in the current window from memory and then loads the specified file.
Save ALT, F, S	Saves the current file to disk after letting you optionally change its name and format.
Send **E**lectronic Mail ALT, F, E or F5	In conjunction with the Electronic Mail application, transmits your document as e-mail.
Print ALT, F, P	Prints the current document.

Autosave   Saves your document to disk at specified intervals.
ALT, F, A

Exit Without Saving   Abandons the current document without saving it
ALT, F, X   to disk.

The Edit Menu

Cut to Clipboard   Deletes or moves text via the Clipboard.
ALT, E, T or SHIFT-DEL

Copy to Clipboard   Copies text via the Clipboard.
ALT, E, C

Paste from Clipboard Inserts text from the Clipboard.
ALT, E, P or SHIFT-INS

Mark Block   Marks a section of text to be cut or copied.
ALT, E, M

Unmark Block   Unmarks a text block.
ALT, E, U or ESC

Delete All Text   Clears all the text in the current window from
ALT, E, D   memory.

Insert File   Inserts the text from a file on disk into the current
ALT, E, I   window, starting at the cursor position.

Goto   Moves the cursor to the specified line number.
ALT, E, G

Spellcheck **W**ord   Checks the spelling of the word the cursor is on.
ALT, E, W

Spellcheck **S**creen   Checks the spelling of the text currently on the
ALT, E, S   screen.

Spellcheck **F**ile   Checks the spelling of all the text in the document.
ALT, E, F or F8

The Search Menu

Find   Lets you specify a text sequence and move the
ALT, S, F   cursor to the first occurrence of it.

Find **A**gain   Moves the cursor to the next occurrence of your
ALT, S, A or F7   text sequence.

Replace   Replaces a text sequence with a different sequence.
ALT, S, R or F6

The Controls Menu

Page Layout ALT, C, P	Sets margins and paper size.
Electronic Mail Page Layout ALT, C, E	Sets margins and "electronic page" size.
Header/Footer ALT, C, H	Sets specified text to print at the top and/or bottom of every page.
Tab **R**uler Edit ALT, C, R	Sets and deletes tab settings on the ruler line.
Save Setup ALT, C, S	Saves current Control and **C**ontrols menu settings as new defaults.
Tab ruler display ALT, C, T	Turns the ruler line display on or off.
Overtype Mode ALT, C, O or INS	Toggles between Insert mode and Overtype mode.
Control Char Display ALT, C, C	If on, displays ENTER, TAB, and SPACEBAR codes.
Wordwrap ALT, C, W	If on, sets words to wrap when past the right margin.
Auto Indent ALT, C, A	If on, makes a new line take on the indentation of the previous line.

Desktop: Outlines

All menus are identical to Notepads except for the following **H**eadlines menu:

Expand Current ALT, H, E	Displays the subheads of the current headline.
Expand **A**ll ALT, H, A	Displays everything in the outline.
Show Level ALT, H, S	Displays headlines at or above the level of the current headline.
Collapse Current ALT, H, C	Hides the subheads of the current headline.
Main Headline Only ALT, H, M	Displays level 1 headlines exclusively.
Promote ALT, H, P	Raises the current headline and its subheads one level.

Demote   Lowers the current headline and its subheads one
ALT, H, D   level.

Desktop: Telecommunications (Modem Directory)

The File Menu

Load   Closes the current directory without saving it and
ALT, F, L or F4   loads the specified directory in its place.
Save   Saves the current directory to disk.
ALT, F, S or F5

The Edit Menu

Edit Entry   Brings up the Edit Phone Directory dialog box for
ALT, E, E or F6   the selected entry.
Create New Entry   Creates a new directory entry.
ALT, E, C
Remove Entry   Deletes the selected directory entry.
ALT, E, R

The Actions Menu

Dial   Dials the selected entry.
ALT, A, D or F7
Manual   Lets you manually dial the selected entry.
ALT, A, M or F8
Hangup Phone   Disconnects; same as its counterpart in the Online
ALT, A, H   Actions menu.

The Setup Menu

Modem Setup   Configures modem settings.
ALT, S, M
Full Online Screen   If on, suppresses the display of status and help
ALT, S, F   information.

Desktop: Telecommunications (Modem Online)
The Actions Menu

Hangup Phone ALT, A, H or F8	Disconnects; same as its counterpart in the Directory Actions menu.
End Transfer ALT, A, E	Ends and saves an ASCII transfer.

The Receive Menu

ASCII ALT, R, A or F6	Downloads text using the ASCII protocol.
XMODEM ALT, R, X or F7	Downloads computer files using the XMODEM protocol.

The Send Menu

ASCII ALT, S, A or F4	Uploads text using the ASCII protocol.
XMODEM ALT, S, X or F5	Uploads computer files using the XMODEM protocol.

Desktop: Telecommunications (Electronic Mail)

The View Menu

View Inbox ALT, V, I or F4	Displays the messages in your inbox.
View Outbox ALT, V, O or F5	Displays the messages in your outbox.
View Sent ALT, V, S or F6	Displays the messages in your sent box.

The Actions Menu

View Highlighted Message ALT, A, V	Displays the contents of the selected message.

Delete Highlighted Message ALT, A, D	Erases the selected message.
Read Mail Now ALT, A, R or F7	Picks up your mail from the selected online service and deposits the messages in your inbox.
Create Mail Message ALT, A, C or F8	Helps automate creating and sending e-mail over the selected online service.

The Setup Menu

Mail Service ALT, S, M	Configures and sets your online service.
Send Mail Schedule ALT, S, S	Sets how often Electronic Mail automatically transmits the messages in your OUTBOX directory.
Read Mail Schedule ALT, S, R	Sets how often Electronic Mail automatically picks up your online messages.
Mail **D**irectories ALT, S, D	Specifies the directories to be used as your inbox, outbox, and sent box.

Desktop: Telecommunications (Send a Fax)

The Actions Menu

Add a New Entry ALT, A, A or F4	Creates a new fax and sends it.
Edit the Current Entry ALT, A, E or F5	Brings up the Fax Details dialog box for editing.
Delete the Current Entry ALT, A, D or F6	Deletes the selected entry from the fax directory.
Send Files to Selected Entry ALT, A, S or F7	Brings up the Fax Details dialog box for fax transmission.
Check FAX Log ALT, A, C or F8	Displays the Fax Log.

The Configure Menu

FAX Drive ALT, C, F	Sets the storage directory for temporary fax files.

Page Length ALT, C, P	Sets the standard fax page length.
Cover Page ALT, C, C	Sets prompting for adding a cover page.
Time Format ALT, C, T	Sets the time format to 24 hr or Am/Pm.
Sent From ALT, C, S	Sets your name, which is printed at the top of every fax page.

Desktop: Telecommunications (Check the Fax Log)

The Actions Menu

Delete the Selected Entry ALT, A, D or F5	Removes the selected entry from the Fax Log.
Search ALT, A, S or F6	Finds specified Fax Log entries.

The Configure Menu

FAX Drive ALT, C, F	Sets the disk directory for storing temporary fax files.
AutoUpdate ALT, C, A	Sets, in seconds, how often the Fax Log window will be updated.

Directory Maintenance

The Volume Menu

Rename Volume ALT-V, V	Displays and lets you rename the volume label of the current disk.
Reread Tree ALT-V, R	Rereads the current disk to update the Tree List and file information.
Change Drive ALT-V, C	Lets you switch to a different drive.
Print Tree ALT-V, P	Prints the Directory Tree or a straightforward list of the directories.

Tree Data Display
ALT-V, T

Sets the information displayed to the left of the Directory Tree.

Exit
ALT-V, X

Exits DM without prompting for confirmation.

The Directory Menu

Make Directory
ALT-D, M or F4

Adds a directory to the root or the selected existing directory.

Rename Directory
ALT-D, R or F5

Renames the selected directory.

Delete Directory
ALT-D, D or F6

Removes the selected directory, and all its subdirectories and files.

Copy Tree
ALT-D, C or F9

Copies the selected directory, and all its subdirectories and files, to the location you specify on the Tree.

Prune & Graft
ALT-D, G or F7

Moves the selected directory, and all its subdirectories and files.

Branch Size
ALT-D, B

Displays the number and total size of files in the selected directory and its subdirectories.

Modify Attributes
ALT-D, A

Displays and lets you change the system and hidden attributes of the specified directory.

Show Files
ALT-D, A or F8

Displays the names and total size of the files in the first level of the selected directory.

Network Rights
ALT-D, N

Displays your access rights to the selected directory on a networked drive.

PC Secure

The File Menu

Encrypt File
F, E or F4

Scrambles files so they can't be read without a password.

Decrypt File
F, D or F5

Unscrambles files using a password.

Exit PC Secure
F, X or F3

Quits PC Secure.

The Options Menu

Full DES Encryption O, F	Performs 16 rounds of encrypting a file's data.
Quick Encryption O, Q	Performs 2 rounds of encrypting a file's data.
Compression O, C	If on, compacts a file so it takes up less space.
One Key O, O	Lets you use the same password, or key, for your entire session.
Hidden O, H	Saves the encrypted and/or compressed file as a hidden file.
Read Only O, R	Saves the encrypted and/or compressed file as a read-only file.
Delete Original File O, D	Overwrites file with its encrypted and/or compressed version.
Expert Mode O, E	Sets a file's encryption to be based entirely on its supplied key (as opposed to the master key).
Save Configuration O, S	Saves your **O**ptions menu settings.

PC Shell

The File Menu

Open ALT-F, O or CTRL-ENTER (B)	Lets you optionally enter parameters, and then runs the selected program file or runs the program associated with the selected data file.
Run ALT-F, R or CTRL-ENTER (B)	Brings up a command line into which you can type a path, program name, and optional parameters (such as the name of a data file).
Print ALT-F, P (I)	Offers the options of Print **F**ile to print text or hex files, and Print File **L**ist to print data on all the files in the current directory.
Search ALT-F, H (A)	Searches for text in your selected files, unselected files, or all files.
View File Contents ALT-F, V or F2 (B)	Brings up View window that displays the contents of selected files in their native formats.

Search ALT-F, H (A)	Searches for text in your selected files, unselected files, or all files.
View File Contents ALT-F, V or F2 (B)	Brings up View window that displays the contents of selected files in their native formats.
Move ALT-F, M (I)	Moves the selected files to the specified drive and/or directory.
Copy ALT-F, C or F5 (B)	Copies the selected files to the specified drive and/or directory.
Compare ALT-F, A (B)	Compares the contents of the selected files against other files for an exact match.
Delete ALT-F, D (I)	Erases the selected files from the disk after prompting for confirmation.
Rename ALT-F, N (B)	Renames the selected files individually or globally (via the DOS wildcards * and ?).
Change File ALT-F, G (I)	Provides the options Edit File, **H**ex Edit File, **C**lear File, and **A**ttribute Change.
Locate ALT-F, L or F7 (B)	Finds files across multiple drives and/or directories based on their names, text contents, creation dates, sizes, and/or attributes.
Verify ALT-F, Y (I)	Scans the selected files for defects and optionally marks bad sectors as unusable.
Undelete ALT-F, U (I)	Runs the Undelete program to locate, examine, and recover deleted files.
Secure ALT-F, E (A)	Provides the three PC Secure options **E**ncrypt File, **D**ecrypt File, and **S**ettings.
Select All Toggle ALT-F, S (B)	Toggles between selecting all files and unselecting all files in the File List.
Exit ALT-F, X or F3 (B)	Brings up the Close dialog box. Pressing ENTER or O, or clicking Exit, then quits PC Shell.

The Disk Menu

Copy ALT-D, C (B)	Copies the contents of a floppy disk to another disk of the same type.
Compare ALT-D, O (B)	Compares the contents of two floppy disks of the same type.
Rename Volume ALT-D, R (I)	Renames the current disk's volume label.
Search ALT-D, S (I)	Finds the sector and offset location of specified data on the current disk.

Make Disk Bootable	Runs the interactive version of PC Format to format

Make Disk Bootable
ALT-D, B (B)
Runs the interactive version of PC Format to format a disk and copy system files to it.

Directory Maintenance
ALT-D, M (B)
Runs Directory Maintenance, which performs such operations as moving and deleting directories.

Park Disk Heads
ALT-D, P (I)
Positions your hard disk's read/write heads over an unused portion of the disk for shutdown.

Sort Files in Directory
ALT-D, T (I)
Sorts display of files in the current directory by name, extension, size, date/time, or selection order, either ascending or descending.

Disk Information
ALT-D, I (A)
Displays technical information about the current disk.

View/Edit
ALT-D, E (A)
Brings up a hex editor for revising sectors on the current disk.

The Options Menu

Confirmation
ALT-O, C
Lets you turn on or off the options Confirm on **D**elete, Confirm on **R**eplace (for when you're replacing old files while copying or moving files), and Confirm on **M**ouse Operations (for when you're copying or moving using the mouse).

File Display Options
ALT- O, F or F6
Sets file characteristics displayed in the File List and criteria for sorting the file display.

Show Information
ALT- O, S
Displays technical information about the selected files.

Colors
ALT- O, O
Runs the PC Config program to let you change color, display, mouse, and keyboard settings for all PC Tools programs.

Change User Level
ALT- O, U
Defines user level of **B**eginner, **I**ntermediate, or **A**dvanced to set the number of menu options shown.

Define Function Keys
ALT- O, K
Assigns new meanings and message bar descriptions to the function keys you specify.

Save Configuration File
ALT- O, A
Saves your current PC Shell settings as the new defaults.

Version 6 Menus
ALT- O, I
Switches PC Shell to displaying the menus used in its previous version, PC Shell 6.

Wait on DOS Screen
ALT- O, W
If off, returns you to PC Shell without pausing after a launched program has exited.

Quick Run ALT- O, Q	When off, swaps current memory to disk before running a program; when on, skips swapping to load programs faster. This option is only adjustable when PC Shell is nonresident; the resident version *always* swaps to disk first to ensure enough memory is available.

The View Menu

Single File List ALT-V, S or DEL	Displays the default Tree List/File List screen.
Dual File Lists ALT-V, D or INS	Displays two sets of the Tree List and File List (useful for copying, moving, and comparing files).
Program/**F**ile Lists ALT-V, F	Divides the screen between the Tree List and File List windows and a Program List window.
Program List Only ALT-V, P or F10	Toggles the display between a Program List screen and the standard PC Shell screen.
Viewer/File Lists ALT-V, V or F2, F8	Divides the screen between the Tree List and File List windows and a View window.
Custom List Configure ALT-V, C	Provides display commands for toggling on or off the **T**ree List, **F**ile List, **P**rogram List, **V**iew Window, Background **M**at, and **DOS** Command Line. Also, provides commands to make the View window horizontal or vertical, and to set PC Shell windows to be static (TILED) or adjustable (CASCADED).
Hide All Lists ALT-V, H	Toggles the display of all windows on or off. Pressing F10 brings back the standard display.
Set Date/**T**ime ALT-V, T	Displays, and lets you change, the system date and time.
Refresh ALT-V, R	Rereads your drive to update the Tree List and File List.
Fi**l**ters ALT-V, L	Provides the options File **L**ist to restrict the File List display to specified files, and File **S**elect (F9) to select specified files.
Unselect Files ALT-V, U or F4	Unselects all selected files in the File List.

The Special Menu

System Info ALT-S, S (B)	Runs the SI program, which provides complete information about your computer system.
DeskConnect ALT-S, C (B)	Connects two computers (such as a desktop PC and laptop) attached by a serial cable.
File Map ALT-S, F (A)	Displays a map showing where each selected file is located on your disk.
Disk **M**ap ALT-S, M (A)	Displays a map of the current disk.
Memory Map ALT-S, E (A)	Lists the names and sizes of programs currently occupying your system's memory.
Remove PC Shell ALT-S, R (B)	Exits PC Shell and unloads it from memory. This option only appears when PC Shell is resident.

The Tree Menu

Expand One Level ALT-T, X or +	Displays subdirectories one level down in the selected collapsed directory.
Expand **B**ranch ALT-T, B or *	Displays all subdirectories in the selected collapsed directory.
Expand **A**ll ALT-T, A	Displays all subdirectories in the Tree List.
Collapse Branch ALT-T, C or –	Hides all subdirectories in the selected expanded directory.

Undelete

The File Menu

Undelete F, U or F8	Undeletes the selected files.
Undelete **T**o F, T	Undeletes the selected files to a different drive and/or directory.
Find Deleted Files F, F or F7	Finds deleted files based on their names, contents, and/or protection status.
View File F, V or F4	Displays the contents of the selected deleted files.

File Info F, I	Displays information about the currently selected file.
Purge Delete Sentry File F, P	Erases beyond recovery specified files or all files in the SENTRY directory.
Advanced Undelete F, A	Provides the options **Manual Undelete, Create a File,** and **Append to Existing** to reconstruct files cluster by cluster, and **Rename Existing File** to rename files.
Exit F, X	Exits Undelete, returning you to the DOS prompt.

The Disk Menu

Scan for Data Types D, D	Finds free clusters containing Lotus 1-2-3, Symphony, dBASE, and/or text data.
Scan for Contents D, C	Finds free clusters containing a specified text sequence.
Scan for Lost Deleted Files D, L	Finds deleted files that belong to deleted directories.
Set Scan Range D, S	Restricts **Disk** menu searches to the specified cluster range.
Continue Scan D, O	Continues an interrupted **Disk** menu search.

The Options Menu

Sort By O, S or F9	Sorts the File List by **N**ame, **E**xtension, **S**ize, **D**eleted Date and Time, **M**odified Date and Time, Directory, or Condition.
Select by Name O, B, or F5	Selects specified files using DOS wildcards.
Unselect By Name O, U or F6	Unselects specified files using DOS wildcards.
Show Existing Files O, H	Displays existing files in addition to deleted files in the File List.
Use Mirror File O, M	For unprotected files, sets Undelete to use the disk's Mirror data instead of its FAT and root directory information.

Appendix **D**

PC Tools Function Keys

This appendix lists the function key shortcut commands for major PC Tools 7 DOS programs with pull-down menus. The programs covered are Compress, CP Backup, Directory Maintenance, the Desktop Manager applications, PC Secure, PC Shell, and Undelete.

Each key is covered in two columns. The first column lists the key and its one-word message bar description, and the second column lists the action performed by the key when you press it or click its message bar description. Only function keys F1 through F10 are listed; PC Tools doesn't support F11 or F12.

For more information on the effects of a key, see Appendix C for a brief description of the menu command the key selects, or see the chapter that covers the command.

Compress

F1 (Help)	Brings up context-sensitive help
F2 (Index)	Brings up the online help index
F3 (Exit)	Performs the same functions as ESC
F4 (Begin)	Selects Compress Begin Compress
F5 (Analyze)	Selects Analysis Disk Statistics
F6 (Techniq)	Selects Options Compression Technique
F7 (Methods)	Selects Options Ordering Methods
F8 (DirOrdr)	Selects Options Directory Order
F9 (Sort)	Selects Options File Sort Options
F10 (Menu)	Like ALT, activates the menu bar

CP Backup

F1 (Help)	Brings up context-sensitive help
F2 (QView)	Displays the contents of the selected file in its native format
F3 (Exit)	Selects File Exit
F4 (NxtDriv)	Displays the Tree List and File List for the next drive when you've selected a multiple drive backup
F5 (Backup)	Selects Actions Start Backup
F6 (Restore)	Selects Actions Start Restore
F7 (Device)	Selects Configure Choose Drive And Media
F8 (Setup)	Selects Configure Define Equipment
F9 (Compare)	Selects Actions Start Compare
F10 (Menu)	Like ALT, activates the menu bar

Directory Maintenance

F1 (Help)	Brings up context-sensitive help
F2 (Reread)	Selects Volume Rename Volume
F3 (Exit)	Performs the same functions as ESC
F4 (Make)	Selects Directory Make Directory
F5 (Rename)	Selects Directory Rename Directory
F6 (Delete)	Selects Directory Delete Directory
F7 (Prune)	Selects Directory Prune & Graft
F8 (Files)	Selects Directory Show Files
F9 (Copy)	Selects Directory Copy Tree
F10 (Menu)	Performs the same functions as ALT

Desktop: Appointment Scheduler

F1 (Help)	Brings up context-sensitive help
F2 (Index)	Brings up the online help index
F3 (Exit)	Performs the same functions as ESC
F4 (Day)	Toggles the display of the Daily Scheduler
F5 (Week)	Toggles the display of the Weekly Appointment Display box
F6 (Month)	Toggles the display of the Calendar
F7 (To-Do)	Toggles the display of the To-Do List
F8 (Usage)	Toggles the display of the Time Usage Graph box
F9 (Switch)	Activates a different open window
F10 (Menu)	Performs the same functions as ALT

Desktop: Algebraic Calculator

F1 (Help)	Brings up context-sensitive help
F2 (Index)	Brings up the online help index
F3 (Exit)	Performs the same functions as ESC
F4 (Clear)	Selects **O**ptions **C**lear Display
F5 (Erase)	Selects **O**ptions **E**rase Tape
F6	Undefined
F7	Undefined
F8	Undefined
F9 (Switch)	Activates a different open window
F10 (Menu)	Performs the same functions as ALT

Desktop: Financial Calculator

F1 (Help)	Brings up context-sensitive help
F2 (Index)	Brings up the online help index
F3 (Exit)	Performs the same functions as ESC
F4 (None)	Selects **R**egisterDisplay **N**o Registers Displayed
F5 (Stack)	Selects **R**egisterDisplay **S**tack Registers
F6 (Fin)	Selects **R**egisterDisplay **F**inancial Registers
F7	Undefined
F8	Undefined
F9 (Switch)	Activates a different open window
F10 (Menu)	Performs the same functions as ALT

Desktop: Programmer's Calculator

F1 (Help)	Brings up context-sensitive help
F2 (Index)	Brings up the online help index
F3 (Exit)	Performs the same functions as ESC
F4 (Stack)	Selects **R**egisterDisplay **S**tack Registers
F5	Undefined
F6 (Data)	Selects **R**egisterDisplay **D**ata Registers
F7	Undefined
F8	Undefined
F9 (Switch)	Activates a different open window
F10 (Menu)	Performs the same functions as ALT

Desktop: Scientific Calculator

F1 (Help)	Brings up context-sensitive help
F2 (Index)	Brings up the online help index
F3 (Exit)	Performs the same functions as ESC
F4 (None)	Selects **Registers No** Registers
F5 (Stack)	Selects **Registers S**tack Registers
F6 (Data)	Selects **Registers D**ata Registers R0 through R9
F7	Undefined
F8	Undefined
F9 (Switch)	Activates a different open window
F10 (Menu)	Performs the same functions as ALT

Desktop: Clipboard

F1 (Help)	Brings up context-sensitive help
F2 (Index)	Brings up the online help index
F3 (Exit)	Performs the same functions as ESC
F4	Undefined
F5	Undefined
F6 (Find)	Selects **S**earch **R**eplace
F7	Undefined
F8	Undefined
F9 (Switch)	Activates a different open window
F10 (Menu)	Performs the same functions as ALT

Desktop: Databases

F1 (Help)	Brings up context-sensitive help
F2 (Index)	Brings up the online help index
F3 (Exit)	Performs the same functions as ESC
F4 (First)	Moves you to the first or last record
F5 (Prev)	Moves you to the previous record
F6 (Next)	Moves you to the next record
F7 (Search)	Selects **S**earch **F**ind **T**ext in Sort Field
F8 (New)	Selects **E**dit **A**dd New Record
F9 (Switch)	Activates a different open window
F10 (Menu)	Performs the same functions as ALT

Desktop: Macro Editor

F1 (Help)	Brings up context-sensitive help
F2 (Index)	Brings up the online help index
F3 (Exit)	Performs the same functions as ESC
F4 (Load)	Selects **File Load**
F5 (Save)	Selects **File Save**
F6 (Find)	Selects **Search Replace**
F7 (KeyNam)	Inserts the macro code of the next key pressed
F8 (Active)	Selects **File Macro Activation**
F9 (Switch)	Activates a different open window
F10 (Menu)	Performs the same functions as ALT

Desktop: Notepads

F1 (Help)	Brings up context-sensitive help
F2 (Index)	Brings up the online help index
F3 (Exit)	Performs the same functions as ESC
F4 (Load)	Selects **File Load**
F5 (Email)	Selects **File Send Electronic Mail**
F6 (Find)	Selects **Search Replace**
F7 (Again)	Selects **Search Find Again**
F8 (Spell)	Selects **Edit Spellcheck File**
F9 (Switch)	Activates a different open window
F10 (Menu)	Performs the same functions as ALT

Desktop: Outlines

F1 (Help)	Brings up context-sensitive help
F2 (Index)	Brings up the online help index
F3 (Exit)	Performs the same functions as ESC
F4 (Load)	Selects **File Load**
F5 (Email)	Selects **File Send Electronic Mail**
F6 (Find)	Selects **Search Replace**
F7 (Again)	Selects **Search Find Again**
F8 (Spell)	Selects **Edit Spellcheck File**
F9 (Switch)	Activates a different open window
F10 (Menu)	Performs the same functions as ALT

Desktop: Telecommunications (Modem Directory)

F1 (Help)	Brings up context-sensitive help
F2 (Index)	Brings up the online help index
F3 (Exit)	Performs the same functions as ESC
F4 (Load)	Selects File Load
F5 (Save)	Selects File Save
F6 (Edit)	Selects Edit Edit Entry
F7 (Dial)	Selects Actions Dial
F8 (Manual)	Selects Actions Manual
F9 (Switch)	Activates a different open window
F10 (Menu)	Performs the same functions as ALT

Desktop: Telecommunications (Modem Online)

F1 (Help)	Brings up context-sensitive help
F2 (Index)	Brings up the online help index
F3 (Exit)	Performs the same functions as ESC
F4 (ASCII)	Selects Send ASCII
F5 (XModem)	Selects Send XMODEM
F6 (ASCII)	Selects Receive ASCII
F7 (XModem)	Selects Receive XMODEM
F8 (Hangup)	Selects Actions Hangup Phone
F9 (Switch)	Activates a different open window
F10 (Menu)	Performs the same functions as ALT

Desktop: Telecommunications (Electronic Mail)

F1 (Help)	Brings up context-sensitive help
F2 (Index)	Brings up the online help index
F3 (Exit)	Performs the same functions as ESC
F4 (Inbox)	Selects View Inbox
F5 (Outbox)	Selects View Outbox
F6 (Sent)	Selects View Sent
F7 (Read)	Selects Actions Read Mail Now
F8 (Create)	Selects Actions Create Mail Message
F9 (Switch)	Activates a different open window
F10 (Menu)	Performs the same functions as ALT

Desktop: Telecommunications (Send a Fax)

F1 (Help)	Brings up context-sensitive help
F2 (Index)	Brings up the online help index
F3 (Exit)	Performs the same functions as ESC
F4 (Add)	Selects Actions Add a New Entry
F5 (Edit)	Selects Actions Edit the Current Entry
F6 (Delete)	Selects Actions Delete the Current Entry
F7 (Send)	Selects Actions Send Files to Selected Entry
F8 (Chklog)	Selects Actions Check Fax Log
F9 (Switch)	Activates a different open window
F10 (Menu)	Performs the same functions as ALT

Desktop: Telecommunications (Check the Fax Log)

F1 (Help)	Brings up context-sensitive help
F2 (Index)	Brings up the online help index
F3 (Exit)	Performs the same functions as ESC
F4	Undefined
F5 (Delete)	Selects Actions Delete the Selected Entry
F6 (Search)	Selects Actions Search
F7	Undefined
F8	Undefined
F9 (Switch)	Activates a different open window
F10 (Menu)	Performs the same functions as ALT

PC Secure

F1 (Help)	Brings up context-sensitive help
F2 (Index)	Brings up the online help index
F3 (Exit)	Performs the same functions as ESC
F4 (Encrypt)	Selects File Encrypt File
F5 (Decrypt)	Selects File Decrypt File
F6	Undefined
F7	Undefined
F8	Undefined
F9	Undefined
F10 (Menu)	Performs the same functions as ALT

PC Shell

F1 (Help)	Brings up context-sensitive help
F2 (QView)	Selects **F**ile **V**iew File Contents
F3 (Exit)	Performs the same functions as ESC
F4 (Unsel)	Selects **V**iew **U**nselect Files
F5 (Copy)	Selects **F**ile **C**opy
F6 (Disply)	Selects **O**ptions **F**ile Display Options
F7 (Locate)	Selects **F**ile **L**ocate
F8 (Zoom)	Toggles between expanding the current window to fullscreen size and shrinking it to half size
F9 (Select)	Selects **V**iew **F**ilters File **S**elect
F10 (Menu)	Selects **V**iew **P**rogram List Only

Undelete

F1 (Help)	Brings up context-sensitive help
F2 (Index)	Brings up the online help index
F3 (Exit)	Performs the same functions as ESC
F4 (View)	Selects **F**ile **V**iew File
F5 (Select)	Selects **O**ptions **S**elect **by** Name
F6 (Unselct)	Selects **O**ptions **U**nselect by Name
F7 (Find)	Selects **F**ile **F**ind Deleted Files
F8 (Undel)	Selects **F**ile **U**ndelete
F9 (Sort)	Selects **O**ptions **S**ort By
F10 (Menu)	Performs the same functions as ALT

Appendix E

PC Tools Menu Maps

This Appendix provides a visual guide to the menus and dialog boxes of major PC Tools 7 programs with pull-down menus. The programs covered are Commute, Compress, CP Backup, the Desktop Manager applications, Directory Maintenance, PC Secure, PC Shell, and Undelete. The programs appear in alphabetical order.

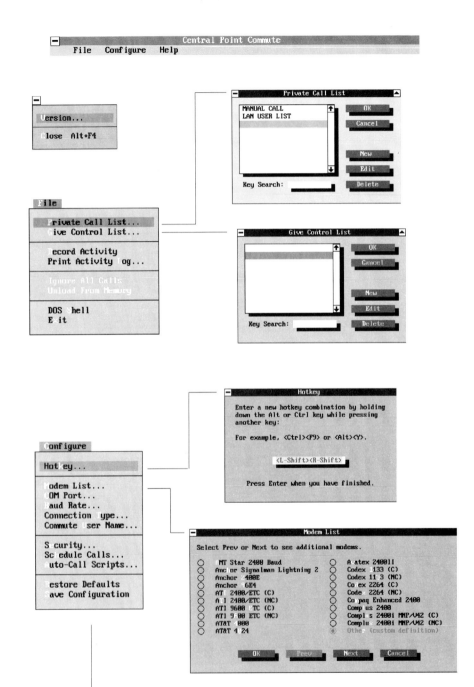

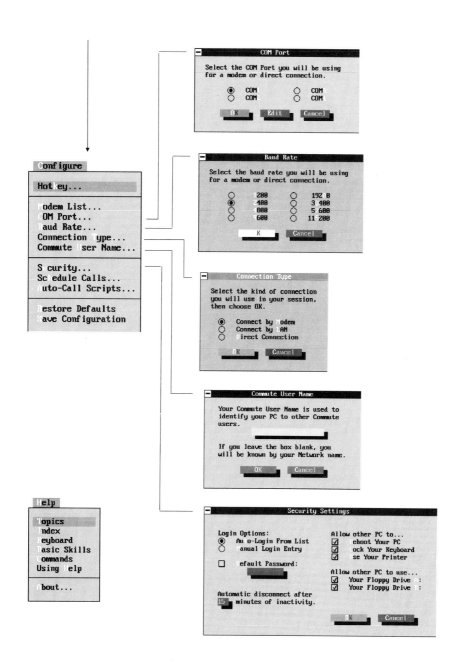

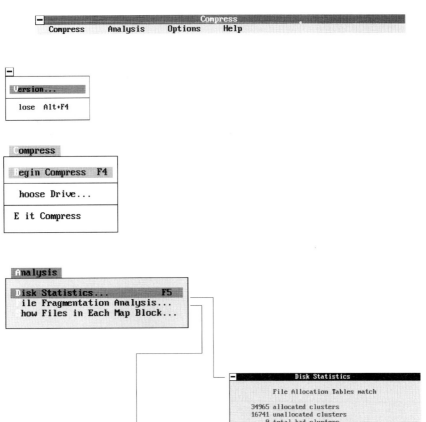

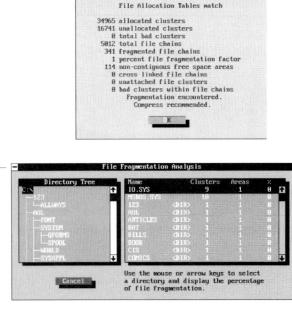

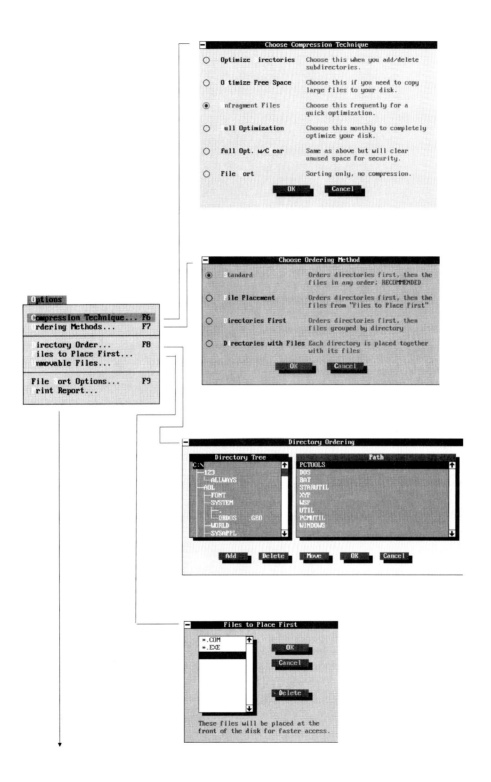

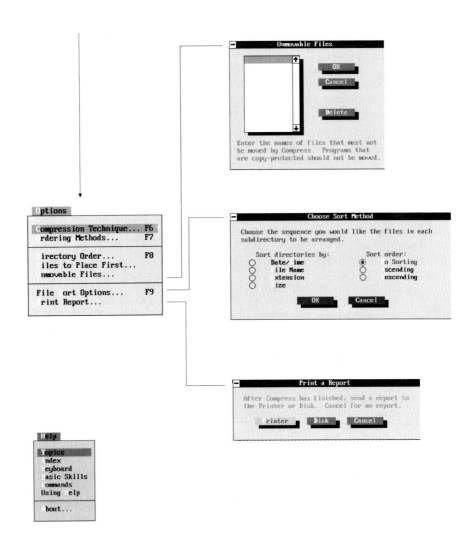

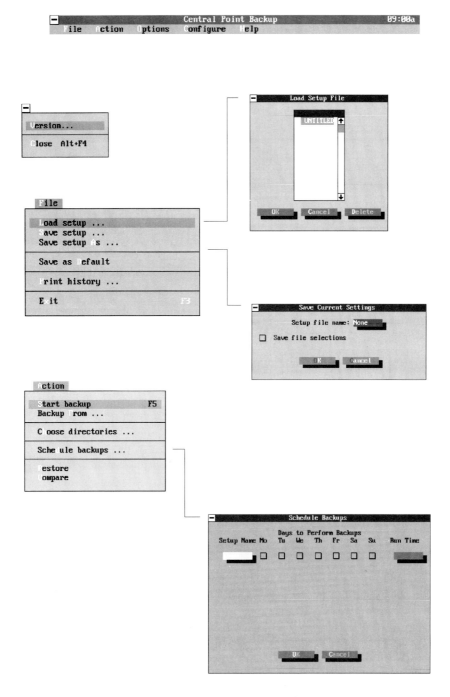

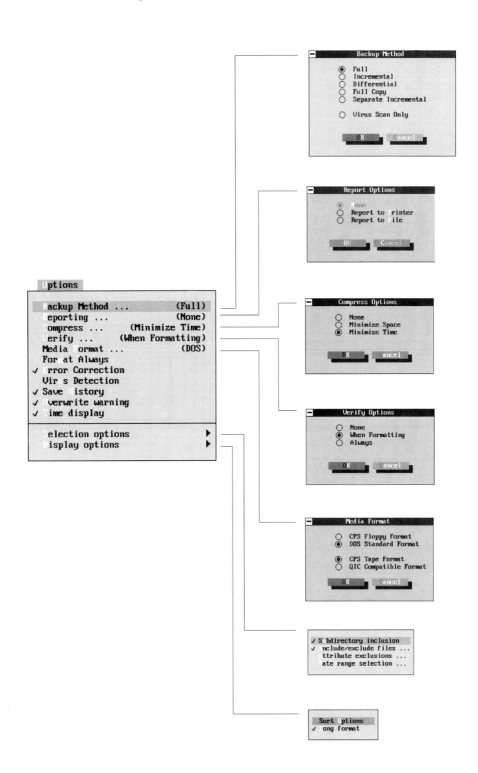

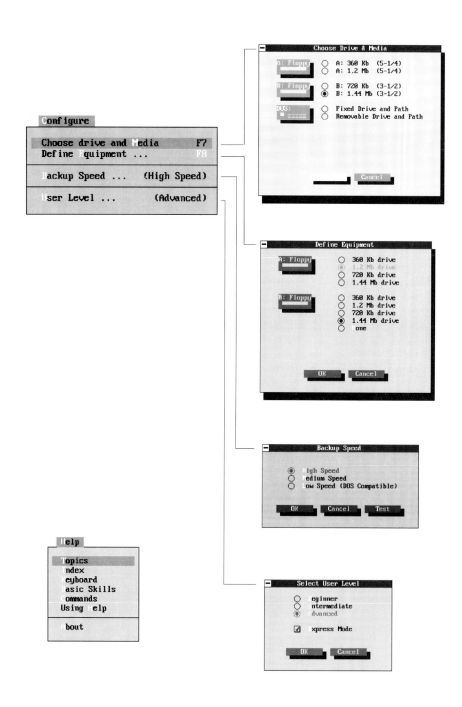

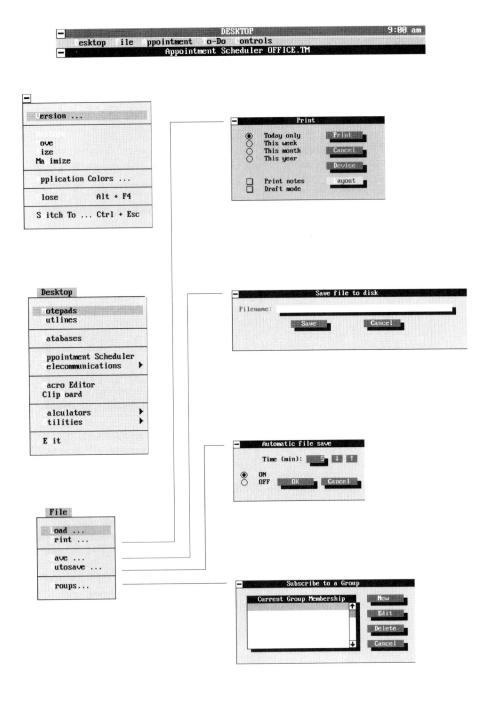

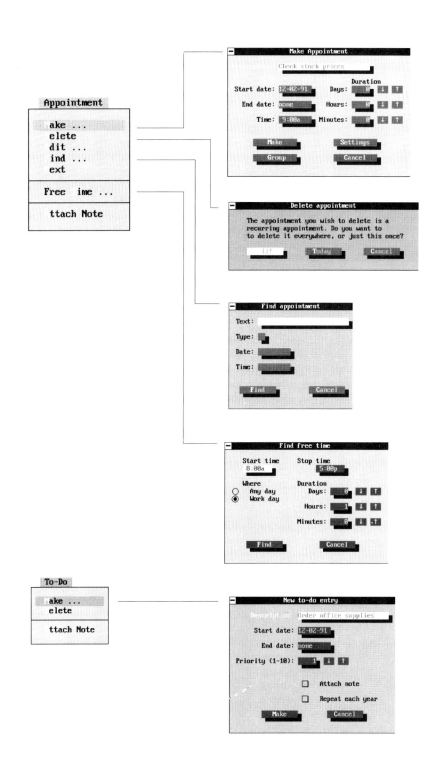

Appointment

ake ...
elete
dit ...
ind ...
ext

Free ime ...

ttach Note

Make Appointment

Check stock prices

Duration

Start date: 12-02-91   Days:

End date: none   Hours:

Time: 9:00a   Minutes:

Make   Settings
Group   Cancel

Delete appointment

The appointment you wish to delete is a
recurring appointment. Do you want to
to delete it everywhere, or just this once?

Today   Cancel

Find appointment

Text:

Type:

Date:

Time:

Find   Cancel

Find free time

Start time   Stop time
8:00a   5:00p

Where   Duration
○ Any day   Days:
● Work day
    Hours: 1
    Minutes:

Find   Cancel

To-Do

ake ...
elete

ttach Note

New to-do entry

Description: Order office supplies

Start date: 12-02-91

End date: none

Priority (1-10):   1

☐ Attach note

☐ Repeat each year

Make   Cancel

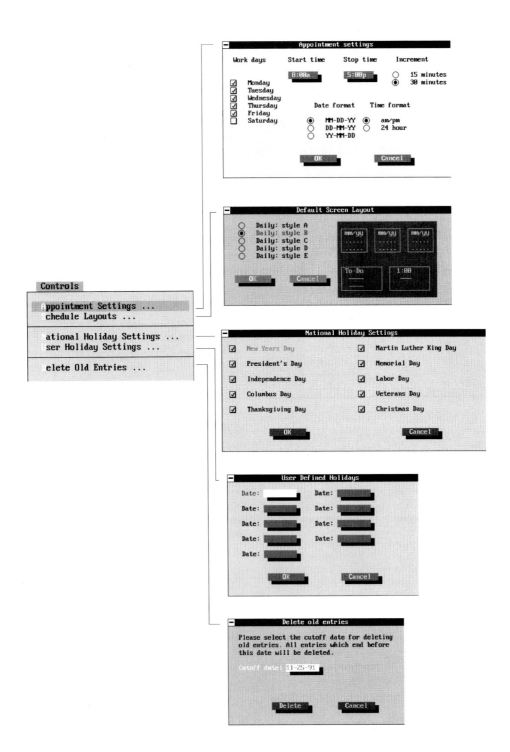

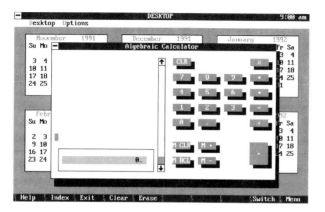

Algebraic Calculator

Financial Calculator

Programmer's Calculator

Scientific Calculator

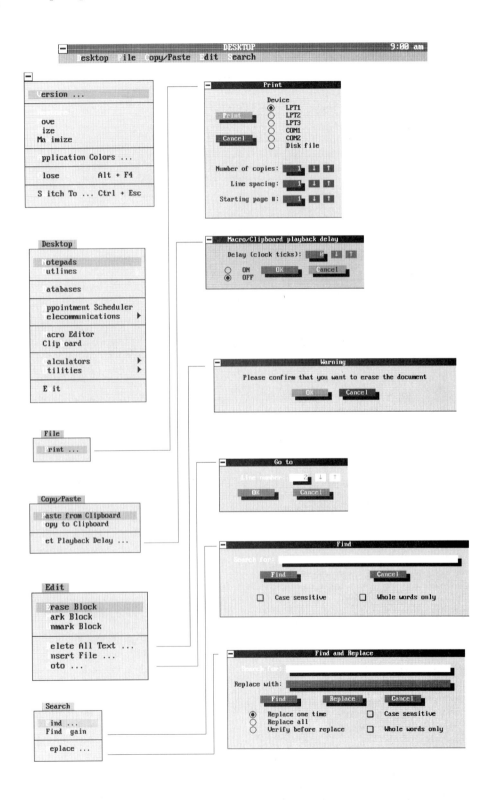

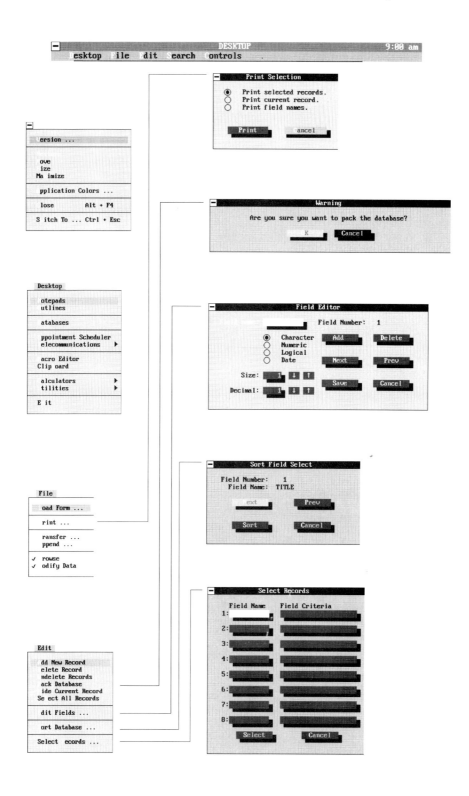

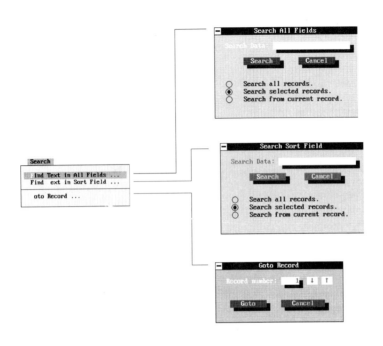

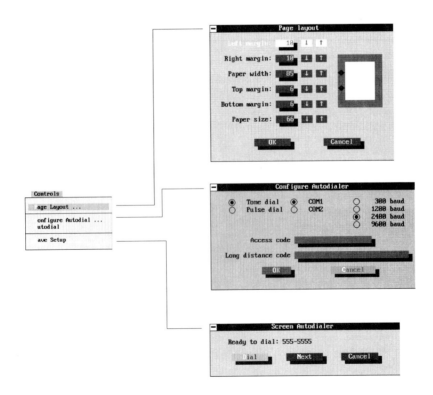

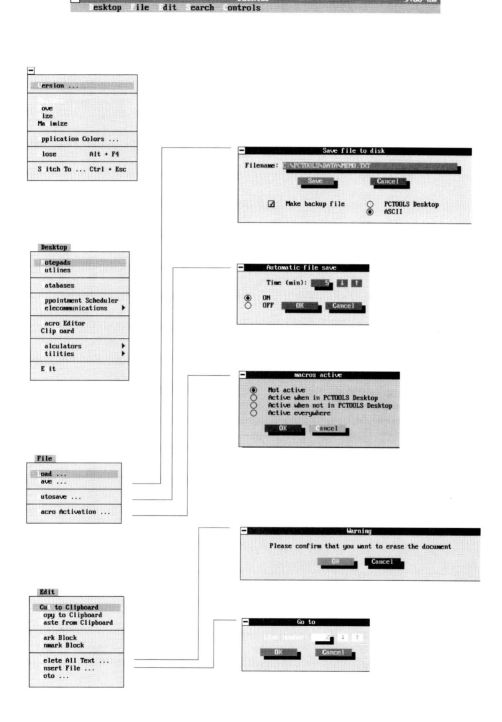

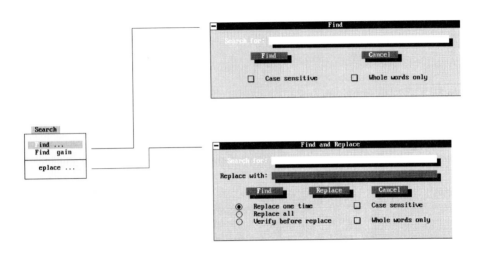

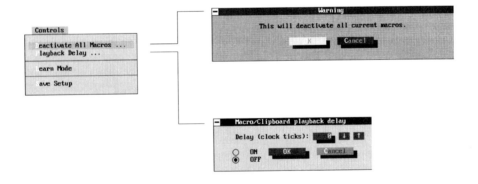

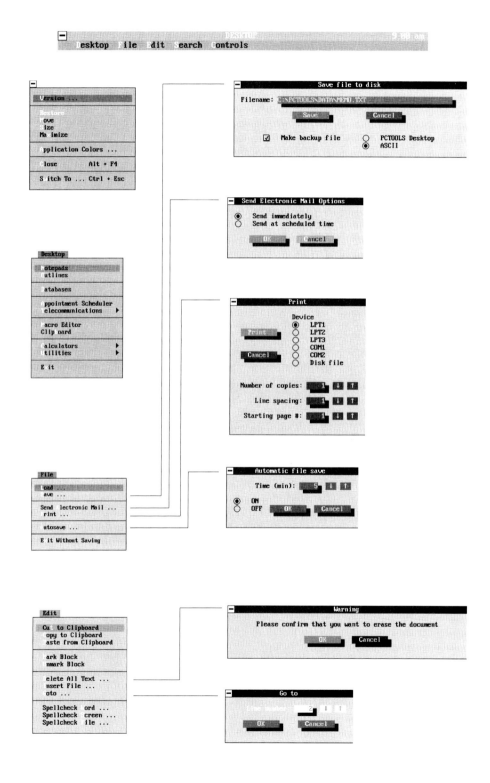

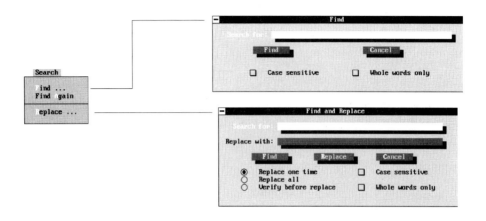

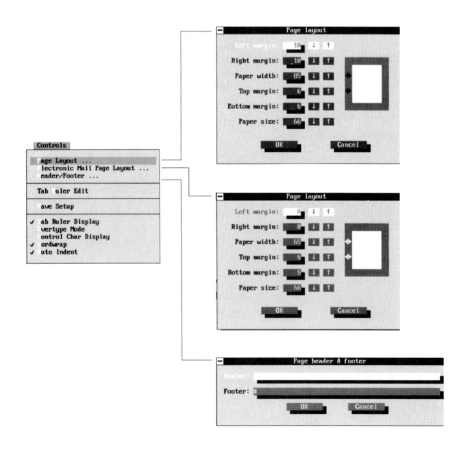

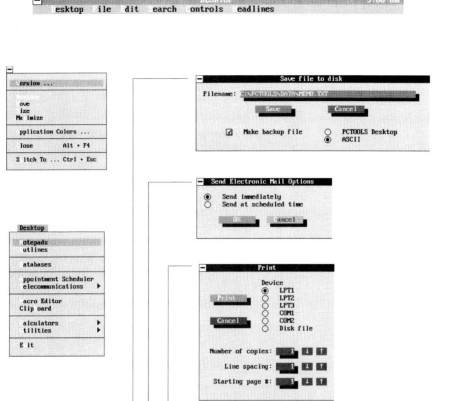

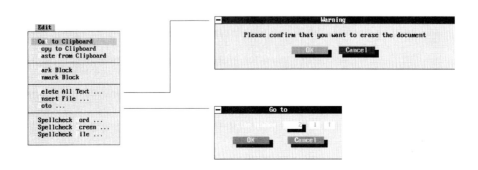

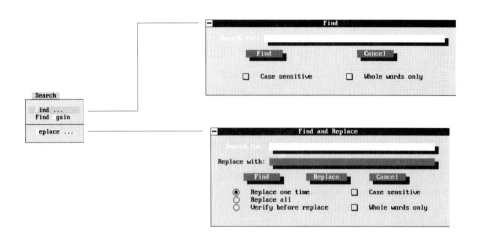

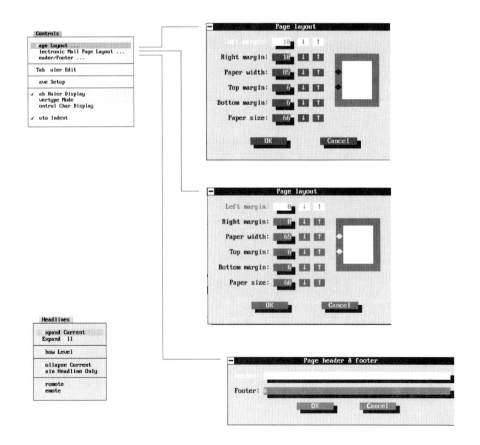

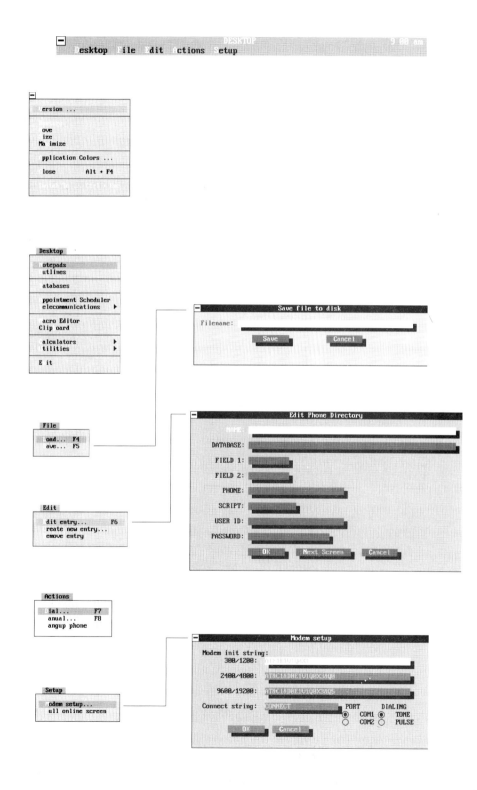

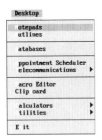

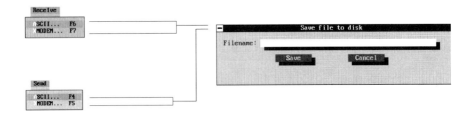

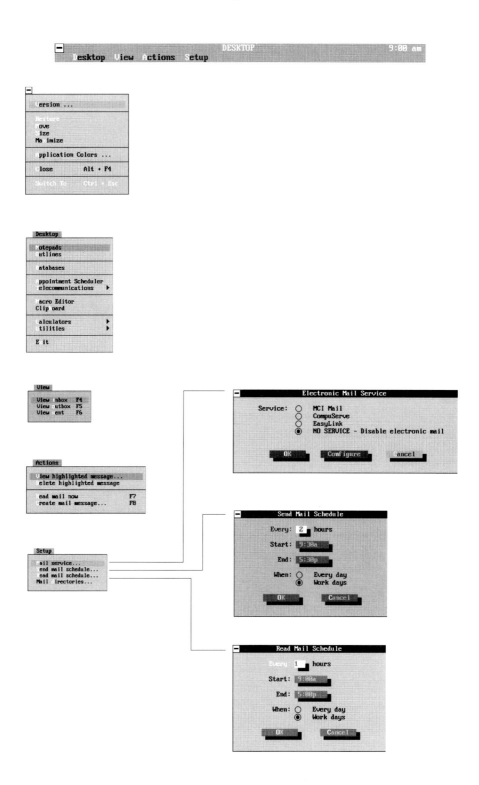

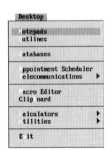

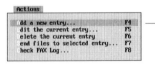

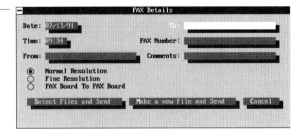

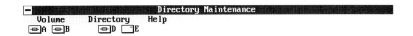

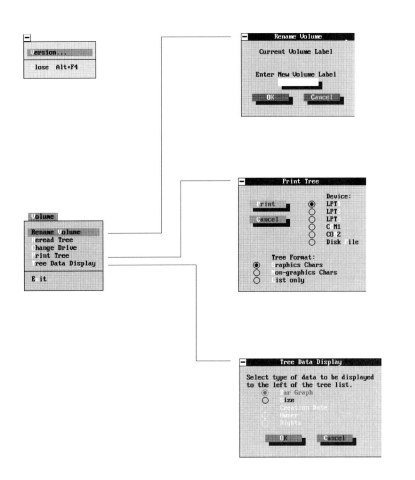

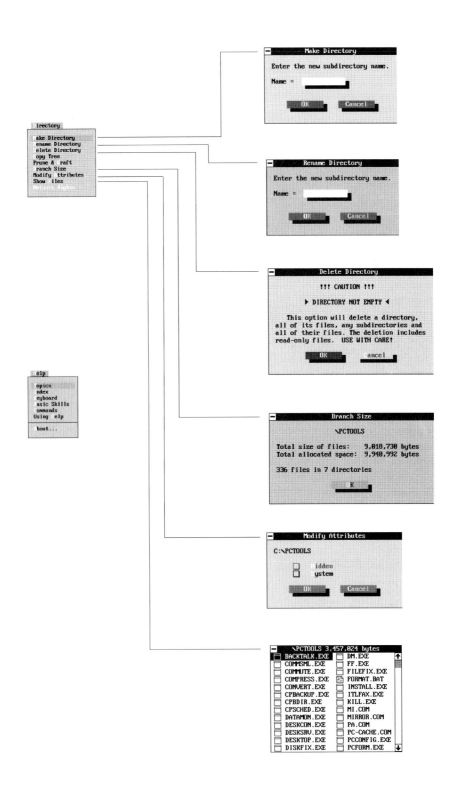

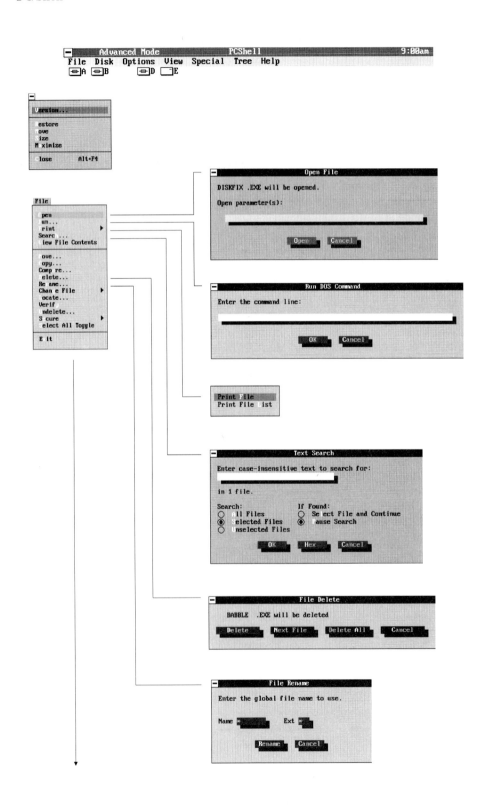

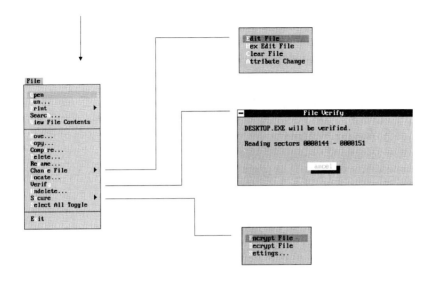

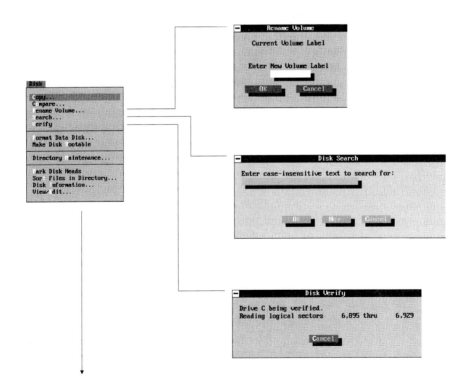

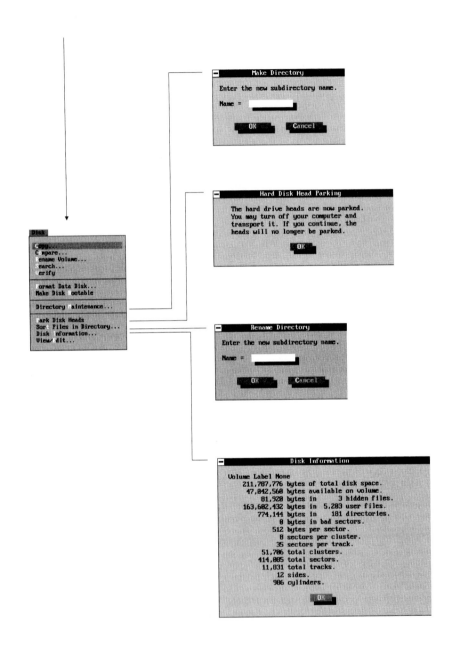

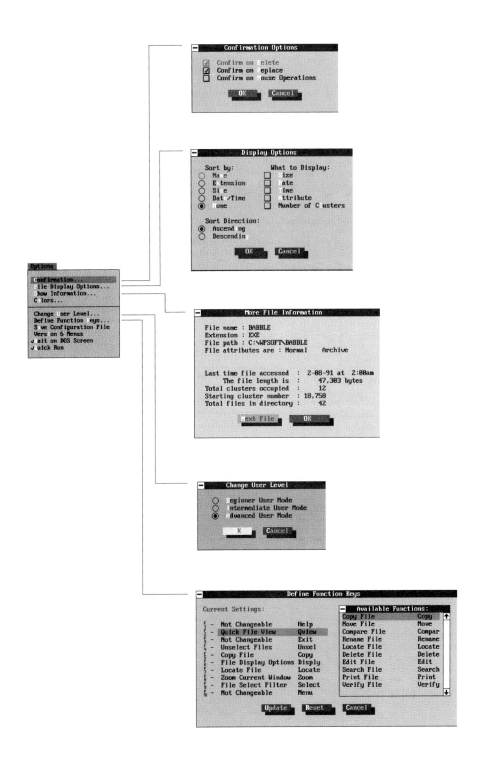

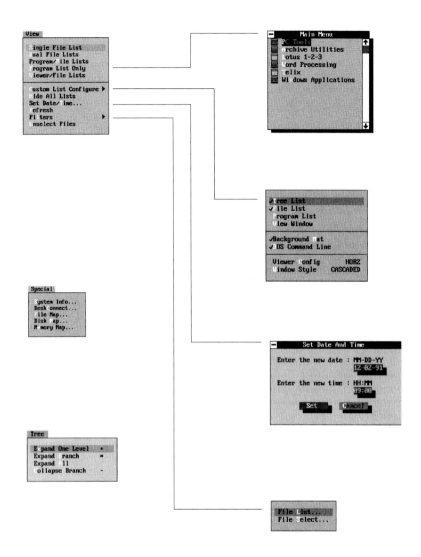

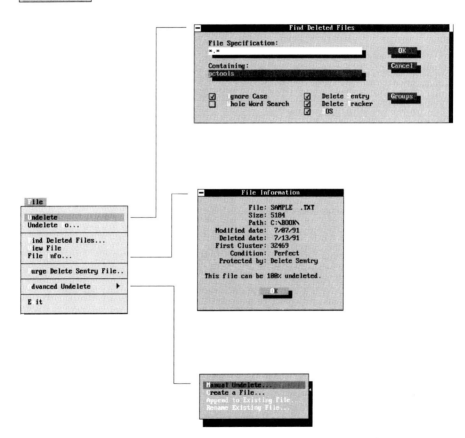

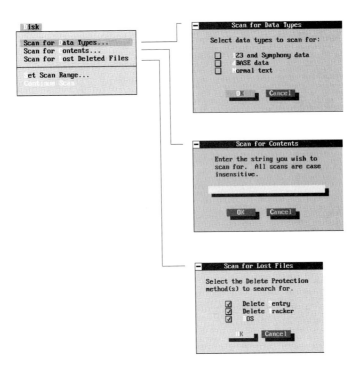

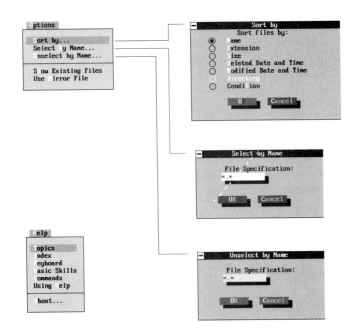

Index

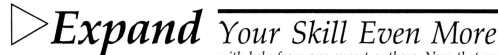

▷*Expand* *Your Skill Even More*

with help from our expert authors. Now that you've gained greater skills with **Harvard Graphics 3: The Complete Reference***, let us suggest the following related titles that will help you use your computer to full advantage.*

Harvard Graphics 3.0 Made Easy
by Mary Campbell

Campbell covers the basics of the latest version of Harvard Graphics before showing you how to create a variety of charts and demonstrating new drawing features. You'll also learn the latest presentation techniques for producing professional slide shows that will make your audience sit up and pay attention.

$24.95 ISBN: 0-07-881746-3 358 pages 7 3/8 x 9 1/4

Quattro Pro 3 Made Easy
by Lisa Biow

After teaching you the basics of building a simple spreadsheet, Biow demonstrates the program's more powerful capabilities. You'll also learn about Quattro Pro 3's new features, including its WYSIWYG environment and three-dimensional graphs.

$19.95 ISBN: 0-07-881735-8 584 pages 7 3/8 x 9 1/4

Covers Versions 2 and 3

Using Quattro Pro 3
by Stephen Cobb

Cobb's outstanding guide takes you through spreadsheet fundamentals, intermediate formulas and file management, then on to advanced commands and macros. You'll find information on significant new features such as the WYSIWYG environment and get productive results fast.

$27.95 ISBN: 0-07-881736-6 839 pages 7 3/8 x 9 1/4

Covers Versions 2 and 3

▶ _____Osborne **McGraw-Hill** ■ Available at local book and computer stores.

Simply 1-2-3
by Mary Campbell

Lotus 1-2-3 beginners will welcome this quick guide to the basics of the world's most widely used spreadsheet. Filled with illustrations and computer screen displays, you'll quickly learn the basics of creating worksheets and performing calculations.
$14.95 ISBN: 0-07-881751-X 208 pages 5 3/4 x 8 3/4
Covers All Releases of Lotus 1-2-3

1-2-3® Release 2.3 Made Easy
by Mary Campbell

Campbell takes you from the basics of spreadsheet organization to more complex functions, including the new WYSIWYG (what you see is what you get) feature that adds presentation graphics and spreadsheet publishing capabilities to your repertoire.
$19.95 ISBN: 0-07-881732-3 429 pages 7 3/8 x 9 1/4
Covers Releases 2.01, 2.2, 2.3

1-2-3® Release 3.1: The Complete Reference
by Mary Campbell

You'll find every Release 3.1 feature, command, and function listed and described in this comprehensive reference. Each entry is explained in detail and demonstrated in practical business applications. You'll quickly find the information you need on new 3.1 features such as the interactive WYSIWYG (what you see is what you get) environment and more.
$29.95 ISBN: 0-07-881699-8 1008 pages 7 3/8 x 9 1/4

1-2-3® Release 2.3: The Complete Reference
by Mary Campbell

Mary Campbell has written a special version of this indispensable reference that covers Lotus' new Release 2.3. You'll find every 1-2-3 feature, command, and function listed and described in this comprehensive reference written for all 1-2-3 users.
$27.95 ISBN: 0-07-881733-1 898 pages 7 3/8 x 9 1/4
Covers Releases 2.01, 2.2, 2.3

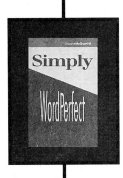

Simply DOS
by Kris Jamsa

Here's the ideal book for everyone who needs to learn the basics of DOS. DOS expert Kris Jamsa makes learning DOS simple, short, and painless. Clear, step-by-step instructions introduce the most essential DOS commands that you need for everyday DOS tasks. All versions of DOS are covered. Filled with helpful illustrations and examples. Plus it has a special binding that lays flat when you open to any chosen page.

$14.95 ISBN: 0-07-881715-3 200 pages 5 3/4 x 8 3/4

Simply PCs
by Bob Albrecht

First-time computer users won't want to miss this short, beautifully illustrated guide that thoroughly explains what a computer system is and how to use it. *Simply PCs* provides a clear overview of software, hardware, peripherals, operating systems, and much more.

$14.95 ISBN: 0-07-881741-2 208 pages 5 3/4 x 8 3/4
Covers All IBM PCs and Compatible Computers

PCs Made Easy
by James L. Turley

If you are a first-time computer user, no other book meets your needs better than this broad, concise, up-to-date introduction to the use of personal computers. It's designed to help you get maximum information with minimal time invested. Turley explains what PCs are, what they can do, and how to make them do it—without relying on jargon or buzzwords.

$18.95 ISBN 0-07-881477-4 319 pages 7 3/8 x 9 1/4
Covers All Personal Computers

The PC User's Guide
by Nick Anis and Craig Menefee

The PC User's Guide offers comprehensive readable documentation for your IBM PC or PC compatible computer. The book begins by acquainting you with personal computer hardware and how to set it up, before delving into operating system software, applications software, and storage media. You'll also learn about servicing your computer system, optimizing its performance, and adding to or upgrading it.

$29.95 ISBN: 0-07-881670-X 700 pages 7 3/8 x 9 1/4, Dvorak*Osborne/McGraw-Hill

Osborne McGraw-Hill

Computer Books

(800) 227-0900

Bookmarker Design — Lance Ravella

Tear off for Bookmark

▼

You're important to us...

We'd like to know what you're interested in, what kinds of books you're looking for, and what you thought about this book in particular.

Please fill out the attached card and mail it in. We'll do our best to keep you informed about Osborne's newest books and special offers.

▶ *YES, Send Me a FREE Color Catalog of all Osborne computer books*
To Receive Catalog, Fill in Last 4 Digits of ISBN Number from Back of Book (see below bar code) 0-07-881 _ _ − _

Name: _____ Title: _____

Company: _____

Address: _____

City: _____ State: _____ Zip: _____

I'M PARTICULARLY INTERESTED IN THE FOLLOWING (*Check all that apply*)

I use this software
- ☐ WordPerfect
- ☐ Microsoft Word
- ☐ WordStar
- ☐ Lotus 1-2-3
- ☐ Quattro
- ☐ Others _____

I use this operating system
- ☐ DOS
- ☐ Windows
- ☐ UNIX
- ☐ Macintosh
- ☐ Others _____

I rate this book:
- ☐ Excellent ☐ Good ☐ Poor

I program in
- ☐ C or C++
- ☐ Pascal
- ☐ BASIC
- ☐ Others _____

I chose this book because
- ☐ Recognized author's name
- ☐ Osborne/McGraw-Hill's reputation
- ☐ Read book review
- ☐ Read Osborne catalog
- ☐ Saw advertisement in store
- ☐ Found/recommended in library
- ☐ Required textbook
- ☐ Price
- ☐ Other _____

Comments _____

Topics I would like to see covered in future books by Osborne/McGraw-Hill include:

_____

IMPORTANT REMINDER
To get your FREE catalog, write in the last 4 digits of the ISBN number printed on the back cover (see below bar code) 0-07-881 _ _ _ − _

Osborne McGraw-Hill

Computer
Books

(800) 227-0900